RACHEL WEEPING

"One might say that such a persuasive dogma is put upon the women that they are not really in harmony with their deepest and most reliable feelings. The forfeiture of one's own unborn finds no melodies in the spirit with which it can sing. There may be a collusive and even coercive force at work, which is in fact inviting women to do violence to themselves in the name of freedom, en route to some sadder enthrallment."
—p. 46—

RACHEL WEEPING
the case
against abortion

James Tunstead Burtchaell, C.S.C.

1817

Harper & Row, Publishers, San Francisco
Cambridge, Hagerstown, New York, Philadelphia
London, Mexico City, São Paulo, Sydney

Acknowledgement is hereby made for the use of the following copyrighted materials:

Passages from *The Ambivalence of Abortion*, by Linda Bird Francke. Copyright © 1978 by Linda Bird Francke. Reprinted by permission of Random House, Inc.

Passages from *Pregnant by Mistake*, by Katrina Maxtone-Graham, published by Liveright Publishers. Copyright © 1973 by Katrina Maxtone-Graham.

Passages from "How Much Should a Child Cost?" by the author. Copyright © 1978 by The Linacre Quarterly.

Passages from "Abortion: Another Point of View," by the author, in *The Ann Landers Encyclopedia A to Z*, edited by Ann Landers, published by Doubleday & Co. Copyright © 1978 by Esther P. Lederer.

A hardcover edition of this book is published by Andrews, McMeel & Parker under the title *Rachel Weeping and Other Essays on Abortion*. It is here reprinted by arrangement.

First Harper & Row paperback edition published in 1984.

Library of Congress Cataloging in Publication Data

Burtchaell, James Tunstead.
  RACHEL WEEPING.

Reprint. Originally published: Rachel weeping and other essays on abortion. Kansas City [Kan.]: Andrews & McMeel, c1982.
  Includes bibliographical references and index.
  1. Abortion—Religious aspects—Catholic Church—Addresses, essays, lectures.
2. Abortion—Religious aspects—Addresses, essays, lectures. I. Title.
[HQ767.3.B87 1984]   363.4'6   83-48986
ISBN 0-06-061251-7 (pbk.)

---

84 85 86 87 88 10 9 8 7 6 5 4 3 2 1

for
Jim Andrews
+1980

A voice was heard in Ramah,
sobbing and loudly lamenting:
it was Rachel weeping for her children,
refusing to be comforted
because they were no more.

Contents

Preface

THE LATE JOHN D. ROCKEFELLER III is responsible for this book. Before my dealings with him in 1976 I wanted nothing to do with the abortion quarrel.

I had been stung a few years earlier. As provost of the University of Notre Dame I was acting president in Father Hesburgh's absence one week when Planned Parenthood / Great Lakes Region had rented rooms in our conference facility for a private meeting. When informed of the meeting in advance I thought we should honor our contract. It was to be a closed gathering for Planned Parenthood people. The three main speakers, in addition to Alan Guttmacher, who had led the organization to abandon its longstanding ban on abortion, included André Hellegers from Georgetown Medical School and William Liu of our own sociology faculty, both articulate critics of abortion. I was impressed that Planned Parenthood would schedule so diverse a program. My only concern was that they not exhibit their use of our premises as an implied endorsement by Notre Dame of their policies. My one instruction to our staff was that there be no publicity. Planned Parenthood I could not instruct; I could only hope they would not take advantage of us. They didn't. But the sidewalk outside was strung with pickets that day, attacking the university for giving the baby-killers the respectability of a welcome to our campus. The president and I both put out statements that a Catholic university was no less Catholic for its being host to many viewpoints. But that gave no comfort to our pickets, who represented a local, conservative Catholic group and a prolife organization. They seemed to me to be unreasonable and a bit nutty—the kind of people whose eyes are too close together. They were a discouragingly antiintellectual crowd with whom I felt no cousinage.

I still had no enthusiasm for this whole squabble in June 1976, when a colleague asked me to write a foreword to a collection of papers from a scholarly symposium on abortion held on campus the previous year. I had no desire to put my name on any document relating to the subject, but agreed to read the galley proofs. The papers all treated abortion at a high level of inquiry. I was especially fascinated, however, with the chapter of Judith Blake, a public opinion analyst then at Berkeley (now at UCLA). Drawing on her analysis of years of surveys, she showed that in all major respects the *Wade* and *Bolton* decisions by the Supreme Court ran contrary to national sentiment. This came as a surprise to me, for my impression from the press was that abortion on demand had majority support. Professor Blake's research was especially credible to me because of her personal agreement with abortion freedom. Her message to fellow believers was that a court-enforced policy is inadequate as a dike to hold back the waters of national will, and that they ought not imagine that the issue had found its quietus. I did not write the foreword, but I was impressed by Judith Blake.

Three or four days later *Newsweek* carried a guest editorial page written by Mr. Rockefeller, berating Catholics for their resistance to abortion. It was a poor piece of journalism, written, I supposed, by some flack on his staff. Those who disapproved of abortion were, the text pointed out, using emotional arguments and political pressure to impose their religious strictures on the rest of the country. Two things caught my attention. First, Mr. Rockefeller was singling out my church for condemnation as an overbearing and regressive villain. And second, virtually every fact he used to stage his accusation was contradicted by what I had just read in Blake. Better use of fact I considered due from a man who, more than anyone alive, had sponsored population control programs throughout the world (not always by popular demand) and had sat in the chair of the Presidential Commission on Population Growth and the American Future. And so, offended more by this well-mannered deception than by the bush-league anger of our erstwhile pickets, I wrote a letter to the editor which appeared four weeks later:

> Three years ago the Supreme Court struck down virtually all state laws controlling abortion. Opponents of that decision, says John D. Rockefeller 3d, are mostly Catholics bent on forcing their peculiar religious beliefs undemocratically upon the nation.
>
> Mr. Rockefeller does not speak the truth. According to the Gallup polls, a clear majority of Americans is of the opinion that:
>
> (1) Human life begins at conception or at quickening, and the unborn are persons before birth.
>
> (2) There should be legal restraints on abortion.
>
> (3) Abortion should be lawful if the mother's health is endangered or if the child will likely be deformed, but *not* if the child is simply unwanted.
>
> (4) Abortion should in any case be unlawful after the third month.
>
> (5) It should also be unlawful without the husband's consent.
>
> (6) It should be lawful only in hospitals.
>
> Each of these views is held invariably by a majority of both Catholics and non-Catholics, both men and women, as shown in surveys commissioned by pro-abortionists and conducted by Gallup before and after the Court decision. It is these views that had been incorporated into laws in every state in the Union.
>
> Those Catholics who do disagree with the minority values imposed by the Supreme Court, who prefer to live according to the national will as expressed by the common law and the statutes of the states, who are willing to put their convictions to the proof by working to amend the Constitution which would require a more

massive consent than any other undertaking in the American political process—these Catholics are mightily exasperated when accused of being a backward minority coercively imposing their religious strictures on an unwilling country. The accusation is simply bigotry. One wonders whether the pages of *Newsweek* would have been available for a similar slur on our Jewish countrymen.

Catholics have invoked no peculiar Catholic dogma against abortion. We are simply raising our voices against a popular form of murder. If this seems unseemly: well, there were times past when life was wantonly destroyed and Catholics were not much heard from. I am proud it is otherwise now.[1]

My letter led me to learn several other things. Mr. Rockefeller was distressed by it, because it showed that Catholic prejudice and unenlightenment had a foothold still even at Notre Dame; he had thought otherwise because of his long association with Father Hesburgh, his eventual successor as chairman of the board of the Rockefeller Foundation. I found myself paying him a visit in his Manhattan office. It was an amiable interview, perhaps due to our common bonds with Father Hesburgh and Mr. Rockefeller's son, Jay, an admired friend of mine. But it was disheartening. The displayed fact that abortion on demand was approved by only a small minority of Americans, and had been imposed on the entire country by seven jurists—this fact seemed to me to be what we had to reckon with, not anything done by fifty million Catholics whose opinions on abortion largely matched those of all citizens. It was the Court's policy, not mine, which seemed politically vulnerable. What struck me most throughout our conversation was that this fact in no way disturbed him. He did not challenge or deny it; he simply let it pass him by. As an ingenuous academic whose vocation and training were to reverence facts and to shape my understanding round their contours, I was appalled. And since the name and word of John D. Rockefeller III were accorded more unquestioning faith than those of any Catholic bishop I knew, I was doubly appalled.

My second lesson came in the mail. Most of the letters ignored the political point I was trying to make and expressed indignation or support regarding my moral views on abortion, which was not the point I was arguing with Mr. Rockefeller. Some wrote, as one did: "Why don't you Catholics quit all the crap about abortions you are putting out? . . . Do you think for a minute that, if the Pope were to threaten ex-communication to the Irish and most catholic people in the world, much of the slaughter in Northern Ireland couldn't be avoided?" In another vein: "I am not a Catholic, I'm sort of a feminist who is opposed to abortion and not for any high blown ideals about the sanctity of human life, but simply because when I see a newborn's eyes I do see a person in there, and it's obvious he's been in there for some time. I'm in nursing and sickened by the sad little plastic bags in the utility room." What gave me most to consider were letters accusing me of hatred and bigotry. "Provost Burtchaell's prejudicial innuendo of some sort of dark media conspiracy between Jews and *Newsweek* doubtless leaves your editors chuckling, along with most of your subscribers. Nonetheless, such canards by the Spiro Agnews and Burtchaell's [sic] of our time manage to scatter portions of their droppings and infect the body politic." I replied to all of these letters, telling the writers that since my own father was Jewish I thought myself free of anti-Semitism. But the letters served to ratify the point I first made. That our Jewish countrymen do not take criticism—real or imagined, bigoted or reasonable—lightly, my mail gave witness. But Catholics, who have not had to suffer oppression and disdain as severely as have Jews, are beginning to lose their polite, thin smile when they are mistreated in public.

I came away from my Rockefeller Center colloquy chastened and thoughtful. I had entered, by only a few paces, the precincts of abortion advocacy and had met with a disrespect for fact, persons, and meaning that I had thought characteristic of the prolife group. It teased me as a challenge, and I resolved to pursue the issue—though quietly—and to give a fuller hearing to the voices which spoke for abortion as an acceptable form of birth control.

I thought it well to inventory my own biases. They deserved at least to be known. Since I was male and celibate and childless and Catholic and a priest and a theologian—viewed by many to be as disqualified from understanding abortion as Tiny Tim was from the Olympic hammer throw—I thought it especially needful to inquire into my early formation. What underlay my quiet conviction that abortion was the killing of an innocent child, a savage crime?

Had I been indoctrinated? We Catholics are thought to labor under heavy thought control. Still, after twenty-four years in Catholic educational institutions before going to Cambridge for my doctorate, I could not recall being taught anything about abortion. Perhaps it had come up, but there was nothing left to memory. What about preaching? The only sermon on abortion which I ever heard, in a lifetime of churchgoing, was one I gave myself to a gathering of college students at their request. Reading? Until reading those galley proofs I had never read a book on the subject. My files, which represented the many interests I followed, held no folder on abortion, not a single clipping. If there had been a concerted policy of thought control, it was either very lazy or very subtle.

The first notice I remember of the awesome subject was occasioned by one or another of the periodic arrests of Dr. Ruth Barnett, our local abortionist in Portland, Oregon. I was a young boy, and in my mind's eye I somehow confused her with a local madame. It does not seem such a violent misunderstanding to think that one lady would make it her business to sponsor the pelvic misadventures of men and also to profit from those of women. Another youthful glimpse was given by several young women who came from various states to live with us, to see their pregnancies through, and bear their children. Abortion was never mentioned. In its way, I suppose, that taught a boy something, as also the easy way we were glad to have them in our family.

Then, when I was moving to the other side of adolescence, I gained some insight into abortion from a nun. Sister Dolores, for years and years, presided over a special ward in a children's nursery where my mother did volunteer work and I sometimes visited. I was welcomed anywhere on the premises except in Sister Dolores's ward, which I knew was for special children. The summer I went away to college she took me in at last to see her little ones: two dozen blighted little children. They were mongoloids, hydrocephalics, microcephalics, children with spina bifida and various sorts of paralysis: all beyond the ability of their families to nurture them. And in that one room, where three women tended their nurselings with so little life to live, I learned what child care is. Love filled that nursery as setting sunlight warmly lights a misty evening. I go back occasionally to refresh that special memory of special love. It was through the nursery that I stood as godfather to a newborn not expected to live, but who went on to live (Sister Dolores meant him to), to be taken into a fine family as a welcome son, and to be a favorite godson over these now nearly thirty years. Of abortion, in a silent way, this all said something.

As a priest I spent some of my early years doing research at Cambridge University. The issue arose there, and not silently. Around 1964, I spent an evening as invited speaker in a circle of the Cambridge Humanists, in search of an exchange with people of more untrammeled mind than I. After we had rambled and wrangled over every imaginable subject, the moderator spoke up. How, she asked, did I defend my condemnation of abortion? Somewhat rattled, I said I could not remember ever mentioning it. But, she pressed on, I was a Catholic and so naturally they knew what I thought. "Why not ask me, instead?" I ventured. To the question finally put, I said that I knew of no transition after conception which appeared to transform one into something notably different from what one was before, but that if there were such a moment, puberty was surely more drastic than birth. Therefore the respect I had for another human being I would have to extend back to his or her beginnings. Birth seemed an unreasonable moment to begin acknowledging another's rights. My statement fared poorly. Rights, stated the moderator, were a flimsy abstraction, a metaphysical nonsense. She was governed in her treatment of others by something more substantial: what she felt towards them. How, then, I asked (turned to this thought for the first time in my life), would she differentiate her position from the Final Solution to the Jewish Problem? For the Nazis it was not enough that one was human; one had to have certain further qualifications in order to survive, and those qualifications were of the party's choosing. My view was that to be human was enough, and that rights were necessary to any humane society. Hitler provided an incendiary end to the evening. In paying my farewells I noted to them that I was well aware of having been their guest because I represented an authoritarian tradition. I had accepted their invitation in order to know their nonauthoritarian ways better. What sent me home confused was that we had discussed perhaps a dozen different subjects—many of them sharply debated in my church—and in this group dedicated to putting down dogma, superstition, and orthodoxy, a group of twenty persons that evening, there had not been a single dissent among themselves on a single subject. That evening, which occasioned the first conversation about abortion which I can remember, ended Humanistically but not well.

My suspicion—faint at first and then hardly to be believed—that there was a sort of crypto-orthodoxy on abortion and perhaps other subjects—was reinforced on another evening at a lecture by Professor A. S. Parkes, known for his work on animal reproduction. His topic was population control, and though he addressed it with enthusiasm warming to evangelical fervor, I did notice that he showed no enthusiasm for abortion, which at that time had been widely established by Americans in Japan. His audience was clearly in favor of anything that would prevent indiscriminate breeding by foreigners, especially those in less cultivated lands. I asked Professor Parkes at question time why he seemed to withhold approval from the Japanese method, since it was so effective. In the face of that audience only a man of abiding conviction could have professed any dissident moral misgivings. "Because," he replied, "it violates the principle of the conservation of matter." It was good for a chuckle. I blushed for the man.

I recall, too, some fleeting images. I stood once, as a graduate student, on a street in Luxor, Egypt, and watched a mother hunkered down, patting dough onto the hard dirt walkway to bake in the sun. The dough was so covered with flies it looked like raisin bread, and her children who awaited it had flies all over their faces. Directly behind them, in one of the more solid buildings of the town, stood the Society for the Prevention of Cruelty to Animals ("Royal" had been effaced). I could look through the doorway and see, in his cool office, a man surrounded by medical provisions, waiting for some farmer's donkey to be brought in with yoke sores. Sister Dolores, I thought, would treat no donkey while children ate off the dirt. Another time, when I was studying in England, word was published of twenty-eight horses en route from Ireland to a mucilaginous destiny in France. They went down in a Channel storm. Tragic descriptions were given of the heart-rending whinnying of the poor creatures as their freighter wallowed in the waves; questions were asked in Parliament about equine and maritime safety. Sister Dolores, I thought, would have heard other cries in the night.

It was something much more explicit that drew me to a more considered view of abortion, however. It was two theological arguments I had. One was with an Episcopalian moralist and one was with the pope. In 1966 Joseph Fletcher published his work on situation ethics. I attacked it because Fletcher was willing to condone virtually any act if it was well intended:

> Despite its name, situation ethics does not revolve on situation at all. . . . The crucial factor in the method is motive. The system really should be called intention ethics. What is novel about it is the claim that any action, in any situation, with any consequences, is good if it is an action of love, and evil if an action of nonlove. Love, urges Fletcher, is the only norm, the only measure. . . . It is essentially indifferent what forms a man's behavior takes, provided this behavior be the outward expression of inward caring. No one can ever be blamed if his intentions were good. In other words, the moral value of a man's deeds is wholly contained in the purpose he brings to them. It is precisely this axiom which I feel to be both the pivot and the weakness of the entire system. The New Moralists are saying that the moral value of an act is what you put into it. They neglect, it seems to me, that it also involves what you get out of the act.

On a phenomenological view, human behavior consists of count-less day-to-day actions scattered across the surface of our lives. Generally we put very little of ourselves into any particular act. We do not manifest our full and true person in any one moment. If we should be voluntarily crucified or something like that, we would most likely be drawing ourselves up to full strength, so to speak—but we are not often voluntarily crucified. Single actions are not expressive of our total character nor utterly decisive in our life. But over a period of time certain characteristic trends and traits appear, personality patterns emerge, an overall direction of our affairs is felt and observed. . . . What I do and what I am are constantly interacting upon one another. My character discloses itself in what I do, yet can be shaped and modified by changes in what I do. My life works from the inside out and *also* from the outside in. In Christian terms, the state of grace and the state of sin refer to this deep level of fundamental option which is forming and stabilizing itself over the course of a lifetime. It would be difficult to localize conversion or serious sin within any singular act, and unobservant to assert that there could be much short-term oscilla-tion between one fundamental option and its opposite. Yet these states are slowly entered and reinforced by the swarm of minor daily deeds. Fletcher, it appears, acknowledges only a one-way traffic: he points out—quite well—how purpose shapes deeds, but neglects that conversely deeds shape purpose.[2]

Fletcher several times argued for abortion as the least troublesome way out of a vexed situation. It seemed, like many of his illustrations, to be a way of convenience (done, of course, out of "love") at the cost of another's life. And as a man who had by then been the invited guest of many people's con-sciences, I was more and more impressed with the way a terrifying pregnancy obliged people to make moral choices that were the making or the breaking of them.

One young wife I knew well worked as a nurse with newborns. The negligence of a fellow nurse exposed her to a child with rubella shortly after she conceived, and the negligence of physicians kept her and her husband waiting through three months of misadministered tests until they were told their first child stood a 60 percent likelihood of being born deformed. That couple saw their pregnancy through and I baptized an unblemished daughter afterwards. But they grew to be great and unselfish parents in those days of waiting, when they reaffirmed that marriage was to serve, not for self. By contrast, I remember so well walking under a high moon late one night with a former student. It was the eve of his wedding, and long hours after the rehearsal dinner only we were still up, strolling together. He told me then that some months earlier he had paid to abort the child of another woman he had impregnated. It seemed simplest, he said. And I had to agree: it seemed simplest. But in my mind's eye he went to his wedding with an undissolved ruthlessness about him. I have dreaded it ever since. Childbearing, I realized better, thanks to Joe Fletcher's pathetic expediency, draws us into untold obligation. There is an intuition at the center of Christian faith which tells that this obligation is not to be shirked by defruiting the womb.

Neither is it recklessly to be begun. That came clear to me in 1968 when I took issue with Pope Paul VI over his letter on contraception. I had just become chairman of Notre Dame's Department of Theology, and as my inaugural act I was hapless enough to call *Humanae Vitae* "disappointingly inadequate and largely fallacious."

The Holy Father, I thought, had rightly known our world for what it is: grudging to children, just as it is grudging toward any claims on its love that strain our generosity. Where he went wrong was in locating the grudge, the evil, in the very use of contraception, which he called artificial and unnatural. He said too little, I thought, not too much. It is the entire course of child-bearing, not the individual acts of contraception, that is crucial to the life of a marriage. He was not, I argued, teaching emphatically enough why we need to have children—particularly as Christians:

> Marriage, like Baptism, begins in faith. . . . It is an open-ended abandonment to an unpredictable person, who is known and cherished enough that one can make the surrender. . . . When you tie yourself to a person, you cannot control your future. Everyone of us has within himself an unbelievable potential for love and for generosity but we do not bring it out very willingly. It has to be torn out of us. And the thing about Christian marriage is that the surprises encountered demand a love and generosity from us that we can in no way calculate or control. If that be so, then the incalculability of the demands of children fits very closely into the generosity a man and a woman share in marriage. . . .
>
> Children are not threats to love or competitors for it—they are new claims upon it, new tugs on the ungenerous heart to force it open further than it felt it could go. . . . Now obviously physical resources are not fathomless, and children must have bread. But in our age and culture, when parents feed their children cake and live in fear of a bread shortage, the church weeps—and rightly so—that the children are starving in a famine of love.

Many who regard all genital matters as the same expected that, as I was willing to approve of contraception within an overall commitment to children, I would naturally do the same for abortion. But I saw the bond holding parent to child like the bond gripping spouse to spouse: carefully to be bound by, relentlessly to be held to.

> Barbara Cadbury, returned from a good-cheer tour in Asia for the Planned Parenthood Federation, wrote enthusiastically in *Family Planning in East Asia* of the "courageous sense of realism" with which Japanese kill their children. But the government, she says, now feels "that abortion is, as a regular method of birth control, harmful to the individual despite its benefit to the nation."

The individual harmed is presumably the individual killing, not the individual killed. (I am reminded of the complaint made by the Commandant of Auschwitz, that the excessive shipments of Jews to be gassed and cremated worked unreasonable hardship on the prison guards.) But Mrs. Cadbury's most telling remark is this: "No other country in the world has so rapidly passed from fertility-motivated habits to producing only desired and cherished children." The two million or so children each year who are not "desired and cherished" are cut out of the womb and thrown away.

[We] should see it just the other way around from Mrs. Cadbury. If a man and woman have brought to life in the womb a child who is not desired or cherished, their problem is not how to murder the child but how to learn to desire and cherish him. The Church would concede that it is often easier to kill your child than to love him. But to the Japanese parents and to Mrs. Cadbury she recommends the latter.[3]

There was hellish controversy after that was published, and I received more abusive letters then from Catholics than I did later from Jews. But I had somehow framed for myself a sturdy conviction that abortion is killing, and that, like all purposeful killing, it requires one somehow to ignore, if only briefly, that the victim is one's own flesh and blood. It was a conviction I drew from the experiences and stories of many people, most of whom I do not speak of here. And it resonated well with my religious belief that God's character was best seen in Jesus crucified, a man come to give abounding life, but a life that grows through self-forfeiture.

After my two encounters, with the prolife pickets and with Mr. Rockefeller, a fascination began to grow about this question toward which I had been indifferent. I resolved to look into it more closely. One endeavor, at the request of Father Hesburgh, was to convene an open conference at Notre Dame that would allow men and women of whatever commitment to discuss abortion at the level of respectful discourse every such great issue needs. That was done in 1979.[4] To prepare for the meeting I began to read extensively in the abortion literature and to pursue a series of questions that emerged. First, I set myself to read the stories of people who had experienced abortion. What I found in those stories was an account substantially different from what abortion advocates were describing. And so, restricting myself to accounts that were most sympathetically and extensively recounted, I tried to analyze what those women and men had to tell, and brought forth the first of these essays.

Then I determined to examine the argumentation on behalf of abortion choice. I studied a few publications on the prolife side, but it seemed far more interesting to listen to people who were unlikely to speak from my perspective. My evaluation of those arguments comprises another of the essays here.

Gloria Steinem recently asked, "If Hitler were alive, whose side would he be on?" Since the Third Reich accorded women so few individual rights, and forbade Aryan women to abort, she identifies him with the prolife side. But more commonly the analogy with the Holocaust has been invoked by those who see abortion to be a similar form of wholesale extermination. It seemed important to study the Holocaust and to see if there were any grounds for fair comparison either way. That issued in my third essay.

Next comes a study I did of the *Dred Scott* case and the proslavery argument it legitimated. It has often been called an ancestor of *Wade* and *Bolton* and the proabortion argument, but I wanted to give slavery a more thorough examination than underlay most of the accusations and most of the denials.

In the course of my inquiry I stumbled upon the fact that birth, which abortion advocates most commonly propose as the threshold of personhood and human rights, is not that rigidly honored by physicians who wish to eliminate handicapped newborn infants. Infanticide is widely practiced in hospital nurseries, and is explained by arguments which, upon examination, I found to move in the same direction as those favoring abortion. This led to my last essay here.

I do not foresee that these essays will bring many readers to a change of mind on the subject of abortion. My own was not reversed by what I learned. It was immeasurably instructed. What I do offer here is, I hope, fair though not neutral, thorough if not exhaustive, and provocative even when not agreeable.

Various persons have been good enough to read portions of this manuscript and it has benefited from their suggestions, though it has not incorporated them all. I wish to thank them here: Elizabeth Christman, Richard Conklin, Vincent DeSantis, James Dittes, Constance Gaynor, Stanley Hauerwas, Donald Kommers, Arthur Kornhaber, Robert Krieg, Mary Ann Lamanna, Kathleen and Stephen Moriarty, Walter Murphy, John Noonan, Mary Ann Roemer, Thomas Shaffer, Thomas Stritch, and Rene Torrado. I am also grateful to James Foley, James J. O'Connell III, and Patrick Trueman for assistance in research. The libraries of Notre Dame, Princeton, and Harvard universities offered every help I ever asked of them. The Albert Zahm Research-Travel Fund gave of its bounty to support my work during the summers of 1978 and 1979. The manuscript has passed more than once through the careful hands of Sandy DeWulf, Amy Kizer, Margaret Jasiewicz, Cheryl Reed, and Janet Wright, typists to whom my colleagues and I at Notre Dame are continually indebted. Lastly, I must acknowledge the support of Jim Andrews, my publisher, who engaged me to write this book well before he could know its shape and sense, and whose recent death has left many of us without an admired friend.

Maritain House in Princeton
December 28, 1980

Essay 1

Rachel Weeping
The Veterans of Abortion

SOME TIME AGO the National Abortion Rights Action League bought the back page of the *New York Times*. The ad advised readers that the "*so-called prolife people* are back at it," compelling women to bear unwanted children.

> "But I'm only 12 years old."
> "I was raped."
> "We'll have to go on relief."
> "My father will kill me."
> "The doctor says it will die before it's two."
> "My IUD failed."
> "I'm 50, I thought I couldn't get pregnant."

The "COMPULSORY PREGNANCY" people "have *one* answer to everything: 'YOU MUST HAVE THAT BABY WHETHER YOU LIKE IT OR NOT!' " Readers who were asked to dig down in their jeans—buttoned be they to the left or to the right—and who know the abortion scene had more to wince at than did the typesetter who had to hustle up all the boldface, caps, and italics.

The ad was, well, a misrepresentation. There are indeed girls who are twelve years old and pregnant, women who would need public aid, women and girls who have suffered rape, and who want abortions. But these situations, desperate and tragic, put forward so strenuously by NARAL and other agencies that make the case for governmentally funded abortion on demand—these cases generally represent only a small fraction (in this instance, perhaps less than 5 percent) of the nearly 1,500,000 legally induced abortions in America each year.

Any public appeal is naturally going to put forward first its Most Needy Cases, but the public also wants to know who the average beneficiaries will be. An appropriations committee deliberating over welfare budgets knows that there are widows out there who have to heat their apartments with their gas ovens; but they will vote no subsidy until they know how much real destitution is going to be alleviated by the cash, and how much flimflam subsidized. Likewise, one outrageous rape-murder has us ready to lock up all young gang offenders for life; but anyone who touches the law had better first learn the full story about this sad traffic of juvenile criminals. Needs must be accurately depicted before sound public policy can be framed.

So with abortion. The American public lacks a reliable sense of who is actually sitting in those abortion clinic waiting rooms round the country. We are told they are mostly blacks; no, others say, there are crowds of suburban

1

white matrons. Most are unmarried; no, there are more married. Their general opinion afterwards is that abortion, while not pleasant, was something they had to have at the time; no, most women will tell you it was rotten, and that they are bothered by some remorse. What is one to believe?

The most influential sources of statistics on U.S. abortion practice are the Alan Guttmacher Institute and the cluster of other agencies linked to Planned Parenthood. But the best single source of statistics on the progress of the Vietnam War was General Westmoreland's office. Eventually some news people thought that it didn't quite tell the full story, and began to wander through the villages talking to the people. What one needs in the case of abortion is an extended visit to the villages, and that is available in Linda Bird Francke's book, *The Ambivalence of Abortion* (New York: Random House, 1978; hereinafter cited as *F*). After reading it one should pick up its natural supplement, *Pregnant by Mistake*, by Katrina Maxtone-Graham (New York: Liveright, 1973; hereinafter cited as *G*).

Both books present interviews. Maxtone-Graham had extended conversations with seventeen women, before abortion on demand was legal nationally but after it was permitted in New York. Francke offers about seventy-five interviews. They are briefer, but more varied: with women, men, and couples; before, during, and as much as fifty years after the abortion experience. Both authors are explicitly sympathetic to abortion choice, and succeed in being relatively fair, inobtrusive interviewers. Francke writes in the aftermath of her own abortion, which she reflected on in a powerful "Jane Doe" piece on the op-ed page of the *New York Times* on May 14, 1976. That column remains one of the most haunting stories of the genre. She has three children by two marriages and, when writing her book, was sans spouse. Maxtone-Graham, also a New Yorker, is married, with four children, and much aware of her own experience of having been adopted and, as an adult, having traced her physical mother and also found her brother.

Their own personal sagas lend intensity to the inquiry without skewing it. Their biases rise up in occasional questions, but the interviewees are quite determined to say it their own way, and they do. In fact, so far do they stray from the conventional wisdom sustaining abortion choice today that Francke's book has gotten a few heavy frowns from fellow feminist *litteratae*.

What makes these two books helpful is that both authors have let the women and men unfold their personal experience of abortion in all its confusion and hurt and courage and isolation. Their stories are rich and varied enough to sustain inquiry beyond (and sometimes athwart) what the interviewers say by way of summary. There is much more to be said on the subject than these people tell about their approximately one hundred abortions. But they do say much that we are rarely told, and what they tell is too large, too irreducible, to be compacted simply into percentages.

What Francke and Maxtone-Graham do not offer is any systematic reflection on what their interviewees have told them. Had they undertaken such an analysis, they would have seen emerging—from the veterans of the abortion experience—a profoundly unsettling story. Their documentation of the abortion experience is strong evidence—stronger in some sense than the indict-ments of antiabortionists—against the portrayal of abortion by its advocates.

The women who seek abortion are described by prochoice advocates as either ordinary, sexually active women for whom contraception has failed or victimized women (victimized by a pathological pregnancy, or rape, or incest, or poverty, or family hostility). Childbirth for either group is an unreasonable burden, more than they should be obliged to cope with. Scholars who have studied women at risk for unwanted pregnancy have for some years disputed that portrayal. The stories studied here, stories recounted by abortion vete-rans themselves, describe a situation so different, so much more complex, that one comes to regard the proabortion portrayal as misleading and evasive. By their own accounts here the abortors are estranged, submissive, and incoher-ent. They are *estranged*: detached from the rooted security of sure family bonds, unaccountable to persons trusted enough that their standards count, alienated individuals without a continuum of generations in which they hold an honored place. They are *submissive*: ready to acquiesce in abuse and neglect by their men, inarticulate in the face of inquiry, unready to take care of themselves even after mistreatment. These women show noticeable hostility towards those who misuse them, but instead of coming forward more asser-tively they make impulsive gestures that do almost nothing to establish their own responsibility, almost nothing that would make them persons to reckon with. Instead of standing up to those who victimize them, by an almost pathetic misdirection they assert their dominance over a creature that lies at their disposal. Just as child battering misdirects parental hostility, away from those dominating persons who are its source and toward others who are helpless, so abortion appears to deflect much rage and frustration. So re-peatedly there is an aggravated helplessness in relation to someone stronger. And so continually that unhappy situation is more reinforced than relieved by abortion, which is an exercise of *incoherent* self-assertion, yet self-injuring and so victimizing. Violence begets more violence. Humiliation stoops instead of stiffening.

Dislocation of Purpose

A theme that runs like a leitmotiv through these tales is incoherence. It establishes itself from the outset in the inexplicable way so many of the women came to be pregnant. Virtually every woman and man interviewed is compe-tent in contraceptive procedures and has access to them. Every birth-control clinic has its in-house stories about contraceptive ignorance, like the one told of the woman who came in, astonished and pregnant, even though her boyfriend had had a vasectomy. He had even shown her the scar. Where? She pointed: right under the armpit (*F*:39).

But the women in these books are not backward or naive about how to contracept. Why, then, do they do it so ineptly? They are so haphazard about it as to seem almost purposeful. In a very few cases conception does result from outright contraceptive failure, no matter what the method. But more typical is the fifteen-year-old, youngest of all the group: "I was going with this

3

guy, you know. It wasn't meant to happen, but it just happened, you know. And I wasn't ready for it. I wasn't using any sort of birth control. I don't know why not. I just wasn't. We were screwing all the time, but I guess I just didn't think about getting pregnant" (F:198). This girl was just emerging from her second abortion in three months. One young woman, when the interviewer noticed that she hadn't seemed worried about pregnancy, mused that she was, "well, kind of ambivalent. I think in a way I wanted to get pregnant." Why? "Sort of as self-punishment. I was in a kind of a 'down' time. And also great curiosity about it. I find it very reassuring to know that I'm fertile" (G:52)

Sandy, who at twenty-one seems not very wise and has had a hysterectomy in the aftermath of her abortion, claims her priest told her it was doubly wrong to use protection when having sex with her boyfriend. So she wouldn't: "At least I hadn't prepared myself to go to bed with the guy that I was going to marry." When her mate told her to go on the pill, "I told him that I just could not force myself to do that, because I felt it was wrong to prepare myself for a sexual relationship" (G:129, 130) (this was after five years of sex). A married woman of thirty, mother of two, who aborted the third, tells that after five years on the pill she began to suspect that it had made her sterile. She wondered, "What have I done? What has happened to my body? And I realized now that this was a part of my getting pregnant. It only happened after the abortion: that I could really see there had been something to being able to say, 'Well, I can get pregnant. I haven't done myself irrevocable harm'" (G:114). Another woman, reminiscing about three abortions during her twenties: "The reason, ultimately, was because I was very self-destructive. But the reason at *that* time seemed to me that if I used my diaphragm I would be *admitting* to a kind of 'lack of spontaneity.' You know, that if I didn't use a diaphragm, it was *his* fault, 'he forced me.' You know, 'I didn't *plan* it ahead of time.' I didn't take responsibility for it, you see" (G:74). Robin Terhune, thirty, single, with two abortions behind her: "I was totally irresponsible about birth control. It was like I was just waiting to be punished. I set myself up for a real shitty thing. I didn't go out to do it, but I didn't do anything to not make it happen. I'm always dangling with fate. I was all hot to get pregnant. I don't know what it is" (F:65). Hans Lehfeldt, NYU professor of Ob-Gyn, discounts contraceptive failure in what he describes as willful exposure to unwanted pregnancy: "These patients have such ambivalent feelings about pregnancy that neither contraception nor pregnancy offers a solution. They want both, so they alternate between contraception and exposure" (F:149, 150).

No single explanation would seem able to account for the curious want of attention to contraception among these women and men who eventually came to the drastic judgment that they did not want a child born of their conceiving. But there is a repeated dislocation of purpose, an implausible hazard even on the part of some who from the beginning had wanted nothing to do with children. One is not quite sure how to understand what "unwanted pregnancies" and "unwanted children" would be, when the very mechanism of wanting, the compass of purpose, has become so demagnetized.

The Subordinated Female

One thing any of us needs in order to pursue our purposes, to define and to know our wants, is a healthy ego. There seems to be some kind of ego deficiency sapping the pursuits of the women that Katrina and Linda asked to explain themselves.

Francke cautions that some of the pregnancies were not nearly as haphazard as one might first think, especially among the older teenagers. "In a 1974 study, 'The Resolution of Teenage First Pregnancies,' fully 72 percent of the white teenagers and 32 percent of the blacks aged fifteen to nineteen interviewed said that they became pregnant to force a marriage. Other teenagers, especially those who were mistreated or came from foster homes, said they were looking for a source of love in a baby, whether they had any affection for the father of the child or not. Another reason was the desire to set up their own household, while others felt that becoming pregnant and carrying the pregnancy to term made them feel more adult and mature. Loneliness was another factor in the pregnancy decision, and among lower-income teenagers the economic carrot of welfare payments to dependent children. For the student whose grades were poor, pregnancy provided a feeling of creative accomplishment, while for teenagers who were not as attractive as the others, pregnancy was a proof of fecundity and sexual desirability" (F:183) As at least some of these women later realized, a child conceived amid stability will tend to draw people even more tightly together, but in an unstable situation pregnancy is a poor remedy; it can alienate rather than rally those who should be together. The women Francke describes are not schemers, or women of purpose; they seem somehow to be ricocheting through life.

So in the interviews. One is struck, for instance, by the hapless way many of them cling to men you wouldn't need your best friend to tell you were schlemiels. There are teenage memories of how girls thought they had to be ready to yield sex indiscriminately to the boys on demand, or else suffer rejection. There is a pervasive acquiescence in these women that does not, however, seem to pass away with adolescence. For example, one meets a professional woman, divorced, with a daughter, living with an eighteen-year-old boy (ten years her junior) who kept walking out on her, yet by whom she had two aborted pregnancies (F:51, 53).

In the matter of contraception, the women note very frequently that the men insisted that it was their—the women's—responsibility. Despite the fact that female contraceptives are either hazardous to health or elaborately cumbersome, it is interesting how often, with the women's acquiescence, the men refuse to use condoms for no other reason than their own convenience. As one woman, the mother of eight, explained, "I guess we were just careless. My husband didn't want me to take pills. My mother has cancer, and no one can prove the pills don't cause it. The IUD? I'm not sold on them. Anything like that can cause something. And the diaphragm. My second one is a diaphragm baby. So I leave it up to my husband, and we both watch the calendar. He hates the rubber. He says it's like taking a shower with his boots on" (F:97). A husband explains, "She felt that it was a one-sided deal, that it

5

was the woman who had to use birth control. I refuse to wear rubbers. Rubbers are very insensitive, and putting them on is the fastest two-handed game in town" (*F*:128; cf. *G*:330). Another man, veteran of nine abortions, feels similarly: "I can't stand wearing rubbers. It's like washing your feet with your socks on" (*F*:143).

And the two books are full of "postponed" vasectomies, enough to keep a clinic going for a year. I was reminded of a psychiatry professor I had years ago, who often told stories of his earlier obstetrics practice. Frequently, he recalled, couples would come in to have the wife's tubes tied. He would explain that this was a fairly tricky surgical operation and would recommend instead a vasectomy, which involved no health risk and was simple enough to be performed during an office call. The husbands always said they would think it over, but no couple ever returned. The male seems to dominate whenever given leave to do so.

The female counteraction to this pattern of male self-concern seems to be covert and even self-destructive. One mother of two, age thirty, got pregnant after the family had moved to accommodate a career opportunity for her husband, at the cost of her teaching position. "I had passed my thirtieth birthday a year before, and here I was, faced with—What am I going to do with my life? That's a very real question to deal with when you've just given up a job that you really like. And I think all of those feelings were tied up with why I got pregnant. I don't know whether one wants to say it was a kind of —almost a hostility toward my husband, almost a subconscious anger that we had left where we were living. Although, in reality, we had discussed all of that" (*G*:115). Another woman, thirty-two, mother of five, who had conceived during an unaffectionate episode, reflected: "Maybe I was saying, 'All right, you bastard, I'll get pregnant and you'll have to pay for it' " (*F*:105).

Acquiescent Yet Angry

The decision to abort is frequently tinctured by a strange acquiescence-cum-anger. One youngster, married a year and now pregnant at eighteen, was faced by her hostile in-laws, who had opposed the marriage and, believing that a baby would preserve it, told the young couple to move out in two weeks if they hadn't had an abortion. "I love the baby. I love my husband. I just think it would be better for him if I have the abortion. I'll get over it. I'm sure there'll be a lot of times when I'll think about it, but we got so many problems now. So many. I know I can have another baby someday. But it's this one I love now. I just love her so much. . . . But my mother-in-law says we got to be off the farm in two weeks—if I keep on having my baby" (*F*:95). Another, about to undergo for a second time a second-trimester abortion, says, "My boyfriend and I decided on an abortion because Andy is going through a divorce and it would have put another trauma on him. This is harder for him than me. He just didn't want a baby. I really did want it, because I didn't think I could mentally handle the abortion, but he talked me into going to Planned Parenthood" (*F*:85).

One girl (one of only two interviewees not to choose abortion) lived years in a fantasy romance with her high school hero-sweetheart who went off to college leaving her pregnant and who, the very night she eventually gave birth to their daughter, was off in Canada in bed with another girl because he "needed somebody" (G:413). She describes her relationship with him: "I wasn't too upset about people finding out. In a way I was kind of proud of it. Because I was having David's baby. . . . It was also kind of an ego thing for me, because David was very popular in high school. Everybody knew David and liked David. And so people used to look up to me, you know, because David cared about me. And the fact that I would be having his baby was kind of impressive, I thought" (G:389) She also describes her father and mother: "Through this whole thing, anything my father said, she went along. She is completely submissive. That's a whole big thing that has to do with my relationship with my mother, too. Anything my father says is right. And so she went along with him" (G:389).

It is there in so many of the women: an absence of personal strength, which Judith Bardwick and others have commented on. "I flew home and thought maybe I'd get married instead, but both of the guys I'd been sleeping with said they didn't feel like it and didn't want the responsibility. They both convinced me I should have the abortion. I wasn't very assertive then" (F:89). "My husband, I don't think was as much concerned, perhaps, as I was. Maybe I—[laughs] you know, maybe I'm a little insecure" (G:334) And a sixteen-year-old: "I get scared real easy, you know. Like I was scared to call that counseling number. You know? It just scared me. Over nothing! Just calling a telephone number! I–I was afraid to do it. And—I don't know, he didn't decide—I didn't even know he was gonna go with me 'til we were talking to the Reverend and he was saying, 'Fly to New York,' and 'You get this and that.' Stig says, you know, 'Yeah, I'm gonna go with her.' And I think, 'Whoa! Far out!' You know. But I didn't say, 'Oh, *before* you weren't gonna go with me.' You know, 'cause he would have been pretty embarrassed" (G:219). The women repeatedly display an unreadiness to assert themselves, to claim fair and fond consideration from their men. Instead, they are uncannily submissive.

The Vanishing Male

As things developed, many women learned that when they became pregnant they found themselves alone. Sometimes the boyfriend would simply hang up the phone. Or he would find some other way to back away. "My boyfriend is twenty-one. I called him this morning, but no one answered. He said he didn't know if he had the time to come with me for the abortion. If he won't be at the house tomorrow before nine, I'm going to leave him a note saying don't bother to see me again. I'm going to be bold" (F:185–86). One young man whose girlfriend, after eight years on-again-off-again and two abortions, won't speak to him, remembers: "When she went for the abortion, I wasn't around. It was frightening to me. I made excuses that I had to be at football practice or something, but in reality it was fear that kept me away. I felt guilty for a long time" (F:146). And a woman who had had an earlier abortion experience with her husband before their marriage recollects how terrible the isolation was. "I can remember just sitting in my apartment on my sofa bed and just not wanting to move. I was aware that some terrible wave of nonfunctioning thing was coming over me and that I needed help. . . . The abortion really was a catalyst that made me start dealing with a lot of s'uit. I was angry at Billy, I had a deep-rooted anger at my sister for always bossing me around and this time being wrong, and there were financial problems. My sister had borrowed money for the abortion and Billy wasn't paying her back, but was going out and buying furniture for his apartment" (F:174).

The resentment of the men is there, but it is so muted. Said one woman: "I think it's going to change our relationship a little. Like he was telling me, it's your fault you're pregnant. You should have done something about it. It's not all my fault. He could have done something about it too. He just says it's up to the girl, and I don't like that at all. . . . He knows that I feel hostile to him right now. He tries to do nice things, and I ignore them. I couldn't be nice back. He told me to call him at home after this thing tonight. I don't even know if I want to talk to him" (F:188). Rarer is the woman who, at forty-one, was looking back across two decades at her abortion and what she considered a very destructive experience: "That was the end of my trust in people. Really, to a great extent. When I saw that both my husband and my father came through at the *last* minute, when it was *safest* to do it—that was it. I have never really trusted anyone since" (G:264).

One has the impression that the pregnancy crisis and abortion disclosed rather than caused the falling away of friends and mates. In case after case there seem to have been no previous bonds generous and giving enough—despite the frequency with which they were anointed as "caring" and "loving"—to sustain much claim on either good sense or energetic support. In so many instances the women simply woke up to find that they had been on their own all along, despite all the couplings. When the emergency erupts, bonds that have been long frayed and rotted simply snap.

Alienation from Parents

One of the very typical responses to this isolation is a repeated unwillingness to confront those who oppose. Parents appear most often in this opponents' role, but the trait is not limited to dealings with them. With a rhythmic frequency, almost that of a refrain, these women describe how unbearable it would have been to suffer parental disapproval or disagreement. "If my parents were dead, then I'd have had that baby. But they're here to remind me of guilt and lay on their disapproval. They're lovely people really, and practice what they preach" (F:61). One boyfriend senses it: "She feels if she does go ahead and have the baby, she's going to miss out on a lot. She wants to go to college, and she can't face telling her mom and dad. That's the worst thing" (F:117).

Mothers in particular loom large. "There's no reason to tell my mother about it. She'd have a fit. She'll never know" (F:201). "My mother doesn't know I'm here. She's sick, and she's been sick for a long time. She didn't know about the first abortion either. I can't tell her because I wouldn't want to upset her. She'd have a fit. I don't think she'd allow me to have an abortion anyway. She'd make me have the baby and then give it up for adoption. If I went through the nine months I wouldn't want to give it up. That's how she had me"

(F:190–91). "I tried to talk to her when I was thinking of having an abortion, but she don't agree with it and she got kind of mad when I was trying to tell her, so I'm going to have to think about what I'm going to tell her after I've had the abortion" (F:57). "I also have a very strict mother who once told me, in high school, that should I ever get in trouble, just to keep going, because she never wanted to see me again" (G:128). And another girl remembered, "I finally broke down and told her. . . . She called me every name she could think of—bitch, whore, slut—which made me feel really terrific" (F:84).

Fathers too are difficult to face in this situation. Several of the mothers concealed their daughters' pregnancies from them. "My father would be shocked if he knew I had slept with anybody. My older sister ran away from home at eighteen. He doesn't speak about her at all. He's very bitter. I was scared" (F:199). For some women, to open this antagonized subject up with their parents would jeopardize the independence they had striven for. "I had made a huge point of not taking any financial assistance from my father after I graduated from college, and I was not about to admit to him that I had made any mistake about anything. It would have been awful to have that child" (F:230). Oddly, this same woman later remarks, "I didn't resent our families for causing us to have the abortion, but then I've always been low on resentment" (F:232). Another gives her predicament: "It would have meant going home to my parents who would—would help me but it—it would crush my grandparents. And definitely everyone in the town would talk. This sort of thing. I don't know how I would be supporting myself; probably to this day I would be depending on my parents for help. It would have meant not being able to finish college. It would have meant a lot of things. I don't know whether—they probably would have encouraged me to give the child up. Although I think they would have supported me in whatever I, you know, finally decided to do" (G:53–54).

As might be anticipated, the parents here described reacted in a variety of ways. Some hastened their daughters off to abortion clinics before the daughters had given that idea much thought. Others seemed more concerned for themselves, or were preoccupied with how they must have raised their child badly. Still others had little counsel to give and simply agreed to whatever their daughter intended to do; in some of these stories one senses more ennui than real support. Some shouted and cursed. But many—very many—simply were never approached. Whatever the outcome, there appears to be a high degree of alienation between these women and their parents, such that they were not often willing to ask their parents in on the crisis. As Francke puts it: "Among the black women I interviewed, some had abortions in spite of their mothers' willingness to take the child. Others had abortions because their mothers wouldn't agree to raise the baby. Among the white women, the role of the parent was more abstract. Over and over again the single women of all ages would admit that they didn't want their parents ever to know about their abortion for fear it would hurt them, although they agreed that the alternative, having the child, would hurt them more. These women didn't give their parents the option to support or reject them. Isolating themselves, the white middle-class single women made their decision alone.

'They wouldn't understand' was a recurring phrase. 'They don't ever need to know' was another" (F:47). It is as she says. The interviews reveal very few women whose maturity stood them well enough to allow a confrontation with parents over this most heartfelt of family dilemmas, with any hope of an agreeable finale.

Resentment of Those Closest

Francke does interview a number of parents of abortees. There are some interesting points to be seen in these conversations. Most of the parents are very solicitous for their children. This arises partly from her sample, which is composed almost exclusively of parents who were accompanying their children through the abortion procedure, and so would not represent the more antagonized. One suspects that the young women may, because of their lack of forthrightness, be painting a prejudiced picture of their parents and may be reporting their reactions as somewhat more irrational than they really were. There is reason to question the fairness and candor of the abortion seekers in their accounts of persons who do not offer them unqualified and uncritical support.

In fact, there is a pattern of need for this support. The women find themselves facing a disaster which, if not uncourted, is at least now unwelcome. They sense inadequate resources of their own to see it through, and look frantically to find who is standing by them. Often there is no one, at least no one of close kinship or friendship. It is a telltale time, and their demand for support is peremptory and urgent.

Many of these women were stung when they encountered rebuffs. One mother of two went to her own obstetrician to ask for an abortion, but was told that in Massachusetts he could not legally perform one at the time. He referred her to Planned Parenthood, who sent her to Pregnancy Counseling Service, who put her in touch with an abortionist in New York, who put her in bed for weeks with a perforated uterus and intestine. "What made me angry was that my own doctor, who's very competent—he's the head obstetrician at the hospital—that he couldn't help me out. Morally he would have, but legally he couldn't. And I know this wouldn't have happened if he had done the abortion. And that's what made me angry. That I had to go and be in someone else's hands, that I knew nothing about, just because I—well—made a mistake and was pregnant" (G:102). One doctor, called on to repair the wreckage of another's botched abortion, said to the woman: " 'I guess you know it's all over,' and all I could think of was don't be like that. Be nicer to me. Help me. I felt really bad. I couldn't stop crying" (F:80).

One woman in her early twenties encountered a put-down from a priest. "After the whole thing was over, I felt very repentant, and I wanted to cleanse myself of my sins. And, you know, 'God has punished me for this horrible sin.' I went to a priest, and he said, 'Well, my dear, but you're excommunicated! You have committed one of the unforgivable sins of the Church and you have to go through the Bishop or the Pope,' or something like that. And I said, to hell with it! That's it, and that was the end of my contact, really, with the Church. I mean, that they could say that to me! . . . In fact, the very fact that they reject me, on the point of this abortion, seems ludicrous to me" (G:149–50). Was the priest insensitive and abusive, or was he telling her this was no petty item she claimed to be confessing? One has no access to his recollection of the encouter. In a sense, though, many of these women feel excommunicated on all sides, at the very time they most crave communion.

One of the male partners gives a clue that some of this experience may have been provoked by the women themselves. He had been opposed to the abortion, but did not discuss his feelings "because it might upset her." He has tried to keep from her how strongly he had been against it. "I was against her for a while, too. Sally is basically a very, very sweet person. She does the things you like to do, because she wants to make you happy. But during the period that she found out she was pregnant, and then she had the abortion, and then for three or four weeks afterwards, she was an entirely different person. She was hard to get along with, she never wanted to do anything. She didn't want to talk about anything, and she acted as if she didn't want me to be around. . . . There wasn't any physical hostility, but the mental hostility was there. It was as if we both hated each other, because when she found she was pregnant, you would gather that I had done something wrong to her" (F:163). One woman herself tells how it was: "When I got pregnant, suddenly my husband and I weren't getting along so well. I was real touchy and oversensitive and I didn't feel so good either. My husband wasn't giving me anything I needed, so we decided to get divorced" (F:110). Another woman, supported by a man other than the one who had impregnated her, recalls: "He was *hurt* by the way I behaved, he said, because I didn't sort of really take him into it, and I didn't feel that he was . . . I mean, to say that he wasn't supportive is not true because he was, terribly. But my feeling, I think, stemmed mostly from resentment. You know, that he wasn't the person who conceived the child, he wasn't the person who had to have the abortion, and *as* such could not possibly understand what I was going through. So, the closer it came, the nastier I got" (G:42).

Women and Men Set at Odds

Other women recollect that their resentment festered over their mates' decision *not* to oppose them. "I was hurt even though the abortion was my idea and it was the only thing to do. I guess I wanted him to talk me out of it, to reassure me we could make it. Instead he was cold. I wish he could have been more feeling" (F:96). And another: "Sometimes I blame him for having let me go through with it. I think he should have said we could have made it with another baby. We made a selfish decision" (F:100). And another: "The night after my pregnancy was confirmed, my husband and I went out to dinner, and my only emotion was anger. I was angry that I was going to have an abortion. He could have persuaded me not to have it, but he didn't. Though I wanted him to talk me out of it, I also didn't want him to. In the back of my mind I wanted to be able to escape from him, to get divorced, to leave him, just to go home alone. I did not want to feel trapped" (F:107). And in their own confused state of attention and expectation, a good number of the women seem to have misconstrued the concern and puzzlement that their men did have towards them. As one of them told it, "the guy harbored deep resentment about it. There was this funny little edge in everything he did, and I thought he thought that the sooner I had the abortion the better. We never really discussed it. It was just understood that I'd have an abortion. He was just kind of a little cruel to me. I have never considered myself an emotionally mature person, and to me it was a rejection thing. It never occurred to me that he was upset that I was having this abortion. It never, never occurred to me. I didn't find out until a year and a half later that he had been very, very upset. He felt rejected and felt that I would never, never have a child of his, that I did not consider him suitable for me, and that it was pointless to love me" (F:53).

The story conventionally told by women is that their men were of less help than they had hoped: they faltered, they drew apart, they were unthoughtful, they left the women on their own. From the men another story emerges: that the men were highly concerned, were finding it difficult to read what the women were feeling, and stifled their own preferences precisely in order to provide the women with the autonomy they seemed to want. One father's comment is typical: "I would rather it not happen, but I don't want to run in and stop it, because it's her body and it's her free will. . . . So I just gotta accept what's happening. If she decided at the last moment not to do it, I would be feeling fantastic" (F:120).

Another man, one of the most deeply moved among all interviewed, later grieved over the abortion and his assent to it.

> She said, "Shall I have an abortion?" and I said, "I guess so." She made all the arrangements for a week later. The whole week I was extremely jumpy and preoccupied. People at work kept asking me why I was so preoccupied. I kept twirling the decision over and over in my head. A lot had to do with the women's movement, of which my wife was a part and which presumed a woman's ability to go out and make a good living without being trapped down by familial obligations. I felt this child would hurt that. She was just beginning to ascend in a good and important job. Pregnancy and all the things that go with it would have knocked the shit out of her career, it just having taken off after the birth of our second child. [After the abortion] I tried to tend to her. I didn't need tending to. I hadn't had an abortion. She didn't need me at that point doing a boo-hoo act. She needed help for herself. In retrospect I think a lot of damage was done to our marriage. My fault was in not articulating sooner that it was a child of mine I wanted born. Mostly I was responsive to her life. . . . In a sense I blamed her for the abortion. Without her requirements for a career, the pregnancy would never have been an issue. I would have said, "Fuck it." I love kids. But there was an intensity about the moment regarding women and careers. I paid too much attention to that and not to what I wanted. I don't know how she would have reacted if I'd said this was a child of mine and I wanted it. Instead, I lost control of my own will and didn't say how much it would affect me. [F:130–32]

His statement seems worthy of long quotation because it presents such an ironic inversion of the inequities and silent frustrations that gave birth to the women's movement. And it recurs in these books. The male senses he is left out; the female, that she is not being supported. She says he wouldn't come with her; he, that she went off without him.

Linda Bird Francke acknowledges: "The right to abdicate future mother-hood is guaranteed. The right to insist on future fatherhood is not. And to some men, that is very disturbing and unfair" (F:114). It also raises questions about a program developed in an Oakland counseling center for males in-volved in their partners' abortions. The men were advised to be unquestion-ingly supportive during the near aftermath of abortion, and only afterwards to encourage their women to talk about it. They were told to expect and to absorb hostility for some time, and then to take the initiative in adopting contracep-tion when their sex life resumed, as a way of assuring the women that they, the men, didn't want the women to have to go through another abortion (F:115). This kind of counseling urges the male to be tenderly supportive of what must be an essentially female decision and experience. It may, however, keep him at a stranger's distance. Even more, like many counseling programs, it may be more intended to alleviate symptoms of distress than to discern what is wrong underneath: coping, not curing.

There seems no reason to believe that the testimony of the male partners in Francke's book (Maxtone-Graham interviews only women) is any less rep-resentative than that of the many women whose stories appear. Yet these men seem solicitous, sympathetic, accommodating, and, at the same time, puzzled by the *dégagé* hostility of the women. They are stymied by it to the point where their own interests are muted—only to emerge later, suffused with anger. These accounts, ironically at variance with the impressions of the women, need not cause any reader to disbelieve what the women narrate, but ought to temper the way they are to be understood. There seems to be some sort of hostility at work which alienates women choosing abortion from even the helpful enjoyment of whatever intimate trust they had previously (and possibly unrealistically) thought they shared with their kinfolk and mates. A decision is produced—apparently the result of freshly independent and straightforward deliberation—yet shadowed by much unspoken and undi-gested thought. Then it is rushed to completion without the sharing of minds and hearts one would hope for even in matters of far less importance.

A Choice of Muddled Choosing

Free and autonomous choice is so valued a feature of the abortion experi-ence that it deserves to be inquired after as purposefully as these stories will allow. One thing quickly noticed is the patterned way in which some of the women tend to assign to others the blame for their unhappy predicament. It is a trait one would more readily expect to find in very young women, and Francke does cite findings to this effect: "Upon learning that she is pregnant, such a teenager is apt to express extensive denial, including disclaiming any responsibility on her part for her pregnancy. She cannot see herself as a mother nor can she see the fetus as a baby. As for the abortion, she accepts it for herself, but does not condone it for others" (F:180). That incoherence again.

But incoherence seems not to be a monopoly of teenagers. The woman mentioned earlier, who decided upon abortion because she had been independent since college days ("and I was not about to admit to him that I had made any mistake about anything") and later observed that she "didn't resent our families for causing us to have this abortion" (F:230, 232), was sixty-two years old when interviewed, looking back over forty years at her abortion. She makes the families "responsible" for what she was unwilling to tell them. Martha Mueller, a Brooklyn Planned Parenthood counselor, sees this as a repeating pattern. Francke summarizes her thoughts:

> Some think that the legalization of abortion has opened a Pandora's box of faulty decision-making. When abortion was illegal, there was a common enemy in the form of the law. Now that abortion is primarily a matter of choice, the decision rests squarely on the shoulders of the woman, a decision many would rather not takes the responsibility for. Some blame their husbands or boyfriends for "forcing" them to have the abortion. Others point the finger at their parents, who have insisted on the abortion or who, the patients maintain, would be furious if they found out their daughter was pregnant. Often it's the doctor who takes the "blame" for the abortion. "He did it to me" is a phrase heard often in clinic or hospital corridors when the doctor walks by. "That's just moving the responsibility," says Mueller. "Women are very good at that." [F:32]

The stories lend substance to her observation. One woman, married, with two teenage children, is a medical student now, and at age thirty-four has gone in for her second abortion. "I was angry. God had to do this again? . . . I was furious, furious, furious. He [her husband] likes to call all the shots, but never to carry them out. I was absolutely furious at him and made him do all the dirty work. I disclaimed any responsibility for the pregnancy. I felt I was absolved of all this. He should have had that vasectomy. I was totally irrational." And then she muses, "The resentment didn't go away. I kept thinking that this was something not everyone has to go through, so why should I. My husband should have said, 'I'm definitely going to have a vasectomy.' In the same way I should have said, 'I'm going to have my tubes tied.' But I haven't. And he hasn't. We all play such destructive games" (F:107, 108).

Another woman, thirty, whose teenage abortion had been followed by a miscarriage and then years of infertility, grieved: "I blamed my husband for making me have the abortion. How could he have done this to me? Our marriage began to fall apart." But earlier she had described how the decision was made: "My sister and Randy and I sat down to talk about it. One of them, I can't remember which, said I should have an abortion. I have a background of not making decisions for myself, but I still said I didn't want to have an abortion. Randy said he wanted to marry me, but he just wasn't ready for children at that time. He just couldn't take on that responsibility. I kind of went along and agreed" (F:81, 78). The young man's reason for urging the abortion is not very impressive, but it is not that different from what motivates most of the abortions in these stories. And characteristically, after a process of muddled collaboration, he is assigned responsibility for the decision.

It is not always the "Randy" who is blamed. Like God, society sometimes serves as an indistinct bogeyman. After two abortions, a marriage and divorce, VD, and then a third abortion after a one-night stand, one woman complained of "great resentment that society was pushing me into feeling that I had to get rid of the child because I was not married. . . . Feeling that I was being pushed by society's values around me, by the social stigma, not to have a child because I am not married" (G:68). One highly confused woman in her middle twenties tells of her abortion at age nineteen. She first describes how it was that she conceived. "I don't like to use birth control. I feel like it sort of destroys the power of my fertility. I don't know how to explain that. But at one time I tried the pill, and it made me real sick, and I didn't want to have an IUD 'cause I think they're very dangerous. So I was using a diaphragm, but I wasn't really using it. A diaphragm makes me feel like I have to keep my cervix or my reproductive organs away from everything" (F:86).

She then had a saline abortion, with no account of any particular ill treatment, and looked back:

> Mostly I felt real brutalized, like I had been treated like a piece of shit by the nurses and by the hospital and by the doctors. Now I want to have a baby. First of all, I'm more stable than I used to be. I have more of an understanding. The reason I had my abortion was because I was a poor working-class woman who was trying to go to school. There was just no way I could have that child. It was society. We live in an antipoverty society where my having that child would have totally ruined whatever aspirations I had. I had no choice. A lot of times we talk about a woman's rights, and I do think we have a right to choose whether or not to have children. But for many of us our class and our economic background pretty much makes the choice for us. We don't really have the free choice to have children when we want them. But right now I really would like to have a child in spite of it. I feel like caring for another human being and seeing this little human being born and raising it, and fighting for this person to survive. It also makes you a stronger person. [F:88]

Among the approximately one hundred abortions accounted for in these books, there are very, very few that appear to have been imposed upon the women. Yet there is a widespread feeling of having been victimized. The phrase "had to have" is a repeating prefix to abortion in the vocabulary. Abortion arrives somehow as an imperative associated with outside forces. It may be that even in cases where a woman is in sole and apparently sovereign control of the decision, there is some dislocation, some short-circuit in that decision experience that leaves her without a full sense of having done a free thing, of having taken her life in her own hands. It is also possible that there is something so denying, so negative—even destructive—in abortion that it is a wrench to have to realize that one has chosen it. Abortion is said to be a symbolically prime choice for women in our time, yet these stories suggest that it is backed into or backed away from, rather than decisively chosen and later ratified.

Hostility to Father, Hostility to Child

These interviews make it difficult to figure out how the male partner participates with (or against) the woman who is struggling with an abortion decision. Much less muddled is the way in which the man enters that decision, not as a codeliberant, but as the one whose relationship with her begets her relationship to the child she is carrying. Francke correctly states, "The most critical factor in the decision to abort . . . is the relationship with the male partner" (F:47).

In some cases a baby is unwanted, not because its father is unwanted, but simply because the man-woman bond is not felt to be strong enough to become a father-mother one. "We're still too early in our relationship to be tied together" (F:157). "My husband and I were fighting about everything and I didn't want to have this baby and bring it up alone. I also thought I might resent the baby because I resented its father so much. I felt bad because all my life I'd wanted to have a baby and suddenly I couldn't have this one. I hated him" (F:110). More often, though, the child of a man disliked or distrusted falls under the same judgment. By what the psychologists call a displacement of affect the women fail to develop an independent bond with the child carried, and instead intrude upon the child the hostility they feel towards the begetting male. "God, you have no idea how much I hated him. And I sure in hell was not going to have that child. I had the abortion to hurt him primarily" (F:241). "I remember thinking it was impossible to have another child, especially one of George's. . . . don't even remember discussing the pregnancy with George. . . . It was part of my shtick not to need him then" (F:105). A young woman whose surfer-type boyfriend grouched at her one night went off the next night and slept with another man, then returned. She was interviewed at the abortion clinic, trying to determine the age of the fetus, to determine which of the men was the father. Said the surfer, "We don't believe in abortion, really, but she didn't want to have the baby of someone she didn't love, and was only with for a night" (F:118). She found it was the boyfriend's baby but went ahead with the abortion anyway.

One teenager doesn't regret her abortion: "I don't know, we really weren't getting along that good. Because being pregnant's a hassle. I was sick to my stomach and I was really bitchy" (G:203). Another woman, mother of two, had lost her job when the family moved to help her husband's career: "What also came out was how I did not want this pregnancy. I had gotten into this situation and the reasons were beginning to appear. I mean, I wouldn't have been able to guess that my hostile feelings toward my husband for having moved here . . . were at work" (G:118). A woman in her twenties, who now has decided never to bear children, looks back: "I never thought about the fetus. . . . It was something that didn't belong there and had no place in my life at that time. I'd hated it before the abortion, but mostly I hated the man" (F:50). One who underwent two abortions says of the second, "Because I was more ambivalent about this baby, being fonder of the father, I waited till I was over two months pregnant. . . . I was more upset about losing that baby than the one before. I thought both before and after the abortion that maybe I should have married the father" (G:233–34).

It is a thing sensed by the men too. One of them put it clearly: "The only man that can totally agree to an abortion is a guy who's just dating a girl he doesn't feel anything about. If he has any feeling at all about her, I would hope that he wouldn't agree to it. If a man loves a woman, I don't think he would agree to it under any circumstances" (F:164). The stories do not quite bear him out, since there do seem to be decisions to abort when mother and father are ostensibly at one. But under these more positive circumstances the offspring seems to have a better chance of surviving. One woman who bore her child explained, "I was proud I was having David's baby" (G:389). Occasionally the alienation helps rather than blocks the mother-sense. A black woman whose husband had walked out on her when she was carrying their first child and then did it again during her next pregnancy admitted: "I was considering having an abortion then, but I couldn't. I kind of fell in love with the baby. His walking out made me closer to my two-year-old and the unborn child" (F:67).

For some women there seems to be almost a disability to establish any bond with the unborn except by borrowing, so to speak, from their relationship with the father. Allison, looking back at three abortions when she was in her twenties, says of the first: "This was a man who, besides everything else, was physically repulsive to me. It was a very sick relationship, and I was a very unhappy person. And at the time that I got pregnant my immediate response was one of utter disgust. . . . I had no sense, really, of the fact that I was pregnant with a child. It was much more as if I had a growth, or a tumor that I just wanted to get rid of, and I didn't want anybody to know about it because it was so 'disgusting.' " Now that she is thirty-two and living with another man, she admits, "I'm not particularly into marrying him, or getting married right now, either. But if I were to become pregnant by him, I think that I'd be very happy and thrilled at the idea of having a child, because he's a beautiful person. And he's exactly the kind of man whose child I would like to have." In retrospect, viewing her three abortions, she explains: "It was very real to want to have a child *then*. But not those children. And those children were defined by my emotional state, and by the man I was involved with, and everything else. I mean it wasn't like I was saying, 'I don't ever want to have a child.' It was, 'I don't want to have *this* child.' For whatever reasons" (G:70, 82, 87).

Women Disengaged

The readiness to disengage from one's offspring at unpleasant moments is not limited to pregnant women, as any parent knows who has been told by his or her spouse, "Your son wrecked the car last night," or, "Your daughter tells me she just flunked out of school." But what functions in these abortion situations seems to be more serious and more ambivalent, to use Francke's title term. One senses a persistently weak ability both to differentiate and to ally. For example, many of the women testify that it was in the critical emergency of undesired pregnancy that they came to a more conscious awareness of their own autonomy. The decision to abort is seen by them as an assertion of rights that had previously gone unrespected and ignored—by themselves and by others. On the other hand, very few of the women seem interested in pursuing the issue of rights. There is meager talk of the rights of grandparents, husbands, or sexual partners, and virtually none of the possibly countervailing rights of the unborn. Girls who are angry at their parents and struggling to dissociate their own welfare from parental authority seem particularly unable to view their own offspring as having any identity with which they themselves should have to come to terms. Women who exert themselves to claim respect for their careers, their health, or their persons from mates who had taken them for granted appear to be unconscious of any correlative claims on them by their own young.

The women speaking here are wary. They have been disappointed in their closest relationships, those of affection and kinship and commitment, which create for people the security of home. Somehow these women have not found—or forged—bonds that are firm attachments yet allow a desirable elasticity of freedom. Most of us find satisfaction when we can count on these closest loyalties as unquestionably secure. It is this commitment to honor claims, to be prepared to sacrifice, to expect to forfeit preference in many ways, that must be balanced with the freedom to extend one's reach to the fullest length of personal maturity and fulfillment. The women in these two books seem not to enjoy such a balance.

Lacking the guarantees of their own individuality, they are weak to acknowledge it in others. Deprived of secure attachment, they seem somehow handicapped in offering it. The unborn, at cost of his or her life, seems to suffer from a failure of personal bonding that the mother also experiences with her parents and with her mate(s), and perhaps with her other children as well. As one woman, describing her own abortion decision two years into her marriage, put it: "That child would have been so fucked up because I was fucked up. Billy was so fucked up, our financial scene was so bad. Everything about our lives was so crazy and so unsettled and so unresolved that a child probably would have been so resented and so not treated well that he would have gotten the shit end of the stick" (F:175).

Reasons for Not Wanting a Child

Obviously, hostility towards the child's father, though salient, is not the only motive or reason which drew these women to wish not to give birth. What are the other reasons? Some, of course, are frivolous. Francke tells of one very young girl who "decided on an abortion because it was football season and her pregnancy would interfere with her baton twirling" (F:180). Some are openly and simply selfish. "There was no question about this pregnancy. I really don't want the hassle. I don't want to be bothered with a baby, and that's the cold, hard truth. I'm simply not interested in bringing one up. Four years ago, yes,

good ✓

but not now. I don't even like babies. Keep them away from me. They are a drag" (F:169).

One man interviewed was an abortion veteran: three apiece by his two wives and three by others. Says he, "I wanted to create a home life, but that didn't include children. I wanted to be the center of attention. . . . What terrified me about having children was that it entailed for me a commitment not to reject them. And I still craved attention for myself" (F:143, 145). His second wife had her own reasons for not wanting to have children by him: "She already had two children by her first marriage and was determined not to have any by me so that I'd be a better father to her children" (F:144). A good number of the married couples explain that before they married they had agreed they did not want any children. One wife says that whenever she had a pregnancy scare, "I went through a lot of hell considering it. I wasn't too sure exactly why. But the idea was that I would be absolutely trapped, that my life would end. I never knew any little kids. I never knew any babies, or children. So it was completely foreign to me. And—it scared me. And there would be days, I do recall, when I thought, 'My God, if I get pregnant, I swear I'll take my bare hands and—claw it out.' I really felt that way. Just [makes scraping noise] dig it out" (G:156).

Some of the explanations are difficult to follow and reflect an inner confusion. One woman explains: "With the pressure of the population explosion, and feeling very sensitive to the social situation—that is, of bringing another child into the world—there were a lot of questions to weigh" (G:114). She also mentions hostility against her husband because the family had recently moved to further his career. Now that her children are of school age there is the question of her own interests to resolve. When she comes to describe the actual decision to abort, however, she is somewhat incoherent. "Our decision was really made on our strengths. For me, it was a matter of having enough confidence in myself as a human being to be able to say: I know that I'll have feelings afterward. How can anybody not? Feeling empty, feeling—But I will cope with these feelings. I don't need to hide from them. I'm pregnant now, but, my God, will I bring a child into the world simply because I am too afraid of having to face my feelings? No, we are too strong. . . . What happened was an error, and I am going to undo it. And undo it out of my feeling of strength" (G:120–21). Then, too, there is the Budapest woman (F:227) who, with two daughters already, had an illegal abortion during the Russian occupation of Hungary because the family was having such a desperate time trying to survive financially. The most peculiar feature of her story is that they were able to pay $10,000 in gold to have the abortion performed.

Some married couples give no reason for their decision other than that "a baby just didn't fit in" (F:151), or, "It's the wrong time for us to have a child. We've talked a lot about having a family, and it will be another year or so. . . . It's not financial, it's just the desire. There would be great interference at this point in our lives. We're both in training positions. I'm a nurse, and John is a psychologist. We're in a very highly pressured environment in our work situations right now, and we feel even though we would like to have a child at some point, we would like to be ready to devote the time to it" (F:152).

As one would anticipate, career requirements, especially for the woman, are often mentioned as the rationale for the decision to abort. "She didn't want to have a baby because of her career as a model. She's doing commercials, and she wants to make a lot of money, and if she had a baby it would sort of put a stop to those plans" (F:119). "She wanted to go to school, and she's working too, and having the baby would mess the whole plan up. 'Cause she'd have to come out of school, and since she's so far in it, it wouldn't make no sense in her coming out, for in a year or so she'd be out of school, she'd have a steady job, we'd have our finances together. Get us a good budget, and we'll see about having a baby then" (F:124).

Sometimes it is the husband's career as much as the wife's which is the key factor. This was the case with a couple living in England, where he was in medical school and she in graduate studies. "Then suddenly he was accepted at medical school [in Connecticut]. And she decided to stay in England to finish up her master's before joining him. Rather than face the complicated mess, they decided it was not the time to have a child. And she had an abortion" (F:219).

In other instances a child is unwelcome because of the financial implications. "Our whole life-style would have been changed. I mean, you buy new furniture—and this all sounds very materialistic, but that's not just it. It's your whole way of life. You know, you get involved in things. I was taking violin lessons, and I was taking courses, and I finally—you know—was out of the mess. I'm not a very good housekeeper; I was brought up in Europe with a lot of servants, and I—it just—it would just have changed my life completely; and that's not the way I wanted it" (G:7). As another explained it, "I was going to school at night, and I have a garden, and I keep busy, and I just didn't want any more children. . . . We like to do outdoor things and this is impossible with a baby, canoeing, and camping, and things like that. So I just feel that it's better for me, and it's better for the children, and better for my husband" (G:94, 104). Francke quotes a Planned Parenthood staffer who observes, "The older you are, especially for women who already have children and aren't desperately strapped for money, the harder the decision is. For women who have completed their ideal family size, the decision to abort can be excruciating. It's a life-style choice, and we are not taught to think in such a self-centered way" (F:92–93).

Increasingly shared, evidently, is an understanding of what an "ideal family size" would be. "The population people have really gotten to me. And I feel very strongly about population control. I just can't see people having more than two children. Also, I know personally, for myself, that emotionally and psychologically it's better for me not to have more than two children. I—I can give just so much. I feel I've reached my limit" (G:281). Another mother of two emphasizes, "I couldn't deal with another one. I had too many oranges in the air. I care so much about children that they are an enormous burden. I just couldn't go through another one and do graduate school besides" (F:105). Those two women were, at the time of their abortions, twenty-five and thirty-two years old respectively. Another, the mother of three, says, "I was thirty-nine, which is not, I feel, a time to bear more children. My husband was forty-two. So this had something to do with our feeling about 'our family's complete, and we don't want to start raising new babies' " (G:230).

For some women, their physical condition has sapped their ability to cope. "At first my husband wanted to keep it, but as the weeks went by and the morning sickness got so bad I couldn't take care of our little girl, he changed his mind. She is just beginning to crawl" (F:99). Another mother had a much longer history of misfortune: "I've been pregnant seven times in my life and only have one living child. My daughter Jennifer died five years ago, and I had three miscarriages before that and two since. I swore with the last one I would never put my feelings on the line again. We had moved to Lexington from Chicago and had rented a house with an extra bedroom so we could try again. But I miscarried again. I can remember lying in the hospital listening as the nurses brought all the babies out to their mothers, and I made the decision if I ever got pregnant again I would have an abortion" (F:109).

One of the most poignant cases is that of a poor woman (not the only one we encounter) who remembered having abused her own child. "I put my hands around her throat like that. And I was just within an ace—of strangling her. And uh—She was then, I guess, just about six weeks. . . . But even at that age she *knew*, and she just *froze*. Just like that. It was the most terrifying thing to see. . . . The fact that the husband rejected her and rejected me has to play a big factor in it too. You become really animal, I think, over the whole process. The civilization drops away completely. . . . I have had absolutely no desire to have children at all. I don't even want to go near children. And I've never gotten over that" (G:339, 342; cf. G:182). One couple's year-old girl suffered from asthma and had been hospitalized several times with critical attacks. Doctors had told them that future children would probably also be asthmatic and that the disorder was likely but not certain to clear up with adolescence. Says the mother, obviously under heavy strain: "If you have two children and they're both asthmatic—a mother could quietly go insane. Also, with two children, I just wouldn't be able to divide my time properly between the children. I would always be being unfair to one, if one were in the hospital. I had seen—when I had been in the hospital with our child—mothers who also had children at home, and who could not be with their child in the hospital because of their responsibilities at home. . . . We could *not* take the chance of having *two* children going through this. It would just be unbearable. I know I—I—my husband felt that I couldn't stand the strain. And I probably couldn't. Because I was so upset with—with her. . . . But even if we had a *healthy* child, somebody would have to suffer; you see? If our daughter were still in and out of the hospital, either the second child, or she would have had to suffer" (G:318, 320, 331). There is hardly a predicament in either book that inspires more sympathy than these two.

The situation is of a different cast when the man and woman are single and unlikely to marry. One man, thirty-one, a mechanic, says: "She wanted to have the kid but it seemed totally unreasonable to me. There was no way I could handle any part of a kid right now. I have enough trouble keeping my own life in a straight direction without taking care of a kid. I just couldn't handle it. I didn't think it was good for her either. If I'd been in love with her, maybe I could have settled down, but it would have been the kid controlling our lives" (F:125–26). And as one young man put it to his pregnant girlfriend: "Lookit, you're just sixteen and I'm four years older than you. So when you're eighteen you might just look around and say, 'Here I am, eighteen, and my whole life's ahead of me, and here I am stuck with a kid' " (G:199). A twenty-one-year-old woman, living with one man with her little boy by another, explains: "We both want a lot of things, and with one child we can get it, but with two, I don't know, because I'm not working. . . . We want to have one, but we don't want to bring a child into the world that can't be taken care of the way it's supposed to be taken care of. I'd rather have an abortion than to make it suffer" (F:56). The problem of a divorced woman was somewhat more complex: "I was also afraid that if I did some crazy thing like going and having an illegitimate child my husband would try to take my daughter away from me because he'd already tried once. He's very puritanical. He would have made fireworks out of it. So I had to protect my own child by not having this child" (she had had three abortions) (F:53).

A Matter of Necessity?

These are the reasons that women and men present as having led them to terminate their pregnancies. In reviewing them one notes several things. First, whichever of the many reasons is put forward, behind it there is most often the dominating matter of an unsettled or, more often, estranged relationship between the woman and either her parents or her partner. Often the "reasons" are not the reasons but the occasions for decision. Second, one would read through all of these stories in vain to find examples—particularly examples that might sustain some critical scrutiny and might be offered as illustrative of the need for abortion on demand—one would, I say, search in vain to find examples that are really compelling, that would justify the expression so frequently used: "We had to have the abortion." In most of the stories both women and men are telling us that they simply did not wish to accept the burden or embarrassment that childbirth would have laid on them. (In most cases the issue is pregnancy and childbirth, not parenthood, because other willing and suitable families are willing to adopt the children.) Fasten your attention on the other cases, those where some sort of predicament is imposed from without on the woman or the couple, and often you will find that there was faint desire for the child anyway. There is a pervasive impression left with the reader that the reason why most of the children were not wanted is simply that they were not wanted.

Most of the interviewees were facing complications in their lives and frustrations and deprivations that were not of a magnitude beyond what ordinary mothers and fathers have found woven through the fabric of their at-times weary lives. Unless one is prepared to argue that all parenthood is a burden beyond what folk should be expected to bear, it is not easy to gather among these cases the wherewithal for any forceful or compelling statement on behalf of elective abortion, let alone subsidized abortion. The most persuasive case would be that of a woman who has been victimized by the very people she should have been able to rely on; one whose energies and generosity are vouched for by a record of service wherein she has already extended herself so much that one could wonder whether she has not approached the limit; and one whose decision not to bear a child is endorsed by a consistent and responsible use of contraception. This is the kind of woman (with her husband or mate) who is so hard to find in these stories. Most of the people who state that they cannot give more of themselves do not appear to have spent themselves much on others, quite apart from the matter of another birth.

My point in making this observation is not to argue that these men and women are therefore obviously qualified to *have* children. They are obviously not. The arguments and explanations offered for these abortions are persuasive in this respect: that they show the persons interviewed to be, by and large, not very desirable as parents. This is a question altogether distinct from their justifications for abortion. But the stories as told will not sustain the commonly held belief that abortion is resorted to by ordinary women who have been victimized innocently by friend or fortune and who must emerge from this untypical moment of trial by resorting to abortion. Folly is too much involved in these predicaments: much of it the folly of the abortors themselves.

Adoption as an Alternative

It is significant that very few reasons *for abortion* are offered by any of the persons interviewed. What reasons they do put forward are reasons not to have a child. They are, then, reasons either to contracept or to discontinue a sexual relationship that is untrue or unwise. In these books there is, it should be noted, scarcely any self-reproach for haphazard or desultory contraception, and virtually none for untrue sex. Since so many of the speakers believe and assert that abortion is a much more drastic procedure than contraception or (possibly) sexual self-discipline, that it imposes some physical hazard on the mother and extinguishes life in a way that raises serious moral concern, it would follow that to decide upon an abortion would require motives and reasons correspondingly more serious. Just the opposite is the case. The reasons that were insufficient to elicit either sexual self-discipline or responsible contraception are now invoked—with none new added—to explain the more chancy choice of abortion. Once again one stumbles into that incoherence, the puzzling absence of its all making sense.

One observes that there is no further set of reasons given for the choice to abort over other choices possibly less drastic. There is one significant exception, however. In the case of many women—and especially those who are single or divorced—one option available would be to bear the child and offer it to couples unable to bear children but willing and indeed anxious to share their homes and lives with sons and daughters. Traditionally this has been the course most recommended to pregnant, unmarried women, especially by those whose experience or observation dissuades them from recommending marriage in that circumstance. It is striking that adoption is so universally and heatedly discounted by the women in these interviews. They repudiate it as something they could not think of agreeing to.

Many of the young women indicate that adoption is simply not anything they had been prepared to think of as an option, like the teenager whose reaction to the suggestion (which she did later follow) was, "I was just so amazed. I had never *considered* that. . . . I never thought of people doing that" (G:388). Francke, in her essay on what single women face, hardly mentions adoption as a possible choice. Since day-care is so difficult to arrange and afford, "the social and financial pressure to terminate her pregnancy by abortion, therefore, becomes so great as to make it almost mandatory" (F:45). Maxtone-Graham, herself adopted, is much more conscious of this as an option (as are the interviewees who were adopted), and her book offers much more frequent comment on adoption.

One finds ignorance, not simply of the possibility, but of the facts surrounding adoption. One woman, not a youngster but forty-four years old, thinks that "most babies that are 'given away' are institutionalized" (G:293). Another thinks that they are put in transient foster homes: "The abortion will be better than having the baby and then giving it up. I've been through foster homes myself, and I couldn't do that to another person" (F:90; cf. F:142). Even one mother who did choose adoption seems to believe that the outcome for her child is unlikely to be very reassuring. "Alex was born and I saw him safely into what I felt was the best situation for him. Yes, he's going to have to deal with the mystery of 'Who are my parents?' and [the counselor] and I talked about that long and heavy. But I think he stands a better chance of dealing and living with that mystery, if he's *got* parents, adoptive parents with him. And no matter how much he will scream at age thirteen, and no matter how many psychiatrists he *may* have to see, he still has the actuality of, 'They wanted me, they came to get me, they kept me. I'm still here, and tomorrow they'll still be there' " (G:182). Another who gave her child in adoption admitted, "Katrina, I *don't* feel good about it. I know that I did the right thing. I don't have to convince myself. There are just little moments of guilt" (G:271).

What little familiarity and satisfaction with adoption is expressed comes entirely from women who have given children in adoption. One is emphatic about it. "I could also give him safely into a home that *wanted* him. And I mean [*hitting table*] *positively, intellectually, emotionally,* the whole bit. 'We want him, we know we want him. We have gone through the hell of the question of infertility, and through the adoption situation. We're clear-headed.' And when this kid spills his milk on the floor and you're about ready to slap his head, 'That's all right, kid, I wanted you.' I didn't want him to have a mother looking at him, no matter how much money she had, no matter how much society has changed, looking at him and thinking, 'Well, are *you* a mixed-up leftover from a mixed-up me' " (G:181). Another, more gentle, is also pleased with her decision: "Also, if you're adopting a baby, you're much more likely to want the baby. Because you wouldn't go to all that effort to adopt her, otherwise. So, I felt she'd be far more secure. And thank God I didn't take her into that second marriage. That would have been unbelievably bad. You know, first with all the trouble she'd had in the early years, and then to have a stepfather who was psychotic. And dangerous" (G:349).

In the eyes of most of the women, though, adoption is an abhorrent idea. "To have unmarried girls go through with it and then give it up for adoption; how—how can you be so cruel?" (G:31). And another: "No, I don't approve of that! Not at all. I have very strong feelings about that. I think you have no right to do that to another human being. I don't think you have any right at all to create a human being and *give it away*. That is not your job in life. Just because it makes *you* feel a little better" (G:292). But apparently most of the women here would not feel better. Says one teenager, "One of the girls that he lives with . . . had a baby last April. And the guy wouldn't marry her. He just told her to fuck off. And he went and enlisted in the Army—in the Marines, for four years. So like she had the baby, and her parents weaseled her into putting it up for adoption, you know? They really talked her into it; they brainwashed her. And like, you know, she sees a little kid and she just—a little girl, about a year old, and she looks at it—and she just flips out, you know? Because like it tore her apart, inside. And I—I've had one nervous breakdown, when my dad split—he split three years ago—and I don't think, mentally, I could handle—you know, cope with giving away—And that girl, she just *wishes* that she'd kept her baby. But she couldn't have kept it because she really couldn't have given it the care that—you know, a baby needs. And so that's why she did it. And like abortions weren't legal then, and otherwise she probably would have, you know. It's really the easy way out" (G:203–4). Another woman, in her early twenties, has similar misgivings: "You would wonder all your life, every little child, 'I wonder if that's mine,' 'What would he or she be like now?' I don't believe that I could ever have a child and give it up. I could have an abortion and forget that, much easier than I could have a child and give it up. Even if I never saw the child, and even if they never told me whether it was a boy or a girl. I would still always wonder. Oh, I wouldn't like to have that on my mind!" (G:108).

Other women put a slightly different cast on the same worry. "I would *never* give up another child for adoption. Because I couldn't go through that again. And knowing I want a child so badly, if there was absolutely no way I could keep the baby, I would have an abortion. . . . I would think, 'What am I doing? Giving away all my children? Will I ever have the chance to have my own?'" (G:422–23). And a woman who had not had the experience says, "To me, the *difficult* thing would be to have a child and give it up. Like, I don't think I could do that. I think I would definitely want to keep my baby" (G:53).

One of the comments labors under its own internal clash of ideas. At the suggestion of giving a child away instead of aborting it, the mother bridles: "Oh my God! I couldn't even consider doing that! . . . I mean I have absolutely no intention of giving it up! . . . I'm simply saying that I feel the child would be rightfully mine, and that I would feel very cheated. . . . The choice to have the child is the choice to be a mother, it's not 'to give it up.' . . . I really feel very strongly that mothers should not give up children, for their *own* sake. . . . After everything I've said it's going to sound very contradictory, but I—I'm not sure it is. I—I don't think it makes that much difference to the child. I think how the adoptive parents handle it is what makes the difference. . . . I really don't feel giving up a child for adoption in terms of the child, is bad. I feel as a *woman* that it's absolutely unfair and ludicrous. I think at times there are real reasons for a woman not to keep a child, but then she shouldn't have *had* it. She should have had an *abortion!*" (*G:*84–86).

It is interesting to analyze the women's understanding of "wanting a child." It seems a proprietary thing: to possess, to be satisfied with, to have. There is only a faint notion of joining one's life to another human being, of accommodating, being prepared to rearrange one's preferences for the sake of another. This Raggedy Ann attitude towards children emerges often in these stories.

"Raggedy Ann attitude" [handwritten marginal note]

But what of this vehemently negative view regarding adoption, this moral outrage that so many of the women express? The women who reject adoption as either hurtful to their offspring or hurtful to themselves reveal in their remarks this tendency to consider children as proprietary objects. They are desired or annulled as the mother wishes, very much to suit her plans and needs. The mothers here may also be projecting onto adoptive parents their own instincts and commitments, neither of which are very reliable.

It is important to observe that this possessiveness, with less regard for the welfare of the child than for the dominant rights one may claim over him or her, is not characteristic only of young, unmarried women. There is another theme to be found here and there throughout the stories: of fathers and of grandparents pushing themselves forward to block adoption and insisting that they, "the family," keep the child. One teenager, facing her boyfriend's parents, was told by both of them that they opposed adoption of the forth-coming child because it would belong to them. She quotes the mother: " 'I do not believe in giving up babies for adoption.' And she points to her son Kenny who's sitting there. 'I never wanted *him!*' she says, 'but I would never consider giving him up' " (*G:*396–97).

There seems to be a general unawareness that adopted children are cared for by paremts whose desire for them is, by and large, more demonstrably keen than that of physical parents. The interviewees would be uniformly astonished to discover that adopted children are emotionally and personally as well integrated as any—and sometimes a little more so. This is all the more telling an item of ignorance in that the rejection of adoption brings many of these women and men most explicitly to the actual abortion decision. It differs from other "reasons" in that it would not serve also as a reason to contracept; it is a reason for aborting what has already been conceived. It is curious that this most salient factor in abortion choices should involve the most widespread misinformation. There is here considerably more ignorance about adoption than about contraception, to make but one comparison.

Is There a Child at Stake?

Whatever the components that combined to bring them to their choice, the women and men interviewed see abortion as a moral issue. This aspect is the subject of copious comment; even those who deny it as a moral problem take pains to say it so explicitly that they too end up entering their own ethical values into the debate. For instance, some say there is no child involved. One abortor recounts her conversation with her mother-in-law: "I told her my reasons, and she said she could understand my reasons but she had just always been taught and always believed that this was—well, I don't know, fetucide, or whatever; that it was a life. And I said that I didn't consider it a life, that it was a mistake. And it wouldn't be a life until the baby was born, and I just didn't want the baby to be born. So she—she's a nice woman and she understood my reasons—and she just said, 'Well, I guess you've made up your mind' " (G:109). Says a man about his girlfriend's abortion: "I went home and drank a couple of beers. I assumed everything was fine, so I didn't worry. I never thought about the baby at all. A baby's not a baby until it's born. And little babies don't do anything for me anyway. I never felt we were doing anything unhumane. It only made me feel guilty knowing she cared and I didn't. I felt guilty for not feeling more about it" (F:126). An eighteen-year-old girl: "I didn't really think of it as a baby. I more or less thought of it as something that was going to be a baby, but not actually a baby. I didn't have any guilt feelings, like I was killing something" (F:205). And a seventeen-year-old: "There was no way I wanted the baby. But I didn't think of it as a baby. I just didn't want to think about it that way" (F:201).

There are repeated hints that one's moral judgment on abortion is correlated to what one finds comfortable. Some women are explicit about this and state that it is their outlook which, simply by being theirs, is decisive of the issue. "I really don't have any strong feelings that when a woman is first pregnant that there's any kind of reality about a 'human being' inside of her. I think that she *makes* it real if she so chooses. I mean I see pregnancy very much as a purely physical state, that's not unrelated to any other physical state. Growing something inside of you—it's no different than a plant, you know. And I really feel that the thing that makes it real is the choice to *have* the child. And the choice to have the child is the choice to be a mother, it's not 'to give it up.' I mean, this is terribly real to me" (G:85). This woman has had the experience of three abortions. Another, who has had two in her early twenties, recounts: "I never felt anything about the fetus. Before the abortion, I'd had one or two thoughts about it, but in my agony I only thought about myself. It's much easier not to think about the fetus, after all. The world would be a lot better place if there were fewer babies in it. That's the important thing" (F:158). Another, now married, says: "To me, it was absolutely a collision between a sperm and an egg, and I don't feel at all that I did away with a human being. Nor does he. The point was that I was able to make a decision as an independent person. I had control over my own life and body. And I think that's really important" (G:125).

Here again, the woman's negative feelings are not unrelated to her determination that the fetus has no human status. When those feelings are explicitly hostile, the moral issue is the more firmly prejudged. "I never thought about the fetus. I had a pre-political feeling of what was inside me and my rights. It was something that didn't belong there and had no place in my life at that time. I'd hated it before the abortion, but mostly I hated the man" (F:50). And an older woman recalls: "I went to Planned Parenthood. I went on my own and had a suction abortion. It sounded exactly like my vacuum cleaner. It was ghastly and graphic, like the hose had something caught in it. I should have put cotton in my ears. But I had no feelings about the baby. I didn't think of it as a baby. I had no emotional attachment to it. Hell, you can make one of those things every month. Once it's born I wouldn't give it up. But a fetus is unique only in the statistical sense" (F:105).

"As far as the baby was concerned, it was like before. I had gotten rid of something that hurt. It was not that I'd gotten rid of a living creature. I didn't feel it before, and I guess that's why I didn't feel it afterwards" (F:102). "To me it was a simple medical procedure, and that's all. It was just more complicated in terms of appointment and traveling and getting there and coming up with the money, and subterfuge—which my husband resented more than I. . . . It was not a question of morality. We had no question of this is immoral, or we were killing a fetus, or any of this mythology" (G:232, 229).

No one among the nearly one hundred persons interviewed addresses the morality of abortion as a serious intellectual issue, or offers a moral defense of having chosen it on grounds other than her or his own feelings. Feelings are invariably the determinant factor, not principles or evidence or facts or even ideas. The woman last quoted evidently considers the contrary position as not intellectually serious. Another states that she has in fact looked at the matter objectively: "So I . . . on a purely intellectual level, I didn't want the child, didn't want to have it, didn't want to keep it. And there was no question of keeping it. I mean it was a decision that had been much *mulled* over, and *discussed*, before the actual question arose. And when it did arise, I realized I still felt the same way. That even though you don't want to do this thing to yourself, you—you don't change your mind on the purely emotional basis. That because you are pregnant, 'you must therefore keep the child because it's a life.' I don't think I really saw it as a *life* in the sense that I was, you know, sort of committing a murder. I certainly did *not* see it that way. At all" (G:36). What the woman has considered intellectually are her reasons for not wanting a child; the issue of whether she has taken life or not she deals with, despite her disclaimer, in terms of what she wishes.

One youngster, after an abortion at the sixth week, remembers, "I just saw a pan full of blood with this little blob in it; that's, that's all it was. But when it's inside of you, it's—it's so different—you know? It really is. But when you see it floatin' around in blood, it's different" (G:198; cf. G:212). A much older woman portrays a similar feeling, but pursues it further: "I never thought about the baby. Having had all those miscarriages and flushed so many fetuses down the toilet, it's not a baby to me. It's just a medical procedure. But then I was only eight weeks pregnant. I could never abort a fetus that moved" (F:109).

The moral attitude, grounded as it is in the complex emotional welcome the woman has or does not have for a child, is affected by whether the fetus stirs within her in a recognizably human way. Francke observes that "many studies point out that first-trimester [abortors] discuss their abortion experience in terms of 'the pregnancy' or 'the fetus.' Late [abortors], on the other hand, use such terms as 'the baby' or 'the child' and refer to the procedure as 'labor,' 'delivery,' and 'childbirth.' Instead of expressing their feelings afterwards as slight grief or loss, the late group often used the term 'mourning' " (F:83). This

FEELINGS

finding is contradicted throughout these stories, where women and men persistently speak of "baby" and "child" (as does Francke herself) and rarely about "fetus," regardless of when the abortions take place. What is applicable in the findings is a reminder that pregnancy summons up some of the most powerful and dominating of emotional forces. When those reactions put on a face that is hostile or unwelcoming they seem to block out any intellectual deliberation on the morality of abortion and to assign the unborn a moral importance proportionate to whatever readiness there is to accept him or her at birth.

Incoherent Reasons, Incoherent Misgivings

One would assume that from an interview sample of persons who had made choices—sometimes repeatedly—for abortion, there would be more moral comment in favor of abortion than on the other side. Curiously, the women and men in Francke's and Maxtone-Graham's books register as many misgivings as affirmations about what they have chosen to do. For some it is not an analytical judgment but a persistent sense of loss or wrong. "I sort of forgot the abortion afterwards, but I always felt guilty" (F:77). "I felt terrible after the abortion. Sean had asked me to call him, and I did. He was reserved but relieved that I was all right. I had a tough time at the ballet. The last dance was a circus scene in which there were a lot of children dancing around. One was a little girl around seven or eight who had strawberry blond hair, pigtails, and freckles. I shed a few tears in the dark and thought, I've just killed my own child. I've always wanted a girl, and she looked just like me. It made me feel really bad. I felt really bad lying on the table right after the abortion too. I felt horribly sad at what I'd done and started to cry. My doctor held my hand and said I'd feel better about it soon. He assured me I could have another child when it was the right time for me" (F:167–68).

Others are more direct and explicit. One woman retells the confrontation between herself and her parents: "He said he did not consider it a grandchild; he never would. My mother said she did not consider it a living thing. And this completely flipped me out. I mean, while she's saying this I can feel the baby moving inside of me. And I kept thinking, 'How can she say that? She's been pregnant; and she knows what it's like to feel the life inside of her.' I just couldn't understand how she—a woman—could say something like that" (G:393).

Karen, a professional woman who has had three abortions, recalls: "I hated myself. I felt abandoned and lost. There was no one's shoulder to cry on, and I wanted to cry like hell. And I felt guilty about killing something. I couldn't get it out of my head that I'd just killed a baby" (F:61). Or, as another woman remembers, "He assured me we could have another baby someday. I want a daughter. All I've thought about is that this is a daughter. I want one so bad. I feel so sad. I feel like my daughter just went down the tubes. I feel like I abandoned her. Oh, I feel so bad. I'd never do this again" (F:96–97). And another: "My feeling at that time was not one of shame, but of sadness. I tried not to think of the fetus as a baby, but I did. I wanted it over as quickly as possible emotionally. Mostly I wanted the option of divorcing my husband.

That was the prime reason for the abortion" (F:107).

Some of the interviews present an even more direct judgment on abortion. To the extent that it is admitted to destroy offspring, it stands in need of justification. The position of a twenty-two-year-old who suffered a hysterectomy in the wake of her abortion is best caught by reproducing a segment of her interview:

> *Katrina:* What would you say on the "murdering" issue? As far as you yourself are concerned, do you feel you committed a murder?
> *Sandy:* Yes. Yes, I do. It's a human being. I really do. I think it's a very technical question: which human being is more valuable or has a greater right to live. But that baby, or that young fetus, or whatever it was, was having a tremendous effect on my body. I mean, there it was, growing.
> *Katrina:* So would a cancerous growth.
> *Sandy:* Yes. But this was not a cancerous growth. This had all the genes and all the potential of being like us. Not just "potential," it was *going to be*. I can't buy the theory that a certain point that unborn becomes human.
> *Katrina:* Could you have, maybe, "killed in self-defense"?
> *Sandy:* Yes, I feel that way. [G:150–51]

Previously in her interview, Sandy had explained: "I really considered abortion wrong. And I still do. I have never said to myself that abortion is the right thing to do. I think now my attitude is that abortion, in my case, saved my life as my life is. It left me so that I could still communicate with my family. I could still have a job. It didn't totally destroy everything I was. And it was sort of a choice between me and that baby" (G:132).

Another woman tells her mother-in-law, who had tried to talk her out of abortion because she would be taking a life, "I just feel that my life is more important to me right now." A woman facing her third abortion states:

> I'd like to get married and have a baby, but I doubt I ever will. I look too much for love and adoration, and I get them mixed up with sex. I guess I do it to get people to validate me. If someone frowns, I always think it's because they're mad at me. I never think about the babies at all. But I fantasize when I'm around little kids. I pretend they are mine. I live vicariously off of other people's children. I have regrets, and that's when they come in. I want. But I keep denying it. Every time I talk about it, though, I want to pound the walls and scream and beat the carpets. I remember a conversation I had with a friend who'd just had an abortion. It's just an embryo, I told her, preferring to use the clinical definition. It's not a being, just a bunch of splitting cells. My friend said, "It's murder. How can you deny it's a life? It's murder, but it's justifiable homicide." Now if I took that as my own philosophy I couldn't follow through with it. I'd have to have the baby. I agree with her, of course, but I just won't admit it. We've gotten very distant now. Maybe I should go to a psychiatrist, but I really don't have the

money or the interest. Truth is hard to take, and I just don't know if I'm ready for it. [F:63]

Some of the women are less assertive and express only a resigned sort of low-level misery about abortion. "I lay on my back with my knees up. I knew inside it was all wrong, but all I could think about was what else could I do" (F:73–74). Another: "I was very much against abortion at the time. I thought I was killing a living thing. And it didn't help much to overhear them talking in the hospital when I had it, saying, 'Oh, it's a baby boy.' I was almost seven months pregnant, and I was born myself two months early. That got to me more than anything" (F:84).

A last kind of negative feeling about abortion comes in garbled form. A professional man reflects on his experience with a former companion: "Ideologically we were both for abortion. But in our own case, there was a great deal of ambiguity. There was the reality of this little person who was mine and hers who probably would have been a good kid. Late at night I thought about killing my own little son or daughter, but I also knew that it was a problem that had to be corrected. . . . In a different world, abortion would be wrong. In this world, it's a necessity of evil. There are too many people, too many fucked-up people. But that's just a rationalization. It could happen again. But it's nothing I could ever feel good about. And that surprised me. With men, I think, there's a confusion between potency and virility. At least I feel more manly for having made a baby. But I still have the residual feeling of having killed something, a life that was already impinging on mine. I've never resolved it" (F:139–41).

Another view, more bewildering than bewildered, is offered by the mother of an abortor. Francke introduces her: "Jessica Kroner, fifty-one, is a vibrantly attractive woman who, after twenty-five years of marriage, divorced her husband and entered the social and political chaos of the sixties with the same energy as her then teenage children. More of a friend to her children than the traditional mother, Jessica insists they call her by her first name. When her daughter, Karen, had her first abortion at fifteen, Jessica was very supportive and indeed pleased to be able to help her. Jessica was equally pleased, when Karen had another abortion last year, that she was mature enough to handle it on her own and to tell her only after the fact. Jessica lives in Philadelphia where she is active in politics" (F:220). And this is what Jessica says: "When she had the first abortion, she said to me, 'I recognize it as murder, and I'm willing to do it.' Boy, was I impressed with that. Really impressed. I hope she won't do it to herself again. But she's still so desperately vulnerable to being hugged. I try to hug her all the time, but I guess it's not enough" (F:222). And a young girl named Betsey offers similarly thwarted reflections: "Once I got the arrangements made, I really looked in the mirror and tried to imagine that there was a child there. I just, with every stretch of my imagination, tried to make myself believe. And I—I do believe there was a child in there. And I, you know, *I'm sorry! I didn't want to* . . . to kill it. And I think I did. But I—I also—you know, I can't honestly say I regret it at all. You know, when you're confronted with a situation like that [she was twenty-one, living with eleven

31

other students, including her boyfriend, in an apartment on a special work-study project], you can't—you can't wish for a possibility that isn't there. That is, that I had never, you know, become pregnant" (*G*:54).

Once again, there is the incoherence one has noticed throughout these stories. Misgivings about abortion are grounded on the same emotionality that is used to justify it. In the end, it is still the mother that is the measure of the child's worth. Even when, in starkest terms, it is said that one has taken her own child's life, that judgment is estopped: it does not carry across with the urgency or force that such moral judgments commonly have. It is canceled out by a statement either that the child is not desired or that its life should go forfeit for that of the mother. When these two lives are weighed in the balance, what is meant by "life" has equivocal meaning. There is never any consideration that the harm to which the woman is liable is of an entirely different kind and magnitude than the harm facing the offspring. The claims of the mother override both consideration and granting of that. Francke observes, "A common phrase many women use in describing their dilemma is 'I want an abortion even though I know it's murder.' To Martha Mueller, a counselor at a Planned Parenthood clinic in Brooklyn, that phrase is a definite sign of ambivalence" (*F*:32). It may signify something more than ambivalence. There is a clean contradiction here, and an unresolved one. The moral issue, so strenuously debated by those at some distance, is dealt with by those closely involved in so incoherent a way that one is pressed to inquire further how this can be so.

A Reluctance about Moral Judgment

The youngest women and men stumble about these pages with a stunted sort of moral sense. Missy, fifteen, says: "I kept thinking about what it would be like. I wanted a boy. My boyfriend and I named him Mark. . . . I don't want to ever have another abortion. It's a very frightening thing. The injection hurt a lot. But mostly I thought about the baby when they were doing it. I thought, I'm killing another human being, but then I'd remember that it wasn't even formed yet. I had two sides going in my mind against each other. But I'm glad for the most part I had the abortion" (*F*:199–200). June, eighteen: "Another thing that makes me feel guilty is my cousin. She's had two abortions and I talked to her Friday, and she said my other cousin had a book showing how the baby looked, and she said if I was to see the pictures I'd really be upset about it. Think it's just best for me because I can't afford another kid right now" (*F*:203). Molly, sixteen: "The abortion sort of bothers me, too. My friend says it's not a baby yet. It's not a baby until after fifteen weeks; then it starts to develop into a baby. She said it's just like tissue right now. It makes me feel a little better about it, but still. . . . It does bother me. And I can't talk to my mother about this sort of thing. We're Catholic, and my dad especially is a strict Catholic. Abortion is just out of the question. I went to a parochial school till eighth grade, so I was taught that it's wrong to destroy a life. Every life has a right to live. So I have that on my mind too, but it's my decision. I couldn't take care of a baby right now, I don't think" (*F*:188). Yet there is an incoherence here that survives youth. Virginia, seventy-three, says (of her abortion fifty years previously): "When I finally came to, I asked what it was. They said it was an 8½ pound boy. It was a beautiful fetus, they said, which made me feel better. . . . He would have had a miserable life. And besides, though his father was a very sensitive lover, he was ugly" (F:238).

It is difficult to evaluate this chiaroscuro of moral judgment. In many of the cases the participants glimpse something unpleasant in the abortion and glance away from it. In others there is an uncanny ability to gaze into the face of chaos and not be confounded. Two men exemplify this. One, now separated from his girlfriend (unmarried abortors tend to separate from their impregnating partners in these stories, and many of the married also go their separate ways), remembers: "There was some kind of tug at the thought of the baby. It was not a fatherly one, but one of unease. We both cracked tasteless jokes about it months later, like how they disposed of it or whether it could have survived in salt water. Neither of us wanted to confront that we had wiped out something alive. So we played games. It's just like war when you end up calling the enemy gooks" (F:137). Another man, a black musician, married, has this memory: "The loss of the baby didn't bother me at all. I didn't think about it. I was more concerned with her welfare rather than having a child at that time. If anything, it was like the child was not there, that we were not going to have a kid; that she was having an operation just to get cooled out. She could have been having her appendix out, and it wouldn't have made any difference to me at that time. I must have blocked it out, because of course it did matter" (F:176).

Catherine, forty-four, looks back to an abortion when she was half that age. At first she seems to equivocate, then seems to adopt an ethical stand. One is left uncertain, however, whether she is clearer when she is unsure or when she is sure:

> Well, many women have more than one abortion. Many women. And if they had enormous emotional hang-ups, if their grief over this particular, quote, "child," was such, they wouldn't do it the second time. . . . And it's pretty apparent that this is a very ambivalent kind of thing; in other words, "This is a child, but it's not a child." . . . Generally, with Catholic girls who are troubled by the concept that they have "a baby that they are now going to murder" (and, of course, a fair percentage of the problem ladies have with abortion would be eliminated tomorrow, if we would all stop referring to this as a "baby"—Where we conjure up this little thing that you're holding in your arms with its blue eyes and its little face.—This is *not* what you're dealing with, when you're talking about an eight-week pregnancy. . . . As you probably notice, I'm a highly rational human being. . . . *All societies, when they are desperate to control the population, reach out to the most extreme methods they can find—including infanticide.* Most people don't realize that, but it's true. When you must control your population and you don't know how to do it, what do you do? You kill the babies that are born. That's the only logical thing to do.

. . . Americans look at me with this look on their faces as if I have just, you know, said the most hideous thing in the world—because I'm prepared to realize that people murder other human beings, *which they must do*. [*G*:301–2, 309, 313, 314]

One notices a frequent distinction between early and late abortions, from an ethical perspective. Many women who see no moral problem in first-trimester abortions would draw the line at those in the second trimester, after they can feel their child moving (some would "draw the line" by refraining from this kind of abortion; the stories suggest that many would go ahead anyway but feel more disturbed later). Says one abortor: "I really couldn't think of it as being, you know, murder, to me. Because I had an abortion before I was quite six weeks pregnant. I had no feeling for the child. I could never have waited until the fourth month or so when the child was kicking. I would have started to have feelings for the child, when the child started to act" (*G*:327). Second-trimester abortions (and, for that matter, third-trimester ones, which are legal and do occur, but are not much mentioned in these interviews) are difficult even for the medical staff, according to Francke's account.

Joyce Craigg, director of a Brooklyn clinic of Planned Parenthood, worked in surgery assisting in late abortions for two months, then quit. "The doctors would remove the fetus while performing hysterotomies and then lay it on the table, where it would squirm until it died. One Catholic doctor would call for sterile water every time he performed a hysterotomy and baptize them then and there. They all had perfect forms and shapes. I couldn't take it. No nurse could.". . . Women undergoing second-trimester abortions have cause to be disturbed. In many hospitals, for example, the fetus is expelled (the medical jargon is "slipped") and left lying on the bed until the afterbirth is also expelled. There is a natural curiosity for the women to look at the fetus, a curiosity the nurses try to squelch. "We tried to avoid the women seeing them," says Norma Eidelman, who worked for a short time with second-trimester patients. "They always wanted to know the sex, but we lied and said it was too early to tell. It was better for the women to think of the fetus as an 'it.' Then we'd scoop up the fetuses and put them in a bucket of formaldehyde, just like Kentucky Fried Chicken. I couldn't take it any longer, and I quit." [*F*:33–34]

The consistent repugnance for late abortions discloses the understructure of all moral statements, pro and con, made by the women and men who speak in Francke's and Maxtone-Graham's books. There is an intensified emotional awareness of one's unborn offspring, because of quickening: the heartbeat is heard about the tenth week, movement is felt in these months, and the swelling begins to be apparent. Also, the procedures for abortion after the first trimester are more palpably violent: the fetus is either poisoned and then delivered dead; or delivered early by inducing or by Caesarean section, and then left to die; or dismembered alive in the womb and evacuated in pieces. Both factors can have a powerful impact on the woman and the attendants.

What is at stake here, however, is not a more advanced fetal development which allows them now to acknowledge that it is indeed a human being (that notion is present throughout but suppressed); it is a more poignant emotional annunciation by the fetus that challenges the emotional denial turned towards it.

The distinction between first trimester and later abortions is more one of instinct and emotion than of the mind. None of the persons expressing distaste for the latter procedure sees the palpable, visible development of the fetus at this advanced stage as evidence of what has been unfolding and present all along. Quickening is not taken as a verification or even a suggestion that, on principle, womb-life is a continuum. Nurses who revolt at hysterotomies and salting-out and prostaglandin abortions simply restrict themselves to vacuum procedures rather than questioning what might be common to all techniques. What is at stake is not the status of the being in gestation, but whether it has broadcast to the woman bearing it or to the persons aborting it enough of an emotional appeal for her or for them to *feel* it as a child. It is as in the many stories that told how the unborn had to be wanted before being accredited as a child. The mother is still the measure of the offspring. The status of humanhood is conferred, and the ethical issue resolved, not by acknowledging the unborn as human, but by deciding whether those who hold the power of life and death wish to confer this status and protection. The visa to life is a grace, not a right.

A Private Judgment

In our time there are several articulated ethical assessments of abortion. It is interesting that no one of these doctrines secures much of a following among the men and women interviewed. It can be no surprise that a prolife position has no champions in the group. But one cannot say, whatever one's expectations, that the more permissive doctrine which animates most abortion facilities, their staffs, and their partisans is heard here with anything like a united voice. One woman's admission seems to represent many: "I don't think for many women abortion is as blithe an experience as women are led to believe. I know I'm not totally unique, but how many women going into it know what to expect? I have no moral handle on abortion—none at all. I've never been able to work it out. Is there a right and a wrong? I don't know what to tell my own children" (F:108).

If there is any common view, it is that abortion is an arduous and often bitter experience, that it may take away child life, but that prompt and ruthless action had to be taken to avoid some unbearable situation. Given such a disorganized mind among these folk on this chief issue, one might assume that they would respond lightly or even tolerantly to other views and opinions, possibly even to some that are critical of abortion. On the contrary: here they close ranks and express a shared vexation with those who question their decisions to abort.

One woman in her forties expresses it this way: "My husband's like me. We were both raised in religious homes, real Protestants. When you're raised that way, you're never really sure you've done the right thing. But the abortions were the best thing for our lives and families. You have to take your own way of life into consideration. You can't worry about what other people think. It's not their lives" (F:98). Opposing views are criticized, not on their merits, but as a personal intrusion of "what other people think." A married woman who recently aborted says: "It's not something I would discuss openly with my friends. I don't want to subject myself to their baggage if they want to tell me that they don't like it, or they think it's wrong, or even if they think it's right. I don't go with their baggage, and I don't expect anyone to go with mine" (F:103). A Hispanic teenager is equally peremptory: "[My sister] said she'd excuse me the first time. But the second time she'd kick my ass in. My mother's dead. My father, I don't know where he is. My older sister died and my little sister is with a foster mother. My boyfriend, he told me he wanted me to have the baby. His mother said no, I shouldn't. My sister wanted me to have it and said she'd take care of it. Her boyfriend said yes, too. But she's already got one and that's bad enough. I told them straight, 'Get off my back. I want to finish school,' and here I am" (F:185). And an older woman says it clearly and tartly: "I think having an abortion should be a woman's choice; you know, it's *her* decision, she carries the child. And if she doesn't consider it killing, then how can someone else tell her that it is?" (G:31).

Moral positions grounded on principles and facts and reasoning are open to trial and to support or denial by others, for arguments can be handed back and forth. Moral positions associated with raw and arbitrary personal choice are different, for whatever validity they have is hidden in a private sanctuary that is inaccessible to others. The attitudes towards abortion displayed in these pages are of this second sort. Not only that, but there is a general assumption by these women and men that all moral evaluations of abortion—and possibly all moral judgments of any kind—are of this private, personal nature. Their position, being essentially unprincipled, is inseparable from their personal selves. It is so personal that any challenge to it is a challenge to their own worth. Opponents are assumed to be pursuing their own self-centered interests, rather than any line of reasoning. Criticism is met, not by pointing out how their position takes a wiser stance than that of others, but by affirming in a slightly more shrill and emphatic way that it is *their* view and so undiscussable.

Those Who Disagree Could Not Understand

These men and women who have experienced abortion are also given to making discrediting assumptions about opponents of abortion. The reader cannot but notice, scattered widely through the stories, a regularly recurring pattern of stereotypes. Opponents are disqualified by categories. The first to come, naturally, is the cohort of parents. Parents who question abortion are "old-fashioned," "early Victorian," "very traditional," "very strict," "so righteous and holy and you know, really holier-than-thou people," "prudes," "God-fearing respected members of the community" (F:70, 230; G:109, 128, 206–7). They are caught within "the confines of their own morality" and anxious to "imbue" their children with their "outdated values" (F:139, 207).

They are "old world" in their attitudes, and they have "drilled" these into their children (F:61). They do not discuss, they give "lectures" (F:59). Physicians, it should be noted, have this in common with parents, that when they do not favor abortion decisions they give "lectures" and are "less understanding" than those who are for abortion (G:274; F:79, 21).

Politicians get poor press here. Those debating abortion funding in Congress do not, we learn, act out of conviction: they "continue to treat a woman's reproductive life as a political football" (F:247, 250). And abortion emphatically should be "a decision that is made *not* by some fink over there in city hall. 'Cause it's none of his business!" (G:47).

Religion is perhaps the most sinister region wherein opponents lurk. Ministers are "stuffy," churches "useless" and riddled with Puritanism (F:15, 75; G:150). It is, however, a distinctly worse thing to be not only religious but Catholic. The noun "Catholic" is more often modified by "strict" than by "Roman" (F:188). Catholic obstetricians are "shocked" (F:105). The hierarchy is "rigid" and believes that the reproductive organs of the faithful belong to the church more than to people (F:250). One woman complains, "My husband didn't help either. He said abortion is murder, but then he's Catholic" (F:112). Another stays away from a Catholic hospital, because "the Catholic women always have to go through it [childbirth] the hard way" (G:345). Best is the mother of a teenage abortor, who remarks about her daughter's boyfriend: "He comes from a Catholic family, but a nice one" (F:223).

Those who speak out publicly against abortion—prolife people—are here subjected to a series of conjectures that will tell little about the prolife movement but possibly something about the interviewees. "I really decry the anti-abortionists, and I suspect if you did a survey you'd find that the people who are against abortion are for capital punishment. They're all for the beginning of life, but not for the continuation of it" (F:160). "I found out that in many cases the loudest spokesmen *against* abortion are those who are *for* our presence in Vietnam. I can't tell you how many times that analogy has gone through my head. Here we, as a country, are dropping bombs on people, and children are getting killed; and I find that absolutely disgusting. And I will do anything in order to help end that war. *That* to me is destroying human life. We have these laws on abortion that are just absurd, and then there are children who are hungry" (G:124–25). "If every Right-to-Lifer kept an unwanted child for a year, then I would have respect for them" (F:239). "The anti-abortion camp is very adept at practicing legislative harassment" (F:250) (proabortion political activity is "lobbying"). And it is well known that the pronatalist people "don't care anything about the feminine experience and just want to control our behavior" (F:252).

Abortion, in the opinion of these women, is a subject that males find at best difficult, and usually impossible, to understand. To begin with, *anyone* else is at an unbridgeable distance, even one's friends. "When my friends and I read something now about abortion or discuss it, I listen to their views and they sound ignorant to me. They have no idea of what happens to you when you find out you're pregnant and you're only seventeen" (F:206). A woman says of a male friend who offered her help during her pregnancy crisis: "He was *hurt* by the way I behaved, he said, because I didn't sort of really take him into it. . . . To say that he wasn't supportive is not true because he was, terribly. But my feeling, I think, stemmed mostly from resentment. You know, that he wasn't the person who conceived the child, he wasn't the person who had to have the abortion, and *as* such could not possibly understand what I was going through" (*G*:42).

Males in particular are disqualified from understanding the mystery of childbearing, birth-giving, child-losing. "I could see him change as soon as I got pregnant. I told him, 'You just don't understand, you just can't understand.' I don't think any male can understand what it's like to be pregnant, what it's like to have an abortion, what it's like to go through the psychological part of it. They go through a certain amount of it, I know. Right now I am feeling I would just like one male to get pregnant so he can know what it feels like. How can they possibly know?" (*F*:194). "Now there's a bill that's coming up in the legislature, in the Massachusetts legislature, to establish the rights of the fetus. Which is completely absurd. . . . And how a man can even talk about a fetus. They haven't got the vaguest notion of what it's like to carry a fetus and what goes through your mind" (*G*:111). "If [a woman] doesn't consider it killing, then how can someone else tell her that it is? Especially people who never had children themselves—like a lot of men, you know! [laughter] How can they judge? They tell you you're so selfish when you don't want a child. Well, God, let them try it!" (*G*:31).

The exclusion of men from initiate knowledge of childbearing is a strong theme here, and deserves serious attention. Each of us is party to a life story that is peculiarly our own. Everyday personal encounters are mystery enough; all the more so those greater moments of rare experience. Most of us see only from a distance what some others know from within: spina bifida, bankruptcy, Soweto, mystical prayer, wounding in battle, a leukemic child, Cook County Jail. Yet it is a persistent human hope that we can speak with enough delicacy and truth to allow a sharing of our privacy, and attend with enough respect to visit another's life and not trample it down. Even the primal and gut-deep mystery of childbearing, the privilege and burden of women, need not be so cloaked in its peculiar purdah that men with their own experiences will be unable to see, to compare, to learn, to know. But these women, in strong and joint utterance, claim that it is beyond men to know of this. Is it possible that the women—the particular women—are somehow handicapped by an inarticulateness so frustrating to themselves that their experience cannot be presented in a way that can be comprehended? Or is it simply that the experience and its construal are both so ineluctably private that there is no use trying to share them (they can only be asserted)?

Rap Groups

The disqualification of men should be assessed in company with the other categorical disfranchisements. Is it the case that parents, clergy, politicians, prolife people, and men are inveterate nay-sayers to the women who carry the unwanted children of our world? Or is it possible that these women in particular have suffered at the hands of the groups they reproach; that they have marched to abortion precisely because, unlike their better-treated sisters, they encountered condemnation when they needed support? Or, third, is it possible that these are simply stereotypes and that the women (and men) implicated in abortion feel they must put down any person who stands against their deed?

To draw near an answer to this, it is helpful to inquire whether there are any groups which, consistently throughout these two books, enjoy general praise and appreciation. There are: feminist rap groups and abortion counselors.

Several of the women mention that they have joined women's support groups; some have been group organizers. Whether the groups maintain any formal affiliation with the women's liberation movement or are informal gatherings of women in a neighborhood, they clearly mean a great deal to those who are describing them. First of all, women have found that in the company of others they are encouraged to articulate their problems because they can count on finding understanding and sympathy. One young unmarried woman, whose abortion had been botched and cost her a hysterectomy, confided: "I think Women's Lib is the first time that I was able to talk about it and really admit a lot of this to myself. Women's Lib has really been a beautiful thing as far as my attitudes about women, particularly, are concerned. For the first time in my life, I began to trust other women. You know, I probably could have told this story maybe to a man. But I could never have told it to you, unless I had been involved in Women's Lib" (G:151). More typically, though, it is their anger with men that women find themselves unfurling in the groups. As one describes it: "What came out was not how *I* felt about abortion, but how I knew society viewed it. And what also came out was how I did not want this pregnancy. I had gotten into this situation and the reasons were beginning to appear. I mean, I wouldn't have been able to guess that my hostile feelings toward my husband for having moved here, or that I was now over thirty . . . were at work. But those things began to come out as I was talking. And I began to realize how, for me, it was very important that I have control over my body and over my life" (G:118).

The rap groups are not just klatsches of friends; in fact, the women say they find the groups helpful because they have some distance from the other members in their personal lives. "It helped me very much to talk about my experience with people who didn't know me then, who didn't know any of the other people involved. It wasn't like they're going to go and see this guy and say, 'Oh yeah, you're the one who got her pregnant' " (G:66). Another woman puts it differently: "The whole idea of going to a psychiatrist, and then having *him* decide what *I* should do—really I find it absurd. . . . My experience in this women's group was that their approach was not at all manipulative. The people just cared for me as a human being, and it didn't matter to them one bit what I did. Whatever I might have decided, they would have supported me. What they were concerned about was me as an individual, and helping me find out what I wanted to do. Never, at any time, did I feel any kind of coercion. . . . There was no sense of judgment, at all" (G:123). She would not have been able to move to her own decision in a previous community, closely surrounded by kin and friends: "The reason, again, is control—that I would have really wanted to do what *we* wanted to do, and not to have it influenced by all kinds of other things; that is, by people who knew us so well that they just couldn't bear the brunt of it: influenced by feelings that were theirs, their own personal involvement, the suffering to *them*" (G:124).

How much thorough independence of judgment and feeling have these groups facilitated? One possible drawback is shown in the preference of the women here who belong to groups for the vocabulary of the movement. The saddest case of this is a seventeen-year-old. "My mother, she's a very strong feminist, too. All our family is. And we're stopping the line right here, at this generation. My cousins on the other side and us were trained when we were very young not to have any children because the world is overpopulated. The world is growing bad. There's no food, the air is bad, there's a lot of radiation, and what good is it to bring up children when you can't even get a job in this world? I'm the oldest on both sides of the family, and I've wanted to get my tubes tied since I was eight" (F:197).

One sees in the women's groups an uncritical support that is needed and appreciated, and helps women reach what they value as independent decisions: more "their own" because they are more able now to discount what other people want or expect of them. They are *détaché* in this double way: in what to think and what to do. The groups are explicitly effective in allowing the women to stand back from their husbands, and to feel the resentments that may have been building up over time. "Things began to go badly between George and me. His work and play always came first. He could get home at five-thirty to play tennis, but not to be at our daughter's birthday party. I joined a feminist rap group and started falling in love with another guy" (F:105).

What the groups may not be doing is helping antagonized women negotiate these grievances, or do so with other strategies than symbolic self-assertion. The number of women in these books is too small and too issue-selected to support broad generalizations about women's rap groups, but the testimony here does raise a question: how much of the freedom is true independence and how much is estrangement? To discover that one has long been used and put upon to another's advantage and then to get up the guts to look after oneself is a significant achievement. But it is somehow still incomplete, transitional, and mostly negative. It is potentially dangerous because it can leave two selfish persons where before there was one. It repeats the experience of many encounter groups under amateur direction: that it is easier to let loose negative feelings than it is to purge them and create something better. In these cases something better might be a further onset of ego-strength, enabling one to address the offensive partner and put it to him how hurtful he has been, and with forgiveness and determination to refashion the relationship more generously than before. This obviously requires a long reach of maturity, possibly more than the rap groups as described would be aware of or resourceful enough to foster.

Abortion Counselors

The women interviewed by Maxtone-Graham and Francke also say that they have been well received and effectively helped by counselors (themselves usually women) in birth-control clinics and abortion facilities. Reports range from "informal and helpful" to "fantastic." "She was really nice, you know. She really relaxed me, because she went into detail of exactly what they were gonna do. . . . That really helped me a lot. They tell the same bullshit to all the patients. That chick down the hall, she got the same thing, 'You're a superb patient.' 'Oh, you're the *best* patient I've had in *years*.' 'You've really been good.' And all this. But like she had her hand on my knee the whole time. I don't know why. It was comforting" (G:210–11). Many of the abortors, especially those interviewed by Katrina Maxtone-Graham, have themselves come back to serve as abortion counselors (G:58–61, 235). A large part of their task is to convey information. "Pregnancy counseling is sex education to begin with; and that's known as 'human physiology' as far as I'm concerned, not 'sex education' which is a stupid word. And human physiology then leads you to conception control. And the failure of conception control leads you to abortion. That's a very simple route; and all three are part of pregnancy counseling. Which is what I think this organization technically was set up to do, but isn't doing; it's doing abortion referrals, a very separate thing" (G:307).

It is a rare woman who does not admit that she went through the abortion ordeal with painful anxiety. Those who come back to counsel seem to be motivated sometimes by a desire to relieve that distressful anxiety in others, but sometimes also by anger. Sometimes it comes from an explicit memory of having been mishandled: "That's what made me angry. That I had to go and be in someone else's hands, that I knew nothing about, just because I—well—made a mistake and was pregnant. I told them that I was angry and that if there was anything that I could do, come in, answer the phone, or whatever, I would do it" (G:102). For others the grievance is framed in more doctrinaire terms: "I was a poor working-class woman who was trying to go to school. There was just no way I could have that child. It was society. We live in an antipoverty society where my having that child would have totally ruined whatever aspirations I had" (F:88).

The experience of counseling is supportive for those who work in it. "I've made a lot of friends here, and it is rewarding. Some people just come in, and all they want is a name and address. But some people are really helped by having somebody to talk to. And you feel as if you've maybe done something to help, you know, made somebody smile that day, or whatever" (G:105). "You have such contact with people, you get such insight, and you learn so much. The more people you talk to—and so many different people and they have so many different views. And the funny thing is that a lot of things that I didn't know—like, for instance, black mothers from the ghetto—there's always the stereotyped idea, you know, 'They're lazy and they don't want to work,' and all this. God, I've counseled several, and I was as scared as they were. [*laughs*] Because I didn't realize I would be able to get through. And I've had the most *marvelous* encounters that way, and I've learned *so* much, you know, from that" (G:26–27). Other counselors, many of whom are themselves undergoing psychotherapy, say that they had found it difficult to unburden themselves of their own abortion experience, and that through their counseling work they have come to be more free to talk about it (G:27–28; F:228).

One cannot come away from these stories with high confidence in the emotional maturity of the women who choose to become counselors. They seem, in fact, to be those who have been least successful in emerging from the tangles and snarls of their own problems. One notable instance is described by Linda Bird Francke: "Life has been more harsh to Leslie English, thirty-two. She has one son, nine, has given up another son for adoption, and has had two abortions, one illegal and one legal. The combination of these experiences caused her to check herself into a mental institution in Ohio in 1969, and later to try to commit suicide. Now Leslie is a counselor at an abortion clinic" (F:71).

What is the quality of the counseling that these women are making available? One woman's explanation tells part of it: "I don't think that anyone's reasons really need to be questioned. If someone is really sincere in—in wanting an abortion. And, with the questionnaire, and just talking, we try and make sure they are; that they're not being pressured by anyone else. You know, find out if it's their decision" (G:103; cf. G:27–28). Says one abortion staffer, "Counselors are just to give the appearance of help. . . . [They] think of themselves as company for the women" (F:25). Professionals in the abortion business admit that there are needs in counseling that are not being met today. "Before, all you could offer to a woman who was really in a state of panic and fear was straightforward emotional support. You were dealing with someone who was in a crisis, and all you had time to deal with was that overt manifestation. The counseling was more of an assurance process. . . . We thought that by moving from an era of something that had been considered both morally and legally wrong the need for counseling would diminish. . . . What we've seen is the need for differences in our approach" (F:30–31).

A professional counseling program at Yale now puts hard questions to women in the clinic, raising rather than lowering their anxiety. "This technique raises stress in making the decision, but we argue that it forms an emotional inoculation. By making the decision a little more stressful you're preventing a great deal of more serious distress in making the wrong decision. We force them to think through the issues" (F:252). What is being tried at Yale is not typical of what is being done across the country, where the counseling is admittedly more reassuring than challenging (F:31). In any case, the counselors interviewed here would appear to be unprepared to do any kind of counseling that would require either participant to work very demandingly to disentangle complex motivation, for they are bedeviled by that persistent incoherence that seems to appear no matter from what angle one chooses to approach this.

For instance, one very enthusiastic staffer at an abortion clinic, Gail, has not ever had an abortion herself. During her teenage pregnancy an illegal abortion seemed not available, and she bore her child and gave her for adoption. Asked about her counseling work, she answers: "I'm very much in favor of abortion. But if I were to become pregnant now, I do not know if I could go through an abortion. I mean I *work* in a clinic, I *see* what abortion is about; there's absolutely *nothing* to be afraid of. But I don't know if *I* could go through with it. I just know that as soon as I got on that table I would picture the entire delivery room, picture childbirth; the whole thing. And know I wasn't having a child. I think it would upset me immensely. Because I know what it's like to be pregnant now, I know what a wonderful experience pregnancy and childbirth is. . . . *Now*, depending on the situation, I would probably consider abortion very seriously. The chances are I would have an abortion. I would *never* give up another child for adoption." The interviewer: "You don't feel you'd direct people toward giving the baby up?" Gail: "Oh, never! Never. No; I don't think I could do that. In fact, I have never yet counseled anybody to have the baby. I'm also doing women's counseling on campus at Albany State; and there I am expected to present alternatives. Whereas at the abortion clinic you aren't really expected to" (*G*:420–22). Gail admits that her biggest fantasy is to be a social worker at the maternity home ("it was heaven") where she had lived during the last months of her pregnancy (*G*:398, 421).

The abortion counseling which is consistently appreciated by the women here interviewed, and is depicted by both clients and practitioners, is not qualified nor intended to challenge. Most abortion clinics have a financial interest in the outcome of these counseling sessions, and in any case the counselors are not without a personal stake in having their own abortion decisions reaffirmed through those of others. There is no suggestion to any prospective abortor that she may possibly be acting selfishly, or striking out unfairly somehow at persons she is bound to. She is encouraged to act in her own behalf: not necessarily in harmony with other persons or interests that might be composed with her own, but subordinating others and their needs to hers.

A further illustration of a problem encountered by counselors (or, alternatively, created by them), one shared generally by other staff in the abortion establishment, appears several times in the course of the interviews. As one staff member puts it, complaining about the mothers of teenage abortors, "You'd think the end of the world had come when they bring in their daughters. But it isn't the fact that the daughter is pregnant that bothers them. It's the fact that she is sexually active" (*F*:179). This parental attitude is a cause of repeated astonishment to abortion counselors. As they see it, parents are simply unrealistic in hoping somehow that their daughters will not become sexually active, and the result is pregnancy. As one volunteer counselor says, "We've just got to educate ourselves and be realistic. I mean, we're going to go to bed with guys" (*G*:144). The conventional policy of the clinics is single-minded: to control births. They abstain, generally, from suggesting that their clients control sex, because that does not seem practical. As another staffer put it impatiently about one seventeen-year-old who has had her third abortion: "She swears every time she has an abortion she won't screw again. I tell her screwing isn't the problem, protection is" (*F*:182). This is elevated to the level of principle by Dr. Lonnie Myers, midwestern chairman of Sex Education Counselors and Therapists: "Most sex is recreational, but we continue to tell kids it's something mommies and daddies do only when they love each other and want a baby. That's lying!" (F:211).

From this perspective, it is easy to see what the counselors would imagine to be unacceptable parental behavior. "Instead of dealing with her problems maturely and encouraging her to use contraception, they pretend this is a one-time accident" (F:211). An example of what drives the counselors to drink is surely the story of Jessie Lomax, whom Francke introduces: "Jessie Lomax, forty-four, was shocked when her thirteen-year-old daughter came to her three years ago to confess she was pregnant. Though it was not uncommon for high school students in the town in Iowa in which they lived to get pregnant, the Lomaxes never thought it would happen to their daughter. They signed the papers for her abortion, as parental consent was then required, and haven't discussed it since." Jessie then goes on to speak: "I was shocked—not that she was pregnant, but that she was having sex. And I was disappointed that she was. All our children know that we don't approve of that sort of thing, but so many girls are doing it nowadays and so many do get pregnant. I guess we shouldn't have been so upset. . . . I told her I'd pay for the abortion, but I didn't want her doing sex again. I don't know whether she's using birth control or not now. I guess you might call it a mental block. I don't think the less of her for it" (F:223). Mrs. Lomax would typify what birth control professionals deplore as an ineffectual communicator with her children. It is those parents, they find, who introduce their children to contraception who are more likely to be approached openly by those children when they become sexually active (F:208).

Mrs. Lomax would not qualify for Mother of the Year. She has obviously not conveyed to this daughter, nor probably to her other children either, any very cogent or consistent understanding of why they should not be sleeping around. But though she has fumbled her duty gravely, Mrs. Lomax and Dr. Myers address themselves to the same problem from enormously different directions. Dr. Myers is soberly and unromantically descriptive: he knows and admits that there is every sort of sexual activity going on among the young, and it is his aim to prevent that sex from generating unwanted children. What he seems not to appreciate is that by doing it the way he does, he forfeits all right to say anything normative to the young clientele he deals with. Having announced that he is willing to service anyone anytime, no questions asked, he cannot plausibly suggest to anyone that any of that sex is wrong (or right). Mrs. Lomax, in her fumbling way, is still a mother, and evidently thinks it important that she be able to tell her daughter that some kinds of sex are good and some bad. She probably also knows that if she stands for any kind of behavior as normative, her children are not so likely to tell her when they fail her teaching. If there were nothing about which they felt uncomfortable in telling her, that would probably be because there was no longer anything she stood for.

A parent cannot tell his or her child that sex means what marriage means, and at the same time instruct that unmarried child in birth control, and then expect to be believed and respected. It would be the same for Mr. Lomax to take young Ralph aside and tell him: "Look, Ralph, using and selling drugs is the worst thing you could do; the kids who are selling smack here are no good, crooked, flakey bums; the one thing I ask you is that you keep clear of drugs. But, Ralph, if you should ever get in trouble, Joe Dobson is the best criminal lawyer in Iowa." The first sentence is a hard saying, and Mr. Lomax has no assurance that Ralph will be wise or strong enough to follow it. The second sentence is realistic, and wants to help Ralph, if he stumbles, not to hurt himself too much. But if he utters that second sentence, Mr. Lomax cancels out the first, and resigns as parent. There is no way Ralph would ever take that injunction against dope as serious and sincere and heartfelt, if in the same breath his father is telling him how to sell dope and stay out of the slammer.

Dr. Meyers and his associates in the contraception and abortion counseling profession seem to misunderstand how important it is to parents not to sign away their ability to instruct their children in what is wise and what is harmful. To instruct poorly or unsuccessfully is one thing; to give up all right to instruct at all is even more drastic. The counselors have chosen fundamentally to follow a counsel of despair: not to stand for anything as right, but to keep whatever sex is occurring from making babies. The policy is not limited to counselors; it is also widespread among educators. The headmistress of a private girls' school in New York, who provides plenty of manuals on the physiology of sex in the library, says, "The church has lost contact with the families. Parents are terrified of alienating their children. And no one is saying sex is a commitment. Instead they are all laying if off on the schools. We try to give the girls factual information here, but I shy away from the morality of it. That simply does not belong in our province" (F:209).

There is a radical cleavage of value and function, loyalties and goals, between those who wish to take any kind of normative position and those who forfeit that possibility. In the interviews with veterans of the abortion experience, one notices that the cohorts of people to whom the abortors resort with least awkwardness are precisely those who forego saying anything normative, and who thus can have nothing to criticize. Having stood for nothing, they cannot be disappointed.

Unquestioning Reassurance

There is a resonance between the feminist rap groups and the abortion counselors, at least as portrayed in these stories. They offer an uncritically sustaining camaraderie. They reassure women who are in the grip of anxiety, fear, and confusion; who, like wounded soldiers in war, have no thought or energy to do anything but survive and escape. They offer them the knowledge that there are other sympathetic women—foxhole buddies—who will not think badly of them no matter how ruthlessly they take care of themselves before all others.

It would seem that strong support would be doubly craved here. First, these are women who show feeble ego strength of their own, who have been victimized in some ways or believe that they have, and who need encouragement to take bold steps to set themselves free. Second, the very act by which they strike out for themselves is one that contends inside them with the primal and fierce mother-call to protect her cubs, her bairns, her nestlings, and is not to be done without some struggle. The curiously improbable rite whereby some of these women would be invited by feminist partisans to enter into the full stature and standing of female adulthood is the sacrificing of their own unborn young, scions also of their helpmates and partners. It is a dread and awesome initiation; strangely thus is a woman blooded and anointed and made a freewoman, at such cost to her own kind.

These resources—the groups and individuals extending this support—leave something to be desired, for they offer the women who turn to them inadequate stimulus to grow. Instead, they soothe and reassure these women that for the moment their misfortune is so severe that, in a compensatory suspension of the everyday respect one must observe towards others, for the present they may rightly think only of themselves. Women who have not managed their lives too well, whose personal intimacies are awry and whose loyalties are in some confusion, who have not thought things out very well or acted very consistently on those thoughts, and who are now in a crisis so urgent that any thought seems hopeless, are talked through the door of expediency.

One is brought to suspect that the impatient rejection of those who question their right to abort and the resolute appreciation for the reassurances of those who stand by to counsel are two faces of a single mood. There is acid resentment of the one and ardent gratitude for the other because each is pointed directly at the personhood of the woman herself. One questions; the other forbears to question. It is not simply the woman's act—or even the reasons for the act, that will be challenged or protected. As we have seen, abortion is often not a matter of reasons. What is at stake is the right of the woman to abort her offspring because she wishes it. It is not her reasons or her story or her misfortune that she ultimately puts forward as pledge for the abortion: it is her self. With antagonists she will not discuss it; with supporters she holds converse that is not really discussion. There is little to discuss, for it is an act of the will in concert, not with its born companion, the intellect, but with those rougher fellows, the emotions.

One may even question further whether the emotions are in fact given free play by this manner of support. One might say that such a persuasive dogma is put upon these women that they are not really in harmony with their deepest and most reliable feelings. The forfeiture of one's own unborn finds no melodies in the spirit with which it can sing. There may be a collusive and even coercive force at work, which is in fact inviting women to do violence to themselves in the name of freedom, en route to some sadder enthrallment.

Medical Personnel

There is one other group, an obvious one, towards which the women of abortion experience harbor definite and judgmental reactions, though their report is mixed rather than uniform: the medical personnel. Reactions here are rarely neutral, except towards the physician who declines to perform an abortion when asked. Because this is usually the regular family doctor or obstetrician, the women—with some exceptions—can generally accept this as a sincere judgment by the doctor and go elsewhere. Usually they return to him after the abortion rather than transferring their regular patronage to the physician who was willing to abort. Expectably, stories that reach back beyond 1973 (or 1970 in New York) find most doctors unwilling to abort; after that they are fewer, but still the majority.

Throughout the interviews, doctors who are appreciated are described as "understanding," "calm," "clean." The classic adjective, which appears over and over, is "nice," modified in special cases to "very nice" or "really *so* nice." There are as many "nice" doctors as "strict" Catholics and "upset" parents (*F*:76, 172, 186, 231; *G*:59, 189, 222, 247, 248, 264, 277). The doctors are helpful because they do not degrade the women in these circumstances, and because they are sensitive to the anxiety and fear the women are suffering. They take the time and the courtesy to explain things. Not all doctors win this accolade. Some (and these are not only the illegals of yesteryear) are "sordid," "hostile," "grumpy and mechanical," "mean," "leery and horrible." "This doctor had me so *intimidated*" (*F*:87; cf. *F*:80; *G*:74, 225, 265, 276, 351). "The abortionist was the most filthy little woman you have ever seen in your life!" (*G*:240). "Mostly I felt real brutalized, like I had been treated like a piece of shit by the nurses and by the hospital and by the doctors" (*F*:88; cf. *F*:233–34).

One thing abortionists are not resented for: their fees. The women report being required to pay $200, $400, $500, $800. It must be cash at the door. Many describe their panic in trying to scratch up the full fare before the doctor would lift a curette. Yet there are no complaints about paying these fees for the work of an hour or so—or, often enough, twenty minutes. In one case a woman is angered that she arrived to find that the quoted price of $400 had been raised $100 more; after useless arguing she had to scour the city and return later with the borrowed money. Another, who had agreed with her lover and housemate of three years that they could not afford a child, paid $200 for her second abortion and then got a second bill of $400 for the excruciatingly painful follow-up required because the abortion had been botched; she furiously refused to pay (*F*:158). But as long as the price quoted is held to, it seems to stir no resentment however much it may be.

Also, although a number of abortionists performed D and C's without any sort of anesthesia, thereby rousing agonies of suffering in the women, the women's willingness to bear the pain is stoic. A few of them even apologized for having possibly embarrassed the doctor by their cries. Cleanliness and efficiency are appreciated, but even aseptic or slovenly practitioners (the dirty ones seem characteristically to be "Middle-Europeans") are forgiven if they are halfway gentle.

A repeated grievance is that the doctors dehumanize abortion clients by not informing them of what is occurring. One woman was less irate at the abortionist in the New York hospital who gave her a perforated uterus and bowel and a $1,000 bill to pay than at her own Massachusetts physician, who criticized the job afterwards but would not "explain to me exactly why he said that" (*G*:100–101). What she resented in the abortionist was not that he had carved her up but that "he treated me like a child when he came in afterward.

He wouldn't tell me what had happened, he just said that 'we ran into complications' " (G:97).

Another woman, pregnant and with her IUD in place, had a difficult time persuading the doctors she was pregnant and then persuading them to abort. Afterwards she learned that they expected the coil to provoke a miscarriage anyway:

> But none of the doctors ever said, "Maybe the reason you're so sick [she was bleeding] is that you're going to miscarry later." And my guess is that this is a possibility that did exist all along and they knew it. But they never said a word. Because they don't want to do it. Well, the second doctor said something to me which I think was fair on his part and very real. He said, "I don't like to do abortions. To do an abortion is abhorrent to a gynecologist who has spent all his life trying to save the fetus. *But*, I will do it." Because, as I said before, he'd seen too many people—who wanted them and then got them illegally—get butchered. But I think that, you know, they—none of them laid the possibilities squarely on the table. And none of them could really tell me why I was bleeding so much, or why I was having pains. I mean I would have miscarried in another month or two months, they must have had some inkling. They could have mentioned it was maybe possible. And I think it would have made my decision much easier, if they had simply said that. [G:279–80]

An older woman is more cynical: "This is, as a matter of fact, the way most physicians handle their patients, for all sorts of procedures. You go in, they say, 'Take off your clothes,' and then, 'Lie down,' and they thump you on the back. They don't tell you why they're doing it or what they're doing. I mean, it's a standard medical way of behaving. So I don't think it's so terribly strange, when you think about it" (G:298).

There is another fault of medical personnel which the women notice but do not resent: their willingness to falsify. Since it is done on their behalf the women are not in a position to criticize. They make a note of it, though, and it costs the medical people some respect in their eyes. "I had to go to see another psychiatrist, which was the only sordid part about it. I walked into the man's office and he sat there saying to me, 'Well, of course, you're a very depressed person.' And I kept saying, 'Well, really, I'm not now. I used to be.' And he kept saying, 'Well, you wouldn't have gotten your self pregnant, right?' And then he'd say, 'You probably, as a matter of fact, wouldn't even want to live if you had this child?' And he kept saying this and writing it down when I'd say yes. And in fact at one point, when I kept saying, 'No, I'm really not, I'm fine,' he finally said, 'Look you'll have to do better than this' " (G:80). The woman later saw this as a sham and, what is more, observed that "everybody admitted it" (G:81). Abortions are entered into the records as "therapeutic" to qualify for insurance payments (G:99). One woman with tuberculosis was assured by doctors that this would qualify her for abortion, though she knew that "actually TBs do fairly well if they're pregnant" (G:343). And abortions were regularly recorded as simple D and C's to evade the law. Several physicians who had previously been unwilling to do abortions and then had swung with the law to become "very active, locally on the abortion scene" incur mild contempt for dishonesty in failing to pursue their true personal convictions.

The medical staff seems in a no-win situation. They are expected to do their patients' bidding; yet if they are less than straightforward in order to do so, this finesse is taken note of—not exactly with disapproval, but with disrespect. Says one abortor: "My own psychiatrist felt that the immediate issue was to deal with my being pregnant. And the secondary issue—which might take years, and which indeed it did—was to find out why I got pregnant and why I kept doing this to myself. But he was not in the least bit moral about it. . . . He was great" (G:80).

Nurses, social workers, and other auxiliary personnel come in for good marks for being characteristically considerate, efficient, pleasant, and, most of all, informative (G:225, 328, 389, 390; G:189). One woman remembers "a nice Irish nurse who held my hand throughout the procedure." Another is grateful to a nurse who "was really, really, *really* wonderful to me. They—they just couldn't do enough. . . . It did hurt, it really hurt a lot. But like if I wasn't *so* scared, I think I could have maintained, you know. But like I was really—I don't know—it just really hurt. And I was squeezin' on her hand and cryin'; and she's like—she was, you know, she *told* me *everything*" (G:216, 215). Another remembers particularly how, when she made an emergency call for the ambulance, the telephone operator remained on the line encouraging her until help arrived.

To gain perspective, one should recall that there are several dysfunctions in the attendance of doctors on women requiring abortion. To begin with, it is usually not a medical relationship. Very few abortions are therapeutic: that is, indicated for the survival or physical health of mother or child. Among the hundred-odd abortions recounted here there are perhaps one or two. This corresponds to the national medical reports. Not only this: the abortion procedure, really and symbolically, thwarts whatever energies of a doctor's being had been roused to minister to life. It is seriously dislocating for a doctor to help a pregnant patient in one examining room listen to the heartbeat of her child and talk about what to do in months to come to ensure the child's healthy growth, and then to step across the hall and suck out of a client's womb "the products of conception" and assure her that this is a matter of negligible personal distress.

Edward Eichner, director of medicine at a Cleveland abortion facility, notices: "No doctor for ethical, moral or honest reasons wants to do nothing but abortions. They are merely willing to fit them in here and there. It's like ordinary shopwork. How many engineers want to do just punch press work? The work is rote and repetitious. Suction abortion is just not stimulating from the point of view of medicine. Women don't like to do abortions over and over for moral reasons. Sometimes our women doctors become pregnant them-selves, which upsets the patients. At the same time, if a woman is carrying a baby, she doesn't like to abort someone else's. We have much more trouble keeping women doctors on the staff than men" (F:40).

It was to be anticipated, when abortion on demand was fully legitimated by the Supreme Court and became openly available, that there would be a disappearance of that shared contempt which had spoiled and left open to exploitation the undercover illegal abortion agreements of the past. But it has not, in fact, vanished. It may be that every medical person has dispositions that have to be crossed before partaking in abortion. Some doctors seem still to withhold from the abortion client the reverence and respect that is ordinarily a patient's due, for typically the abortion seeker is not a patient and is paying the attending physician to secure a convenience for herself (it does not appear so to the client, but the doctor may see it as the reason he is being paid to put aside his doctor's oath).

Once again, we see that women in search of freedom from the terrifying distress of unwanted pregnancy do lay heavy requirements on others. Doctors, nurses, psychiatrists, all of whom in the course of their service make sensitive and awesome judgments about the welfare and survival and comfort of their patients (a responsibility that tempts them often to ignore the patients' feelings, as women testify), are in these circumstances to use their skills and license and equipment for death, not life; for a relief that is not a healing. The high fees may be paying, no longer for a criminal risk, but for an indignity.

A Matter Unresolved between Man and Woman

For what some call a "simple medical procedure," the abortion experience proves by most testimony to be a deeply personal event. Many of the women, including some for whom it was painful in the extreme, and fearful, look back on it as an event that rearranged their lives. One of the positive aspects is their expressed belief that they had, often for the first time, seized control of their own affairs in a way they had previously found impossible. Many came to the crisis with a sense of frustration, of being trapped. "I had this *incredible* need for freedom. And freedom to me was the day I went to the hospital. And I think it was a physical freedom, too. I think there was a sense of a tremendous physical burden. Plus the one thing of—of starting my life again" (G:250–51). To have decided, to have survived; this is an accomplishment. "The decision to have the abortion was no decision, really. I had made it in the hospital the year before. And at thirty-seven I didn't feel capable of starting the bottle-and-diaper routine all over again. But mostly I decided not to take that risk again. With so many miscarriages, I decided to be in control of the situation this time. . . . [Afterward] I was proud of myself that I had gone through with it. I had made a big decision and followed through with it. I was definitely proud" (F:109). For some it is felt to initiate a thorough change of self. "What happened was an error, and I am going to undo it. And undo it out of my feeling of strength. . . . And interestingly enough—also during this time—it was not a decision that we would *never* have any more children. We absolutely acknowledged that probably our feelings were such that it would be very, very nice to have a third child, but that it was going to be done the way it had been done before. And with those same kinds of feelings. . . . The point was that I was able to make a decision as an independent person. I had control over my own life and body. And I think that's really important" (G:121, 125).

The independence shows in different ways. One woman begins to stand up to her boyfriend: "He said he didn't know if he had the time to come with me for the abortion. If he don't be at the house tomorrow before nine, I'm going to leave him a note saying don't bother to see me again. I'm going to be bold." Another is pleased to find that she has thrown her weight around and been taken seriously: "It was really such a *great—victory* on my part, I felt. That I had all on my own convinced some, you know, big-shot doctor, to do this for me. He must have seen great value in me, you know; and I was never that self-assured about my own capabilities or anything. 'My gosh, I really did this. Now,' you know, 'if I can do this, then I can do anything.' . . . I'm now involved in a seminar at one of the universities, and we discuss adolescence. And they're all educated women and I'm not; I quit pretty early, when I came to this country. But sometimes I say things that they don't dare to say" (G:29–30).

The portrait of women acquiring self-possession, growing to assertive control, is blurred by other features. Some of the women, cited before, later realized that they would have wanted their partners to take a larger part in the abortion decision. They misunderstood at the time the reluctance of the males to intervene. "Inside, I really didn't want to have another baby, but I really didn't have enough courage to make the decision. I—I felt I needed some outside force and obviously these doctors weren't going to give it to me. And my husband—I think rightly so—said it was completely up to me and he would go along with whatever decision I made. [*laughs*] Which really didn't help. [*laughs*] Because I wanted him to say, you know, 'Do one thing or the other' " (G:277). Linda Francke observes that, after summoning up their determination to strike out independently, many women present themselves at the birth-control clinics and really want the personnel there to take over from them, to carry them through the decision and the abortion together. Coming away from female-male relationships they describe as overly submissive (G:278–79), they then submit to the abortion professionals, as if autonomy were more craved than captured. One woman alludes to a like feeling: "I resent the fact that I've got an IUD in me now. I resent that I can't get pregnant. Maybe I just want the decision taken out of my hands, like a woman raped" (F:100).

Another countervailing trait is the repeated failure to discuss this highly significant decision. Many fathers, it has been observed, felt stifled in not being able to tell how strongly they wanted the pregnancy to go forward to birth. Many couples came to their choice the way this one describes theirs: "The second baby was planned. And then we decided no more after that. When this pregnancy came along it was a surprise. But we decided, just with no discussion at all, that this baby wasn't going to be born and raised" (G:95).

It may be that within the perceived yet undiscussed agreement there lay some measure of unconfronted dissent. The men speak of it repeatedly. "I knew she was real afraid when she found out she was pregnant, but I didn't know what of, so I tried to be real nice to her. She's kind of stubborn, anyway. She really wanted this abortion. We both cried, I guess. It was real important to me for her not to have the abortion, but I didn't let on. I didn't want her to feel she was hurting me" (F:122).

A grandfather whose son and daughter-in-law told him of their abortion says he was crushed by it: "It's a special thing, you know, a grandchild. It's continuity. And if you have a strong family, which we do, then it's the first dividend. It's more than a loss of family continuity, too. Jews are being screwed out of existence. Who uses birth control? Who gets all these abortions? We're being physically wiped out. Now there's one less. But even more, we lost our option for personal continuity. I feel dreadful" (F:219–20). So does another man: "I didn't discuss my feeling with her then or now because it might upset her. I just walk around and keep it to myself. We had discussed abortion about a year ago, and she knows I don't believe in it, but as far as she knows, she thinks I was in full accord with this abortion" (G:163). The woman says, however: "Reginald and I haven't talked about the abortion at all. We've talked around it, like I'm still bleeding and all, but we never say why. I was thinking about that today, like coming in here. Even being in here today, I still feel real detached from anything here. It's just like coming to the doctor for any old checkup and just not thinking about it" (F:162).

Particularly strong in many men is the desire to have a son. Many of them resist abortion out of this hope, which they do not always share with their women. "I'd like to have a son to do things with. When I make love to her now, I try to keep it out of my mind as much as I can" (F:117). "A boy, that's what I kinda want. Just one boy, that's all I want. It's going through my head now. I believe if she hadn't come down here today, I wouldn't have let her come down" (F:124). "If it could have been a boy, I would have said I very much wanted a child. If she had insisted on an abortion anyway, I would have been very upset and fought to have the child. If she had needed my consent for the abortion, for example, I wouldn't have given it" (F:129).

Even more, they admit that post-mortem discussion does not come naturally. "We never discussed the first abortion at all. In fact, we never have" (F:146). "I blocked out everything about the abortion. It was just another thing we had to do. We never talked about it then or now" (F:227). "I thought afterward it would hurt more. But my husband and I decided not to talk about it, and it worked. I regret the abortion even though I know it was right. It's hard. I admitted it to my husband last night. I still have doubts. He told me not to think about it. He doesn't want to talk about it. He's sure it was a boy" (F:100).

This craving-and-blockage of discussion that leads many into abortion counseling may have a common root. The strenuous and costly struggle to take and follow up a decision, thus reinforcing one's powers of choice, seems not in fact to turn out as an accomplishment that satisfies, as a composed and proud deed. It seems not to have been faced and looked full in the eye. Many have blinked and glanced away. The experience seems to be one of those which are never wholly past or done with. It continues on with a long half-life. One thinks of radioactive wastes buried in subterranean storage. Any tremor of the earth may crack the reservoir and let the seething deposit leach out to poison the ground around. Abortion, like these burning wastes, seems something one cannot easily dispose of.[1]

Are These Interviews Reliable?

These are the accounts that women and men have given of their abortion experiences—some close to the event, others looking back at it (or at them) over a length of time. Is their story fairly told? Do these roughly one hundred abortions tell fairly the tale of the nearly fifteen thousand times that number which affect—to relieve or to afflict—the lives of Americans each year? The interviewers should receive no criticism for their interrogatory techniques. They are sympathetic and shrewd at the same time, and rival one another (and Robert Coles) in their knack for enabling strangers to offer them their confidence.

There is one significant skewing in their sample. Both Maxtone-Graham and Francke used abortion clinics and birth-control centers as recruitment points for finding most of their interviewees. Each also benefited from a grapevine as word of her project spread. Missing from their group is an entire sector of abortion witnesses. These are women and men who, having decided upon abortion, now repudiate that choice; who regard themselves as having slain their offspring; whose sorrow has emerged, not in persistent depression or a sadness that eventually atrophied, but in great bawling cries and grief-stricken mourning; who eventually asked for pardon and removed the shrapnel and purged the fever; whose experience leads them to condemn what they did, not defend it; whose sexual lives are now composed and committed within family; and who would have no values shared with the clinics nor relish for them nor need nor desire to talk out their experiences more; and who therefore do not take their proportionate place in either of these books. It would have filled out the story had these chapters also been included. One cannot know whether the pervasive incoherence there would have been modified by their inclusion.

Also, Francke's very valuable interviews with seven parents of abortors include six mothers who had accompanied their daughters to the clinic. The one father, whom she met and interviewed on a train, evinces attitudes different enough from theirs to make the reader wish other parents had been sought out. One would like to hear from some whose daughters and sons reported them as hostile or hysterical. How would the story sound from their side? The male partners here present themselves in ways that suggest the women have in part misperceived them. Did they also misread their parents?

Another drawback in Francke's book is her presentation of research data. Gail Sheehy's dust-jacket blurb hails her as "a thorough researcher," but she is no more that than is Gail Sheehy. She is still a student at it. She gets an F in history, for pushing poor Martin Luther back into the fifteenth century (F:15), and for telling us that "it is only within the last hundred years that abortion was decreed illegal in the United States and deemed a mortal sin by the Roman Catholic Church" (F:13). Common law, rights at equity, and statutes in the Anglo-American tradition had long maintained a thicket of restraints against abortion before the enactment of the laws to which she refers. The condemnation of abortion as grave sin dates back to first- and second-century Christian authorities. Indeed, it was one of the radical departures from tradition of the earliest Christians, who condemned the dominant Roman culture for both abortion and infanticide even more than had their Jewish forebears, who forbade abortion but in less stern terms. In social science Francke gets no better than a D. She tells us, for instance, that "a twenty-year study in Sweden followed the lives of 120 children born to women who had been denied abortion matched up with a control group of 'wanted' children; the results of the study indicate that children from the former group 'were registered more often with psychiatric services, had engaged in more antisocial and criminal behavior and had received more public assistance' " (F:45). She is obviously citing the 1966 Forssman and Thuwe study, unaware that it is inconclusive because it counts among the "unwanted" children a large number born out of wedlock, an added circumstance which by itself would have affected the child outcomes independently of their being "unwanted." Francke continues: "Another earlier study done in Czechoslovakia charted the first seven to nine years of life of 200 children whose mothers had also been denied abortion; this study suggested that 'unwanted' boys in particular had fared less well than their 'wanted' counterparts. The 'unwanted' boys had a greater incidence of illness, poorer grades in school, and more difficulty with peer-group relationships, and they were 'at seemingly greater risk for future delinquency' " (F:45). The Czech study, by Dytrych et al., which is later, not earlier, than that in Sweden, mingles among "unwanted" children many who are living with stepfathers, thus complicating the issue of the original "unwantedness." Also, as Lamanna has pointed out, Dytrych emphasized all the differences which favored his conclusion, ignoring the more numerous points of comparison that failed to yield statistically significant differences, or even stood in favor of the "unwanted." "Unwanted" girls, for instance, scored higher in initiative and self-confidence than "wanted." Francke does not seem conversant with the work of Pohlman, Furstenberg, and Sears, Macoby, and Levin, among others, which suggests that attitudes of "wantedness" and "unwantedness" towards children are so fluid and changeable as to make them exceedingly unreliable bases for these kinds of comparison.

It is possible that Francke, whose indebtedness for her data is attributed in her acknowledgments to staff work at Planned Parenthood, has been unwarily handed some in-house reading of research that would not survive critical scrutiny elsewhere. She cites, for example, a finding of Christopher Tietze, chief statistics forager for the abortion movement, that "70 percent of the legal abortions now performed in this country have merely replaced the illegal abortions that historically have been readily available in many parts of the country for those who could afford to pay for them" (F:17). Scholars have noticed that Tietze's figures have a way of rising to meet whatever argument he is making. This particular statistic, now commonly cited, is based on a supposition that rests on a series of unproven assumptions: its validity measures about two notches higher than that of a barroom assertion.

Francke's presentation, then, of many of the "findings" she relates from

statistical misuse

social research must be read with caution, for so much of that research has been finding what it wanted to find. Also, Francke's medical statements need some care in the reading, as, for instance, when she uses the term "therapeutic abortion" to include abortion because of physical defect or undesired sex in the fetus (F:24).

Apart from these two caveats—a somewhat selective sample in both works, and inadequate research in the Francke book—both stand as the best first-person accounts of the abortion experience, undistorted by any purposeful editor's pencil. And they are, simply as human stories, revealingly sincere.

Women of Alienation

After hearing these people out, and reflecting on their testimony, what does one see? I was struck by how sad they were, especially the women. They use some very harsh expressions in describing themselves: "a pretty screwed up kid"; "terrified"; "like a piece of dirt"; "hurting"; "a little insecure"; "rattled"; "never very mature"; "completely fucked up"; "emotionally crippled"; "neurotic." Even apart from the self-invective that sometimes erupts, these women and men do not seem very proud of themselves.

One sees them deprived of secure interchange with the ones whom we all most need to bear us up. They are estranged from their parents. Ellie remembers: "I was totally rejected by my father. He was nearly fifty when I was born. And he didn't know anything about children. Couldn't *stand* me, you know. He just wanted to sit in a corner and read and smoke all the time. And at the age of three, I remember I'd always be pestering him, trying to get some affection out of him, you see. And he would usually cuff me—or throw me halfway across the room if he thought Mother wasn't looking" (G:355). And Patti: "And like, my mother, you know; I walk in the house and I come home—you know, I've been gone for *two* hours—'Where were you? Out peddlin' your ass? Tramping, you little slut? You fucking bastard.' That's my name, 'fucking bastard'" (G:206). And Fritz: "My father was a frightfully irresponsible ne'er-do-well who saw me around five times in his life. He deserted my mother when I was three, and the only memory I have of him is being terrified of his booming voice. I rarely saw my mother either and can only remember her kissing me good night. I lived with my nanny while my mother was being supported by her various boyfriends. I was sent away to boarding school at the age of six and always had a terrible feeling of rejection" (F:145).

Of course, most stories have no such Eugene O'Neill scenes. Besides, every adult knows it takes work to make relations grow with one's own father and mother. But the women and men in Maxtone-Graham's and Francke's books are, person for person, very much without the security and trust and understanding one would like to share with parents. Their alienation during the pregnancy and abortion crisis shows how badly this is so.

There is sorry and abundant evidence that the security of the interviewees with their mates—husband or wife, girlfriend or boyfriend or percale partner—is not well established. For the unmarried, Francke's observation is borne out: "Almost every relationship between single people broke up either before or after the abortion" (*F*:47). Whether the abortion was a wedge or a weapon or of little significance in their parting, the bonds from the outset are described as flimsy. What they have conceived together often grows from no union of two in one flesh. And in a sense the husbands and wives have misbegotten also. The ties that lash them to one another seem already frayed. Abortion does not usually sunder them, of itself, but it calls for more candor and consideration than many of the couples seem to enjoy. Alternatively, it bonds some fast together in a collusion of qualities that are not becoming, not promising.

Despite the set topic of conversation, I expected more comment on and interest in their born children than is actually to be found. It is difficult to gauge how full are the hearts of the parents for the children who do receive life and home and haven from them.

There is also widespread alienation from church and the community of belief: the bittersweet company that calls for virtue and forgives sin. Less noticed is the estrangement many women in the stories undergo from their own obstetricians, since most will not perform elective abortions. It is hard to know how much the women may stand to lose by this. Everyone knows about, but few can adequately fathom or appreciate, this relationship, distinct from others in medical ministry, which women engender with the persons who deliver them of their children.

In the place of this inner group of familiars, the female abortors in our stories are supported by an outer group of replacement comrades in rap groups, peer counselors, and the professional personnel of the abortion establishment. This cadre endeavors to help women discern and follow their own personal feelings and preferences. They often see it as their duty to encourage their clients to disengage from those in the first group and to disregard "what they want." As these narratives tell it, however, the second group carries heavy ideological freight. One is left with the distinct conviction that the female clientele, though urged to lay hold of freedom, is given a pretty precise notion of what the agenda for freed persons must be.

There is a received dogma that has little in-group challenge. For coercive, orthodox uniformity it far exceeds anything, say, that a church could impose. Possibly the ecological movement or one of the hypnotic religious cults would offer a fair comparison.

Are these women freed from the people who seem to demand much—often too much—of them, and do they then find support from other people who have nothing to demand, who will help them to discharge from their lives some oppressive burdens? Or are these women unmoored from the kinfolk and professional sustainers who are pledged to stand by them no matter what may happen, only to be delivered up to other people whose interest in them is more programmed than personal? The latter way of construing the stories is true, but I have a sense that there is truth in the former also.

Women of Snarled Instinct

The women here, unhappy in so many ways, do not present themselves attractively. Nor do the men. As with anyone who lets others into the privacy

[handwritten marginal note: Good follow-up on the women's movement]

of his or her life story, they are appealing, but more as persons in disorder than as persons you would care to have to rely upon. They do not come across as great mothers or fathers . . . or spouses.

We meet abortors who display the instincts of motherhood, as women do, yet in some flawed way. "After they're born I love to nurse them, to hold them, and let them sleep on my stomach" (F:104). One who had already decided to abort recalls, "I didn't want to do anything to hurt the baby. I did dumb things, like driving slower in the car" (F:192). And another, during the abortion itself: "All I could think was that I was going to be a mother. And that this child would love me and I was hurting it. I lay on the table and kept cradling my arms as if there was a baby in them. I swear I could hear it crying" (F:64). They are also women who carry the counterinstincts of motherhood; who wonder, as one does, "Would I end up someday holding his head over the gas jet?" (F:182). The joy of it and the fatigue of it coexist in any woman. In these there seems to be a snarling of the instincts. It is said that the choice for abortion is made when a woman finally gets a clear sight on her own feelings. Which set of feelings? Most people carry within them powerful instincts and feelings that pull in opposite directions. Whence the arbitration between them? In these stories it is not so often the woman's feelings which prompt her choice, but "reasons," a way of looking at her life which does not so much rise up from within her as it does offer itself for her belief.[2]

A point of hesitation here. How fair or reliable is it to look in on people at a traumatic and untypical moment of their lives, and then come away with an impression of them? The abortion crisis naturally is not going to give a balanced display of a person's full self. The women and men are at their worst, in fact: unstrung, defensive, anxious, with no time for the luxury of thinking calmly. Yes, but there is also something very specially disclosive in exactly such moments. Aquinas said that character is revealed in unexpected emergency. We respond to crisis and threat, with no chance to reflect; this is telltale. The person we are from day to similar day has another face that only shows in hasty peril. Faces of this sort look out at us from these stories.

Disrupted Bonds of Blood and Promise

Antecedent to abortion is sex, and there is much sex in these chronicles. There is impotence too. It is scripted in among the dramatis personae as much as is casual promiscuity. So also are the many less forthright ways of drawing back from the sexual embrace. Those things antecedent to committed sex—kinship, home, promises, and the confidence that promises will be kept—do not abound here. In fact, what emerges from the narratives is a palpable sense of how naturally and insistently sex draws one forward into childbearing: not as Russian roulette draws one to death by the fortune of the odds, nor as robust appetite can draw one into obesity; but as courting leads to marriage, and study to discovery. Or, to put it differently, when one witnesses abortion concentered within the forfeiture of so many commitments one is prepared to believe that love, fidelity, sex, marriage, childbearing, parenthood—all these—grow and wither together.

To embark upon one is to be set already for the far port at the other end.

the true and good use of sexuality is a commitment to the other and a surrender of the self — in which

good

re

Many of the wayfarers in this log seem to have embarked upon a treasure hunt instead of a journey. They are uncommitted to what childbearing essentially requires and what sex already asks: a surrender to the potential unexpected, and to what is uncontrollable in another person who has love-claims from you and on you. Childbearing, the sexual union, and the oaths of marriage emerge alike as calling for this jeopardy to others. The women and men of these tales are chary about jeopardy to others.

Two primal ties, one of marriage and one of descent, one of commitment and the other of blood, are concelebrated in the sexual union that ratifies one and begets the other. One cleaves to a person she or he is sure of, but to yield to other emergent persons one can never be sure of. It is odd: when one demands that the outcomes be known beforehand and closely calculated, this intercourse tends to lose the surety it should have, and loses the promise to raise up new life. One closes these two books with a sense that abortion was a sad sequel to many miscarried unions between parties whose kinships and commitments, bonds of blood and promise both, were radically disturbed. Companionship, sex, conception, response to pregnancy, abortion, birth, and rearing—all seem so similarly haphazard, so poor of purpose.

What of the autonomy, the accession to equality, the rejection of imposed norms, the control over their bodies and their selves which women here speak of as abortion benefits? Barbara Grizzuti Harrison, in her review of Francke's book for *Ms.*, comments: "I was even more appalled by the women who routinely use abortion as a contraception device—and astounded that these same women could righteously mouth clichés about 'control of their bodies,' when the idea of exercising 'control' never seemed to occur to them before having intercourse."[3]

It is difficult to see much real gain in control of any significance. The abortors do not emerge from their experience noticeably stronger than before. They are on no more healthy terms with their families. They had previously found it difficult to speak their minds, especially in the face of contradiction, but so often they still avoid confrontation, simply by seeking a more sympathetic audience. They had been obliged to acquiesce to men, to sacrifice career, the arts, public life, or to compress their designs within whatever fragment of time and energy their partners would declare available. Yet most of the rearrangements that occur seem to be at the cost of the partnership itself. Some ground is gained but the body count is frightful. There are words and gestures of defiance, but they are often stealthy and furtive, done behind the backs of those who should be faced and changed. To tell the truth, one of my favorite moments in either book was when a woman, sixty-four, was describing an episode during her pregnancy exam. "There I was still in the stirrups and suddenly he began groping around again, and it was definitely not medicinal. That bastard was making a pass at me. I sat bolt upright and said, 'Cut it out,' and he mumbled something and stopped" (*F*:234). It was that sort of spunk and guts which seems in short supply in these stories. The reader does not see the women coming from abortion with appreciable new strength, or with anyone close enough now for them to use it on. They are strong enough often to do what they please but not to make others differently pleased; strong enough to be aggressive but not strong enough to make the aggression unneeded.

Perhaps this asks too much. Take a more realistic goal. Suppose that abortion need not be a growth experience. Grant at least that some people, overwhelmed by more than they feel able to cope with, at least rescue themselves from chaos, or even buy time to get their affairs in order. Is this not enough? Well . . . buying time is not always right, at the price, and sometimes not right at any price. There are, in the affairs of humankind, some disagreeable crises which we must go to meet rather than elude, because the better day for which we save ourselves will not abide us save with the honor and sacrifice we must sometimes throw into hazard before reaching it. There may be a more turbulent disorder in one's life, at its deepest parts, brought on by forfeiting the life of a child conceived, than any of the disturbances that child's birth could bring on. At least that is what these stories intimate.

Who Are the Abortors?

What are the situations of the women who speak here? Do they justify the public presentations made on their behalf? "But I'm only 12 years old." No twelve-year-olds or subteens among them. "I was raped." No rape victims, though one woman was set upon by a priapic and sodden husband one night. "We'll have to go on relief." No one here is quite in this situation. "My father will kill me." All the teenagers say this; although in some instances one might cheer the father on, it is not a serious fear. "The doctor says it will die before it's two." No doctor says that here. "My IUD failed." Once here. "I'm 50, I thought I couldn't get pregnant." No fifty-year-olds here; only one who is in her forties; a dozen plus in their thirties; the typical age is the early twenties. There are certainly women in the land who come to abortion in the circumstances described by the NARAL advertisement with which this essay began, but they are very few. And they are not the clientele for whom abortion is provided. The clientele in these pages, more representative, is a group of women relatively unsettled with their men, pushed a bit by pressures, and bold in the company of those who will not say them nay. They have not yet sorted out well the give-and-take of life shared, and they choose now to take more and share less. Their abortions have not wrecked their lives. They have not resolved them. The same disorder, the same incoherence, seems to continue. The abortions do not deal with the problems investing their lives and, in fact, may even distract them from these problems.

One of the women sums it up: "Abortion, be it legal or illegal, paid for or not, is here to stay. It is not up to men to tell women what to do under these circumstances. Nor is it up to women to tell each other what to do. Solving the dilemma of an unwanted pregnancy is probably the single most important decision an individual will ever have to make. And regardless of whether she chooses to continue her pregnancy or to terminate it through abortion, it is her decision alone. So it falls to all of us to support that decision with grace, safety, and understanding—and to live with it, and each other, as best we can" (F:257).

Those are Linda Bird Francke's closing words. What she describes as the ambivalence of abortion, however, is not really ambivalence. It is incoherence: the crazy incoherence that comes when one tries to walk through a contradiction. Like declaring a nation based on rights to life, liberty, and the pursuit of happiness, guaranteed to all, and at the same time denying these rights to slaves. That is not ambivalence. Like providing equal protection under the law for all citizens, and denying the vote, the jury, and the bar to women. That is not ambivalence. Like saying that it is one's child one carries in the womb, and disposing of it at will. That is not ambivalence. These are contradictions, and experience shows that we are capable of living incoherently, putting off justice, for a long time indeed.

The testimony of those women and men who recount their personal experiences of abortion compels strong human sympathy. The last thing in the world it does is to sustain an acceptance of abortion. It tells, story after story, the tale of how unborn young lives have been the wastage of an incoherence, disaffiliation, self-indulgence, and repugnance for truth that afflicts their parents. Here is testimony to a most dismal, even an uncannily spiritual, extinguishing of fertility, of life planted and unable to grow from withered stock.

One final word. The movement for women's rights is composed of many strands and fibers of issue and interest. I expect that they will be unraveled and braided again into new combinations in years to come. At this time those who see abortion as a tragedy tend to hold themselves at some distance from the women's movement because some of its vocal leaders are partisans for abortion choice. This might be otherwise.

Anyone who understands abortion as part of a complex convulsion within family should be mighty and vigorous in defense of equality for women. There will always be some abortion, as Francke says; there will also always be infanticide and parricide and rape. But the colossal number of abortions sought now in our country seems in some respects to be epidemic. It is not due simply to the contemporary hostility towards children, nor to a resolute campaign of public persuasion, nor to the recent legalization, nor even to the irresponsible use of contraception. It is due in some measure to the fact that age-old patterns in the family have been abruptly repudiated. Women are chafing under denials of appreciation, opportunity, and freedom that hurt much more now, after the inadequacy has been drawn to our attention but before it has been remedied. Men, who were for all that time as unwitting as women in perpetuating the inequities, come in for hostile treatment they do not want to accept as merited. It little matters; there must be change. It will require clout, for advantage is rarely given up without a push. But much more than clout, it will require great wisdom.

Equality is not that hard to come by; it is equality in family that is the problem. The family needs to be renegotiated: not in the clumsy, life-depriving ways described in these stories, but in ways that will produce fewer sullen and selfish women or impotent men. When that comes, many then will be too wise and too committed to choose abortion.

Essay 2

Very Small Fry

Arguments for Abortion

THE ARGUMENTS ON opposing sides of any issue rarely seem to grapple directly with one another. They start from different presumptions; they locate emphasis differently; they advance toward their conclusions from diverse angles. And there is another way in which arguments can be elusive. Sometimes an argument will not only fail to meet its adversary squarely over their points of disagreement, but will also shift the ground of its own development of the issue. Thus explanations after the fact may take a shape and a sense that tell little about why the choice that is now being defended was made in the first place.

An inquiry into the public arguments on behalf of abortion freedom needs to be at least alert to these two possibilities. Does the explanation counter and resolve the challenges that abortion opponents have erected as the armatures of their argument? And does it lay out the reasons which really lead women and men to abortion clinics? Whatever one's answer to these two questions, of course, the case for abortion freedom needs to be taken on its own terms. It need not be the diametrical match of what prolife arguments are saying, and it may indeed be an improvement upon the motives and thinking of abortion clientele. It has a public life and status of its own, and that is what I set myself to study and what stands forth in this essay.

What are some of the principal arguments advanced by those who defend abortion, particularly abortion on demand, which is presently the legally protected right of every woman in our land? Do those arguments, if rapped soundly, ring true?

Ethical Argument: Abortion Is a Medical Matter

The United States Supreme Court has characterized abortion as "a medical procedure," a "surgical procedure," related to the "preservation and protection of maternal health." The Court states, in its summary of the 1973 cases, *Roe* v. *Wade* and *Doe* v. *Bolton*, that "the abortion decision in all its aspects is inherently, and primarily, a medical decision, and basic responsibility for it must rest with the physician." It follows upon a "medical judgment," the doctor's "best clinical judgment."[1] The Court is only following the American Medical Association, which in 1970 had asserted "that abortion is a medical procedure," to be performed on grounds of "sound clinical judgment."[2] The American Civil Liberties Union in 1968 had called for repeal of criminal sanctions for abortion that would forbid doctors, in accordance with their

61

As a Medical Procedure

"medical opinion . . . to perform what their professional judgment may dictate as a necessary medical procedure."[3]

(1) What might this mean? At the very least it might mean that abortion is responsibly left to an obstetrician, who is adept, surgically and medically, at evacuating the womb, and who is capable of treating any maternal complications which could follow. It might mean, second, that if abortion is inevitable, (2) legalization lessens the dangers to maternal life and health (mortality and morbidity) caused by illegal, and therefore covert, operations. In this sense, legalized abortion would provide health advantages. Third, and most directly, (3) it might mean that abortion is a measure used by a doctor to treat some health disorder threatening a pregnant mother.

Abortion as a health-care measure is advocated in proabortion literature on all three counts. A conclusion quickly follows. Since this is a doctor's work, it should enjoy the professional immunity of any other medical matter. "Religious or philosophical objections to abortion, therefore, must have no more influence on medical or clinical considerations than objections by certain religious sects have on transfusion or any surgery."[4] Considerations of right and wrong, particularly if they clothe themselves in the law, are out of bounds if they intrude into the privacy of medical judgment. "Morality," testified a Planned Parenthood obstetrician-gynecologist, "is not the issue for consideration; . . . whether to continue or not continue a pregnancy is a medical decision, therefore should be decided privately between a patient and her physician."[5] Since a decision to abort arises from an obstetrician's skilled assessment of his patient's health needs, that medical judgment ought to stand beyond the reach of review or criticism on any but clinical grounds.

We must ask: is this valid? To what extent is abortion, as practiced in our land today, a medical matter? In the strict sense, how many abortions are medically indicated to preserve a mother's life or physical health? The evidence varies. In 1978 Illsley and Hall estimated that less than 2 percent of current abortions were performed for maternal health reasons.[6] This estimate may be high. Surveys of reasons alleged for abortion do not show "medical reasons" for abortion to be significant. For instance, Steinhoff, Smith, and Diamond's Hawaii study after abortion law repeal there indicated no "medical" reasons cited by their respondents.[7] Cutoffs of tax-subsidized abortion through the Hyde Amendment, which did permit Medicaid payments for abortions when there was serious threat to maternal health or life (as well as when the pregnancy resulted from felonious intercourse or the offspring was handicapped), caused a reported 99 percent reduction in Medicaid abortions. One may infer that very few of those abortions had serious clinical grounds. No studies are conclusive, but the evidence suggests that perhaps 1 percent, or perhaps slightly less, of the abortions presently performed in America are prescribed by a physician because pregnancy is threatening the mother's physical health.

1% are true medical procedures

This may be partly explained by medical advances in the treatment of many health disorders that can be aggravated by pregnancy: toxemia, diabetes, high blood pressure, pulmonary tuberculosis, acute rheumatic fever, and congenital heart defects. One year following the American Medical Association's proprietary claim over abortion as a health measure, the chairman of the Department of Obstetrics and Gynecology at the medical school of the University of California, Davis, himself an abortion advocate, explained at the AMA annual meeting how difficult a claim this was:

> Few abortions need to be performed for organic disease in a well-conducted contemporary practice if the traditional demand of hazard to life is followed. Cardiovascular disease, for example, has long been known to increase the risk of maternal health during pregnancy. Yet "recent research" has shown that nearly every pregnancy of a cardiac patient can be completed successfully with little risk of maternal health. . . . A small number of pregnant patients with severe renal disease and decompensating renal function seem truly threatened by pregnancy. Even in this instance, however, heroic measures such as the use of a dialysis unit may see these women through severe life-threatening episodes. . . . Neurologic disease is an occasional indication for abortion. The patient with multiple sclerosis, for example, sometimes is, indeed, made worse by pregnancy. The effect in this instance is unpredictable, however, and the condition of some patients actually improves. The effect of pregnancy on epilepsy is equally uncertain and pregnancy itself does not increase the risk of death for the pregnant women. . . . Tuberculosis accounts for nearly all of the pulmonary conditions thought to indicate therapeutic abortion. But with the advance of drug therapy, abortion rarely seems necessary for this disease. . . . Malignancy is occasionally an indication for legal abortion. There is little convincing evidence, however, that pregnancy in any way adversely affects the outcome of neoplastic disease. Even with cancers known to be endocrine dependent, such as cancer of the breast, the survival seems unaffected by pregnancy interruption.[8]

Are we perhaps being too narrow, construing "health" in the traditional physical sense? The Supreme Court has viewed it in a much broader sense: "physical, emotional, psychological, familial, and the woman's age."[9] In this sense, of course, every abortion serves a woman's health because it serves her perceived well-being. On this understanding of health the denial of any strong desire would provoke distress and thus constitute a health problem. But health in this Court-preferred, broad sense is so widely splayed as to lose any correspondence to what physicians and surgeons do or are trained to do. And when, in two out of every three abortions performed today, the pregnant woman has paid her fee, received conclusive encouragement and instructions about contraception from the counselor, been sedated, laid prostrate, draped and disinfected, on the surgical table with her feet in the stirrups prone beside the sterile instruments laid out in readiness—all this, before the physician ever enters the room—it is perhaps unrealistic to speak of his "best clinical judgment" being brought to bear in the short seconds before he injects the anesthetic.

Another strictly medical indication for abortion might concern the health of the offspring. Children handicapped by congenital defect or by certain maternal diseases such as syphilis or rubella will surely face the need for extensive and sometimes costly medical treatment, after birth and possibly before it. Also, mothers who are extremely young, unwed, poor, or pregnant from haphazard sex cannot always be expected to give their unborn adequate prenatal care. Unhappy medical sequelae follow from this. These mothers tend to bear more children who, because of low birth weight, succumb in infancy.

Soon after abortion became readily available, some reports began to note its public health benefits for children. Infant mortality rates began to descend.[10] This is a claim which merits some attention. Clearly, selective abortion does tend to eliminate many unborn who are at relatively higher health risk. Dr. Philip Handler, president of the National Academy of Sciences, drew this fact toward further but logical application in a speech he gave to the American College of Surgeons in 1971. If abortion could be applied massively, he explained, to weed out the unfit, who would otherwise be born with prenatal defects and illness, then medicine would have an easier time coping with disease. "The responsibility of medicine is not merely to the individual but to the human species," he told the surgeons, and the welfare of the individual now may be less important. Calling the surgeons to a new kind of ethics, he spoke of medical care, in a remarkable but perhaps unreflective turn of phrase, as "a birthright of all Americans rather than a privilege."[11] The snarl in his argument is lodged, not in its facts, but in its ethics, which would reduce medical problems by eliminating the patients. As one sociologist has commented: "Presumably we could also improve the health and lower the death rates of our over-65 population if we undertook a policy of selective termination of 64 year-olds."[12]

What about abortion as a medical matter in a less direct sense? Where abortion is outlawed it is performed by the unskilled, with high risks of mortality and morbidity for the mother. Legalization will at least ensure that the procedure is performed professionally and aseptically, and will eliminate the health dangers to pregnant women. Lower maternal death rates have followed the elimination of the quack abortionist.

This has been a potent argument. Indeed, one of the most persuasive arguments on behalf of abortion law repeal was the high death rates that were ascribed to botched abortions. Abortion advocates have commonly estimated that from 5,000 to 10,000 American women perished annually in desperate attempts to avoid childbirth.[13] Typically, though more conservatively, the *New York Times* gave an editorial accolade to the first permissive abortion law—Colorado's—in 1967: "It offers dignity and decency in place of present pitiless restrictions throughout the nation which have resulted in more than a million illegal abortions and the needless death of four thousand mothers each year."[14] If one compares these declarations with a recent estimate that after the legalization of abortion there are only about nineteen reported deaths caused annually by induced abortion (legal and illegal combined), one is invited to appreciate how many women owe their lives to the banishment of the coathanger.[15]

These dramatic savings in mothers' lives become less compelling when they are examined. The most significant reduction in abortion-related maternal mortality is due, not to legalized abortion, but to the development of the sulfa drugs and later antibiotics. The most dramatic declines occur in the 1940s. By 1967, the year the *Times* was declaring 4,000 women dead annually from abortion, there were 133 such deaths on record. The *Times* had allowed itself an editorial adjustment of slightly more than 3,000 percent. By 1967 there were numerous states, including some where maternal mortality was used as a strong arguing point in the campaign for abortion law repeal, where not a single such death was reported. Even these relatively low figures dropped again during the subsequent decade, but much of the credit attributed to legalization is dubious. This was the decade when the suction machine for vacuum extraction was introduced. Its use, legally or illegally, has been most responsible for the reductions in maternal mortality and morbidity related to abortion in these latter years. As far as reported statistics indicate, then, the repeal of abortion laws in our land cannot reliably be said to have saved the lives of thousands of women. Bernard Nathanson has written:

> How many deaths were we talking about when abortion was illegal? In N.A.R.A.L. [the National Association for the Repeal of Abortion Laws, later the National Abortion Rights Action League] we generally emphasized the drama of the individual case, not the mass statistics, but when we spoke of the latter it was always "5,000 to 10,000 deaths a year." I confess that I knew the figures were totally false, and I suppose the others did too if they stopped to think of it. But in the "morality" of our revolution, it was a *useful* figure, widely accepted, so why go out of our way to correct it with honest statistics? The overriding concern was to get the laws eliminated, and anything within reason that had to be done was permissible.[16]

But perhaps these mortality rates are understated. It is widely known that a doctor, rather than risk his own or a colleague's legal safety, or a woman's reputation, would be likely to falsify a death certificate in order to conceal the true cause of death from illegal abortion.[17] Abortion advocates have used this unreliability of death reports to justify their much higher estimates. One means of evaluating those figures—both the published reports and the conjectures—is provided by the obstetrician-gynecologists of Minnesota, who from 1950 onward deployed medical teams to conduct an exacting, case-by-case double-check of female deaths that might be maternal. They corrected considerable errors and omissions in the official reports, and found that during twenty-four years criminal abortions accounted for a total of twenty-eight deaths in Minnesota: an average of 1.2 deaths per year. This would equal about 1 percent of the death rate from illegal abortion then being claimed by abortion advocates.[18] Even if this searching examination had missed some undisclosed abortion deaths, its baseline statistics are of an entirely different magnitude than those presented on behalf of abortion law repeal.

It is also possible that today's reports on abortion-related maternal mortality are unreliable. When the case for nationwide abortion freedom was being argued a decade ago, much attention was given to the effects of legalized abortion in New York State. Proponents pointed to the fact that since the new, permissive law had been in force there, maternal mortality (from abortion and all other causes) had declined in the state by 37 percent. But what abortion advocates overlooked or ignored was that when legal abortion came to New York the maternal mortality rate there had been twice the national average. One physician remarked: "We see a picture of a metropolitan system of health care delivery registering what must rank as one of the worst obstetrics records in modern American medicine. We are then asked . . . to believe that large-scale abortion has transformed it into a system of great safety, efficiency and 'high calibre health care.' " In their reports of high abortion safety in New York, advocates evidently contaminated their equations. First, they calculated deaths against abortions performed, though 65 percent of them were on women from out of state about whom the follow-up data were unreliably scanty. Then the deaths that did come to light were excluded whenever a way could be found. One early notice described "an 18-year old who committed suicide three days after a suction procedure, because of guilt feelings about having 'killed her baby,' before she could be informed that she had not been pregnant." Her death, which would ordinarily have been classified as abortion-related, was excluded from the statistics on the ground that she had not in fact been pregnant.[19]

After abortion on demand became lawful in all states it was assumed that mortality and morbidity statistics would become more reliable, since there was little criminality to cover up in health reports, and since women would no longer be traveling far from home for the procedure and then breaking off contact with the clinics and their follow-up studies. This seems to have been a wrong assumption. Abortion, though everywhere legal, remains for most abortors something to be concealed. An enormous proportion of today's legal abortions are essentially clandestine. License plates of cars in clinic parking lots are often said to be from other localities, where identical facilities are available but identical anonymity is not. The abortors and the complications they experience are not known to the physicians who perform the abortions, and who then publish abortion-related statistics that are unreliable.[20] The chief of the Family Planning Evaluation Division of the Bureau of Epidemiology, Center for Disease Control, has testified to the difficulties in verifying reports of abortion-related deaths.[21] One obstetrician reported treating fifty-four teenagers for significant abortion complications which, because the patients had not returned to the physicians who performed the abortions, never appeared in their data.[22] The total number of abortion complications treated in American hospitals has, in fact, been reported to have increased since abortion was legalized nationally. In 1969, 9,000 cases were reported; by 1977 it had almost doubled, rising to 17,000.[23] As regards maternal deaths, a study of four large abortion clinics by the *Chicago Sun-Times* disclosed 12 abortion-related deaths that had previously been unknown to state officials.[24]

In brief, just as the incidence of abortion-related death and dangerous complications was inflated for propaganda purposes before abortion law repeal, so also the figures for mortality and morbidity from legal abortion since then seem to have been understated. It is possible that in either case they cannot be refined to the point of meticulous accuracy. But they certainly do not presently support the claim that wholesale deaths of aborting women have been averted by the change in our law.

When the Congress withdrew Medicaid subsidies for abortion in 1977 the Center for Disease Control, whose officers had taken a partisan position strongly supportive of abortion choice, predicted a bloodbath. Later the director of its Abortion Surveillance branch admitted that such had not occurred.[25] Even if abortion should once more be declared a criminal act, it is unlikely that a wave of maternal carnage would ensue. Suction curettage has made early abortion much more simple; in many countries it is performed by paramedics. All evidence shows that even when abortion was illegal the enormous majority of procedures were performed by physicians. In the future, even in abortions administered by nonphysicians outside the law, the coathanger will have vanished. Its significance at present is only to add vividness to proabortion rhetoric.[26]

Close observers of the abortion scene have all along discounted the claim that abortion was a health measure. In Great Britain, Cambridge biologist Charles Goodhart noted in 1970 that "the vast majority of cases are not primarily medical at all, but social, whatever the certificate may say about risks to the physical or mental health of the mother and her children; and what the mother wants is much the most important factor, if not the only one, to be considered in coming to a decision."[27] More recently the London *Times* commented on a High Court opinion that the bench should abstain from reviewing the clinical judgments of doctors associated with abortion. "The satisfaction with which that opinion will be greeted in the medical profession would be more widely shared if there were confidence that in all or in very nearly all cases the doctor's judgments as to whether the statutory medical conditions for a lawful abortion have been met are genuinely clinical judgments and are not substantially influenced by their own ethical or social convictions about abortion. . . . And if that medical opinion is to any extent founded on the preference rather than the health of the mother or even on the preferences of the doctors, then it becomes less unreasonable to ask that preferences of other interested parties, which would include the father, be taken into account also."[28]

An American medical journal, after polling 40,000 American physicians about abortion in 1967, quoted Dr. David Decker of the Mayo Clinic as saying that there were "few, if any, absolute medical indications for therapeutic abortion in the present state of medicine."[29] Psychiatrist Thomas Szasz is more astringent: "Abortion is a moral, not a medical, problem. To be sure, the procedure is surgical; but this makes abortion no more a medical problem than the use of the electric chair makes capital punishment a problem of electrical engineering."[30] And Daniel Callahan, permissive of abortion as is Szasz, puts it most sharply: "Abortion is not notably therapeutic for the fetus. . . . It may be merciful and it may be wise, but, unless I am mistaken, the medical profession does not classify procedures with a 100% mortality rate as therapeutic. Perhaps, then, abortion is therapeutic for the woman. . . . But is it proper to employ language which has a very concrete meaning in medicine—the correction or amelioration of a physical or psychological defect—in a case where there is usually no physical pathology at all? Except in the now-rare instances of a direct threat to a woman's life, an abortion cures no known disease and relieves no medically classifiable illness."[31]

Abortion is undeniably a surgical procedure. But the Supreme Court speaks in blurred meanings when grounding it upon "clinical judgment" and clothing it in the immunities which the people wish doctors to enjoy in their professional ministry to their patients' health. Abortion, legal or criminal, serves no one's health, and is no medical matter—unless those words be stretched beyond their ordinary meanings. In perhaps 99 percent of present cases it is medical only in virtue of being performed by a physician. It is no more medical than is the implantation of silicone in a hopeful lady's bosom.

Ethical Argument: Abortion Is Psychically Therapeutic

The notion of health which the Supreme Court brought to bear in 1973 actually gave more play to the welfare of the spirit than to that of the body. Abortion, Justice Blackmun said, could be indicated by many factors: "physical, emotional, psychological, familial, and the woman's age."[32] The Court did not pursue this observation consistently and authorize psychiatrists, clergy, psychologists, or professional counselors to participate in legal abortion alongside their medical colleagues. Nor did anyone expect this, for it was clear that the physicians were given exclusive jurisdiction over abortion, not because they knew how to diagnose the need for it, but because technically they had the knack for it. And, in any case, psychiatrists had had, for the previous decade, a widespread involvement with abortion that had made everyone uncomfortable.

Around 1960 it became common in most states for obstetrician-abortionists to protect themselves from legal jeopardy by making stable arrangements with one or two psychiatric colleagues willing to certify that their unhappy patients might take their own lives if not delivered of their pregnancies. They could and did thus circumvent the laws which forbade abortion except to save the life of the mother. Throughout the 1960s the preponderance of legal abortion traffic was certified as psychiatrically necessary: estimates vary between 80 and 95 percent.[33] Those involved knew that the psychiatrists were simply vouching, for a fee, for a conventional pretense.

For some time psychiatrists took this task in stride. One explained, "While I may recommend abortions, it's easier to say it's OK for somebody else to do them."[34] But eventually the custom of diagnosis on demand began to chafe. It became well known that the suicide rate was lower for pregnant women than for the general population nationally. As a psychiatric indication for abortion the alleged danger of suicide was shown to be insignificant.[35] Indeed, studies indicated that even among women who had sought abortions and been refused, the risk of suicide was almost nil.[36]

As the plausibility of suicide risk came into eclipse, the law was changing to allow threats to psychic health as indications for abortion. Psychiatrists were not lacking to certify that women with unwanted pregnancies faced severe trauma if made to bear their unborn to term. But research in the area overwhelmingly showed these diagnoses to be as contrived as their predecessors. All pregnancy, it was pointed out, even when willingly undertaken, tends to involve a likelihood of emotional stress, with not infrequent anxiety and depression.[37] Numerous studies have reported that pregnant women, especially adolescents, who want to abort tend as a group to have had fractured and chaotic life experiences.[38] Those most vulnerable to distressed pregnancy are said to have emotional problems, conflictual relationships with sexual partners, negative relationships with their mothers, and unhealthy dependencies on their fathers. In short, abortion seems to have been resorted to typically by women in psychic distress.[39] It was hardly a means of preventing emotional disorder. It was, however, a measure which some practitioners hoped would keep existing troubles from aggravation. Comparisons between women who continued originally unwanted pregnancies to term and those who aborted do not support the belief, though, that the former group suffered psychic damage which the latter was spared.[40] Generally, psychiatrists began to object that there were no common and meaningfully severe emotional risks for women who bore the children of undesired pregnancies. The diagnoses were being fabricated as a convenience for women anxious to circumvent the law, and voices began to be raised against a practice some felt to be degrading to their profession.

Seymour Halleck, a Wisconsin psychiatrist, wrote in 1971: "No psychiatrist, if he is honest with himself . . . can . . . describe any scientific criteria that enable him to know which woman should have her pregnancy terminated, and which should not. When he recommends an abortion, he usually lies. It is a kind lie, a dishonesty intended to make the world a little better, but it is still a lie."[41] In 1972 California psychiatrist James Ford stated: "A review of some of the most oft-quoted, and presumably quite authoritative, psychiatric literature on the subject of abortion appears to substantiate the posited fact that most honest and knowledgeable psychiatrists have now come to admit that they find themselves out of their depth in this matter of the psychiatrically-indicated abortion decision." Even abortion advocates were admitting that abortion was not serving medical or psychic health; it was, they said, "therapeutic" in a sociologic way since it solved the problem of unwanted pregnancy. Ford's opinion: in the absence of consistent, valid criteria on which to base a psychiatric recommendation for abortion, "the current practice of performing innumerable, mechanized, elective abortions can only be considered unethical."[42] In 1974 Dr. Irving Bernstein of Minnesota, a professor of both psychiatry and obstetrics and gynecology, summarized his testimony before Senator Bayh's subcommittee in this way:

> There are no psychiatric indications for therapeutic abortion because: (1) therapeutic abortion is not effective treatment for the

patient or for the situation, and just kills babies; (2) the abortion will not solve the battered child syndrome; (3) suicide is less of a risk in pregnant women than in nonpregnant women; (4) it is impossible to predict who will develop a post-partum psychosis; (5) therapeutic abortion has its own psychiatric morbidity; (6) adequate treatment methods are available to handle psychiatric difficulties occurring during pregnancy.[43]

Psychiatrist Stephen Fleck of Yale, who has vigorously advocated abortion freedom, expresses a consensus of his profession, whatever its individual members' ethical judgment in the matter: "This phrase [therapeutic abortion] compounds the ethical confusion and intellectual dishonesty which are characteristic of popular and professional attitudes and notions about abortion. Obviously abortion is not a treatment for anything unless pregnancy is considered a disease, and if it were that, it is the only disease which is 100 per cent curable by abortion or delivery at term."[44] Some in the profession would go further. Women who display the most severe stress symptoms during unwanted pregnancy, according to some studies, seem to develop the most psychiatric complications after abortion.[45] "It therefore could be deduced," says Bernstein, "that these patients who can tolerate a therapeutic do not need it in the first place." Psychiatrically, he believes, patients are often much helped when reassured that they are not so ill they could not have another child. "Being told that one is too sick emotionally to tolerate a pregnancy can be extremely upsetting to a patient."[46] Halleck is of a similar mind. "Granting excuses to emotionally disturbed individuals may, in the long run, harm them. Although there probably is little danger of depression following therapeutic abortion, the process of securing a psychiatric excuse from meeting an obligation may be psychologically damaging; the patient may learn to use 'illness' as a means of avoiding other obligations, insist that she should not be held responsible for her actions."[47]

Concern among abortion advocates regarding psychiatric aspects of abortion has undergone redirection during the last decade. There is now virtually no serious debate about whether abortion is emotionally therapeutic. The question has now been turned around: is abortion itself a cause of psychic disorder? On this issue there has been a cascade of research, though of a partisan nature. Psychiatrist Sidney Bolter "has never seen a patient who has not had guilt feelings about a previous therapeutic abortion or illegal abortion."[48] Psychiatrist James Welch says that in his postabortion interviews, "I can remember only one woman who regretted the abortion."[49] These two statements illustrate a clear conflict of interpretation and report. Most of the literature on psychiatric sequelae to abortion emanates from studies under proabortion auspices. They are hampered by the difficulty in following up abortors after two or three months; they rely often on hastily posed telephone interrogatories; and in general they have not been impressive in their methods or their findings. Much depends on the measures one uses. Henry David, echoing most studies, asserts "that postabortion psychosis is practically unknown, whereas postpartum breakdown is quite familiar to psychiatrists."[50] It does seem clear that women very rarely report for psychiatric hospitalization or formal therapy in the aftermath of abortion. Most studies report that a third to a half of the women admit to grief and guilt afterwards, but they also report that these feelings are transient, and disappear after about three months.[51] Counselors associated with abortion clinics or referral agencies believe that their clients surmount an early period of depression, then integrate the experience and emerge with an overall feeling of relief. Yet counselors with agencies that urge alternatives to abortion claim to see women who confess profound and unresolved grief, sometimes coupled with suicidal thoughts, even years after their abortions.[52]

Many critics have raised questions about research that depends on abortion personnel to ascertain psychological sequelae of abortion, after a brief lapse of time. A few have noted that within the literature there is frequent confusion between the presence of psychological illness and subjective feelings, particularly those of guilt.[53] It may well be that there are recurring guilt feelings about abortion which arise beyond the short time limits of most follow-up studies, do not involve the kind of pathological disablement that might bring them to the attention of the psychological or psychiatric professions, yet do represent a serious and unstudied grieving over abortion long past.[54]

As they are now reported, women's emotional adjustments after abortion are heavily subject to partisan interpretation. To illustrate: a nineteen-year-old was interviewed while awaiting her third abortion in less than three years:

> "I feel comfortable and calm. I have no regrets at all. But in six or eight months I will look back and think, 'My child would have been born now.' I write the date down on the calendar in a code that only I can understand. I guess that in a way I feel sad. . . .
>
> "It's my fault," she said. "I have used contraception—the pill. But I forgot to take them. After all, I don't take vitamins or anything else every day so there's nothing to remind me. I want something that's safe and not too difficult to use."
>
> To the suggestion that the man might take some responsibility for contraception, she responded, "My boyfriend has said that maybe he could withdraw. He says next time."
>
> All of Cheryl's pregnancies were fathered by a 26-year-old automobile mechanic with whom she has had a long-term relationship. "Each time this happened to me, he wanted to get married and have the kid," Cheryl said. "He tried to talk me out of the abortions. At first I was tempted, but I wasn't even out of high school, and I couldn't imagine what I would do with that poor kid. I tell him that I will get married someday but now I'm working and enjoying myself. . . .
>
> "I think it all through before I make appointments. It's not an easy thing to do, and I don't think people should use abortion just because it's handy."
>
> Still, when asked whether she considered an 8-week-old embryo to be a human being, she said, "I feel it's a baby all the way, so there is a little guilt."

And if she were to become pregnant again? "No matter what, I would have it. Three abortions is the limit for me," she said.

"I just can't keep on destroying babies. After all, my mother didn't destroy me," she said. To bolster her resolve, she said, she is having her third abortion under local anesthetic instead of the general anesthetic she had had in the past. "I want to be awake during this one, I want to see how it feels, to feel the pain. Maybe that will convince me not to come back again."[55]

From one perspective she could be seen as realistically coping, and expected to emerge rather stably after some ephemeral unsettlement. From another view she would be seen as a profoundly disturbed and incoherent adolescent.

Psychiatrists and psychologists generally concur that most of the abortions for which their colleagues vouched as therapeutic were in fact indicated by none of the emotional disorders with which they are professionally competent to deal. They know of very few psychic complications in unwanted pregnancy for which abortion is an appropriate treatment. Indeed, they now express misgivings because true emotional disorders that call for serious therapy are being given swift and apparent relief through abortion, but a relief that may be deceptive, since the unwanted pregnancy itself is so often not the human problem but an aggravation of problems which then are left to fester. The psychiatric sequelae of abortion seem to involve different sentiments which are confused by those who report them: unresolved estrangements which preceded abortion and may be its cause rather than its effect; and moral guilt (a psychically healthy repudiation of one's behavior, not to be confused with neurotic guilt). In short, whereas elective abortion was once associated with bogus psychiatric diagnosis, it can now be seen to be entangled with serious emotional problems that have yet to receive adequate study or treatment, and for which abortion is offered sometimes as a placebo.

Ethical Argument: No Unwanted Child Should Ever Be Born

When one has stripped off the claims of medical and psychiatric need for abortion—claims that were generated with an eye to legal clearance and public approval—there remains the one innermost indication, or reason, for abortion as currently practiced: that children are sometimes not wanted. The prevailing motive for abortion, *au fond*, is that the mother, on her own determination or through the intervention of persons persuasive with her, does not welcome the unborn she is carrying. The argument on her behalf is that no woman ought be forced to give birth to a son or daughter whom she does not welcome.

This claim takes several shapes. Sometimes it is pled on the child's behalf. "Without legal and affordable abortion," editorializes *Time* magazine, "many lives in progress are hopelessly ruined; the unwanted children very often grow up unloved, battered, conscienceless, trapped and criminal. A whole new virus of misery breeds in the accidental zygotes." Without available abortion, "the women (often young girls) who cannot raise the money must presumably . . . bear their unwanted children—thus bringing many thousands of new customers to welfare."[56] In this appeal, as in others, there is a clear implication that it is the poor who typically lack the wherewithal to raise their children decently and therefore also lack the willingness to bear more of them. Minnesota Abortion Rights Council president Betty Benjamin presses the point: "Among the 800,000 unplanned, unwanted children born every year in the U.S., many become loved and wanted. Unfortunately, many others end up as battered children, delinquents, and criminals. Studies of battered children reveal a high percentage of unmarried and unwanted pregnancy, or forced marriage among the abusive parents."[57] Mrs. Benjamin does not refer us to these studies, but her impression is widely shared. It is contradicted by the research of E. F. Lenoski, pediatrician at the University of Southern California Medical School, who found that 90 percent of the battered or abused children he studied were the result of desired pregnancies, compared with only 63 percent of children in a matched control group. Also, battered children were much more likely to be born of legitimate birth, and to mothers who displayed satisfaction with their pregnancy.[58]

The argument for abortion to spare the child does not repose simply on the likelihood of physical abuse. "It is a low form of cruelty to insist ruthlessly on bringing into the world a child for whom there is no welcome, no proper care and nurture, and no chance for a decent life. It is all very well to argue about the rights of the fetus. But what about the rights of the child? There is no virtue in a legal insistence on bringing into the world unwanted children doomed to poverty, disease and delinquency."[59]

One notes a recurring association with the lower classes. It is present also in the forceful testimony of Ms. Bella Abzug on this matter:

> Although it is certainly not inevitable that the child unwanted at birth will be rejected and unloved in life, research into the etiology of mental illness, criminality and mental retardation has singled out parental deprivation as perhaps the single most important causal factor. The number of grossly deprived, abused, and neglected children is so large that for every child who may be helped by the intervention of child welfare agencies, hundreds go undetected until it is too late. Child abuse, in which the children are beaten, tortured, maimed, or even killed by their parents, has become such a widespread problem in our society that we have even had to enact a national law to attempt to deal with it.[60]

All this, she urges, might somehow be alleviated had these children been aborted. Abzug and others who make this argument have turned much attention to two major studies on the outcome of unwanted children. In Sweden, Forssman and Thuwe traced 120 children whose mothers had sought unsuccessfully to abort them (study group) and compared them to 120 other children (control group). Study children at age twenty-one were found to have had a more insecure childhood (70 percent vs. 34 percent), more psychiatric care (28 percent vs. 15 percent), more reported delinquency (18 percent vs. 8 percent), more drunken misconduct (16 percent vs. 11 percent), less higher education (14 percent vs. 33 percent), more welfare payments in their later teens (14 percent vs. 3.5 percent), more rejections among males for military service (15 percent vs. 7 percent), and more subnormal grades in school (11 percent vs. 5 percent). James Prescott of the National Institutes of Health, testifying on behalf of abortion, concludes: "Unwanted children suffer over twice the social, emotional and mental disabilities than do wanted children on a variety of measures. The costs to society in increased crimes; welfare recipients; poorly educated citizenry and drunkenness constitute a clear and present danger to a well-functioning society."[61] Dr. Leonard Laufe, an obstetrician and consultant to Planned Parenthood, draws a more vigorous conclusion: "There was an overwhelming significant portion of antisocial behavior among these children—the common criminal crimes that we all know, plus a very significant incidence of schizophrenia in those offspring."[62]

The Sweden study has not enjoyed as much credit among social scientists as it has among abortion advocates. Forssman and Thuwe neglected to control, or isolate, the factor of illegitimacy. Many children in the "unwanted" study group were reared out of wedlock, a factor not matched in the control group, and one which by itself would heavily influence the children's welfare and development. The study, therefore, has been seen as inconclusive.[63]

A second and more careful inquiry into the fortunes of unwanted children has been conducted in Czechoslovakia. The study children there number 220 and they were born to mothers who were denied abortion twice: their requests had been turned down, appealed, and again turned down. The control group, for comparison, was carefully assembled and matched. The unwanted children, over the years, have fallen behind the control children in a number of comparisons, leading Dr. Prescott to state that they "experienced quite varied and usually more unfavorable consequences in their subsequent lives than wanted children," and thus to argue "that denial of abortion leads to undesirable consequences for the unwanted child and society."[64]

But here again the research is too exuberantly put to use. While advocates recount all comparisons disfavorable to the study group they fail to point out that on most comparisons the differences between the groups are too slight to be statistically significant, while on some scales the "unwanted" children rank higher, leading the researchers themselves to observe that the study children had not fared so badly. "The idea commonly held among psychiatrists and clinical psychologists that eventual difficulties in the behavior of an unwanted child are inevitably linked with the originally rejecting attitude of the mother toward his existence is not wholly supported for both boys and girls. On the other hand, the view commonly entertained by the lay public that the birth of the child changes everything and every mother comes to deeply love her child is apparently also invalid."[65]

The Prague researchers began with the knowledge that "in child psychiatry and psychology the opinion is generally accepted that an unwanted pregnancy can have a very negative influence upon the development of a child." After straining to confirm this assumption, they admit that between these two meticulously studied groups of "unwanted" and "wanted" children, "the differences remain to be not very pronounced and not very dramatic." The most that they can conclude about unwantedness is that it "is a factor not nearly negligible in the life of the child."[66]

Indeed, when one reflects that these were children whose mothers strove to be rid of them, not just by a possibly unstable request for abortion, but through the more resolute procedure of appeal, only to be denied twice, one might expect that these children, more than any, would have to face extraordinary parental animus. One would anticipate that their lives would be marked by neglect and by bitterness strong enough for some to think that the children would better not have survived. But as Lamanna observes, "An interpretation of this study to suggest that 'unwanted' children will almost surely have a poor future would be misleading; the study children seem to be leading relatively normal lives."[67]

The most rigorous research into the ups and downs in the lives of children rejected during pregnancy does not show them to be blighted by adversity. They seem, on an honest reading of the studies, to be in arrears in some aspects of their lives, but far less than one might have anticipated, and decidedly less than would reasonably support the thought that society and the children would both be better off had the children been denied birth. Presumably even those willing to entertain the view that the unborn are being done a favor by extirpation would need evidence of a more dreadful destiny for them than these studies describe.

But even if the force of the "unwantedness" argument for abortion as an intervention on behalf of the child is stymied for want of evidence, it needs to be examined further. As many have pointed out, a woman who does not want the child she is carrying cannot be relied upon to continue in that attitude: "The ability of mothers to accept infants after they are born is underrated and underestimated. We also are much too quick to accept trite statements and poorly controlled studies about the influence of so-called sick mothers upon their children."[68] An unwanted pregnancy does not lead regularly to an unwanted child. Dytrych, Matějček, and their Czech colleagues have also observed this.[69] Evidence is surfacing that women (and men) who did not want to carry their unborn to term have later reported that they were satisfied as parents of those children. It is interesting to note what social scientists, especially those sympathetic towards abortion, do with this evidence. Some tend to disbelieve the reliability of the mothers' memories.[70] Others disbelieve mothers who say they came to love their children, and conjecture that they must still be harboring unconscious hostility.[71]

Perhaps the most interesting reaction—and an influential one—is shown by the authors of a Princeton study of "unwanted fertility" among Americans: Westoff, Ryder, and Bumpass. Setting zero population growth as the desirable goal, these social scientists asked what would happen to reproductive patterns if couples retained their present preferences regarding how many children to bear, but possessed "perfect fertility control," the ability never to bear any child except by choice. Their study disclosed one fact and two interpretations that bear on "wantedness." They found that the desire for children was not constant: it enlarged as women grew older and had fuller experience of motherhood. In other words, women (and their spouses) near the end of their childbearing years stated that they were pleased to have a larger number of children than they had originally intended or, had they been provided with fail-safe contraception, than they would have begotten. The authors discount this later measure of "wantedness":

> We suspect that the number of children desired as conventionally measured in fertility surveys contains a considerable amount of post factum rationalization of children who at the time of conception had never been wanted but whose presence had been subsequently accepted and who, by the time of the interview, had been redefined and included in the total number of children desired. One suspicion of such rationalization stems from the fact that desired family size increases with age and marriage duration. Another suspicion stems from the fact, noted above, that about one-half of the women who reported an unwanted birth also reported, in a different part of the interview, that they did not prefer fewer children than they had had. Not all of this should be regarded as inconsistency since the two measures refer to different points in time—one the time of conception and the other a varying period of time later when the woman was interviewed. For many women the additional child may now really be desired. The critical measurement for some purposes, however, is not the capacity to accommodate oneself to the unintended consequences of sexual union but rather the number of children that would have been born if perfect fertility control were available, that is, the number of children the couple would have had if the only determinant of this number (with existing levels of fecundability) were the preferences of the parents at the time of conception.[72]

This interpretation seems influenced by the authors' distrust of the women's more mature perspective and their preference for the women's originally desired family size. "It must be difficult for a woman retrospectively to report a birth as unwanted since such a report reflects on her ability to control her fertility, and perhaps also on the status of the child who is now a member of the family."[73] Dissatisfied with at least half of their respondents, who were pleased that they had *not* enjoyed totally effective fertility control, the Princeton social scientists argued for a policy which would assure families of a size that satisfies newlyweds, rather than one acceptable to the more mature. The "wantedness" to be served is not allowed to come after the fact.

This leads to their second interpretation. An "unwanted" birth is defined as one that follows from any conception which was not purposely sought. The notion of "unwantedness" is not associated with any hostility or avoidance. Between the two clear categories of actively desired conception and resolutely resisted conception most people are aware of a wide middle ground: conceptions that are neither premeditated nor unwelcome. In the Princeton study all these pregnancies are transferred over into the "unwanted" column. To be wanted, a child must positively have been intended at the moment of conception. Any desire which rises to meet the child afterwards is "rationalization."

Recent developments in the Princeton research have displayed "a disturbingly high frequency" of women who related positively to an unwanted pregnancy. The researchers were disconcerted to find "that 42 percent of women who said in 1970 that they wanted no (more) children reacted positively to a subsequent pregnancy." Of those whose last pregnancies were unwanted, only a third reported negative reactions when they did conceive. Between 19 and 27 percent reported that they were "thrilled," "happy," "glad"—that it was "nice." And, by what the authors continue to call "retrospective rationalization," women continue to accept their children when conceived and to forget that they had been unwanted.[74]

This notion, given a strong introduction by Westoff and his colleagues, that unintended conception yields an unwanted pregnancy and a repudiated child, has gained strong acceptance. It is the background of the creed of Planned Parenthood: "We believe that the birth of every child should never be an accident."[75] It has led to casual estimates, well beyond theirs, of how many unwanted children see the light of day in America. And, as an arguing point on behalf of abortion, it has also influenced how many children do not see the light of day.[76]

An obvious question of method arises when a study systematically writes off the accumulated experience of parenthood as an increasing deviation from a younger, less accommodating wisdom. But it also invites some meditation on the widespread American belief that the finest possible preamble to a childhood that is happy, well provided for, and well adjusted is a pregnancy that is purposeful. A Canadian psychiatrist has speculated, for example, that it is abortion, not unwanted birth, which is associated with child abuse. Philip Ney, chief of psychiatry in a Vancouver Hospital, noticed that an increase in child deaths from social causes in Canada coincided with the introduction of elective abortion; that provinces with high and low abortion rates rank similarly in child abuse; and that individual women who abused their children were reported to have higher abortion rates. "Having to treat so many battered children, I began to worry that using abortion to make every child a wanted child might be backfiring. When I examined the evidence, I became convinced that most of the abused children resulted from wanted pregnancies and that elective abortion is an important cause of child abuse." Ney offers several hypotheses to explain the relationship between elective abortion and the battered child syndrome:

> Having an abortion can interfere with a mother's ability to restrain her anger toward those depending on her care. Abortion might also weaken a social taboo against harming those who are defenseless. With wholesale abortions discarding nondefective unborn children, the value of children might diminish, resulting in less care and protection. . . . An aborting person, having already repressed her instinctive caring for her unborn young, might be less inhibited in giving vent to her rage at a whimpering child. . . .
>
> Only two decades ago parents were willing to suffer major deprivation to have and raise children. It seemed like a sacred

obligation or a great privilege. Nowadays, people balance having children with wanting a country house, another car, better vacations and early retirement. This might be observed by children in such families. As a result they might feel less confidence in their parents' true concern for their welfare. They might then become so importunate in their demands for care and attention that their parents feel threatened. Not infrequently, the parental response to those attention-demanding children will be physical violence. . . .

Society is beginning to believe that a child has no right to exist and is therefore valued only when it is wanted. If it is permissible to kill an unwanted, unborn child, then one can defend killing children already born when they are no longer considered valuable. . . .

Recent evidence indicates many woman harbor strong guilt feelings long after their abortions. Guilt is one important cause of child battering and infanticide. Abortion also lowers women's self-esteem and there are studies reporting a major loss of self-esteem in battering parents. . . .

Some women resent their male partners impregnating them and then coercing them to have an abortion. Fathers, on the other hand, might feel hostility toward women because they have no rights in decisions about which infant gets aborted and when. The "battle of the sexes" aggravated by elective abortion can all too easily be turned violently against children.

There is increasing evidence that previously aborted women become depressed during a subsequent pregnancy. Depression interferes with a mother's early bonding with her infant, and children who are not bonded to their mothers are at a higher risk of being battered.[77]

Ney's suggestions enlarge a doubt that "wantedness" best describes what healthy parenthood requires. Some time ago Dr. Elizabeth M. Whelan published a book describing the lengthy considerations she and her husband, attorney Stephen T. Whelan, were engaged in. The book, A Baby? . . . Maybe, was followed after some years by a daughter, Christine. Dr. Whelan, who runs a preparenthood counseling service, joined her husband in explaining this to the public. "After we looked hard at the pros and cons and weighed all possible alternatives as scientifically as we could, we finally realized that what we were dealing with was basically an emotional decision. We felt—for no fully rational reason—that we didn't want to miss the experience of having at least one child."[78] The obvious embarrassment of the Whelans, whose defection from rational and scientific contemplation to parenthood seemed to call for public apology, is a reflection—and an only slightly risible one—of a dogmatic tenet of our time: that parenthood had best be planned and purposeful. As Rabbi Balfour Brickner, spokesman for the Religious Coalition for Abortion Rights, expresses it: "We call for the right to life when wanted—not under biological roulette."[79]

The most profound question to be raised in this matter is this: is good parenthood—zestful, generous, expansive, resilient—most reliably vouched for by planned and purposeful pregnancy, if children inevitably require of their parents a continual acquiescence—a delight, even—in so much that is unplanned and unpurposeful? How ideal a welcome is it for a child to be born to parents at exactly the time and into exactly the life circumstances they have wished for him or her? Is it not a small step from there for them to decide further, when the choice is open to them, that they will welcome a him but not a her?

Several years back, when amniocentesis and late abortion were beginning to find popular use as a means of eliminating unborn of undesirable gender, it brought transitory misgivings to the doctors who complied. Doctors at Yale, UCLA, and George Washington universities, when interviewed, indicated that they regarded the process as immoral but were prepared to do it for two reasons. First, they expected it to be infrequent. Second, having agreed to let women control their "reproductive future," they would feel obliged to cooperate with whatever choices that entailed.[80] Dr. John Fletcher, who writes from within the National Institutes of Health to advise physicians on moral issues, confesses that he too finds this procedure unjustified, but would feel himself a hypocrite were he not to comply. "The existence of some trivial reasons should not deter us from the larger goal of protecting the right of women to make such decisions in the first place. . . . It is inconsistent to support an abortion law that protects the absolute right of women to decide and, at the same time, to block access to information about the fetus because one thinks that an abortion may be foolishly sought on the basis of the information."[81] Instructive in Fletcher's view is not simply the fact that he is prepared to let the Supreme Court provide him with ethical as well as legal doctrine, but that he sees that the absolute right of decision, once conferred upon women regarding their offspring, cannot be quibbled with. What one must ask is whether an absolute right to decide is what parenthood is all about.

Once one has got the fit and feel of it, one easily expects that she or he has a right to get the sort of child one dreams of: unblemished, right sex, high IQ—all that a parent could require. The snag in this is that the parental vocation knows no other phase or moment when children can or should conform absolutely to their parents' requirements. The mindset of untrammeled choice, of "wantingness," is at odds with true and hopeful parenthood, where there is much more coping than choosing to be done.

If children are to be welcomed only by choice and design, we easily invite ourselves in to make better choices than others might. "Abortions should be required of every woman on welfare and all mothers of illegitimate children. . . . If there are no abortions, I believe it would not be against the law to starve to death unwanted children. . . . If 'educated' Americans can't control it so well, how can we expect those blacks and yellows to control their birthrates? . . . Most of those unwanted births are to irresponsible and ignorant women of minorities. . . . Nine out of 10 unwanted babies turn out on welfare or in prison."[82] With this sort of reaction in mind, columnist Sidney Callahan wrote in 1971:

The powerful (including parents) cannot be allowed to want and unwant people at will. . . .

It's destructive of family life for parents even to think in these categories of wanted and unwanted children. By using the words you set up parents with too much power, including psychological power, over their children. Somehow the child is being measured by the parent's attitudes and being defined by the parent's feelings. We usually want only objects, and wanting them or not implies that we are superior, or at least engaged in a one-way relationship, to them.

In the same way, men have "wanted" women through the ages. Often a woman's position was precarious and rested on being wanted by some man. The unwanted woman could be cast off when she was no longer a desirable object. She did not have an intrinsic dignity beyond wanting.[83]

In marriage, in childbearing, in all tightly bonded human relationships, it is a brittle and feckless attitude which orders up all things according to one's wants, and expects to see the adventure through on the same terms. Abortion because a child is unwanted has no ground to stand on that is truly in the child's favor. The only referent for the rejection is oneself: one does not want this child to live, to impinge. Some psychiatric researchers have seen this as profoundly selfish. One study, for instance, observes: "Contrary to the popular belief that shame over pregnancy out of wedlock is the major motivation for abortion, we observed that . . . much more important was the woman's rejecting of motherhood with all of its attendant demands. Our impression is that these women tend to be narcissistic and regard the fetus as a competitor for the succorance and dependent care they themselves obviously require."[84] Another study noticed that women who approached abortion as an issue related to concerns of justice involving a weighing of two lives were more likely to continue their pregnancies, while women who approached abortion as an issue related to the self-determination of the individual were more likely to terminate their pregnancies.[85] Arranging one's children for one's wants is hardly the model to put forward for nurturing parenthood. Indeed, some research has suggested that parents of battered children think of them very possessively, as positively "wanted." Child abuse expert Ray Helfer points to something like this when he describes the "World of Abnormal Rearing Cycle":

> Although the advent of abortion interrupts a large number of pregnancies, it seems to interrupt less pregnancies of W.A.R. children. Girls who are reared in this unusual atmosphere have a strong desire to become pregnant. They often refuse the use of birth control and dismiss any thought of abortion. . . . Unfortunately, the pregnancy is wanted for very selfish reasons, i.e., to resolve some special problem for the mother. The new baby is supposed to get her away from an unhappy experience in her home, or will keep her company or even take care of her and

comfort her in her loneliness.

As the pregnancy comes to completion, the child may or may not have the capability of meeting the expectation that the parent(s) have developed through the W.A.R. years. Many young mothers who had every desire to get pregnant, with great expectations that the baby would resolve one of their many problems, find themselves even worse off than before. Their baby does not—or is not able to meet these needs.[86]

Helfer's colleague, C. Henry Kempe, who coined the term "the battered-child syndrome" and has done extensive research in the abuse of children, has observed: "Basic in the abuser's attitude toward infants is the conviction, largely unconscious, that children exist in order to satisfy parental needs."[87] This is why doctors in this field have been pointing out that prospective battering parents *want* children, and in this they stand apart from aborting parents. If the two groups have anything in common, it is "the assumption that the rights, desires, and ideas of the adult take full precedence over those of the child, and that children are essentially the property of parents who have the right to deal with their offspring as they see fit, without interference."[88] While it is obviously desirable that children be wanted when conceived, "unwantedness" fails as a convincing argument for abortion. Many children who were not wanted originally cause a change of heart in their parents. Children born in the face of hostile animus from their parents are not crippled by that original unwantedness. There are no clear signs that children first unwanted face abuse. Indeed, some forms of pathological child treatment involve a possessive "wantedness." Healthy, adaptive parenthood must be prepared from the start to make one's own wants second to one's children's needs—including the need to go on living.

Ethical Argument: The Unborn Are Not Our Human Peers

I began this essay about the case for abortion with an observation that came clear to me only well along in my inquiry. Adversary arguments are rarely symmetrical: they do not grapple directly with one another. This is conspicuously so with respect to the status of the unborn. Opponents of abortion dwell often and at sometimes tedious length on this matter. In the proabortion literature, by contrast, it typically receives a treatment that is oblique, nonchalant, elliptical. I was puzzled to find that although virtually everyone agreed with Justice Blackmun that the entire ethical and legal truth about abortion pivoted on this one question of whether the unborn are fellow persons with ourselves,[89] those who thought it obvious that they *were* human persons devoted much of their energy to expounding what they considered evident, while those who found the matter *unclear* made no substantial efforts to resolve it.

Discussion about the unborn, when unattended by anyone's readiness to be rid of them, has ordinarily acknowledged conception as the commencement of the human individual. Thus Alan Guttmacher's book, *Life in the Making*, published in 1933, devotes itself entirely to a study of human fertilization. In a series of essays entitled "How Life Begins," Guttmacher reviews the progressive scientific discoveries about mammalian and human procreation. This research reached a crescendo in the nineteenth century (Guttmacher's account is as masterful as any I have seen), when impregnation could finally be known and observed: "The nucleus of the sperm-head, bearing all the hereditary factors which come through the father, becomes indissolubly united with the nucleus of the ovum, bearing all the hereditary material which comes through the mother—and a new life, a composite of them both, is begun."[90] Thus, when the author refers interchangeably to "the fetus," "the unborn child," "the unborn infant," he is not simply conforming to a convention of speech. He is asserting what science only a century ago had plucked free from prior misunderstanding.[91] Guttmacher's book on the beginning of life is a book entirely about conception, for he is at pains to argue that the human individual is then created and composed. Thirty-five years later, as president of Planned Parenthood / World Federation, he initiated the process that led the organization to reverse its policy, to endorse the repeal of legal restrictions on abortion, and to sponsor abortion as a means of birth control. In 1967 he publicly advocated abortion in an essay which is doubly fascinating when one compares it with his earlier work. His argument for abortion begins with a historical survey that touches on most of the same influential traditions of the past—religious, legal, medical—but whereas in 1933 he had criticized those traditions as obscurantist and unscientific about creation, in 1967 he cited their acceptance of abortion as good reason for making it legal in the present. Second, his call for abortion freedom is totally silent about when human life begins.[92]

Dr. Guttmacher chose a common way of dealing with the established view that what abortion destroys is a human individual: he simply did not discuss it. In some respects this has been the simplest gambit in proabortion *Realpolitik*. Other approaches seemed to end in an embarrassing morass, for they were all variants on the "magic moment" argument.

Abortion protagonists have very rarely been ready to acknowledge that the unborn to be eliminated is an infant human being. And so they have sponsored a series of suggestions—novel since the particulars of conception had been confirmed in the last century—that humanhood, or personhood, begins sometime after the unborn is conceived. These suggestions have come to be known as "magic moment" arguments.

Probably the most serious suggestion of an onset of humanhood after conception is one that is not widely discussed: the implantation of the unborn in the wall of the womb. Bernard Nathanson has argued for this as the rightful cutoff point for abortion. Only after implantation, he points out, does the unborn dispatch endocrine signals that he or she is present, that pregnancy is underway. There is little principle sacrificed in adopting this as a policy, he maintains, for implantation is the earliest that one can test positively for pregnancy anyway.[93] The obvious attraction of this argument is that it would meet the objections to the IUD and menstrual extraction as birth control methods: They are generally thought to work by preventing implantation and by aborting the very young unborn. Other supporters of this view argue that the human soul may not be established within the unborn during the first fortnight between conception and implantation, since twinning and the reconjunction of twins are still possible during that first phase.[94]

Nathanson's argument does not really serve as a guideline of principle: the fact that the unborn can now be detected as nestled in the womb suggests no principle to explain why it could be considered another sort of being during its earlier, silent journey towards that nest. The argument that individuation is not decisively settled until implantation is a more serious one, though it implies gratuitously that a single unborn organism destined shortly to divide into two has, not one soul, but none. For those impatient with all talk about souls, this argument will have little appeal.

The next magic moment, or point of crucial status-change, is that of quickening. Cyril Means has made much of the fact that Anglo-American common law, and some early statute law, treated abortion as a serious felony only after quickening—that is, after the mother had felt the unborn stir within her and thus knew that she was pregnant, or "quick with child."[95] Opinion surveys show that even today some persons believe that this is when the unborn commence to be alive, and some argue that this is the rightful watershed between moral and immoral abortion. Sissela Bok's argument, for example, would find some such time, generally thought to be about midway through pregnancy, to be the beginning of human status: "Because there is no semblance of human form, no conscious life or capability to live independently, no knowledge of death, no sense of pain, words such as 'harm' or 'deprive' cannot be meaningfully used in the context of early abortion and fetal research."[96]

The moment of quickening is very difficult to recognize as the onset of humanhood. For one thing, quickening no longer occurs at the midway point of pregnancy, when a mother feels the first kick. It was always a twofold event: factual, in days of uncertain knowledge about procreation, in confirming that one was indeed pregnant; and emotional, in that the unborn was felt and acknowledged. Today a woman can test chemically for pregnancy within two weeks of conception, and can make emotional contact by listening to her child's heartbeat at about the eighth week (it begins about the fourth week, but beats too softly to be heard), or by watching the unborn move from about the same time (ultrasound has revealed that the unborn are much less animated in later pregnancy, when their movements can be directly felt, than at an earlier stage, when they are less crowded and are free to cavort energetically in the amniotic pool).

As regards jurisprudence, Dellapenna and Byrn have shown that the hesitancy of ancient law to inflict severe punishment for early abortion was due, not so much to a firm belief that the unborn stir to life when their first kick is felt, as to the difficulty of convicting without sure evidence that a woman was pregnant and knew that she was.[97] Thus quickening offers scant reason to be honored as a crucial beginning point of the human individual. Indeed, if quickening be the moment when pregnancy can be verified and the unborn acknowledged, then ironically today it is the invariable prelude to all surgically induced abortion.

Others have spoken of viability as a threshold of human status. The Supreme Court has gestured in this direction. "With respect to the State's important and legitimate interest in potential life, the 'compelling' point is at viability. This is so because the fetus then presumably has the capability of meaningful life outside the mother's womb. State regulation protective of fetal life after viability has both logical and biological justification."[98] The protection allowed by the Court is specious, of course, since it must always yield to maternal "health," defined as including a mother's sense of her well-being. The Court has not secured much praise for either its biology or its logic here. Biologically, viability, like quickening, moves forward as ever younger offspring can be sustained after premature delivery. And logically, there is little one can see in placental nourishment that would differ starkly enough from lactation (or, for that matter, intravenous infusion of invalids or the itinerant nourishment of astronauts) to make the former prehuman. An adult undergoing open heart surgery is thrown upon others for the sustaining of all life systems as thoroughly as is the unborn before or after viability. Possibly the most gaping inconsistency in the viability-as-threshold argument is the most recent: the "test-tube" babies were all viably outside the womb *before* implantation.

The magic moment most commonly designated is birth. Most advocates of elective abortion agree with the present law that this is the decisive event after which one is reckoned to be human. The unborn, says the Court, possess "potential life." Some speak of a "potential person," or of "potential human life."[99] Much puzzlement has followed from this usage of "potential." The passages from acorn to oak, ovum to fetus, unborn to adult, and caterpillar to butterfly are all quite different, and insight has only been blurred by smearing the designation "potential" across them. In any case, though a fetus, an infant, and an adolescent are all "potential" adults, one individual passing through these developments is obviously not "potentially" his or her future self, for stages pass while selves endure. What we honor in humans is not their stages but their selves. The unborn is not a potential human, but a human with potential.[100]

Garrett Hardin has attempted to rescue the birth moment as crucial by comparing unborn and adult to blueprint and house. Neither blueprint nor embryo is very valuable, he contends, because neither is so unique that it cannot quickly and easily be replaced by another copy. Hardin's argument has done little to shore up the case for birth as an onset of humanhood. For one thing, a blueprint is not a house, not even an incipient house; designs do not grow into artifacts in the way that living beings organically develop while retaining identity. Further, what he says about the nonuniqueness and replaceable value of the embryo is also true of the grown adult.[101]

The point can also be made more coarsely, and without wit. Natalie Shainess calls the unborn a parasite.[102] It is improbable, however, to suppose that the suckling newborn has graduated into independence. Indeed, parents of college students attest that they can now identify the stage at which filial parasitism takes its heaviest toll.

One embryologist has this to say:

These first reflex movements [intra-uterine] are probably mediated by the spinal cord; the brain is not yet well enough organized to control them and will not be so organized until after birth. When the fetus is ready to leave its dark and silent first home in the uterus its organ systems are, however, sufficiently developed to carry on the activities necessary for survival in the outer world, while the child is still protected and nourished by the mother. But the child is not yet an independent individual. The complicated muscular coordination necessary for walking and talking has to wait a year or more after birth until the nerve fibers of the brain have developed sufficiently to carry specialized impulses. A newly hatched chick or a newborn guinea pig trots off almost at once in search of food. The parents of a human infant, on the other hand, have the privilege and duty of watching with their own eyes the final stages of fetal development.[103]

Likewise, when one reads that the unborn "is an extension of the mother's uterus" one is at a loss how to understand it. One might say that the nursing infant is by equal logic an extension of the mother's breast. Or one might even enter a biological corrective by pointing out that not only the fetus, but even the placenta is a foreign being lodged in the womb.[104]

One looks in vain for significant transformations at birth which would give some plausibility to the view that it is the initiation of human existence. Some abortion advocates have felt this way, and accordingly have relocated the moment of humanification sometime in infancy. "A person, to speak very roughly, is an entity that has the (actual, not merely potential) capacity for self-consciousness, complex and sophisticated perception, rationality, self-awareness, and self-motivated behavior. Such entities have rights by virtue of the fact that they have definite, preconceptualized preferences with respect to their own present and future states; they have desires, hopes, plans, and fears. Above all, they normally desire to go on living, or at least not to be killed in a way not of their own choosing."[105] A Presbyterian clergyman sees it similarly. "Those who view an embryo or fetus as a 'person' in the fullest sense, who project it as a 'child' in the same sense as the neighbor's little boy out in the yard, albeit yet unborn, will never accept the concept of abortion. . . . Those of us who find abortion acceptable (in certain circumstances) do not share this view, of course, but see the development of a child in organic and progressive terms. . . . Medical science teaches that the 'person' develops as the requisite structure of human life (body) enters the experience of human life and becomes both aware and responsive."[106] Geneticist Joshua Lederberg is somewhat more explicit: "Even the newborn infant must undergo further development to achieve the full measure of humanity. An operationally useful point of divergence of the developing organism would be at approximately the first year of life, when the human infant continues his intellectual development, proceeds to the acquisition of language, and then participates in a meaningful, cognitive interaction with his mother and the rest of society."[107]

In their denial that birth is the crucial turning point these persons, who are logically obliged to allow infanticide as liberally as they would allow abortion, have replaced birth with an even more elusive magic moment. "Thus, though they deny that a day-old infant is a person, they admit that its life cannot be forfeited for any reason that would not equally apply to a two-year-old."[108] Another reflection upon these descriptions of beginning humanity is that Professor Lederberg and the rest have not spent adequate time observing infants. The sophistication they expect by the first birthday must, in some lives, await adolescence or later. But the fact is that they are not truly describing and honoring the onset of human life. They are really saying that when a youngster has begun to take our fancy, to have taken a station functionally close enough to our own to awaken our sense of kinship, then we clothe him or her with human dignity, or "personhood."

Roger Wertheimer has shown the impossibility of designating any moment after conception as the instant when a human *individual*, invested with human rights, begins to exist. "Going back stage by stage from the infant to the zygote one will not find any differences between successive stages significant enough to bear the enormous moral burden of allowing wholesale slaughter at the earlier stage while categorically denying that permission at the next stage."[109] In the end, he admits, we are drawn to define matters according to how we are willing to deal with them. A slaveholder looks at blacks, sees uncontrovertibly that they are inferior—in fact, less than human—and regards all talk of resemblances and species-solidarity as unrealistic raving. Wertheimer's comparison, one can see, sheds light on this feature of the abortion argument. Blacks were inferior in the eyes of those who wanted to use them. Human offspring are inferior in the eyes of those who want rid of them. It is not the development of embryo or fetus or newborn that is determinative, but his or her own desirability. As one young man remembered the abortion decision made by him and his companion at age eighteen, there was little moral or ethical or religious soul-searching. "None of that had any bearing on our situation. As far as I am concerned, there was just a bunch of cells there, no little human being."[110]

Joseph Fletcher admits: "I am very much afraid of all the attempts to establish some specific point on the continuum and invest the developing life at that point with some kind of sacred or imponderable, irreversible value."[111] His criterion for protecting the unborn: "desirability." The unborn is human if wanted, subhuman if not. One very active New York abortionist explains: "What is human? Consciousness. Pain. Desire. When a baby loves its mother. When it smiles. . . . You won't get me to say I'm sorry for the fetus. I feel sorry for a starving cat. I feel terrible about a mistreated child. An unloved child— that's sad. If you lose a baby you want—that's sad. A fetus that nobody wants—that's not sad."[112]

The status of the unborn, it is clear, is being made dependent upon whether or not they are desired. Thus the same *New York Times* which berated the prosecutor in the Edelin trial for his "deliberate effort to confuse the jury by using interchangeably the terms 'fetus' and 'baby,' " could editorialize about the unborn who was recently carried by a Mrs. Thrane as surrogate mother for Mr. Noyes, by whose sperm the offspring was sired: "Baby Thrane, who is still residing in a rented womb, may on delivery be moving to a foster home." The

Noyeses, in the *Times*'s view, were "taking a chance on love."[113] As Dr. William Lynch of Boston has said, "You can't have it both ways. Medical scientists claim they are creating human life in a test tube. You can't call it something else in the womb."[114]

After dutiful attention to the various intricate expositions of when the unborn or newborn comes into his or her rights as a fellow human, one is reminded of the terse comment someone made about the lengthy debates and studies and lawsuits over school integration, when the hardships of transport to school beyond one's neighborhood were being elaborated: "It ain't busing, it's the niggers." Abortion advocacy, in its graduated attempts to dehumanize the unborn, is not scrutinizing their credentials. If it were, the arguments would foul themselves on two fallacies. First, human and civil rights must be conferred or assured, not on grounds of performance, but on grounds of identity. Second, development for an organic, living being must not be understood as development for any other sort of being. The passage of an oceanic archipelago from protectorate to territory to commonwealth to state represents a series of status changes; the passage of a human from unborn to infant to adolescent to adult represents the unbroken, continuous development of a single human individual. We accord to the human being, unlike the islands, a consideration that transcends his or her transient status. But, as I say, there is a prior difficulty with the abortion argument about magic moments that disqualifies it before one need look into these other fallacies. There is here no objective inquiry, no sense of free search for the truth such that one would be ready to forgo abortion if the argument should collapse. This is because the decision to abort comes so obviously before the arguments, not after them.

This does wrench the trajectory of human and civil rights out of its ancient course. Traditionally, the vulnerable have been defended and protected in the teeth of hostility simply because they were our human peers. The proabortion argument has worked to strip them of this equality, not for any new discoveries about their status, but only because, now that they are more easily dispatched, they are the more easily disregarded. The unborn are decategorized as human young for one reason only: it is a preliminary to their extinction. They are, for those who wish them so, very small fry.

Isaac Asimov describes the great continuum of youthful development: "Birth . . . is only the moment you emerged from the womb. You existed as a genetically distinct individual from the moment of conception some nine months before. And you did not become an independently functioning member of society (a functional kind of birth) until you 'came of age' some years after you emerged from the womb."[115] This, for someone with no curette to grind, is the natural view of life's beginnings, as it was for a younger Dr. Guttmacher. Likewise for the Inter-American Convention on Human Rights, which affirms that the right to life shall be protected by law "and, in general, from the moment of conception."[116]

When the issue is really not the rights of the unborn but the preferences of those at whose disposal they lie, then this picture goes dark. Tristram Englehardt, noting that "there is nothing personal about the fetus," suggests that "viability" as a cutoff point for abortion ought be a social, and not a biological, event. It is the mother's acceptance of her child, before or after birth, which renders the offspring socially "viable" and confers on him or her a "new measure of worth." "This justifies the difference in attitude towards a very premature infant for whom much energy is expended to insure survival, while the late abortus [of the same age] is allowed to die. The first is valued in terms of its promise to the parents or guardians involved; the second is not valued because of the mother's decision not to have that fetus be a child for her."[117]

It is this ominous readiness to assign status and value to individuals, young or old, according to whether those in power wish "to have them be human for them," which sweeps aside all the meticulous talk about "beginning moments" and discloses them to be what people really have in mind as "ending moments."

One misunderstanding in proabortion arguments, in particular, has caused me to reflect longer than some others. The question of when life begins, it is said, is a philosophical or religious issue, and cannot be verified medically or scientifically. In particular, it cannot be resolved by the display of photographs of fetuses. Both segments of this argument miss important points.

The question of when human life begins is interesting to compare with the question of when it ends. Our ability to detect life's onset and its quittance has in modern times become more knowledgeable. Once one held one's finger to the artery or a mirror to the mouth; when pulse and breath were no longer there one knew that life had fled. Now we can measure electric activity in the brain, a more subtle index of life's presence. Once one took a woman's sense of movement in her womb, after a lapse of menses, to signify quickening, or the start of life. Now we have knowledge of female and male germ cells, and the concert of endocrine activity that attends their union. In the detection and measurement of these subtle surges we have a more reliable sign that life has been inaugurated in the womb.

There are some differences in this knowing when a human begins and ends life, differences not affected by our improved capacities for detection. First, we can have more direct observation of an individual human at life's end than at its beginning since our species, like many others, reproduces by fertilization and initial growth within the mother. Second, by contrast, we have a more elaborate knowledge of the process of life's initiation than of its termination, since we begin by one same way but we end by many.

These times when life springs up and when it gives out are more interesting in their similarities. Each may be attended by a gradual growth or decline of form and function. Yet each is discerned as a point along the continuum of a human life: either the point at which growth begins (all prior events being preparatory) or the point at which decline ends (followed only by decay). The first moment is irreversible without death. The last moment is irreversible to life. That is why we have always called them moments, or points in time.

Also, we are in each case less able to define life's start and end than we are to ascertain or verify that they have occurred. This is because, while we can point to living human beings—ourselves and our fellows—we easily come to grief when we try to set forth (let alone come to agreement about) life's constitutive qualities, its specific essence or properties, its characteristic acts. These are not matters impervious to inquiry or matters of light importance, but to determine the occurrence of life and death is not grounded on such analyses. It is prephilosophical. We can much more surely know when life is than what it is. We detect life's end by those earliest certain signs after which no amount of nurture will restore an individual to what we point to among ourselves as human life. We detect life's start by those earliest signs after which nurture alone will bring into our midst an individual with what we point to among ourselves as human life. To verify life's start or its conclusion—a work of physical observation—is antecedent to and independent of a thorough understanding of what that life is or how it ought be valued.

Human life is sometimes thought to end "truly" at the time of the last exercise of some human characteristics which we esteem, or to begin "truly" at the point when these same characteristics are mature enough for exercise. But this appreciation of life as ripe or rotten is not the same as detecting life's presence or its absence. This kind of appreciation, so often intended to segregate out those living humans who are less desirable, springs more from what we wish than from what we know.

We must keep quite distinct these different activities. To detect the start or the end of life is a work of those skilled in the science of zoology or its engineering cousin, medicine. For inquiry into what life is, we all look to philosophy, and some of us to theology. For an understanding of what is valuable in human life and human beings, the philosopher and the theologian are joined by those in other humane and social disciplines. How human life and human beings are to be husbanded and nurtured is the concern of medicine and nutrition and education and a healthy social order. And when we consider whether or in what fashion such life is to be protected from human harm, then we expect those in law and governance to offer special insight.

The photographic displays that prolife advocates employ are misunderstood if one imagines that they are intended to resolve any kind of scientific or philosophic debate about the status of the unborn. They are powerful precisely because they are not arguments. They move in to motivate people at precisely the point where arguments are inappropriate. So also with the accounts of early development in the unborn: heartbeat, brain waves, sensation, circulation, digestion, excretion, movement are all described as beginning rather early in fetal life. None of this is *evidence* intended to accumulate into a scientific argument, because the point at issue is prescientific.

There is a difference between *arguing* and *showing*. When the three Christmas ghosts gave Ebenezer Scrooge his three visions they were not arguing with him; they were showing him what he knew but did not wish to see. Hamlet's play within the play was the thing wherein he caught the conscience of the king because, instead of presenting evidence that Claudius was guilty of fratricide, he *displayed* what needed really no argument. When people who are prejudiced against blacks or Jews or women or Americans are converted from their prejudice, it is never on the strength of social science evidence or arguments: they come to know, in a personal and admiring way, a few members of the odious group, and the prejudice is done in. When the

German and Allied troops came to the mutinous point of playing furtive soccer games between the trenches during Christmastime in World War I, it was not because pacifist literature had been distributed at the front; it was because the Tommies and the Jerries had been dug in so close to one another for so long that they came to *see* one another as fellows.

The discovery that an individual or a group whom we had previously disenfranchised from human fellowship is indeed our own flesh and blood is not something which we conclude. It is something which dawns on us.

Thus the fetal photographs.[118] They are to abortion what the My Lai photographs were to Vietnam: persuasive in a different way than the revealing dispatches of reporters like Harrison Salisbury, for they revealed something we already knew but did not want to see.

After considering the four weightiest arguments for abortion as an ethically justified procedure—that it is medically indicated, that it is psychically therapeutic, that unwanted children are best not born, and that the unborn are not our fellow humans—one emerges with the conviction that the arguments are not only contrived, but if inspected seriously raise the most serious moral difficulties about abortion. Also, one is drawn to admit that these arguments are precisely that: arguments, not reasons. And being such compromised arguments, they eventually collapse to disclose behind themselves a much simpler justification. That is raw rejection, a form of self-preference which is difficult to criticize because it offers no rationale. Most unborn aborted in America are eliminated, not to save or relieve anyone's health or to assure anyone's psychic composure or to spare child and society one another. They are eliminated because their parents are unwilling to extend to them their first foothold in the world. Were that made clearer in the abortion debate today the exchanges would be clearer. But when raw self-interest clothes itself in the crisp uniforms of professional service or the soft garments of altruism, it assumes a guise that many are too polite to strip away.

Possibly the strongest argument for legal approval of any action is a moral one: what is just and fair and reasonable and humanly needed is precisely what ought to enjoy the permission and sometimes the encouragement of the law. Accordingly, the case for abortion on demand commonly sets forth its moral arguments first, some of which we have reviewed. But there is a second echelon of argument. Several explanations are given why, aside from whether it is justified and desirable, abortion still ought to be free of any legal restraint. These arguments have standing in their own right, and they have next claim upon our attention.

Political Argument: Legal Abortions Replace Illegal Ones

If a certain large number of pregnant women are determined to abort, whatever the law may say, and are likely to prevail in their desire, then is it not wise, for reasons of public health alone, to make abortion legal so that at least it can be performed by competent physicians instead of by quacks with coat hangers or by the women themselves with knitting needles?

This argument, of course, gains or loses force depending on how many abortions would inevitably occur in the face of a legal ban. To evaluate its cogency in the hands of abortion advocates, one needs to study three very commonplace statistical claims.

In 1955 the Planned Parenthood Federation of America convened a conference at Arden House in New York on the subject of abortion. One interest of the conference was to estimate how many criminal abortions were being performed in the United States. The principal data base presented to the conference was provided by Alfred C. Kinsey, whose interviews regarding sexual behavior had yielded a sample of about 5,300 women who had disclosed, among other things, their past involvements with abortion. Was it possible to extrapolate from this sample some reliable estimate of how many abortions occurred among American women at large? The statistical committee, including Alan Guttmacher and Christopher Tietze, stated explicitly that it was not possible. The Kinsey women were not a representative sample of the general population, nor one dependably free from biased selection. The committee disallowed the personal conjectures that had been put forward by various conferees (750,000; 1,000,000) as unreliable, and concluded as follows:

> Taking into account the probable trend of the abortion ratio since the interwar period, a plausible estimate of the frequency of induced abortion in the United States could be as low as 200,000 and as high as 1,200,000 per year, depending upon the assumptions made as to the incidence of abortion in the total population as compared with the restricted groups for which statistical data are available, and upon the assessment of the direction and magnitude of bias inherent in each series of data. There is no objective basis for the selection of a particular figure between these two estimates as an approximation of the actual frequency.[119]

The statisticians at Arden House explicitly forbore to base their guess on statistics from Dr. Kinsey or anyone else. They offered no grounds for their supposition beyond what has been quoted above. It is instructive to see what befell this original, unevidenced conjecture.

A decade later Lawrence Lader, campaigning against abortion laws, recalled that it had been "estimated that U.S. abortions could run from 200,000 to 1,200,000 annually," and stated that Dr. Tietze (who had been chairman of the committee that produced the estimate) "considers 1,200,000 the most accurate figure today. Dr. Harold Rosen, of the Johns Hopkins University Hospital, editor of an authoritative study, *Therapeutic Abortion*, recently raised the estimate to 1,500,000."[120]

Tracking Lader back to his sources, one finds that they contradict, rather than support him. In a paper delivered while Lader was writing his book and published just as Lader went to press, Tietze had quoted verbatim the 1955 conjecture of 200,000 to 1,200,000 and the conclusion that no objective basis existed for preferring any figure within that range to any other. "No new data," he stated, "have become available since 1955 on which a more reliable estimate could be based."[121] As for Rosen, in his authoritative book published twelve years earlier, he simply endorses the guess of Russell S. Fisher, not of 1,500,000 abortions annually, but of 330,000. Nowhere in his 1954 book or its

1967 edition does Rosen suggest the figure Lader attributes to him in 1966.[122] In Lader's hands not only has the conjecture been boosted upwards considerably, but it has also been reinforced as "expert, authoritative, accurate." What had begun only ten years before as a bashful conjecture had now ripened into a "careful estimate."

Lader's next book, *Abortion II: Making the Revolution*, published in 1973, refers simply to "an estimated 1,000,000 secret abortions." A footnote cites the reader to the very page where, in the midfifties, this estimate was presented as groundless. Lader nevertheless vouches for it as "accepted by most public health authorities." Since, by 1972, so many abortions had been legalized in a number of states, in his footnote Lader pulls back his figure on criminal abortions to 750,000. The figure now had a sturdiness of its own and could be adjusted with time and change.[123]

By the next year, 1974, the estimates had become commonplace knowledge. In testimony offered before a subcommittee of the U.S. Senate Judiciary Committee, they make repeated appearances:

> *Congresswoman Bella Abzug*: "It has been generally estimated that all throughout the period when antiabortion laws were on the books, about 1 million American woman were having abortions each year."
>
> *Planned Parenthood of Washington, D.C.*: "Although there is no way of knowing the total number of illegal abortions that were performed throughout the country, estimates range from 1–1½ million."
>
> *Senator Charles H. Percy*: "We know that prior to that decision [*Wade*-and-*Bolton*], about one million abortions were performed annually in the United States."
>
> *Congressman Ronald V. Dellums*: "The medical profession estimates that 1 million illegal abortions were performed annually in the 1960's."
>
> *The American Jewish Congress*: "Prior to the Supreme Court's decisions, it was estimated that from one to 1½ million abortions were performed each year within the United States."
>
> *Reverend Alfred B. Starratt* (a Baltimore clergyman, in a sermon submitted as testimony): "May I remind you that the best estimates are that there were about one million illegal abortions each year before the Supreme Court decision."
>
> *Dr. Michael M. Levi* (OB / GYN Associates, New York City): "It is estimated that 1.2 million abortions are done illegally or were done illegally in the United States."[124]

By the end of its second decade of existence the estimate has come into considerable dignity. It has now lost its statistical ranges (200,000 to 1,200,000), or has had them escalated (1,000,000 to 1,500,000); it has acquired the endorsement of the "medical profession"; and it has gained public acceptance enough to be set forth in congressional testimony without question. Indeed, most recently it has risen beyond all credible limits. In a publicity flier drawn up in March 1981, Planned Parenthood of New York has made what is hitherto the most extravagant of all claims: "EVERY YEAR before New York legalized abortion in 1970, an estimated 1 million women in New York State sought and had abortions."[125]

In a much softer voice Dr. Tietze, the original conjecturer, in his own senatorial appearance, declines to endorse any of the national estimates about the frequency of illegal abortion. "For obvious reasons, this is an area in which reliable statistics are not available and in which some extraordinary estimates have been made."[126] Three years earlier his fellow abortion statistician, Henry P. David, had written: "Incidence data compiled from a variety of sources do not yield a single figure which can be substantiated as more accurate than another. For example, the often cited number of one million annual illegal abortions in the United States cannot be readily verified."[127]

Thus one witnesses the process by which a simple, rough conjecture, proposed without any supporting evidence, can acquire at the hands of its partisan users an inflated size and a public acceptance without ever having the reinforcement of a single fact. It is interesting to note that no abortion advocate seems, during this period, to have compared these conjectures of abortion frequency with reported abortion-related deaths. In England, where the conjecture of 100,000 abortions annually was similarly canonized without the benefit of evidence, Charles Goodhart did make the comparison. He concluded that either criminal abortion was one of the safest surgical procedures practiced, or illegal abortions were likely to be only about 15 percent as numerous as claimed. His remark deserves reflection in light of the American estimates: "It would therefore seem that the professional competence of criminal abortionists has been very seriously underrated or else, and surely more probably, that their numbers have been much exaggerated."[128]

This leads to the story of a second widely enunciated statistic: the number of women who have died in the course or aftermath of criminal abortion. Here was a statistic that would have a sharp bite, for the bid of the proabortion movement has been to eliminate or at least to minimize these sad deaths by irresponsible butchers.

The actual reported nationwide figures on abortion-related deaths (presumably only a few of them from legal abortion) throughout the decade of the 1960s averaged about 225 annually.[129] Surely there were other abortion-related deaths, of undeterminable number, which did not find their way into these figures, but these are the reported, published statistics from which one must begin. How have they been used?

In 1966 Lawrence Lader warned: "One recent study at the University of California's School of Public Health estimated 5,000 to 10,000 abortion deaths annually. Dr. Tietze places the figure nearer 1,000."[130] Here, as always, it is enlightening to consult the sources to which Lader refers the reader. No University of California study is cited. Instead, Lader refers to a source that depends on a deputy medical examiner of Los Angeles, who simply passes on a conjecture of 5,000 to 10,000 deaths annually.[131] As for Tietze, the article to which Lader refers contains no estimate of or comment upon national abortion mortality.[132] The reader is left to infer that Lader has once again had to fabricate a statistic. There is some hint, however, of a method that may have been employed. One might have been expected to begin with the one statistic that was publicly available, the death reports, next try to correct it for error (by calculating abortion-related deaths that had been reported under some other category), and then somehow extrapolate this mortality figure into an estimate of how many abortions were occurring. Curiously, abortion advocates seem to have done the opposite. Ignoring the death reports almost entirely, they began with a statistic of their own manufacture, the "estimate" of how many criminal abortions occurred. They then applied to this a conjectural mortality rate, and produced their "estimate" of how many women must have been dying annually. Their starting guess was 1,000,000 to 2,000,000 abortions annually. For their mortality rate they went to Taussig's very unreliable work in 1936 (he reckoned there were 681,600 criminal abortions annually, that 1.2 percent were maternally fatal, and that 8,000 deaths therefore resulted), reduced his fatality rate from 1.2 percent to .5 percent because of the advent of antibiotics, and thus produced the conclusion that there were 5,000 to 10,000 deaths (1,000,000 to 2,000,000 times .005) each year. (Besides being entirely ungrounded, this conjecture incorporated two mistaken assumptions: that most abortions were performed by amateurs, and that, being illegal, the procedures were performed carelessly.)

In any case, whatever its lack of credible underpinnings, the statistic which Lader and the abortion movement proposed to the public enjoyed rapid acceptance. As has been pointed out earlier in this essay, at the time Lader was setting the death toll at 5,000 to 10,000, published reports spoke of 133. The reports were ignored and the proabortion figure became established. Senate hearings brought it out repeatedly: Congresswoman Abzug reported 400 to 1,000 deaths; Congressman Dellums (citing the "medical profession"), 5,000; the American Jewish Congress, 5,000 to 10,000; Reverend Starratt, 8,000; Dr. Leonard Laufe, of International Planned Parenthood, 3,000 black women alone.[133] Once again, a strategic statistic had been minted expressly for purposes of the abortion movement, and it became powerfully persuasive in moving the public to support the movement's aims.

A third such statistic which has also enjoyed wide acceptance is the claim by Dr. Christopher Tietze that 70 percent of present legal abortions replace illegal ones: that is, if one applied this figure to recent reports of 1,500,000 abortions, about 1,050,000 would be taking place anyway—illegally—if they were once again to be made criminal. This is a contention which has been repeated so often that it too has become a commonplace in the literature.

On April 10, 1974, Congressman Ronald Dellums testified: "Passage of an antiabortion amendment would mean a return to the deplorable conditions of illegal abortions. A study in New York, reported by Dr. Christopher Tietze, indicates that if abortion were again illegal, of every 10 women now having legal abortions, 7 would resort to illegal abortion rather than be forced to bear an unwanted child."[134] The 70 percent figure cited then by Mr. Dellums has become part of the conventional wisdom about abortion. Tietze arrives at it by a formula that combines statistics on present legal abortions, the birthrate, and the maternal mortality rate, and then extrapolates backward to a conjecture of how many abortions previously occurred and how many would be likely to occur illegally if the law were changed.[135] His argument, which was sketched out in 1973–74, is elaborate. He acknowledges that "the numbers of illegal abortions and total pregnancies were unknown before the legalization of abortion, and remain unknown after the fact."[136] But in extending his conjecture backwards, several times he inserts into the construct some ciphers or values which he simply assumes, or fabricates. In a sequential construct where facts are not available for each segment, this may be legitimate if cautiously and openly done, and when the resulting conclusion is designated as conjectural. But when it has been done as much as six times one ends with an hypothesis, not a finding; still less a dogma. The end product of this construct, however, is a public-relations slogan. It is simple and clear but unfounded—and it is put about publicly as if it were a fine-tuned calculation, much as if astrology were being marketed as astronomy.

At the time when his 1975 paper was still in draft form, Dr. Tietze was invited to present it at a conference on abortion at Notre Dame. One commentator noted that several segments of the argument were simple assumptions, and asked whether it would not as easily yield a conclusion of 20 percent as of 70 percent by small adjustments in those assumptions. At best, the commentator suggested, one could conclude that "many" legal abortions would have been performed anyway without the change in law. Dr. Tietze did not dispute this, but explained that American readers like numbers, and that he wanted to supply a numerical estimate by way of conclusion.[137]

American readers have their numbers, and the numbers have cogently supported the cause of abortion freedom. But some are contrived and unreliable numbers. Three examples have been offered: statistics which have been confected for a purpose, and which do not bear careful scrutiny. In time they have come to be brandished by many citizens who have no slightest notion of where they came from, who developed them, or how partisan they are.

Other sides of this issue are darkened, not by the manufacture of information, but by its absence. Let two examples suffice.

When the Hyde Amendment, denying federal payment for Medicaid and other abortion services, was first being debated, it was widely assumed that Medicaid abortors would henceforth be obliged to "find some way, however dangerous, dark and filthy, to kill the fetus more cheaply. Such methods have had the result of sometimes disposing of the mother as well."[138] Then, when the Supreme Court upheld the Hyde Amendment as constitutional, Justice Thurgood Marshall raged in dissent: "By definition, these women do not have the money to pay for an abortion themselves. If abortion is medically necessary and a funded abortion is unavailable, they must resort to back-alley butchers, [or] attempt to induce an abortion themselves by crude and dangerous methods."[139] Further, officials at the Center for Disease Control predicted a bloodbath, especially because even indigent women who would finally be able to pay for abortions would seek them in later stages of pregnancy, when dangerous complications are more likely.

In this discussion two relevant facts have not come to light: one is old, one new. First, it had long been known during the days before legalized abortion that most criminal abortions were being performed by physicians. Various studies reported this at 87 percent, 56 percent, 75 percent, 94 percent, 91 percent, 70 percent. Kinsey's sample, though not representative, reported abortions by physicians 84 to 87 percent of the time; self-induced, 8 to 10 percent; and by "others," 5 to 6 percent.[140] Even under a different law, this would suggest that resort to an illegal practitioner is likely to find the same sort of doctor who runs abortion clinics legally today, under conditions not less sanitary than those in clinics which have processed Medicaid trade in greatest numbers. And, as a Princeton survey has shown recently, after federal Medicaid funds for abortion were withheld, 80 percent of the women paid for abortions themselves at an average cost of $162, with an average time delay of three days, with no significant incidence of maternal mortality.[141]

Here we can see that the case for legalized abortion has spoken with conviction on two issues without evidence for the assertions. There are no grounds from which to argue honestly that a denial of abortion subsidies for abortion will send indigent women to be victimized by butchers and quacks. The point one draws from this, most of all, is that no reliable case has yet been made that legalization has made safer for American mothers the abortions they would in any case have. What one can see, from looking closely at the evidence, is that abortion advocates have fabricated a case that is contrived, and dissembling, and boldly filled with putty just where the cracks and fissures run.

Political Argument: Abortion on Demand Is Approved by Most Americans

A second reason for permitting abortion legally, quite apart from whether it be right or wrong morally, would be that it enjoys majority support among the public. Abortion advocates have insisted, with but few exceptions, that public opinion surveys show consistent approval of the prochoice position. How the polls have been used, and what they report regarding citizen opinion, affords another issue that will permit insight into the integrity of the proabortion argument.

Abortion advocates sometimes assert, without supportive reference, that there is majority support for legal abortion. Karen Mulhauser, for example, writing in the *Newsletter* of the National Abortion Rights Action League, of which she is executive director, states: "We are undisputed winners in the public opinion polls—we are the majority."[142] Those who oppose are "the vociferous and fanatic few."[143] Planned Parenthood speaks of a "well-organized, well-financed minority [trying] to impose their narrow moral standards on an unwilling society."[144] Arlie Schardt, erstwhile executive director of the American Civil Liberties Union, has stated for the public record: "Despite the fact that polls show most citizens—including Catholics—favor the right to abortion, and despite the Supreme Court's finding that women have the constitutional right to abortion, the issue frightens Congress."[145] Beverly Harrison, an abortion advocate who teaches social ethics at New York's Union Theological Seminary, refers in argument to "the large number of polls which show that slightly over half of the public support the Supreme Court decision."[146] This sort of general, unreferenced claim to majority support is not in itself objectionable . . . unless it happens to be trumped up. In this instance, as one finds, the evidence not only fails to sustain the claim; it consistently suggests the contrary.

A second misuse of opinion surveys is to falsify their findings by distorted restatement. Ellie Smeal, president of the National Organization for Women, gives a typical example of this. Describing "the overwhelming feeling of the majority," she asserts that "81% of all Americans and 76% of all Catholics support the right of women to choose a safe and legal abortion."[147] This, as we shall see below, takes considerable liberties with the reported data.

A third snag is in the polls themselves. The correct calculation of public sentiment on abortion has repeatedly been stymied by poll questions that are poorly framed. A large measure of distortion is caused, for instance, when a question is couched in terms that warm the respondent toward a particular answer. The Harris Surveys are sometimes spoilt by this sort of editorializing. When Congress was first moving to deny Medicaid funding for abortions, Harris announced that public support for the Hyde Amendment was weak. When asked, "Do you favor or oppose a ban on the use of federal Medicaid funds for poor women who couldn't otherwise pay for them?" 47 percent favored the ban, 44 percent were opposed, and 9 percent had no opinion. But when Harris reshaped the question in biased form its survey produced a different result:[148]

	YES	NO	?
"The U.S. Supreme Court in its original decision was right to say whether a woman has an abortion is a decision she and her doctor should make, and the new ban interferes with the right of a pregnant woman to make that decision."	55%	34%	11%
"The ban is wrong because poor women who cannot afford legal abortions will be forced to have unwanted children or to have dangerous illegal abortions."	51%	37%	12%
"Such a ban is unfair, because it means that rich women, who can afford abortions, will have them while poor women, who can't afford them, will not."	51%	40%	9%

The NARAL, which gave prominence to the more agreeable but less reliable results, described the reshaped questions as having "personalized the funding issue."

Poll results are even more obviously coached when solicited by nonprofessionals. Congressman James W. Symington of Missouri canvassed his constituency to ascertain their views on a prolife amendment. His question was as follows:

> The Constitution is the basic document of our American political system. From this fundamental document our laws are derived. In our nation's history it has been altered only 26 times, and only after long debate and serious thought. Recently, several new amendments have been proposed; which, if any, would you support? An amendment to prohibit abortion under any circumstances except to save the life of the mother?

Here, besides a strongly cautionary preamble which communicates to the voters more of the congressman's attitude than their responses are likely to convey to him of theirs, Symington skews the inquiry further by specifying only one of the amendment formulae under discussion, and that the most restrictive. Predictably, responses showed very little support: men, 18 percent; women, 21 percent.[149]

In November 1978 the ballot in Oregon included an initiative measure to cut off state funding of abortions. Before the vote a NARAL poll sought public reaction to this statement: "The service should be available to poor women who depend on public welfare, rather than have taxes raised to pay the costs of those extra children if abortion were not permitted." Fifty-eight percent agreed. The statement, however, is obviously more appropriate as a public relations tactic than as a legitimate opinion survey instrument. It is distorted by three assumptions: (1) that abortions for which tax-supported subsidy is denied will not take place anyway; (2) that children born after such denial of funded abortion will draw state welfare payments; and (3) that tax increases will result.[150]

A most egregious example of an opinion survey-cum-coaching was provided by the Planned Parenthood Federation of America. At the federation's annual meeting in Houston, November 1979, delegates learned from Dr. Michael Rappeport and Ms. Patricia Labaw of a survey designed to go beyond yes-or-no questions. Of the 1,500 adults interviewed nationwide by telephone, at first 34 percent thought a woman should have an abortion only if her life were in danger, and 45 percent said they disapproved of abortion. "But you ask them about the 45-year-old woman with three children whose contraception did not work or the sixteen-year-old rape victim and suddenly they favor abortion." By the end of his survey, which Planned Parenthood had commissioned, Dr. Rappeport said that 90 percent favored abortion under certain circumstances, which the story headline cited as: "Survey Shows Most Adults Favor Abortion."[151]

Other opinion surveys yield contrived results by asking questions that are more overtly misleading. Some, for instance, have asked whether respondents support the Supreme Court decisions of 1973, but then include some misstatement of what the Court actually decreed. Most frequently a poll will describe the Court as having legalized abortion during the first three months of pregnancy. There are many examples of this, but the Harris surveys provide the most widely known example. For years Harris has asked respondents whether they favored "the U.S. Supreme Court decision in making abortions up to three months of pregnancy legal." The results, which are discolored by the question, have been widely cited on behalf of abortion freedom.[152]

When Harris's findings are reported by the NARAL they lose their original, disqualifying detail. They become simply: "Favorable Harris Polls Demonstrating 60% Support for Legal Abortions." "According to Mrs. Mulhauser, the latest figures from a Harris Poll in March show that 60 percent of Americans now support the Supreme Court decision on abortion."[153] Lawrence Lader used the Harris Survey to show "that 52 percent of Catholics approved the Supreme Court's legalization of abortion."[154] The United States Commission on Civil Rights, in its 1975 proabortion report, cites a 1974 Gallup Poll (identical with the erroneous Harris Survey) wherein 52 percent agreed and 48 percent disagreed that "abortions through the third month of pregnancy should continue to be legal," and concludes that "the Court is supported by a majority of the population."[155]

Congressman Thomas M. Rees of California, an advocate of abortion choice, polled his district, "a district of good, God-fearing middle-class people," whom he described as intelligent and highly educated. His question was: "A recent United States Supreme Court decision legalizes abortions which are performed by qualified physicians during the early stages of pregnancy. This allows an abortion to be a decision made by a woman and her doctor, rather than regulated by the government. Do you favor the Court ruling?"[156] Besides coaching his respondents towards a particular answer and misrepresenting the Court, Mr. Rees crippled his survey by a third kind of blunder that has become an unfortunate commonplace in proabortion opinion reporting: the woman-and-her-physician formula.

What *Wade* and *Bolton* handed down was exactly what the abortion movement had asked for: total freedom for abortion on demand throughout pregnancy. Since that state of affairs has never since 1973 enjoyed broad public approval as either morally justifiable or legally desirable, those disposed to preserve and defend it have been at pains to identify some finding in the opinion surveys which might be construed as a blanket endorsement of what the Court had decreed, without putting too fine a point on it. One such finding lay in the consistently positive response to this (or a similar) question: "If a woman wants to have an abortion, that is a matter for her and her doctor to decide, and the government should have nothing to do with it." This question, in a preelection survey conducted by the Knight-Ridder newspapers, elicited an 81 percent agreement. At first sight, a positive response would seem to endorse a complete absence of legal restrictions on abortion. Ellie Smeal, of the National Organization for Women, has presented it as such: "81% of all Americans and 76% of all Catholics support the right of women to choose a safe and legal abortion." Likewise, in November 1979, when the *New York Times* / CBS News Poll posed the thesis, "The right of a woman to have an abortion should be left entirely to the woman and her doctor," it drew Catholic approval of 64 percent and Protestant approval of 69 percent (down from 69 percent and 76 percent, however, in 1977). The *Times* headline summed up: "Catholics in Survey Endorse Abortion."[157] Louis Harris, who has asked this question repeatedly, sees the positive response as reflective of "the majority view favoring abortion."[158]

As Peter Skerry has pointed out, however, the woman-and-her-physician question and its interpretation in proabortion literature are both misleading: "these high rates of approval do not stand up to scrutiny." In other, very reliable, polls there have been contradictory responses. In Gallup polls of 1972 and 1974 respondents said that the law should specify when abortion is justified, rather than leave women under no constraints (54 percent vs. 39 percent in 1972; 53 percent vs. 40 percent in 1974). Numerous Gallup polls have shown strong public demand for some form of local regulation (76 percent in 1975; 74 percent in 1977; 73 percent in 1979; 71 percent in 1980).[159] Furthermore, in several surveys from 1970 through 1975 about one-third of the public said it should be lawful for a woman to obtain an abortion without her husband's consent.[160] In these two respects the Court and its law are at variance with the public opinion thus expressed. The public appears to wish two exceptions to the woman-and-her-physician sovereignty: it wants abortion allowed under certain conditions (thus with some purview by the government through law) and it wants a decision shared by the husband. It is difficult therefore to accept that the woman-and-her-physician responses are quite that reliable in their own right. It is still more difficult to conjure them into serving as blanket endorsements for the present law of unrestrained abortion. Possibly they are taken by respondents to disapprove of some imaginable involvement in abortion by government officials.

There is yet another presentation of poll results which would strike an observer as directly dishonest if the data were not openly displayed by the very advocates who do them violence. In May 1979 *Redbook* published an analysis of its own abortion poll, conducted through the Gallup Organization. Its principal conclusion was that "the law of the land still accords with the will of the majority," since "80 per cent of Americans say abortion should be legal under any or certain circumstances."

The chief *Redbook* question was: "Do you think abortion should be legal under any circumstance, legal only under certain circumstances, or illegal in all circumstances?" The responses were as follows (to which I add other responses received by Gallup to the same questions):

	Redbook				
	1975	1977	1978	1979	1980
Legal under any circumstance	21%	22%	22%	26%	25%
Legal under certain circumstances	54%	55%	54%	54%	53%
Illegal under any circumstances	22%	19%	19%	17%	18%
No opinion	3%	4%	5%	3%	4%

These responses show a stable and consistent pattern, and agree largely with other comparable surveys. Invariably they have been construed as support for *Wade* and *Bolton*, whereas they most clearly are the opposite. Citing a similar but older poll, Joseph O'Rourke, a dismissed priest who heads Catholics for a Free Choice, declared that a majority of the country, Catholics, Protestants, Jews, Democrats, and Republicans, were in favor of abortion under certain circumstances.[161] Betty Benjamin, president of the Abortion Rights Council of Minnesota, argues: "Public opinion polls reveal that 60–88 percent of people in this country think abortion should be legal either in all or some circumstances." Those who oppose abortion freedom oppose "the rights of the majority of Americans."[162] What O'Rourke, *Redbook*, and Benjamin, with many others, have done is to coalesce the two groups ("always" and "sometimes" legal) into what they see as a majority in support of the present law and the prochoice position. But what the polls relentlessly reveal is that neither the prochoice position nor the prolife position (in its strong form) enjoys more than minority support.

There are presently two polar positions on abortion being actively advocated in this country. One position asserts that abortion is immoral and ought to be illegal, except possibly to save the mother's life. This position is satisfied by only one response: "illegal under all circumstances" (though if danger to the mother's life were specified as one appropriate legalizing circumstance this reponse would be significantly enlarged). This position consistently enjoys the adherence of about one respondent in every five. The other polar position asserts that abortion is an entirely individual moral issue for the pregnant woman and that she ought to be legally unrestricted in obtaining it (except as her own health and safety require). This position is satisfied by only one response: "legal under any circumstances." It enjoys the adherence of about one respondent in every four. This is presently the law of the land.

The majority of Americans surveyed do not subscribe to either polar position—prolife or prochoice—as presently preached. The majority will countenance abortion in certain circumstances. And the polls are clear and consistent in disclosing what those circumstances are. Basically, the "middle group" considers what are commonly called the "hard reasons" as justifying abortion and it rejects the "soft reasons." To get some sense of this we may put the *Redbook* findings alongside the two most recent comparable Gallup polls.

Question (asked of those who replied they would make abortions legal under certain circumstances): "Now, thinking about the first three months of pregnancy, under which of the circumstances do you think abortions should be legal?"

	Redbook 1979	Gallup 1979	Gallup 1977
Woman's life is endangered	85%	78%	77%
Woman's physical health is endangered	50%	52%	54%
Woman's mental health is endangered	45%	42%	42%
Chance baby will be deformed	52%	44%	45%

	Redbook 1979	Gallup 1979	Gallup 1977
Rape or incest	75%	59%	65%
Family cannot afford to have the child	14%	15%	16%
Don't want child	14%	—	—
No opinion	—	9%	2%

Several things must be noted here. First, this is not the total national sample responding, but that portion of the sample, the "middle group," which would allow abortion "under certain circumstances." Second, these responses hold only for first-trimester abortions. Approval falls off sharply for later abortions, as these same polls show (1977 and 1979 responses beside each other; the *Redbook* survey did not include this information):

	First Trimester	Second Trimester	Third Trimester
Woman's life is endangered	77%/78%	64%/66%	60%/59%
Woman's physical health is endangered	54%/52%	46%/46%	34%/33%
Woman's mental health is endangered	42%/42%	31%/31%	24%/22%
Chance baby will be deformed	44%/45%	39%/37%	28%/28%
Rape or incest	56%/59%	38%/32%	24%/19%
Family cannot afford to have the child	16%/15%	9%/6%	6%/4%
No opinion	2%/9%	9%/9%	20%/21%

What can we learn from these responses? There is clear allowance for abortion to save the mother's life. There is considerably less allowance for abortion on behalf of her physical health. For abortion after rape or incest there is fairly strong allowance, but only during the first trimester. There is increasing rejection of abortion to eliminate a deformed child (especially since most such abortions require amniocentesis and must await the second trimester, by which time few would allow it). For reasons of mental health or economics there is little feeling that abortion is ever justifiable.

Obviously the largest segment of the public, the dominating swing group that wants to discriminate among reasons justifying abortion, is sympathetic towards endangerment of a mother's life and (much less emphatically) physical health, and towards pregnancy from rape or incest. Other reasons lack the approval of a majority of even this middle group. The only position, then, which this configuration of judgments comes near to approving (though it is less permissive) is that of the American Law Institute's Model Penal Code, which in its abortion provisions had been adopted by a growing number of states before 1973. This middle group does not agree with the present law of the land, enunciated in *Wade* and *Bolton*, which forbids state and federal legislatures to restrict abortion at any time during pregnancy, even the last three months if the woman claims it is for her health (understood in the widest sense). And since well over 95 percent of abortions currently performed are truly elective—that is, they occur because a child is unwanted, rather than for one of the "hard reasons" accepted by this group—this group of respondents stands at odds with current abortion law and practice.

Although the advocates of abortion on demand correctly identify their active opponents, the prolife group, as a minority no larger than themselves and perhaps a little smaller, they have failed to acknowledge another group, twice as large as either polar faction, which does not accept present abortion law. It is this group, not just the prolife faction, whose political weight can explain the various legislative frustrations the proabortion group has endured of late, and whose stable convictions regarding abortion explain its unreadiness to acquiesce in what the Supreme Court has done.

Judith Blake, the UCLA professor who has most persistently examined survey results on abortion, has long noted this. While tracing the differentiated opinions of this middle group through Gallup, NORC, and National Fertility surveys back into the 1960s, she has noted various majority opinions that go contrary to the teaching of the present Court: that human life begins at conception or at quickening, and that the unborn are persons before birth; that abortion should be unlawful without the husband's consent; that it should be lawful only in hospitals; and that it should almost never be permitted after the third month.[163]

The fact that a national majority does not believe in unrestricted abortion has not been admitted by its advocates throughout the years of dispute over abortion funding. Indeed, the doctrine of the abortion advocates was that the legislative branch of the government was being manipulated by a vociferous minority. That the Congress should deny funding for abortion (except in the "hard" cases) simply because it was reflecting the national sentiment was something they have not been able to accept. Only lately have abortion advocates begun to admit that they represent a minority view.

In his indignant dissent from the Court's vindication of Congress's right to withhold Medicaid funds for abortions, Justice Brennan called the Hyde Amendment "a transparent attempt by the Legislative Branch to impose the political majority's judgment of the morally acceptable and socially desirable preference." Many political observers reflected that this was precisely what they thought Congress was authorized to do. Justice Blackmun, author of the *Wade* and *Bolton* opinions, took the same occasion to regret what was happening: "the Government 'punitively impresses upon a needy minority its own concepts of the socially desirable, the publicly acceptable, and the morally sound.' "[164] Karen Mulhauser of the National Abortion Rights Action League, looking back to *Wade* and *Bolton* in 1973, has quietly acknowledged that "the country wasn't with us at that point."[165] Patricia Roberts Harris, at the end of 1980, when her tenure as Secretary of Health and Human Services (formerly

HEW) was drawing to a close, spoke out against telling young people, "in really medieval terms, you must control your sexuality," and advocated abortion freedom. She acknowledged, however, "that the cutting edge of public opinion is probably contrary to what I am saying."[166] Linda Greenhouse, commenting on *McRae* in 1980, noted that *Wade* and *Bolton* "was as far in the van of a national consensus on abortion as the Court should prudently get."[167] It seems, on the contrary, that the real national consensus does not think of the Court as its vanguard, and is securing for itself a belated recognition.

Before leaving this subject of public opinion on abortion, there is one constituency about whose opinion something needs to be said: women who have aborted. The female personnel of abortion facilities and of advocacy groups tend to include significant numbers of women who are veterans of abortion and whose comradeship in this experience binds them together. It may be their presumption—at least, this seems to recur in the literature of abortion advocacy—that women who have undergone elective abortion will uphold the right of other women to do the same. There is some evidence that this is not so.

Perez-Reyes and Falk report on a group of unmarried adolescent abortors who harbored opinions about the justifiability of abortion that were not entirely permissive. One third of the girls (34 percent) disapproved of abortion except for "hard" reasons—e.g., to save the mother's life or health, to avoid a handicapped child—or for serious medical need. "Apparently in a number of cases, the experience of having a[n abortion] did not result in a generalized more liberal attitude but forced the girls to rationalize their guilt by considering themselves 'exceptions' to the rule."[168] Zimmerman's later study of a group of abortors noticed a similar phenomenon. "Abortion . . . is legal but, from the standpoint of public acceptance, it is not moral. . . . The women we studied tended to approve only under very restrictive circumstances. . . . Thus, the women appeared to retain the idea that they had committed an immoral act. In order to rescue the inconsistency between this and their moral character, they talked in terms of being forced to have an abortion, of not having had a choice. . . . They cut themselves off from future negative implications by viewing themselves as having changed. They took the position of being a different person now from when they had the abortion."[169]

A third item for reflection comes from Japan, where, since American occupation days, abortion has been the most widely used form of birth control. One could expect that the women of a nation which may have between two and three million induced abortions annually, most of them performed for married women, would have made their accommodations of conscience on that subject long ago. Some public opinion surveys taken during the 1960s suggest it may not be so. Various polls, for example, yielded these responses:[170]

Aichi:	59%	felt that abortion is something "very bad"
	16%	felt that it is considerably bad
	17%	felt that it is somewhat bad
	8%	thought that it could not be called something bad

Nagoya: 67%   "I think it [the fetus] is a human life from the
                    moment it is conceived in the womb"
           42%   [The abortion situation in Japan] is not good
           52%   [The abortion situation in Japan] is bad, but it
                    cannot be helped
            1%   "I don't know whether it is good or bad"
National: 11%   [Abortion] should be prohibited completely
           29%   "I think it is something bad"
           48%   "I think it is not good, but it cannot be helped"

These few slips of evidence are only suggestive, not conclusive. The question they arouse is: does the massive incidence of elective abortion produce mostly partisan, sympathetic female (and feminist) veterans of the experience, or does it also produce, by abreaction, women who would not willingly send others into the experience? It is a question too difficult to answer at this time, but one cannot simply presume that abortors are, as a public opinion cohort, notably more liberal or permissive towards abortion than others.

After one has set aside the opinion polls that are valueless because the questions they ask are too vague, or invite certain responses, or misstate the issues, or draw on an unrepresentative sample; and after one has disregarded presentations of these survey results that are skewed or selective or blundering or dishonest,[171] one confronts two facts. First, the only situation at law which would do political justice to polled majority opinion in this country over the last fifteen years would be one in which state laws permitted abortion in some circumstances and forbade it in others. The second fact is that, whether through guile or bias or self-deception, the advocates of abortion on demand have not acknowledged the first fact. It does not follow that they need agree with this majority view, but it does follow that in propounding their own more permissive views and in lobbying for them politically, they may not claim with any honesty to be representing a view that prevails in the minds of their fellow citizens.[172]

Political Argument: Opposition to Abortion Imposes Religious Dogma through Law

The persisting claim by abortion advocates that theirs was the conviction of most Americans has encountered, as we have seen, some embarrassment. How was it that elective abortion fared so poorly in public opinion surveys and in so many elected legislatures during the nineteenth and twentieth centuries? In particular, advocates have suffered frustration during the abortion funding debate that has occupied Congress and state governments during the past five years. How explain the repeated failure of the proabortion cause to muster support against the Hyde Amendment if the cause is truly as popular as alleged? Under prodding by the Hyde dispute, abortion advocates have characterized the prolife effort as a maneuver by the Catholic church (specifically, the Catholic bishops) to impose their sectarian moral theology on the nation through law; as a well-financed, well-organized political organization; and as a coalition of socially regressive, reactionary groups that oppose every move on behalf of the disadvantaged. This portrayal of its opposition has become so imbedded in the abortion movement's apologetic that each of its claims deserves some evaluation.

The religious defense of abortion in the political arena (the venue in which this particular complaint is most often filed) is proposed in several ways. The first grieves that the prolife movement is largely a front for the Catholic church (read: clergy, bishops), which means to foist this component of its sexual-marital dogma on the national citizenry. Second, even if the prolife lobby is not the Catholic church *contra mundum*, the abortion debate does represent an intramural dispute between various religious traditions, one in which it is inappropriate for the government, through law, to take sides. Third, whatever its church patronage, abortion is essentially a moral matter, and the law ought not be used to regulate morality. Lastly, the basic question (whether the unborn are our human peers, and thus rightful claimants to protection under law) is one resolvable only by appeal to religious faith, and therefore it is not one whose solution should be given civil application.

The first assertion is the most common. The American Jewish Congress has declared that "today opposition to abortion and particularly governmental financing of the procedure for the economically disadvantaged reflects religious rather than secular values, and for all practical purposes only the religious values of the Catholic Church."[173] This point is made frequently by pro-abortion clergy. Methodist John M. Swomley, Jr., seminary professor in Kansas City, has seen the Catholic bishops' hand in attempts to surmount *Wade* and *Bolton*:

> The Roman Catholic bishops of the United States are currently campaigning for passage of an amendment to the Federal Constitution which would write Catholic doctrine into constitutional law. They want to change the traditional American position that a person legally exists at birth to their theological position that a person exists from the moment of conception.

The constitutional amendment introduced by then Senator James Buckley, he notes, comes "directly from Catholic sexual and medical ethics," which deny parents the freedom to choose the number of children they will have. "By contrast, the major Protestant Churches do not view sex as necessarily sinful. . . . If Vatican legalism with respect to fetal rights were inserted in the Constitution it would triumph over the rights of the husband, wife and children of an existing family."[174]

The late Fred Jaffe, president of the Alan Guttmacher Institute (research arm of Planned Parenthood), also criticized Catholic involvement in the abortion issue. "The Right-to-Life movement, while organized formally into lay groups, draws most of its sustenance from a few religious groups, the largest and most influential being the Catholic Church, which has carried out an unprecedented mobilization of its clergy, dioceses, and parishes on the abortion issue."[175] There seems to be little denial that abortion has become, to a high degree, an activist cause for American Catholics. The former executive director of the National Right to Life Committee, Mormon Ray L. White, states: "The only reason we have a movement in this nation is because of the Catholic people and the Catholic Church."[176] On the other hand, some do seem willing to project Catholic presence, and even dominance, where it might not exist. One Oregon journalist, reporting on the state's Right-to-Life organization, notes that it describes itself as nondenominational and identifies its leaders as a Mormon layman and Baptist, Lutheran, and Bible church pastors. She nevertheless characterizes it as a Catholic enterprise.[177]

There has been considerable resistance to the idea that this Catholic tradition and animation are the sole explanation for prevailing national trends regarding abortion. For one thing, there has been more overt Protestant prolife involvement than has been noticed. One of the most eloquent public presentations, a million-dollar film entitled "Whatever Happened to the Human Race?" was financed and produced by Francis A. Schaeffer, a well-known Swiss Presbyterian churchman, and Dr. C. Everett Koop, a Protestant pediatric surgeon practicing in Philadelphia.[178] Protest has been vocal within communities whose authoritative bodies have endorsed abortion freedom and subsidy: critics include Paul Ramsey, Stanley Hauerwas, and Albert Outler among Methodists; Richard Neuhaus and John Strietelmeier among Lutherans; Harold Brown among Congregationalists; Baruch Brody and David Bleich and Hadley Arkes among Jews.[179] The Christian Action Council, one of the largest prolife organizations, is virtually all Protestant. Baptists for Life has strong presence in the movement. Two of the last three presidents of the National Right to Life Committee have been Protestant women. The board of American Citizens Concerned for Life comprises Lutheran, Jewish, Catholic, Methodist, and Baptist clergy, and laity of similar ecumenical diversity. A number of conservative religious-political groups which entered the movement abruptly during the 1980 electoral campaign are not party to the prolife movement but may have had some impact in influencing some voters. Some of the most influential authorities ranged against abortion are venerable in the Protestant tradition: Jean Calvin, Karl Barth, Dietrich Bonhöffer, Helmut Thielicke, Emil Brunner.

Some members of other traditions than Catholic have had a change of mind on the subject. Professor C. Eric Lincoln of Union Theological Seminary had at first given his support to liberalized abortion, but later reversed his stance:

> I took the position that in America, at least, the notion of a woman's complete personal autonomy over her own body is, or should be, so elementary as to preclude debate, and that to require a woman to be an incubator for a child she does not want is barbaric and tyrannical and in violation of the most basic expectations of a civilized society. But I also insisted that "any liberalization of the abortion laws [should] serve a constructive interest of those who are particularly disadvantaged by the consequences of isolation and poverty," and that "their economic and social vulnerability should not be . . . exploited by other interests masquerading as abortion reform." . . . I considered abortion a draconian measure of last resort for a limited class of people who, after having considered the vast implications of what they were about to

do, would proceed with fear and trembling and a prayer for forgiveness. I was not prepared for the bloodletting which has, in fact, ensued.[180]

In Congress, abortion opponents have been annoyed to be told they were pawns in the hands of the Catholics. In the House, when the Hyde Amendment was first being considered in 1976, the votes in its favor, by religion, were: 167 Protestants, 76 Catholics, 5 Jews, 3 Mormons, 5 unaffiliated.[181] When the U.S. Civil Rights Commission issued its 1975 caveat against amending the Constitution on abortion because it would violate the First Amendment, it drew a sharp response from then Senator James Buckley: "I do not know precisely what the Commission has in mind when it refers to 'one set' of religious views. But if this is meant to be a code word for Roman Catholic doctrine then the Commission should know that six out of seven cosponsors of my amendment are not Catholics."[182] An attack by Lawrence Lader drew response from then Senator Richard Schweiker of Pennsylvania (later Secretary of Health and Human Services):

> This obvious effort to link the growing anti-abortion movement in America to the "Catholic Church" and "the right wing" is a gross distortion of the political realities of the abortion situation in this country today. To label the abortion issue as solely a "Catholic concern" first of all overlooks simple basic facts; for example, many of the outspoken opponents of abortion in Congress, such as myself and such fellow Senators as Orrin Hatch, Mark Hatfield and Jesse Helms, are non-Catholics.[183]

Voices raised from within the religious and political arenas confirmed what the polls had been saying throughout the decade: that the segmentation of opinion within various Christian and Jewish denominations was quite diverse in most groups, and did not clearly reflect official statements of religious authorities.

Prochoice advocates have also been grieved, they explain, by the prospect of the law affiliating itself with one side of a dispute among religionists, no matter how the lines may be drawn denominationally. Since opposing views about abortion have been advanced among religious groups, a law that agreed with one view would grant it "establishment" and deny its opponents "free exercise" of religion. In matters touching on religious dissent, they say, should not the churches and synagogues deny themselves the temptation to reinforce their particular doctrines with the coercive hand of the state? One group of abortion advocates deplored legal opposition as "a serious threat to religious liberty and freedom of conscience. . . . If successful, it would violate the deeply held religious convictions of individual members and official bodies of so many other religious groups about when human personhood begins, the relative rights of a woman and a fetus, and responsible family life."[184] Theologian John Bennett has argued that abortion is different from other social issues wherein Catholic advocacy is allowable. "In those cases broad issues of opinion are not to any degree based on religious presuppositions that are dominant in one church but not in others."[185] Rabbi Balfour Brickner of the Religious

Coalition for Abortion Rights objects: "I cannot believe that the state has the right to foist, through legislation, the religious conviction of any one group upon all the citizens of the country."[186] Many partisans have compared prospective legislation against abortion to the Eighteenth Amendment. Prohibition, then heavily supported by evangelical Protestants, was imposed upon the country but the citizenry took it as a violation of their personal rights and eventually threw it off.[187]

Some criticism had less to do with the position of churches on abortion, and argued in general that it was not the law's task to govern the moral behavior of citizens. But response was quick. There is hardly any major issue regarding human behavior, it was pointed out, that is not seriously a moral issue, and on which there has not been division of opinion among religious thinkers. Were the law to be forbidden to deal with these matters it would be left with only frivolities to regulate. Daniel Callahan objects: "I have seen nothing to convince me that abortion is inherently a more religious issue than justice, peace or the general social welfare. . . . One might as well say that the Vietnamese war is a religious issue, not subject to legislation because there are some churches which declare war immoral on religious grounds. Religious groups have taken religious stands on many social issues, including war, race, poverty, population, and ecology, without exempting those problems from public legislation or turning them into 'theology.' "[188] *Commonweal* magazine editorializes: "Whatever the mixture of beliefs behind it, Congress's decision to protect fetal life is as secular on the face of it as its decision to protect tracts of wilderness from spoliation, unknowing consumers from toxic drugs, or laboratory animals from cruel experimentation."[189] To the claim that opposition to abortion stems from religious beliefs and cannot be cast into law without abridging the separation between church and state, Rice philosopher Baruch Brody replies: "Remember that opposition to torture in Brazil does not become a religious moral position just because that opposition is now being led by the Catholic bishops."[190]

One of the most comprehensive statements on the subject has come from Robert Hoyt, a veteran journalist in the liberal Catholic tradition, serving as managing editor of the Protestant journal *Christianity and Crisis*:

> When the issues of policy must be resolved—the death penalty, racial segregation, chemical warfare, the rights of labor—it is absurd to argue that legislators may not enact or that courts must not respect laws reflecting their constituents' ethical beliefs, no matter how derived. . . . [The] insistent emphasis on Catholic influence is misleading (and prejudicial) in two ways. . . . That influence is born out of two facts of no possible judicial concern— the number of Catholics in the country and the tight structure of their church. If there were 30 or 40 million Quakers and Mennonites in the population, the Pentagon would be no more than a triangle, our foreign policy would be very difficult (and much better), and the Quaker-Mennonite impact on policy would not be improper, much less unconstitutional. . . .

It is ironic in the extreme that even while the ACLU is attacking the Hyde Amendment because it is "religious," it is also sending urgent appeals to church bodies asking money to help promote abolition of the death penalty. Suppose the churches respond and the effort succeeds; would not the result be vulnerable to the McRae doctrine? Or consider the Wagner Act. It was authored by a Catholic Senator, and it embodies ideas he drew from papal encyclicals on social justice. The hierarchy supported it strongly; dozens of "labor priests" lobbied for it; hundreds of pastors endorsed it, as did scores of diocesan newspapers. Those are precisely the kinds of activities that are given a sinister tone in the McRae brief's argument with respect to abortion law. If that argument prevails, what is to prevent the National Association of Manufacturers from challenging the Wagner Act as being fatally tainted with "religion?" So also with the Civil Rights Act; Hubert Humphrey wrote for the record that religious influence was the most important factor in its passage.[191]

The *New York Times* took an editorial position that "if churches insist on maneuvering public laws by their conformity to religious doctrine, they only drive society toward choosing one doctrine and suppressing the others." "Not so," insisted Donald Shriver, president of Union Theological Seminary. "On the one hand, people of faith lose their integrity if they refuse to measure social policy by perspectives rooted in their faith. On the other, a pluralistic society protects its citizens' rights to disagree with each other's faith assumptions, reading of fact and preferred public actions."[192] Freedom of speech, he says, allows us to provide a religious argument for or against public policy.

The assertion that morality, above all morality at issue between churches, should not influence legislation was not an assertion that fared well in the public forum, especially since it offended some weathered liberals whose careers had been spent wrestling the laws into some sort of morally acceptable shape. The argument then backtracked several paces and ventured off on a slant, though still in the same general direction. Granted that some laws may embody moral viewpoints, even viewpoints that enjoy church sponsorship, surely they should not give coercive sanction to any conviction that is grounded on an act of faith. This point is put squarely by Philip Wogaman:

> Of course, all might agree that fetal life is *potentially* possessed of that inherent worth that the state properly recognizes in human personhood—and both ordinary experience and the sciences can be mustered to demonstrate the connection. But, as the Supreme Court said, ordinary experience and the sciences cannot confirm the existence of human personhood in that sense in fetal life, at least in the first few months. It takes a venture of faith, having the rational status of conjecture, to bridge that gap between the known and the unknown. Everybody is entitled to take such ventures, but it is arguably unconstitutional to abridge anybody's freedom of choice on such a basis.[193]

Civil libertarian Aryeh Neier insists that the only motive alleged for resistance to abortion is that the unborn are actually human and alive, a view that is "exclusively rooted in theology and supportable only by an act of faith."[194] Harvard law professor Laurence Tribe agrees. The only way legal control over abortion could be justified would be that this would protect living human beings from destruction. This premise, that there is a crucial moment after which actual human life must be aknowledged in the fetus, has never (at least in this century) been advanced except by organized religious doctrine. It is an inherently religious notion, claims Tribe, undiscussable in purely secular terms.[195] Rabbi Balfour Brickner defends the claim that "determining when life begins is a medical and theological matter—not a legal one."[196] Though he would allow it as a question that others besides divines might discuss, he would still declare it out of bounds to legislators. Fred Jaffe, whose statements have served as canons of orthodoxy in the abortion movement, asserted that since science cannot determine that a fetus is a person, "this belief can only be based on religious values, or metaphysical values that are religious in nature if not in expression."[197]

This complaint has been met from several different directions. One cadre of debaters—including many who are sympathetic toward abortion—has replied that whatever the purpose of legislators may be, the defense of human persons is not the only legislative purpose imaginable for antiabortion laws. One may advance for them the much more modest—and constitutionally agreeable— secular purpose of preserving the unborn whatever their status. Professor Monroe Freedman has used this counterargument against Neier:

> About two decades ago, in a debate in support of woman's right to choose an abortion, I outraged my adversary by pointing out that a fetus in the early stages is, biologically, a fish. Assume with me that a fetus is nothing more than a fish. Does that mean that Congress could not constitutionally legislate to protect it? Of course not. On the contrary, Congress has enacted valid legislation to protect not only whales but snail darters.[198]

Quite a different reply was given by those who turned the argument on its head and accused the proabortion position of being grounded on a faith tenet:

> It is possible to defend abortion from a religious position; a particular religion may hold that the unborn is not a human life in the first months of pregnancy. This is also the belief expressed in the Supreme Court's decision on abortion.
>
> I maintain that this view cannot be held except as a matter of faith. All the biologic evidence indicates that the unborn from the moment of conception is a unique individual, genetically human and different from the parents.[199]

Others have pointed out that in *Wade* the Supreme Court has already effectively subscribed to a specific side of the argument (whether the unborn are human persons). Noting that this was a point of debate within several disciplines (medicine, philosophy, and theology), the Court stated it "need not resolve the difficult question of when life begins." At the same time it conceded that if it *is* the case that the unborn are human persons, then they would certainly deserve the law's protection and the abortion issue would be resolved. Then, however, the Court rebuked the State of Texas for "adopting one theory of life" and devising a law (as had every other state) that implied both mother and offspring to have rights and provided for which rights would prevail in various conflicts.[200] But the decision whereby all possible rights of the unborn would invariably be overridden by the mother's simple preference was not a neutral one, since it did not allow of any benefit of doubt to a being in jeopardy of extinction. As the *New Republic* observed, "For the government to take a truly agnostic position on the issue of when human life begins, it would have to protect fetuses from the moment of conception in case Roman Catholics are right: you don't walk away from a flooded mineshaft because there's only a 50-50 chance someone's trapped at the bottom."[201] The nation's law now is no more neutral than were the abortion statutes of the fifty states: it is firmly grounded in the conviction—theological or not—that the unborn are indubitably not human. Says Daniel Callahan: "A decision to remove abortion laws from the books is no more ethically neutral than a decision to put such laws on the books or keep them there."[202]

Yet another rejoinder to the proabortion plea that the unborn's status as human depends on religious tenets beyond scientific or rational verification questions the criterion itself:

> What in the realm of opinion *is* scientifically verifiable? Are minorities and women equal? Should abortion be funded? Are the Democrats the party to vote for? Should the war in Rhodesia continue? Is the neutron bomb a weapon which should be deployed? Should aid be given to Israel, or to the Arabs? The opinions which would inform a judgment regarding the answer to each question noted above depends to a great degree upon the consciousness, philosophy and personal opinion of the answering party. None are peculiarly "secular."[203]

Similarly:

> Throughout history, there has been no "scientific consensus" that individuals, or races, are fundamentally equal. If anything, the "scientific consensus" has been the other way. (And in many times and places—colonial America, Nazi Germany, South Africa today—there has been no "religious consensus" either.) To conclude that society must therefore abstain from judgment on these questions is nothing less than disastrous.[204]

The many-pronged religious argument on behalf of free and funded abortion has not fared very well in the forum of public debate. To date it has not been any more successful at the bar. No segment of the argument has been given high patronage by the courts, and several have been either explicitly rejected or disregarded. Courts have held, or observed in *dicta*:

> (1) that no law is infirm simply because it incorporated moral values that derive from religion;[205]

(2) that laws somehow restrictive of abortion funding [or freedom] would not be invalid if they sanctioned one among many religious views, namely, that of the Catholic Church;[206]

(3) that there are grounds and purposes for legislation touching on abortion freedom or funding which are not exclusively theological or religious;[207]

(4) that, since abortion laws have on their face a sufficiently secular purpose, there can be no warranted search by the judiciary for further "true purposes" of the lawmakers or their constituents.[208]

There seems, then, to be no public acceptance for the claims that abortion law would enshrine sectarian dogma (principally that of the Catholic church), legislate morality on a matter disputed among the churches, or rest on nonsecular beliefs about unborn humanhood. But some observers of the debate see this matter as extending beyond the specific grievances that have been made. They see this religious argument as expressive of a prejudice against Catholics. The *New Republic*, in an otherwise proabortion editorial, makes such a suggestion: "The most unfair argument against the anti-abortion movement is the smear of guilt by association with the Catholic Church."[209]

There is throughout the literature a general yet restrained contempt for Catholic convictions. Some incidents are, on the most generous reading, difficult to account for except as dyspeptic bias. Several years back, for example, in its report on roll calls on the Hyde Amendment, the *Congressional Quarterly Weekly Report* identified each Catholic senator and representative by an asterisk. One columnist erupted: "Can one imagine the fire storm if CQ placed a little yellow star of David beside the name of all Jewish members of Congress voting against F-15s for Saudi Arabia?"[210] About the same time coverage in the *New York Times* incurred professional censure by the National News Council for "implying that Catholic Congressmen can be expected to respond almost automatically to the abortion issue on the basis of religious pressure." A check of voting patterns in the House of Representatives had shown the implication to be unfounded. The *Times* earned further censure for referring to the City Council of Akron as "Roman-Catholic dominated" in a story on that city's controversial abortion ordinance. The reference was found to be misleading because, though seven of thirteen councilors were Catholic, one of them had declared against the ordinance, and "therefore the issue of 'dominance' was debatable."[211] A coarser approach to the same issue was employed by a cartoon in the *Reproductive Rights Newsletter* which portrayed the Akron City Council as four males in clerical garb.[212]

Cartoons were the medium of another attack on Catholics that drew national attention. In the spring of 1978 Planned Parenthood / Chicago Area secured from its Denver affiliate a packet of cartoons commissioned there and prepared, with accompanying scripts, for national distribution. The packet was reproduced and sent by Planned Parenthood to college newspapers, with instructions to use the materials without attribution. The contents are described by Joan Beck:

The six-panel strip shows an official-looking seal of the Department of Health, Education and Welfare. The words, presumably spoken by HEW secretary Joseph A. Califano, Jr., read:

"I was raised in a very devout family. So was my wife. Of course we have a very religious home and accept the teachings of the church about birth control and abortion. When we had all the children we felt we should, my wife and I talked it over. She chose total abstinence for the rest of her fertile years. I respect her choice.

"Of course my mistress feels differently about it."

Another of the half-dozen cartoons pictures a Catholic bishop holding matches and a can of gasoline. Slyly he says the church is not worried about abortion because "we've got the faithful out burning down the clinics."

The package also contains blatant and nasty anti-Catholic and anti-religion blasts editors are urged to use as "background material for your editorials." . . .

With the bishop cartoon, for example, additional copy reads, "Yes, they're burning down the clinics. In Minnesota. In Ohio. In Vermont. Fanatics, stirred into activity by the bombast of 'churchmen' are running about with matches. Why?

"Because some people, some religious and semireligious groups dominated by elderly men, simply cannot deal rationally with sex. They can't talk about it rationally, can't think about it rationally, and above all can't give up the power which controlling other people gives them. They control other people through sex.

"What groups? The Roman Catholic Church . . . the Mormon Church . . . certain fundamentalist churches. . . . All of these groups control people through controlling their sexual activity. . . . They want to force their beliefs on you and they are very likely to succeed."

Beck then describes first reactions.

Queries to Planned Parenthood / Chicago first brought a defense of the package (it was time "to take the offensive against the Catholic Church in desperation because of its severe and sustained attacks on Planned Parenthood" and Califano's view on abortion justified the snideness against him).

A spokesman for Planned Parenthood Federation of America agreed the material is tasteless, unfortunate and offensive, but pleaded local jurisdiction.

Noting that Planned Parenthood is a major recipient of federal funding, and a beneficiary of United Way in many communities, Beck deplored the bigotry and hatred shown in the materials. Eventually the chairman of the board of Planned Parenthood / Chicago Area reassured the public that they realized the package was tasteless and offensive, but disclaimed responsibility. "The package came into our office where a departing staff member [the public education director] made a unilateral decision to send it to a list of campus newspapers."[213]

A similar sort of jibe, though less crude, was published by columnist Georgie Anne Geyer. In a column headlined "Abortion Fight Now a Religious War," she designated the Catholic church and certain fundamentalist faiths as the only opponents of abortion on demand. Then she posed a query: "But one has to wonder about all the religious 'pro-life' groups that are precisely behind the fanaticism—and the violence." She answers the query: it is the Catholic dioceses, with their contributions to the National Committee for a Human Life Amendment, a Washington lobbying office. The bishops, one is given to understand, are sponsoring the firebombing of abortion clinics.[214]

The Catholic bishops are made fair game for much gratuitous comment. In the aftermath of John Paul II's visit to this country, Congressman Paul McCloskey of California rose in the House of Representatives to deplore the pope's appeal: "To destroy those innocent unborn children is an unspeakable crime—their right to life must be recognized and fully protected by law." McCloskey first recalled how the pope's predecessors had presided over the Inquisition, the torture and execution of thousands, a tradition brought by the Spaniards to New Mexico. Not so in eastern America, he said, which offered haven to refugees from religious persecution (he neglected to mention the only colony which observed religious freedom for all sects: Catholic Maryland). The message: "We have chosen to separate our laws and our religious beliefs. . . . In fact, whenever religious views disagree, it is an accepted restraint in our system of delegated governmental powers that one religion's view not be written into law at the expense of others."[215] The remarks were a conventional criticism of the Hyde Amendment, but Catholics took it as offensive that their leader, who had come to preach justice, should be decried as one ready to command with rack and screw.

The abortion issue also served to bring down criticism on the pope's head in exactly the opposite direction. Carl Rowan has made abortion advocacy one of the frequent themes of his syndicated column. "Solely on the basis of dogma," "an arrogant minority," "a passionate clique" "holier-than-everybody-else" (Catholics are mentioned), has insisted "on imposing their religious convictions on everyone else." Rowan objects to Catholic convictions wielding clout in the political order. Yet after John Paul II had visited Latin America, Rowan saw his pastoral message to be mostly "opiate" because he had not stirred the poor to anger and political violence. His comment on the papal journey to the United States: "We are left to ask where hope lies if organized religion has so little influence on the social and political behavior of the people."[216] On abortion the pope was to be silent. On issues Rowan favored he was to be a political lion. The pope, it appears, was to be held in contempt no matter how he comported himself.

But there was a *frisson* of astonishment when Mother Teresa of Calcutta was savaged by abortion advocates. In her Nobel Peace Prize acceptance remarks she had said:

> Our poor people are great people, a very lovable people. They don't need our pity and sympathy, they need our understanding

love. They need our respect. They need that we treat them with dignity. . . .

The greatest destroyer of peace today is the crime of the innocent, unborn child. . . .

To me, the nations which have legalized abortion, they are the poorest nations. . . . They don't want to feed one more child, to educate one more child. And so the child must die.[217]

One critic in Los Angeles wrote: "After awarding the Nobel Peace Prize to Henry Kissinger, spreader of war, the committee has given it to Mother Teresa, propagator of poverty. . . . She takes care of child mothers. No child should be a mother. She exemplifies the evil good people do when they hand their brains over to an 'authority.' "[218] Liz Smith, columnist in the *New York Daily News*, explained: "Well, insiders know that Mother Teresa received her speech direct from the Vatican, and a papal nuncio was in constant attendance to be sure that she did not deviate from the point of view of the Church."[219]

There is enough anti-Catholic odium in the general atmosphere to explain much of this. One need not imagine that abortion advocates are more given to this bias than anyone else. But Bernard Nathanson has recounted how, in the founding days of the abortion movement, the Catholic hierarchy was explicitly assigned the role as villains of the piece.[220] Daniel Callahan has warned proabortion activists that purposeful public abuse heaped on Catholic bishops will not, as hoped, secure abortion support from liberal Catholics, who enjoy wide freedom to dissent within the church. It will, he predicts, be taken by them as an insult to themselves. "The most obvious test of bigotry is not that of outright persecution; it is whether representatives of one's group are always singled out for a religious identification."[221]

Catholics have not failed to notice how, and have wondered why, their coreligionists are always the ones pointed out. The *National Review* took exception to what it sensed to be anti-Catholic discrimination in the ACLU brief submitted in the *McRae* case:

> In order to establish the "unconstitutionality" of [the Hyde] Amendment, the ACLU has inspected Congressman Hyde's mail and had him followed to a Catholic Mass, where its informant reported he actually received communion. This kind of snooping is not generally associated with civil liberties (certainly not when the FBI does it), but then, as we know, the price of liberty is eternal vigilance. . . . (The ACLU has never asked to read Senator Javits' mail or followed him to his synagogue.)[222]

In poring over the detritus of the debate one does not find much by way of retaliation expressed on the part of Catholics. For instance, one cannot help but take note that the book in which Lawrence Lader most vituperates Catholics about their antiabortion activism is one of a series of proabortion books issued by the Beacon Press under the auspices of the Unitarian Universalist church.[223] There was some kind of double standard here that could bear mention.

In particular, there has been not even a whisper of antagonized comment about the differential treatment accorded to Catholics and to Jews in this matter. To my knowledge no Catholic has ever pointed out in print how proportionately numerous are Jews among the leadership of proabortion agencies and organizations, while it is a commonplace to note and deplore Catholic presence in prolife groups. A telltale incident took place a decade ago. In 1970, *New York Times* coverage of the passage of an elective abortion bill in the New York Assembly made extensive references to Catholic involvement: which assemblymen were Catholic, which districts had Catholic majorities, what comments had been made in which Catholic parish churches on Sunday, how Catholic legislators voted and why. The measure passed by one vote when George M. Michaels of Auburn changed his vote, explaining that he did so under pressure from his two sons, one a rabbinical student. Portrayed in news stories and editorial as a profile in courage because he represented a largely Catholic district, Michaels was given much attention during his subsequent unsuccessful electoral campaign (*Times* headline: "Michaels, Whose Vote Passed Abortion Bill"). Catholic readers and others could not help noticing that Catholics were expected to vote out of conformity, while a Jewish legislator was praised for having voted out of conscience against his constituents' presumed wishes. When they vote against abortion because of their own convictions, Catholics are dogmatic; when they do so to accommodate their constituents, they are craven. When non-Catholics vote against abortion because of their own conviction, they are unintelligible; when they do so to accommodate their constituents, they are under intense pressure. Put otherwise: when a majority want abortion from their legislators, that is democracy; when a majority do not want abortion, they follow what the *Times* calls "the politics of punishment."[224]

In one very specific sector of the abortion literature Catholics are the objects of a systematic discrimination that seems to have aroused no concern. Virtually all public opinion surveys report separately on how Catholics respond. Sometimes they are the only subgroup singled out. Poll analysts have for years noted that responses do not tend to differentiate Catholics from Protestants by significant intervals, yet the segregation of the Catholic cohort persists. There is no comment upon the fact that the Catholic population shows much internal diversity of opinion about abortion, while there is least contour of opinion among Jewish respondents. Nor has anyone pursued the implications of poll results that classify together "Jews, Episcopalians, None." What is there in the experiences of these two religious-ethnic groups which provides them with the same values on abortion, and possibly other subjects, as those who have no religion at all?[225]

What, in sum, might one say about the religious argument on abortion's behalf? Advocates have unjustifiably succeeded in persuading some of the American public that the religious interests which surround abortion policy and the religious activists who have taken a public hand in the struggle are inappropriate. If anything, the blundering and offensive manner in which accusations of bigotry have been made has stirred more serious reflection on the question of abortion than would have arisen had the accusations not been made. It is not at all clear that this reflection will enlarge the national sympathies for abortion on demand.

I come away from this part of my inquiry with several more personal observations.

First, the political structures of America are under no strain, through the course of this debate, taut enough to weaken or fatigue them. In fact, I see them as invigorated by the impassioned yet astute advocacy this moral issue is receiving.

Second, the question of when human life begins will continue to be discussed with the same admixture of biomedical information, legal concern, and philosophical and theological overview that attends the question of when life ends.

Third, it is true that the abortion controversy marks the debut of Catholics in America as an unabashed political force. This is due in large part to *Wade* and *Bolton*, which dealt so airily with the traditions and convictions of the citizenry and its legislative interests. But it is also due to the fact that now, unlike in the days when Catholic influence worked powerfully on behalf of organized labor, liberalized immigration, or racial integration, church leaders cannot bring much direct influence to bear on civil officials. What is distinctive about the Catholic activism against abortion is not that masses of laity march to the bishops' orders. Quite the contrary, the prolife presence of Catholics is mostly lay, and such populist support as rallies to it comes less from any conformity to authority than from deep persuasion. Other future social causes will find Catholics more practiced in this style of citizenship.

Fourth, the divide between religionists on abortion is not one which cleaves one set of communions from another. The cleft follows two older fracture lines, and does not conform exactly to church boundaries. Most significantly, the religious groups that resist abortion are the same groups that traditionally have placed high value on the marriage bond. Those who advocate protection for the unborn, even at sharp sacrifice, are the same who have advocated fidelity in marriage, for better or for worse. They are prepared to withstand a cultural sympathy for abortion because they have long withstood a similar sympathy for divorce and remarriage. Those who have defended the bond of promise are, not surprisingly, also defenders of the bond of blood.[226]

It has been said, but erroneously, that the precise point where religion properly enters the abortion debate is where the question arises: when does human life begin? Religion has much less to say to the question "Lord, who is my neighbor?" than to the distinctly different question of what to do with that neighbor. Christianity, in particular, has much less to say about the value of human life than it does about the value of human beings to our life. For it teaches that we have nothing better to do with our lives than to share them with others. The beam of insight in Christianity about human value is more focused on our own life than on that of another. For Jesus' teaching is that when one human eliminates another, worse damage befalls the killer than the killed. Christian teaching on lifetaking centers less on the value of human life in the abstract than on the need we have of sustaining others' lives lest we perish ourselves. The Christian stake in the status of the unborn is not simply that the unborn is human, but that he or she is our brother or sister; and, even more, it is that we shall thrive only if we nurture our brothers and sisters. The doctrine is about me more even than about him or her. Christianity does not have its own peculiar answer to the question of whether the unborn are human. But it does have its own characteristic address to that question, for we aspire to be a community that is fit to welcome children into the world.

As Stanley Hauerwas has so eloquently put it:

> Christians are thus trained to be the kind of people who are ready to receive and welcome children into the world. . . . The Christian prohibition of abortion is but the negative side of their positive commitment to welcome new life into their community . . .
>
> It is, of course, true that children will often be conceived and born under less than ideal conditions, but the church lives as a community which assumes that we live in an age which is always dangerous. That we live in such a time is all the more reason we must be the kind of community that can receive children into our midst. Just as we need to be virtuous, not because virtue pays, but because we cannot afford to be without virtue where it does not pay; so we must learn to be people open to new life. We can neither protect our neighbors from that suffering nor deny them the joy of participating in the adventure of God's kingdom.
>
> . . . From the world's perspective, the birth of a child represents but another drain on our material and psychological resources: children, after all, take up much of the energy that we could use in making the world a better place and our society a more just one. But from the Christian perspective, the birth of a child represents nothing less than our commitment that God will not have this world "bettered" through the destruction of life.[227]

Fifth, I anticipate that the liberal, social activist cadres among Protestants and Jews will reexamine their "religious establishment" charges against Catholics, in the abortion context. This will be prompted from within their own ranks. When the National Council of Churches asked its religious liberty committee whether it should file a brief in the *McRae* case, a number of the attorneys and First Amendment experts "asked how one church body could impugn another church body for doing what both believe to be right and moral and best for the whole society." They argued that it would be "suicidal" for a church organization that had been so active in public policy struggles to claim that church advocacy invalidates enactments of law.[228] The fact that the liberals' strategy, whether from anxiety about being on the losing side of the abortion issue, or from anti-Catholic bias, or from some other motive, has undercut their longstanding social activism will be brought home to them in other forums. American Lutheran Church executive Edward Schneider takes a proabortion Protestant editor to task: "He says abortion is not a proper concern for regulation, yet other items that he cites as proper for political deliberation—'hunger, social programs, military spending'—also clearly involve theological considerations. Many church people opposed our nation's involvement in Vietnam precisely for theological reasons." Another Protestant extended the critique: "According to the editor, single-issue politics based on theology is wrong when there exists a difference of theological opinion with regard to the issue. Were the Christians who founded the Free Soil Party (out of which grew the Republican Party) wrong, since probably a majority of Christians at the time believed that slavery was in accordance with the divine will? Would single-issue politics have been wrong in Nazi Germany to oppose the systematic murder of Jews? Incidentally, no group has practiced single-issue politics more than the proponents of the ERA, despite the fact that there are strong religious convictions on the part of the amendment's opponents."[229] Veteran activist Richard Neuhaus says, "The abortion debate is leaving an anemic liberalism on the wrong side. . . . It is an atomistic liberalism obsessed with individual rights to the exclusion of corporate rights or responsibilities (except when corporate rights are affirmed in collectivist terms or state control). But the liberalism Christians would embrace is one that is community-building. We would expand rather than contract the definition of the human community for which we accept responsibility. . . . Christian liberalism must reject the *moral logic* of the Supreme Court's 1973 *Roe* v. *Wade* decision . . . that the possession of a right depends on the power to assert that right."[230]

Sixth, I doubt that many Americans on either side of this issue derive their most basic convictions about it from their religious faith or teaching. People come down either acknowledging or denying that the unborn is a fellow human. They do not receive this from faith as a principle, and then act accordingly. It is the other way around. People either are or are not disposed to eliminate undesired offspring—and they form their conscience accordingly. I am quite sure that the Afrikaaners in South Africa do not first imbibe the belief that blacks are negligible, and then proceed to treat them that way. They habituate themselves first to exploitation and then they have no comfortable alternative but to harbor prejudice. The treatment generates the attitude. And all manner of contempt for women, for adversaries in war, for slaves, for foreigners, for the poor, for infidels, has arisen, not from the doctrine that they are contemptible, but from the advantages one has first enjoyed by treating them contemptibly. As regards abortion, church and synagogue have been more reinforcers than originators of the disposition either to cherish or to dismiss the unborn.

Last, though the advocates of abortion do at times appear to be bigoted and prejudiced against the religious groups they see as opponents, I do not reckon the proabortion movement to be essentially anti-Catholic. Their uncivil and sometimes intemperate fusillades against bishops and dogma and thoughtless conformity do not issue, as one might be forgiven for thinking, from a studied opposition to the Catholic church. Let a comparison serve here. It is normal in Latin America for the affluent to revile efforts by Catholic clergy and activist laity on behalf of land reform and democratic government and the elimination of torture: they say this is all Communist inspired. It is not that the affluent, whose ease comes from the subjection of most of their countrymen, know much about Catholic doctrine on justice (or Marxist doctrine on it). They simply cannot fathom why anyone could wish to favor peasants at their expense, and so they suppose that only Communism could inspire such a thing. So also, many people who are sensitive to the sacrifices that women— especially very young or very poor or very embarrassed or very unresourceful women—would have to make if they gave birth to their children, and who are used to the advantages of being able to eliminate those children at will—these people cannot fathom why anyone would wish to favor the unborn at their expense. And so they suppose that only dogmatism could inspire such a thing.

Political Argument: The Prolife Movement Is Well Financed

For some years now the case for abortion freedom has had to cope with one inconvenience of its own making. Advocates had been claiming that the abortion movement spoke for a national majority. The challenge to this came, not so much from the opinion polls, which were not being closely read, but from political reversals. If indeed unrestricted abortion were the wish of America's people, then why was it so repeatedly unsuccessful when put to the test politically? Why was it that the legal rulings of the Supreme Court had never been acceptable to a single legislature? Why were so many legislatures enacting statues that tried to curb the permissiveness of the Court's law? And why, if this were the public will, was the call for tax-subsidized abortion across the nation meeting with conspicuous defeat? Why were many legislators prominent for their support of elective abortion—Brooke, Bayh, Clark, Culver, Fraser, McGovern—not being reaffirmed at the election booth?

Instead of questioning the claim that abortion was so politically popular, advocates offered an explanation. Their opponents, though a minority, were "well-organized and well-financed."

From the bench of the Supreme Court itself, Justice Marshall deplored the fact that public officials were "under extraordinary pressure from well-financed and carefully orchestrated lobbying campaigns."[231] Judith Randal, in a column in the *Washington Star*, described the prolife movement as "ominous" and "heavily subsidized by the Catholic Church."[232] The Religious Coalition for Abortion Rights warned that mass mailings to conservatives were soliciting funds. "Clearly the campaign to end legal abortion is not purely a grassroots effort funded by the nickels and dimes of concerned citizens. Anti-abortion activities are being escalated with an infusion of big money supplied by the power brokers who have little personal concern for the issue, but who view it as a means to manipulate political events."[233] The *New York Times* described the movement as enjoying "a dollar investment well into the millions," raised by "highly organized, increasingly broad-based and generally well-financed campaigns."[234] As the 1980 elections approached, organizations on each side anticipated sizable expenditures. Planned Parenthood and the National Right to Life Committee each projected an investment of a million dollars in the campaign.[235] After the election's finale Gloria Steinem reiterated the warning about political takeover by "a small, well-organized, and well-financed faction."[236]

Alerted by such descriptions of bulky wealth quietly at work on the political scene, one is encouraged to delve for facts. Whether the prolife movement is "well-organized" is difficult to measure. The major organizations do not seem to enjoy a tradition of mutual collaboration such as one sees between the veteran proabortion groups. But organization is much less calculable than are finances, and if one wishes to ascertain whether the movement has within it resources that will magnify its voice in the political arena, one should look for money.

My first inquiry was in 1977. A manifesto which blamed Catholic churchmen for Congress's refusal to vote abortion subsidies was published in several Protestant journals, signed by a large group of predominantly Protestant churchmen and churchwomen. It denounced the "heavy institutional involvement" of the bishops and dioceses of the Catholic church, and in particular the "massive financial contributions by those dioceses to the National Committee for a Human Life Amendment."[237] Curiosity piqued and nostrils flaring at the scent of cash (something the bishops were not known to dole out lavishly), I determined to learn just how massively the Catholic dioceses were bankrolling this organization. What I found was disappointing—at least, it must have been to the committee. That fiscal year the total diocesan contributions amounted to $280,000: half a penny per Catholic; an average contribution of $1,590 per diocese; less than one-half of 1 percent of what they were budgeting for Catholic Charities, not to mention health care, inner-city schools, overseas relief, and other social services. This did not satisfy my sense of massive support, and was my first discovery of how modest the movement's financing actually was.[238]

The elections of 1980 supplied an ideal context in which to witness prolife financing at work. Early alerts pointed to the campaign of Oregon's Senator Bob Packwood as a cameo example of it, for he had been given prominence on the prolife movement's "hit list," and there were reports of big money moving to Oregon.

In his previous campaign Packwood had benefited financially from renown as an environmental protectionist. He had been the sponsor of several population-oriented bills. One bill would have limited to two the number of children who could be declared as federal income tax exemptions.[239] Another would have authorized abortion on demand in the District of Columbia; it was followed by a bill that would have permitted it nationwide.[240] At election time a solicitation letter, written over Paul Ehrlich's name, was sent to a national Zero Population Growth mailing list and brought in numerous donations.[241]

But by 1980 his stature as an environmental-population activist had been diminished. True, the Packwoods had secured national attention by announcing that, instead of begetting children, they were adopting two, both of whom, as one responsive commentator observed, "were brought into the world by others who perhaps were not so well informed or motivated about controlling the population."[242] The senator also attracted sympathetic notice when he was "very disheartened" and "outraged" over the death of some cattle due to a pump failure in eastern Oregon, and called for a thorough investigation into the tragedy.[243] More recently he had even been honored by Greenpeace for sponsoring a prowhale amendment that would save "those great, great creatures" from being killed.[244] But in 1980 the Oregon League of Environmental

Voters, explaining that they were tired of "an election year environmentalist," withdrew their endorsement from Packwood and gave it to his Democratic opponent. Noting in the polls that, in any case, the environmental issue had lost its public following and was unlikely to raise much support for his forthcoming campaign, the senator turned to another national constituency: abortion advocates.[245]

Two years before the election, Packwood made his first overture in this direction when he summoned up the specter of prolife militancy. Expecting "abortion opponents to mount a well-financed campaign" to dislodge pro-abortion leaders in Congress, he spoke of "$10 to 15 million" as a modest estimate of what they might raise.[246] In the summer of 1979, well before most campaigns were organized, Packwood's committee sent out a letter of solicitation, this time over Gloria Steinem's name, directed to a variety of national proabortion mailing lists (Packwood later said it went into every county of every state). The letter was reissued again in 1980, and was to prove immensely successful. "At this early stage," the letter warned, "even before the primary, $200,000 has already been earmarked for the campaign against him. . . . that does not include the army of volunteers that will pour into Oregon. Without our help, Bob Packwood is in danger of drowning in a sea of 'Right-to-Life' money and zealots." Recipients were invited to subscribe on the contribution form: "Yes, I agree we must not sit back and let the 'Right-to-Life' forces punish Bob Packwood for his outstanding leadership on the abortion issue. I understand the 'Right-to-Lifers' have earmarked $200,000 to defeat him."

The storm warnings had been run up the staff early. Clearly a tidal wave of prolife money and choler was threatening the shores of Oregon. As it turned out, the only prolife challenge to Packwood came from a Brenda Jose, one of four unsuccessful contenders in the Republican primary election. At the end of her campaign Jose reported total contributions of $39,286. How much had come from the prolife warchests? She had received two loans from national and state prolife groups ($1,000 and $5,000 respectively), which she repaid, but not a dollar in straight contribution. No out-of-state commandos were recruited for doorbell punching. In short, there was no "sea of Right-to-Life money," hardly a puddle. And a group which, out of an entire state, could not produce one serious prolife contender at election time was not easily to be accused of being "well organized."

This began to be noticed around primary time. Packwood's press secretary, Mimi Weyforth, admitted that she had produced the $200,000 figure. What was her source of information? It was, she said, "based upon predictions being made in Washington, D.C. by veteran political observers."[247]

How successful was this prudent and timely advisory raised against prolife money? Bob Packwood's senatorial election campaign was one of the most abundantly financed in the nation. His campaign committee has reported total receipts of $1,566,175 to the Federal Election Commission. Reportedly, $750,000 came in response to the Steinem letter, $528,500 of it already in hand at primary time in April. Generous support had come from various commercial interests, since Packwood sat on the Senate Finance Committee and was ranking minority member (later chairman) of the Committee on Commerce, Science, and Transportation. Nevertheless, the appeal to the nationwide antiabortion lobby was to be his most lucrative strategy. Curiously, his support for abortion went unmentioned in the lengthy exposition of Packwood's credentials his staff put in the *1980 General Voters' Pamphlet*.[248]

There was another feature in Packwood's proabortion appeal which in retrospect raises a serious question. The letter explained how badly some start-up cash was needed. "Right now, Bob's biggest problem is money. He must raise funds to open a campaign office and pay for other campaign expenses. He must raise a minimum of $78,000 within the next 30 days to get his re-election campaign in full swing." That letter went out in August 1979. Packwood's campaign committee had taken in receipts of $314,613 during the first six months of that year alone, and had spent only $91,125. On August 3 his campaign, which had been gathering funds as far back as 1975, purchased $122,070 in treasury bills so that the excess money could earn interest until it could be spent. (His financial report shows a repeated series of investments in short-term paper, a luxury which is not the lot of candidates who are underfinanced.) Whatever Packwood's problem was, it was not money.[249] By the end of September 1979 he had taken in $494,512; by the end of the year, $824,408.

Here then was an electoral struggle where the well-organized and well-financed war chest of the prolife forces was to open wide. On inspection, one sees a proabortion candidate who, with an utterly bogus scare appeal, succeeds in drawing his largest funding, three-quarters of a million dollars, from abortion advocates across the country. One prolife leader told the press that spring, "Sen. Bob Packwood is an absolute liar—and you can quote me on that." Not only had $200,000 never been earmarked for his defeat; "There isn't $200,000 among all the prolife PAC's [political action committees] combined." The claim of abundant funding within the prolife movement, in this case, proved not only to be untrue, but to have been contrived as a gambit that was immensely successful, both as propaganda and as an entrée to affluence.[250]

A third way of assessing prolife financing is to inspect the size of the national prolife organizations' annual budgets. There could be little hope of calculating the total sum generated across the country, for prolife groups in cities and counties handle their own funds. But surely some dependable measure of the movement's resources could be ascertained by reviewing the cash flow of its flagship offices. In order to gain some perspective on these statistics I sought comparable figures for the leading advocacy organizations on either side of the issue. This is how they look.

ANNUAL BUDGET TOTALS (1980)

Leading Prolife Organizations

American Life Lobby	$ 980,000
National Right to Life Committee	$ 677,000
Life Amendment Political Action Committee	$ 380,000
Christian Action Council	unavailable[a]
Americans United for Life / AUL Legal Defense Fund	$ 325,000
National Committee for a Human Life Amendment	$ 300,000

Leading Proabortion Organizations

Planned Parenthood Federation of America	$24,200,000[b]
Population Council	$14,536,000
National Organization for Women	$ 3,200,000
Alan Guttmacher Institute	$ 2,700,000
National Abortion Rights Action League	$ 1,788,500

[a] *Several inquiries into the funding of prolife organizations were unsuccessful because officials were hesitant to have it known how modest their finances are.*

[b] *This figure represents the budget of the national office only; the total reported budget of this and the affiliates together is reported to be $146,200,000.*

These figures tell only part of the story. A fuller calculation might include the financial outlay during an election year by various Protestant activist groups that explicitly aligned themselves, for this time at least, with prolife interests. On the other side, one might try to calculate the cash value of the legal counsel provided to the abortion movement by the ACLU. Also, some organizations which have a wide assortment of programs must be considered differently from those organized about a single purpose. The Bishops Committee for Prolife Activities, for instance, had a 1980 budget of $285,203, of which $154,000 was supplied by its parent organization, the National Conference of Catholic Bishops, from its total budget (NCCB and U.S. Catholic Conference combined) of $14,550,481. But as a closecut, inner measure of the flow of money within these two contending movements, these budget figures tell an interesting tale. The picture is not, however, one of affluence on the prolife side. Quite the contrary. To view this in scale, one must note that Planned Parenthood has set aside for 1981 a budget item of $3,700,000 to promote legalized abortion; one series of ads cost the New York City affiliate alone $400,000.

There are other possible comparisons. Among the top one hundred political committees in the nation during the 1980 election campaign, three were abortion-related. On the prochoice side, the National Abortion Rights Action League PAC reported receipts of $407,918 and the Voters for Choice PAC gathered in $333,277. The two proabortion groups totalled $741,195. On the prolife side, the Life Amendment PAC reported receipts of $590,847.[251] Another possible comparison is provided by salary levels. The annual salary of the chief executives of the prolife organizations mentioned here is, on average, less than one-third the salary paid their counterpart at Planned Parenthood. Indeed, one of the largest of the prolife organizations had no paid chief executive until 1980. The smallest of the leading proabortion organizations here is financially nearly twice the size of the largest of the prolife groups.

Is the prolife movement awash with cash? On inquiry I found no way to sustain the accusation. Indeed, wherever I looked I found the very opposite of abundance: frugal budgets, numerous volunteers, modest annual increments. By the only reasonable measure available, a comparison with their opposite numbers across the great divide (who were telling the tales of opulence), the prolife organizations would consider themselves fortunate to sup from the leavings that fell from their adversaries' table. By comparison with its own steadily effective work in marshaling citizen sympathy against abortion, the prolife movement is one of the most scantily capitalized populist endeavors of our era.

Political Argument: The Prolife Constituency Is Indifferent to Other Human Needs

One consistent and forthright feature of the movement to legitimate abortion on demand under law has been the charge that abortion opponents, beyond being a sectarian, bullying minority, are not really motivated by humanitarian compassion. Their cause is an inconsistent one, for they turn a blind eye to other social needs which, were they sincere, they could not ignore.

Accusations of this sort are among the most common provender of the abortion cause:

> . . .it seems likely that this view of humanity, like so many others, has been adopted for limited purposes having to do with the prohibition of induced abortion, rather than from a real belief in the full human rights of the first few cells after conception. [Sissela Bok, Harvard ethicist][252]

> The tactics and literature of those who oppose legal abortion make it clear that most are concerned only with fetal life. They are openly callous about women, unwanted babies, and the quality of life. [National Abortion Rights Action League][253]

> We have never gotten any help from them in caring for children after they are born. They do not care about that. [Minnette Doderer, defeated candidate for Iowa lieutenant-governorship][254]

> The absolutist position does not concern itself about the quality of the entire life cycle, the health and well-being of the mother and family, the question of emotional and economic resources, the cases of extreme deformity. Its total preoccupation with the status of the unborn renders it blind to the well-being and freedom of choice of persons in community. ["A Call to Concern"][255]

> Just as important and fundamental as the right to choose who [sic] to marry, is the right to choose the number of children you want. When you want them. Or to have none at all. The "right to life" movement wants to deprive you of your freedom of choice by imposing its belief on everyone. Some of your most important rights are being challenged. The right to use contraceptives. [Planned Parenthood of New York City][256]

> Make no mistake about it, much of the controversy reflects not just religious scruple but a yearning for moral punishment. [Karen Mulhauser, executive director of National Abortion Rights Action League][257]

> If they really cared about equity and fairness in life they would

say that as long as abortion is legal in this country, poor people should have the same access as the rich. But instead they say: "Poor people are the most unorganized, they're the most vulnerable, that's where we can strike at the system first." [Faye Wattleton, president of Planned Parenthood Federation of America][258]

What about people starving in the South? What about all the deaths in Vietnam? Where were the right-to-lifers then? Don't tell me they've got reverence for life—they don't give a damn! [Dr. Howard I. Diamond, abortionist][259]

It is my impression that the "right to life" people were not generally so deeply concerned about the killing of thousands of "innocent inconvenient" human beings in Vietnam—including old men and women, young men and women, children, infants, lactating mothers and, no doubt, hundreds of fetuses. Ninety percent or more of those deaths were due to United States military action; the United States used 450 times the firepower of the enemy. But I heard no protest from the "right to life" groups. [Clifford M. Turner][260]

Supporters of the anti-women position include not only the traditional so-called "right to life" groups but an unlikely axis of other groups including The Christian Crusade, The John Birch Society, The Ku Klux Klan, and the National States Rights Party. [Eleanor Smeal, president of the National Organization for Women][261]

They come in with such self-righteous arrogance. These people who are putting out the right-to-life issue; they act like God has revealed himself to them and to them alone. . . . The right wing is at war with the whole Judeo-Christian ethic in the sense that they're against feeding the hungry, against health care for the afflicted, against housing for the needy. [Senator George McGovern, during unsuccessful campaign for reelection][262]

These accusations are about prolife people. These people lack political and moral credibility, the charge maintains, because they lack consistency and principle. They are not visibly devoted to the needs and feelings of women unhappy with pregnancy; they have not validated their advocacy of the threatened unborn by service to the disadvantaged newborn; they are not notable in vindicating other rights that our society brushes aside; they have found themselves allies among the most antisocial reactionaries of our time.

In one sense these accusations are earned. There is an urgency about life-or-death situations that suspends other cares. During civil war in Nigeria, outside agencies rushed food and medical care to starving Biafran Ibos—without concern for whatever might be the mutual political grievances between the tribes. Freighter captains who encountered boat people foundering in the South China Sea rescued them—without concern for how many other refugees might be encouraged to follow. Military medics with a conscience push themselves to the utmost to save all the wounded they can—without concern for the fact that some are their foes, for in these tents there should be no enemies. When we are roused to rescue people from imminent death, there comes an overriding concentration on that duty which suppresses other concerns, no matter how reasonable. When some shipowners instructed masters of their vessels to ignore the boat people, they were howled down in an international furor. Lifesaving may suspend other life-serving. Some prolife people, whose overriding concern is that the unborn young in their thousands and their millions are awash on a sanguinary tide, are distracted from other cares. As advocates some do indeed seem to have little word for the many motives of misery that bring women to forfeit their unborn. But that is to be understood in context. If a man's health is broken, his children taken from him; if he is evicted from his home and fired from his job and hounded by all the powers of the land, he will understandably be desperate. But if, in his desperation, he seizes hostages and begins to slay them, people's thoughts will not be turned to his miseries and the outrages he has suffered. They will rise in alarm and rescue the captives whatever the cost. They will not be moved by his crazed outburst to make his life more bearable. When he is no longer a threat (if he has survived), then they may turn their minds and hearts to him. But while he kills, they will have care only to prevent him. And from his point of view they will seem to be more heartless than ever, with never a care for his sorrows. So must the prolife people seem to those from whose hands they are bent on rescuing the unborn. It is so sad that men and women who might otherwise be the most compassionate towards women with unwanted pregnancies are driven to become their adversaries . . . because death's hand is raised.

One of the most interesting things about the discrediting remarks about the prolife constituency is that they have their echo among prolife activists themselves. Immediately after *Wade* and *Bolton*, the liberal magazine *Commonweal* had this to say editorially:

> If the abortion debate continues on the present—women's exclusive right-to-decide vs. "It's murder"—level, and if the public continues to view abortion in isolation from other social and moral problems, the anti-abortion cause will become the political tool of the right wing, . . . of those who have consistently backed a murderous war, opposed gun control, and fought labor, health and welfare legislation designed to enhance the dignity of society's weakest members . . .
>
> What should the church do now? Radically re-educate itself on both the value of *every* human life and its own need to take a less compliant and more prophetic stance against the trend toward egoism and selfishness in our government, culture and church. Support responsible birth control so people will learn to decide about a child before it is conceived. Take women seriously and give them real status in the community of the church so that childbearing is not seen just as a woman's joy-burden but as a community responsibility. Make it socially acceptable and finan-

cially possible to have a child outside of marriage. Really be
pro-life: champion all those whose lives are still in progress, whose
future is still precarious, whose true potentials are still struggling
to be born.[263]

The *National Catholic Reporter*, which calls itself a radical Christian newspaper, has called for a similarly broad alliance of prolife interests. "Having a
preferred activity or a favorite cause should not preclude moral, political and
financial support for the rest of the pro-life spectrum. On the contrary. To
work for the fetus without supporting the child, sadly unwanted, carried to full
term, is to make mockery of celebrating life. To work for the fetus without
supporting the adolescent, the unemployed woman and man, is to subdivide
Christ's message."[264]

Most critics would accept these as credibly consistent, humanitarian con-
texts for a prolife position. The question is, however, whether those who serve
as typical activists in the movement live up to such a call or whether they are,
in fact, social reactionaries? Members of the Indiana Right to Life organization
asked themselves that question recently. Do Right-to-Lifers care only about
the unborn? They canvassed their most active members, those who came to
the regional convention (229 persons). They found that:

> 81 distributed food and clothing
> nearly one-fourth donated blood regularly
> 37 worked in support groups (drugs, alcohol, suicide)
> 17 worked in programs for abused women
> 28 worked in hospitals, clinics and hospices
> 38 worked in volunteer fire and police departments and neighbor-
> hood associations
> 116 worked in scouting, youth work and meals on wheels
> 176 worked in schools: tutoring, aiding teachers, etc.
> 67 worked in voter registration
> 52 worked in political campaigns
> 100 worked in Sunday schools
> 45 worked in a crisis pregnancy phone line
> 75 worked distributing maternity and infant clothing
> 47 have shared their homes with pregnant strangers, elderly,
> refugees, sick, or foster children.[265]

It is not the actual survey which tells most; it is the concern of the organization
to draw the kind of people who spend themselves on those in need. Similarly,
when the *National Right to Life News* picked up a story about a research
project in California that claimed female abortors favored the death penalty
more than females in general, it was obviously reported in order to discredit
abortors as having less regard for life, but at the same time it dissociated the
publication from a favorite rightist cause: capital punishment.[266]

Observers of the prolife movement claim to see among its ranks a variety of
zealots who have won their spurs in liberal causes. Feminist political scientist
Mary Segers says: "In actual fact, there are a considerable number of abortion

opponents on the left who have a broad respect-for-life ideology extending to such issues as disarmament, nuclear energy, gun control, capital punishment and food for peace."[267]

There seems to be a new literary genre emerging: the liberal who is against abortion, interviewed. Bill Raspberry describes a thirty-year-old who had trekked from San Diego to Washington, D.C., to march and rally. His credentials: "deeply moved by the plight of the Cambodian children," pro–civil rights, pro-ERA, cohabiting for two years with a woman (one looks for the glint of a golden earring). "A lot of my liberal friends who are in the anti-nuclear movement will acknowledge that there are a lot of uncertainties about nuclear energy, but they still insist that we ought to be on the side of safety and shut 'em (nuclear plants) down. Why can't they reach the same conclusion with regard to abortion clinics? I remember what one of the Save-the-Whale people said when they cut open a dead whale and find [sic] a rather large baby whale inside; 'Those SOBs killed two whales, not one.' Why can't they look at human beings the same way?"[268] Another journalist interviews a number of young abortion protesters: "Some are anti-nuclear activists whose concern for the next generation grew from studying the effects of radiation on the unborn. Some work for the rights of the disabled or retarded, and fear that infanticide will be practiced on those born with mental or physical handicaps. Others are pacifists who find that they can no longer support abortion while opposing war and capital punishment."[269] Barbara Grizzuti Harrison tells of her conversations with leaders of Feminists for Life, who support both the Equal Rights Amendment and a Human Life Amendment. The head of the D.C. chapter is a black, working, welfare mother of six, supportive of ERA, daycare centers, shelters for battered wives, and sex education in the public schools. "Abortion," she says, "is not an alternative to sharing jobs and wealth. Abortion does not cure poverty." The president of FFL says, "Feminism grew out of the anger of women who did not want their value to be determined by men. How can we turn around and arbitrarily devalue the fetus? How can I support a Nestlé boycott and turn around and support the destruction of life *in utero*?"[270]

The twenty-three-year-old president of American Pro-Life University Students, it turns out, came to the movement after being involved in environmental advocacy. The twenty-six-year-old president of the National Youth Pro-Life Coalition was broken in through work for the United Farm Workers, women's liberation, the environmental movement, and world hunger projects. The twenty-nine-year-old leader of Pro-Lifers for Survival founded it in order to bring peace activists to see that the prolife movement was not right-wing.[271]

Mary Meehan has observed that the prolife leaders are concentrating on the wider social theme of corporate responsibility:

> Senator Hatfield says that "belief in life's fundamental right to be has inevitable corporate consequences." He notes that, in opposing American intervention in Vietnam, "I did not merely believe it would be wrong for me, as an individual, to fight there. I

believed that no American should fight there, which compelled me to propose legislation expressing the conviction." Juli Loesch, a pacifist and pro-life feminist, speaks of women in the peace movement: "It would never occur to us to say, 'For private moral reasons I don't personally condone *nuclear arms*, but I really can't impose my feelings on my fellow citizens who don't hold the same religious beliefs—and certainly each nation has the right to choose to incinerate its enemies if it wishes.' " And Jesse Jackson says that the idea that life is private and that one may do with it as one wishes "was the premise of slavery. You could not protest the existence or treatment of slaves on the plantation because that was private and therefore outside of your right to be concerned."

The other growing conviction that liberals have brought to the prolife movement is feminism:

> Daphne de Jong, a pro-life feminist of New Zealand, writes: "Of all the things which are done to women to fit them into a society dominated by men, abortion is the most violent invasion of their physical and psychic integrity. It is a deeper and more destructive assault than rape." . . . She views abortion as "merely another way in which women are manipulated and degraded for male convenience and male profit. This becomes blatantly obvious in the private abortion industries of both Britain and America, and the support given to the pro-abortion lobby by such exploitative corporations as the *Playboy* empire." She refers to the women's movement as "processing women through abortion mills to manufacture instant imitation-men who will fit into society made by and for wombless people. Accepting the 'necessity' of abortion is accepting that pregnant women and mothers are unable to function as persons in this society."
>
> Juli Loesch, like de Jong, sees abortion as a great convenience for men. She notes that, before abortion-on-demand, the father of a child born out of wedlock was expected to be accountable and to provide support. But now, she says: "the responsible thing is to put up the cash for an abortion ('No hard feelings, OK?'); and if the man actually goes to the clinic with the woman—if he holds her hand—why, he's a prince. . . . And if the woman, for some reason, ends up having the baby after all, the man may feel perfectly justified in saying, 'Hell, I did my duty. I offered to abort it. Don't expect me to help support it.' "[272]

Aligned with the unborn are many who need not apologize for their social service record. One thinks of Cesar Chavez, Graciela Olivarez, Dolores Huerta, Dick Gregory, Richard Neuhaus, Daniel Berrigan, John Noonan, Theodore Hesburgh, Gordon Zahn. Chicago's black newspaper, the *Chicago Defender*, is on record: "Many young blacks have adopted the popular theory that the unborn are a burden and they may be killed easily in hygienic

conditions without any sense of guilt or responsibility. That is an evil, inhumane, devastating view. Blacks ought to know more about that subject than
any other racial group in America."[273] One supposes that Mother Teresa's
humane credentials need no review. John Paul II has stood his ground as
resolutely on abortion as on civic freedom and human rights. In his homily on
human life in Washington, he said:

> When freedom is used to dominate the weak, to squander
> natural resources and energy, and to deny basic necessities to
> people, we will stand up and reaffirm the demands of justice and
> social love. When the sick, the aged, or the dying are abandoned in
> loneliness, we will stand up and proclaim that they are worthy of
> love, care and respect.
>
> I make my own the words which Paul VI spoke last year to the
> American Bishops: "We are convinced, moreover, that all efforts
> made to safeguard human rights actually benefit life itself. Every-
> thing aimed at banishing discrimination—in law or in fact—which
> is based on race, origin, color, culture, sex, or religion is a service
> to life. When the rights of minorities are fostered, when the
> mentally or physically handicapped are assisted, when those on
> the margin of society are given a voice—in all those instances the
> dignity of life, and the sacredness of human life are furthered."

This seemed no narrow program.

Respect Life, the large booklet issued annually by the Catholic Bishops
Committee for Pro-Life Activities, alongside its content on behalf of the
unborn, presents strong advocacy for help for the handicapped, support for
pregnant teenagers, racial justice, care for the dying, provision for the elderly,
and against capital punishment. This seems no narrow agenda.[274]

The ecumenical Christian journal *Sojourners,* which gained high respect
among Christian social activists in the 1970s, has devoted an entire issue to the
subject of abortion. Editor Jim Wallis explained:

> In the process of our reflection and reevaluation, we have noted
> two significant occurrences. First, some radical voices in the peace
> and justice movements are reaching the same pro-life conclusions
> about abortion. Second, we have met and had very encouraging
> dialogue with people who represent a whole new generation of
> leadership in the pro-life movement. They are mostly young men
> and women whose opposition to abortion is leading them also to
> oppose nuclear weapons and power, genetic engineering, and
> capital punishment. Some are now questioning the kind of global
> economic system that starves children after they are born and
> makes expendable whole classes of human beings.
>
> There is clearly an opportunity here for a convergence of con-
> cern. . . . For some conservative Christians, abortion has become
> a "threshold issue" opening the door to wider concerns. For some
> radical Christians, abortion is emerging as a "consistency issue"
> which reveals basic differences with the cultural and sexual values

of the Left. There is the real possibility of some highly creative and unexpected new alignments.[275]

Some who oppose the prolife movement are giving it some credit. The *New Republic* calls it "inspiring, in a way. Since the end of the antiwar movement, these misguided people represent the only major pressure group on the political scene whose cause is not essentially self-interest."[276] Michael Harrington, veteran socialist leader, dampened a celebratory fete sponsored by Planned Parenthood to honor founder Margaret Sanger when he spoke complimentarily of the organization's opponents. "The long-time socialist drew a gasp from the largely female crowd when he commented that his travels had convinced him that the anti-abortionists' 'right-to-life' movement is 'one of the few genuine social movements of the 1970's.' "[277]

Those who hold the prolife movement as suspect see very few committed social activists in its ranks. Those who sympathize see them there in plenty. What is one to think in so unmeasurable a matter?

Clearly the movement was roused and brought along, in the wake of *Wade*, by a membership and a leadership that were conservative: socially, morally, politically. This need cause no surprise. There is hardly a controversy involving family and childbearing which does not attract partisans instinctively into two camps: on the one side, those who hold for personal freedom and individual self-realization; on the other side, those who argue for fidelity to duty and mutual accommodation. It was natural that the abortion issue would segregate partisans by instinct into the camps of advocates and adversaries. But there is reason to expect that this rallying of first instinct will not much longer hold. For this is no ordinary tussle over emphasis and right balance. Death is here. And when a struggle leads to death, parties to that struggle often feel their instinctive loyalties subordinated to a dread but more thoughtful choosing.

Many citizens of tried and proven compassion are enlisting in the prolife effort. They will be the movement's next leaders. They have come *because* of other commitments, as did a former student of mine. At Notre Dame he had puzzled over the war and finally signed and served as a conscientious objector. During the Michigan referendum on abortion law he felt compelled, out of consistency with his earlier stand, to canvass on behalf of the unborn. It was a painful and awkward initiation into sitting at booths and handing out leaflets. One woman glanced at a broadsheet he handed her, crumpled it up and threw it at him, saying, "Why don't you just go and adopt some of those black kids?" (He is black.) "I will," he said. And he did. People like him come to this issue as to a heartfelt one. Yet it is not for them one issue which puts all others into eclipse, as population growth or nuclear hazard are for some knell-sounders.

In general, the prolife movement has been amateur and blundering. It has mobilized people who had no previous experience in citizen activism. They tend to be short-tempered, they lack the sense for public appearances which older campaigners learn, and they lose patience easily because of what called them out of their houses: a deep dismay that their neighbors are killing children. It takes years of experience to address that concern calmly. Prolifers are often short of breath, and not good at hearing people out to the end of their paragraphs . . . or sentences.

The liberals are coming. But they have been sorely missed and long in coming. Why? Movements that rock us usually start with mavericks, or monomaniacs. They rarely state their case fully enough to do justice to all the human needs that their project is going to send sprawling. And their first followers are often a scruffy lot: strident, narrow, not self-possessed. The movement for contraception, for instance, would surely have found easier acceptance had it been joined to any decent vision of marriage. And it might have had that if its founder, Margaret Sanger, had not originally enthused over birth control and sterilization as ways of weeding out racially inferior, poverty-blighted strains in the population (an idea she had to mute when the Nazis later made much of it), and had her own sexual life been less of a public debauch.[278] But without Margaret Sanger there might have been no movement. The resistance to the war in Vietnam lost credibility in the hands of shrill, hedonistic youngsters of intemperate speech and greasy hair. But without them the war might be spilling blood still.

Liberals are as fashion-conscious as any, and they have not hastened to ally themselves with a movement which, however strongly they might have warmed to its defense of the undefended, had such bad manners and humorless personnel.

At the close of this inquiry I have come to wonder how much difference it ought to make whether a cause is served by credible and consistent folk. Rosa Parks's act of fatigued courage was right, when she refused to move to the back of the bus in Montgomery. It mattered not a bit that she did not also solicit funds for cancer research. Martin Luther King, Jr.,'s act of courage in her defense was also right. His cause was made no more just when he joined his civil rights struggle to the antiwar movement, for it had already been just. Nor would it have been any less just if J. Edgar Hoover's allegations about his private life were true. His cause was just. It is the cause and its justice, not the orientation or the manners of its adherents, which most matter. The gaucheries of the prolife leaders have, one would think, served overlong to deflect the consciences of the fastidious.

Misjoinders along the Way

There is little wit and no humor in the abortion debate. It is deadly earnest. Even professional cartoonists and comedians, whose jesting can jar our vision of the most vital concerns back into true focus with comic glimpses of incongruity, have left this subject largely untouched. It is no laughing matter.

Yet, as months and years of attentiveness to the proabortion argument drew me to this point of comment, I could recollect that strewn throughout that argument there was much matter for musing, even occasional humor. Not the guffaws or hilarity of comedy, but the sadder softness of tragedy and farce. There is, I came to notice, a measure of incongruity there too absurd for serious rejoinder and yet too telling to be ignored. I found myself often provoked to a sort of mirth *de profundis*.

I remember no occasion more absurd than when I sat one day listening to a private interview recorded by one of my research students with an abortion counselor. Shortly before, I had witnessed a broadcast interview with her mentor, the executive director of Planned Parenthood in South Bend, Indiana. According to the director, the cadre of volunteer counselors who helped women with unwanted pregnancies was composed of ministers, teachers, social workers, and professionally trained counselors. They were readied for this work by a series of workshops and training sessions. Their main purpose was "to help a woman recognize that she has some options, that there isn't only one way, and to get her to really consider what are these options. . . . The only real position for a valid counselor is objectivity, and taking no stand on any of these options." For those whose abortion proves to be upsetting, good counseling could help to make it "a very rich experience. That is, a problem pregnancy handled well and a woman getting the full, better understanding of herself and how she reacts, and working this out on her own, can be an extremely helpful period of her life. . . . In seven years I cannot really say that I have seen a remorseful woman. Never."

From this description by the director of competent, sensitive, and dispassionate counsel, I turned to listen to one of those who provided it. She was a college student (and had been an abortor herself). Her training for abortion counseling had been acquired back home. During summer vacations she worked in an abortion clinic:

> After the mother had aborted my job was to take the fetus and weigh [it], put it in a bag, like a lunch bag . . . after I made sure the placenta was intact I weighed the placenta . . . we did like 16 a day, you know, it was just like one after the other . . . after everything was weighed and bagged and a disposal card was signed for the fetus I took everything downstairs to the morgue. I took it down in a grocery cart, which was pretty gory, and just put it in another laundry bag and from there it was thrown in the incinerator. That job was a little hard to handle but from that I got experience on how to handle the girls, how to read into their emotions and their feelings . . . yet maintaining a professional distance from them.

She dwelt at length on her own views:

> I see more of murder the further along they get. Although inside me I know it's murder from the beginning, because there is the fact that when it is conceived it is a potential human being, potential person, potential life, potential organism or whatever you want to call it. There's just so much terminology: is it a human, is it a person, is it a being, is it a life or organism or whatever? I believe that, yes, it is a potential life or being, person, but at the same time it is not independent of the mother and it's not able to live by itself. Until we can reach that point where we can really say that, yes, there is a unit out there that will maintain its life, it's really the mother that has the decision over the life, and when technology reaches the point that I think that it can handle preg-

135

nancy outside the uterus at an early stage, then there won't be a solution to the abortion issue. Does that make sense?

These views, however, were to be withheld behind the veil of counseling objectivity:

> We have personal biases about a lot of things in our life and these are just things you don't let conflict with another person's interest. . . . I'm not there to change her mind. [Question: Does one ever suggest that a child is killed by abortion?] I've never asked them that question, but from my standpoint from just talking to the girls it's just something that's there that's got to be gotten rid of because it's in the way, and it is an "it." It's not a human being. . . . No, you never throw that out to them. You use just "abortion" and lots of times I don't even use the word "abortion." I use the word "terminate." When I tell people I do counseling I don't say, "I do abortion counseling or problem pregnancy counseling." No, it's just "counseling," just to lessen the impact of "abortion." . . . You don't say to a girl who's going through an abortion that it's a murder. Just like delivering the fetuses in the hospital back at ———, I used to get a mother who would say, "What sex is it?" . . . But I say, "Lay back, you really can't tell." These are things you do to relieve the anxiety within the mother.

The counselor was less ready than her director to reckon abortion to be "a very rich experience." Was there guilt in a lot of cases? "A lot of guilt." Why, then, was she involved? "It was an easy job. It didn't take a person with education to do what I did. I could handle it emotionally and stably and, to tell the truth, it doesn't bother me. You know, I mean it's gory, and it's a really sad situation to see the abortions and I have my own opinion about how I feel about abortion. . . . To me it's a job and it's the closest I could get to what I wanted to do . . . I want to be a nurse-midwife."

I encountered some of the same dark and dreadfully humorous incoherence in some of the sleeker language of the argument. Abortion is described as "cessation of life support."[279] Some young unborn are described as "nonviable," meaning that if extirpated from the womb they would die; this, it is said, makes it legitimate to extirpate them. Other unborn, mature enough to be "viable," cannot morally be extirpated, for they are old enough to survive.[280] Former Senator Gruening testifies: "I realize and fully appreciate that there is something distasteful about abortion—the killing of nascent human life." He then subdues his sense of taste and urges that the law allow abortion.[281] When an Arizona abortionist failed to estimate correctly the age of the unborn and, instead of destroying her, delivered an eight-month live child, his partner apologized: "We can't always be perfect."[282] A pediatrician explains the benefits of prenatal diagnosis that allows parents to eliminate their handicapped offspring: "The potential for service to very many families who care deeply about the children that they bring into the world is enormous."[283] Another pediatrician, who also recommends aborting the handicapped (doing "nothing more than correct an oversight of nature"), feels called upon to explain how this could possibly square with the "reverence for life" associated with his former mentor, Dr. Albert Schweitzer, with whom he had spent time as an African medical missionary. "Who," he replied, "is allowed to impose such prospective suffering on another individual? Is it not more humane, and more ethical, to prevent such tragedy? Similar thoughts also apply to the unwanted."[284] A geneticist, also in favor of aborting the handicapped, testifies: "I emphasize the right of a child to be born free of any serious disease or deformity that could be prevented by an abortion, and to be born into a home where it is wanted, loved and well cared for."[285]

One cannot help but be startled by this play of thought and language. One marvels at parents who *care deeply* enough, and doctors who are *reverent* and *humane* enough about blighted children to eliminate them. One staggers at the thought of how, if the *right to be born disease-free and wanted* could be assured to the unborn by eliminating those who lacked these benefits, we might by the same strategy guarantee other rights: the right to medical care, the right to old-age support, and the right to humane circumstances for the imprisoned. An entirely new approach to human and civil rights—less expensive and less fumbling than our present attempts—offers itself to one's imagination . . .

One is then reminded of another turn of phrase much relied upon to resolve the unanswered moral indictments directed at abortion: it is said to be a "tragedy." Granted, it may annihilate the young; granted, they are innocent and lie within our protection; granted, they are often sacrificed to convenience. Still, we must accept this sadness and live with it as tragedy.

Hitherto, one had always thought that only victims or their sympathizers could call their sufferings tragic. If I go on a drunken joy ride and kill your four-year-old daughter on the sidewalk, you could speak of it as a tragedy, and so could any friend, but I could not. For me it must be a crime. No one would allow me the use of "tragedy" as a sort of moral cop-out. But now, on this new and clever use of the word and its power, the rightist assassins of San Salvador's Archbishop Romero might speak of his death as a tragedy. Hiroshima as tragedy could put America's guilt to rest. The Gulag, the scattered toxic chemical wastes, the atomic inferno we daily risk—all, if designated as official tragedies, can then be lived with by their makers. It offers an unrepentant and costless sort of peace.

There is another contrivance of words which catches one's sense of incongruity. The welfare of mother and child are, by those advocating abortion, thrown upon the pans of a balancing scale. "The physician . . . has to decide which life to sacrifice—that of the mother who is needed by her children, her husband, and society around her, or that of the severely abnormal fetus."[286] Similarly, the *New York Times* admires abortion freedom because "the health of mothers" and "the health of fetuses" can both be balanced on the scales.[287] Protection of the unborn, on the contrary, would be barbarous and repugnant, for it would give the rights of the fetus an advantage over the rights of the mother. Here, one must admit, is a fresh and bracing use of language. The life and health and rights of mother and of offspring are fairly and democratically balanced. One could almost ignore the fact that, applied to an unwanted pregnancy, this meant that what the mother stood to lose was, at the most, incomparable with her offspring's loss: the child stood to lose his or her life.

As one makes one's way through the abortion literature, at every turn there are things to ponder. One finds that the Association for Retarded Citizens has recently roused itself to address the abortion issue. An Ad Hoc Task Force on Abortion reported its majority view that the abortion of a damaged fetus should be both legal and appropriately funded. Lest anyone be startled at this as a policy of the unfortunate against their own kind, "the Task Force *agrees* that a policy which permits parents to select abortion as a method of preventing the birth of a baby who will be handicapped from birth need not, and certainly is not intended, to imply any derogation of any person presently living or to be born in the future with any type of handicap, including one which might have been detected prenatally."[288] How right that is, one reflects. In much the same way, a total withdrawal of military aid to Israel need not, and certainly would not be intended to, imply any derogation of any Jews presently living with that handicap. . . . My puzzlement at this attitude towards the handicapped eventually resolved into good-hearted appreciation when I finally realized that this was the Association *for* Retarded Citizens, not *of* them. The retarded themselves would have lacked the mental capacity and the detachment needed to draw up such a policy.

This is not the only instance where one learns, with bleak humor, that the reading of public statements requires some finesse. One day I was confronted by a dramatic, full-page advertisement by Planned Parenthood of New York City in the *New York Times*. There was a poignant photograph of a girl, with a powerful text in large print:

> WHAT IF YOUR BABY IS GOING TO HAVE A BABY?
>
> In 1978, over 63,000 teenagers became pregnant. In New York State alone.
>
> Each is somebody's daughter. With her entire life in front of her.
>
> Yet the "Right-to-Life" movement wants to force her to have a baby. No matter how young she is. No matter how she, her doctor or her parents feel. . . .[289]

I could not suppress a sense of incongruity. Here was Planned Parenthood, taking out space for a series of advertisements costing nearly a quarter of a million dollars, to issue an exhortation on behalf of family solidarity. How many readers of the *Times*, I mused, could enjoy the boldness and derring-do of Planned Parenthood, or relish their splendid sense of humor in representing themselves as solicitous for the parents of pregnant minors? It has long been the policy of Planned Parenthood to provide contraception and abortion to minors without the consent or knowledge of their parents. As plaintiff, Planned Parenthood secured from the Supreme Court the ruling which struck down parental consent required by state laws for abortions on minors, *Planned Parenthood* v. *Danforth*. They had filed *amicus* briefs in *H.L.* v. *Matheson*, asking the Court to strike down laws that required even notification of parents. And the roster of suits brought to diminish parental involvement in minor children's abortion decisions sounds like a chorus in their honor: *Planned Parenthood League of Massachusetts* v. *Bellotti, Planned Parenthood Association of Kansas City, Mo.* v. *Ashcroft, Planned Parenthood Association* v. *Fitzpatrick*, and so on. No institution in the United States has worked more indefatigably or consistently to market abortion to the immature woman, "no matter how her parents feel." The dark humor in it is that Planned Parenthood would have her parents (and her family doctor) feel nothing about it at all, because they would never learn about it.[290]

The abortion literature abounds in incongruities. The Department of Labor considers guidelines to protect women workers from exposure to substances hazardous to their "unborn babies," while across the mall the Department of Health, Education and Welfare is considering guidelines that would give aborted "nonviable fetuses ex utero" the status of laboratory animals. On the Hill, meantime, the House Agriculture Committee approves a bill that would extend early meat-packing rules on "humane" slaughter by requiring animals to be knocked unconscious before being killed.[291]

Feminist NARAL abortion advocates have denounced local "informed consent" ordinances that require a one- or two-day waiting period before abortion, because they are "designed solely to frighten patients out of having an abortion." They have angrily demanded, at the same time, a federally imposed thirty-day waiting period before sterilization, "so women would not be coerced."[292]

The research work of Dr. Patrick Steptoe, the English doctor who devised *in vitro* fertilization as a remedy for sterility due to blocked Fallopian tubes, was subsidized by his earnings as an abortionist.[293]

Harvard-Radcliffe ethicist Sissela Bok has called for elective abortion to eliminate damaged offspring, and has also called on the government to ban drug use (nicotine, alcohol, sprays, creams, etc.) involving pregnant women, to protect fetal development.[294]

When one follows the work of Amnesty International to dampen the violence in our society, and reads of their recent struggle to eliminate capital punishment, one cannot help reflecting that in one hour and a half the same number of unborn are aborted throughout the world (5,000) as convicted criminals were executed in the past ten years.

As never before, we are put on the alert about inhumane suffering that we could help to relieve. Greenpeace calls on us "to personally bear witness to atrocities against life," to fight "injustice" against the whales, seals, the forests, the seas, insisting that "the whole earth is part of our 'body' and that we must learn to respect it as we respect ourselves." Outraged at the "tragedy of slaughter"—"every 26 minutes a great whale dies in agony at the hands of men"—Greenpeace activists go out "to place ourselves between the hunters and the hunted, between the harpoons and the largest relative of mankind." One is reminded of mankind's smallest relative, 1,500 of whom die every 26 minutes at the hands of men. Whales are highly intelligent: "their kinship with man at the level of neurological development holds us in awe and fascination." One thinks of other creatures with a pretty nifty neurological development and kinship. We read of different killing methods: the explosive harpoon ("deep within the whale's spine the shock of the explosion does its work quickly, tearing through the inside of the creature") and the cold harpoon ("more inhumane . . . because it causes agonizing death lasting sometimes more than an hour"). This too is not without its comparisons, curettage and saline poisoning.[295]

Then we read of another instance of "animal rights, [which] just may become one of the most important moral issues of our time." A major cosmetics firm tests the potential harmfulness of chemicals on rabbits' eyes, "blinding and poisoning innocent animals for the sake of greater profits." The tormented rabbits (2,200 in 1979) "suffer hell."[296] Our humane instincts are mobilized by the Humane Society itself, on behalf of dogs and cats. "They can't ask for help. So we must do it for them." With our help they have "a chance for a good home. . . . Without us, their fate would be heartbreaking—abandonment, starvation, abuse . . . and worse."[297] One knows what is worse, and remembers that it is the destiny of more unborn children in this country than of its cats and dogs. Mostly, one meditates on this need to be "humane," and wonders whether that word ought to be loaned out to defenders of the whales, rabbits, and cats before it has worked its proper power upon us and drawn out compassion for its first, endangered referent, the humans.

A final incongruity to catch our eye and heart was the most piquant of all. Here was no animal story suggesting oblique and darkly ironic comparisons with human wastage. Here, in one brief and miserable story, was the perfect and diametrical match for abortion, a crime which had its clone at last. A woman, sixty five, and her son, thirty-four, were found guilty of murdering the man's twenty-six-year-old wife: he as killer, she as accomplice. The man admitted strangling his wife, dismembering her body, bagging the remains, and disposing of them in a lake. "He said he had been planning the killing for up to a year because of marital problems. A divorce, he said, might have meant the loss of custody of his two children. . . ." When he informed his mother of his plans, she replied, "It will be for the best." Later she observed, "You had to do it for the sake of the kids."[298]

At the conclusion of this inquiry into the case usually put forward on behalf of abortion in our country, one finds, not only that its individual arguments will not sustain serious inspection, but that this inspection leads one to the opposite conclusion. Rarely has an argument for a major social policy led the inquisitive so uncannily to its own disproof.

Die Buben sind unser Unglück!
The Holocaust and Abortion

THE WORD "HOLOCAUST," given to us from the biblical Hebrew through Greek and Latin, designates a specific kind of sacrifice wherein the offering is wholly consumed by fire. In our time it has clothed itself in a second sense: the destruction by Nazi Germany of large groups of people, especially of Jews, who were by a dread sort of irony commonly consumed by fire. Most recently, this unspeakable memory has been summoned up as a term of execration in the abortion controversy. It is a word of sad rage. The question I wish to explore here is whether that rage, that usage, is legitimate in the present dispute over abortion.

A retired woman who has coped successfully throughout her lifetime with spina bifida has deplored the fact that according to a survey most parents whose unborn children had this handicap, and most doctors attending them, would abort the offspring. "Presumably aborting of a spina-bifida fetus is done because no one can either prevent or correct the defect, and letting a spina-bifida child live is a particularly expensive nuisance. Aborting of such fetuses, however, takes us a long way down the road called genocide. Who can forget Nazi Germany's attempts to insure that the country be inhabited by a master race of individuals with perfect health in perfect bodies?"[1]

A professor of law has construed the abortion decisions of the Supreme Court as a threat to free government, where the laws should be used to protect the weak from the predatory powerful. "As the corrosive jurisprudence of raw utilitarianism gains ascendancy, as we continue, with the law's blessing, to kill upwards of a million children a year, can we say with confidence that we shall not reach the point where the shared values of the American commitment 'are no longer vigorous enough to restrain the passions and shatter the selfish inertia of men'? . . . To say it cannot happen here is to ignore the lessons of Nuremberg."[2]

In these and many other ways, those who reject abortion have compared it to the Holocaust. Those who advocate abortion as a free choice, however, resent the comparison. Roger M. Williams, senior editor of *Saturday Review*, in an article entitled "The Power of Fetal Politics," observes: "Some of the [antiabortion] rhetoric is positively venal, and there are instances of its apparently leading to violence. Two years ago, the St. Paul, Minnesota, diocesan newspaper conducted an editorial campaign against a local planned parenthood / abortion clinic, labeling it 'little Dachau.' Not long afterward, the clinic was fired upon and burned."[3]

Mary Peek, defeated candidate for the Minnesota legislature in 1972, appeared in *McRae* v. *Califano* to testify that Catholic opposition to her stand on behalf of abortion had been an intrusive denominational involvement in politics. When asked on the stand whether she would likewise have found a Catholic bishop's opposition to murders in Auschwitz intrusive, she retorted: "The kind of questions you have been directing to me in this courtroom are exactly the kind of badgering questions that are leveled against everyone who advocates freedom of choice and they are made to seem to condone murders in Auschwitz, the death penalty, euthanasia and all those kinds of things when we are not talking about that at all."[4]

In a précis of arguments on legal abortion, the National Abortion Rights Action League fends off the antichoice argument that "pro-abortionists are mass murderers, just like Hitler": "Hitler tried to eliminate certain groups of people. There is absolutely no similarity between genocide and the worldwide movement toward assuring an individual's reproductive freedom." To the assertion that the Nazis started with abortion, there is the response: "Quote from Hitler: 'The use of contraceptives means a violation of nature and a degradation of womanhood, motherhood and love. . . . Nazi ideals demand that the practice of abortion shall be exterminated with a strong hand.' " Gloria Steinem has argued that it is the prolife movement, authoritarian and antifeminist, which is reminiscent of Nazism.[5] Eugene Fisher, in charge of Jewish relations on behalf of the American Catholic bishops, deplores comparisons between abortion and the Holocaust, because the latter was "the practice of conscious, societally-planned genocide on racial grounds alone."[6]

Dr. Bernard Nathanson, a founder of NARAL who later apparently reversed his attitude on abortion, nevertheless dislikes the Holocaust comparison. "I must protest that the waving of the Nazi flag . . . is inexpressibly unfair to pro-abortion citizens and to my former colleagues. They are not Nazis. And as a Jew, I cannot remain silent at this facile use of the Nazi analogy, though I realize that some anti-abortion Jews use it. If this argument is so compelling, why do Jews remain generally favorable toward abortion?"[7] In fact, the epithet is cast back by some abortion advocates. In an essay entitled "Know Your Enemy," the *Reproductive Rights Newsletter* reports that a conference studying "the rightwing onslaught against abortion rights, the right to organize, the ERA, affirmative action, and the Panama Canal Treaties (to name but a few battles)," explored the work of "Young Americans for Freedom, the John Birch Society, the National Right-to-Work Committee, the so-called Right to Life groups and the neo-NAZI organizations."[8]

There is a particular satisfaction in identifying one's adversary as a Nazi. The Third Reich has served these decades past as practically the only historical moral absolute within reach. There is none of the ethical give-and-take about Hitler's doings that one hears, say, in discussions of capital punishment, of foreign investment by multinational corporations, or of the dangers of nuclear holocaust. We shall not be reading in either popular or scientific journals anyone's arguments that the Gypsies really were a lawless, unhygienic people, or that the Jews did constitute an unpatriotic minority in Europe. These matters are not discussable. Hitler's evil is seen to be so exemplary, unqualified, and malicious that it is unthinkable for there to be two sides to this question. He provided our own country with one of the very few wars we are not ashamed of.

It is not easy, however, to look back at the Holocaust without a certain distortion of vision. In the real affairs of mankind we tend to romanticize when we portray to ourselves what sorts of people actually bring such outrage and devastation upon their fellows. We imagine cunning, and fury, and malice, and sadistic savagery. But evil actually incarnates itself in more ambiguous forms and folk. If we go looking for it with an identi-kit image that is more mask than human visage, we shall find no evil men. One must avoid framing one's notions and memory of Nazi destruction so melodramatically that we arrive at the belief that this magnitude of evil is not to be seen again, at least not in our time. It may be.

If mighty evil once was done, then it is likely to rise again in newly tragic forms; for those who remember, it will be recognizable by an ancient stench and spirit. The Nazi Holocaust ought not be disallowed as moral metaphor simply because it can be hurled as a clumsy curse at some who do not deserve it, or because those who do deserve it may not, when viewed close-up, appear all that monstrous. What I should like to do here is to look rather closely at the record and to discern there, in this most sadly documented of the modern world's massacres, the track and traces of it all. Among all that we know of the Holocaust, which so resists understanding, are there patterns that would likely reemerge as recognition clues if this same spirit possessed the hearts of other men and women to do this same tormenting work? Only if we work to see and understand this past catastrophe will we know, with any responsibility, whether any feature of our abortion struggle bears true comparison with Auschwitz, Treblinka, and all that they enshrine.

How Count Deaths When One Is All-Tragic?

What we see and lament in the Holocaust is not unique in its body count or in its savagery. Frederic Wertham observes:

> We should not regard the Nazi mass killings of civilians in isolation. Many extensive massacres and exterminations have occurred in the past: the Crusades (a million victims); the massacre of St. Bartholomew's Day; the Inquisition (a quarter of a million); the burning of witches (at least 20,000); the subjection of colonies in South America (more than 15,000,000); the Island of Haiti (14,000 survivors out of 1,000,000 inhabitants after thirty-five years of colonization); the extermination of the Indians in Argentina and Uruguay; the Island of Mauritius (the work slaves died so fast that 1,200 had to be imported annually); Java (the Dutch East India Company extorted in twelve years $830,000,000 from the slave labor of 5,000,000 natives, untold numbers of whom perished); the Congo (of 30,000,000 inhabitants at the time of its colonial takeover, 8,500,000 were still alive in 1911); India (open violence such as the Amritsar Massacre: during the dispersal of an assemblage, 379 were killed and 1,500 wounded, in an episode which had a lasting effect on Nehru's political development); the Indians in the

United States . . . ; Nanking (the massacre by the Japanese); the
Hereros in Southwest Africa (40,000 men, women, and children
were surrounded, driven to the desert, and left to die of hunger
and thirst. Neither the German parliament nor the traders or
missionaries protested. Report of the German General Staff: the
Hereros had ceased "to exist as an independent tribe)."[9]

What seems to be new about the Nazi massacres is that they were so
thoroughly planned and efficiently carried out. "Never before in history had
people been killed on an 'assembly-line' basis. The killing centre . . . has no
prototype, no administrative ancestor." What were the results? Besides the
military casualties of warfare, the Germans are reckoned to have exterminated
between 7 million and 8 million persons. There were groups entirely marked
out for destruction. These included Jews, Gypsies, Jehovah's Witnesses,
homosexuals, conscientious objectors, Soviet political commissars, the chronically or mentally ill, handicapped children, and politically active socialist,
communist, or Christian opponents. By far the most numerous victims were
the Jews; between 5 million and 6 million perished.[10] Nearly a third of a
million mentally ill were killed; at the close of the war mental institutions
housed only slightly more than 10 percent of the number of patients they had
had in 1939.[11]

The way of their perishing is well and sadly known. Victims were shot in
ditches; beheaded; burnt alive; gassed by carbon monoxide or by Zyklon B
(prussic acid); hanged; injected with phenol or gasoline or carbolic acid or
virulent infectious matter; blown to bits with dynamite; dismembered or
frozen or diseased or poisoned in various experiments; starved, suffocated, or
worked beyond survival; castrated, sterilized, garroted, disemboweled;
yielded up to typhus and other camp diseases. Their bodies were at first
buried in mass graves; later, burned in great open pyres or cremated in
high-temperature ovens. Some were rendered for their fat. Their property
was confiscated, their labor enslaved, their hair shorn for felt, their teeth
broken out for gold, their clothes, spectacles, and shoes taken from them.
They went naked and despoiled to their deaths. They had been taken from
their homes and immured in ghettos without room, work, or freedom; then
transported for days in sealed livestock cars without food, drink, or sanitation;
then, after separation from their kin, imprisoned for as long as they were able
to labor without diet, medicine, or rest; then destroyed. There were no
hearings or trials, for none was accused of crime. They were simply not
wanted.

Who did this to them? The SS, the Gestapo, the German Wehrmacht,
military and civilian medical and hospital personnel, conscripts from subject
countries like Lithuania and the Ukraine, the police of Germany and its
tributaries, the governments of cooperative regimes, and the German government in its many ministries: military, Reichsbank, Propaganda, Interior,
Transport, Economy, Food and Agriculture, Finance, Labor, Security,
Foreign Affairs, and Justice. Many tens of thousands of people—mostly but
not exclusively Germans—merged their wits and their efforts that many

millions of their fellow humans—not as soldiers nor as criminals—might be destroyed.

How, if the predators were not all simply berserk, did this happen?

I have found seven factors in the Holocaust which may help us to understand it as an archetype of massacre that is acknowledged only after the fact. Those guilty of Holocaust:

1. depersonalized their victims
2. euphemized their public and private vocabulary of death
3. discharged responsibility for their acts onto others
4. disavowed vicious intent
5. once initiated, killed indiscriminately
6. found it an occasion to acquire wealth
7. were encouraged by a temporizing opposition.

1: "They are not really human"—Depersonalization of the Victims

One of the SS officers who had commanded a mobile extermination unit, when standing trial at the war's end, was asked how his work of killing had been the fruit of National Socialist doctrine. "I am of the opinion," he replied, "that when for years, for decades, the doctrine is preached that the Slav race is an inferior race and Jews not even human, then such an outcome is inevitable."[12]

A theme repeated throughout the record is that the Germans were dealing with a variety of racial groups, most of which were designated as inferior. For example, when Dr. Eugen Haagen, professor of hygiene at Strassburg University, was receiving prison inmates in batches of two hundred to be injected with typhus, a question was raised whether some of the experimental subjects might be Alsatians. Haagen's assistant explained reassuringly that "the experiments would not be conducted with prisoners but only with Poles," as "Poles really are not human beings."[13] Slavs, in the National Socialist racial scale, were classed as subhumans, *Untermenschen*, only one grade above Jews.[14] Thus Hans Frank, governor-general of occupied Poland, could say in 1944: "Once we have won the war, all those Poles, Ukrainians and anything else that may still be running around here can be turned into mincemeat as far as I am concerned, unless anyone has any better ideas for them." Four years earlier he had been quoted in the German press as saying, "In Prague, for instance, big red posters were put up saying seven Czechs had been shot that day. I said to myself that, if we had to put out a poster for every seven shot Poles, the forests of Poland would not be sufficient to provide the paper for such posters."[15]

Already in *Mein Kampf*, written in 1923, Hitler had foreseen that the racial groups of eastern Europe would have to be made a "service population" for the "superior races" (those of Germany, Scandinavia, Britain, Holland, and parts of France).[16]

Under the patronage of the SS, Dr. Sigmund Rascher, a medical officer in the Luftwaffe, was freezing scores of prisoners to death in his research to preserve German aviators who had to bail out into the cold northern seas. SS chief Heinrich Himmler had ordered that if any subject should by chance revive after being frozen he should be spared further treatment and be "pardoned" to life imprisonment in a concentration camp. Rascher then explained that his victims had all been Poles and Russians; did Himmler mean his ruling to extend even to them? Himmler wired back that Poles and Russians were a different matter and, of course, qualified for no such amnesty.[17] Conti, Hitler's secretary of state for civil health services, had earlier drawn up a plan for the extermination of the entire Polish intelligentsia through sterilization.[18]

From this perspective inferior races would become even more dispensable in the strain and struggle of war. Hitler spelled it out to President Rauschning of the Danzig Senate: "Nature is cruel, therefore we, too, may be cruel. If I don't mind sending the pick of the German people into the hell of war without regret for the shedding of valuable German blood, then I have naturally the right to destroy millions of men of inferior races who increase like vermin."[19]

Ironically, when other peoples classified as inferior were coopted into the liquidation work itself, they were seen as savage. Early in the war German soldiers had been seen watching and photographing Rumanian death squads carrying out mass executions of Jews. The Wehrmacht commander, General Wöhler, issued a public order: "Because of the eastern European conception of human life, German soldiers may become witnesses of events which they cannot prevent at this time but which violate German feelings of honor most deeply. To every normal person it is a matter of course that he does not take photographs of such disgusting excesses. . . . To gaze at such procedures curiously is beneath the dignity of the German soldier."[20]

Gypsies, regarded as parasites and as probably related to the Jews, were low on the roster of inferior peoples, and were elaborately classified as "Z" (*Zigeuner*: full Gypsy), "ZM+," "ZM," or "ZM−" (*Zigeuner Mischling*: Gypsy mongrel with more, equal, or less Gypsy blood mixed with German). Thus the stigma of inferior race could be partly relieved by admixture of a less tainted racial texture.

Notoriously the most odious racial group was the Jews. Possibly the mildest reproach against them (acknowledged by German Jewish leaders; quite untrue, however, about the immensely more numerous Jews of eastern Europe) was that they were "abnormal" in their occupational structure: top-heavy in trade, commerce, and the professions, and underrepresented in agriculture and industry. More ominous was Hitler's accusation that Jews, holding a racial loyalty above patriotic ties, were plotting the disintegration of Germany. "If international-finance Jewry inside and outside of Europe should succeed in plunging the nations into another world war [he said in 1939], then the result will not be the Bolshevization of the earth and, with it, the victory of the Jews, but the annihilation of the Jewish race in Europe."[21]

Like Gypsies, but with even more complexity and an increasing confusion caused by subsequent definitions and different decrees from country to country, Jews were classified as Jew, *Mischling* first-degree (two Jewish grandparents, not practicing Judaism, and married to a Gentile), or *Mischling* second-degree (one Jewish grandparent). Ultimately, any Jewish kinship beyond one great-grandparent would bring one to destruction.[22]

Most simply, Hitler asserted that "the Jew is no German."[23] It made more effective propaganda to say, as he was quoted apropos of the exterminations in Poland, that if the Jews "there did not want to work, they were shot. If they could not work, they had to succumb. They had to be treated like tuberculosis bacilli, with which a healthy body may become infected. This was not cruel, if one remembers that even innocent creatures of nature, such as hares and deer, have to be killed, so that no harm is caused by them."[24]

Hilberg writes:

> A number of Nazis, including the chief of the German SS and Police Himmler, the jurist and *Generalgouverneur* of Poland Hans Frank, and Justice Minister Thierack, inclined to the view that the Jews were a lower species of life, a kind of vermin, which upon contact infected the German people with deadly diseases. Himmler once cautioned his SS generals not to tolerate the stealing of property which had belonged to dead Jews. "Just because we exterminated a dead bacterium," he said, "we do not want, in the end, to be infected by that bacterium and die of it." Frank frequently referred to the Jews as "lice." When the Jews in his Polish domain were killed, he announced that now a sick Europe would become healthy again. Justice Minister Thierack once wrote the following letter to a worried Hitler: "A full Jewess, after the birth of her child, sold her mother's milk to a woman doctor, and concealed the fact that she was a Jewess. With this milk, infants of German blood were fed in a children's clinic. The accused is charged with fraud. The purchasers of the milk have suffered damage, because the mother's milk of a Jewess cannot be considered food for German children. The impudent conduct of the accused is also an insult. However, there has been no formal indictment in order to spare the parents—who do not know the facts—unnecessary worry. I will discuss the race-hygiene aspects of the case with the Reich Health Chief.[25]

Hans Frank's medical and propaganda offices jointly sponsored a political hygiene program in Polish schools, highlighting a slogan: *Juden—Läuse—Fleckfieber* ("Jews—Lice—Typhus"). And SS Gen. Friedrich Uebelhoer, chief of one region in Poland, explaining that the ghetto would only be a temporary measure, stated: "In the end, at any rate, we must burn out this bubonic plague."[26] That this was a view held widely may be illustrated by Ernst Biberstein, first a Protestant clergyman, then a functionary in the government's church ministry, and eventually an SS and Gestapo officer involved in the deportation of Jews and commander of an extermination squad in Poland. When he later stood trial in Nuremberg the judge asked whether, as a former clergyman, he had not wished to offer some comfort to Jews about to be slain. His reply: "Mr. President, one does not cast pearls before swine."[27]

Dr. August Hirt, a former professor of anatomy who was requesting several hundred skulls of Jews for his laboratory, explained to Himmler: "By securing the skulls of Jewish-Bolshevist commissars, representing a repulsive but typical species of sub-humanity, we stand to acquire tangible scientific research material."[28] Once, when the gas generator at the Belzec annihilation center broke down, leaving seven to eight hundred naked Jews freezing in the gas chamber for hours, they began to wail. An SS visitor listening at the door quipped: "Just like in a synagogue."[29] Perhaps Paul Karl Schmidt, press officer for the Foreign Office, put it most crisply when he explained, during a tour of Slovakia: "The Jewish question is no question of humanity, and it is no question of religion; it is solely a question of political hygiene."[30]

Under this prevailing attitude it was possible for Jews whose only involvement with the law was a traffic ticket to be designated as "antisocials" and arrested. Other victim groups were similarly depicted and considered as of negligible human value. For instance, pursuant to an agreement between the SS and the Justice ministry that "asocial" prisoners would be transferred to concentration camps and there exterminated, the judiciary had to meet to discuss "ugliness." The summary of the conference reports:

> During various visits to the penitentiaries, prisoners have always been observed who—because of their bodily characteristics—hardly deserve the designation human [Mensch]; they look like miscarriages of hell [Missgeburten der Hölle]. Such prisoners should be photographed. It is planned that they too shall be eliminated [auszuschalten]. Crime and sentence are irrelevant. Only such photographs should be submitted which clearly show the deformity.[31]

When Hitler adverted to the elimination of handicapped and retarded children, he referred to them as "racially valueless," not in the sense that they were of inferior racial stock but that they were unworthy of the race he wished strengthened and purified.[32] One woman whose husband had commanded an extermination clinic for those children, though he never told her until the end what his work was, later reflected:

> Well, I must tell the truth: however really terrible I felt about the people they killed in Treblinka and Sobibor, I didn't feel like that about Hartheim. He told me all about it that day; who they were, how ill they were; how nobody could be killed without the four certificates from the doctors. I never knew exactly how these killings were done—not in Poland either; I somehow thought they assembled people and then exploded a gas-bomb. I thought at Hartheim they had given them injections. But I often imagined how I would have felt if I had had a baby who was so terribly abnormal; I know I would have loved it as much, perhaps more than my normal children and yet . . . no, I cannot say in all honesty that I felt as badly about Hartheim.[33]

One of the strategies at the camps was to depersonalize the arriving victims by terrorizing them to the point where they acted addled. Sereny describes the process: "The killings were organized systematically to achieve the maximum humiliation and dehumanization of the victims before they died. This pattern was dictated by a distinct and careful purpose, not by 'mere' cruelty or indifference: the crammed airless freight-cars without sanitary provisions, food or drink, far worse than any cattle transport; the whipped-up (literally so) hysteria of arrival; the immediate and always violent separation of men, women and children; the public undressing; the incredibly crude internal physical examinations for hidden valuables; the hair-cutting and shaving of the women; and finally the naked run to the gas chamber under the lash of the whips."[34] At Treblinka, for instance, one Jewish *Oberkapo* would meet the trains. "He didn't just carry an ordinary whip—he had one of the long ones and he'd stand there swinging it and shouting in his broad Viennese, 'You pigs, you shit sows, get on with it, let's see how quick you can learn to be.' He behaved as if he wanted to outdo the worst of the Ukrainians."[35]

Franz Stangl, SS commandant of Treblinka and other extermination camps, was given extensive and searching interviews as a postwar prisoner by Gitta Sereny, who drew from him some most revealing recollections about this process of dehumanizing:

> "*What was the worst place in the camp for you?*" I asked Stangl.
> "The undressing barracks," he said at once. "I avoided it from my innermost being; I couldn't confront them; I couldn't lie to them; I avoided at any price talking to those who were about to die; I couldn't stand it."
> It became clear that as soon as the people were in the undressing barracks—that is, as soon as they were naked—they were no longer human beings for him. What he was "avoiding at any price" was witnessing the transition. And when he cited instances of human relations with prisoners, it was never with any of those who were about to die. . . .
> "*Would it be true to say that you finally felt they weren't really human beings?*"
> "When I was on a trip once, years later in Brazil," he said, his face deeply concentrated, and obviously reliving the experience, "my train stopped next to a slaughterhouse. The cattle in the pens, hearing the noise of the train, trotted up to the fence and stared at the train. They were very close to my window, one crowding the other, looking at me through that fence. I thought then, 'Look at this; this reminds me of Poland; that's just how the people looked trustingly, just before they went into the tins. . . .'"
> "*You said 'tins,'* " I interrupted. "*What do you mean?*" But he went on without hearing, or answering me. " . . . I couldn't eat tinned meat after that. Those big eyes . . . which looked at me . . . not knowing that in no time at all they'd all be dead." He paused. His face was drawn. At this moment he looked old and worn and real.
> "*So you didn't feel they were human beings?*" "Cargo," he said tonelessly. "They were cargo." He raised and dropped his hand in a gesture of despair. Both our voices had dropped. It was one of the

few times in those weeks of talks that he made no effort to cloak his despair, and his hopeless grief allowed a moment of sympathy.

"When do you think you began to think of them as cargo? The way you spoke earlier of the day when you first came to Treblinka, the horror you felt seeing the dead bodies everywhere—they weren't 'cargo' to you then, were they?"

"I think it started the day I first saw the *Totenlager* in Treblinka. I remember Wirth standing there, next to the pits full of blue-black corpses. It had nothing to do with humanity—it couldn't have; it was a mass—a mass of rotting flesh. Wirth said, 'What shall we do with this garbage?' I think unconsciously that started me thinking of them as cargo."

"There were so many children, did they ever make you think of your children, of how you would feel in the position of the parents?"

"No," he said slowly, "I can't say I ever thought that way." He paused. "You see," he then continued, still speaking with this extreme seriousness and obviously intent on finding a new truth within himself, "I rarely saw them as individuals. It was always a huge mass. . . ."

"What is the difference to you between hate, and a contempt which results in considering people as 'cargo'?"

"It has nothing to do with hate. They were so weak; they allowed everything to happen—to be done to them. They were people with whom there was no common ground, no possibility of communication—that is how contempt is born."[36]

Over and over again the point is made: there are some subhuman kinds which a strong and superior Germanic people must subdue or eliminate. Arthur Guett, director of public health in the Reich, published his policy on this point in 1935:

> The ill-conceived "love of thy neighbor" has to disappear, especially in relation to inferior or asocial creatures. It is the supreme duty of a national state to grant life and livelihood only to the healthy and hereditarily sound portion of the people to secure the maintenance of a hereditarily sound and racially pure folk for all eternity. The life of an individual has meaning only in the light of that ultimate aim, that is, in the light of his meaning to his family and to his national state.[37]

Who were the people who would stand head-high in the new order? The authentic Teuton, whom the SS *Rassenprüfer* (race examiners) were to be selecting, was characterized by a party theorist as "tall, long head, narrow face, well-defined chin, narrow nose with very high root, soft fair (golden-blond) hair, receding light (blue or grey) eyes, pink white skin color."[38]

The elimination of lesser elements was often called a purification.[39] As an army indoctrination booklet explained it, "The fight against Jewry is a moral fight for the purity and health of God-created humanity and for a new, more just order in the world." Himmler, to a group of generals, asserted that the struggle to rescue a "healthy elite" was for the sake of beauty and culture, creative power and "the heritage of our ancestors."[40] In a personal address to officer cadets, Hitler himself explained in 1944 what it meant to be of stronger stock:

> Nature is always teaching us . . . that she is governed by the principle of selection: that victory is to the strong and that the weak must go to the wall. She teaches us what may seem cruel to us, because it affects us personally or because we have been brought up in ignorance of her laws, is nevertheless often essential if a higher way of life is to be attained. Nature knows nothing of the notion of humanitarianism which signifies that the weak must at all costs be surrounded and preserved even at the expense of the strong. Nature does not see in weakness any extenuating reasons . . . on the contrary, weakness calls for condemnation.[41]

Ten years earlier the point had been spelled out in a syllabus for the philosophical education of SS and police personnel:

> It is an untenable position when the relationship between the efficient and the ineffective in a State assumes an unhealthy form. The nation has to spend a great deal of energy and money in dealing with the feeble-minded, the criminal and the anti-social. If these examples of poor heredity were eliminated, large sums of money would be saved and could be diverted to other, more productive ends. A responsible State leadership should devote all its attention to plans for maintaining and increasing those of sound stock. In primitive societies, the community rids itself of its weaklings. In so-called civilised nations, a false attitude of brotherly love, which the church has been especially assiduous in fostering among the broad masses, operates in direct opposition to the selective process.[42]

The Third Reich was in debt to the earlier theorists of Social Darwinism, like Wilhelm Schallmayer, who had argued that the principle of social usefulness was a better guide for legislation than was the "untenable" notion of human rights. The unfit and weak, proposed Schallmayer, should be either barred from marriage or sterilized. Also important to this intellectual movement was the early teaching of the French nineteenth-century orientalist Paul de Lagarde, whose advice about Jews was: "One does not have dealings with pests and parasites; one does not rear them and cherish them; one destroys them as speedily and as thoroughly as possible."[43]

It was not from out of nowhere, then, that a deputy would argue in the Reichstag in 1895: "The Jews, who operate like parasites, are a different kind of problem. . . . Gentlemen, the Jews are cholera germs . . . beasts of prey . . . the Jew is no German." And in 1920 a distinguished jurist, Karl Binding, with an eminent psychiatrist, Alfred Hoche, would publish an immensely influential little book on the elimination of the mentally ill, whose title gave Germany a new technical phrase and slogan: *The Permit to Destroy Life Not*

Worth Living [*lebensunwertes Leben*]. Even in the Holocaust's smoking aftermath, when one group of criminals called to justice was given acquittals or light sentences for mass murder, a Cologne court explained that some of the dead—those mentally ill—had, after all, been "burned-out human husks." Another court called them "poor, miserable creatures." A court in Hamburg, dismissing charges against one group of child-destroyers, noted that disposal of "life not worth living" was something obvious and reasonable to classical antiquity, and that the ethic of Plato and of Seneca ought to claim as much respect from the law as that of Jesus Christ.[44]

The record consistently shows that the Nazis saw their target groups as of some lower nature, inferior to the Germans and even subhuman, parasitic upon and threatening to the state, which for its own progress and purity had to require its citizens to join in eliminating these others whose claim to live was inconsiderable, even impertinent. It was necessary to degrade, to dehumanize, to depersonalize in order to kill.

2: The Euphemisms of Torment—Language Turned Inside Out

To disdain and to discredit the several categories of Nazi victims, the German language was canvassed for some of its harsher and more vilifying terms. Quite the opposite is the case when the government must find words to prescribe what should be done with these people. The common outcome was death, but, to avoid all open mention of death and its violent forms, official documents developed an elaborate, almost elegant, euphemy. Virtually everyone involved at every station in these people's procession to their deaths knew what was to happen. Still, their language walked in great circles to detour round the staggering truth.

Here is a partial glossary of extermination:

Aussiedlung	evacuation
Umsiedlung	resettlement
Aufräumung	clean-up
Entfernung	removal
Judenfrei gemacht	cleared of Jews
Evakuierung	evacuation
Arbeitensatz im Osten	labor in the East
Säuberung	cleansing
Desinfektion	disinfection
Sonderbehandlung	special treatment
Grossäuberungsaktionen	major cleansing actions
Rückkehr unerwunscht	return undesirable
weg	departed
Verlegung	transfer
Sonderaktionen	special actions
Massnahme	measures
Invaliden-Aktion	invalid-action
Exekutivmassnahme	executive measures
der Sondermassnahme zugeführt	forwarded for special measures

sicherheitspolizeiliche Massnahme	security police measures
sicherheitspolizeilich durchgearbeitet	worked over by security police methods
abgempft	inoculated off
abgespritzt	injected off
durchgeschleusst	dragged through
eingeschläfert	put to sleep
entsprechend behandelt	treated appropriately
Vollzugstätigkeit	drawn to a conclusion
gesondert untergebracht	separately quartered
Ausschaltung	removal
Beseitigung	elimination
Aktionen	actions
Durchgangslager	transit camp
Kriegsgefangenenlager	prisoner of war camp
Konzentrationslager	concentration camp
Sammelstellen	assembly points
Arbeitslager	work camp
Stiftung	foundation
Spezialeinrichtungen	special installations
Badeanstalten	bath houses
Entlausungs Aktionen	delousing actions
Ostland	the East
Entlassungen	discharge certificates
Lösungsmöglichkeiten	possible solutions
Bereinigung der Judenfrage	clean-up of the Jewish question
endliche Lösung der Judenfrage	final solution to the Jewish question[45]

Euphemism ran through the corridors of justice also. There was the 1933 Law for the Prevention of Hereditarily Diseased Posterity (which effected prevention through sterilization or death); the Reich Committee for Children (which destroyed them); the Reich Committee for Research on Hereditary Diseases and Constitutional Susceptibility to Severe Diseases (which identified those to be eliminated); the Non-Profit Patient Transport Corporation (which conveyed them to the clinics where they would die); the Charitable Foundation for Institutional Care (which paid for it); and there was "euthanasia" and "mercy death" (which was what it was all about).[46]

As noted above, in 1920 Professors Binding and Hoche had legitimated, in German medical and legal circles, the notion of *lebensunwertes Leben*, life not worth living. This was any life afflicted with physical handicap or deformity, mental retardation or derangement, or chronically incapacitating illness; or, to put it another way, any life that required extended custodial care without any prospect of advantage to the state. The currency of the expression may be appreciated from the fact that when the extermination program was condemned by the Vatican in 1940, the statement from the Holy Office incorporated the very terminology fashioned by the Nazis, declaring that "the extinction of unworthy life by public mandate [was] incompatible with natural and divine law."[47] These victims were characterized as "useless eaters" and "socially unfit." Their treatment, as one book described it, posed "The Problem of Abbreviation for Worthless Lives."[48]

The rationale for their elimination or "abbreviation," though really arising from social notions about cleansing the national health-stock and curtailing medical expense that would not aid the national struggle, was publicly portrayed as serving the advantage of those who would be killed. As one Nazi official in Franconia described it in a directive, residents in mental institutions were to "be released from their sufferings." Dr. Karl Brandt, major general in the SS, personal physician to Hitler, and coordinator of the "euthanasia" program, specified that this undertaking was designed for persons of "fully extinct spirit." At Nuremberg he was to explain that this was "a measure dictated by purely human considerations," so that those who "could no longer take any conscious part in life were to be given relief through death. . . . The doctors were of the opinion that there was no justification for keeping such a child alive."[49]

Brandt's attorney, Dr. Robert Servatius, portrayed Brandt's work in more forthright fashion:

> Karl Brandt considered the motive of pity for the patient to be the decisive one. . . . Who would not have the desire to die while in good health rather than to be forced by all the resources of medical science to continue life degraded to an animal's existence! Only misguided civilization keeps such beings alive; in the normal struggle for existence nature is more charitable. . . .
>
> If healthy human beings make great sacrifices for the community and lay down their lives by order of the state, the insane person, if he could arouse himself mentally and make a decision, would choose a similar sacrifice for himself. Why should not the state be allowed to enact this sacrifice in his case and impose on him what he would want to do himself? Is the state to be forbidden to carry out such euthanasia until the whole world is a hospital?[50]

Pastor Bodelschwingh, a clergyman who managed one of these clinics, explained, "You must not picture Professor Brandt as a criminal, but rather as an idealist."[51]

The ideals pursued in the "euthanasia" program in the clinics seem not to have differed in substance from those that later inspired "cleansing actons" in the concentration camps. During a staff banquet held at Treblinka, SS Lt. Col. Pfannenstiel, professor of hygiene at Marburg University, told his coworkers: "Your task is a great duty, a duty useful and necessary." To a visitor he later spoke of "the beauty of the task" and the "humane cause," and to the staff he said, "Looking at the bodies of those Jews, one understands the greatness of your work!"[52]

Throughout the literature the theme of "favor" is repeated. Just as the destruction of mentally or physically defective persons was called "an act of grace" and the "privilege of a mercy death," when it was later agreed at a conference called by Adolf Eichmann that "mongrel Jews" were to be offered their choice of deportation or sterilization, it was anticipated that "therefore sterilization should be considered a favor and should impress people as such." This was a program wherein anything but death had become a favor; under that light death itself was easily transformed into a favor also.[53]

The concern that this should be a humane work showed itself in different ways. For instance, when one mobile killing unit, *Einsatzgruppe* (Special Detail) *D*, was liquidating all Jews in a sector of the occupied Crimea, the officer in charge checked to see that the victims were shot "humanely," since in "the event of other killing methods, the psychic burden would have been too great for the execution *Kommando*." Another unit commander prided himself on having court-martialed some soldiers who poured gasoline over some civilian suspects and burnt them alive to the approval of a crowd of shouting comrades. This he found particularly cruel and inhumane.[54]

The same theme can be discerned in a petition to the Interior Minister from the Central Jewish Council in Budapest during the roundup of Hungarian Jews: "We emphatically declare that we do not seek this audience to lodge complaints about the merit of the measures adopted, but merely ask that they be carried out in a humane spirit." Once extermination becomes inevitable, one can think of the methods used as humane or inhumane. It is possibly this standard of humane treatment that led one witness, describing a Jewish roundup by a killing unit, to report: breaking into the houses, the Germans threw hand grenades into the cellars, and some "especially sadistic persons" fired tracer bullets point-blank at the victims."[55]

What is this "humane" way of sending people to their deaths, in which one is not "especially sadistic" if one merely kills by gas, garrote, or grenade? What are we to make of this extraordinary contortion of language? Beneath all of this euphonious and graceful talk nearly eight million men, women, and children were ruthlessly seized and slaughtered.

Clearly some of the language is sheer camouflage. In this spirit, new arrivals at Auschwitz would walk through blossoming orchards, often to music by the inmates' orchestra, with an eye on the famous motto hung over the portal: *Arbeit macht frei* [Liberty through Work].[56]

It is true that in a few documents, usually towards the end of the war, a blunter vocabulary is occasionally found:

Ausrottung	annihilation
hingerichtet	executed
ausgemerzt	exterminated
liquidiert	liquidated
Liquidierungszahl	liquidation count
erledigt	finished off[57]

So in one sense all the euphemisms are, as one might expect, a grisly glossary of intentional doubletalk. These people aimed to kill: they knew it but chose not to say it. When, for example, the exclusion of Jews from public facilities (in the early days) was decreed "to alleviate overcrowding," to promote the "convenience" of the German public, and when the later herding of the Jews into the ghettos was described as a "health-political" measure, that was clearly public cant.[58]

But from another angle this seems not simply to have been the straightforward mendacity of clearheadedly evil men. Gerald Reitlinger has observed that to do this work one had somehow to dull one's own mind:

> Cruelty and unreason were implicit in the system that had brought them employment and advancement, and to both they had to do lipservice. After they had occupied their desks for some years, they had to invent a mumbo-jumbo language about biological material, inferior strains of blood, "asocial" and "unlabourworthy" types, and so forth—to hide from themselves what they were doing.
>
> Like the aerial bomber, the bureaucrat does not see his kill. It is possible that Eichmann never saw a single one of the millions of Jewish corpses of which he boasted, and Himmler, after the experience at Minsk . . . probably never wanted to watch another execution. Ordinary Germans were able to see more. Towards the end of the war in particular it must have been hard to avoid seeing something of the plight of the concentration-camp victims pouring into the last pocket of the Reich. The lowest depths of human misery were on public view. Yet Professor Marc Klein has described how the German crowds in the railway stations in February, 1945, watched with absolute indifference the passage of the train from Gross-Rosen to Buchenwald, an immense procession of open trucks, in each one of which a hundred living skeletons crouched in their ragged prison pyjamas under the guns and rubber truncheons of the SS guards and *Kapos*. So, too, the Norwegian witness Hans Capellen declared that the Dachau internees, who worked on bomb-disposal in Munich, were cursed and blamed by the crowd for the bombing.[59]

This penetratingly deep perversion of language gave expression to the Holocaust in some extraordinary ways. Field Marshal Jodl, in the dock at Nuremberg, when accused by the prosecution of having ordered the murder of a certain group of civilians, retorted with exasperation: "But they were not murdered at all; they were given the last rites and shot according to martial law." An SS commander who slipped a word of warning to Jewish leaders in his brother-in-law's home town and then, after they failed to take it seriously enough and came out of hiding, exterminated them all, spoke of the episode as a "misfortune." He later described a proposal to kill 30 million Slavs as "the question of the excess birthrate in the East." An official of the propaganda ministry wrote in his diary of a town where two barns full of executed civilians had been burned, but incompletely, so that pigs were found feeding on the corpses. This failure to incinerate "made a very bad impression on the remaining population."[60]

What we are witnessing seems to have been a self-preserving affliction of participants at all levels. Hannah Arendt comments on this with respect to Eichmann. Throughout his memoirs, depositions, and testimony he spoke in unrelieved clichés, describing matters of thundering tragedy with limp and bureaucratic stock phrases. When taken to task for this by the judges, he apologized: "*Amtssprache* (officialese) is my only language." Was he merely refusing to address what would bring him to his own doom? Arendt doubts this. "The longer one listened to him, the more obvious it became that his inability to speak was closely connected with an inability to *think*, namely, to think from the standpoint of anyone else. No communication was possible, not because he lied but because he was surrounded by the most reliable of all safeguards against the words and the presence of others, and hence against reality as such."[61]

Arendt sees this as no Nazi monopoly. She records one striking example of it in the courtroom, from the expert in tax and business law who had been called from Cologne to defend Eichmann:

> Servatius declared the accused innocent of charges bearing on his responsibility for "the collection of skeletons, sterilizations, killings by gas, and *similar medical matters*," whereupon Judge Halevi interrupted him: "Dr. Servatius, I assume you made a slip of the tongue when you said that killing by gas was a medical matter." To which Servatius replied: "It was indeed a medical matter, since it was prepared by physicians; *it was a matter of killing, and killing, too, is a medical matter.*"

The attorney, she wryly notes, knew about these "medical matters." He was Robert Servatius, who two decades earlier had pleaded for Karl Brandt, chief defendant in the "doctors' trial" at Nuremberg.[62]

It appears that these men, convinced of the inferiority and undesirable weakness of large classes of fellow humans and resolved to eliminate them, simply were unable in their own minds to acknowledge that they were massacring men, women, and children by tens, hundreds, thousands, millions. They did not lie by euphemizing; the truth was now extinct in them. It would kill them to know.

3: "I was not responsible"—Dislocation of Responsibility

A third theme that rises repeatedly from the Holocaust record is the denial of responsibility. This is a fugue scored in several keys. The first way of putting it is for each person to account for his killing work by pointing out that he acted under law, having submitted his judgment to those empowered to make decisions of state. In Germany at that time, as is well known, with the suspension or dissolution of all forms of representative government, all authority emanated from Adolf Hitler, whose single title eventually was *Führer*, "Leader." As one official memo put it: "The Führer gave the order, the law is made."[63]

Defense counsel for the SS chief of hygiene, who had directed many lethal experiments on prisoners, explained at Nuremberg: "If the experiment is ordered by the state, this moral responsibility of experimenter towards the experimental subject relates to the way in which the experiment is performed, not to the experiment itself."[64]

In the public mind the wishes of the Führer and the laws of the state and the orders for the armed services were the same: Hitler was the unique source of legitimacy for all public policy. Thus the argument of the army's chief of medical services: "I was a soldier. I was in charge of the medical administration of the *Wehrmacht*, but had no power and no right to issue orders, and whatever may have happened, I am not responsible for it." He refers to the same plea by Field Marshal Wilhelm Keitel, chief of the High Command of the Armed Forces, who one year earlier had explained that he had no authority to issue orders.[65]

In practice, of course, orders and policy were formulated up and down the line, and were clothed in the same high authority as if they had come from the Führer. Thus the commandant of Auschwitz could address his work with the same tranquillity of spirit as if sent to it by Hitler himself:

> By the will of the Reichsführer SS [Himmler], Auschwitz became the greatest human extermination center of all time.
>
> When in the summer of 1941 he himself gave me the order to prepare installations at Auschwitz where mass exterminations could take place, and personally to carry out these exterminations, I did not have the slightest idea of their scale or consequences. It was certainly an extraordinary and monstrous order. Nevertheless the reasons behind the extermination program seemed to me right. I did not reflect on it at the time: I had been given an order, and I had to carry it out. Whether this mass extermination of the Jews was necessary or not was something on which I could not allow myself to form an opinion, for I lacked the necessary breadth of view.[66]

As a matter of fact, some of the most devastating directives of the Holocaust were elaborated by relatively low-grade officials. The 1935 Nuremberg Law for the Protection of German Blood and German Honor and its sequels, whereby German Jews were categorized, dispossessed, and disenfranchised, came basically from the pen of a fifth-level bureaucrat.[67] The Final Solution to the Jewish Question was actually devised by a conference of civil servants and military officers of comparatively modest rank. The least among them, Lt. Col. Eichmann, who had earlier harbored doubts about "such a bloody solution through violence," now had his conscience put at ease. "At that moment, I sensed a kind of Pontius Pilate feeling, for I was free of all guilt. . . . Who was I to judge? Who was I to have my own thoughts in this matter? . . . The most prominent people had spoken, the Popes of the Third Reich. Not only Hitler, not only Heydrich, or Müller, or the S.S., or the Party, but the elite of the Civil Service had registered their support."[68]

Eichmann, interestingly, derives more reassurance from the compliance of middle-level bureaucrats than from the explicit orders of the Führer—of which, it must be noted, there were, for the Holocaust, very few. For the extermination of the Jews, Hitler seems to have given hundreds of cues but no direct command. Likewise for the Gypsies. Likewise for the Soviet commissars. Likewise for the medical experiments. Likewise for the other condemned classes. The only apparent exception is the order signed by Hitler on his personal notepaper, as of September 1, 1939:

> Reichleader Bouhler and Dr. Med. Brandt are responsibly commissioned to extend the authority of physicians, to be designated by name, so that a mercy death may be granted to patients who according to human judgment are incurably ill according to the most critical evaluation of the state of their disease.
>
> *Adolf Hitler*

Frederic Wertham comments: "The note does not give the order to kill, but the *power* to kill. That is something very different. . . . The note is not a command but an assignment of authority and responsibility to a particular group of persons, namely, physicians, psychiatrists, and pediatricians. This assignment, far from ordering it, did not even give psychiatrists official permission to do what they did on a grand scale, *i.e.*, kill all kinds of people who were not at all incurable or even mentally ill, making no attempt to examine them first. . . . It certainly cannot be construed as an order to kill people with no serious disease or with no disease at all." Thus one official in the program (which killed almost a third of a million persons) later insisted, "No doctor was ever ordered to participate in the euthanasia program; they came of their own volition." This was an echo of Himmler's own clarification: "What happens in [this psychiatric institution] is carried out by a commission of physicians. . . . The SS furnish only help in vehicles, cars, etc. The medical specialist, expert and responsible, is the one who gives the orders."[69]

This, however, was not the view of those who did the killing. Dr. Brandt, on trial, made much of the Hitler memorandum, arguing rather meticulously that, though unpublished, it was embossed with the golden eagle and the authority of the state.[70] He then went on to invoke this authority, not simply for the elimination of invalids, but for all killing done by medical personnel, including experiments on prisoners.

> I am of the opinion that, when considering the circumstances of the situation of the war, this state institution . . . takes the responsibility away from the physician. . . .
> [Question: Does it take away that responsibility from the physician, in your view, or does it share that responsibility?]
> In my view, this responsibility is taken away from the physician because, from that moment on, the physician is merely an instrument maybe in the same sense as in the case of an officer who receives an order at the front and leads a group of three or four soldiers into a position where they are certain to meet death. . . . I don't believe that the physician as such, from his ethical and medical feelings, would carry out such an experiment without the assurance of the authoritarian state.[71]

The argument for another health official ran thus: "If these laws and government orders were crimes against humanity, very well, then the statesmen and ministers who introduced such laws can be held responsible. . . . But it would be unfair today to try to impose the moral guilt for this development upon a man who was always a mere subordinate executive agent with no independent authority to give orders . . . never one of the fanatical and ruthless types of the Hitler regime."[72]

The appeal to higher orders was no courtroom invention at Nuremberg. As Raul Hilberg summarizes the situation of the German soldier: "If for any reason he was instructed to help the SS and Police in their task, he was expected to obey orders. However, if he killed a Jew spontaneously, merely because he *wanted* to kill, then he had committed an abnormal act, worthy perhaps of an 'eastern European' (such as a Rumanian) but dangerous to the discipline and prestige of the German Army. Herein lay the crucial difference between the man who 'overcame' himself to kill and one who wantonly committed atrocities." Thus army orders could read: "The number of transgressions by military personnel against the civilian population is increasing. . . . It has also happened lately that soldiers and even officers independently undertook shootings of Jews. . . . The officer has to see to it that there are no unpleasant excesses by the troops."[73]

When Franz Stangl accepted an offer to enter extermination work in the SS, he was partly persuaded to do it by being told that "euthanasia" was already being done by law in America and Russia. Pastor Schlaich, director of a nursing facility, having received word that he was to hand over 150 of his patients within four days, protested: "Is it possible for such a measure to be carried out without a pertinent law having been promulgated? Is it not the duty of every citizen to resist under all circumstances an act not justified by law, even forbidden by law, even if such acts are carried out by state agencies?" His vigorous complaint continued: "If the state really wants to carry out the extermination of these or at least some of the mental patients, shouldn't a law be promulgated?" Both SS officer and clergyman found moral repose in legislation.[74]

By universal testimony, the Nazi extermination programs were accomplished under the cloak of firm authority. Equally universal is the testimony that it was always by someone else's authority. This was true, not just afterwards, when those involved were on trial for their lives, but earlier, at the crest of their power. The medical people claimed to be working at the behest of the law people; the government stated that the doctors were making their own professional decisions. Lower officials invoked directives from their superiors; higher officials claimed that their subordinates were always exceeding their warrants. All things were done in the name of the Führer; yet the Führer's signature never appeared on any death orders. Like the "grace" and "privilege" that death was often said to be, "responsibility" and "authority" became somewhat unusual realities.

It is interesting to note that this is so even in the SS, the Nazi organization intended to be most authoritarian. There were twelve ranks in the SS officers corps. Every rank, from *Untersturmführer* up to *Reichsführer* (second lieutenant to field marshal) included the designation *Führer*, "leader." Yet, instead of leadership being the hallmark of the organization, it was obedience. As Höss, commandant at Auschwitz, put it: "An SS man must be able to destroy even his closest dependents should they commit an offense against the state or the ideals of Adolf Hitler. 'There is only one thing that is valid: Orders!' That was the motto which he used in his letterhead." This was the officer who claimed that everything in his camp was done on orders that he had received, and who also complained that most of what went on in his camp was decided by lower officers on their own say-so. The commandant claimed to be the source of no commands.[75]

It appears that within an authoritarian society, where giver and taker of orders do not share responsibility, everyone acts like a giver while feeling like a taker, and this produces the schizoid attitudes towards law which we see at work killing the enemies of the Third Reich. Insofar as this has engendered crime, crime which all disclaim, then all must be, by those who bring later truth to bear, "forthwith transformed back into perpetrators, that is to say, human beings," in Hannah Arendt's words. She observes that "the essence of totalitarian government, and perhaps the nature of every bureaucracy, is to make functionaries and mere cogs in the administrative machinery out of men, and thus to de-humanize them. One can debate long and profitably on the rule of Nobody."[76]

Mitscherlich and Mielke similarly observe: "The individual, the more forcefully he seeks to emerge from a world rooted in collectivism, stubbornly undermines his own qualities, by means of a doctrine of man assigning each feature and peculiarity in turn to non-individual forces that in the end become dehumanized."[77] Both comments describe the Nazis as dehumanized and thus a brutal irony emerges—the Nazi appeal to law had in it a twist that turned those in command into *Untermenschen*, the subhumans they had sought to extirpate.

Beyond this forfeiture of responsibility in the name of lawful command there lay another disclaimer: necessity. Various reasons were urged whereby deeds otherwise unthinkable were imposed on men by this or that imperative.

One story was that the controlling position of Jews in Germany had become insupportable. The chief of the Charitable Foundation for Institutional Care (which liquidated the ill), reminiscing years later, admitted that in the early Nazi days, "if you had said to somebody in Germany, a man in the street *or* an SS officer, 'We are going to kill the Jews,' he would have said, 'The man is mad: have him locked up!' " What was originally expected, he recollected, was that only one-third of the Jews were to be killed; one-third were to be resettled, possibly in Madagascar; and one-third allowed to assimilate. "I think it was only when nothing else worked out that they decided. . . ." Asked if he now regretted what had been done, he said:

> Well yes, that goes without saying. But, on the other hand, if one realized what the situation was in Germany in the early 1930s: I remember when I said I wanted to study law, somebody in my family took me to the Ministry of Justice in Berlin. We walked

along a corridor and he told me to read the names on the office doors we passed. Almost all of them were Jews. And it was the same for the press, the banks, business; in Berlin all of it was in the hands of Jews. That wasn't right. There should have been *some* Germans.

[Question: Of course, they *were* Germans, weren't they?] Well yes, but you know what I mean. . . .[78]

Another imperative that the Nazis claimed was forcing them to act was the threat of Bolshevism. As one Fascist newspaper explained it to the Hungarians: "To remove the Jews was necessary, not only because they were the blood-suckers of the Hungarian nation, but also because they reduced the Hungarian officials and peasants to the level of coolies. Their removal was further necessary, because they were an obstacle to our final victory, on which the fate of every Hungarian depends."[79]

Lazlo Endre, Nazi-installed secretary of state in Hungary, made the same point:

> In Hungary the Jews have openly become the stronghold of Bolshevism. In the interest of our country's defence it was necessary to adopt protective measures against them. The Jews assisted the enemy not only by demoralising the country, but actively by means of sabotage and espionage. In the eastern district, which has become a war zone, we were compelled to adopt the most rigorous measures against the Jews and to set up concentration camps. Steps were however taken to ensure that the treatment of the Jews would be above criticism. The solution of the Jewish question is not an end in itself, but a real and unconditional necessity. And only this can establish the basis for the solution of other Hungarian problems.[80]

There were also imperatives of a more personal nature. Franz Stangl, concentration camp chief, recalled that he had first transferred from the Austrian police to the Gestapo to save himself. He had, it seems, arrested a poacher who turned out to be a high party member, and Stangl feared retribution after his country was annexed.[81] Karl Gebhardt, major general and chief staff surgeon in the SS, only began vivisection and induced-gangrene experiments on female prisoners to clear himself of suspicion that he had negligently or deliberately let Reinhardt Heydrich die of gangrene developed from assassination injuries.[82]

Some saw their work as a necessary evil done to avoid something worse. Viktor Brack, physician and SS lieutenant colonel, explained that his X-ray device designed to sterilize 150 to 200 Jews a day, without their knowing it, was "less of an evil" than Himmler's taking those Jews and "doing something worse to them. . . . The same way a troop commander sacrifices a few thousand people somewhere if he can save a hundred thousand somewhere else."[83]

Dr. Hermann Pfannmüller, director of an infant medical facility, explained to a visitor that his work was to relieve the nation of a burden:

"These creatures—" he meant the children just mentioned—"I consider, as a National Socialist, to be a mere burden on our population. We don't kill them—" or he may have said, "We don't do the job—" —"by poison, injections and so on, as then the foreign Press and certain people in Switzerland—" he probably meant the Red Cross— "would only have a fresh pretext for worrying us. No! Our method is a much simpler and more natural one, as you see." With these words he pulled one of the children out of its cradle with the aid of a female nurse who was apparently regularly entrusted with this sort of work at the Station. He held up the child for our inspection as though it were a dead hare, at the same time making some such remark, with a knowing and cynical grin, as: "This one, for instance, will only last another two or three days." I shall never forget the look of that fat, grinning fellow with the whimpering little skeleton in his fleshy hand, surrounded by the other starving children. The murderer then went on to say that it was not the practice to deprive the children suddenly of food but gradually to reduce their rations.[84]

The most imposing necessity invoked was the survival of the state itself (not of the German people, who could only be eliminated by the thitherto unprecedented measure of total genocide they had themselves devised, but of the German government). This was the root of the political imperative: *raison d'état*.

According to that theory, the actions of the state, which is responsible for the life of the country and thus also for the laws obtaining in it, are not subject to the same rules as the acts of the citizens of the country. Just as the rule of law, although devised to eliminate violence and the war of all against all, always stands in need of the instruments of violence in order to assure its own existence, so a government may find itself compelled to commit actions that are generally regarded as crimes in order to assure its own survival and the survival of lawfulness.[85]

By 1936 all SS units in training were indoctrinated thus: "The Jew is a parasite. Wherever the Jew flourishes the people die. . . . Elimination of the Jew from our community is to be regarded as an emergency defense measure." The "right of emergency defense" was the rubric in *Mein Kampf* under which Hitler had urged the gassing of "twelve or fifteen thousand" Jews.[86]

The court at Nuremberg heard this as a frequent plea. In defense of Mrugowsky, who had infected prisoners with typhus: "The experiments were a form of research work necessitated by an extraordinarily pressing state emergency, and ordered by the highest competent state authorities. . . . The number of fatalities [142 at Buchenwald] amounted to one percent of the toll taken *every day* by typhus in the *Russian prisoner camps alone* in winter 1941–42."[87] In defense of Gebhardt, who performed vivisection on prisoners and infected them with gangrene: "The leaders of the German Wehrmacht would have neglected their duty . . . had they not attempted to solve, at any price, the problem as to which chemical preparations were capable of preventing bacterial wound infection and, above all, gas gangrene. . . . In a state of self-defense and emergency, even such actions are permitted which violate the laws of warfare and therefore international law."[88] In defense of Sievers, who collected Jews to be converted to skeletons for research: "Justice cannot insist with utter consistency upon the individual respecting foreign rights and sacrificing his own at all costs and under any circumstances. A Frenchman [Pradier] says to this question: 'This theory is admirable for saints and heroes, but it is not for common humanity.' "[89] In defense of Brandt, chief of both the "euthanasia" and the prisoner experiment programs: "Ethical obligation has to subordinate itself to the totalitarian nature of war. . . . The question is how great a sacrifice may the state demand in the interest of the community? The decision is for the state alone."[90]

Much the same message was given by the Vichy government's chief of Jewish affairs, in response to a leading rabbi's remonstrance for having accepted the Nazi policies of anti-Semitism: "Let me point out that in the government's attitude there is no anti-Semitism, simply the application of reasons of state. Please be assured, Rabbi, of my genuine regard."[91]

At variance with this is the testimony of Dr. Andrew Ivy, an American expert witness at Nuremberg: "There is no justification in killing five people in order to save the lives of five hundred." Servatius, Brandt's attorney, was dumbfounded by this view, and suggested to the court that it was a personal view of Ivy, unsupported by public opinion.[92]

It seems, then, that just as the Nazi appeal to state authority in fact resulted in the withering of truly responsible authority, so the appeal to unlimited defense by the state against savagery from without wrought within a savagery more sinister than any an enemy could have devised. The claim "I was not responsible," pled by individual or by state, was not a defense. It was a self-imposed sentence.

4: "There was certainly no vicious intent"—Savagery from Normal Folk

There is a fourth trait to be discerned in the Holocaust, another dislocation of the human soul. It is that few of these mass murderers were, with obvious malice, purposely evil. It is difficult for us to imagine the spirit and character of those who would do the work of killing infants, Jehovah's Witnesses, Jews, Poles, or whatever other group might be designated for liquidation. Robert Coles writes of this apropos of Charles Whitman, the young man who shot dozens of people from the library tower at the University of Texas:

> Curiously enough, it is easier to deal with a mass murderer such as Whitman than with the concentration camps and battlefields this century has witnessed. We can call one man a lunatic (for what he has done, if not for what doctors can discover in him). That is, we can understand why he may have *felt* violent (and violated) even if we still do not comprehend why those feelings prompted in him the particular action he took. In contrast, what can we say about those many thousands who a few years ago killed millions in gas ovens or through bombing? . . .

How do we analyze the thinking of inscrutable leaders who would sacrifice a country's entire generation to forced labor, prisons and hunger in the name of an abstraction like "dialectical materialism," an ideology whose meaning and purpose cannot really be debated in such countries save by a very few? While "primitive" people have given something like *amok* a cultural form (among the Malay, Iban and Moslem groups of Borneo and elsewhere), mighty and "civilized" nations threaten to destroy everyone alive on this planet. The mind shudders before the prospect of looking at it all, the awful carnage of which man is capable. [93]

There were women like Ilse Koch, the "Red Witch of Buchenwald," who had lampshades made of prisoners' tatooed skin, and Irma Grese of Auschwitz and Belsen, who was said to have bound together the legs of prisoners in labor so that mother and child would perish together. There were surely others like those. There were men like Heinrich Himmler, SS chief, who had this to say to those managing a program whereby two hundred thousand blond, Aryan-appearing Polish children were kidnapped from schools and off the streets to be put up for adoption in Germany:

A member of the SS must be decent, fit, loyal and a good comrade to his fellows, but not towards representatives of other countries. For instance, he is not interested in the fate of a Russian or a Czech. We take those among these peoples who are of good blood, we steal them just as we steal their children, and we shall see to their education. The conditions in which these peoples live, or whether things go well or badly with them, are a matter of complete indifference to us. They interest me only to the extent that we need them as slaves for our culture. Otherwise they do not interest me at all. If 10,000 Russian women die of exhaustion in digging an antitank ditch, that interests me only to the extent that the ditch is ready for Germany. We Germans, who are the only people in the world who have a correct attitude towards animals, will also have a correct attitude towards these animal human beings. [94]

Yet this same Himmler, a devoted family man, took a warm interest in children, stood as sponsor for scores of them in the ceremony the Nazis had created to replace baptism, and was always sending anniversary cards and gifts to them.

And there was Dr. Sigmund Rascher, a close and favored protégé of Himmler, who was not only associated with the latter's *Lebensborn* program (dozens of homes across Germany housed racially selected young women who, serviced regularly by SS men, were to breed especially fine stock for the nation), but was also detailed to Dachau, where he conducted aviator clothing tests by freezing prisoners to death, and trials of parachute function by suffocating others in high-altitude chambers, and experiments on blood coagulants by shooting prisoners and noting how long it required for them to bleed to death. Rascher, when confronted by his uncle one day, admitted, "I dare not think; I dare not think."[95]

There was Karl Brandt, chief of both the "euthanasia" and prison experiment programs, who as a young doctor had made plans to join Albert Schweitzer in his mission hospital work at Lambaréné. And there was Karl Gebhart, of the castration and sterilization project, who also worked on surgical techniques to rehabilitate handicaps of birth and injury.[96]

The monstrous work of these men seems not to have made them bestial off-duty or in the course of their usual human relationships. Let us look at three for whom the evidence is abundant: Höss, commandant of Auschwitz; Stangl, commandant of Sobibor and Treblinka; and Eichmann, in general charge of the SS office for Jewish affairs. Each of the three was a high agent in death programs that yielded in the magnitude of one million exterminations.

As Bertrand Russell has written, Rudolf Höss "was a very ordinary little man. He would never have been heard of by the general public had not fate decreed that he was to be, perhaps, the greatest exterminator of all time."[97] During service in World War I, when he shot his first enemy, an Indian, he was upset as any newly blooded soldier would be. Reflecting on a brief spell in prison, he was revolted by one inmate's story of killing a pregnant mother, her four small children, and servant girl. As a junior SS man he observed: "The block leaders who hastened to these whippings, and whose taste for these spectacles I learned to know, were almost without exception sly, rough, violent, and often common creatures, whose behavior toward their comrades and their families was in character with their natures. They did not regard prisoners as human beings at all. . . . I was certainly not one of these." Appointed camp commandant, he "shuddered at the prospect of carrying out exterminations by shooting," and was relieved when he found that death came so quickly in the new gas chambers.

His principal solace were his wife and exquisitely blond children, who lived with him on the camp grounds in a "paradise of flowers." "No former prisoner can ever say that he was in any way or at any time badly treated in our house. My wife's greatest pleasure would have been to give a present to every prisoner who was in any way connected with our household. The children were perpetually begging me for cigarettes for the prisoners. They were particularly fond of the ones who worked in the garden. My whole family displayed an intense love of agriculture and particularly for animals of all sorts. Every Sunday I had to walk them all across the fields, and visit the stables, and we might never miss the kennels where the dogs were kept. Our two horses and the foal were especially beloved."[98]

As an Austrian policeman in the troubled days before the *Anschluss*, Franz Stangl recalls, "All I wanted was just to close the door of my house and be alone with my wife. I was mad about her. I really wasn't political you see." When someone testified that on one occasion when the whips of the Ukrainian staffers were not emptying the boxcars fast enough Stangl impatiently fired into the crowd with a pistol, "Stangl, insisting that he had never shot into a crowd of people, appeared to be more indignant about this accusation than about anything else, and to find irrelevant the fact that, whether he shot into the group or not, these very same people died anyway, less than two hours later, through actions ultimately under his control."

Throughout, both he and his wife insisted that he had taken no part in any killing; his responsibility was "merely administrative." He vigorously denied the claim that he had frequently had floggings and hangings carried out in his sight. "Not one," his wife insisted. On leave, the two of them would stay at the home of a priest friend, and go to Mass every morning. Stangl's claim in prison that his family believed in him and stood by him is borne out by his middle daughter's avowal: "All I can say is that I have read what has been written about my father. But nothing — nothing on earth—will make me believe that he has ever done anything wrong. I know it is illogical; I know about the trial and the witnesses . . . but he was my father. He stuck to me through thick and thin and he saved me once when I thought my life was in ruins. 'Remember, remember always,' he once said to me, 'if you need help, I'll go to the end of the moon for you.' "[99]

Adolf Eichmann was another faithful family man who seems sincere in his claim that he went to lengths not to be mean or vicious. When asked whether it was not ironic for him to prescribe "no unnecessary hardships" when involved in mass killings, he

> did not even understand the question, so firmly was it still anchored in his mind that the unforgivable sin was not to kill people but to cause unnecessary pain. During the trial, he showed unmistakable signs of sincere outrage when witnesses told of cruelties and atrocities committed by S.S. men—though the court and much of the audience failed to see these signs, because his single-minded effort to keep his self-control had misled them into believing that he was "unmovable" and indifferent—and it was not the accusation of having sent millions of people to their death that ever caused him real agitation but only the accusation (dismissed by the court) of one witness that he had once beaten a Jewish boy to death.[100]

One Eichmann anecdote deserves retelling because it shows that the apparently humane side of this man was available, not simply to his family away from his work, but in a mystifying way even to his victims. In the course of his dealings with the Austrian Jews he had come to know many of their leaders at first hand. One appealed to him after being shipped to Auschwitz.

> I went to Auschwitz and asked Höss to see Storfer. "Yes, yes [Höss said], he is in one of the labor gangs." With Storfer afterward, well, it was normal and human, we had a normal, human encounter. He told me all his grief and sorrow: I said: "Well, my dear old friend [Ja, mein lieber guter Storfer], we certainly got it! What rotten luck!" And I also said: "Look, I really cannot help you, because according to orders from the Reichsführer nobody can get out. I can't get you out. Dr. Ebner can't get you out. I hear you made a mistake, that you went into hiding or wanted to bolt, which, after all, you did not need to do." [Eichmann meant that

Storfer, as a Jewish functionary, had immunity from deportation.]
I forget what his reply to this was. And then I asked him how he
was. And he said, yes, he wondered if he couldn't be let off work, it
was heavy work. And then I said to Höss: "Work—Storfer won't
have to work!" But Höss said, "Everyone works here." So I said:
"O.K.," I said, "I'll make out a chit to the effect that Storfer has to
keep the gravel paths in order with a broom," there were little
gravel paths there, "and that he has the right to sit down with his
broom on one of the benches." [To Storfer] I said: "Will that be all
right, Mr. Storfer? Will that suit you?" Whereupon he was very
pleased, and we shook hands, and then he was given the broom
and sat down on his bench. It was a great inner joy to me that I
could at least see the man with whom I had worked for so many
long years, and that we could speak with each other.

Six weeks after this normal, human encounter Storfer was shot.[101]

The bloody task of mass murder, it appears, can be the work of men who in
some respects remain gentle, friendly, and quietly attractive. We should view
these individual vignettes also against the background of a wider society that
supported their work and sympathized. There were, it is reckoned, about 350
medical doctors who willingly participated in the works of death. Only rare
instances are recorded of a physician who turned down the invitation. Scores
of these doctors assumed respected positions in the medical and academic
world of postwar Germany.[102]

In anticipation of the liquidation of defective children, a survey was done of
parents which disclosed that they mostly acquiesced in it. An analyst reported
that "most of the relatives agree to it; it is characteristic that many disagree but
declare that they do not wish to be asked and that the matter had best be secret
and covered up (death should come unexpectedly, not influenced by the
wishes and interests of others, and should not burden the relatives)." The
policy therefore was to leave the release form signed by parents quite vague,
"in order that their conscience should not bother them later."[103]

Throughout the record is strewn a miscellany of signs that the bearing of
these killing folk was generally not mordant or macabre. One thinks of the
remark of Otto Ohlendorf, extermination squad commander in Russia, that he
inspected the shooting sites personally to be certain that they were "humane
under the circumstances."[104] One thinks also of the day in 1941 when the
psychiatric hospital at Hadamar observed the occasion of the cremation of its
ten-thousandth patient. There was an evening celebration. "Psychiatrists,
nurses, attendants, and secretaries all participated. Everybody received a
bottle of beer for the occasion."[105]

Is the record to be trusted when it tells us that the most devastating
massacre of history was largely accomplished by men and women whose inner
lives were immune to the murder whereby they earned their bread? As I read
them, these descriptions are, for the most part, not just self-serving and
desperate, intended to exculpate prisoners at the morrow's bar of justice.
They fairly portray a most puzzling state of spirit. One mobile unit member
who had personally presided over the liquidation of at least fifteen thousand

people explained that he had always been "inwardly opposed" to what he was doing. An occupation governor testified in court that only his "official soul" carried out the crimes for which he was to be hanged; his "private soul" had always been against them. Perhaps these men were, in some ironic sense, telling the truth.[106]

We do not easily believe such inconsistency to be bearable within one human character. But what these persons displayed and claimed was that they led an inconsistent life, regrettably, and that it was the gentle moments of domestic and comradely *Gemütlichkeit* that were expressive of their true and authentic character. In support of this they maintained that their work was very difficult.

Höss, who thought of himself as obligated to "perpetual self-mastery," admitted that the Gypsies were his "best-loved prisoners," and that he frequently joshed with them. (He noted, though, their habits of vagrancy and regretted that they produced a strange moral attitude that did not regard stealing as wicked.) It was all the harder on him when he was ordered to have the doctors dispose of them, starting with the sick and the children. "And it was precisely they who had such trust in the doctors. Nothing surely is harder than to grit one's teeth and go through with such a thing, coldly, pitilessly, and without mercy." By contrast, he saw the work of the mobile killing units as even more grueling. "Many members of the *Einsatzkommandos*, unable to endure wading through blood any longer, had committed suicide. Some had even gone mad. Most of the members of these *Kommandos* had to rely on alcohol when carrying out their horrible work."[107]

In his own camp it was the rare person who could bear the burden impassively. About one such person, a detail leader, Höss reported:

> P was always there at executions; he generally did his killing with a shot in the nape of the neck. I have often watched him and I could never see the slightest sign of emotion. As he carried on his fearful job he was calm and relaxed, unhurried and expressionless. Even when he was on duty in the gas chambers, I could never detect a trace of sadism. His face was always impassive and emotionless. Psychologically he had become so callous that he could go on killing uninterruptedly without a thought in his head. Of all those who actually had to do the killing P was the only one who never once took me quietly aside and poured out his heart over this fearful business.[108]

In Stangl's camp the men went to bed early after their shifts, tired from the work and strain. There was, he knew, much drinking in the barracks. He drank himself to sleep every night.[109] Staff at the Hadamar psychiatric killing center were said to drink themselves to oblivion nightly in the local *Gasthof*. Men who worked on the mobile units complained of chronic headaches after each unloading, associated with what one adjutant called "moral strain." One commander admitted that "nothing is worse for people spiritually than to have to shoot defenseless populations." Another, in the midst of a series of working luncheons to plan a changeover from shooting to gassing, had to go on sick leave twice. One soldier, describing how he sat for four hours steadily shooting Jews until they lay layers deep in a pit, said: "During this time we drank a lot of Schnappes to keep our spirits up." An SS man complained that "it wasn't exactly pretty to spray with machine-gun fire ditches crammed with thousands of Jews and then to throw earth on the bodies that were still twitching."[110]

Karl Brandt grieved, "Do you think that it was a pleasure for me to receive the order to permit euthanasia? For 15 years I had toiled at the sickbed and every patient was to me like a brother. I worried about every sick child as if it had been my own. My personal lot was a heavy one. Is that guilt?"[111] One killing unit commander, stung by criticism from above that the Jews (at least those sent from Germany, "from our own cultural level") were human beings and that he and his killers were maniacs and sadists who satisfied their sexual lust while shooting, expressed annoyance that "we, in addition to having to perform this nasty job, were also made the target of mudslinging."[112]

An entirely different way of construing these difficulties was to take pride in them. Hitler, when the war opened on the eastern front, had already forewarned his generals: "One of the sacrifices which commanders have to make is to overcome any scruples they may have."[113] When SS Major General Odilo Globocnik was asked whether it was wise simply to bury his victims and thus leave traces of his massacres behind in Poland, he replied with some heat: "Gentlemen, if there ever came a generation of such weaklings and spineless persons that they could not understand our great task, then indeed, National Socialism had been created for nothing. I am, on the contrary, convinced that we ought to bury bronze tablets there on which it would be perpetuated that we had the courage to accomplish this great and necessary task."[114]

Himmler adopted the same tone when addressing a group of SS leaders in 1943 on the "extermination of the Jews." "Eighty million worthy Germans and each one has his decent Jew. Of course, the others are vermin, but this one is an 'Al' Jew. Not one of those who talk this way has witnessed it, not one of them has lived through it. Most of you know what it means when a hundred corpses are lying side by side or five hundred or a thousand. To have stuck it out and at the same time—apart from exceptions caused by human weakness—to have remained decent men, that is what makes us hard. This is a page of glory in our history which has never been written and is never to be written."[115]

One detachment setting off for its duty post was exhorted by Himmler to be *übermenschlich-unmenschliche*: "superhumanly inhuman." Hannah Arendt sees Himmler as having governed human instinct in his troops by reconstruing it, turning it round: "So that instead of saying, What horrible things I did to people!, the murderers would be able to say: What horrible things I had to watch in the pursuance of my duties, how heavily the task weighed upon my shoulders!"[116]

One question inevitably comes up: if the work of liquidation was so ugly, why was it not somehow avoided? Some maintain that any person recruited to do the killing would himself have been done away with had he declined. The evidence does not support this. Physicians and nurses, for example, had the "mercy death" program explained to them and were then asked to cooperate.

Most did, but there seem to have been no severe reprisals against those few who did not.[117] Some SS men did leave the extermination camps; the greatest risk they ran, it seems, was denial of promotion.[118]

There was indeed some bluster about noncooperation. When Rascher's experiments encountered some foot-dragging, Himmler grumbled that this was probably due to religious backwardness. "It will take at least another ten years before we have rooted out this narrow-minded approach from our people." Later he became sharper: "I regard as traitors to their country those people who even today reject these human experiments and would rather see brave German soldiers die of the effects of chilling. I shall not hesitate to pass on the names of such gentlemen to the authorities in question." Basically, though, the claim that one might with impunity have withdrawn as a minister of the Holocaust is difficult to verify for want of examples of those who did.[119]

Another common defense is that had one refused to take part it would have made no difference: someone else would have done the deed. But this is not a claim made by everyone. Indeed, those involved often went out of their way to capitalize on their participation. The medical experimentalists, for instance, were publishing in professional journals the results of their lethal treatment of prisoners. The medical guild throughout the land was invited to take note.[120]

Loathsome though the works of death were said to be, resistance to them was supine. The hope instead was that they might be endured, perhaps even proudly, without their becoming characteristic of their doers. Those who killed do not so much argue that they were coerced into doing so. They point out that they remained, throughout the bloody business, decent fellows, not savages, and that like any good soldier they would one day put down their arms and go home to a peace won at tragic but needful cost. The question an outsider must ask, of course, is: Who is the survivor who goes home? What manner of man then is he? Has he really survived? Psychiatrist Leo Alexander offers comment on this. The members of the SS had been successfully trained to abandon their normal, earlier ethical standards. "Yet not only did they undergo a complete change of their superego ideals in their adult life, sometimes even in their late adult life, but after committing crimes in accordance with these new superego notions, most of them remained completely free from guilt feelings." Himmler eventually complained that his own people had become untrustworthy, filing reports he could not rely upon, filching confiscated goods for themselves, etc. "What Himmler did not understand was that what he himself deplored as a deterioration of the sacredness of property, honesty, and probity was an inevitable and inexorable result of the policy of spoliation, trickery, robbery, and murder which he and his henchmen had themselves instigated, but which they wanted to be directed against the Jews and the nationals of occupied territories. But the destructive principle had, as inevitably it must, gotten out of hand."[121]

In what is surely the strongest page in her study of Eichmann, Hannah Arendt speaks to this, and also to Robert Coles's query about the mind and motives of any mass murderer. Eichmann was, she judges, not demonically evil, not an open villain, no purposeful or malicious predator:

Eichmann was not Iago and not Macbeth, and nothing would have been farther from his mind than to determine with Richard III "to prove a villain." Except for an extraordinary diligence in looking out for his personal advancement, he had no motives at all. And this diligence in itself was in no way criminal; he certainly would never have murdered his superior in order to inherit his post. He *merely*, to put the matter colloquially, *never realized what he was doing. . . .*

He was not stupid. It was sheer thoughtlessness—something by no means identical with stupidity—that predisposed him to become one of the greatest criminals of that period. And if this is "banal" and even funny, if with the best will in the world one cannot extract any diabolical or demonic profundity from Eichmann, that is still far from calling it commonplace. . . . That such remoteness from reality and such thoughtlessness can wreak more havoc than all the evil instincts taken together which, perhaps, are inherent in man—that was, in fact, the lesson one could learn in Jerusalem.[122]

5: A Readiness to Kill—The Unlatching of Self-Preference

The agents of the Holocaust, as we have gazed at them, appear to have maintained towards their victim groups one attitude—of ruthless hostility and alienation—while fostering an entirely different attitude—one of close loyalty—towards their kinsfolk and comrades. From this one might surmise that these were people generally inclined to be peaceable, though prepared to strike out at particular groups who represented a threat to their people, their peace. Whether or not a given group fell afoul of the Nazi force would have been determined by the stance (or at least the perceived stance) of the adversary group. The evidence, however, is not very supportive of this surmise. The killers do not, in fact, appear to have been discriminating. What characterizes them is not so much a defensive readiness to destroy all major enemies of the state as it is a tempered willingness, once they had blood on their hands, to eliminate any person or group that constituted even a relatively mild frustration.

The first major Holocaust program was that of "mercy death" for chronic mental and medical patients. Originally scheduled to be eliminated were schizophrenics, epileptics, the senile, those with multiple sclerosis, polio, encephalitis, Parkinson's disease, Huntington's chorea, brain tumors, and similar serious disorders. Once the program was well underway the indications were, without any discernible previous expectation, enlarged. Originally, only those confined to hospitals had been listed; later, in northwestern Poland, the SS sent out mobile X-ray units, and anyone who showed traces of tuberculosis was sent off to an extermination center. When it became clear that the German people were more acquiescent in the elimination of the sick than in political or socioeconomic liquidations, psychiatrists and doctors were used to legitimate these other killings. Alexander records:

So-called "psychiatric experts" were dispatched to survey the inmates of camps with the specific order to pick out members of racial minorities and political offenders from occupied territories and to dispatch them to killing centers with specially made diagnoses such as that of "inveterate German hater," applied to a number of prisoners who had been active in the Czech underground.

Certain classes of patients with mental diseases who were capable of performing labor, particularly members of the armed forces suffering from psychopathy or neurosis, were sent to concentration camps to be worked to death, or to be reassigned to punishment battalions and to be exterminated in the process of removal of mine fields.[123]

Reitlinger presents evidence that already in 1941, before the Final Solution to the Jewish Question had been formulated, an early batch of three hundred Jews was shipped off to extermination under authority of contrived certifications of insanity. Thousands of others followed.[124] In the same year a commission of psychiatrists was sent to study inmates at Dachau, to winnow out a good number for extermination. Criteria were: (1) ability to work; and (2) political reports. When one such expert was later asked in court how it was that psychiatrists could make judgments interchangeably on medical and political grounds, he responded: "One cannot separate them."[125]

In time, doctors and nurses began to weed out, not the most crippled, but those patients whom they found more disagreeable. As for the children, soon they were being gassed or killed by injection for such things as having "badly modeled ears" or being chronic bed-wetters.[126]

The memorandum from Hitler initiating the process had prescribed "the most critical evaluation" of the diseases of its victims. The record shows an elaborate procedure. Local medical staff were to fill out extensive questionnaires on any handicapped or chronically ill persons. Each questionnaire was then examined by four expert psychiatrists, who indicated their evaluation by annotating it "+" or "−". No expert was allowed to evaluate patients from his own institution. Final judgment was then made by a chief expert. The entire process assumes another character, however, when one learns that one expert typically processed a batch of 300 questionnaires in two or three days (in addition to his ordinary workload). On other occasions he rendered 258 "most critical evaluations" of life or death in one day, and 2,190 in two weeks.[127]

The first of the killing programs, once initiated, soon began to shed the professional and discriminating caution it had been invested with at the start—or, perhaps, it began to show that all precautions had been a purposeful disguise for a work of death that would not willingly suffer itself to be restrained.

The technological developments, the evaporation of mild public unrest, and the blooding of camp staffs led to the second major extermination program, that of Bolshevik political commissars among the Soviet prisoners. They were an early group of victims at Auschwitz, dealt with by personnel who had served their apprenticeships with "mercy death" units.[128]

When the Jews' turn came, there was a progression in their torment.

First their "social disparity" was dealt with by a series of decrees excluding them from participation in the marketplace and in the professions, and in the civil and military services. Then they were removed from academic life. Then a series of incidents of staged thuggery was used as a pretext for imposing massive fines and exacting tributes from the Jewish community. Emigration was encouraged, but only if all property and currency were left behind and a stiff "flight tax" was paid. Then Jews were herded into ghettos as a "health measure." Then they were deported "for work" to "the East." Then they were gassed. Nora Levin remarks that in the summer of 1940 (at the ghetto stage), "no Jew in Poland could have known what lay ahead." But it may also be the case that most Germans, including even those who were to gas and cremate those Jews, could not then have known what lay ahead, or would have disbelieved it if told, for the work of killing moved by steps, not by a sudden lurch. Yet from the start there seems to have been a readiness to eliminate, an attitude of spirit which, once developed, stayed. And festered.[129]

As the Nazi state asserted itself to send people to their deaths, it simultaneously proposed to govern births. Reproduction policy would consistently and naturally harmonize with death policy. Already in the early 1930s it was state policy to encourage Germans (Nordic Germans) to increase and multiply. The Order of the Rabbit was awarded to mothers of large families: bronze for four children, silver for six, gold for eight. Women so decorated were entitled to public honors and provisions allowances and, later, household help from imported forced labor. It was not until 1943 that German women had to leave their homes to help in the factories, so high a national priority was the rearing of children. A wife's sterility or refusal to bear children became, in 1938, grounds for divorce. Laws against prostitution and homosexuality were energetically enforced (the death penalty is what "energetically" often meant). Abortion was severely proscribed. A doctor who under the Weimar Republic faced a token fine of forty marks for performing an abortion was now sentenced to six to fifteen years in a concentration camp.[130]

On the other hand, the Nuremberg Laws forbade marriages with Jews and facilitated the divorce of such existing unions. The terms of the Final Solution worked out by Eichmann's Wannsee Conference moved to obstruct marriages between Germans and Jewish *Mischlinge* ("mongrels"). Later laws made sexual intercourse between Germans and Jews (called *Rassenschande*, "racial shame") a grave crime. And abortion was made legal when either party suffered from an hereditary disease. Also, at this time Hitler had different intentions for his subject territories with respect to abortion. In a conversation in 1942, he made this clear:

> If any such idiot tried to put into practice such an order [forbidding abortion] in the occupied Eastern territories, he would personally shoot him. In view of the large families of the native population, it could only suit us if girls and women there had as many abortions as possible. Active trade in contraceptives ought to be actually encouraged in the Eastern territories, as we could not possibly have the slightest interest in increasing the non-German population.[131]

Himmler saw to it that in the eastern territories a reverse fertility program was instituted. Propaganda was put abroad that large families were undesirable, and multiple births dangerous to a woman's health. Abortion was made easily available and hygienic, as was sterilization.

For Germans, extramarital reproduction was no longer to suffer moral frowns. One man wrote to the woman who was then carrying his child in a *Lebensborn* (SS breeding establishment):

> When you say in your letter that it would be a great disgrace to bring an illegitimate child into the world, I must remind you of what you once said. Or do you change your mind from day to day, as I am almost beginning to think? My view of the matter, and also that of the Reich, is different. It is clear and straightforward, and not half-hearted. Nowadays there is no shame in a mother having an illegitimate child. On the contrary, it is the greatest happiness of a German mother. Those who take a different view have nothing in common with the present age. Heil Hitler![132]

On the other hand, blighted children of such unions were destroyed by infanticide. "No need was felt to exercise any tact or sympathy in informing the child's parents of the decision to 'disinfect' their offspring. . . . There was no need to explain to volunteers in the Führer's service that the abnormal child had died of a bad cold or an inflammation of the middle ear. They did not care how it died, for it rid them of a taint."[133]

As has been mentioned, two hundred thousand Aryan-looking Polish children were kidnapped and brought anonymously into the Reich for adoption, to augment the national genetic wealth. This program is difficult to understand, given all that was being said about Slavs as subhumans. A particularly bewildering instance is the Germanization of some of the children from the village of Lidice (everyone else in the village was killed in retaliation for the assassination of Reinhardt Heydrich).[134]

Sterilization was also a strategic instrument for genetic control. The 1935 law allowing parents with any hereditary disease to abort had, in fact, been an adjusting amendment to a 1933 law requiring such people to be sterilized.[135] It should also be known, though, that there were tentative and unrealized plans to castrate three million Jewish "mongrels," and also to liquidate English males and Germanize English females. Planned also was the sterilization of three million Bolshevik prisoners, so that they could be freed for war work.[136]

The record suggests that the Nazi *Züchtungsziel*, or "breeding drive," was akin to the *Vernichtung des lebensunwertes Lebens*, the "destruction of life not worth living," and the *endliche Lösung der Judenfrage*, the "final solution to the Jewish question." They all converge together into a consistent, spiraling ambition to evaluate and permit human life only on terms agreeable to the desires of those in power.

The result was a rapid cheapening of life. One thinks of the judge investigating a charge that a doctor had been poisoning several of his fellow SS personnel at a concentration camp. The judge called in four Russian prisoners and had a poison in the doctor's possession fed to them. They died with the same symptoms as had the SS personnel. Thus was murder established by murder. One also thinks of a group of girl prisoners at Treblinka who, as "work-Jews," had been befriended by the soldiers. They ate together and sometimes slept together. One day, after months of this camaraderie, when the camp was being dismantled, one of the noncoms got up from the table after lunch with the girls and said, "Well, girls, just one more trip for you [to the 'showers']." These are but two vignettes illustrative of a single, untrammeled, almost naively innocent readiness to kill.[137]

At Nuremberg the prosecution argued that the killing programs unfolded from one another, that the genocide of the six millionth Jew was somehow unleashed by the morphine overdose given the first harelipped child. Later commentators have agreed with this. Arendt writes, "The gassing in the East—or, to use the language of the Nazis, 'the humane way' of killing 'by granting people a mercy death'—began on almost the very day when the gassing in Germany was stopped. The men who had been employed in the euthanasia program in Germany were now sent east to build the new installations for the extermination of whole peoples."[138]

The story is told that when Abe Reles, a hit man for Murder, Inc., was asked by the prosecutor whether his conscience bothered him he replied: "How did you feel when you tried your first law case?" The district attorney answered that he had been nervous, but that later he got used to it. Said Reles: "It's the same with murder. I got used to it."[139]

The conclusion that each chapter of the Holocaust was a sequel to the prior one involves questions of interpretation that will remain open to debate. Indeed, there may be some Jewish objection to my including any victims but Jews under the very sacred title of Holocaust. One may, however, derive a devastating sense of how this was all a single, extended massacre by pondering two strikingly different reactions to the first killing project, the "mercy deaths."

On November 25, 1940, the wife of Walter Buch, president of the Supreme Nazi Party Court, received an agitated letter from her friend, Frau von Löwis (described as a "Nordic goddess come down from heaven"). The letter read:

> Nothing has so far shaken my confidence that "Greater Germany" will successfully overcome all difficulties and dangers standing in its way; believing in the Führer, I have been able to thread my way unerringly through all obstacles. But, as was said to me yesterday by a young one-hundred-per-cent enthusiastic Party member working in the Racial Policy office, what is now happening simply cuts the ground from under one's feet.
>
> Undoubtedly you know of the regulations under which the incurably insane can be got rid of. Probably, however, you have no idea how this is being done, nor on what an immense scale, nor of the deplorable impression it is making among people in general. *This tragedy is taking place* here in Württemberg in Grafeneck auf der Alb and the place now has a frightful reputation. At first people instinctively refused to believe it and thought that the rumours

were at least much exaggerated. In mid-October, at our last regular meeting at the *Gau* school in Stuttgart, I was assured on "well informed" authority that the regulations were applied only to absolute incurables and that "euthanasia" was used only after very careful verification of each case. This story can now be made credible to no one, since completely reliable evidence to the contrary is mushrooming. . . .

The frightful thing, the dangerous thing is not so much the fact that it is happening; if a law had been passed like the sterilization law, applicable only to a definite category of the insane people who really had no spark of human understanding or feeling, and if the law had prescribed the strictest possible professional control, then I am convinced that, after some initial reaction, people would have calmed down and accepted it, perhaps even more willingly than the sterilization law. . . .

There may be differing opinions as to how far men have the right to assume power of life and death over their fellow men; one thing, however, is certain: this right must be strictly circumscribed by law and used only with the utmost sense of responsibility, otherwise the door will be wide open to the most dangerous passions and crimes. After all, a favourite method of ridding oneself of embarrassing relatives has always been to have them certified as mad and send them to the lunatic asylum. . . .

The rule is now being applied not merely to the hopelessly imbecile and the hopelessly deranged. Apparently it is now gradually being interpreted to include *all* those sufferng from incurable mental illness—including even epileptics who are not mentally deranged at all. Among the victims are to be found many who can still take part in life, still do their modest bit of work. . . . What recruiting propaganda for the Catholic Church! . . .

I am convinced that we shall reap a bitter reward if we try to suppress or silence the popular feeling of revulsion against these goings on; it testifies to a sense of right and justice without which a people has set its foot irretrievably upon a slippery slope.[140]

In stark contrast with this is the story told of the reaction by the Dutch medical profession to the same program about one year later:

When Seyss-Inquart, Reich Commissar for the Occupied Netherlands Territories, wanted to draw the Dutch physicians into the orbit of the activities of the German medical profession, he did not tell them, "You must send your chronic patients to death factories," or "You must give lethal injections at Government request in your offices," but he couched his order in most careful and superficially acceptable terms. One of the paragraphs in the order of the Reich Commissar of the Netherlands Territories concerning the Netherlands doctors of 19 December 1941 reads as follows: "It is the duty of the doctor, through advice and effort, conscientiously and to his best ability, to assist as helper the person entrusted to his care in the maintenance, improvement and reestablishment of his vitality, physical efficiency and health. The accomplishment of this duty is a public task." The physicians rejected this order unanimously because they saw what it actually meant—namely, the concentration of their efforts on mere rehabilitation of the sick for useful labor, and abolition of medical secrecy. Although on the surface the new order appeared not too grossly unacceptable, the Dutch physicians decided that it is the first, although slight, step away from principle that is the most important one. The Dutch physicians declared that they would not obey this order.

When Seiss-Inquart threatened them with revocation of their licenses, they returned their licenses, removed their shingles and, while seeing their own patients secretly, no longer wrote birth or death certificates. Seiss-Inquart retraced his steps and tried to cajole them—still to no effect. Then he arrested 100 Dutch physicians and sent them to concentration camps. The medical profession remained adamant and quietly took care of their widows and orphans, but would not give in. Thus it came about that not a single euthanasia or nontherapeutic sterilization was recommended or participated in by any Dutch physician.[141]

Frau von Löwis abominated the killing she saw. Many of the victims were not truly incapacitated. Many were dear to their families. The whole thing was done so publicly and uncontrollably. If only they could have made do with sterilization, or perhaps eliminated only the thoroughly insane, it would not be such a discredit. Amid all the "differing opinions" about men rightfully killing fellow men, Frau von Lowis looked to the one source of certainty, the law, to clear up, "with the utmost sense of responsibility," just what killing was acceptable. Her basic principle was that she did not regard it as a crime to kill the innocent. She echoes the cry of Rudolf Höss at Auschwitz: "What is right? And what is wrong?" She was standing on the same slippery slope as were the SS men whose work she so deplored. All she had to steady her was her sense of good taste.

As for the Dutch doctors, they did not look to the laws to resolve for them the differences of opinion about killing. They simply preferred dying to killing. Killing, it seems from this Holocaust record, is a thing hard to condemn in one fashion if you have already accepted it or committed it in another.

6: There Was Profit in It—Where Blood Ran, Money Flowed

A sixth observation about the Holocaust is a brief one. A great deal of money was let loose by it. A final accounting would probably disclose that in the end it was a financial drain on the German state and economy. Billions of marks of earning power were sacrificed. Most victims were from outside Germany proper, and their assets had to be forfeit, not to the Germans, but to their subject governments. But what I wish to observe here is that the destruction of so many people released into nearby hands massive amounts of real and personal property, bullion, and currency. Some of the troves were prodigious. One estimate would locate 20 to 25 percent of the total wealth of prewar Hungary in Jewish hands. Some of Germany's largest industrial concerns, such as I. G. Farben and Krupp, were enabled to build immensely profitable plants inside the concentration and labor camps, utilizing the slave labor of hundreds of thousands of prisoners at a cost of little more than their eight-to-ten-pfennige daily keep. At every stage of the process Jews were being compelled to pay: special taxes, fines, penalties, expatriation fees, etc. Jewish money financed the *Lebensborn* breeding centers. Jews were made to pay the costs of their own deportation. And, in the last disgusting violation of their bodies at the moment of death, after hair had been shaved and spectacles taken and rings wrenched off and gold teeth broken off, their clothes were allotted to the national welfare agency for distribution to the unfortunate.[142]

At the operational level, where people were being tormented, ghettoized, deported, or exterminated, there was money flowing: wealth in loot or bribes or confiscation or labor or extortion. Some of the income was a matter of record. Doctors in the death camps, for instance, earned a monthly stipend of twelve hundred Reichsmarks, in view of their special duties, and for a young doctor that amount of income would indeed be an incentive. But most of the financial incentives were more furtive. Despite Himmler's attempts to control corruption (for him this meant personal profiteering), everyone who worked the Holocaust was party to an economy wherein there was considerable financial opportunity that did not have to be closely accounted for. Owners who disappeared left all behind. The Third Reich did not get rich from the plunder of the Holocaust, but there were lucrative possibilities for those who did this work for the Reich.[143]

7: The Disarming of the Sentinels—A Temporizing Resistance

After the Allied war crimes trials adjourned, the world was ostensibly left only with mourners of the Holocaust. Everyone, it seemed, had either been ardently opposed, paralyzed by horror, or ignorant of the carnage when it was taking place. Apart from a few rather misbegotten groups that wear the swastika at supermarket demonstrations, or the rumored gatherings of ODESSA, everyone is against the Holocaust. The documents of the time, however, persuade us that while the Holocaust was in progress it met with remarkable tolerance and even acceptance.

Just before Christmas of 1940, Heinrich Himmler, uneasy at the public unrest over the putrid, smoking chimney of one of the "mercy death" homes, suggested to Viktor Brack that he close the place and "disseminate information in a clever and sensible manner by showing motion pictures on the subject of inherited and mental diseases in just that locality."[144] A film was accordingly produced: *"Ich klage an,"* "I Accuse." The film presents the story of a woman suffering from multiple sclerosis. Her husband, a doctor, kills her, accompanied by a sympathetic colleague who plays soft piano music in the next room.[145]

For younger people these same ideas could be presented in school materials. One mathematics textbook offers an example:

> Problem 94. In a province of the German Reich there are 4400 insane in state mental institutions, 4500 under the care of public welfare, 1600 in district mental institutions, 2000 in homes for epileptics etc., and 1500 persons in Welfare Training Homes. The State alone pays out at least 10 million RM per annum for the said institutions.
>
> (a) Therefore, what does a patient cost the State on an average per annum? In the State mental institutions:
>
> I. 868 patients remained more than 10 years.
> II. 260 patients more than 20 years
> III. 112 patients more than 25 years
>
> (b) What does a patient of Group I (II, III) cost the State during the whole period of his accommodation according to the minimum average figures stated in (a)? (Compare with problem 96)
>
> Problem 95. The construction of an insane asylum required six million RM. How many new housing units at 15,000 RM each could have been built for this sum?
>
> Problem 96. According to various calculations an insane person costs the State about 1500 RM per annum, a pupil in school for the mentally deficient 300 RM, an elementary school pupil 100 RM, a pupil in secondary schools or colleges about 250 RM. Illustrate the amount graphically by stripes (rolls of coins).
>
> Problem 97. An insane person costs about four RM daily, a cripple five and a half RM, a criminal three and a half RM. In many cases a civil servant has only about four RM, an office employee barely three and a half RM, an unskilled laborer not even two RM per head in his family. (a) illustrate these figures graphically.
> According to cautious estimates there are in Germany 300,000 insane persons, epileptics, etc., under institutional care.
> (b) What is their total annual cost at a figure of four RM? (c) How many marriage-allowance loans at 1000 RM each, subject to renunciation of repayment (for each living born child of a marriage one-fourth of the original loan is written off) of the money later, could be paid out from this money yearly?[146]

Another effective propaganda device was the slogan. Perhaps the best known of these was original to the Nazis, but was struck first by Heinrich von Treitschke, a Berlin history professor, in 1893: *Die Juden sind unser Unglück*: "The Jews are our misfortune." A leading anti-Semite of the next generation would write that this phrase "became a part of my body and soul when I was 20 years old; it essentially influenced my later political work."[147]

The various Nazi propaganda initiatives, particularly those against Jews organized by Julius Streicher, are widely enough known not to need much citing here. What is worthy of note is that very important established and powerful groups seem to have yielded to them and acquiesced in the Holocaust. Three establishments in particular require attention in this regard: the medical profession, the churches, and the leaders of Jewish communities.

Dr. Servatius is somewhat to be pardoned for his lapse in Jerusalem, where he referred to the extermination activities as "medical matters." There was nothing medical about the slaughter, but it did require the active interest and cooperation of many medical professionals. Doctors were from the outset responsible for victim selection, for legitimation documents, for the execution process, for the torturous and lethal "experiments," for castration and sterilization and breeding, and for the technological development of newly efficient death procedures. As Alexander sums it up, "The physician gradually became the unofficial executioner for the sake of convenience, informality and relative secrecy."[148]

Other medical personnel participated also. Nurses took a hand in scheduling patients and prisoners for liquidation, and often in the actual killing. Red Cross trucks delivered the gas. The German Red Cross, in fact, once advanced one million Reichsmarks to the SS to fund the initial expenses of the death programs. There were also the "desk murderers"—medical administrators who rarely if ever killed a patient directly but who presided indirectly over the murder of hundreds of thousands.[149]

Alexander speculates that Gebhart, Rascher, and other physicians were drawn into this perversion of their guild's healing arts when their loyalty was questioned. They then exerted themselves to vindicate it in the eyes of the government.

> These cases illustrate a method consciously and methodically used in the SS, an age-old method used by criminal gangs everywhere: that of making suspects of disloyalty clear themselves by participation in a crime that would definitely and irrevocably tie them to the organization. In the SS this process of reinforcement of group cohesion was called "Blutkitt" (blood-cement), a term that Hitler himself is said to have obtained from a book on Genghis Khan in which this technic was emphasized.[150]

The entire medical profession had for some time been softened up for this work. The record shows little sagacity on their part about where they were being led. One interesting vignette from the past is found in the minutes of the annual meeting of the Union of Bavarian Psychiatrists in 1931. A paper was presented, "On the Question of Sterilization of the Mentally Abnormal." The introductory paragraphs point out that mental patient care costs the government 150 to 200 million Reichsmarks per annum. After this financial observation and overview the speaker recommends (with the support of serious researchers, he expects, and against opposition begotten of emotional hesitancy or legal or ethical scruples) widespread eugenic sterilization.

In the discussion that followed this presentation, Dr. Otto Bumke of Munich got to his feet. After extensive and detailed comments on the paper he offered two observations:

We cannot address this [genetic] problem either from the standpoint of some instant scientific data or under provocation of a temporary economic crisis. If we can prevent the spread of mental illnesses by sterilization, then we surely ought to do so—not because it saves the government money, but because every mental illness means endless distress for the sick person and for his relatives. Economic considerations here would be not only inappropriate but positively dangerous. One needs only to think through a proposal to eliminate on financial grounds all men who are suddenly expendable, and figure out its implications, to realize the rather staggering result: we would then have to slay not just all the mentally ill and the psychopaths, but all the cripples, including war veterans, all elderly spinsters who have no occupation, all the widows who no longer have children to raise, and all persons living on investments or pensions. That would surely save us money, but we are not likely to do it.

Secondly, may I suggest that propaganda for sterilization be presented with a certain restraint until the political atmosphere in our country has somewhat improved, and scientific racial theories can no longer be employed for political advantage. Introduce the discussion on sterilization into the battlefield of politics today, and there will likely be little talk about mental patients, but much more about Aryans and non-Aryans, of the blond Germanic race and less valuable round-headed ones. It is surely not apparent that anything positive would result. Instead, science in general and heredity and eugenics in particular would suffer mischief which we could not later easily undo.

This excerpt is interesting, but not because it takes a stand on principle. Dr. Bumke had forsworn principle when he accepted eugenic sterilization. What he does stand on is a realistic understanding, before the Nazis had yet come into power, of what kinds of service his profession was likely to be summoned to give—and was already preparing itself to give. What makes his remarks memorable is that, unprincipled though they were, they constitute as bold a public rebuke as the Nazi program was to sustain from a German physician. It was rare—almost unique—and it was before 1933. It was unheard.[151]

There was a special stake in the Holocaust for medical researchers so inclined. Some instances have been mentioned; there are many others. All bodies of defective children born and then destroyed in the *Lebensborn* homes, for example, were dissected out of scientific curiosity. It mystified German science that such carefully chosen Nordic stock could produce infants with genetic blemishes.[152]

There was also a scramble for bodies and bones. When anatomy professor August Hirt set about assembling a collection of body casts for his institute, he requested that captured Russian Jews, both men and women, be brought to Strassburg alive so that he might arrange for a "subsequently induced death" in such fashion "that the heads not be damaged." They were not; the U.S.

Army arrived unexpectedly to find 150 bodies still floating in formaldehyde.[153]

Some German laboratory people also harbored a scientific curiosity about the Polish intelligentsia. When Dr. Witasek of Poznan and a group of his comrades in the resistance movement were executed, their heads were removed and sent back in gunnysacks to Germany for study.[154] Professor Julius Hallervorden, who was shipped six hundred preserved brains of "mercy death" victims for his research in neuropathology, testified after the war: "There was wonderful material among those brains: beautiful mental defectives, malformations and early infantile diseases. I accepted these brains, of course [he had requested them]. Where they came from and how they came to me was really none of my business." One American professor commented that Hallervorden "merely took advantage of an opportunity."[155]

Possibly that is the most appropriate post-mortem to the hundreds of medical personnel who agreed to kill for the Third Reich: they merely took advantage of an opportunity.

The resistance, or lack thereof, of the Christian churches to National Socialism, particularly to its Jewish policies, has been the concern of a vast and still unconcluded literature which need have no recapitulation here. But there are several assertions that can be made and substantiated. When Nazi anti-Semitism moved from talk to action, the party kept a wary eye peeled to see what Christian leaders would do. There were some early and vigorous remonstrances to the Nuremberg Laws. But the Nazis noticed then that the German churches took their stand, not on the pure issue of the human or civil rights of all Jews, but on an expedient and self-serving concern for Christian Jews. The church-state struggle at that time concerned whether "Jew" was an ethnic or a religious category. The next time the churches were aroused came when the "mercy death" massacres occurred almost in public view. Here the protests eventually caused Hitler to draw back awhile, but not before he had determined that the Christian churches enjoyed quite limited influence in the political order. So, when the liquidation program moved east, turned genocidal, and swept away millions, it was beyond the ability of the churches to oppose Hitler publicly and effectively. Nor did they try.

There were individually brave men, such as Pastor Martin Niemöller and Pastor Braune and Bishop Preysing of Berlin. There were also clergymen who helped with the Holocaust, like several Protestants already mentioned, and Albert Hartl, an unfrocked Catholic priest who worked in the SS Reich Security Office, and Josef Roth, another former priest, who worked in the Reich ministry that dealt with the churches. There were courageous and anonymous clergy and members of religious orders here and there who sheltered victims and helped them escape. There was, however, no concerted, public, official stand taken by any major Christian church in Germany against the Holocaust. After the war the Protestant *Evangelische Kirche in Deutschland* confessed: "Before the God of mercy we share in the guilt for the outrage committed against the Jews by our own people through omission and silence."[156]

It is instructive to review Christian reactions in Hungary, first an Axis ally and later an occupied satellite. In 1938 Christian deputies in parliament gave noisy support to the repressive and disabling Second Jewish Law (à la Nuremberg). The Jewish community appealed openly to their Magyar Christian fellow-citizens to support them in their calls for justice. When more legislation was being prepared in 1941, the churches did protest, though to no effect. When Jews were being tormented and ghettoized in 1944 the papal nuncio, the cardinal primate, and the chief bishop of the Reformed Church all protested. But what they objected to was the inclusion of Christian Jews, even clergy and members of orders, in the persecution. They were accordingly appeased . . . for the moment. Then they protested again, this time for all Jews but especially for Christian Jews. The Catholic bishop of Kassa, in full pontifical garb, led a procession of protest to a local concentration camp.

More loudly now the bishops objected, spurred by calls from the Jewish community. The nuncio again intervened. Cardinal Serédi prepared a pastoral letter; but most copies were confiscated by the government and a medley of threats and promises persuaded him to withdraw it entirely. After that old Serédi avoided all requests for a joint protest with Lutherans and Evangelicals. At lower levels the parish churches started baptizing Jews to provide them with some immunity. The nuncio actually went out on the highways with a few cooperative and courageous Red Cross officials and strove desperately to rescue Jews from deportation, having atrocities filmed and issuing Vatican passports and identity cards.[157]

The Hungarian saga, compared with the more subdued German story, suggests two things. First, the appeals, though repeated and strenuous—and sometimes brave—never overcame the early perception that the churches had a more authentic interest in the religious rights of their own members than in the human rights of all mankind. Even when this position gave way to a straightforward outcry on the Jews' behalf, it was addressed to a government that had found the churches' range. Second, the fearless ventures of the middle leadership can be dishonored by the foot-dragging of their superiors; yet the superiors are generally more exposed to threats of reprisal, not so much against themselves as against those they wish to shelter.

Many Jews also collaborated with their own destroyers, partly under duress, partly under the impression that they might forestall worse treatment, partly to save their own skins. Jewish councils ruled the ghettos under Nazi orders, and often arranged for deportation roundups. Jewish auxiliary police patrolled the ghettos. Jewish *Kapos* policed the camps. Jewish workers despoiled and burned their brothers' and sisters' bodies.

The largest questions raised are two. First, why did the Jewish leaders not rise, revolt, resist? Why was the battle of the Warsaw Ghetto not accompanied by many others, fought by desperate and angered Jews? Possibly the best response is offered by Raul Hilberg. For two thousand years Jews, as a vulnerable and oppressed minority, had always survived precisely by not revolting. There were age-old strategies that had helped them weather ugly storms: emigrating, presenting appeals, complying with minor impositions, playing for time. Hilberg sees that during the Holocaust all of these maneuvers failed, though they had served so well so long. This time the Jews were duped, paralyzed, overwhelmed.[158]

Perhaps Hilberg's most insightful observation is that the compliance of the victims may have been an evil gradually succumbed to, like the rapacity of their destroyers.

> Let us not suppose, however, that compliance was easy. If it was difficult for the Germans to kill, it was harder still for the Jews to die. Compliance is a course of action which becomes increasingly drastic in a destruction process. It is one thing to comply with an order to register property but quite another to obey orders in front of a grave. The two actions *are* part of the same habit—the Jews who registered their property were also the ones who lined up to be killed. The Jews who lined up on a killing site were the ones who had registered their property. Yet these two activities are very different in their effects. Submission is altogether more burdensome in its last stages than in its beginning, for as one goes on, more and more is lost. Finally, in the supreme moment of crisis the primeval tendency to resist aggression breaks to the surface; resistance then becomes an obstacle to compliance, just as compliance is an obstacle to resistance. In the Jewish case the cooperation reaction was the stronger one until the end. The Jews consequently dealt with their resistance in much the same way as the Germans dealt with their consciences.[159]

A second question is why some Jews turned on their fellow victims. Some of the Jewish councils took the occasion to put on high and prideful airs. Jewish police enjoyed exemption from deportation for their families, "but that exemption depended on slavish obedience to Jewish authority. One policeman, trying to wrest a child from its father, responded to the father's plea: 'What makes you think I'm human? Maybe I'm a wild beast. I have a wife and three children. If I don't deliver five heads by five P.M., they'll take my children. Don't you see, I'm fighting for the life of my own kids?' "[160]

Jewish council members explained that they might be able to make things easier on their people. One council president wrote: "When the question arose whether Jewish orderlies should pick up Jews for deportation, I took the position that it would be better for them to do it, because they could at least be more gentle and helpful than the Gestapo and make the ordeal easier. It was scarcely in our power to oppose the order effectively."[161]

Another explanation was that by negotiation at least some Jews would be saved. Hannah Arendt is not persuaded by this:

> Dr. Kastner, in Hungary, for instance, saved exactly 1,684 people with approximately 476,000 victims. In order not to leave the selection to "blind fate," "truly holy principles" were needed "as the guiding force of the weak human hand which puts down on paper the name of the unknown person and with this decides his life or death." And whom did these "holy principles" single out for salvation? Those "who had worked all their lives for the *zibur*

[community]"—i.e., the functionaries—and the "most prominent Jews," as Kastner says in his report. . . .

By being asked to make exceptions, and by occasionally granting them, and thus earning gratitude, [the Nazis] had convinced their opponents of the lawfulness of what they were doing.[162]

What might we see here, in the sad and simultaneous cooptation into this great and savage blood bath of these three groups we would like to think of as unlikely aides to the Nazis: those who served by healing and comforting the sick; those who spoke for Jesus, the Jew of Nazareth, who died for all mankind; and those who were the chosen spokesmen and caretakers of the Jewish communities? What might we say? That all three stumbled in the same way. Confronted with clear hatred and grave injustice at the very start, they temporized. They thought they might go some modest distance with National Socialism to win a point, to await a better day, to avoid disaster, to save some leverage. No one, it is true, could know what was coming eventually. But the disposition to destroy was there from the first. The enemy which all three groups were sworn to oppose came onto the field with pennants showing. All three groups folded theirs. No one who acquiesced in the Holocaust can say that any good was served, in the outcome, by all their cleverness.

Post-Mortem on the Holocaust

It is dispiriting to pass in review so compact an encyclopedia of depraved and perverse blood-crime. It is necessary, however. We are not trying to analyze a single outburst of killing rage. We are trying to understand a massacre wrought over years by thousands of persons who would at the time have resisted the accusation that they were depraved and perverse criminals. It was a massacre beheld by millions of acquiescent citizens who, in the troubled rush of events, the urgency of the national conflict, the lack of familiar precedent, the disagreement among authorities, by contrast with the assertive certainty of those who did the killing, withheld their condemnation. It was a massacre which in its aftermath was seen by all to be an unspeakable and revolting tragedy. Our endeavor here, since these tragedies seem so difficult to recognize while underway, is to disengage some characteristic traits of the Holocaust that would serve to alarm us if we found them reoccurring in our own time.

Let us recapitulate briefly.

1. *It was necessary to depersonalize in order to kill.* Preliminary propaganda and in-group recruitment stressed that the target groups were inferior creatures, or so crippled by nature that they would be fortunate if released from the life that stretched before them. Later, when the victims were actually undergoing destruction, their treatment was by design so bestial, so undignifying, that the practitioners of death were rarely to have their composure shaken by glimpses of the truth: that those perishing at their hands without outcry were their silent, subdued, contorted brothers and sisters. The victims, it was said, were not only subhuman themselves. They would drag down the life quality of the rest of the people: economically, by draining the economy and its medical resources; genetically, by contaminating the

healthy, striving population with an admixture of uncontributory dependents. The question was never posed as involving the human rights of the victim, but always as regretting the toll they took on society's aspirations. At other junctures of history, perhaps, this burden might have been borne, but in a time when resources were short and there were vital needs that could be met only through the efforts of those of untrammeled strength, it would be too much of a drain, too fruitless an effort, to divert massive wherewithal simply to help these inferior and dependent ones to survive. At a time when some achievements are urgent but not all are possible, people of lesser or nil human status cannot be given the luxury of equal treatment.

2. *Murder*—the elimination of groups of innocent persons, not for any alleged crime or militancy—*had to be clothed in a counterfeit language.* A campaign, barbaric at every step, to torment and kill millions of people was exposed and construed in a vocabulary as ersatz as wartime coffee. It was not a coy or elusive or indirect vocabulary: it was totally mendacious. "To be cleansed" meant to be mangled in one's own blood; a "discharge certificate" was a death order. The perversion of language dragged down bystanders, so that even churchmen began babbling about "unworthy life" and Jews began to be grateful for being "humanely" trucked to their executions, and lawyers could talk of purposely murderous procedures by doctors as "medical matters." Despite the absurdity of this double talk when heard from the record, it does not seem to have been devised primarily as an adroit cover-up for what savage men and women wished to conceal from the world. Worse, it allowed them to conceal from themselves the blunt and dirty fact that were committing murder.

3. *Everyone who was responsible had a clear and careful theory about who was responsible.* There was no haphazard guessing about who was responsible for all these deaths. Those involved had often worked out—in writing, before any killing began—a line of accountability that always led away from themselves. Subordinates said it was the decision of superiors; superiors, of subordinates; the doctors, of statesmen; statesmen, of doctors; Germany, of barbaric Easterners; Easterners, of their German masters. Before the demands of the law, the commands of the military authority, the desperate needs of the state, the emergency of the time, or their own peril, men took up the garrote, the syringe, the machine gun, the can of gas pellets—and all, as they thought, were free of the responsibility. One cannot really contradict them. They had, by killing innocent men, women, and children because "they had to," actually forfeited and lost their responsibility. By a "strange interdependence of thoughtlessness and evil" they had yielded up that authority over one's own life which is characteristic of free humans.

4. *This work was thought to be one of duty and committed service, not of preference or pleasure; hence it was neither vicious nor typical of those who did it.* The agents of extermination contrast themselves with squalid and unnatural killers who slay with enjoyment. Their moral sense, they point out, is intact: they are concerned about corruption, stealing, laziness. Almost compulsively they cleave to their families, protect their children. While somewhat regretting what they must do, bringing other homes into mourn-

ing, they find solace from the burdens of duty in their own homes. They are decent, sometimes religious, gentle to animals, and especially sensitive about their stake in their professional guild. In a word, they are mass murderers who believe that their work is somehow sequestered from the rest of their lives. Here, once again, the claim is probably to be allowed: not to exculpate them, but to acknowledge that by some bizarre disintegration they had come to lead lives of no coherence, no integrated sense or value. Without that coherence there could be no piercing of the abscess, no repenting, no truth.

5. *Once having disposed of a first victim-crop, one had lost all ground for objection when others were presented.* There is a sort of virginity about murder; once one has violated it, it is awkward to refuse other invitations by saying, "But that would be murder!" And there seems to be an uncanny sense of powerful achievement when one's first victims are removed, with no cry from them and little from any defenders. The "slippery slope" does not entail blooded killers looking actively for other categories of victims. What it does mean is that a primicide is particularly unlikely to argue about a second request for his services; more unlikely still, about a third. The Holocaust began with murder, but with wary, secret, and cautious murder. By some sort of inner momentum it became unhesitant, voracious, omnipotent. Population policy, which was an amalgam of birth incentives, breeding establishments, and kidnapping to secure the right sort of youth, and contraception, sterilization, castration, abortion, and infanticide to eliminate the wrong sort, laid dictatorial claims on life-giving that were matched by those asserted over life-ending. Invasion of a neighbor's life is, apparently, a compellingly progressive kind of art.

6. *Those who kill many do not go unrequited.* They are paid for their pains. The call of burdensome duty was assuaged by opportunities for wealth. Despite much talk about dull and wearying work, conformity to orders, and routine, the staff of the Nazi killing organization virtually all enjoyed a level of luxury previously beyond their means. This became even more the case when the rate of death was greatly increased.

7. *Timid and temporizing resistance, as unprincipled as the crime itself, was able to be outwitted, appeased, quashed.* The fear of those who conceive such a program of destruction, which makes its way in stealth and ambiguity and muddle, is that some sentinel will let fly a sharp shout in the darkness, and cry aloud the name of what is being done. In the Holocaust the sworn sentinels never did that.

A murderer is someone who has committed murder and never purged himself of it. An accessory to murder is someone who has seen it done and has cooperatively kept silent. Complicity, like crime, has a deflowering at its start. The attempts to blunt the prongs of savagery, or to bargain for fewer victims, or to acquiesce in some crimes while negotiating to stop others, or to have the crimes done less painfully, or to await some "later" moment of strategic influence: all this meant defeat during the Holocaust. The medics, the clergy, the Jews themselves all began by selective objection, by calculatedly partial outcry, which was doomed to become less vociferous as the killing became more so. It was too late at the start. To save one victim by yielding another is implausible. At the end your saved victim will also go, and you too. No one can count on outwitting those ready to kill.

Is the Pattern Unique?

After studying the Holocaust and probing for its features, I wondered whether this pattern of man's inhumanity to man allowed of other instances. Could these same characteristics be found in other programs of human destruction and exploitation that we commonly regard as tragedies in our past? One such comparison I resolved to explore was with the program Americans called "internment" for Japanese from the western United States during the Second World War. From 1942 until 1945, 110,000 persons were arrested in the Pacific coastal states and imprisoned, without regard for the fact that 70,000 were citizens of the United States. Their property, real and personal, was in most cases lost without fair compensation. The only avenue of release was enlistment in the armed forces. The Japanese Americans were not killed or physically tortured or enslaved. Their treatment was such, however, as to make one fear the possibility of its recurrence. In a concurring opinion in one of a series of Supreme Court decisions which denied these Americans equal protection under the Constitution, Justice Frank Murphy noted "the melancholy resemblance to the treatment accorded to members of the Jewish race in Germany." There is much to sustain his observation.[163]

The Pacific coast had earlier been populated by Chinese, before the Japanese immigrants came. By the late nineteenth century, the Chinese settled in California had been subjected to much mistreatment:

> Subject to physical persecutions and cheating at the hands of rougher elements in the frontier population in California, the Chinese had no recourse to the courts. They were ineligible for citizenship, and since they were "heathens" they were considered unfit to testify truthfully in their own or others' behalf or to take court oaths. In the eighteen-seventies laws were passed in California prohibiting corporations from employing Chinese. There was a special tax on Chinese miners and a head tax, and licenses to do business were often denied. Agitators portrayed the Chinese as Asiatic hordes bent upon overtaking and destroying the white populace. In 1879 President Hayes vetoed an act of Congress that would have stopped Chinese immigration, but three years later Congress succeeded in passing the Chinese Exclusion Act. In the meantime, Japanese immigration had begun, and anti-Japanese prejudice was superimposed on the already existing anti-Chinese feeling.[164]

The "Yellow Peril" persecution was largely inherited by the newly arrived Japanese in this country. On St. Patrick's Day, 1900, a San Francisco paper had this to say about both Oriental groups:

> Chinatown with its reeking filth and dirt, its gambling dens and obscene slave pens, its coolie labor and bloodthirsty tongs, is a menace to the community; but the snivelling Japanese, who

swarms along the streets and cringingly offers his paltry service for a suit of clothes and a front seat in our public schools, is a far greater danger to the laboring portion of society than all the opium-soaked pigtails who have ever blotted the fair name of this beautiful city.[165]

From that time until World War II, the Japanese in this country, by birth or immigration, faced unrelenting vilification. The war naturally intensified it. A federal judge, shortly before the war, had ruled that a Washington law forbidding Japanese even to lease land was not discriminatory because Chinese were bound by the same restriction. "Further, he found yellow or brown skin to be the 'hallmark of the Oriental despotisms'; people possessing it were not able to adjust to a republican form of government." As General DeWitt, who was put in charge of the arrest and deportation of Japanese Americans, said, "A Jap's a Jap. . . . You can't change him by giving him a piece of paper." And Governor Chase Clark of Idaho elaborated in a speech: "The Japs live like rats, breed like rats and act like rats."

One member of Congress suggested that Negro and Japanese blood donated through the Red Cross be labeled so as not to contaminate Caucasians. One VFW post commander said he would not want any Japanese blood, and he didn't think any serviceman would. In some areas there was resistance by veterans to the burial of fallen Nisei soldiers in national cemeteries. A California assemblyman, chairman of a legislative committee dealing with Japanese Californians, received from a friend a clipping announcing that three Nisei boys had been killed in action in Italy, with this added note in the margin: "Here are three Japanese who will not be coming back to California." The assemblyman returned it with his own note: "Glory! Hallelujah! Hallelujah! Hallelujah!" One pamphlet in circulation, entitled *Slap the Jap Rat*, advised that "no Jap is fit to associate with human beings."[166]

Close observers believed that the arduous existence of Japanese on the coast made them both withdrawn and misunderstood. "The effect on the Issei [first-generation immigrants; Nisei were children of Issei born in America as citizens] of the series of drastic prohibitions in the form of alien land legislation, the exclusion law, and ineligibility for citizenship was to thwart their desire to merge in the general American community and to increase ingrown tendencies among them." They accepted imprisonment as they had all previous misery, with a restrained submission, but the intolerable strains they underwent in the camps led to the bitter quip that the camps should be run as mental institutions.[167]

There is a clear pattern of depersonalization by word and by treatment, after which the victims begin to act strangely and to confirm their tormentors in their original judgment.

As for euphemisms, they were common. After President Roosevelt had made a slip of the tongue in a 1942 news conference and referred to "concentration camps" for Japanese Americans, this too-suggestive phrase was quickly denied. As one cynical UCLA professor put it, they were not concentration camps, "just a place where you got shot if you stepped outside." They were called "wartime communities," or "relocation centers," and the prisoners were "colonists" or "residents." A pamphlet of definitions and vocabulary was issued by the government.[168]

Responsibility for the imprisonment was laid upon the necessities of war. At the start of hostilities the Department of Justice said it would deal with Japanese Americans individually. Their care was then transferred to the War Department, which dealt with them as a racial group, invoked the president's war powers to extinguish their constitutional rights, and had this act sustained in the courts both during and after the war. All this was done in a climate of invasion fear. Martin Dies, chairman of the House Un-American Activities Committee, claimed knowledge of a spy ring of 150,000 members. Senator Stewart stated: "There is no such thing as a Japanese not being a subject of the Emperor of Japan." Hollywood produced a series of propaganda films on espionage and sabotage by Japanese Americans. A columnist in the *Los Angeles Times* wrote: "I am for immediate removal of every Japanese on the West Coast to a point deep in the interior. . . . Sure, this would work an unjustified hardship on 80 percent or 90 percent of the California Japanese. But, the remaining 10 or 20 percent have it in their power to do damage— great damage to the American people. They are a serious menace and you can't tell me that an individual's rights have any business being placed above a nation's safety. If making 1,000,000 [*sic*] innocent Japanese uncomfortable would prevent one scheming Japanese from costing the life of an American boy, then let 1,000,000 innocents suffer. . . . Personally, I hate the Japanese."[169]

How justified was this appeal to necessity? That may be judged by two facts: there was not a single instance on the mainland of espionage or sabotage by Japanese American citizens or residents during the entire war (though many Caucasians were apprehended); the 442nd Regimental Combat Team (a segregated Nisei outfit serving in the European theater) received the highest percentage of Purple Hearts ever awarded an American unit, while in the Pacific MacArthur's intelligence chief credited Nisei soldiers with having shortened the war by two years.[170]

It is difficult to document any disavowal of vicious intent by those who mistreated the Japanese Americans. On the one hand, those who imprisoned them did not regard the detention as a serious imposition: Japanese, after all, were accustomed to live in squalor. Besides, this treatment seemed increasingly lenient as stories of war atrocities began to circulate in America.

There is much evidence, however, not just of a "slippery slope," but of an avalanche of victimization. First, there was a legacy from the past. Orientals were denied by law the possibility of naturalization. In 1913 California denied aliens who were ineligible for citizenship (meaning Orientals) the right to own land and provided that land already owned could not be transmitted to heirs. In 1920, by public referendum, California removed even the right to lease land, and in 1922 the right to be tenant farmers or sharecroppers. Similar laws were then adopted by every state with a substantial Japanese American population, with the exception of Utah. In Oregon and Washington fishing was forbidden to Orientals. Then Japanese were denied admittance to theaters, swimming pools, barbershops (their hair was "too coarse"), many labor unions, and virtually all skilled employment. In Oregon a fruit-stand proprietor who employed alien help was obliged to warn the public of this by a large placard.[171]

This process of victimization simply continued during wartime. At the very start General DeWitt had dismissed the suggestion of group imprisonment as "damned nonsense." He began to speak of contraband raids, then of alien naturalization, then of removal from around defense installations. Then, without warning, the Japanese Americans were quickly evacuated—so quickly that they could not secure their property. A custodian of their assets was to have been appointed, but none was. They were not allowed to vote by absentee ballot. Measures were introduced in Congress to annul the citizenship of native-born Americans of Japanese ancestry. In the meantime they were compelled to serve in the military. Proposals were made to disenfranchise them, to deport them all, even to sterilize them, or at least to intern the sexes separately so as to prevent reproduction. As late as February 1945 a congressman was suggesting appropriations to sterilize them all. Much of this sort of thinking was sponsored by Charles Goethe, a wealthy Californian whose two principal public concerns were the expulsion of Orientals and the Eugenics Society. One of his pamphlets noted with pleasure that the Immigration Acts of 1921 and 1924 were some of the earliest eugenics legislation by a world power, though Nazi Germany was the "first nation of prime rank to enact a complete program of both negative and positive eugenics."[172]

The disposition to mistreat, once established, had a clear run. Since earlier injustice had been inflicted with impunity, there was little ground for objecting to later abuse.

Was there much wealth at stake? Besides the expectable adversaries of the Japanese Americans, both patriotic (American Legion, United Spanish War Veterans, Disabled American Veterans, Military Order of the Purple Heart, Veterans of Foreign Wars) and xenophobic (Native Sons and Daughters of the Golden West, Oriental Exclusion League, Joint Immigration Committee), there was another group of predators with an obvious orientation: the California Farm Bureau Federation, Western Growers' Protective Association, California Real Estate Association, California Grange, American Federation of Labor, Associated Farmers (an antiunion group) . . . yea, even the California Baby Chicks Association.

Whence all this agribusiness interest? Japanese Americans, who could not own land until the second, native-born generation had come to adulthood, had, back in 1920, controlled (though not necessarily through ownership) only 1.6 percent of California farmland. On this land, often scrub and vacant before they were permitted to work it, they had succeeded in raising 13 percent of the state's produce, including 92 percent of the strawberries, over 80 percent of the celery and asparagus, and 66 percent of the tomatoes. Since that day, in the face of withering legal disabilities and social exclusion, this people had showed it had no equal in the fertility of its agriculture. Once the Japanese Americans had been uprooted from the coast, their farmlands were purchased at ridiculous prices and the other growers closed in to occupy their share of the market—never so lucrative as in wartime. Thus these powerful and greedy groups were not disposed to have the Japanese Americans come back. No one has calculated how many tens of millions of dollars of damages this would all represent, for the courts never allowed them to be claimed.[173]

What kind of advocacy did the Japanese Americans have on their behalf? Not much. The courts ruled continually against them. The American Civil Liberties Union, potentially a natural and formidable ally, took a compromised stance. Though willing to dispute various actions taken by local or subordinate authority, the ACLU was unwilling to challenge the basic order to imprison them. "The fact that the Executive Order was issued by Roosevelt significantly altered the protest. Roosevelt was a figure of great personal appeal with a deserved reputation as a champion of the underdog. It seemed inconceivable to civil libertarians, some of whom were his personal friends, that he could be taking such a drastic action on inadequate evidence." The national office therefore restrained its local offices from very vigorous advocacy.[174]

The churches tended to take no notice nationally. Locally they canceled each other out. The Los Angeles Federation of Churches advised against the return of Japanese Americans. The Catholic Interracial Council wanted the ban lifted. The *American Baptist Home Mirror* called for fair play, and the General Council of the Methodist Church, as well as the Christian Church in Los Angeles and San Jose, strongly supported the deportees. But the only aggressively active ecclesiastical friend was the Friends, the Quakers, through the American Friends Service Committee.[175]

The victims had their own protection group, the Japanese American Citizens League. It had a distinguished history of service, but its work on behalf of the community during the war was short and controversial. Girdner and Loftis write:

> JACL leaders . . . met with West Coast officials and learned that the die was cast. A Nisei, returning home from the meeting, summed it up for his family in two words, "We lost." But they had snatched a concession from the defeat. In exchange for a promise of their active cooperation with the projected evacuation, they would be allowed to confer with General Dewitt's staff on how it was to take place in order to lessen the hardship for the people.
>
> Some Japanese-Americans continued to protest. "Has the Gestapo come to America?" asked James Omura, an editor. Lincoln Kanai of the San Francisco YMCA said that to confuse Nisei with enemy alien groups was "diametrically opposed to the Constitution and the objectives of the war." The capitulation of the JACL was to be an underlying cause of the hatred many evacuees expressed toward the organization once the gates of the relocation centers closed upon them. They felt that a small group of Nisei spokesmen had betrayed them. Mike Masaoka claims that the JACL, the only organized Japanese-American group to step forward at the time, had no choice but to accept the dictates of the Western Defense Commander. The Army had two evacuation

plans, one to be used if the Nisei cooperated, and a second, to be enforced with guns and bayonets, if they did not. JACL officers had considered courting arrest as a means of protesting, but decided that such action would leave the communities leaderless.[176]

There were, then, opponents of internment, but they were timorous and temporizing.

The pattern of the Holocaust, emergent in the features we see on the face of Germany in those years, can be seen in American treatment of its Japanese American citizens and residents. It was, of course, not so horrible. They were dispossessed, disenfranchised, deported, but they were not tortured and killed. Yet if in our country tens of thousands of innocent citizens were stripped of their rights and made subject to whatever the War Department wished to do with them, would they have survived if the War Department had chosen to exterminate them instead of imprisoning them? It was a time of stress here as it was in Germany. The same notice was taken of this tragedy here as was taken there of Treblinka and all it stood for. Would it have intensified if we had also built gas chambers and ovens? One is haunted by a statement of one American imprisoned in his youth because he was of Japanese extraction: "There is no question in my mind that if the United States Government wanted to run death ovens we would have marched quietly to our doom with only slight hesitation."[177]

The pattern is there. I fear too that it was there as the United States set about the destruction of Vietnam. One thinks of all the euphemisms. Michael Herr describes "the cheer-crazed language of the MACV Information Office, things like 'discreet burst' (one of these tore an old grandfather and two children to bits as they ran along a paddy wall one day, at least according to the report made later by the gunship pilot), 'friendly casualties' [shooting one's own troops or allies] (not warm, not fun), 'meeting engagement' (ambush), concluding usually with 17 or 117 or 317 enemy dead and American losses 'described as light.' . . . We consider this a real fine kill ratio, real fine." Herr also recalls:

> Once I met a colonel who had a plan to shorten the war by dropping piranha into the paddies of the North. He was talking fish but his dreamy eyes were full of megadeath. . . .
>
> [Another] colonel explained the war in terms of protein. We were a nation of high-protein, meat-eating hunters, while the other guy just ate rice and a few grungy fish-heads. We were going to club him to death with our meat; what could you say except, "Colonel, you're insane?" It was like turning up in the middle of some black looneytune where the Duck had all the lines. I only jumped in once, spontaneous as shock, during Tet when I heard a doctor bragging that he'd refused to allow wounded Vietnamese into his ward. "But Jesus Christ," I said, "didn't you take the Hippocratic Oath?" But he was ready for me. "Yeah," he said, "I took it in America."[178]

Most Americans are uncomfortably conversant with the unsettling change which overcame us (we like to think it was a change) when we tried to "terminate" the Gooks, Slopes, Dinks, vermin. Less fresh to memory but far more horrible to it is the enslavement of blacks in our land, by our white people, in the past. The model fits, and well. The economics are clear. "For what purpose does the master hold the servant? Is it not that by his labor he, the master, may accumulate wealth?" As one southerner grumbled about the abolition movement: had any people in history ever voluntarily surrendered two billion dollars worth of property?[179]

The enslaved black was property, not a person. One owner lamented the loss of a slave who had committed suicide: "I had been offered $900 for her not two months ago, but damn her . . . I would not have had it happened for twice her value. The fates pursue me." Another grieved at the birth of a stillborn child: "She has not earned her salt for 4 months past. Bad luck—my usual luck in this way." To protect this property white men whipped their slaves, salted their lashes, pulled out toenails, cropped ears, branded, gelded, burnt hands, hunted with buckshot and dogs, then burnt their slaves to death or hanged them. "Let every tree in the county bend with negro meat."[180] They were bought, sold, bartered, deeded, pledged, willed, auctioned, awarded as prizes in lotteries and raffles, wagered at gaming tables and horse races. "A lawyer, searching for legal precedents which might justify a claim of 'unsoundness' in a slave recently sold, cited past judicial opinions 'as regards horseflesh.' "[181]

Negroes, according to South Carolina legislation, were "of barbarous, wild, savage natures, and . . . wholly unqualified to be governed by the laws, customs, and practices of this province." They had to be controlled by special laws "as may restrain the disorders, rapines, and inhumanity to which they are naturally prone." No black survived a trial for rape of a white woman; no black could be tried for rape of a black woman, because such a crime was unknown "to common or statute law."[182]

Who stood up for the slaves? The churches baptized and married them, but did not object when Christian families were then sold apart. Blighted advocacy.[183]

It is a miserable story, and those who inquire into it will see there the general pattern of human sacrifice, of Holocaust. So too if one looks at the way Turkey in 1915 resolved "The Armenian Question": by massacring 1,500,000 men, women, and children in a few months.[184]

There are many other stories which, if told, would be reminiscent of that savagery we have seen in the Holocaust. I have touched lightly on but a few of them here simply to head off any supposition that the dark spirit which inspired the Third Reich is something peculiar to Germany, or that it roams free only under dictatorship, or that it always puts its victims to death. The Holocaust spirit can be seen in our own country, our own people, our own time, our own mirror.

Is the Abortion Movement a Holocaust?

Now we must look into that mirror. Can the face and features which we saw in the Holocaust fairly be identified in what is being done today? I have

195

explored and set forth at some length the profile of what transpired between 1933 and 1945 because it is a story that has already begun to fade from public memory. And it also is a story that can grow distorted by time. We are likely to imagine that the savagery we recognize now was similarly perceived at the time when it was happening. And, by seeing it only as the burden of another people's conscience (since we ourselves were fighting on the other side), we can be tempted to make the memory more a solace than a warning.

My own judgment is that the movement advocating elective abortion in the world today, and especially in this country, bears the features of the movement that effected the Holocaust.

1: "They are not really human"—Depersonalization of the Victims

There has been a systematic effort made to dehumanize and depersonalize the being which abortion eliminates. Garrett Hardin, biologist at the University of California, Santa Barbara, and a forthright publicist for the abortion movement, noted in 1974 that a new neutrality of expression had helped people think more clearly on the subject of abortion. For example, since 1960 "the word *abortion* is no longer censored. (As of 1960 the stylebooks of many newspapers did not allow the word to be printed. 'Illegal operation' was the commonest euphemism.) [Also,] the word *abortion* is no longer tabooed. (Most 'nice' people—even women who had had abortions—couldn't bring themselves to speak the word in the old days.)" Hardin set himself to use, in this controversy, only words bare of connotation. Thus he uses "embryo" and "fetus" but excludes "unborn child" as a "sneaky way of implying that the powers, privileges, and rights of a later stage belong also to an earlier one. . . . We give a child the right to life. Until we have decided that we want also to give an embryo the very same right, unconditionally, we should not call it an *unborn child*, for that would prejudice inquiry."[185]

There has been a transformation of nomenclature for the unborn. Whether it has been in the direction of neutrality one may question. The unborn has been designated as "protoplasmic rubbish," "a gobbet of meat protruding from a human womb" (Philip Wylie); "a child-to-be" (Glanville Williams); "the fetal-placental unit" (A. I. Csapo); "gametic materials," "fallopian and uterine cell matter" (Joseph Fletcher); "a part of the mother" (Oliver Wendell Holmes), or "a part of the mother's body" (Thomas Szasz); "unwanted fetal tissue" (Ellen Frankfort); "the products of pregnancy" or "the product of conception" (HEW); "sub-human non-personhood" (F. Raymond Marks); "child Who-Might-Have-Been" (James Kidd); "so much garbage" (Peter Stanley); "defective life"; "the pregnancy" (*Family Planning Perspectives*); "live human material"; "a collection of cells"; "the conception" (Malcolm Potts); "potential life" (Mr. Justice Blackmun); "a chunk of tissue"; "the fertilized ovum" (Sarah Weddington).

Some of the new expression carries an undeniable animus, as when the unborn is called a "parasite" (Havelock Ellis). Natalie Shainess, a New York psychiatrist, exclaims: "Medically, physicians recognize that pregnancy is a kind of parasitism. A parasite can commit murder. What attention has Catholic thinking of the law given to the fetus's capacity to murder its mother?"[186] Others have compared the unborn to a tumor on the uterus, a wart on the nose, a hamburger in the stomach.

Bernard Nathanson, an obstetrician who helped found the National Abortion Rights Action League and ran its New York clinic, where, he said after his defection in 1974, "I am deeply troubled by my own increasing certainty that I had in fact presided over 60,000 deaths," now continues in his private practice to perform abortions (though reluctantly) for individual patients (he has now supervised a total of 75,000). His nomenclature, like his present conviction, is ambiguous. As an absolutely neutral term to designate the unborn he has chosen "alpha." "Pro-abortion spokesmen too often treat alpha as merely a chunk of tissue or an ordinary organ of the mother's body, rather like an appendix that is snipped off. . . . This whole line of argumentation is biological nonsense, unworthy of the people who have advocated it." Nathanson speaks of "human life" within the womb.[187]

A similar concern for nomenclature has been provoked by an anomaly of law. The law of the land now permits a physician to destroy the unborn at the mother's request at any time before birth. If, however, the procedure should fail to kill the unborn before it is expelled or removed from the mother, then the laws of the states recognize it from the moment of emergence as a born live child, and oblige the same doctor who was unsuccessful in his efforts to destroy the unborn now to bring to the newborn every help that medicine can provide to help him or her survive. That this turn of events should go against the grain of the medics who abort is understandable. Hence they have devised new expressions which, although they are medically absurd and of no defense against present law, show an attempt to extend beyond birth the disqualifying language that the abortion movement has used to depersonalize the unborn. The living abortion survivor is called "a living fetus" by Malcolm Potts, and a "non-viable fetus ex-utero" by the National Commission for the Protection of Human Subjects of Biomedical and Behavioral Research.[188]

Henry P. David, a distinguished protagonist for abortion, proposed in 1971:

> I wish to make a plea for aborting the word "abortion." For far too long and for too many people its image has been associated with misguided ideas of sin and murder. Birth planning has become a social necessity, whether through foresight or hindsight procedures. Just as the term "family planning" overcame the negative connotations of "birth control," an acceptable substitute for "abortion" is needed. With the new prostaglandins we may begin talking about "postconception planning" or "pregterm suppositories."[189]

Although the aim of the movement was to disqualify the unborn as human persons from conception to birth, and the force of present law offers no protection against the determination of a mother to abort at any stage of pregnancy, there has still been a disposition to describe the younger unborn as even more "non-human," so to speak, than those more developed. Lord Riddell observed that "the destruction of a full-grown child is a revolting affair, whereas the abortion of an early fetus differs but little from the removal of a uterine tumour."[190] The U.S. Supreme Court similarly, in *Roe* v. *Wade* and *Doe* v. *Bolton* (1973), classified the unborn as "non-viable" and "viable," the latter being those who are developed enough to survive if delivered at that point. This more mature category enjoys some qualified security in that the state, "in promoting its interest in the potentiality of human life may, if it chooses, regulate, and even proscribe abortion" except when the mother and an abortionist agree that the birth of the unborn would threaten her well-being.[191]

The language traditional in medicine had referred to the unborn as zygote, blastocyst, embryo, and fetus—with fair if not universal consistency of application to successive phases of growth. The convention in the law, as in ordinary usage, was to call the unborn a "child." A woman was "with child" in Anglo-American law. In that tradition "to kill a child in its mother's womb" was a straightforward way of describing a felony, and "if the child be born alive" and then die, it was murder. In England "any person who, with intent to destroy the life of a child capable of being born alive, by any wilful act causes a child to die before it has an existence independent of its mother" was liable to life imprisonment.[192]

So widespread a custom, so ingrained an attitude, would yield with difficulty to a newer nomenclature. It was natural that even among those committed to elective abortion there would be slips, thoughtless fallbacks into the old usages. Thus Justice Blackmun, when speaking for the Supreme Court of the United States in *Wade* and *Bolton,* and denying that there is protectable life before birth, inadvertently adopts the parlance of the statutes he is invalidating and refers to "the woman," "the pregnant woman," "the mother," "the pregnant mother," "the mother's womb." The Court, then, speaks as if a woman might be a mother without ever having had a child. Judge Clement Haynesworth, giving judgment for a bench of federal judges in South Carolina in an abortion-related case, laid the old and the new usages side by side: "Until the child is viable, the mother's constitutionally protected right to choose to terminate her pregnancy or not to do so must be allowed by the state to prevail over any interest it may have in the preservation of fetal life. Indeed, the Supreme Court declared the fetus in the womb is neither alive nor a person within the meaning of the Fourteenth Amendment."[193] And during the celebrated trial of Dr. Aleck Bourne in England for abortion in 1938, the judge referred to that which could be destroyed as "the unborn child," if abortion be the need of "the mother."

Similar lapses occur elsewhere. The story is told of Robert and Sherri Finkbine, the Arizona couple whose unborn was feared to have been affected by thalidomide. The Finkbines went to Sweden for an abortion.

> When she came out of anesthesia, Bob was standing by her bed. "Did you hear what the doctor said?" he asked. "The baby was deformed." He repeated it over and over again to make sure she understood. "It was not a baby," the doctor told her. "You must think of it as an abnormal growth within you."[194]

Various churches, in their endorsements of abortion freedom, have referred to what was dealt with as "the sanctity of life," "the conceptus," "life no less human," "a potential person," "the beginning of new human life," "children, including the unborn," "the sanctity of unborn human life." From an entirely different source, a New York City waitress and singer who had been referred by her drug source to the city's largest abortion clinic for her second termination, comes this explanation:

> "Medically, they were fast and efficient. The whole thing gives you a sens of well being. But I'd never do it again. It's painful to talk about," she blurted, choking on her words. "It bothers me that I made a decision to not let my baby live. But what else could I do? Both times, the fathers didn't want the babies, and I didn't believe in single parenthood. Women I know who have done it deliberately get no help at all. It's self-defeating for them and the baby."[195]

Despite reversions to the old way of words, it has been a reasonable policy of those sponsoring abortion freedom to discontinue all references to the unborn that would accord them humanity or personhood. Once learned, this nomenclature would need to be held fast. Thus, for instance, after the 1973 decisions the Department of Health, Education, and Welfare, noting that the Social Security Act's provision for assistance to dependent children had always entitled women to help for unborn as well as born children, cut off all aid for the unborn since, as of 1973, they were no longer to be considered children. Courts in nineteen jurisdictions disagreed with this denial of funds, but in 1975 the Supreme Court, under obligation of consistency with its own nomenclature, reaffirmed the cutoff.[196]

The literature on abortion discusses and categorizes the many kinds of unborn. Besides the designations of "viable" and "non-viable," one also speaks of fetuses blighted by congenital illness or handicap; conceived by rape or by incest; conceived in adultery or fornication; conceived in such a way as to incur a serious health threat to the women carrying them. All of these categories and concerns derive from some objective fact. But behind the assertion that these and other unborn are expendable, that they are either not human or less human, lies another principle that is subjective. The unborn's status and value and consequent treatment are all established in direct relation to the needs and proposals of those who hold them at their disposition. The status of the unborn is determined, in the last analysis, not by any imperatives of their own condition, but by whether or not they are wanted.

Joseph Fletcher, testifying before the National Commission for the Protection of Human Subjects of Biomedical and Behavioral Research, has argued that "a fetus is 'precious' or 'has value' when its potentiality is wanted . . . [and] this means when it is wanted by the progenitors, not by somebody else." If it is not wanted, Fletcher sees it as avilable for any sort of medical experimentation before abortion and disposal.[197] Fletcher rejects the various "objective" categorizations of the fetus: "I believe that it is as impossible to select any point on the continuum as the moment of life as it is to select any point as the moment of death. My more precise view is that the decisive consideration in determining whether or not to induce an abortion should not be inviability or quickening or viability but desirability."[198]

Glanville Williams, in a similar vein, has maintained that the law on abortion should accommodate itself to personal preference instead of curbing it. "Why does the moral theologian now draw the line at impregnation rather than some time else—say, the time of quickening, or of viability? If the line is to be drawn by reference to social considerations and human happiness, then pretty obviously the time of impregnation is the wrong one to take. . . . Infanticide has been all but suppressed while abortion is still rampant. The reason for the difference is not far to seek. The infant child is felt as a human being, so that protective feelings are easy to arouse: but the embryo is not. The question to be considered is whether it would not be wise to . . . fix some lesser limit of protection that is more in accordance with human needs, public opinion, and the possibilities of enforcement."[199]

Williams's point that abortion is less unattractive than infanticide is illuminated by Charles Mercier, an English physician whom he commends and quotes:

> The procuring of abortion with the consent of the woman wrongs no one. It prevents the foetus from attaining complete development, but the life of the foetus is scarcely begun, and it is yet far from being conscious, and has not even an independent existence. It would strain the meaning of words intolerably to look upon the action as a wrong done to the foetus, nor can it be considered a wrong to the mother, who freely and eagerly consents to it. . . .
>
> No, the only ground upon which the procuring of abortion can be held to be a crime is that it infringes the racial principle. It deprives the community of a potential citizen. . . . As the potential citizen is farther from the stage of actuality than the infant, it should seem that the crime is of less gravity than infanticide.

But on infanticide Mercier has this to say:

> In comparison with other cases of murder, a minimum of harm is done by it. . . .
>
> The victim's mind is not sufficiently developed to enable it to suffer from the contemplation of approaching suffering or death. It is incapable of feeling fear or terror. Nor is its consciousness sufficiently developed to enable it to suffer pain in appreciable degree. Its loss leaves no gap in any family circle, deprives no children of their breadwinner or their mother, no human being of a friend, helper or companion. The crime diffuses no sense of insecurity. No one feels a whit less safe because the crime has been committed.[200]

A doctor at Yale–New Haven Hospital, which had shortly before announced its program of withdrawing medical care from handicapped infants (thus eliminating 43 of them), explained to a television audience that to have a life worth living a baby had to be "lovable." The physicians who assisted parents in reaching what they called "management decisions," which generally resulted from the parents' fear that "they and their children would become socially enslaved, economically deprived, and permanently stigmatized," explained to their colleagues that these young patients had little prospect of "meaningful humanhood": "for example, they have little or no capacity to love or be loved."[201]

Further back behind the welcome or rejection offered by the conceiving couple is the interest of the state, which has often displayed a particular attention to the reproductive inclination of groups such as the poor, blacks, and other classes that are a heavy charge on the public purse. Support for abortion, notably initiated from within the upper-middle socioeconomic classes, has been especially ready to restrain its enthusiasm for high birthrates among the poor.[202]

Within all of this concern for the welfare of the victims born or unborn, Paul Ramsey perceives that what separates "meaningful life" from "wrongful life" is the personhood which society chooses to confer on those candidates who present themselves in a timely and attractive manner. Anyone who is not wanted is depersonalized.[203]

Daniel Callahan comments:

> The great strength of the movement against abortion is that it seeks to protect one defenseless category of human or potentially human life; furthermore, it strives to resist the introduction into society of forms of value judgments that would discriminate among the worth of individual lives. In almost any other civil rights context, the cogency of this line of reasoning would be quickly respected. Indeed, it has been at the heart of efforts to correct racial injustices, to improve health care, to eradicate poverty, and to provide better care for the aged. The history of mankind has shown too many instances of systematic efforts to exclude certain races or classes of persons from the human community to allow us to view with equanimity the declaration that fetuses are "not human." Historically, the proposition that all human beings are equal, however "inchoate" they may be, is not conservative but radical. It is constantly threatened in theory and subverted in practice.[204]

Callahan's observation notwithstanding, the new nomenclature of abortion has been effective and persuasive. One law professor writes: "I think I really might have supported abortion if I had not met one woman who supported abortion [and] admitted that abortion-on-demand involves the taking of human life without having to give a reason, but said that the value of total sexual freedom (the freedom from any worry about pregnancy) was sufficient to her to outweigh the value of the child's life. Or, again, a law student at Yale who wrote to me: 'Faced with an undesired slavery, I would kill. I understand it to be killing, and I would do it.' " Few see the issue so clearly drawn.[205]

The *New York Times*, which shapes both its editorial and its reportorial copy to conform to its aggressively proabortion policy, has displayed what might be called a double standard in its vocabulary of the unborn. When the *Times* is either editorializing on behalf of abortion freedom, or presenting news stories in furtherance of that end, there is talk only of "the fetus," "the unborn," "the embryo," and other terms which consistently avoid any acknowledgment of human peerage in the womb. But when the *Times* is reporting or opining on medical efforts to rescue the unborn from various misfortunes, its vocabulary enlarges to speak of "the endangered baby," "the baby destined to be born," "the unborn baby," "the baby still residing in the womb," or, simply, "the baby." The clear inference from this usage is that when a child is welcomed, he or she is a baby from the start. When there is no welcome, there is only an embryo. Instead of treating a subject as his or her status deserves, one decides whether or not one is prepared to make room for him or her, and assigns status accordingly. The implications of such usage in any area of human rights are evident and ominous.[206]

On the face of it, there seems to be a policy from within the abortion movement to withdraw from the unborn such accreditation as they had previously enjoyed as fellow human beings, and to efface from our vocabulary the familiar ways we had of referring to the unborn child. There are lapses in this program, but there are also reinforcements: the simultaneous movement to sponsor nontherapeutic research on unborn who are awaiting abortion and another movement supportive of infanticide for handicapped children both provide further incentives to confer the designation of "human person" even more sparingly at life's dawn. As in the case of the Holocaust, victims are designated by classes according to their lack of appeal, and then given the attention of a public relations campaign. The aim of this campaign is to allow for their destruction without alarming anyone ordinarily concerned about human rights.

2: The Euphemisms of Torment—Language Turned Inside Out

The Holocaust required a bizarre yet purposeful distortion of normal language in order to camouflage the extermination of eight million unwanted people. The abortion movement has also been semantically creative.

The leading protagonist for abortion on demand in Britain, Cambridge law professor Glanville Williams, acknowledges that "many doctors attempt to avoid what they consider to be the unsavory connotations of the word 'abortion' by speaking instead of termination of pregnancy."[207] George Will, writing in *Newsweek*, has noted the same turn of phrase:

> Abortion advocates have speech quirks that may betray qualms. Homeowners kill crabgrass. Abortionists kill fetuses. Homeowners do not speak of "terminating" crabgrass. But Planned Parenthood of New York City, which evidently regards abortion as just another form of birth control, has published an abortion guide that uses the word "kill" only twice, once to say what some women did to themselves before legalized abortion, and once to describe what some contraceptives do to sperm. But when referring to the killing of fetuses, the book, like abortion advocates generally, uses only euphemisms, like "termination of potential life." Abortion advocates become interestingly indignant when opponents display photographs of the well-formed feet and hands of a nine-

week-old fetus. People avoid correct words and object to accurate photographs because they are uneasy about saying and seeing what abortion is.[208]

Bernard Nathanson comments on this new sequence of appropriate expressions. "On Operating Room schedules, the pre-Blackmun term that was written down was 'therapeutic abortion'; after Blackmun it became 'elective abortion.' Now it is 'termination of pregnancy,' the ultimate euphemism, almost Huxleyan in its finesse. To the gynecology residents, it remains 'scraping it out.' "[209]

"Therapeutic abortion" was a term much used before 1973 in the days when elective abortion had to be given credibility (and legal protection) by contrived medical or psychiatric "indications." As Callahan has remarked, the term itself is contrived. "Even in the instance of a fetus with a grave defect, abortion is not therapeutic. It may be merciful and it may be wise, but, unless I am mistaken, the medical profession does not classify procedures with a 100 percent mortality rate as therapeutic." The term has most often borne no reference whatever to the health of anyone, offspring or progenitor.[210]

Typical indications for "therapeutic abortions" in a group of unmarried teenagers include: "They did not feel ready to raise a child; they feared the social repercussions of an illegitimate pregnancy; the putative father offered little support; it would be much more painful for them to give the baby up for adoption."[211] One practitioner, after reviewing the literature, concludes: "No psychiatrist (or anyone else, for that matter) can pretend to any expertise in predicting a *therapeutic* outcome for abortion."[212]

Since 1973 no pretense of medical need has been required (except to invoke the "danger to health" proviso that can override state statutes forbidding abortions after the point of viability). As the atmosphere of abortion centers has been transformed from that of medical facility to that of salon, other, more demure words have come into the usage. Some clinics speak only of "treatments." For physicians it is a "life-rationing," rather than a "life-taking" activity. Others offer a "procedure," or "post-conception planning." Mechanized abortion during the first twelve weeks of pregnancy can be called "menstrual extraction"; when done chemically it is "menstrual regulation" (in each case, of course, it is used when the menses have not occurred) to "insure non-pregnancy." Outsiders to the medical profession have also found suitably indirect language. Former Supreme Court Justice Tom Clark, for example, in an article advocating abortion on demand, asked: "If an individual may prevent conception, why can he [*sic*] not nullify that conception when prevention has failed?"[213]

The institutions which offer this service also have titles that invite reflection. In Pittsburgh there is *Women's Health Services*, where the services have little or nothing to do with women's health. In Florida there is the *Orlando Birthing Center*, which will handle second-trimester abortions but no births. In Leiden one finds the *Center for Human Reproduction*, which is concerned to arrest reproduction, as also the *Water Tower Reproductive Center* in Chicago. In Missouri, *Parents Aid* aids women to avoid being parents, while in Chicago *Family Guidance* guides people to prevent families. *Pre-Term* in

Cleveland and *Pre-Birth* in Chicago preclude full-term births. Other sense-inverting titles include *Family Foundation, Midwest Population Center, Biogenetics Center, Master Health,* and *Resolve, Inc.* The *Center for Reproductive and Sexual Health* in New York evoked comment from its former director: "In retrospect, such a name for an abortion site is one of those ultimate euphemisms that our century uses to hide the enormity of what mankind is actually doing. Auschwitz as 'resettlement camp.' "[214]

Another style of rhetoric is employed in the polemic literature. An illustration of this may be found in *Abortion II,* published just after the abortion decisions of 1973 by Lawrence Lader, founder of the National Abortion Rights Action League. In recounting the story of his struggle for unrestricted abortion freedom, Lader employs two distinct vocabularies. One describes his allies; the other he draws on to depict those who oppose abortion on demand:

Proabortion People	*Antiabortion People*
tough, shrewd	dogmatists
jovial, pink-cheeked	Catholic hierarchy, political
handsome, poised, literate	wreckers, and medical
soft-voiced, sandy-haired	reactionaries
winsome, freckle-faced	ridicule, public vilification and
prestigious, with impressive	danger
credentials	puritan ethic
dedicated	violent
stormy petrels	bitter harassment
gentle, persuasive	cruelty
aggressive	hypocrisy, prejudice
dynamic	harsh
courageous	unbending
inspiring	attack
a wild, unorthodox zest	an orgy of frenzied invective
modest, highly efficient	scurrilous
vision	hysterical
aura of passion and joy	fury
flamboyant	blatant
boldness	vitriolic
frail, wispish figure	repulsive
humanitarianism and medical	extremist
skill	prim
folksy, idiosyncratic rebel	venom
like the words of the biblical	religious tyranny
prophets	frenzy and vituperation
serene, appearance of grace	authoritarian control
and gentility	crude and shocking
compassion and sweetness,	lash out
resolution and strength	furious lobbying

The case Mr. Lader has to make is, so to speak, helped along. Thus, a colleague of his (she of the winsome, freckled face) who had left her husband to cohabit bigamously with a friend is said to live with her "common law husband." By a similar turn of phrase, "abortion was not murder, as Catholic dogma claimed, but a humane solution to a critical social problem."[215]

There has also emerged, within the abortion movement, a glossary of expressions that are now of classical usage in arguments made to the public on behalf of abortion. While they are drawn from common coinage, they have, in this context, highly specialized meanings and overtones.

To illustrate: a phrase almost technical in its use is "meaningful life." Although it was introduced by the philosophers of the movement, it was hoisted to higher respect when Justice Blackmun said, in *Wade*, that states might raise a hand against elective abortion only when the unborn was capable of "meaningful life outside the mother's womb."[216] Three years later the Supreme Judicial Court of Massachusetts reversed the manslaughter conviction of abortionist Kenneth Edelin, noting that the child he may have failed to destroy by abortion could not in any case have enjoyed a "meaningful survival."[217] What the phrase has come to designate in the abortion argument is not so much the appraisal that the one to be aborted might put upon his or her life later were it to continue, but the meaning it has for those entitled to make the abortion decision. Thus one can understand the remark of Rabbi Balfour Brickner to fellow clergy who led a march on the Washington Capitol in June 1979 on behalf of federal funding for abortion on demand: "We call for the right to life when wanted." Like meaningful life, wanted life must be wanted, not by its holder, but by him or her who has the freedom to destroy it.[218]

The sense is the same when one reads of the "deep concern of most Americans that their children should be born when they are wanted, when they can be loved and cared for by their parents."[219] Or, as one doctor reacted to the 1973 court rulings: "I feel that to have a child born without continuous maternal care or father or family upbringing is an injustice to the child." The usual meaning, that family nurture should rise to meet the needs of arriving offspring, is replaced by its obverse, that offspring ought to be eliminated if burdensome . . . but in the name of justice. The injustice is removed by removal of its victim.[220]

Dr. Jane Hodgson, abortionist and clinic director, testified in federal court in 1977: "In my medical judgment every one that is not wanted by the patient, I feel there is a medical indication to abort a pregnancy where it is not wanted. In good faith, I would recommend on a medical basis you understand, that, and it would be one hundred percent . . . I think they are all medically necessary."[221]

Bernard Nathanson writes: "At some point in pregnancy, many children are temporarily 'unwanted.' For that matter, offspring are often 'unwanted' at certain moments after they are born. An unwanted [unborn] does not always end up as a resented baby. . . . The 'unwanted child' is also a myth . . . because of the hopeless shortage of babies available for the long list of childless couples who earnestly want to adopt them."[222]

When the unborn is not wanted, the language can be turned around to make him or her an aggressive offender. Thus, Rabbi Seymour Siegel has justified using the unborn as research material by comparing them to enemies in war who forfeit their right to live: "In the same way, the fetus' right to our concern for its life is mitigated when the fetus threatens someone else's life or health."[223]

The entrance into one's life of an unwelcome human creature who needs nurture and support which one is unhappy to provide is thus seen as a "wrong." In 1975 Agnes Glasper underwent an abortion to discharge her third offspring. Seven and a half months after this ineffective operation she was delivered of a six-pound girl. Now that her daughter is three years old, Ms. Glasper has sued the abortionists for $100,000 for "wrongful birth."[224] Ethicist Paul Ramsey reports the suggestion that handicapped persons be invited to sue their parents for "wrongful life," for having allowed them to survive. H. Tristram Englehardt, Jr., has published an article that develops this theme: "Euthanasia and Children: The Injury of Continued Existence."[225]

Another expression important within the abortion movement is used to define the issue as a matter best resolved "between a woman and her doctor." This is not because abortion often affects health, but because doctors have the license, the equipment, and the skills to perform it. Thus, one might likewise state that a misunderstanding among the Mafia would be a matter best resolved "between a man and his gunsmith." Thomas Szasz, a proponent of abortion, has admitted: "Abortion is a moral, not a medical problem. To be sure, the procedure is surgical; but this makes abortion no more a medical problem than the use of the electric chair makes capital punishment a problem of electrical engineering."[226] A similar comment comes from a physician: "Abortion is no more purely a medical problem just because the physician wields the curette than chemical warfare is purely a problem for pilots because they press the lever releasing the chemical."[227]

The Supreme Court has ruled that the physician is sovereign in making the abortion decision (though in response to a woman's request), and that what is, "primarily, a medical decision" rests on his "medical judgment," his "professional judgment," his "best clinical judgment."[228] The ambit of that unreviewable clinical judgment is then described as including all relevant factors in emotional welfare, mental health, family relationships and values, economic planning, and religious obligations and convictions. Matters of life and death are to be resolved between a woman and a physician who is professionally untrained and incompetent to deal with what is at stake in more than 95 percent of today's abortions, which have no bearing on the health that a physician is medically trained, licensed, and experienced to serve. The logic here could as well entrust the policy of the United States on nuclear weaponry and warfare to the unreviewable control of the physicists at Los Alamos. Doctors are, by this slogan, given a deputation no less absurd or ominous.

Another linguistic device is the specialized use of the word "privacy." This too, though a common enough word, has acquired a technical meaning that is not easily understood. On the one hand, the sexual union and the intimacy that bind husband and wife, parents and offspring together are invoked and supported. The American Civil Liberties Union is on record as defending "the marital right to privacy."[229] The Supreme Court, in the abortion decisions of 1973, refers to the guarantee of privacy in matters referring to marriage, the marriage bed, and the begetting and rearing of children.[230] Lawrence Lader of NARAL has from the start justified abortion and contraception as bounded by the enclosure of "marital privacy."[231] Justice Douglas, in a concurring opinion, even stated that the privacy between married people is anterior to the Bill of Rights, and "intimate to the degree of being sacred." One must therefore be free to marry when and whom one chooses and then, with that person, to procreate, to rear, and to educate children.[232]

Privacy within marriage, then, has been presented as a sacred sharing between husband and wife, a sharing from which children are to proceed and within which they would be helped to mature. This was a privacy into which the state would not sponsor or allow intrusion. But then, abruptly, a new and curious meaning of privacy was introduced. Judge Arnold Gesell, striking down the District of Columbia abortion statute in 1969, noted that a woman's right of privacy extended to "family, marriage and sex matters and may well include the right to remove an unwanted child at least in the early stages of pregnancy."[233] And by 1976 it was clear that the privacy the Supreme Court would really respect was not *within* the family but *apart from* the family. Husbands could not claim a share in the decision to destroy the unborn they had fathered; parents could claim no say-so in a minor daughter's decision to seek an abortion. Indeed, the judges thought, it was often just as well that neither father nor parents know about it. Privacy, in this transformed sense, was to be ultimately a possession of the individual. It was not something that people came to share; it was what held them free of one another. The law has proved itself more protective of the purchased privacy between a woman and her physician than of the pledged privacy between a woman and her husband or her rearing parents.[234]

The vocabulary of the abortion campaign has developed a series of expressions that are somehow contorted, as did the vocabulary of the Holocaust. Some of it is just ordinary nonsense, as when columnist Georgie Anne Geyer confides that "now, I personally have never approved of abortion-as-contraception," which she considers a deplorable "new sexual abuse." Abortion, by definition, can, of course, never be contraception.[235] The self-contradiction here is matched by that of a phrase of emerging popularity, "preventive death." Abortion has been justified as a necessary "backup" for contraceptive failure, a second chance for family planning; now a Virginia doctor who has been eliminating handicapped children in the hospital nursery has, by the same logic, described this practice as providing a second chance for an abortion.[236] An expression used by the Nazi apologists is now in common circulation: "passive euthanasia." It means that the unwanted are eliminated, not by drugs or gas, but by the denial of medical care and / or nourishment.

The unborn who are chosen for abortion and then made available as subjects for medical experimentation are said, by Dr. Marc Lappé, an ethical researcher, to "ennoble that death" they will shortly undergo. He explains that the unborn is "doomed to death anyhow, but perhaps its death can be ennobled because it served those more fortunate." The traditional concept of ennobling service, with its assumption of benefit to the *less* fortunate, seems, in Lappé's view, to have undergone a singular transformation: now the less fortunate are to be ennobled by service to those luckier than they. It is in accordance with this new, inverted understanding that mothers are described as coming forward to offer their unborn for experimentation and then abortion "because they wanted something beneficial for mankind to result."[237]

One researcher at Yale, Dr. Maurice J. Mahoney, points out that not to use the unborn for experimentation would be a failure in duty: "To eliminate the participation of human fetuses from experimentation because they are unable to consent, denies fetuses as a class the right to benefit from medical progress and directly contradicts the presumption that the human fetus is a legitimate participant in the human community." The fetuses who are experimented with and destroyed, presumably because they are not welcome as participants in the human community, owe this to fellow fetuses who will be given entrée.[238]

Other statements rise from the debate as memorable for their perspective. In 1973 the Supreme Court declared that during the entire course of pregnancy, from the first to the last day, no effective legal restraint could thenceforth be raised against any woman who desired an abortion for her well-being. Chief Justice Burger, concurring with this judgment, expressed his confidence that the abortionists would "act only on the basis of carefully deliberated medical judgments relating to life and health. Plainly," he wrote, "the Court today rejects any claim that the Constitution requires abortions on demand."[239]

Another remarkable perspective is enjoyed by the *New York Times* as it views the abortion issue. On February 19, 1975, for example, the *Times* ran two editorials immediately next to one another. In the first, headlined "Abortion Error," the paper deplored the conviction of Dr. Edelin (not for abortion, but for the manslaughter of an abortion survivor). The "cause of rational abortion" had been set back by a "misguided jury," twelve laypeople who, the *Times* judged, were incompetent to decide the fact of whether an infant, delivered from its mother and apparently breathing, was a human. The jury was "confused" by "intolerable" references by the prosecution to the word "fetus" and "baby" (manslaughter, as prescribed by criminal law, must have a "baby," not a "fetus," as a victim). The second editorial, "Bird Massacre," begins:

> Although the United States Circuit Court of Appeals for the District of Columbia has upheld the legality of killing millions of starlings, grackles, and redwing blackbirds that roost near military installations in Kentucky and Tennessee, the Army has shown commendable sensitivity in accepting the court's suggestion that it delay this ruthless and questionable procedure. . . .
>
> The city of Paducah, Ky., however, acted on its own. It hired the pilot of a small plane to make repeated passes over the birds' roosting area and spray them with a detergent. . . . 'Sprayed birds benumbed by the cold dropped from their roosts and skittered

along the ground. Later the birds huddled together for warmth and some hours later began dying by the thousands.'

The editorial deplores "the poignant spectacle . . . this hideous project . . . this mass slaughter," and proposes "the self-evident solutions": thin out the pine trees in which they roost. "It is as simple as that." One is drawn to imagine how the editorials might have read if the indignation, moral concerns, and solutions had been reversed.

But enough. One is in danger of being amused by ironies that are too serious for chuckling. The rhetoric and vocabulary of the abortion movement have swerved around direct reference to what is actually being done to the unborn, and why it is being done. It has been rare for anyone to say, straight out, as one physician did, that "abortion as it is currently practiced is necessary, but also that it is, in essence, homicide, although whether for social or other reasons, justifiable or necessary homicide. The true denial of the value of life is more likely to stem from the denial that one is killing than from the actual act of a necessary killing in itself."[240]

The parallels between the Holocaust code and abortion speech are not subtle. The resettlements and cleansing actions and special treatments of the SS are echoed in the terminations and procedures and treatments of Planned Parenthood. The work of the Reich Committee for Children is repeated by Parents Aid and the Family Foundation. The victims who had a life not worth living are succeeded by victims who lack meaningful life, or even lead wrongful lives. The medical matters to which Dr. Servatius referred in court are what Judge Gesell referred to as family, marriage, and sex matters. The necessary and useful duty to which the Treblinka personnel were exhorted is matched by the justifiable or necessary homicide that is discussed in the *New England Journal of Medicine*. The sacrifices for the benefit of the community offered by Karl Brandt's medical experiment victims were made by the less fortunate for the more fortunate, and the victims were ennobled in death to the same degree as the aborted unborn praised by Dr. Lappé. Just as German mental patients were released from their sufferings in Franconia, in Washington Dr. Englehardt urges us to spare from birth those who face the injury of continued existence. And, as motive for it all, Karl Brandt's measures dictated by purely humane considerations are no more greathearted than Lawrence Lader's humane solution to a critical social problem.

3: "I am not responsible"—Dislocation of Responsibility

There has been no Nuremberg for abortion in America, nor is there likely to be. No court will sit in judgment over a destruction of the unborn which was authorized by the courts themselves. Yet, even without the prospect of facing the bar of accountability that the workers of the Holocaust faced, those who do the work of abortion display a similar unwillingness to accept responsibility for it.

On one view of it, abortion is the responsibility of the physician. Malcolm Potts, a British leader in Planned Parenthood / World Federation, states that "the woman chooses and requests abortion but the medical profession, at all levels, has been unwilling to diminish its power of decision and veto."[241] This power, however, is not one that physicians easily confess they have. Potts's British coadvocate of abortion, Glanville Williams, concurs with the opposite view, that "doctors are a timorous group. They do not wish to be responsible for an abortion that does not comply with the law, even if they are morally convinced that such an abortion should be done."[242]

Do physicians wish to accept responsibility for the abortions they perform? In some instances they appear ready to attribute this responsibility to the law. In 1973 the Supreme Court stated that it was taking no stand on the question of when human life begins. Seeing no consensus on the matter within the disciplines of medicine, philosophy, and theology, the justices declined even to speculate on whether it was a living, human being that had sprung up in the womb and was at risk by abortion. They agreed that the entire issue, moral as well as legal, would be decided if in fact the unborn could be defined as a human being and thus a person to be protected by the law. They withheld both ethical judgment and legal protection. But immediately after the Court had restrained itself from taking a moral stand, its legal decision began to be used as a reliable moral premise. If the Supreme Court allowed abortion, one need harbor no ethical misgivings about it. One obstetrician put it this way in an interview:

> Q. Have you ever performed an abortion?
>
> A. Oh, yes, not one of the illegal abortions. . . .
>
> Q. Would you be adverse to performing an abortion for someone whose health wasn't in question, who simply wanted an abortion?
>
> A. No, I wouldn't if it's been declared legally in the United States that a woman may have an abortion if she wishes. We have religious and moral aspects in that decision but that has been the decision.
>
> Q. That's what I'm trying to get at . . . the religious and moral aspects. Do you consider the baby when you abort it to be alive, to be fully human, partially human, or how do you look at that?
>
> A. That's a very difficult question. I don't think that enters my mind.[243]

Joshua Lederberg of the Stanford Medical School insists that the crux of the moral issue is whether the fetus is a person, and that this "has already been decided at law by the Supreme Court."[244] Gaylin and Lappé, physician and ethicist, take the same stand. Discussing the ethics of nontherapeutic experimentation on the unborn, they see the Supreme Court as having laid the moral issue to rest. The Court has ruled that there is no person in the womb; therefore, with the mother's permission (since the unborn is, by her decision, never to be born), one may rightfully do any reasonable kind of research with it. The logic here has a certain elasticity. Justice Blackmun, for the Court, though he had stripped the unborn of status *before the law* as a person, emphatically shied away from giving this opinion a moral justification by denying that human life was present. His restraint, rather than curbing the conclusions to be drawn from the ruling, seems to have invited wider liberties.

Gaylin, Lappé, and others want to take legal rulings as moral warrants. Do they then consider themselves completely free to use the unborn at pleasure? No, the researcher is bound by other limits, they say. "Whether we allow ourselves the special privilege of using the dead body as 'material' depends on the motives and purposes for so doing." The doctor, now that the law has left the area, will encounter no possible moral reproach. For all that he does will be good, since good is what he intends.[245]

Doctors are also of a mind that the abortion is the responsibility of the woman who asks for it. Nathanson in 1974 wrote: "Certainly the medical profession itself cannot shoulder the burden of this matter. The phrase, 'between a woman and her physician' is an empty one since the physician is only the instrument of her decision, and has no special knowledge of the moral dilemma or the ethical agony involved in the decision. Furthermore, there are seldom any purely medical indications for abortion. The decision is the most serious responsibility a woman can experience in her lifetime, and at present it is hers alone."[246]

Dr. Kenneth Edelin had routinely performed abortions before his trial for manslaughter and indicated that he intended to continue them. He explained that he did not like abortions, but felt he was obliged to serve the choice of women who desired them.[247] A Yale physician, interviewed about his program for eliminating handicapped infants, was asked whether mongoloid children could ever enjoy "meaningful humanhood," and thus be exempted from extermination. "He seemed to hedge, leaving the decision to parents who 'pay the fiddler to call the tune,' while the physician and hospital policy need only sometimes decide 'whether the family's God is fair to the child.' "[248] And Dr. Edmund Overstreet, an abortion advocate in California, even though he persists in calling abortion "therapeutic," acknowledges that it is no medical matter, "since physicians increasingly use it simply to solve the problem of unwanted pregnancy."[249]

There is, then, a recurring desire by physicians not to bear the responsibility for this one kind of work. It was shown also in Great Britain in 1969. Two years after legal abortion had become freely available, two-thirds of five thousand doctors polled said that they wanted the law repealed or modified to provide that the "social ground" offered for most abortions be evaluated by local nonmedical committees or authorities, rather than by themselves.[250]

There is some ambivalence, however, about whether pregnant women wish to assume the full burden of choice for abortion. "An Appeal to Congressional Conscience," a manifesto presented by a group organized by NARAL and the Religious Coalition for Abortion Rights, makes the claim that in the matter of abortion, conscience ought to be decisive (except that they were unhappy at the prospect of legislators voting according to theirs). "We call upon these lawmakers to refrain from legislating their own beliefs on the matter of abortion, but urge them to ensure true government neutrality by supporting legislation which would allow every individual to seek health services consistent with his or her own moral and religious conscience."[251]

The full onus of choice is not entirely acceptable, however. Some cities have required that women seeking abortion be given an explanation of the stage of fetal development of their unborn, in order to provide for a more considered decision. Karen Mulhauser, executive director of NARAL, objects: "In many communities the zealots have succeeded in passing so-called 'informed consent' ordinances designed solely to frighten patients out of having abortions."[252] Her colleague Lawrence Lader sees a similar advantage in allowing pregnant women to procure abortions without full knowledge and clear choice. He sees a particular benefit in women's taking prostaglandins after a missed menstrual period (thus preventing both implantation and any sure knowledge of whether conception and abortion ever took place): "The woman need never know if she is pregnant or not. . . . Particularly for some Catholic women, who may still feel guilt over vacuum abortion, the prostaglandin approach removes any knowledge of the existence of a fetus. More importantly, it should undercut in large part the Church's objections to potential 'murder,' when even the most determined theologian could not prove that conception had taken place."[253]

Many have advocated strongly that women be left free to make abortion choices. It is not clear, however, how seriously these choices are meant to be reflective or responsible.

What of the view that law, or the government, has made the basically responsible decision about abortion? This view too encounters some muddling. When the *Chicago Sun-Times* ran an extensive exposé of the four most active and lucrative abortion centers in Illinois, reporting that they were unsterile, unprofessional mills run by venal racketeers, government officials at city, county, and federal levels were appealed to. Government was asked, most notably by abortion advocates, to intervene: to reform or to close the clinics. Yet 95 percent of the abortions in these facilities were performed during the first trimester of pregnancy, and the Supreme Court had ruled that no public authority could intrude between a woman and her physician to prevent such abortions.[254] The view of the law was, not that it condoned abortion, but that it simply had no involvement in the matter. "[The obstetrician], perhaps more than anyone else, is knowledgeable in this area of patient care, and he is aware of human frailty, so-called 'error,' and needs. The good physician—despite the presence of rascals in the medical profession, as in all others, we trust that most physicians are 'good'—will have sympathy and understanding for the pregnant patient." With abortion in such charitable hands, the state need assume no supervisory responsibility.[255]

Indeed, so impotent is the government to intervene that, in the 1976 abortion cases, it confessed it could not "delegate" to a husband any responsibility in the matter, nor "give" to parents any authority over their minor daughters regarding abortion. As in wartime Germany, the only acknowledged font of responsibility is the state (even the family is said by the court to derive its parental authority from the state). Yet the state has contrived both to authorize widespread abortion and to disclaim any say-so over it. The fathomless state power is exercised, but is not deemed accountable.

Father Robert F. Drinan, former law school dean and onetime member of the House of Representatives (where he held chief responsibility in the Judiciary Committee for revision of the U.S. Criminal Code), reads the law to say that the medical profession is now the "sole regulator" of what standards should be followed, with "virtually exclusive jurisdiction" over who will live and who will die. This he finds a clear and desirable result.[256] Harriet F. Pilpel, chief attorney for Planned Parenthood, would have the professional determination of the physician ascendant over control by state or family in the matter of abortion.[257] And ethicist Paul Ramsey is one of several who, on close reading of *Wade* and *Bolton*, believe that the liberty they award is not for women but for doctors.[258]

Some have argued that the law has no responsibility for abortion because it is none of its business. Glanville Williams exclaims: "It is not for lawyers and priests to dictate to doctors and patients how to deal with suffering." He draws a poetic analogy:

> "The toad beneath the harrow knows
> Exactly where each toothpoint goes.
> The butterfly upon the road
> Preaches contentment to that toad."[259]

The American Civil Liberties Union has held "that every woman, as a matter of her right to the enjoyment of life, liberty, and privacy, should be free to determine whether and when to bear children. The Union itself offers no comment on the wisdom or the moral implications of abortion, believing such judgments belong solely in the province of individual conscience and religion. We maintain that the penal sanctions of the state have no proper application to such matters."[260]

Responsibility for abortion has been a hot potato tossed to and fro. The law folk say they are simply leaving doctors free; doctors say they do only what the law permits; both say they are respecting free and rightful choices of pregnant women; and women are only doing what both lawyers and doctors approve of.

Other voices also comment on the assignment of responsibility. Joseph Fletcher says doctors are now to be exempt from the scrutiny of his fellow moralists. "Medicine must be delivered from the kinds of ethics which follow principles when following them means we have to condemn and nullify the acquisition of useful know-how in medicine's effort to save and improve human life."[261] Other clergymen of Fletcher's persuasion had banded together in 1967 to form the Clergy Consultation Service in various major cities. Ostensibly this was a counseling resource. "We do not tell a woman what to do. Rather we urge a woman to make her own decisions." The sessions, which "ran from ten minutes to an hour or so," led 95 percent of the clients to make decisions to have abortions, and then to accept referral to abortion clinics in areas where they were legal and available. When threatened with prosecution for running an unlawful abortion referral service, the CCS angrily called it "a first and very threatening infringement of ministerial rights." The service was able to be neutral or committed, secular or religious, as required.[262]

Meanwhile psychiatrists began to disavow their liability for abortions. Kenneth R. Niswander, professor and chairman of Obstetrics and Gynecology at the University of California, Davis, insisted that there were virtually no psychiatric grounds for abortion (in his state at the time more than one hundred thousand abortions per annum were being performed, more than 90 percent of which were registered as "psychiatric"). He concurred with a colleague: "If society wants abortion to be easier, it should have the courage to campaign for it honestly and not exploit the psychiatrist who, I contend, has no factual basis for being associated with the problem."[263]

Seymour Halleck noted in 1971 that most abortion clientele were of the community elite, with questionable need for abortion. "No psychiatrist, if he is honest with himself, will claim to be able to distinguish between selfish, practical, idealistic, and irrational motivation. Nor can he describe any scientific criteria that enable him to know which woman should have her pregnancy terminated, and which should not. When he recommends an abortion, he usually lies. It is a kind lie, a dishonesty intended to make the world a little better, but it is still a lie."[264]

The national establishment of abortion on demand, in the face of citizen and government objection and resistance, has required the collaboration and involvement of many groups, especially professional organizations. It appears that, while this support has been willingly given, there is a characteristic reluctance to accept responsibility for abortion. Even very energetic advocates are liable to state that they are struggling to make others free to pursue what seems best for them. Like the Holocaust, it is a massive achievement for which very few are anxious to accept authorship.

Also, like the Holocaust, it is a policy that many regard as having been imposed by necessity. This is a sort of necessity so imperative that people feel they are relieved of the otherwise normal duty to verify that their undertakings are morally unobjectionable. There are, for abortion on demand, two principal kinds of necessity strong enough to overwhelm moral concern. One, of course, is that abortion has been and inevitably will be practiced. Since there is no imaginable way to interdict this determination of so many women, or to thwart their acting upon it, one has simply to suspend all ethical questions and provide that the abortions can at least be performed safely and hygienically.

A second kind of necessity—this one derived largely from the policy of the Planned Parenthood Federation—is that widespread extramarital sexual activity, particularly among teenagers, is an inevitable fact: a fact so axiomatic that all moral comment on it is stifled. Millions of men and women unprepared to raise children *will* conceive each year, and in the face of this unacceptable and engulfing emergency one must act differently than one would in the best of worlds.

A third kind of necessity—a *raison d'état* for abortion on demand—is the compelling threat of overpopulation. This is, of course, rarely a motive that affects the sexual or reproductive habits of couples, but it underlies governmental policy and appropriations, and is then available as a motivational overlay for whatever reasons individuals may act upon.[265]

Although the abortion movement has not had the jolting retrospect of a Nuremberg, the dislocation of responsibility suggests itself in ways parallel to the Holocaust. A national process of experimentation and liquidation is authorized by the highest authority in the state—yet by no positive order.

Instead, a simple ruling is issued that doctors are free in this matter to act on their best judgment. From the medical personnel involved there comes the explanation that they are prepared to do only what the state acknowledges as rightful. From those obliquely involved there are clear reminders that their role is but to remove obstacles from the way of what others must have their reasons for doing. There are reassurances that this is well-established practice in other respectable nations. It is seen as a necessity for individuals and for the state, an otherwise unattractive measure which, when these emergency times pass, may no longer be appropriate. It is a policy for which there is clear authority and widespread responsibility, but everyone locates these with someone else.

4: "There was certainly no vicious intent"—Savagery from Normal Folk

A signal difference between the Holocaust and abortion is that in the latter case the unborn destroyed are not on view as victims. Much less effort at emotional suppression is required when one can destroy without actually seeing or hearing or, in frequent fact, even touching the one to be eliminated. Late abortions do disturb, of course, in a way that early ones do not. Williams writes that in late pregnancy abortion is "more repulsive because one is dealing with a fully-formed baby." Potts describes it as "aesthetically offensive."[266]

Female medical personnel seem to have been even more alienated by this than men. As Mt. Sinai Hospital in New York moved into high-volume abortion work ("pregnancy interruption service"), the director of nurses reported: "Most nurses find the destruction of life the very antithesis of what they believe. . . . Nurses in delivery rooms had been accustomed to every conceivable effort to save babies, even those of one to three pounds, and they found that sometimes they were 'salting out' bigger babies than those they had worked to save." The hospital promptly hired a psychiatrist to bring them round, to help them see that "physicians help people in what they need, and a nurse should feel that way." Eventually the head nurse of the prenatal clinic, "who was 'all in favor of abortions,' said she prided herself on the fact that she did not make moral judgments." A Catholic nurse, who would "never have an abortion" herself, decided to work with abortors because of her belief that "a woman has rights over her own body," but she obtained a transfer to the recovery room, where "we don't see the fetus passed."[267]

Some doctors also speak of being disturbed. Nathanson tells about this:

> Curiously, abortion appears sometimes to have had a more profound effect on the people who were doing them than on those on whom they were being done. . . .
>
> I also recall well being cornered by the wife of one doctor at the cocktail party we gave when the 62nd Street clinic opened. She drew me aside and talked in a decidedly agitated manner of the increasingly frequent nightmares her husband had been having. He had confessed to her that the dreams were filled with blood and children, and that he had latterly become obsessed with the notion

that some terrible justice would soon be inflicted upon his own children in payment for what he was doing. Another time, the wife of a second doctor, who had done at least 2,000 abortions at the place, phoned to report that her husband had developed a serious drinking problem over the past year that, in her view, was precipitated by the clinic work. Yet another doctor walked into my office after three weeks on the job and submitted his resignation. He declared that he had absolutely no feelings on the morality of abortion as such, but "when I'm up this close to it, it's just too much for me. Too bloody, too much pressure. You guys are turning out abortions here like an assembly line, and you expect us to work at this with no feelings at all."[268]

Nathanson himself, as his clinic attained an output of one hundred abortions a day, seven days a week, began to be upset at the recitation of these figures at weekly staff meetings: "As Pyle read off her statistics, all of us forgot that these were little human cataclysms, bloody and often unforgettable to those involved." This conflict became critical as he involved himself in perinatology, the medical diagnosis and treatment of the unborn. "What began to erode the NARAL dogmas was the daily realization of the 'intrauterine patient' that we were treating, tracing, sampling and observing through electric monitoring of the flickering images on an ultrasonic screen. To a physician, *that* is reality."[269]

Dr. Anthony Shaw, who allows disappointed parents of handicapped newborn children the right to have them deprived of medical care and thus eliminated, reports: "As a surgeon whose natural inclination is to use the scalpel to fight off death, standing by and watching a salvageable baby die is the most emotionally exhausting experience I know. It is easy at a conference, in theoretical discussion, to decide that such infants should be allowed to die. It is altogether different to stand by in the nursery and watch as dehydration and infection wither a tiny being over hours and days. This is a terrible ordeal for me and the hospital staff—much more so than for the parents who never set foot in the nursery." Shaw later observes: "It seems to me that a society which does not provide for its defectives is less than humane."[270]

The moral issue, however, is not raised by disturbance or disgust at human carnage, but by the way otherwise decent people incorporate a work of destruction into their lives without persistent distress or visible coarsening of other ethical behavior. Norma Rosen, who interviewed abortionists for the *New York Times*, found some who derived great gratification from their work. "Apparently feeling guiltless, these doctors are positive about what they do. For them, much of the idealism associated with delivering babies has gone into their fetus-aborting skills." Dr. Howard Diamond of Beth Israel Medical Center explained the reticence of some doctors: "Cultural—it's all cultural. Like eating snake meat. If you tell yourself it's disgusting, you'll get sick." His colleague, Dr. William Rashbaum, veteran of thousands of abortions, had for years suffered during each removal the fantasy of the fetus resisting, hanging on to the uterus walls with its tiny fingernails, fighting to stay inside. How, he was asked, had he managed while enduring this fantasy? "Learned to live with it. Like people in concentration camps." Did he really mean that analogy? "I think it's apt—destruction of life. Look! I'm a person, I'm entitled to my feelings. And my feelings are who gave me or anybody the right to terminate a pregnancy? I'm entitled to that feeling, but I also have no right to communicate it to the patient who desperately wants that abortion. I don't get paid for my feelings. I get paid for my skills. . . . I'll be frank. I began to do abortions in large numbers at the time of my divorce when I needed money. But I also believe in the woman's right to control her biological destiny. I spent a lot of years learning to deliver babies. Sure, it sometimes hurts to end life instead of bringing it into the world."[271]

Part of the intention of the abortion movement has been to alleviate moral concern and distress. As Fletcher explains it to the medical profession, what is called for is "a quality-of-life ethics instead of the sanctity-of-life ethics in the classical Western tradition." Any appeal to a reverence for others' lives is "metarational" and "undiscussable." All alleged rights (which are unreliable because "genetic and embryologic investigation" fails to justify them) are at best imperfect and relative. "But what is there, then, to appeal to, to validate our humanistic concerns to our person-centered values? My answer is: needs. . . . If human rights conflict with human needs, let needs prevail."[272]

According to this imperative view of needs, one is invited to isolate abortion from the rest of one's life and work. Georgie Anne Geyer writes with conviction that "it must be clear that abortion is necessary in an industrial society, while working out the rules of its new sexuality." Dr. Marcia Kramer, on the companion issue of life or death for handicapped infants, proposes that cost-benefit analysis might go a long way towards producing a moral decision.[273]

It being a fact one must accept, abortion is better not fretted over. Dr. Henry P. David, a psychologist long active in the international abortion movement, disagrees with the view of a woman who, after a year of interviewing abortion veterans, had written that it was a uniquely important choice an individual must face. Most commonly, he says, the decision to have an abortion ("a surgical procedure") "represents a healthy coping with reality, a maturing experience," and he argues that "it is time to move the focus of the debate from adversity to successful coping."[274]

Yale psychiatrist Stephen Fleck expresses a similar impatience with those who pause overlong for moral reflection:

> There is much discussion about the destruction of the fetus, called murder by some. This is an important legal and ethical question, and abortion could be said to reflect an expression of unconcern for life and its value. But physicians and health professionals as a whole, being preoccupied with the preservation of life and health, are hardly guilty of any such lack of concern. Also, this particular form of murder, if it be that, seems a somewhat hypocritical concern in a society that does little to prevent some 30,000 annual criminal murders and that condones, as do most societies, murder in the service of the national goals determined by its leadership.[275]

In some quarters the issue has been successfully freed from moral misgivings. At a New Orleans fund-raiser for the Louisiana Civil Liberties Union in 1977, for example, an abortion was auctioned off. It went for thirty dollars.

There is, at least in the published literature, little consistent evidence at this time that any of the classes of people responsible for abortion on demand have been visited by disabling questions. It is not, understandably, a work that many cherish or delight in. Potts writes: "No doctor enjoys performing abortions any more than he would enjoy carrying out limb or breast amputations. But it is his appreciation of the improvement in the social and emotional health of the woman that can be expected to follow abortion which encourages him to embark on an intrinsically disagreeable task." Somewhat unrealistically, he describes the doctor and woman as establishing the same sort of link that binds an obstetrician to a mother whom he or she is seeing through pregnancy and delivery. Then, in full flight, he continues:

> The decision of a woman, or a couple, to have an abortion is not necessarily made because they dislike children, it is normally an expression of the fact that at this particular time in their life they feel that they cannot offer a child the love, security and physical support which would meet their ideals: the young unmarried girl feels that she cannot give her baby the life she sees as necessary for its proper healthy development; the married woman often feels that another child would take away from her existing children too much of the physical and emotional resources available and would mean that in the future all her children would be to some extent deprived. Abortion is usually an altruistic decision.[276]

Possibly closer to the mark are the remarks of Dr. Schwartz, a New York physician who, at lower rates than most, had himself performed fifteen thousand abortions: "God knows, I don't wear a halo. God knows, there are more skilled practitioners. But I think in the mix, you could do a helluva lot worse than if you come to me for what I claim to know how to do."[277] One of the contentions frequently made about abortion is that, however bad it is, it is still the lesser evil. Glanville Williams urged it in this way as a measure to eliminate the handicapped: "To allow the breeding of these defectives is a horrible evil, far worse than any that may be found in abortion; yet neither Church nor law perceives any offence to society in it."[278]

By and large, intent ethical concern has been deflected by framing the question as one of conflict of interests. James J. Kilpatrick, the columnist, writes: "There are rational arguments in behalf of the woman who is pregnant with an unwanted child; and there are rational arguments in behalf of the unborn infant capable of survival beyond the womb."[279] The Rockefeller Commission has reported: "The Commission believes that a wise and sound decision in regard to the abortion question requires a careful balancing of the moral problems relating to the woman and the child along with those concerning the fetus."[280] And John Fletcher describes a couple requesting amniocentesis in order to detect and abort a handicapped offspring as "caught between loyalty to the life of their child and loyalty to the norm of 'healthy' life."[281]

Ordinarily, when moral claims or loyalties are measured in the balance, human death weighs more heavily than human distress. To avoid the abortion question's being decided in this customary way, advocates find it helpful to speak of the balance pans as still hanging in swing.

There are a few anomalies in this proabortion position, however, which have begun to attract some notice. It was expected that women who had sought out and experienced abortion and felt no guilty reaction would naturally approve of abortion on demand. Perez-Reyes and Falk, after follow-up studies on young abortors in North Carolina, were surprised to find that although virtually all abortors had had abortions of convenience, a significant proportion of them, after emerging from depression, crying spells, anxiety, guilt, and anger, and eventually declaring themselves glad to have had abortions, did not believe that elective abortion was justified; some even voiced strong opposition. "Apparently in a number of cases, the experience of having [an abortion] did not result in a generalized more liberal attitude but forced the girls to rationalize their guilt by considering themselves 'exceptions' to the rule."[282]

Potts, deploring opposition to abortion on demand from Roman Catholics and from nurses, notes with satisfaction that both groups were well-represented among those who resorted to it.[283] But the inference that people will be ethically consistent enough to approve of what they have been implicated in may not be reliable. For many participants in abortion there is a preliminary obstacle: they consider it a destruction of innocent human life. Some set this moral barrier aside systematically; others may do so for a time, but not thoroughly or permanently. Persons regularly involved in abortion suppose that their clientele must either suffer from residual, religiously induced guilt feelings or go away convinced of the beneficial nature of abortion. But human beings, as the Holocaust shows, are capable of holding in suspension indefinitely the resolution of moral conflict, without either confessing their guilt or deciding that they did no wrong.

A second anomaly has been noticed by a female physician:

> Ideally, the reform is designed to encourage women to take responsibility for this most important aspect of their lives, to give them freedom of choice, and to remove the decision from (usually) male authority figures. Unfortunately, this is not necessarily what happens. . . .
>
> Now that abortion is not only possible but fashionable, many young women do not experience themselves as having a choice in the matter any more than they did before. Whereas society once told them that they must have their babies whether they wanted to or not, it now seems to be telling them that they *may not* have their babies even if they wish to. Before the laws were liberalized in Massachusetts, Nadelson wrote of the mother applying for therapeutic abortion, "we rarely attend to her welfare or that of her children; we do not consider her needs, her capacities or aspirations as she sees them." Now that the laws have been changed, Nadelson's statement unfortunately still stands.[284]

The advent of mass abortion has not, it seems, eradicated exploitation by the abortion mills. Just after the 1973 rulings Robert Hall, whose Association for the Study of Abortion had striven so hard to bring about the change, looked into the future. Would "abortion specialists" pop up everywhere? "Not very likely. We're expecting to see about a million and a half legal abortions a year—about triple the number now. But instead of being concentrated in a few states, they'll be distributed evenly among M.D.s in every state— probably about 20,000 in all. That's an average of only a couple of abortions a week per doctor—hardly a big enough figure to constitute a new specialty." It would, he was sure, mean the end of the commercial abortion clinic.[285]

But it has been otherwise. Five out of six hospitals in the country will not permit abortions except as a truly emergency procedure to save a mother's life. Most obstetricians and the overwhelming majority of other physicians and most nurses choose not to participate in abortions. Most of the nearly million and a half abortions are performed in clinics heavily advertised in the classified pages, with commissions paid to referral "counselors," and toll-free telephone numbers advertised in the yellow pages to attract business from other towns. The enormous volume of abortion work is, for the most part, handled by doctors and nurses who no longer deliver children, either because their patients have left them or because the income from abortion work is more attractive. These practitioners, it now appears, although they have equipment and techniques that involve less material risk than even ten years ago, tend to run clinics with only the thinnest veneer of professional care for their customers. There are no patients, only clients. It seems to cause some wonder and astonishment to investigative reporters sympathetic to the abortion cause that this kind of mercenary person should have been attracted to—indeed, should now dominate—the purveying of this "surgical procedure."

Comparison with the Holocaust is suggested less by the venal and septic proprietors of abortion mills than by the other folk who are involved in abortion and who have not ostensibly integrated their ethical lives with human alienation or exploitation. Most apparently do not suffer the nightmares of Franz Stangl or Dr. Nathanson's colleague. The medical experiments on the unconsenting unborn are openly performed and the results published in professional journals as were those undertaken at Dachau and Treblinka on unconsenting inmates. Most of the establishment physicians, who abort only their private patients, disdain those of their colleagues who are able to satisfy themselves with this disagreeable work day in, day out. They can say, "I was certainly not one of these." Humane, under the circumstances. Potts's "no doctor enjoys performing abortions" evokes Brandt's "do you think that it was a pleasure for me?" In neither case is there any vicious intent.

5: A Readiness to Kill—The Unlatching of Self-Preference

In 1964 Garrett Hardin was one of the few publicly avowed advocates of abortion on demand. One of the objections he had then to contend with had been raised by Norman St. John-Stevas, a member of Parliament: "Once the principle of the sanctity of life is abandoned there can be no criterion of the right to life save that of personal taste . . . once exceptions are made the whole structure of human rights is undermined." To disallow this "camel's nose" argument Hardin cites the use of automobiles and of alcohol. Both are dangerous, both can kill, yet we do not think the wise way to cope with either hazard is to outlaw it. "Abortion, like alcohol and speed, is a danger, and we want to minimize it."[286]

Hardin either misses or sidesteps St. John-Stevas's point, which was not that abortion was hazardous and therefore to be managed carefully, but that it leapt entirely over the principle that human life is to be reverenced simply because it is human life. Once one is prepared to destroy another for one's own satisfaction, what principle is left to protect any other possible victim?

Glanville Williams, in the lists for abortion even before Hardin, had (like Hardin) disavowed infanticide. Both regarded it as violating "the sanctity of life." Apropos of infanticide in pre-Christian Greece and Rome, Williams in 1957 quoted his predecessor, Cambridge jurist J. R. Seely:

> "Habit dulls the sense and puts the critical faculty to sleep. The fierceness and hardness of ancient manners is apparent to us, but the ancients themselves were not shocked by sights which were familiar to them. To us it is sickening to think of the gladiatorial show, of massacres common in Roman warfare, of the infanticide practiced by grave and respectable citizens, who did not merely condemn their children to death, but often in practice, as they well knew, to what was still worse—a life of prostitution and beggary. The Roman regarded a gladiatorial show as we regard a hunt; the news of the slaughter of two hundred thousand Helvetians by Caesar or half a million Jews by Titus excited in his mind a thrill of triumph; infanticide committed by a friend appeared to him a prudent measure of household economy."[287]

It is interesting to note just what each abortion advocate has to say in these earlier days with respect to infanticide. Hardin writes: "Who would recommend infanticide, open or covert, as a remedy for failure in birth control? I would not; and I know no one who would. So let us pass on." Williams, reflecting on the ancient practice, writes: "What seems appalling to the modern mind about the behavior of the Athenian Greeks of the classical age, and of the Romans, too, is perhaps not so much their custom of getting rid of newly born children for whom they could not provide, as the means they adopted for doing so. The practice of exposing the baby meant that death was the most merciful fate that might befall it; often the child might be picked up by someone, and reared for slavery or prostitution."[288] One notes that both writers avoid the more basic comment: that it is wrong to destroy children. Hardin thinks the question is moot, and he has no principle whereby to deal with it if it is raised. Williams wishes that the Greeks and Romans had dispatched their young more efficiently, and admits the ominous thought that some people would be better off dead. Each writer has let slip the dogs of death.

The Holocaust, as one can see in the record, was not a program fully planned which proceeded as foreseen. Each phase begot the next. The first set of victims were mental patients, eliminated to free hospital facilities for the war. Then it was the turn of those being cared for at home, for as useless eaters they were also a burden. Next came the handicapped children, for they would bring no strengthening to the national stock, the enhancement of which was of the highest priority. Then came the conscientious objectors and Jehovah's Witnesses, who refused to serve the nation's most urgent need. Then Gypsies, and homosexuals, and Soviet political commissars. Then the Jews, country by country, as possible. Then their own most badly wounded soldiers. As it became clear to those involved that they really could with impunity dispose of humans as they wished, and as they got the feel of it, they introduced breeding establishments for Germans and sponsored abortion for inferior peoples. They let loose their physicians on the prison populations as on a whole new supply of laboratory animals. The science of death, as one observer later said, had become a sinister newcomer among the life sciences.

Step by step the procedures, the personnel, the policy, the political acquiescence, the disposition to destroy—all moved forward together, given appetite by each feeding. We have no evidence that any planner of the Holocaust or any participant in it saw or intended what they would willingly be doing at its crest. Yet from the autumn of 1939, when first they fell upon innocent human beings whom they found undesirable, *because* they found them undesirable, no principle was left to bridle their expansive appetite to rid the world of the unwanted.

The abortion story is not dissimilar. Since developments in the United Kingdom preceded those in the United States, and were not without influence here, they merit mention. The English law, common and statutory, considered abortion a crime. In the 1930s the College of Obstetricians and Gynaecologists supported abortion for rape victims, and in 1938 the Birkett Committee recommended that it be rightful if needed to save a mother's life. That same year, in the celebrated case of *Rex* v. *Bourne*, a physician was acquitted of aborting a girl of fourteen, pregnant by rape. Various bills were then introduced in Parliament: in 1952–53 and in 1954, to allow abortion "for the purpose of preventing injury to the mother in body or health"; in 1961 and 1963, in case of rape or risk of child deformity; in 1965, to relieve injury to physical or mental health, or in case of deformity, social inadvisability, or pregnancy through sexual offense. None of these bills passed. The Abortion Act of 1967 permitted abortions in hospitals, authorized by two doctors, to relieve risks to physical or mental health of mother or family, or risk of child handicap. Abortions thereafer rose to one million per annum from an estimated ten to one hundred thousand. The restraint of dual authorization was eased by the creation of abortion hospitals, wherein doctors could countersign for each other's clients. The requirement of health risk has, in fact, been neutralized into abortion on demand, as the statistics show. A conscience clause which allowed medical personnel to abstain (the medical profession and its societies had raised opposition to the bill in 1967) was noted by the Lane Committee, formed to review the law in 1974; the committee then gave its approval to the device whereby only students who were proabortion would be admitted into gynecological practice. The need for the conscience clause would thus eventually be obviated by excluding from the profession those who were conscientiously opposed to abortion. As the 1970s progressed, earlier medical resistance to abortion yielded. There were disturbances over trafficking in the corpses of the unborn, but they came to nothing. An attempt to tighten up the law failed in 1975. Bills have now been introduced to decriminalize "euthanasia."[289]

In the United States the legal situation has developed differently. Instead of a single rule of law in the land there are fifty states and a variety of federal jurisdictions, each with its own code. The old Anglo-American tradition was modified in all of those jurisdictions in the nineteenth century by the combined efforts of the newly formed American Medical Association and a coalition of influential Protestant clergy. Discoveries in the early 1800s had revised the understanding of life's origins. Abortion laws, accordingly reformed, protected the unborn no longer from the time of quickening in the womb, but from conception onward. Provision for therapeutic abortion was made within the law, however. This usually required the services of a licensed physician, in an accredited hospital, with the concurrence of a specified number of other physicians, to save a mother from death or from grave threat to her health.

During the early 1960s the American Law Institute, which had been drafting a model penal code for use by the states, suggested a law on abortion that would allow it not only to preserve the mother's physical or mental health, but also to avert birth of a child with grave physical or mental defect, and when pregnancy resulted from rape or incest. This scheme was endorsed by the American Bar Association in 1967, the same year that a similar plan received support from the American Medical Association. Colorado, California, and North Carolina had conformed their laws to this model by the end of the year, and seven other states followed by 1969. Reported abortions sharply increased. In 1969 a federal court swept away all legal restrictions on abortion in the District of Columbia, and in 1971 the Supreme Court restored the law but said that the "health" provision was to be interpreted elastically as "psychological as well as physical." Abortion reports swelled, and then Hawaii, Alaska, and New York saw movements to repeal, not rewrite, the abortion laws. By 1972 the ABA was calling for abortion through the twentieth week of pregnancy; New York allowed it until the twenty-fourth week. The American College of Obstetricians and Gynecologists agreed to the abandonment both of medical grounds for abortion and of the need for concurring medical opinion. In 1973 the Supreme Court struck down abortion laws in every state of the Union, permitting abortion on demand throughout pregnancy, on the private agreement of woman and abortionist. Three years later husbands and parents of minor daughters were excluded from the abortion decisions of their partners and children, and litigation was begun to oblige the public treasuries to pay for elective abortions for the poor. In 1978 authority to allow a minor child to have an abortion was still withheld from parents, but was granted to local judges. Reported abortions now exceed a million and a half annually, outnumbering live births in the District of Columbia and certain other cities.

Meanwhile, in the same year as *Wade* and *Bolton*, medical journals carried reports on systematic programs to destroy handicapped infants in hospital nurseries. The March of Dimes fund for elimination of birth defects facilitated amniocentesis studies to allow couples the choice of eliminating an unborn who carried such defects. Because amniocentesis could also be used to determine the sex of the fetus, couples were then able to abort on the basis of gender preference. Infanticide was offered as a postterm abortion decision in the same way abortion had been offered as an ex post factum contraception decision. In 1975 a national ethics panel commended virtually unrestricted experimentation on the unborn before, during, and after abortion.[290]

One could say that the nation has traveled some distance between 1963, when Planned Parenthood discouraged abortion because, unlike contraception, it destroys "the life of a baby after it has begun," and the present, when a researcher may, without legal or other hindrance, decapitate a batch of living second-trimester abortuses in order to study the rate of oxidation in their brains.[291]

While there has been considerable change in practice there has been none in principle. From the start the governing principle has held that one may eliminate inconvenient life, by category and by individual. Once that principle of expendability had been embraced, "inconvenient life" began to be seen in many forms. Neither the status nor the merits of the lives judged eligible for elimination had any bearing on that determination; what was to be measured was not worth but desirability, with status under the law to be revised accordingly. This was done under the aegis of what the Constitution calls "due process."

When this course was predicted early on, the observation was resented. Sharon Robbins and Bruce Granger commented on the debates before the British Abortion Act of 1967: "All the dreary, pompous arguments were brought out. The authoritarian thundering of the Vatican Council was heard throughout the land: 'Life must, from its very conception, be guarded with the greatest care. Abortion and infanticide are abominable crimes.' (Note the dishonest dialecticism. Of course, infanticide is an abominable crime, but why couple it with abortion? You might as well couple child beating, or torture to death. But if you did that, of course, it would be ridiculous; and so would the logic in the Vatican's statement become!)"[292]

Bernard Nathanson, discussing the "slippery slope," is of two minds: "Where is the evidence that abortion produces a generally lowered regard for life in democratic societies? . . . The linkage with mercy-killing, also common, does not credit human intelligence with the ability to distinguish between two issues which are separable and highly complicated on their own terms. . . . Strangely, they seldom mention the one instance in which abortion may produce a slide down the moral slope: the question of infanticide."[293] Williams, as we have seen, simply did not think infanticide would come to be desired or practiced. But he did view it as an issue that stood on the same principles as abortion. "Law," he wrote in 1956, "has been called the cement of society, and certainly society would fall to pieces if men could murder with impunity." There were, however, three forms of killing, of murder, which had been prohibited without consideration for the security of society: abortion, infanticide, and suicide. He saw no advantage in laws against any of the three.[294]

Others were quick to see that infanticide posed no substantially new problem for those who had accepted abortion. In 1972, when the courts were ruling that humans became persons at birth, Stanford philosopher Michael Tooley objected that this cutoff point had no obvious moral relevance. Looking elsewhere, he argued that an individual becomes a person, and thus has a serious right to life, only when psychologically mature enough to desire consciously to have that right. Thus infanticide is allowable, as is abortion.[295]

Quite a number of abortion people saw it the same way. Milton Heifetz, chief of neurological surgery at a Los Angeles hospital, reported his practice of eliminating infants whose lives he did not think adequately meaningful, who did not have enough of what he calls "salvage value." The newborn, he argued in 1975, was hardly less potential in its humanity than a fetus. "Is life at birth any more significant than at the second, fourth, or sixth month of pregnancy? It is not."[296] A Virginia medical professor argued in the *New York Times* that denial of surgical treatment to a handicapped infant was a woman's second chance to have an abortion.[297] An attorney with the Childhood and Government Project at Berkeley, F. Raymond Marks, pursued the suggestion mentioned above, that infanticide serve as a backup for abortion just as abortion is a backup for birth control. Any squeamishness about accepting the "fiction of non-personhood," Mark says, could be alleviated by "briefly withholding birth certificates and names from high risk infants and those in certain categories." "How different," Marks asks, "is the decision in the nursery from that of the pregnant woman?" Not much, if one looks at the reasons for infanticide that are acceptable: "if the infant is defective and unwanted by its parents and unneeded by society"; if it would avoid emotional burdens for his or her brothers and sisters, or financial strain for the father and mother. One even hears repeated the formula so familiar from the early days of abortion on demand: many "would never consider" infanticide for themselves but "would not condemn" others who resorted to it.[298]

One is drawn to contemplate a comment by Dr. John M. Freeman, whose curiosity was roused by reports that from 1958 to 1962, exactly when surgical techniques to treat myelomeningocele had made doctors more optimistic about the future of babies born with this defect, the "stillbirth" rate for children so afflicted had fallen from about one-half of those born to zero. Freeman sees this statistic as implying that obstetricians had previously eliminated many such children and falsified the death certificates. This would suggest that infanticide, in the experience of doctors, had actually preceded abortion as a covert but accepted practice.[299]

An idea whose time has come is not slow to beget its successor. When abortion on demand was being legitimated across the United States, Florida was considering a bill to allow doctors in state hospitals to eliminate retarded patients. The bill's proponent, a legislator who was also a physician, stated that 90 percent of the fifteen hundred retarded in Florida institutions should be allowed to die. "Why not let them die, when the money for their care could be used for such good social purposes? Five billion dollars could be saved over the next fifty years in Florida if the mongoloids in our state institutions were permitted to succumb to pneumonia."[300]

As *Time* magazine stated in that same year, 1973: "While legal purists complain that euthanasia and the right to die peacefully are separate issues, the fact is that they are converging." It was a year for many convergences and few purists.[301]

It is only recently that laws allowing the states forcibly to sterilize or to castrate the retarded (it is called a "medical intervention") and those incapable of providing for themselves have begun to disturb black and Hispanic leaders. What if the visionaries guiding social policy saw *their* poor as particularly shiftless, the sort that should not reproduce?[302] One columnist, seeing these things as harbingers of the future, waggishly imagined a memo that might issue from an HEW-funded clinic to a couple who had just had twins:

> Our records show you have two more children than is morally defensible. While we certainly would be reassured to know you have taken steps to produce the 2,000,000 gallons of fresh water, 600 head of livestock, 300 acres of crop land, 5,000,000 cubic yards of oxygen and 500 tons of manufacturing your brats will squander in their long, prodigal lifetimes, we understand that accidents will happen.
>
> Meanwhile, won't you and your wife report to the clinic 8 A.M. sharp Tuesday for surgical alteration. To save a trip you might as well bring your extra children to the Surplus Children Home next door so we can place them with a family which hasn't used its quota.[303]

The humor here ought not distract from the fact that only a few years have intervened since one of the strong objections to abortion was its likeness to infanticide. Now that abortion advocates have no principle with which to disavow infanticide and have overcome their earlier distaste for it, the arguing point gives them no pause or difficulty.[304]

Advocates of medical experimentation on the unborn argue that if abortion be rightful, what they propose can hardly be objected to. "In abortion, we condone procedures which subject the fetus to dismemberment, salt-induced osmotic shock, or surgical extirpation. No experimentation so far imagined would do the same. If society can condone abortion procedures which subject the live fetus to these unimaginable acts of violence, how can it balk at [using the occasion for research that will benefit wanted babies]?"[305]

There are other comparisons which could be recounted. These suffice to evoke comparisons with the Holocaust, which began, not with the Final Solution to the Jewish Question halfway through the war, but with the first decision, dated the day the war began, to eliminate humans whose lives were considered to be unmeaningful because burdening. The abortion avalanche dates back, not to *Wade* and *Bolton* in 1973, but to the conversations held by the American Law Institute in the 1950s, when the idea took hold that some unborn should be destroyed, not for any serious danger they presented, but simply because they were undesirable. From that all followed. And we do not yet know what that all will be.

Two sequences began, each requiring that those to be eliminated be selected by "the most critical evaluation" by physicians. Each would ultimately exterminate wholesale victims whose doom had absolutely nothing to do with health, medicine, or anything else doctors had been trained or licensed to know or serve. Two programs unfolded under the supervision of men of the law, whose chief service was to find legal grounds for decreeing the prospective victims out of the human community, group by ostracized group. Each program, though meant to reduce the population, had its curious obverse: Hitler's Order of the Rabbit is congruent with Doctor Steptoe's financing of his fertility research from the proceeds of his abortion practice. Hitler's belief that "nature is cruel" has an echo in Glanville Williams's remark about the bitch killing her puppies: both are ready to help the natural order of things. The skulls of Jewish commissars sent by the SS to Strassburg for study are lamentably like the heads cut from the unborn for NIH research at Helsinki: both yield a sadly wrought science. The reassuring silence of the German parents who asked no questions about why their handicapped youngsters came home as envelopes of ashes has its counterpart in the reaction of those who gave the word that their children should perish in the Yale–New Haven nursery: "Although some have exhibited doubts that the choices were correct, all appear to be as effective in their lives as they were before this experience."[306] All could say with Abe Reles, "I got used to it." John Noonan remembers John Updike's comment after the abortion in *Couples*: "Death, once invited in, leaves his muddy bootprints everywhere."[307]

6: There Was Profit in It—Where Blood Ran, Money Flowed

By the time abortion on demand was regularized in 1973, the decline in childbirths had already caused concern among obstetricians. One specialist's reaction was pragmatic: "A lot of doctors who previously depended on obstetrics rather than gynecology have found their incomes curtailed. They think they're going to make up for it by doing abortions." One salesman reported receiving twenty orders for suction machines from a single city on the day of the 1973 decisions.[308] Another obstetrician-gynecologist comments: "I must decide whether I should get rich or watch my colleagues get rich from my rejects."[309]

The picture is not clear, but it appears that all those who have abortion as their main practice can expect incomes that are considerable, even for physicians. Nathanson remembers that doctors in his clinic could clear more than a thousand dollars on an eight-hour shift, and that some worked double shifts to earn more.[310]

At the low-price, high-volume operations in Chicago, one doctor alone billed Medicaid $792,266 for abortions in 1974—and this for only his welfare customers. One large abortion center promised a prospective abortionist in a recruitment letter: "Salary and fringe benefits will be extremely attractive. Imagine the opportunity to make at least $80,000 a year for no more than ten hours work each week." A woman running a telephone abortion referral and "counseling" facility made up to $5,000 per week on commissions from abortionists. A pathology lab supplying reports on abortion remains charged

Illinois Public Aid $735,000 in 1977 at $8 per report, twice what private clients were charged. "Business is business," said the owner, "and the way you bring in business is to give good prices." Some clinics ran as many as nine different want ads in the classified pages, with nine different names and telephone numbers, to attract more business. One investigator estimated that 12 percent of the women serviced in one clinic under observation were not pregnant and had had negative pregnancy tests. The key to the entire business was given by Judith Widdicombe, president of the National Abortion Federation, whose post-exposé statement was: "We just want the safest possible conditions for the consumer." Women in these circumstances had clearly been transformed from patients into consumers: the transformation in the physicians was comparable.[311]

Another aspect of the financial gain associated with abortion is the savings entailed by eliminating the unborn. As one hot-line agent was overheard to say while impatiently trying to make a sale to an undecided woman over the phone, "Having a baby is a $410,000 question. Do you have that kind of money to raise a kid?"[312] Glanville Williams also pointed out an economic advantage in abortion for the British National Health Service: "It is also to be noticed that an abortion if properly performed results in a considerable saving of hospital time; whereas a woman who gives birth to a child spends about ten days in a hospital, between two and four days are enough for a medical abortion [this was in 1964]."[313]

James Neel, sympathetic towards elimination of the handicapped through abortion, observes: "Any one of us can document instances in which the prolonged care of such individuals as these . . . has entailed exorbitant cost to some agency or institution, with the ultimate result—loved though he or she may be—a very marginal performance in our complex society. While I do not for one moment wish to place a price tag on a human life, I cannot help wondering how that same sum spent on normal children might advance the interests of society."[314]

The same economic cost-benefit analysis, writ large, is used to sustain the use of tax monies for abortions of the poor. Dr. Louis Hellman, veteran abortion strategist, pointed this out after he had been deputy assistant secretary of HEW. An abortion, he said, "costs only about $350 at most while pre-natal care through the first year of a baby's life costs $2,200. It is estimated to cost $35,261 to raise a child to the age of 18."[315] The Population Resource Center reported that the 600,000 births to teenagers in 1979 would cost taxpayers eight billion dollars over a twenty-year period. If abortion were to be outlawed, or no longer financed by tax funds, "the increase in the number of births . . . would send government costs skyrocketing."[316] Congresswoman Shirley Chisholm, in a letter to congressional colleagues in 1977, urged abortion funding lest "unwanted children increase such program outlays considerably."[317]

So reasonable a view is it that elimination of the offspring of the poor is the equivalent of a tax-relief measure, that when suit was brought in a federal court to compel the government to pay out funds for elective abortions which Congress had refused to appropriate, the solicitor general of the United States and the general counsel for HEW, charged with defending that congressional prerogative, admitted to the court that abortions for the poor would constitute a governmental economy, by saving "monies that would otherwise have been expended for childbirths and post-natal care if women were to carry unwanted pregnancies to term."[318]

Abortion has been called an alternative that could help poor women to avoid being drawn down further into the vortex of indigence. Others not so poor have also found it financially meaningful. The poor have learned to view with healthy skepticism the advice of the affluent concerning ways in which they might economize. Or, as the hostess at a gala benefit to raise funds for Planned Parenthood, given by the social leaders of Palm Beach, explained: "It's the charity that makes other charities unnecessary."

7: The Disarming of the Sentinels—A Temporizing Resistance

When the fires of the Holocaust were first lit, the social forces within Germany that might have denied it its victims were notable. We have seen that three of them—the medical profession, the churches, and the leadership of the Jewish community—were effectively neutralized because the objections and resistance they did put forward were oblique. They temporized. The heart of the outrage, the willful destruction of human beings because they were considered undesirable, was not condemned. Instead, the greatest annoyance the Third Reich had to put up with was a series of impotent maneuvers. The SS was willing to haggle over details, but all the while the boxcars were being loaded.

In the later 1960s it was becoming clear that the medical profession in this country was facing a major crisis in professional ethics. There was a flurry of efforts to legalize abortion on demand. In 1967 a large poll by *Modern Medicine* showed 87 percent of physicians to be in favor of some kind of abortion law change.[319] That same year a survey of the OB-GYN staffs in teaching hospitals in North America showed that, in order to evade laws to the contrary, those hospitals were accepting nontherapeutic indications for "therapeutic" abortions, and the staffs wanted the laws either changed or abolished. Despite the practice of abortion for social, emotional, and economic indications, all institutions required consultation with or approval by other colleagues. In one more intensive survey the researchers found that only one out of forty-four abortion requests was actually being granted.[320]

That same year the AMA accepted its Committee on Human Reproduction's recommendation permitting abortion on substantially the same indications that the American Law Institute and American Bar Association had approved: mother's life or health, child's deformity, rape or incest. It laid heavy stress on having abortions performed by a physician, in concert with professional colleagues, in an accredited hospital. Three years later, with allusions to "sound clinical judgment," "due concern for the patient's welfare," and "informed patient consent," the AMA resolved that abortions should be performed by duly licensed physicians, in consultation with specially selected colleagues, in conformity with high medical standards and personally held moral convictions. There was now no further mention of grounds for abortions. That year the American College of Obstetricians and Gynecologists abandoned its consultation rule and its norms for proper medical indications for abortion. Simultaneously, the American Public Health Association called for easily available counseling, facilities, referral, and treatment.

Throughout this transforming period two concerns run continuously: the medical profession is anxious to retain professional control of the process—and equally anxious to free itself from the threat of prosecution. The doctors wish, on the one hand, to prevent the burgeoning abortion practice from becoming the exclusive domain of their disreputable abortionist colleagues, and, on the other, to be left unvisited by the costly intrusions of the law as they take up this new work themselves.

Within the deliberating chambers of the medical fraternity there was virtually total silence about the norms and professional criteria that its members, once unrestrained by the law and freed to abort on nonmedical grounds, should rightly follow. Moving into a swirl of such vital issues as family fidelity, economic inequality, the liberation of women, philosophical principles, criminal sexuality, population management, religious ethics, domestic relations, welfare policy, adolescent sexual liaisons, inheritance law, and much besides—they address the single concern that this be treated in an accredited hospital. And while they sit voting on consultation with especially competent specialists, the new chains of abortion clinics in rented offices are handling two-thirds of the trade.

The churches meanwhile were alerted to abortion as an issue on which they would have to take a stand. The American Baptist Churches, the American Friends Service Committee, the American Jewish Congress, the American Lutheran Church, the B'nai B'rith Women, the Central Conference of American Rabbis, the Disciples of Christ, the Church of the Brethren, the Episcopal Church and the Women of the Episcopal Church, the Lutheran Church in America, the National Council of Jewish Women, the National Federation of Temple Sisterhoods, the Presbyterian Church in the U.S., the Reformed Church in America, the Reorganized Church of Jesus Christ of Latter-Day Saints, the Union of American Hebrew Congregations, the Unitarian Universalist Association and Women's Federation, the United Church of Christ, the United Methodist Church and Women's Division, the United Presbyterian Church, USA, the United Synagogues of America, the Women's League for Conservative Judaism, and the Young Women's Christian Association—all of these groups published official statements supportive of the new abortion liberty.

The churches had spoken out. Doctors had shied away from the social and moral issues as being none of their medical concern. But this was precisely the churches' métier. Here in this rich loam of family and childbearing, love and treachery, life and life-taking, parents and offspring—here the churches could make a thousand flowers bloom.

But no. Almost to a synod, the churches spoke to the question of law. Some—the Jewish groups especially—made explicit and endorsing reference to the 1973 court decisions; virtually all were focused on the one legal issue of the liberty of women minded to have abortions. There were very rare allusions to "the sanctity of unborn human life." Most, however, spoke out for the "individual" right of the woman to make the abortion decision. Due mention was made of prayer, of clerical counsel, and of "a properly licensed physician." About what might arouse prayer, or guide the counselor, or authorize the physician besides his license, there is not a whisper. In substance, there is little in these documents that would differentiate them from similar declarations of the American Civil Liberties Union, the American Humanist Association, the American Law Institute, the National Organization for Women, or the Isaac Walton League. They are no tablets of stone. As soon as the Supreme Court went further, to deny to parents any authority in the abortions of their minor daughters, the United Presbyterian Synod of the Northeast hastened to endorse it as a good idea.

The vigor of these churches has been aroused: to support judicial decisions giving individuals a great liberty. The state has been addressed by the churches. That done, what principles—with, were it imaginable, something distinctively Jewish or Christian about them—do the churches offer to their communicants about how to use this great liberty? Is there even a hint that it might best be forgone in favor of some more imposing obligations or duties or ideals? To all of this, the churches offer no solid guidance. It is enough for them that there be no law.

Ranged on the other hill are the Southern Baptists, the Orthodox, the Mormons, the Orthodox Jews, the Roman Catholics. Their statements against abortion have also been colored by the contemporary political struggle. Yet, possibly because theirs is a position whereon religious leaders can take a stand and not simply acquiesce in a secular policy, the statements on this side do have a little ring to them. For instance, the Catholics recur often to the abortion doctrine of Vatican II:

> Furthermore, whatever is opposed to life itself, such as any type of murder, genocide, abortion, euthanasia or willful self-destruction, whatever violates the integrity of the human person, such as mutilation, torments inflicted on body or mind, attempts to coerce the will itself: whatever insults human dignity, such as subhuman living conditions, arbitrary imprisonment, deportation, slavery, prostitution, the selling of women and children; as well as disgraceful working conditions, where men are treated as mere tools for profit, rather than as free and responsible persons; all these things and others of their like are infamies indeed. They poison human society, but they do more harm to those who practice them than those who suffer from the injury. Moreover, they are a supreme dishonor to the Creator. [321]

Following that, the American Catholic bishops in 1968 had taught:

> At this tense moment in our history when external wars and internal violence make us so conscious of death, an affirmation of the sanctity of human life by renewed attention to the family is imperative. Let society always be on the side of life. Let it never

dictate, directly or indirectly, recourse to the prevention of life or to its destruction in any of its phases; neither let it require as a condition of economic assistance that any family yield conscientious determination of the number of its children to the decision of persons or agencies outside the family.[322]

Antiabortion statements by official church groups have been chiefly concerned with abortion as one of many instances of human abuse. Those favoring abortion choice have been concerned with the narrow issue of legal abortion liberty. Both, though, have been unduly fixated on what the government does or does not do.

Church membership does not always graze where official shepherds beckon. All public opinion analysts—Blake, McReady, Gallup, Harris, and their peers—have for years been pointing out that differences between Protestants and Catholics on this subject have been reduced to insignificance. Both constituencies agree, contrary to Catholic official statements, that abortion should be permitted for the mother's life or health or when pregnancy results from rape or incest. Both constituencies agree, contrary to Protestant official statements, that abortion should not be available for other reasons, and certainly not on demand.

There are other anomalies in the commitments of church people. Three of the most distinguished theologians ranged against abortion are Paul Ramey, Albert Outler, and Stanley Hauerwas. All three are Methodists. After the United Methodist Church published an abortion statement accepting that in conflicts of interest a mother might prevail, Outler had this to say:

> The essence of the [Christian] tradition is that no human life has a right to its own *self*-enhancement at the cost of other human life. And it is all of human life that is sacred, from its mysterious origins to its equally mysterious ends. In the sex-procreation-fetus-infant-family syndrome we see a paradigm of human obligation at every level: freedom of choice issuing in consequences that are then accepted as personal and collective responsibility. Care for the unborn is a mutuality between weaker and stronger. It is the essence of every relationship of unselfish love.[323]

Strong condemnations of abortion had come from Protestants like Karl Barth, Dietrich Bonhöffer, Emil Brunner, Helmut Thielicke. It is the view of evangelical journalist-theologian Harold O. J. Brown that "the natural constituency of the pro-abortion group is elitist. The natural anti-abortion constituency is populist: blue-collar and other Catholics, Bible-belt and other Protestants, Mormons. So broad a group cannot be hypnotized by a constitutional doctrine, especially as it has come to realize that it is: a) not what the Founding Fathers meant by the First Amendment; b) not what the nation has practiced for most of two centuries; c) not what the words actually say; and d) not what the majority of the people want today."[324]

On the other hand, a Catholic, Charles E. Curran, has offered this view:

> Abortion could be justified to save the life of the mother or to avert very grave psychological or physical harm to the mother with

the realization that this must truly be grave harm that will perdure over some time and not just a temporary depression. From my theological perspective there is also another theoretical justification for abortion in some conflict situations based on a theological notion of compromise. The theory of compromise recognizes the existence of human sinfulness in our world because of which we occasionally might be in a position in which it seems necessary to do certain things which in normal circumstances we would not do. In the case of abortion, for example, the story as reported about women in Bangladesh who were raped and would no longer be accepted in their communities if they bore a child out of wedlock illustrates a concrete application of the theory of compromise. . . . I am adamantly opposed to any position which does not recognize some independent life in the fetus and which justifies abortion as just another form of contraception [sic].[325]

There are, of course, churchmen like Joseph Fletcher, who serve as chaplains to the abortion movement. Fletcher writes:

The ethical question—to whom do we owe our prior obligation, to the few or the many, the one or the several?—affects live research. Absolutizing or tabooing fetal life, even when a fetus is not wanted, is an obvious form of radical individualism (selfishness and narcissism), because it would deny the research uses of a live fetus which could provide lifesaving substances for living persons or yield lifesaving information.[326]

Also, there has been the contribution of the Anglican bishop of Winchester, John Taylor. The church should simply recognize, Bishop Taylor teaches, "that medical terminations of pregnancy are taking place and that the parents, doctors and nurses involved in them are often in deep perplexity." How minister to that perplexity? Taylor wants to "deepen in society the sense of reverence for life," and has composed a prayer so that "those who take upon themselves such a decision may commit to God what they have done and the life that has been brought to an end":

Heavenly Father, You are the giver of life,
And you share with us the care of the life that is given.
Into your hands we commit in trust
The developing life that we have cut short.
Look in kindly judgment on the decision that we have made
And assure us in all our uncertainty
That your love for us can never change. Amen.

The prayer was not adopted by the Church of England.[327]

Two campus chaplains in California, when the new state law sent many of their coeds to unburden themselves of pregnancy, stated that they understood abortion to be the destruction of children. They asked themselves in 1970: "What happens when a culture makes a radical shift from affirming life in the womb to permitting or even encouraging the destruction of that life?" Their answer: the church must assume the responsibility for "helping to integrate abortion into our culture." The suggested strategy: develop a pre- or postabortion ritual, a celebration that "this is a time to end life"; a rite that will satisfy the male partner's need symbolically to partake in the deed; "an act of confession, an affirmation of the preciousness of life, and an acknowledgement that it is human life which has been or is to be ended." The padres wished especially that the rite stress the theme of sacrifice, "giving up something or someone for what is more valuable." Clearly they were on their way, before the English bishop, to christening everything the culture might conceive, if not all that humans might.[328]

The churches, like the medical profession, have supped with a short spoon at the table of the abortion advocates, and supped badly. The doctors have asked only to be left alone to provide abortion for women who pay them for it. The churches have either blessed the change or blamed it on the government.

Some of the physicians and churchmen who were early sympathizers with what they thought of as a generous cause have later had second thoughts. Dr. Aleck Bourne's name is a benchmark in English history because of *Rex* v. *Bourne*, his 1938 trial for an abortion he performed in so public a way as to provoke a test of the law. Bourne later became a member of the Society for the Protection of the Unborn Child in response to the 1967 Abortion Act. He said that abortion on demand would be a disaster for women. "I've had so many women coming to my surgery and pleading with me to end their pregnancies and being very upset when I have refused. But I have never known a woman who, when the baby was born, was not overjoyed that I had not killed it."[329] A more celebrated defection was that in America of Bernard Nathanson, charter member of NARAL and director of the largest abortion clinic in the country, who professed public dismay at having presided over more than sixty thousand deaths.[330]

Dr. Russell L. McIntyre, medical school professor in New Jersey, reports that the rise of abortion-repeaters, for two, three, or four operations, has rattled the principles of some physicians. Many can understand the need for an abortion. "Once conception has occurred, however, very few physicians accord the product of that conception 'zero' value. It may be less valuable than other concerns surrounding the woman's life, but it is never totally valueless. The conflict is thus between 'reasonable' justification for abortion and the woman's apparent lack of any regard for the fetal life that has been begun in her. Physicians facing these 'repeaters' in abortion clinics often develop the very uncomfortable feeling that their own value system has been co-opted by a valueless system."[331]

C. Eric Lincoln, black social theologian and seminary professor, withdrew his earlier support for the abortion movement. In the 1960s his advocacy of "a woman's complete personal autonomy over her body" made abortion an undiscussable liberty; in the 1970s his mind had changed. "I considered abortion a draconian measure of last resort for a limited class of people who, after having considered the vast implications of what they were about to do, would proceed with fear and trembling and a prayer for forgiveness. I was not prepared for the bloodletting which has, in fact, ensued. I, for one, am sick of blood and bloodletting—in the streets, on the battlefields and in the safe aseptic privacy of a doctor's office. In our continuing retreat from responsibility, we are too ready to wipe out the consequences of our private and public acts with a shrug and a resort to blood."[332]

In December 1978, after the *Sun-Times* exposé of scandals in Chicago abortion mills, the reporters sought a statement from Spencer Parsons, the Protestant minister who had organized that city's Clergy Consultation Service ten years earlier to refer women to abortionists. "The state," he replied, "has to do a better job of regulating and supervising the abortion clinics."[333]

There was a third group that might have resisted the abortion movement: the women. It was not to be so. In fact, the most persuasive constituent behind the movement in the season of its satisfaction was a coalition of women's organizations.

The women's movement directed its grievances at familiar targets: husbands, children, employers, educators, clergy, physicians, officials, communications people, all who had unfairly and unthinkingly burdened women with stifling inequalities. But the new leadership of the late sixties, typified in the founding and the founders of NOW, handled these grievances differently. First, unlike their counterparts in older feminist groups, they were not women mostly satisfied in their own lives and ready to push for others less well settled. Many of these new women had experienced personal disappointments which they believed to be evidence of the society's mistreatment of their sex. When they told their resentful stories, crowds of women identified with them, and push came to shove. Second, instead of claiming independence as a public strategy and equality as a domestic one, the new leaders pushed an indiscriminately alienating policy that sought freedom, in family as elsewhere, by individual and even overtly self-centered withdrawal from the jeopardy that commitment to husbands had conventionally put them in. Third, these women made this alienation such a loyalty test within the movement that feminists who saw it as corrosive to the family were either excluded from the movement or made silent within it. Also, men who supported the causes of female liberation were expected to give the salute to this policy and its strategies, one of which was abortion advocacy. Myths collapsed at this time. One which was due to fall anyway was that of the woman as she-tigress, instinctively protective of her cubs to the point of risking her own life. With tens of millions of women across the world extirpating their offspring every year, mother-love had to be something besides instinct.

The case for abortion on demand, then, was argued by women who maintained that sexual fertility, once thought a prime social value, was a very private thing: an intimacy possessed, managed, controlled rather than shared. A woman's special time of vulnerability being when with child (an economic, emotional, physical vulnerability), advocates for women proposed free access to abortion as a means of lessening the control of others over women's lives. The sexual embrace and the springing of life within—in other eyes, what cleaved man and woman, old and young, together—was now to be an arena that woman entered armed, with her native nearest, spouse and child, as potential adversaries.[334]

Women anxious to struggle for equality, both newcomers and veterans, were expected by the new leadership to prove their loyalty by supporting abortion on demand, by pleading its cause as a conflict of interests, of rights. The question being put that way, the woman's interests were sure now to prevail. As has been noted, "All of those who oppose abortion are already born."

The unborn, in these two decades, have been *personae non gratae* to their three traditional tutelaries. The doctors found that the unborn was no longer their patient, and took pains to assure that the mother not go elsewhere for services they could provide, services no longer medical but no less lucrative. The churches were concerned that the government not impose on all a rule that many had come to doubt. They exhorted the government to impose no ethic on their adherents. And this took so much of the churches' energies that they themselves failed to give the moral teaching they fought to be free to give. The women were struggling for opportunity themselves, and took the abortion movement as an ally. If the child was an undesirable burden, he or she must pay the forfeit of the mother's freedom. In a macabre footnote to abortion-as-for-women came the revelation that after a new sex-disclosure test for the unborn was discovered in China, twenty-nine of the first thirty women to learn that they were carrying daughters aborted them.[335]

The Holocaust and the Abortion Movement

The Holocaust gave off a moral stench that should linger in our nostrils. The flesh-hungry barbarity which enjoyed, then, its freedom to stalk the land cannot be killed. It can only be caged. It creeps abroad in other guises, at other times, on other errands. But there are telltale features on its face by which we can be warned. The resemblances I have set forth above suggest to me that the putrid decay in the open pits at Babi Yar and the sacrificial smoke that rose from Auschwitz were the effluvia of a spirit that now leaves like offerings in the pails of Pre-Term and the incinerators of the Center for Reproductive and Sexual Health.

The reader will want to have a further look, to ask for herself or himself whether it be so. The author's finding was brought home to him one afternoon when he was studying the law of another land—almost the only developed, industrial country in the world that has curbed the aborting of its unborn.

In that land, an article of the Basic Law, or constitution, reads: "Everyone has the right to life." It also provides: "Everyone has the right to the free development of his personality to the extent that he does not infringe upon the rights of others and does not violate the constitutional order or the moral law."

In that land, representatives of both major parties approached the question of abortion by agreeing that "the legal value of unborn life is to be respected in principle equally with that of born life."

In that land the highest court, charged with interpretation of the Basic Law, has ruled:

> Where human life exists, human dignity is present to it; it is not decisive that the bearer of this dignity himself be conscious of it and know personally how to preserve it. The potential faculties

present in the human being from the beginning suffice to establish human dignity. . . .

Human life represents, within the order of the Basic Law, ultimate value, the particulars of which need not be established; it is the living foundation of human dignity and the prerequisite for all other fundamental rights. . . .

Were the embryo to be considered only as a part of the maternal organism the interruption of pregnancy would remain in the area of the private structuring of one's life, where the legislature is forbidden to encroach. . . .

Since, however, the one about to be born is an independent human being who stands under the protection of the constitution, there is a social dimension to the interruption of pregnancy which makes it amenable to and in need of regulation by the state. The right of the woman to the free development of her personality, which has as its content the freedom of behavior in a comprehensive sense and accordingly embraces the personal responsibility of the woman to decide against parenthood and the responsibilities flowing from it, can also, it is true, likewise demand recognition and protection. . . .

A compromise which guarantees the protection of the life of the one about to be born and permits the pregnant woman the freedom of abortion is not possible since the interruption of pregnancy always means the destruction of the unborn life. In the required balancing, "both constitutional values are to be viewed in their relationship to human dignity, the center of the value system of the constitution." . . .

Abortion is an act of killing. . . . The description now common, "interruption of pregnancy," cannot camouflage this fact. No legal regulation can pass over the fact that this act offends against the fundamental inviolability and indisposability of human life.

In that land, the president of that high court, himself a Protestant sitting amid a majority of Protestants, later explained that "developing life participates in the protection of human dignity because human dignity is present where human life exists regardless of whether there is consciousness of this dignity or not."

In that land, that court explained to its people—and to a world wherein most courts, countries, and peoples might not understand this persistent interest in the unborn—that its present law could only be understood as the result of a previous, very sad, time in their land, and of a "spiritual-moral" confrontation they had endured:

In opposition to the totalitarian state which claimed for itself limitless dominion over all areas of social life and [in] which, in the prosecution of its goals of state, consideration for the life of the individual fundamentally meant nothing, the Basic Law . . . has erected an order bound together by values which places the individual human being and his dignity at the focal point of all its ordinances. At its basis lies the concept . . . that human beings possess an inherent worth as individuals in the order of creation which uncompromisingly demands unconditional respect for the life of every individual human being, even for the apparently socially "worthless," and which therefore excludes the destruction of such life without legally justifiable grounds. This fundamental constitutional decision determines the structure and the interpretation of the entire legal order. Even the legislature is bound by it; considerations of socio-political expediency, even necessities of state, cannot overcome this constitutional limitation.

And in that land, in a city where another court had sat to visit some small measure of judgment on the high destroyers of that previous, very sad, time, a new code of ethics in medical research had then been drawn up to ensure that the horrors of that time would not again find other victims. That code enjoined:

The voluntary consent of the human subject is absolutely essential. This means that the person involved should have legal capacity to give consent; should be so situated as to be able to exercise free power of choice, without the intervention of any element of force, fraud, deceit, duress, over-reaching, or other ulterior form of constraint or coercion; and should have sufficient knowledge and comprehension of the elements of the subject matter involved as to enable him to make an understanding and enlightened decision.

That these things were done and these things said in the Federal Republic of Germany is a sign to me that those who knew the Holocaust best best know its foul and ugly offspring in our time.[336]

Essay 4

Eliza and Lizzie Scott, and Infants Roe and Doe: How They Fared

Slavery and Abortion in America

ON MARCH 5, 1857, the Supreme Court of the United States of America gave judgment that Dred Scott, his wife, Harriet, and their daughters, Eliza and Lizzie, as slaves of John Sanford, were to remain at his disposal. In the opinion of the Court, delivered by Chief Justice Roger Brooke Taney, it was constitutionally inevitable that people of African descent, whether bondsmen or their freed descendants, had "never been regarded as a part of the people or citizens of the State, nor supposed to possess any political rights which the dominant race might not withhold or grant at their pleasure." In the mind of the founders of the Republic, "a perpetual and impassable barrier was intended to be erected between the white race and the one which they had reduced to slavery, and governed as subjects with absolute and despotic power, and which they looked upon as . . . far below them in the scale of created beings. . . . This stigma, of the deepest degradation, was fixed upon the whole race."[1]

On January 22, 1973, the Supreme Court gave judgment that Infant Roe, as the unborn child of Jane Roe, was to remain at her disposal. In the opinion of the Court, delivered by Associate Justice Harry Blackmun, no protective reference in the Constitution to "persons" "has any possible pre-natal application. . . . In short, the unborn have never been recognized in the law as persons in the whole sense."[2]

It has become commonplace to discredit the *Wade* decision, along with its companion case, *Doe* v. *Bolton*, by likening them, in temper and spirit, to the *Dred Scott* decision. My undertaking in this essay is to explore the two judgments to discover whether their resemblances lie only upon the surface or run deep. Beyond that I am further drawn to inquire whether there be larger ways in which the abortion conflict in our century has trod along the traces of the struggle over slavery in the nineteenth century. Lastly, with only an oblique eye of comparison glancing at our abortion conflict, I want to study more thoroughly the different courses taken by two different statesmen regarding the earlier contest between asserted freedoms. The curiosity that led me on, and the interesting documentation I offer here, are of course more extensive regarding the elder and now less familiar of the controversies. Readers will be able to pursue the comparisons I have investigated with further knowledge of their own.

Two Great Lawsuits

Breadth of Decision

The lineaments of the *Dred Scott* case are as follows. Scott was suing for his freedom from enslavement on the grounds that his former master had taken him to live for about two years in the state of Illinois, where state law prohibited slavery, and thereafter for another two years in the Minnesota Territory, where, by virtue of laws passed by Congress in 1820 (as part of the Missouri Compromise), slavery was also prohibited. The black man was seeking recognition of his claim that, since he had lived on free soil, he had acquired his freedom. The Supreme Court, after the case had been through three lower tribunals, ruled:

(1) that it would exercise its discretion beyond those aspects of lower court treatment which Scott was arguing to be in error, and would overturn even matters decided in his favor and not appealed;

(2) further, that even if Scott were a free negro he would not be entitled to claim recognition of it, because negroes of both slave and free status were not "citizens" within the meaning of the Constitution, and therefore not capable, as are full members of the political community, of bringing suit in the federal courts;

(3) further, that the Constitution gives Congress no radically larger governing authority over the people of the new territories than over the people of the states, and hence the federal law forbidding slavery in Minnesota was invalid;

(4) further, that since slaves are private property, the only laws Congress can make in their respect are laws which protect the rights of their owners;

(5) and further, that within its borders Missouri need pay no heed to Illinois law, and once Scott returned there he would revert to being again the private property of John Sanford.

The lineaments of the *Wade* and *Bolton* cases are as follows. Jane Roe, a pregnant single woman, sought relief from a Texas law prohibiting abortion except to save the life of the mother. Mary Doe, pregnant, married, and indigent, sought relief from a Georgia law which allowed abortion to protect the mother's life, or to avoid a seriously defective child, or after rape, but which required abortions to be performed only on Georgia residents, in accredited hospitals, with the concurring recommendation of two additional physicians and with approval by a staff committee. The Supreme Court ruled:

(1) that it would lean beyond ordinary bounds to resolve certain issues of legal standing and procedure in favor of the plaintiff-appellants;

(2) further, that neither Infant Roe nor Infant Doe, being unborn, was to be considered a "person" within the meaning of the Constitution, and that they were therefore incapable of being protected as full members of the political community would be;

(3) further, that since the unborn are held within the constitutionally protected enclosure of maternal privacy, the only laws which Congress or the states can make in respect of the unborn are laws that protect the health and interests of their mothers;

(4) and further, that within the ambit of her relationship with her physician,

a woman need pay no heed to any outside medical judgment or legal restrictions, and within these precincts of maternal jurisdiction Infant Roe and Infant Doe were the private concerns of their respective mothers.

Both decisions, *Dred Scott* and *Wade*-and-*Bolton*, reached beyond the parties at suit to heave aside great and weighty blocs of existing legal tradition. Taney and his brethren took the occasion to strike down the power of Congress, exercised throughout the nation's existence and even before the Constitution was ratified (in the Northwest Ordinance of 1787, under the Articles of Confederation), sovereignly to govern all nonstate lands. It was the first time in the history of the Republic that the Supreme Court declared a major act of Congress to be unconstitutional, and the law it chose to knock down was but one post in a fence that had stretched back across the lifetime of the country's rule of law. The upheaval in jurisprudence was massive.

It was no less so when the recent Court, speaking through Justice Blackmun, struck down every existing abortion law in the Union, voiding a statutory tradition that extended back into the early nineteenth century, and a holding of the Anglo-American common law which has restrained abortion since the memory of man runneth not to the contrary. Rarely has the American judiciary attempted to set aside so much traditional law, in matters so grave and so disputed, as in these two judgments. In this they stand as twins.

A Claim of Restraint

In each of the cases the Court professed it had confined itself to a narrow judgment. Chief Justice Taney wrote: "It is not the province of the court to decide upon the justice or injustice, the policy or impolicy of these laws [treating negroes as a subordinate and inferior class of beings]. The decision of that question belonged to the political or law-making power; to those who formed the sovereignty and framed the Constitution. The duty of the court is, to interpret the instrument they have framed, with the best lights we can obtain on the subject, and to administer it as we find it, according to its true intent and meaning when it was adopted."[3] Had the Court really followed its professed instinct of judicial restraint it would, however, have avoided the issues of Scott's citizenship and Congress's power over the territories, and would never have needed to determine those troubled constitutional issues. Indeed, even had it denied his citizenship and right to sue, the Court need have gone no further, since traditional restraint would forbid a court that had disqualified someone as a suitor before it to go on then to judge the merits of his case. Taney and his brethren, particularly those partial to slavery (five on the bench were from the South; seven were Democrats; Taney, a Jackson Democrat, came from a family of Maryland Catholic slaveowners), seem in fact to have welcomed the case and wrung from it far more extensive and creative a judgment than Taney's modest disclaimer suggested.[4]

The *Wade*-and-*Bolton* decision was also quite limited, as Justice Blackmun explained. The argument was made, he wrote, "that the woman's right is absolute and that she is entitled to terminate her pregnancy at whatever time, in whatever way, and for whatever reason she alone chooses. With this we do not agree." Chief Justice Burger concurred: "Plainly, the

Court today rejects any claim that the Constitution requires abortion on demand."[5] Despite these avowals the Court proceeded to remove from the states and from the Congress all practicable authority to restrict abortion, beyond requiring that the abortionist be a physician who agrees that an abortion would serve the mother's interests, and that the abortion be performed in medically safe circumstances if the unborn is more than three months old. In this case the Court displayed a zeal, even an appetite, to cut the widest possible swath through the law, though it announced that it was dealing with the issues in a limited way.

An Attempt at Court-given peace—and the Outcomes

Each decision, in 1857 and in 1973, was intended by the Court to bring to an end an increasingly bitter controversy. By 1787, when the Federal Constitution was ratified, five of the founding states had abolished slavery, either outright or by gradual emancipation. The eight states which had legal slavery constituted a majority in every way: in population, land area, economic strength, and political dominance. By the time Missouri was admitted to the Union in 1820, free soil and slave states stood about even: twelve each. That represented a balance in other respects as well: in population and in economic clout. But large new tracts of land, which would more than double the size of the country, would later have to be organized and admitted: the remainder of the Louisiana Purchase, the Oregon Territory, the Mexican conquest. Through a series of compromises new states made their way into the Union under one of the two flags, slave or free. But in their contest to claim future states for their separate ways of life, the two camps came into even sharper conflict, never more hostile than during the 1856–57 struggle over Kansas. By this time the South was in every way a minority power in the land—in every way, that is, but politically, because they had long continued to control government by dominating the majority Democrats (ironically helped, in the House and the Electoral College, by their slaves, who increased their apportionment by three-fifths representation). This hegemony, however, was just about to collapse, and many proslavery people, knowing they could no longer have their way in the national legislature, looked for support to the Supreme Court, still clearly in southern and proslavery hands. The judiciary was the last hope for a badly outnumbered proslave minority to ensure a protected future. As Justice Wayne, from Georgia, put it in his concurring opinion: "The case involves private rights of value, and constitutional principles of the highest importance, about which there had become such a difference of opinion, that the peace and harmony of the country required the settling of them by judicial decision."[6]

About Taney, Thomas Shaffer has written:

> His generalization about the status of black people under the Constitution was horrible, but it was hardly unusual in his generation of Maryland lawyers, and was, as Taney wanted, being dissipated politically. (Taney opposed slavery and regularly went to mass and confession with black people; Catholics in Maryland appear to have been among the rare Christian congregations who

did not segregate their worship services.) Taney's mistake was in supposing that an institution such as the Supreme Court was able to rule a democracy. He supposed that, whatever the Court said about slavery in the American territories to the West, the people of the country would regard the issue as settled. He was mistaken when he concluded that America had already decided to be a slave republic, and he was wildly deluded when he supposed that it could be.[7]

The proslavery people's need for protection was more than economic, more than political. For since the 1830s a growing abolition movement had been eroding the long disposition of the North to acquiesce in the extension of slavery for the sake of peace in the Union. The abolitionists, who had at first been ignored as a crowd of overheated eccentrics, were insisting that slavery should be outlawed throughout the land, and immediately. This for two reasons: first, the South's plea that slavery would gradually disappear after the negroes had been patiently prepared for civilized freedom was simply a hoax to gain more time and more slave states; and second, yet more important, no man could rightly own another. It was this claim that slavery was a moral outrage, a claim sweeping aside all other arguments, which stung the proslavery partisans the most. From a seesaw struggle over political or economic ascendancy the slavery contest had been transformed into one of moral condemnation on the one side and resentful impatience on the other. It was into this aggravated and unresolved conflict—political, economic, and ethical—that Roger Taney and his eight brethren, using *Dred Scott* as their entrée, betook themselves as rescuers of the Union and composers of the peace.[8]

The Taney Court failed in every way. As regards Dred Scott himself and his family, the Court's ruling was not determinative, for the next year they were purchased by friends and given their liberty. Scott died months later.

What was the effect of *Dred Scott* on the larger political scene which Taney hoped to influence? The Liberty Party, abolition's pathetically insignificant political incarnation in the campaigns of 1840, 1844, and 1848, had given way in the fifties to the Free-Soil party, which was still a splinter group with less clout even than the Know-Nothings. At a stroke *Dred Scott* and the Kansas scuffle swept the Free-Soilers into control of the new Republicans, recruited the antislavery Whigs (Lincoln had crossed over just months earlier),[9] fractured the North-South Democratic alliance, and created a truly one-issue political group. In 1858 many proslavers and even neutrals lost their seats in Congress and in the statehouses. In the election of 1860 antislavers were given the rule of the nation. "It may fairly be said that Chief Justice Taney elected Abraham Lincoln to the Presidency."[10]

And the war came. In its wake a cascade of statutes and constitutional amendments undid—or tried to undo—what the now ascendant and assertive majority saw as the war's cause: the Emancipation Proclamation in 1863, freeing slaves in rebel territory; the Thirteenth Amendment in 1865, abolishing slavery throughout the Union; the Fourteenth Amendment in 1868, acknowledging freed negroes as citizens and assuring their equitable treatment by the states; the Civil Rights Acts in 1866 and 1875 and the Fifteenth Amendment in 1870, confirming the right of citizens to vote, regardless of race or previous enslavement. It was this concerted response by the executive and legislative branches together which justified Derrick Bell in calling *Dred Scott* "the most frequently overturned decision in history."[11]

There then followed, however, nearly a century wherein all branches of the federal and state governments segregated the negro, withheld many of his civil rights and protections, and made him free game for private mistreatment. It little availed Dred's descendants that they were now citizens. Many have hailed the Warren Court's 1954 desegregation decision, *Brown* v. *Board of Education of Topeka*, reversing *Plessy* v. *Ferguson* of 1896, as the final voiding of *Dred Scott* v. *John F. A. Sandford*, but the still incomplete application of even that more recent ruling has manifested the deepest truth of the matter—a truth which neither Taney nor many of his adversaries knew. The "dark and fell spirit" which begets bondage and other forms of human subjugation is a moral derangement that has no adequate political remedy. *Dred Scott* did not really create the degradation of blacks in America; and neither the new amendments nor *Brown* really abolished it.

In 1973 a national conflict had also harrowed the mind of the nation. Since the previous century, when statutes had replaced and tightened the older common law on the question, every jurisdiction in the Union had prohibited abortion. Some state laws and judicial custom made an exception when a mother's life was at stake. That there were violations of these laws no one doubted. That most of the abortions were performed clandestinely by physicians was common knowledge. Relatively few prosecutions were initiated. Like most criminal acts, abortion was relatively uncontroversial. In 1962 the American Law Institute, following the counsel of Professor Glanville Williams, president of the British Abortion Law Reform Association, proposed to the states a model abortion law which would allow abortion to avoid danger to the mother's physical or mental health, or the birth of a handicapped child, or a birth resulting from rape, incest, or other felonious intercourse. Largely through activist support of the American Civil Liberties Union, Planned Parenthood, and some medical organizations, aided by newly organized proabortion societies, bills to conform state penal codes to the ALI provisions were introduced into most of the state legislatures. The issue quickly became one of sharp contest. Between 1967, when political action broke out in earnest, and 1973, fourteen states altered their laws, more or less according to the ALI model. Four states went further, virtually dropping all need for "reasons" to legitimate abortion (Hawaii, Alaska, and New York by legislation; Washington by referendum). Thirty-two states had chosen not to make abortion permissive. This balance of statistics does not convey the keen struggle that went on in many capitols. New York, after securing passage of abortion appeal by the changed vote of one assemblyman, later voted to reinstate the law, but Governor Rockefeller blocked this with his veto. Florida had a permissive law imposed by court action, and Connecticut, Massachusetts, Wisconsin, New Jersey, and the District of Columbia had their abortion laws dismantled by courts. In three states the matter was taken to the people by referendum: Washington loosened its abortion restrictions by a vote of 56 percent; Michigan and North Dakota reaffirmed theirs by 61 percent and 77 percent, respectively.

Clearly this was a matter far from settled in the many theaters of political struggle. A scatter of antiabortion organizations quickly came into being. The advocates of easily available abortion, despite success in some legislatures, still were far from their goal. Every single state which allowed abortion set some fetal age limit after which it was prohibited. In most of the permissive states a danger to the mother's health had to be invoked, and since in most abortion clients there was no such danger, psychiatrists had to be found (and paid) who would vouch for one. The only places where abortion on demand was effectively available were New York, Washington, D.C., and California, and those locales were serving as the abortion clinics for the entire nation. Though advocates of abortion on demand were finding that court injunctions could bring down abortion laws when the elected legislatures could not be persuaded, still, after great exertions for a decade, there were less than half a dozen places where the flag of victory flew unchallenged, and there had begun to arise a resistance more vigorous than had been expected. Also, the opponents of abortion, whom everyone had at first underestimated as ingenuous and disorganized, were making arguments remarkably reminiscent of those framed by the abolitionists: that the prochoice plea that abortion would gradually diminish after contraceptive know-how had been patiently inculcated was a hoax (a very large proportion of abortors were women versed in contraception who chose not to use it); and second, but more important, that no human rightly holds the right of life and death over his or her offspring. It was this accusation—that abortion was a moral outrage—which swept aside all other arguments and galled abortion advocates the most.

The controversy quickly became embittered on both sides. It was into this hostile and alienated atmosphere, this unresolved contest—political, economic, and ethical—that Justice Blackmun and his eight brethren stepped, offering to bring the hostilities to a close. Very much like Justice Wayne a century and a quarter earlier, Justice Blackmun expressed the assurance that a judicial ruling might bring a tranquilizing objectivity to bear. "We forthwith acknowledge our awareness of the sensitive and emotional nature of the abortion controversy, of the vigorous opposing views, even among physicians, and of the deep and seemingly absolute convictions that the subject inspires. . . . Our task, of course, is to resolve the issue by constitutional measurement, free of emotion and of predilection."[12]

Not nearly years enough have passed for us to evaluate *Wade*-and-*Bolton's* aftermath. As in *Dred Scott*, the Court's holding was not really determinative for the immediate parties with most at stake. By January 1973, Infant Roe and Infant Doe no longer existed.

Politically, there has been a flexing of antiabortion muscle that could only have been stimulated by Justice Blackmun's dicta. Both candidates for the presidency in 1976 went out of their way to clarify their antiabortion credentials; in 1980 Mr. Carter disavowed the proabortion segment of his party's platform, while Mr. Reagan brandished the antiabortion segment of his.

Congress has six consecutive times withheld subsidy from abortions for the indigent (and several times also for federal employees and dependents). And Congress has been stripped at election time of many of its most outspoken abortion advocates. Lawmakers at the state, city, and even county level have been doggedly framing ordinances that might possibly survive court review (nearly two hundred state bills were introduced the first year after *Wade*-and-*Bolton*).[13] There have been the beginnings of a call to amend the Constitution; since no concerted push for that has yet come, it is difficult to assess its chances for success. But clearly the Supreme Court did not bring the national mind with it when it imposed an abortion policy more permissive than any one of the states had framed for itself. Whereas the majority of public opinion polls show a consistent willingness to abide abortion for the so-called hard reasons (danger to maternal life or physical health, rape / incest, or handicapped fetus [though this last "reason" has been losing its previous majority support]), they also show that the nation does not accept abortion on demand as authorized by the Court. In fact, public rejection of abortion on demand has been stiffening in the latter 1970s.[14]

It probably remains to be learned that neither a constitutional amendment, nor a reversal by the Supreme Court of its 1973 decisions, nor the withdrawal of public funding, nor any other governmental act will remove abortion from the land. For, like slavery, it is a measure of moral choice that has no adequate political remedy. Like slavery, it too has a variety of like but lesser acts that hold the unborn and newborn at cheap value. The "dark and fell spirit" which withholds a welcome to the world for new life will need many years to be exorcized, surely no fewer than it is taking for America to receive blacks fairly.

A Legal Excommunication: From Citizen to Property; From Person to Private Potential

Thus, with remarkable similarity, the Supreme Court attempted in each of these quarrels to resolve an embittered standoff, and found that the highest bench in the land did not have the wherewithal to dissipate so much controversy, or to substitute its judgment for the political and moral meeting of minds that alone could bring peace. But the Court tried. And it is worth noting that its method was almost identical in the two cases. In both *Dred Scott* and *Wade*-and-*Bolton* the judges were presented with a class of beings who had been dealt with inconsistently by the law. Blacks could own and purchase and bequeath property, enter into contracts, complain or be tried in criminal proceedings, sue or be sued in civil proceedings, serve in the military or the maritime, give evidence, and marry. On the other hand, they could usually not vote, serve on juries, give evidence against whites, marry whites, or, in some jurisdictions, even enter the territory. It was this inconsistent standing before the law which made their status unclear—and their redress against abuse perilous. The unborn had been protected against abortion by criminal law since the thirteenth century, and since the seventeenth century against battery, and in civil proceedings during the twentieth century against torts; they could inherit property, qualify their mothers for aid to dependent children, sue to protect their welfare against maternal neglect (through appointed conservators), and cause the execution of a condemned mother to be postponed until their safe delivery. On the other hand, their destruction, while considered a form of homicide, was never classified as murder; some of their legal protections were assured them only if they were subsequently born alive; and in many extralegal ways an infant was acknowledged as having arrived in the world and come into possession of his or her human dignity only at birth.[15] The status of the unborn before the law was, like that of the black, inconsistent—even equivocal—and in any conflict of interests would need clarification.

Clarify the Court did: by removing from blacks and from the unborn even such equivocal legal standing as they had had. And the Court did this in the two cases in identical ways. In *Dred Scott* Chief Justice Taney defined them out of the category "citizen":

> The words "People of the United States" and "citizens" are synonymous terms, and mean the same thing. They both describe the political body who, according to our republican institutions, form the sovereignty, and who hold the power and conduct the Government through their representatives. . . . The question before us is, whether the class of persons described in the plea [of African slave descent] compose a portion of this people and are constituent members of the sovereignty? We think they are not, and that they are not included, and were not intended to be included, under the word "citizens" in the Constitution. . . . On the contrary, they were at that time considered as a subordinate and inferior class of beings, who had been subjugated by the dominant race, and, whether emancipated or not, yet remained subject to their authority, and had no rights or privileges but such as those who had the power and the Government might choose to grant them.[16]

But were there not to be found in the nation's founding documents some basic acknowledgments of human right that might serve to defend blacks against such treatment? It was the traditional task of the highest bench in the land to stretch out these fundamental rights to shelter any beneficiaries who had been inconsistently treated. Taney did the reverse. Rather than notice a longstanding inconsistency and grant redress, he asserted that the nation's founders were incapable of having two minds on the subject. The sweeping claim in the Declaration of Independence that all men are created equal, and are endowed by their Creator with certain inalienable rights

> would seem to embrace the whole human family, and if they were used in a similar instrument at this day would be so understood. But it is too clear for dispute, that the enslaved African race was not intended to be included, and formed no part of the people who framed and adopted the Declaration; for if the language, as understood in that day, would embrace them, the conduct of the distinguished men who framed the Declaration of Independence would have been utterly and flagrantly inconsistent with the principles

they asserted; and instead of the sympathy of mankind, to which they so confidently appealed, they would have deserved and received universal rebuke and reprobation. Yet the men who framed this declaration were great men—high in literary acquirements—high in their sense of honor, and incapable of asserting principles inconsistent with those on which they were acting.[17]

The only category into which Taney could comfortably put black slaves was that of "property." Within the Constitution "the only two provisions which point to them and include them, treat them as property, and make it the duty of the Government to protect it. . . . The Government of the United States had no right to interfere for any other purpose but that of protecting the rights of the owner."[18]

The *Wade*-and-*Bolton* judgment very similarly clarified the ambiguous status of the unborn, by erasing any acknowledgment of them as vested with rights. Justice Blackmun did this by defining them out of the category "person." Those defending Infant Roe, he writes, "argue that the fetus is a 'person' within the language and meaning of the Fourteenth Amendment. . . . If this suggestion of personhood is established, [Jane Roe's] case, of course, collapses, for the fetus' right to live would then be guaranteed specifically by the Amendment."[19] But he notes that neither does the Constitution "define 'person' in so many words," nor does it go out of its way anywhere to say that fetuses are persons. The obvious facts that judicial and statutory precedent as old as the common law had implicitly treated the unborn as only persons are treated, but had not done so uniformly, suggest an inconsistency. This inconsistency Justice Blackmun then flattens simply by eliminating one of its components: "the word 'person,' as used in the Fourteenth Amendment, does not include the unborn."

What Taney had done with the category of "property" Blackmun did with the cousin category of "privacy" (both words sprung from nigh ancient roots): he made of it an enclosure within which one party may hold another at her pleasure, an enclosure wherein the state may have entry, never to protect the underling, but only to reinforce the welfare of the one in domination. As Dred Scott was property which the state might approach only to safeguard the interests of John Sanford, Infant Roe lay within a privacy which the state might approach only to safeguard the interests of Jane Roe.[20] Personhood the Court declined to allow to Infant Roe because the Constitution does not mandate it *expressis verbis*; privacy, which appears *expressis verbis* nowhere in the Constitution, it allowed to the mother.

The parallels may be extended still further. Mr. Chief Justice Taney, in speaking of "the degraded condition of this unhappy race," "that unfortunate race," makes it clear that the white man's will is not only the source of that degradation and unhappiness and misfortune, but also the only measure of worth for black people, "so far inferior, that they had no rights which the white man was bound to respect."[21] Pursuing a like insight, Mr. Justice Blackmun notes that if the state had any interest in protecting Infant Roe, it would arise only if he or she had "the capability of meaningful life outside the mother's womb." The sole arbitrage of that meaning, as the ruling makes clear, is whether Jane Roe desires her offspring or rejects him or her.[22]

In fact, just as Chief Justice Taney makes a negro out to be a property *especially* protected more than most, so Justice Blackmun gives to a mother more arbitrary authority over her unborn offspring than over most other protected private holdings. Each decision made clear that in a contest of interest and survival between what Taney called "a member of the political community" and a member of the disadvantaged class, the party at risk need not look to those more powerful for tutelary protection, or even for some imperfect and inconsistent rampart of legal shelter. He or she will lose even the ambiguous protections of the past and will be consistently, unobstructedly put at the disposal of those in power. To be unguarded is not to have fewer rights; it is to have no rights at all. It is to be subject.

A Treatment of History

There is one other notable feature of comparison between these two judicial decisions. Both lay down lengthy preambles of historical justification. And both treatments of history have fared poorly with historians. *Scott*, in fact, encloses two historical essays. The first is a long but selective review of restrictive and discriminatory treatment of blacks in the thirteen founding states since the beginning of the Union. Strong emphasis is laid upon the fact that even in those states which had outlawed slavery the attitudes towards free blacks were proof that the abolition reflected no readiness to receive them as fellow members of the people. The second historical survey supports the view that Congress was never meant to govern the territories (the survey overlooks an unbroken precedent since the 1780s), nor might territorial governments adopt any laws that would put at a disadvantage arriving citizens from any of the states (say, if they were slaveholders). Both histories were cut to fit the classical and frequently formulated partisan proslavery arguments of the Southern Democrats.[23]

In *Wade* and *Bolton* the ground is also ploughed and harrowed historically, and here also two stories are told. The first attempts to review the past jurisprudence on abortion. Construing the distant annals of medicine, Justice Blackmun finds that the prevailing attitudes in Roman and Greek antiquity were permissive of abortion: so much so that the Hippocratic Oath, whereby new physicians swear never to abort, really embodied a minority view that was probably perpetuated only because it was acceptable to Christian teachings. Then, in his review of the Anglo-American legal tradition, he finds that the older common law did not generally punish abortion before "quickening" because of the medieval theological belief that the unborn came to life only late in pregnancy, when movement began to be felt. Later statutes against abortion, dating from the nineteenth century, came to outlaw abortion at any stage of pregnancy. The chief reason for this, he believes, was to protect women from the health hazards that abortion then presented to maternal health and life.

The Court's historical conspectus here, it has been noticed, is no more original than was that of Roger Taney. Justice Blackmun reproduces intact the interpretation of Cyril Means, Jr., legal counsel to the National Association for the Repeal of Abortion Laws (NARAL became, after vindication by *Wade* and *Bolton*, the National Abortion Rights Action League), and the argument of Lawrence Lader, NARAL founder: together they are cited fourteen times by the Court. The history they offer has not been flattered by critical scrutiny. As for antiquity, an overwhelmingly more influential antecedent for western medicine and jurisprudence than Hippocrates or the Pythagoreans was Christianity. And it was a distinctive and emphatic teaching of Christianity, from the first century onwards—in a clean break with both pagan and Jewish doctrines—that abortion at any stage was a serious sin and crime. Of this much more significant historical precedent there is no mention in *Wade*.[24]

The Court's review of the common law has also been criticized. The reason why early abortion was not generally a civilly punished crime was not because of theories about the beginnings of life, but because the penalties for abortion were so severe that only cases allowing of undeniable proof could be prosecuted. Early abortion was held to be a crime, but it had been dealt with in the church courts where both rules of evidence and penalties were less severe. The reason for excluding "post-quickening" abortion after the civil courts took jurisdiction over all crimes following the Reformation was still grounded on the difficulties of proof, not on theories of ensoulment.[25] In his examination of nineteenth-century statutes Justice Blackmun overstresses the reformers' concern for maternal health and virtually ignores their explicit desire to rescue the unborn.[26] New discoveries in embryology had recently made it certain that the young unborn is the result of conception (the mammalian ovum was first seen in 1827), and not simply a growing but unanimated deposit of the father.[27]

The Court's conclusion, standing on these struts, is that past abortion law was utterly permissive with respect to that early span of pregnancy during which virtually all abortions now occur. This conclusion is as unsure as the borrowed reading of history on which it stands. The only constant which this history resolutely discloses is an unbroken disposition, from the first century of Christianity until the past fifteen years, to consider abortion a crime.

Justice Blackmun's other great historical survey treats the jurisprudential notion of privacy. Here he drives most of his precedents from the domain of marriage, childbearing, family relationships, and parental care. Having established that this is a sector of human affairs into which the people have traditionally not allowed the state to roam, he appears to miss the large historical fact that it is entirely a corporate privacy: it is a complex of intimate bonds between people which are reserved to them. It does both historical and juridical violence to this tradition to invoke it for what the Court has defined as something that does not involve marriage (Jane Roe is single), childbearing (Infant Roe is not to be borne), family relationships, or parental care—or, indeed, any relationship at all, since the Court concludes that what Jane Roe is free to expel is no person. Here too history is called on by the Court to strain the evidence beyond its credibility.[28]

Constitutionalist Dissent

Both decisions, in 1857 and in 1973, were rendered by a division of seven to two. In each case the two dissenting justices were tart in their disagreement. Wrote Justice Curtis:

> To engraft on any instrument a substantive exception not found in it, must be admitted to be a matter attended with great difficulty. And the difficulty increases with the importance of the instrument, and the magnitude and complexity of the interests involved in its construction. To allow this to be done with the Constitution, upon reasons purely political, renders its judicial interpretation impossible—because judicial tribunals, as such, cannot decide upon political considerations. . . . And when a strict interpretation of the Constitution, according to the fixed rules which govern the interpretation of laws, is abandoned, and the theoretical opinions of individuals are allowed to control its meaning, we have no longer a Constitution; we are under the government of individual men, who for the time being have powers to declare what the Constitution is, according to their views of what it ought to mean.[29]

His brother on the bench, Justice McLean, was more pointed: "All slavery has its origin in power, and is against right."[30]

In *Wade*, Justice Rehnquist objected:

> The fact that a majority of the States reflecting, after all, the majority sentiment in those States, have had restrictions on abortions for at least a century is a strong indication, it seems to me, that the asserted right to an abortion is not "so rooted in the traditions and conscience of our people as to be ranked as fundamental." . . . To reach its result, the Court necessarily has had to find within the scope of the Fourteenth Amendment a right that was apparently unknown to the drafters of the Amendments."[31]

His colleague, Justice White, was more sharp:

> I find nothing in the language or history of the Constitution to support the Court's judgment. The Court simply fashions and announces a new constitutional right for pregnant mothers and, with scarcely any reason or authority for its action, invests that right with sufficient substance to override most existing state abortion statutes. . . . As an exercise of raw judicial power, the Court perhaps has authority to do what it does today; but in my view its judgment is an improvident and extravagant exercise of the power of judicial review that the Constitution extends to this Court.[32]

The dissents could be interchanged between the cases. So could the protest of old John McLean, senior even to Roger Taney on the high bench: "A slave is not a mere chattel. He bears the impress of his Maker, and is amenable to the laws of God and man; and he is destined to an endless existence."[33]

An Accommodation of Others

In a sense, though, these two decisions were both out of the ordinary in that they gave voice to others beyond the nine sitting justices. In the case of *Dred Scott* there was a persistent rumor around the Capitol that Roger Taney had been in collusion with James Buchanan, whom he had sworn into office only two days earlier, and who, though from Pennsylvania, had come down on the slave-state side of the great issue. It was only many years later that evidence emerged to show that Buchanan—quite in defiance of the bounds of propriety—did have his hand in the *Dred Scott* judgment through clandestine correspondence with several members of the Court. In *Wade* and *Bolton* it is already clear in the record that Justice Blackmun was indebted, for the innards of his argument, to two of the major strategists of the abortion movement. What is now only a persistent question which must await a later resolution is how much Harry Blackmun, who for nine years provided legal services to the doctors of the Mayo Clinic, drew upon their particular perspective in making the law of the land.[34]

Four Great Movements

Thus far through our inquiry, one can see a curious and persistent parallel between the *Dred Scott* case and those of *Wade* and *Bolton*. As it fell out, each of them enunciated an attempt by the judiciary to pacify a national quarrel. Neither succeeded in laying the issue to rest. Indeed, each inflamed it. But the full freight of a controversy rarely comes to court even when its central issue is tried there. We should proceed further and look beyond the judicial decisions. Are the resemblances we have seen there confirmed or discounted when we look beyond the courtroom to the larger movements and convictions that collided there?

An Inevitable Institution or an Outrage?

One of the arguments put forward on behalf of slavery was that history showed it to be inevitable. This was a strong feature of the case argued against Dred Scott, and it appeared constantly in proslavery treatises. Typical of it was a report submitted by a committee of the South Carolina General Assembly in 1857:

> That slavery has always existed, is recorded in the world's history. That it always will exist, in some form, however modified by the several circumstances of race, climate, civilization and tradition, may be inferred:—from the evident necessity of a menial class of duties to be performed by no other than a menial class of individuals; from the natural inequalities existing between the several races, classes and conditions of men; from the accumulation of wealth, on the one hand, which gives patronage and power, and the continuance of poverty, on the other, which needs protection and seeks service; from the necessity of social order and civil government; and from all the other universal evidences which God has manifested in the economy of his creation.[35]

The argument from inevitability has also been raised in respect of abortion. Abortion restrictions have often been likened to those which were levied against alcohol. An editorial in *Time* asserted: "The statutes forbidding abortion were a kind of Volstead Act, so widely (and often dangerously) violated as to be worse than useless."[36] Daniel Callahan has elaborated the point further:

> A policy to prohibit abortions would certainly encounter a number of obstacles: an unwillingness on the part of many state law enforcement agencies to carry out the letter of the law, or a tendency to put the investigation and prosecution of abortion cases so far down on the list of priorities as to render them meaningless; the willingness of many physicians to risk breaking the law because they would know that the opinion of the public and of their medical colleagues was divided, and that the enforcement of the law would be minimal at best; the willingness of many desiring abortions to break the law because they would feel it was their moral right, or would be led by desperation, to do so, or would know—given the divided state of popular and professional opinion—that they could always find significant support for their actions.[37]

Advocates of slavery, though they elaborated a series of arguments in defense of that institution, really preempted them all by the assertion that to eliminate it was unthinkable, impossible. William Drayton of South Carolina told the U.S. House of Representatives:

> Slavery, in the abstract, I condemn and abhor. I know no terms too strong to express my reprobation of those who would introduce it into a nation. I know no language of crimination too unqualified to be applied to those who are engaged in the African slave trade. An African slave ship is a spectacle from which all men would recoil with horror. . . . But, when we live in States in which slavery existed before we did . . . it has become so inseparable from, and interwoven with our condition, as to be irremediable.[38]

Slavery, so the plea went, "originated in, and is perpetuated by a social and political necessity, and its continuance is demanded equally by the highest interests of both races."[39] As a professor at William and Mary College explained, "Every plan of emancipation and deportation which we can possibly conceive, is total impracticable."[40] A lecturer in New York City, one year before the outbreak of the Civil War, rebutted the insistent call of the abolitionists:

> They assert that negro slavery is unjust. . . . Our negro bondmen can neither be exterminated nor transported to Africa. They are too numerous for either process, and either, if practicable, would involve a violation of humanity. If they were emancipated, they would relapse into barbarism, or a set of negro States would arise in our midst, possessing political equality, and entitled to social equality. . . . It is in vain that this could be endured.[41]

Emancipation was unthinkable politically because it would flood the country with free negroes:

> The Slave States adopted opinions, as to the negro character, opposite to those of the freed States, and would not risk the experiment of emancipation. They said, if the Free States feel themselves burdened by the few persons, of African descent, they have freed, and whom they find it impracticable to educate and elevate, how much greater would be the evil the Slave States must bring upon themselves, by letting loose a population nearly twelve times as numerous. Such an act, they argued, would be suicidal— it would crush out all progress in civilization; or, in the effort to elevate the negro with the white man—allowing him equal freedom of action—would be to make the more energetic Anglo-Saxon the slave of the indolent African. Such a task, onerous in the highest degree, they could not, and would not undertake—such an experiment, on their social system, they dared not hazard.[42]

As for deportation, it was doubly impossible. For one thing, it would be too costly. But the second reason had a more altruistic color to it:

> The slave trade, which takes off 100,000 human beings from Africa, for the slave markets of the West Indies and South America, has, by its operations, quickened the procreative powers of society in Africa to such an extent, as not only to keep up her numbers, but to furnish besides 100,000 souls for exportation. Could we suppose it possible for this slave trade to be annihilated at a blow; repugnant and shocking as it is to every feeling of humanity, it would be found that its sudden cessation would plunge the whole of Western Africa, for a season, into the most dreadful anarchy and appalling distress.[43]

Either prospect, emancipation or deportation, was unimaginable. Abolitionists might as well propose, one proslaver grumbled, freedom for convicts, Irish Catholics, foreigners in general, and the poor.[44]

A similar sense of the unthinkable has invested the defense of abortion on demand. For those who are prochoice, it is not imaginable that so many women be expected to give birth to the unwanted fetuses they are carrying, whether to raise them later or to give them up for adoption (two alternatives that correspond to emancipation and deportation for the proslavery advocates). The sense of impossibility was conveyed in a memorandum written for Joseph Califano, then secretary of Health, Education and Welfare, by Connie Downey, who headed a study group he had asked to report on alternatives to abortion: "Abortion is but one alternative solution to many of the 'problems.' It is an option, uniquely, which is exercised between conception and live birth. As such, the literal alternatives to it are suicide, motherhood and, some would add, madness. Consequently there is some confusion, discomfort and cynicism greeting efforts to 'find' or 'emphasize' or 'identify' alternatives to abortion."[45]

Abolitionists had from the first charged the slavers with raw self-interest.

For this reason a cascade of rebuttals issued from the South, itemizing the numerous ways in which slavery redounded to the benefit of the slaves themselves. It had stimulated the birthrate of the blacks, compared with that of free blacks in Africa. One could see how beneficial their situation was by contrasting it with that of the American Indians. "Had the race of the North American Indians been reduced to slavery, as they might have been, they, like the negro, would have increased and multiplied, and instead of numbering by thousands, would have numbered by millions. The few of them that remain, indeed, are scattered over the Far West, and in the still onward progress of civilization must ultimately become extinct. The same, or a similar fate would await the emancipated negro living in juxtaposition with the white."[46]

If emancipated, the negroes would perform "just labor enough, in addition to what they could rob from the whites, to live a lazy, dancing, dissolute, savage life, till the whites, finding it impossible to live among them, would abandon every thing and fly with their families to the Free States; then the negroes would fall upon and butcher one another!"[47] Some partisans noted that since a higher proportion of blacks in the free states were certified insane than in the slave states, slavery must somehow be beneficial to mental health. Crime too seemed to be a problem among freed blacks.[48] Roger Taney himself, in private correspondence after *Dred Scott* was published, recalled that when his own slaves had been given their freedom thirty years earlier, they had adapted well and not disappointed his expectations. But for most slaves, "usually cheerful and contented," emancipation would spell "absolute ruin."[49]

William Scott, sitting on the Missouri Supreme Court and delivering judgment against Dred Scott and his family at an earlier stage in their struggle for freedom, expressed similar concern for black welfare in the final sentences he spoke for the court:

> When the condition of our slaves is contrasted with the state of their miserable race in Africa; when their civilization, intelligence and instruction in religious truths are considered, and the means now employed to restore them to the country from which they have been torn, bearing with them the blessings of civilized life, we are almost persuaded, that the introduction of slavery amongst us was, in the providence of God, who makes the evil passions of men subservient to His own glory, a means of placing that unhappy race within the pale of civilized nations.[50]

Should black slaves be exposed to the give-and-take of civilization, though, they might fare ill. "The slave is certainly liable to be sold. But, perhaps, it may be questioned, whether this is a greater evil than the liability of the laborer, in fully peopled countries, to be dismissed by his employer, with the uncertainty of being able to obtain employment, or the means of subsistence elsewhere. . . . If slaves have less freedom of action than other laborers, which I by no means admit, they are saved in a great degree from the responsibility of self-government, and the evils springing from their own perverse wills."[51] But if the blacks were emancipated and were not given a share in the "responsibility of self-government," then they would have to share the land with whites continually conscious of their own natural superiority and exclusive grip on political power. "They would still have *masters*, though not *proprietors and owners*. Instead of one master, as at present, they would have a thousand. Instead of having, as at present, in their owners a master, engaged by various and powerful motives of both sympathy and interest to care for and protect them in their health, welfare, and preservation, they would have in the whites, now *no longer their owners*, a thousand tyrants; not only feeling no sympathy for them, and taking no interest in them, but entertaining for them, on the contrary, a positive dislike and sympathy, not to say hatred."[52]

The argument tended to shunt back and forth. In one mode it was upbeat and assertive. The blacks were treated kindly and were abundantly fed. "We have no doubt but that they form the happiest portion of our society. A merrier being does not exist on the face of the globe, than the negro slave of the U. States."[53] In another mode, the tone was apologetic and resigned: "It is said slavery is wrong, in the *abstract* at least, and contrary to the spirit of Christianity. . . . if, as really is the case, we cannot get rid of slavery without producing a greater injury to both the masters and the slaves, there is no rule of conscience or revealed law of God which *can* condemn us." "Our fathers left it to us as a legacy, we have grown up with it; it has grown with our growth, and strengthened with our strength, until it is now incorporated with every fibre of our social and political existence. What you say concerning its evils *may* be true or false, but we clearly see that your remedy involves a vastly greater evil, to the slave, to the master, to our common country, and to the world."[54]

The abolitionists were undercutting all proslavery arguments about the history of slavery, the comfortable circumstances of the slaves, and the permanence of black inferiority by their limpidly simple claim that no human could rightly own another. Period. But the proslavery apologists had a comparable point. They undercut all antislavery arguments based on principle by citing pragmatic necessity:

> I am aware, that however often answered, it is likely to be repeated again and again—how can that institution be tolerable, by which a large class of society is cut off from the hope of improvement in knowledge; to whom blows are not degrading; theft no more than a fault; falsehood and the want of chastity almost venial, and in which a husband or parent looks with comparative indifference, on that which, to a freeman, would be the dishonor of a wife or child?
>
> But why not, if it produces the greatest aggregate of good? Sin and ignorance are only evils, because they lead to misery. It is not our institution, but the institution of nature, that in the progress of society a portion of it should be exposed to want, and the misery which it brings, and therefore involved in ignorance, vice, and depravity. In anticipating some of the good, we also anticipate a portion of the evil of civilization. But we have it in a mitigated form. The want and the misery are unknown; the ignorance is less a misfortune, because the being is not the guardian of himself, and

partly on account of that involuntary ignorance, the vice is less vice—less hurtful to man, and less displeasing to God.[55]

The configuration of the primary proslavery apologetic is fairly well pronounced. It is conceded that, in the abstract, enslavement is inhumane and undesirable. (The concession is, however, emphatically limited to the echelon of principle; in fact, the negroes were said to be a contented and uncomplaining lot.) The slavers are free of moral fault because the system was already established before they entered it. What could be done to abolish it? To set the slaves loose in American society would devastate them. Their native shiftlessness would cast them to the bottom of the labor scale or, more likely, into unemployment. Their native inferiority would make them fair game for resentful white folk. Their native inability to care for the common good would show up in high crime rates. Their native inability to cope with stressful freedom would make many of them demented. And, if one chose to give them the franchise of citizenship and political equality, they would become a destructively powerful menace. The only alternative to having the emancipated blacks as the social and political companions of whites was to deport them back to Africa, and the costs of such a mass migration (among which the costs of indemnifying their owners were always calculated as heavier than the costs of transport) were too great to allow of serious consideration. A significant component of the argument at this point is one of silence. It was virtually never suggested that the freed negroes might be given preferential access to any of the yet unsettled western lands.

The conclusion was direct. Whatever might be said in a theoretical way about the injustice of slavery, a hardheaded, pragmatic realism which did not allow one principle by itself to predetermine any complex ethical choice, but balanced all the alternatives in order to reckon which one would workably yield the greatest good for all concerned, slave and master alike—that approach would be the only valid moral approach.

This apologetic is rather closely followed by the lineaments of the primal prochoice argument on behalf of abortion. It is granted without argument that abortion is undesirable, tragic, never to be welcomed—in theory. Says Bella Abzug: "I believe that abortion is the least desirable method of birth control. No woman prefers it. It is generally regarded as a method of last resort."[56] The declaration by the 1976 General Conference of the United Methodist Church is not untypical: "Our belief in the sanctity of unborn human life makes us reluctant to approve abortion. But we are equally bound to respect the sacredness of the life and well-being of the mother, for whom devastating damage may result from an unacceptable pregnancy."[57] The inevitability of abortion is central to its political and moral justification. The late John D. Rockefeller III argued that, "as a practical matter, legalization of abortion is a much more sound and humane social policy than prohibition. Banning abortions does not eliminate them; it never has and it never will."[58]

If allowed to survive, the unwanted unborn would confront devastating disabilities. Because they are unwanted they will be more likely to suffer emotional injury and abuse, which will in turn make them more prone to crime. Garrett Hardin, an early and forthright proabortion spokesman at the

University of California, has testified: "The condition of unwantedness also makes it probable that the child will be poorly cared for, economically, physically, and psychologically. Many people find it distasteful to make a comparative evaluation of adult and embryo, but the very real conflict of the interests of a woman and her unwanted embryo call [sic] for such an evaluation." Abortion, he urges, can be owed to the unborn if one realistically contemplates what they are being spared.

> *Abortion for the children's sake*—this is paradoxical but true.
> And society wants children to be wanted so they have a reasonable chance of growing up without twists. (If they grow up physically or psychologically twisted, society pays grievously for their unwantedness.) . . .
> What would be the consequences if the number of psychologically warped adults could be reduced to a tenth the present population by seeing to it that no mother ever was compelled to bear an unwanted child, and every child born was a wanted child?
> We have no historical model of such a world. The mind boggles when it tries to take in the momentous consequences of producing only wanted children. . . .
> Right-to-Lifers see abortion as a purely negative thing, a killing, a murder, a loss of potential.
> *How wrong they are.*
> The unborn lives that are put to an end before the time for recognition as members of the community—which occurs at birth, in our society—by their disappearance contribute in a positive way to the psychological health of the surviving community. . . .
> Only if tiny unwanted beings are removed before society confers on them the status of human beings (and thus right-full members of the human community) can all those who are born into the community be endowed with the psychic strength that comes from knowing for sure that they were wanted. Such knowledge must be nearly universal among its members if a society is to have a decent chance to become fully sane.[59]

The unwanted are also portrayed as at risk themselves for mental disorder. Ms. Abzug speaks of this danger. "What happens even to the well baby born to a scared, unmarried teenage girl, herself virtually a child? What happens to the child born into abysmal poverty or into a family already too large? Or to the child born to a sick or disturbed mother? Although it is certainly not inevitable that the child unwanted at birth will be rejected and unloved in life, research into the etiology of mental illness, criminality and mental retardation has singled out parental deprivation as perhaps the most important single causal factor."[60] So ominous, testified one physician, are the handicaps faced by the unborn who is unwanted or blighted, that "we have the responsibility to advocate the fetal right not to be born unless the physical, mental, emotional, and environmental well-being of its mother is assured."[61]

Vivian and Eric Lindermayer, writing in *Christianity and Crisis*, also portray abortion as a choice that can be altruistic. They take issue with the view "that for women the choice to terminate a pregnancy is necessarily a *selfish* choice between their quality of life and the well-being of the fetus. What this ignores is that for many—we would venture most—women there is a *crucial* third element that enters into their deliberations: the well-being of the child that would be. And that quality of life—not their own—is a major reason for terminating the pregnancy."[62] This closely parallels the concern expressed in the last century that the emancipation of slaves was undesirable because of the quality of life that faced the freedman that would be.

A similarly impatient and similarly moralistic concern for the welfare of children not aborted was declared by Justice Thurgood Marshall when the Supreme Court decided in 1977 that it could not force Congress to fund certain abortions:

> The enactments challenged here brutally coerce poor women to bear children whom society will scorn for every day of their lives. Many thousands of unwanted minority and mixed-race children now spend blighted lives in foster homes, orphanages, and "reform" schools. Many children of the poor, sadly, will attend second-rate segregated schools. And opposition remains strong against increasing Aid to Families with Dependent Children benefits for impoverished mothers and children, so that there is little chance for the children to grow up in a decent environment. I am appalled at the ethical bankruptcy of those who preach a "right to life" that means, under present social policies, a bare existence in utter misery for so many poor women and their children.[63]

Justice Blackmun agreed with his Brother Marshall, as he had in all the abortion cases, and accused his colleagues (who this time formed a majority against him) of sharing with antiabortionists a naive neglect of the realities of the social misery that abortion is needed to cope with. It was reminiscent of the accusation against the abolitionists that they were unpragmatic and doctrinaire. "There is another world 'out there,' the existence of which the Court, I suspect, either chooses to ignore or fears to recognize. And so the cancer of poverty will continue to grow."[64]

If the unwanted were to survive, they would face overwhelming disadvantages. The only other alternative to allowing these unborn to share one's domestic community is to offer them in adoption, and like deportation for blacks that is rejected as too costly, either financially (for the teenager who aims through pregnancy at an independent income from welfare) or emotionally (for the woman who prefers to eliminate her offspring rather than yield him or her to other parents).

Basically, the prochoice argument is that whatever might be said in a theoretical way about the injustice of abortion, it would be doctrinaire to let that single consideration decide the entire issue. Any unwanted pregnancy is dramatic and complex, and one must balance all alternatives in a pragmatic way to find which would workably yield the greatest good for all concerned, parents and child alike.

Inferior, Therefore Disfranchised?

Simply denying that the abolitionists' primary argument was conclusive did not, of course, relieve defenders of slavery from having to present other defenses. One which lay close to hand was that negroes were inferior. Dr. Josiah C. Nott of Mobile, Alabama, stated the belief of many that blacks and whites did not belong to the same species.[65] Not all made so strong a claim. It was more commonly observed that since white people constituted the norm for humanity, black people had not (or not yet) arrived at that standard:

> Humanity *alone* could not belong to [negroes], for it is an attribute of man alone created in the image and after the likeness of God; but a degree of it is their due, *inasmuch* as they resemble the white man, for in so much they are *accountable*, and no more. . . . As there is a vast *difference* in the *mental* and physical organization of the progressive existences of colors and man, . . . so there *is* in *humanity*; hence a *difference* in *humanity*, or a *degree* of *humanity*, is not humanity itself; therefore they cannot bear fully the term *human*, but *intermediate-human.*[66]

The relative status of blacks and whites was to be reckoned, not by principle, but by fact. And the facts demonstrated that blacks were inferior. "I take it for granted," insisted John Campbell in Philadelphia, "that no dark race of men has ever been equal to a white race. . . . I speak not here of the justice or injustice of the matter, I only speak of the fact! The whole history of the world proves it. . . . How I loathe the hypocrisy which claims the same mental, moral and physical equality for the negro which the whites possess."[67]

From this inferiority of performance one argued directly to an inferiority of status and of rights:

> It is the order of nature and of God, that the being of superior faculties and knowledge, and therefore of superior power, should control and dispose of those who are inferior. It is as much in the order of nature, that men should enslave each other, as that other animals should prey upon each other. I admit that he does this under the highest moral responsibility, and is most guilty if he wantonly inflicts misery or privation on beings more capable of enjoyment or suffering than brutes, without necessity or any view to the greater good which is to result.[68]

The almost universal application of this theory was that throughout America blacks were exploited and persecuted. This did not mean that whites were, from their superior standing, awarding blacks lesser or inferior or limited rights. They awarded them no rights. Whoever depends on another for all of his rights emerges, not with less, but with none. This was Roger Taney's argument from the bench. Says Fehrenbacher: "Negroes had equal rights with white men in *all* respects or in *none*. And Taney rightly assumed that most Americans of his time, if restricted to such a choice, would answer 'None.' His purpose was to exclude Negroes from all rights guaranteed in the Constitution."[69]

It was not necessary, then, to excommunicate blacks from humanhood in order to put them entirely at the disposal of the dominant whites. It was enough to declare them inferior in potential and performance, and to put their protection at the pleasure of their superiors, for them to be left with no more status than if they had not been human. They were declared outside the enclosure of the political community, and that practical inferiority became as telling as anything theoretical. One speaker, on the brink of the Civil War, said it all: "As a white nation, we made our Constitution and our laws, vesting all political rights in that race. They, and they alone, constituted, in every political sense, the American people."[70]

A reinforcing consideration for proslavers was that white superiority laid on them the burden of higher tastes and wants: a further reason to use the blacks for their own (the whites') betterment. "It seems to be in the order of nature that those races of the human family who have the highest intellectual and moral organization should have also the most numerous and various wants, or that those races should have the most numerous and various wants who have been endowed by nature with the superior faculties and ingenuity which are necessary for obtaining their gratification."[71] One of the accomplishments rendered appropriate by their superior ingenuity was to assume power over the inferior blacks, for "laws, manners, religion, arts, science, or manufactures, *have no existence among them*."[72]

No violence, then, to the natural order was done if whites assumed sovereignty over blacks. The only fault one might find with a slaveholder was not the enslavement itself, but any mistreatment of his slaves. Immediately after the Civil War a Georgia pastor made this point to his congregation. The South, as he saw it, had been divinely judged by its recent defeat: not for slavery, but for abuses of it:

> There are many who question the existence of such right of [slave] property, but assert that slavery begins in the perpetration of a *wrong*, . . . and that no legal enactment can ever cause that to be right which was once in itself *wrong*. . . . On the other hand there are those who contend that the relation is *right in itself*, that it has its sanction from God, that the institution as it has existed among us, both in *principle* and *practice*, is *jure divino*, that it is a divine institution, and beneficial to society. . . .
>
> The relation of master is established in the Bible. . . . But to this relation there is annexed a corresponding duty, a moral obligation. The neglect of that obligation determines the moral character of slavery.[73]

A Presbyterian pastor in Virginia had made the same point before the war:

> The grand mistake, as we apprehend, of those who maintain that slave-holding is itself a crime, is, that they do not discriminate between slave-holding in itself considered, and its accessories at any time or place. They have a confused idea of chains and whips, of degradation and misery, of ignorance and vice, and to this complex conception they apply the name slavery, and denounce it as the aggregate of all moral and physical evil.[74]

The position, in brief, was that although blacks were of the same species as whites, they had no ability to act as peers or partners, and hence could not be awarded equal status. What their status amounted to was subjection, a subjection so complete that it could be abused only by wanton assault. Inferior potential and performance argued for inferior status, which argued for totally subordinated rights, which amounted to no rights.

The argument subtending abortion choice has followed somewhat similar lines. As with blacks, so with the unborn: there are some who exclude them from humanity. This, for instance, is the assumption of Sissela Bok, an ethicist at Harvard. Speaking of the youngest unborn, she says:

> This group of cells cannot feel the anguish or pain connected with death, nor can it fear death. Its experiencing of life has not yet begun; it is not yet conscious of the interruption of life nor of the loss of anything it has come to value in life. Nor is it tied by bonds of affection to others. If the abortion is desired by both parents, no grief will be caused such as that which accompanies the death of a child. Almost no human care and emotion and resources have been invested in it. Nor is such an early abortion and consequent research [on the aborted] brutalizing for the person voluntarily performing it, or a threat to society. Because there is no semblance of human form, no conscious life or capability to live independently, no knowledge of death, no sense of pain, words such as "harm" or "deprive" cannot be meaningfully used in the context of early abortion and fetal research.[75]

Just as the negro had been judged inferior by the measure of the white's self-understanding, the adult is made the measure of the unborn. Robert Veatch, another ethicist, asks at what point an individual is vested with equal rights, equal sacredness. It is, he says, at "the point where there is a quantum change in the value or meaningfulness of the living organism so that it includes that which is significantly valued as essentially human." This would come, he surmises, with development of the nervous system adequate to allow "social interaction." After the youngster has that social capacity, he or she is "vested with a sanctity uncompromisable to the interests of lesser claims." But beforehand, due to inferior status, the young have "intermediate value" which would recede before the interests of adults.[76]

The unborn is not excommunicate from the species, but within the species he or she is not a peer, and hence is denied equal status. "Since the fetus is the organic beginning of human life, the termination of its development is always a serious matter. Nevertheless, a qualitative distinction must be made between its claims and the rights of a responsible person made in God's image who is in living relationships with God and other human beings." This is an official Lutheran statement. A Presbyterian one makes the same point: ". . . the unborn fetus must be respected for its own worth regardless of the period of gestation. However, the needs of the mother may at times take precedence over the needs of an embryonic and unformed child."[77]

The result of human disfranchisement for the unborn, as it was for the negro, is the debarring of any claim to rights other than those which the dominant parties might choose to award. Hence the unborn have, in effect, no rights which would keep them from being utterly at the disposal of their mothers. Exclusion from the social and political community converts inferiority into annihilation.

An Economic Bloc?

The political and social issues touching on slavery, as is well known, branched off an economic taproot. One of the arguments consistently raised in its defense was the claim that only with slavery could the American South hold its own in the world agricultural market.[78] During the mid–nineteenth century the "peculiar institution" of the South had become more crucial to its economic well-being than before. A series of technological developments had transformed the textile industry: the carding machine, the spinning jenny, steam-driven spinners, the power loom, and the cotton gin. U.S. cotton exports had, in the course of a few years, quintupled.[79] In brief, slavery was transformed from an economical means of tilling marginal land into a source of considerable wealth.

> The use of slaves in southern agriculture was a deliberate choice (among several alternatives) made by men who sought greater returns than they could obtain from their own labor alone, and who found other types of labor more expensive. "For what purpose does the master hold the servant?" asked an ante-bellum Southerner. "Is it not that by his labor he, the master, may accumulate wealth?"[80]

But while true, this was oversimple as an explanation of the ardent proslavery resistance to abolitionism. It was the entire South that went to war on slavery's behalf, even though only a small fraction of the grey army had any direct stake in the institution. About three out of every four white southerners had no personal or familial ownership of bondsmen in 1860.[81] Actual slaveholders in South Carolina, the state with the highest proportion of them, amounted to 9.3 percent of all whites in 1850.[82] Yet their sectional comrades saw slavery as a right to be defended—and one by which the South, which for so many years had labored at a disadvantage, might somehow be able to assert itself and deal with the North, which had enjoyed the ascendancy, on equal terms.

A comparable financial picture emerges when one regards the institution of abortion in our day. Recent developments in technology have made it much more obviously attractive. Public health improvement has reduced the infant mortality rate so that numerous births are no longer required to produce the desired number of children in a family. The widespread availability of effective contraceptive techniques has resulted in a world of conscious "family planning," wherein the notion of free choice reigns supreme. Vacuum aspiration has made the abortion procedure itself both less expensive and less hazardous for women. Socioeconomic developments have given women much more generous access to careers in public life. Advertising technology has stimulated the desire for material comfort to a point where, for many, this exceeds the desire for children or for more children. This convergence of developments has abruptly made abortion seem to offer more advantages than it once did.

The advantages are not without financial components. On the level of public policy abortion is promoted as a way of keeping welfare payments down, or reducing support for the handicapped.[83] For medical practitioners, especially obstetricians faced with lowered birthrates, the practice can be financially significant. And, of course, for the individual woman considering abortion there can be a double motivation: to avoid the burdens of supporting a child, and to retain the career and income that pregnancy and childbearing could obstruct. All of these are economic factors which make abortion more attractive to all parties involved.

Yet, like slavery, abortion has had an enlarged constituency. In the middle of the last century there were probably as many persons in Boston involved in the slave-sustained textile industry as there were major slaveholders in any southern city. And there were some abolitionists in the South and some proslavery partisans in the North. Yet the South as a section rallied to the "peculiar institution" as representative of the status and aspirations of half of the nation. Likewise with abortion. Only 2.5 percent of women aged fifteen to forty-four abort each year, and about a fourth of them are repeat abortors.[84] Relatively few women have a direct stake in abortion, yet abortion freedom has been taken up in a particular way as a feminist cause, a right to be defended and one by which the ability of women, a half of the people who have long suffered disadvantage, might somehow assert itself on equal terms with that of men. The prospect of women attaining financial parity with men has caused many women who have no personal involvement in abortion to identify with the cause. Thus abortion, like slavery, has drawn into its support group a sizable number of persons who hold for it: not as desirable in itself, but as a partisan issue they believe they must rise up to support.

Religion or Churches

What part did the churches play in the abolition struggle? There was, from the South, an appeal to northern Christians for understanding. One minister assured his coreligionists: "Believe me, Christian masters seek to act conscientiously in this matter [the treatment of their slaves]; they apply the *law of love* in retaining their slaves in bondage, and *good men* here are the very last men, who will practically be influenced by abolition principles." The context for this appeal, made in 1837, was the unanimous adoption by the Presbyterian clergy of South Carolina and Georgia, during their 1834 synod, of an antiabolition resolution which declared emancipation "inconsistent with the best interests of the slaves." Support of slavery by the churches was put forward as a claim upon Christian respect. "I ask my Christian friends of the abolition Society—is not the opinion of the whole southern Church of some important weight in the matter? . . . Can you easily believe that these thousands of ministers of the Gospel, who 'count not their lives dear to them,' . . . can you believe that *they*, and the tens of thousands of Church members associated with them, are recreant to their Master and his cause on earth . . .?[85]

Antislavery opposition, however, was also religious in motivation. Charles K. Whipple, abolitionist, stated: "The Anti-Slavery movement . . . was at its commencement, and has ever since been, thoroughly and emphatically a religious enterprise." William Jay, son of John Jay and a leader in the movement, claimed: "I do not depend on any man as an abolitionist who does not act from a sense of religious obligation."[86] Indeed, whereas proslavery theology was arguing *permissively* that slavery was allowed by the Bible (and most of this seems to come from the Bible churches: "our purpose is to introduce no question on which the Bible does not give us specific instruction"[87]), their opponents preached abolition as a religious *imperative*.

Abolitionists were accused of being chiefly from one religious denominational tradition (Presbyterian-Congregationalist), but in fact they coalesced from many churches, including Quakers, Baptists, Methodists, Episcopalians, and the smaller perfectionist sects.[88] They noted some glaring inconsistencies in their proslavery confreres' treatment of Christian slaves. Slavers abided by laws which forbade bondsmen to convene for religious purposes; they insisted that slave marriages be celebrated religiously and adhered to with religious fidelity, but had no objection when owners separated husbands from wives, parents from children.[89]

When antislavery religious arguments pressed too strongly, they were met with the southern defense that Christians should not be proposing too strongly any specific measures with respect to slavery "because it requires the Church to obtrude herself into the province of the State."[90] This did not go down well with the abolitionists, who were insistent that the writ of Christian concern ran as far as any serious moral issue.

The religious aspect of the antislavery case serves to show that it was no phalanx of tightly unified thought. There were people opposed to the institution who stood off from others in the same camp. The Reverend Francis Wayland, for example, who served as president of Brown University in Rhode Island and had published denunciations of slavery, was not radical enough to suit the abolitionist minister Henry C. Wright, who recounted a conversation they had:

> The conversation turned on the question—*Can a slaveholder be a Christian?* . . . I asked him—"Can a man be a Christian and claim a right to sunder husbands and wives, parents and children—to compel men to work without wages—to forbid them to read the Bible, and buy and sell them—and who habitually does these things?" "Yes," answered the Rev. Dr. and President, "provided he has the spirit of Christ." "Is it possible for [a man] to be governed by the spirit of Christ and claim a right to commit these atrocious deeds, and habitually commit them?" After some turning, he answered, "Yes, I believe he can." "Is there, then, one crime in all the catalogue of crimes which, of itself, would be evidence to you that a man has not the spirit of Christ?" I asked. "Yes, thousands," said the Dr. "What?" I asked. *"Stealing,"* said

he. "Stealing what, a *sheep* or a *man*?" I asked. The Doctor took his hat and left the room, and appeared no more.[91]

Though the abolitionists were from many churches, they dominated in none. The mainstream religionists wrote them off as fanatics. Still, those of religious conscience had to frame their views on slavery. How was this resolved within the councils of a church that was national, wherein the various factions somehow had to come to terms with one another? The deliberations of the Methodists may serve as a case in point. Most of the early Methodist leaders had condemned slavery: John Wesley himself, Watson, Clarke, Bradburn, Coke, Asbury, Garretson, McKendree. In 1784 the General Conference ruled slaveholding and slave-trafficking out of the church. Very shortly thereafter the execution of that rule was suspended to allow for reconsideration (because of resistance from the South). Then in 1796 the antislavery rule was stiffly reasserted. The General Conference of 1800 changed it: only clergy were to have no slaves; as for laymen, they were to plan for a gradual emancipation. In 1804 the conference exempted North Carolina, South Carolina, Georgia, and Tennessee from that rule, instead telling the clergy there to exhort slaves to respect and obedience. The General Conference of 1808 told each local annual conference to formulate its own rules on slaveholding, since it was unprepared to issue any general ones. In 1820 the old rule forbidding clergy to own slaves was set aside. A proposal was made in 1828 to publish a caution about the inhumane treatment of slaves; it was tabled. In 1836 the church rejected abolitionism. In 1840 it ruled that in church trials blacks could not testify against whites. Slaveholding by clergy was affirmed if local laws forbade emancipation. In 1844 came a crisis. James O. Andrew, the first bishop to ignore the unwritten rule that bishops should not be slaveholders, was asked by the General Conference to refrain from the exercise of his duties (his rank and salary were left intact). The southern component of the church forthwith separated itself to become the Methodist Church, South.[92]

How the church receded from its original outlawing of slavery, first through a long process of fitful acquiescence to slaveholding interests, and eventually by a schism, received, as might be expected, diverse comment. A northern Methodist commented in 1857 that "notwithstanding the stampede of slaveholders in 1845, we are now, as a Church, more deeply and criminally involved in slaveholding than at any former period in our history."[93] A pastor in the South interpreted these events in 1865:

> The language of the rules was objected to in Virginia and in the states further south, as calculated to embarrass the operation of the ministry in preaching the Gospel to the blacks. They were afterward abandoned and others adopted in their place, still censuring the practice of slaveholding, but allowing the retention of the slaveholder in the church. This was a mere concession to the slave power, not a surrender of the principle. Several modifications were made subsequently, all concessions to the slave power, but never for one moment was the principle abandoned. . . . [After the division in 1844] the Northern branch receded toward

abolitionism, and the southern toward proslaveryism, until the one adopted a rule to exclude all slaveholders from the church, and the other expunged from the discipline every rule relating to slavery.[94]

A student of the religious arguments composed in defense of slavery in this period does come away with the conviction that neither reverence for the Scriptures nor pastoral concern for the blacks was the true motivating insight behind them. It was the economic stake of the more prosperous church members in the South. The abolitionists had no stake in slavery, and seem to have looked to Christian principles in a more dispassionate fashion. In the end it was not the churches but certain churchmen and churchwomen who developed the religious case against bondage. In their policy-making councils the churches were least likely to grasp the nettle.

The modern movement on behalf of abortion—especially for the repeal of legal restraint upon abortion—has had prominent support from the Christian churches, and also from Jewish groups. Early in the movement a national network of Protestant and Jewish clergy formed the Clergy Consultation Service on Abortion, which was able to use the traditional legal immunities of clerical confidentiality to refer women to abortionists before the practice had been legalized.[95] Sometime thereafter many religious bodies began to issue statements in favor of abortion choice: Lutheran, Episcopalian, Unitarian, Quaker, Baptist, Presbyterian, Methodist, United Church, Reformed and Conservative Jewish, and others.

Religious motivation has been prominent also on the antiabortion side. It has been a movement with more lay leadership than was the abolition movement, but it has been similarly broad in its base. Prochoice forces have asserted the belief that opinion against abortion on demand is predominantly Catholic, but social scientists have tended to discount this.[96] It has lately come out that in the early strategizing by proabortion advocates, the Catholic bishops were designated in advance as target villains in the public relations efforts that were to follow, as being a group sufficiently unpopular to allow even the Catholic laity and lower clergy to dissociate from them.[97]

There is a difference between the rhetoric of religion as wielded on either side of the dispute, a difference reminiscent of that which sundered the churches on slavery. Whereas most abortion defense is permissive—arguing not that abortion is morally good but that one should be allowed it as a choice—the charge on the other side is imperative: that abortion is the killing of the innocent, a moral crime. On behalf of abortion choice the fact of church endorsements itself is offered as a religious warrant. Senator Bob Packwood, for instance, told the U.S. Senate: "Timorously at first, and then in greater quantity, and finally in almost an avalanche, religious leaders and a great, great number of religious organizations passed resolutions in favor of legalized abortion. . . . These are not organizations unconcerned with life, or unconcerned with morality. These are organizations in every sense as moral and as concerned with the rights of individuals as those who are sincerely opposed to abortion."[98]

Frequent too is the warning that religious cautions against abortion ought not intrude too specifically into the civic plaza. Shortly before primary elections in the fall of 1980, Cardinal Medeiros of Boston published a pastoral letter to his fellow Catholics, advocating for the unborn "what the Declaration of Independence proclaims as a fundamental human right—the right to life." Restating his opposition to legalized abortion as an "offense against God and humanity," the prelate encouraged his readers "to exercise your right and duty to vote in the upcoming elections and to bring your own conscience—the voice of God within you—to the ballot box with you." Those who vote, he said, have a share in the legislation of those they elect, and if their representatives deprive the unborn of legal safety, they "cannot separate themselves totally from the guilt."[99] The *New York Times* called the letter a "setback for the American political process. It is not the church's view of abortion that gives offense; churches have every right to address moral and social issues that also figure in political debates." But they should not try to influence elections.[100] The editorial accused the cardinal of intimidating his coreligionists, and then noted that the proabortion candidates were elected.

How have the churches, exposed simultaneously to those who claim an overriding priority for women's interests and choices over those of their consorts and their offspring and to those who defend the rights of men to share and children to survive, steered their principles through the midst of it all? The United Methodist Church is not unrepresentative. The church's abiding doctrine had forbidden abortion. Then, promptly after the movement to decriminalize it had gained its first public strength, at the behest of its women's issues group, in 1968 the church's most authoritative assembly reversed itself and by resolution endorsed the legal proposal exactly as formulated by the American Law Institute. Abortions to avert threat to a mother's health (physical or mental) or to prevent the birth of handicapped offspring or those conceived through rape or incest: all these abortions were said to be permissible. Four years later, in an even more fundamental document, the church's Statement of Social Principles, in the portion entitled "The Nurturing Community," the church elaborated its own standpoint on abortion. Reluctantly, despite "belief in the sanctity of unborn human life," it now would countenance abortion without any restrictions, save only that the pregnancy be "unacceptable" and that searching and prayerful inquiry should precede the abortion. In 1976 this statement was amended. Since at that time, conformably to the church hope, virtually no legal restrictions remained on abortion, the church stated that "governmental laws and regulations do not necessarily provide all the guidance required by the informed Christian conscience." Most recently, in 1980, the statement was left unchanged except that prayerful consideration, to be followed by medical and pastoral advice, was now to be supplemented by "other appropriate counsel." As to what reasons there might be for abortion, how it is consistent with the sanctity of unborn human life, what question should be pursued by prayerful inquiry, what alternatives to law exist to enlighten the Christian conscience or to offer it counsel—of all this the church utterances offer no suggestion. Although the documents are unquestionably religious, in that they proceed from the high-

est authority of a major church body, they do not display any religious
principles upon which one might ground or challenge or encourage a decision
to abort. [101] The adjustment of the church's stand—or, rather, the withdrawal
of the church from taking a stand of religious import beyond endorsing legal
freedom—was hailed by communicants who had worked hard to avert their
denomination's being offensively opposed to the abortion constituency. An
alternative estimate was offered by the church's best-known ethicist:

> Churchmen seem to have a penchant for saying today what the
> surrounding culture said twenty-four hours earlier. Clearly, that
> word is "feticide upon request." It has already been spoken.
> Possible warrant for this position, however, in Christian
> morality—the law's permission ought not primarily to concern
> us—cannot be imagined. Instead, one cannot imagine a clearer
> case of acculturated Christianity, or rather the abolition of Chris-
> tian teachings and their replacement by secular timeliness and
> social problem-solving (i.e., solving other problems by means of
> abortion) in a medical-technological and an increasingly pagan
> age. [102]

The role of religion in the abortion dispute is reminiscent of its earlier effort
to deal with slavery. Those who condemned the two institutions appealed to
religious principles of justice and compassion towards fellow humans at risk.
They were met by religious counterclaims: not so much that slaveholding or
aborting were things Christians were encouraged to do, but that they could
not be un-Christian if so many churchmen endorsed them. Advocates of the
two institutions defended themselves from religious reproach in other, similar, ways. They urged the impossible predicament for the dominant parties if
the institution should be withdrawn and their claims of justice in maintaining
their lives as they were previously. They cast discredit on the opposition by
identifying it for the most part with a single denomination. They raised the
church-state issue, criticizing those who would turn a religious argument into
a civil issue. One can notice a similar meeting of diverse religious rhetorics.
The defenders claim, at the most, not that the institution is specifically
Christian, but that (though tragic) it is not incompatible with their faith; the
opponents call it religiously deplorable and civilly criminal. Church policy
bodies, especially if beholden to the constituency whose lives would suffer the
most disarrangement if those others whose lives were forfeit to the institution
went free, showed themselves capable of doctrinal reversal, though not
capable of giving a theological account of the grounds for reversal.

A Higher Law?

Another aspect of each struggle, while not directly religious, was religiously
related and significant. When one examines the moral case made on either
side of the slavery issue one notices that as argued for the defense it seems
more prima facie Christian, with abundant reference to slavery in the Bible
and in the behavior of churchmen ever since. The cogency on the abolition
side is less explicitly Christian, though deeply religious and held by commit-

ted Christians. It was an appeal from the authority of the law to an appellate moral standard, a "higher law," as it was known in debate. William H. Seward, U.S. senator from Ohio, invoked it when arguing against the Fugitive Slave Law:

> I know that there are laws of various sorts which regulate the conduct of men. There are constitutions and statutes, codes mercantile and codes civil, but when we are legislating for states, especially when we are founding states, all these laws must be brought to the standard of the laws of God, and must be tried by that standard, and must stand or fall by it. This principle was happily explained by one of the most distinguished political philosophers of England in these emphatic words: "There is but one law for all, namely, that law which governs all law; the law of our Creator, the law of humanity, justice, equity, the law of nature and of nations. So far as any laws fortify this primeval law, and give it more precision, more energy, more effect by their declarations, such laws enter into the sanctuary and participate in the sacredness of its character. . . ."
>
> The Constitution regulates our stewardship over the national domain. . . . But there is a higher law than the Constitution, which regulates our authority over the domain, and devotes it to the same noble purposes. The territory is a part . . . of the common heritage of mankind, bestowed upon them by the Creator of the universe. We are his stewards, and must so discharge our trust as to secure in the highest attainable degree their happiness.[103]

The "higher law" was kin to the divine law of Christian ethics, the natural law of the philosophers, and the law of nations of the jurists. It was a notion of more than Christian provenance, yet was brandished by very explicitly Christian partisans. It appealed, not to isolated passages in the Scriptures, but to the emergent message and spirit of Jesus' teaching. Theodore Parker, a Congregationalist minister in Boston, drew on it a few months after Seward:

> I have sometimes been amazed at the talk of men who call on us to keep the fugitive slave law, one of the most odious laws in a world of odious laws—a law not fit to be made or kept. I have been amazed that they should dare to tell us the law of God, writ on the heavens and our hearts, never demanded we should disobey the laws of men! . . . Talk of keeping the fugitive slave law! Come, come, we know better. Men in New England know better than this. We know that we ought not to keep a wicked law, and that it must not be kept when the law of God forbids!

When standing trial five years later for just such civil disobedience, Parker pled to the jury:

> Is this law just? That is, does it coincide with the Law of God, the Constitution of the Universe? There your own conscience must decide. Mr. Curtis [Judge Benjamin Curtis; later he would sit on

the U.S. Supreme Court and enter a strong dissent in *Dred Scott*] has told you there is no morality but Legality, no standard of Right and Wrong but the Statute, your only light comes from this printed page, "Statutes of the United States," and through the sheepskin covers. Gentlemen, if your conscience is also bound in sheepskins you will think as those Honorable Judges, and recognize only Judge Curtis' "Standard of Morality,"—no Higher Law.[104]

Such high claims antagonized opponents, as might be imagined. A South Carolina editor reproached Parker in an anonymous letter: "Are you aware, Sir, that, in your crazy opposition to, and warfare against, slavery, you are arrogating to yourself a wisdom and a righteousness which not only exceed those of the scribes and Pharisees, but which are superior to those of God and patriarch, and of Christ and apostle?" Roger Taney himself was exasperated by this appeal to a "higher law" (understandable in a chief justice of a Supreme Court) and the resultant "fanaticism against slavery."[105]

In some respects such an appeal does not arise within our contemporary abortion controversy. For one thing, slavery was an institution sustained by the law, while abortion is an institution sustained by the removal of law. The opponents of both were disappointed by Supreme Court decisions, respectively, to uphold and to overturn the law. But whereas the former deplored the law as it stood, the latter have been asking for redress through law. In fact, much of the sophisticated antiabortion literature has come from the pens of attorneys, and has tended to appeal to no law higher than the Constitution rightly read. Little polemic as strident as what rose from William Lloyd Garrison's followers has marked our abortion debate, at least as published.

It may be, however, that at the yeoman's level things are said differently. There is a level of defiance more explicit than what one finds in the more cultivated literature. Abortion facilities are picketed, prospective abortors approached, and clinics burnt. Some of this is illegal; all of it is bitterly resented. But it has an interesting precedent in the energetic efforts many antislavery believers made to thwart their racist adversaries. Some forced their way into "Jim Crow" accommodations in order to demonstrate their opposition. Others sheltered runaway slaves on free soil. Others, even more given to the cause, worked in slave territory to send the fugitives on their way. People vouched for having sped four hundred, six hundred, as many as twenty-seven hundred, to their freedom. For the slaveholders this represented a staggering loss of capital investment. And it was not without risk. The Reverend Charles Torrey of Boston, dead in a Maryland jail cell, was one martyr to the cause and a hero to slave liberators. When one calculates the financial loss this represented to owners one can understand their fury at the general refusal of northerners to execute the laws for the rendition of escapees. In a way, the freeing of the slaves and the burning of the clinics displayed—more clearly than published remonstrances—the smoldering vehemence of feeling against slavery and against abortion.[106]

Intrusion or Rescue?

There is evidence of persistent self-questioning about the "peculiar institution" in the slave states. "The attitude that slavery was deplorable was common enough to qualify a good many slaveholders as being antislavery in sentiment. The mark of the true reformer, however, was his compulsion to probe, to question, and to agitate. In the eyes of less dedicated individuals he might well seem 'arrogant,' 'malignant,' 'belligerent,' and, above all, 'impractical.' "[107] It was this readiness on the part of some to move beyond misgivings to unwelcome conclusions that helped solidify and arouse proslavery sentiment. They could abide indecisive regret, but not a move towards consequences.

One common grievance they nourished was that their critics were too remote from the slave scene and from southern agriculture to speak with any credibility. *Uncle Tom's Cabin* was met with a cloud of scorn from southerners who derided Harriet Beecher Stowe's ignorance of realities in the slave areas.[108] Having honored the many practical and unresolvable arguments on either side of the case, those who saw no workable way out of slaveholding became angered at the flippant way abolitionists turned a blind eye to all the evidence:

> There seems to be something in this subject which blunts the perceptions, and darkens and confuses the understandings and moral feelings of men. Tell them that, of necessity, in every civilized society, there must be an infinite variety of conditions and employments, from the most eminent and intellectual, to the most servile and laborious; that the negro race, from their temperament and capacity, are peculiarly suited to the situation which they occupy, and not less happy in it than any corresponding class to be found in the world; prove incontestibly that no scheme of emancipation could be carried into effect without the most intolerable mischiefs and calamities to both master and slave, or without probably throwing a large and fertile portion of the earth's surface out of the pale of civilization—and you have done nothing. They reply, that whatever may be the consequence, you are bound to do *right*; that man has a right to himself, and man cannot have property in man.[109]

When Congress was wrangling over whether to admit Utah and New Mexico as slave or free, antislavery forces could not understand why the South was shouldering the issue so heavily. All knew that slavery could have no financial survival in that terrain. Congressman Brown of Mississippi explained that for his people it was more than a symbolic contest: "Ask yourselves if it is right to exasperate eight millions of people upon an abstraction; a matter to us of substance and of life, but to you the merest shadow of an abstraction."[110]

The apparently irresponsible way antislavery people pushed aside their arguments and harassed them took away all patience from proslavers in the debate:

> Suppose your brother should come to you, and declare that your

nose is freckled, and insist on skinning it, or that your head is deformed, and undertake to scalp you;—would you readily submit to the operation? No sir; you would not submit. . . . Suppose he should get impatient and knock you down;—would that have any tendency to *convince* you? Would it not enrage you, and drive you farther from him? He must first convince you that what he says is true—that there was a mistake in your formation and that he can rectify it.[111]

Franklin Pierce, in his annual message to Congress on the eve of New Year's Day, 1856, lay the blame for nationwide alienation on the intrusions of the antislavers. "While the people of the Southern States confine their attention to their own affairs, not presuming officiously to intermeddle with the social institutions of the Northern States, too many of the inhabitants of the latter are permanently organized in associations to inflict injury on the former, by wrongful acts [aiding fugitive slaves], which would be cause of war as between foreign powers."[112]

A congressman had earlier addressed the House: "To understand how slaves ought to be treated, we must be among them. . . . One not living among them, would be as unfit to prescribe rules for their government, as could be an ignorant empiric to prescribe a remedy for a disease which he knew only by name. . . . We would as soon permit others to invade the sanctuary of our dwellings, as to touch [slavery]. We would as soon permit Congress to dictate to us in our domestic concerns,—in our social intercourse—to prescribe to us a system of religion, or a code of morals. We should receive any extrinsic interposition as an injury, and resent it as an insult."[113]

Soon the slavery advocates were asking why they owed their critics any accounting for how they lived their lives. Slaveholders were urged to "put aside all care or thought what *Northern* people say about them. Let us be independent in this at least!"[114] A brochure on "The Morals of Slavery" asked: "Why should we account to that people? What are they that they should subject us to the question? We are their equals; sprung from the same stocks, in possession of the same authorities, learning at the same schools, taught from the same books, by the same great masters of thought and language, and in the full assertion of an equal civilization and freedom."[115]

Abolition meant money—enormous money—and it was doubted that its partisans would speak with the same enthusiasm were it their own fortunes at stake. "But if slavery be an evil, as they alledge [*sic*], and the South have had it thrust upon them by old England and New England, are they now to be told they are pirates, thieves, and robbers! . . . If wrong has been done, who ought to right it? Heaven doubtless would decide, old England and New England, if it takes every dollar and every thing they possess on God's earth! And until prepared for this discretion, it seems to me, would require they should not be quite so brazenfaced with their accusations.[116]

Since the case made by antislavers seemed to them to have no force, their opponents surmised that something besides logic lay behind their persistence. Some saw a design to dominate the South financially. "We can distinguish no great difference between the trade in American negroes, and the trade in any other article of property. Nothing but sectional malice and narrow bigotry prevents the trade in slaves from being left to the greatest laws of commerce, which can best adjust the relation between supply and demand."[117] More often, abolitionists were seen as "knaves and demagogues who care nothing for the happiness of either Negro or white, provided they can accomplish their own selfish purposes."[118]

> It is well known that, with few exceptions, the Abolitionists give themselves very little care about the comfort or happiness of the negro. Their business is, I am sorry to say, not happiness to the negro, but *trouble*, as much as may be, to the Negro's master. Their vocation is *destruction*. They would *pull down*. . . . The *thorough* Abolitionist is a radical, and that in the worst sense of the word. He is for uprooting everything which stands in the way of his own pet notion of universal equality; but, he is far more anxious to bring down those who are above him than to raise up those who are below. He is far more proud and intolerant than compassionate and humane.[119]

A similar resentment is expressed by prochoice partisans in the abortion conflict. For one thing, they see themselves as facing opponents with little stake in or knowledge of rejected pregnancy. Karen Mulhauser, executive director of the National Abortion Rights Action League, writes, after an unsympathetic hearing from congressional subcommittees: "I suppose that if a male Congressman or Senator wants to believe women enjoy rape, he might also believe that women should carry through a pregnancy that results from rape. . . . Make no mistake about it, much of the controversy reflects not just religious scruple but a yearning for moral punishment. Congress spent months last year weighing how much misery and shame should fall on the poor and pregnant before Federal help would be offered."[120]

Congresswoman Bella Abzug, testifying against a prolife amendment to the Constitution, reminded her male auditors that they were dealing with an issue in which they could never know personal involvement:

> I appear before you as a Member of Congress, but also as a woman who is aware that in the consideration of this proposal, the fate of women is once again to be decided by men. I recognize that views both for and against the right to abortion are found in both sexes. The fact remains, however, that these are amendments aimed exclusively at women, which have been introduced by men and submitted to a legislative body consisting entirely of men. . . .
>
> Man and woman are equal in the act of conception, but after the single act has occurred, it is the woman's body that carries and nurtures the embryo and the fetus.
>
> It is the woman who experiences the physical and psychological changes of pregnancy.
>
> It is the woman who has the discomforts and sometimes the medical complications that accompany pregnancy.
>
> It is the woman who feels the pain of childbirth. It is the woman

who may have the postpartum depression.

And in our society, it is still the woman who bears the major responsibility of caring for and raising the child and who often must leave school or her work to do so.

Childbearing and childraising is a great experience for most women. For some it is not. For some it is sometimes. The point is that it is a totally individual experience, the most highly personal process in a woman's life.

And yet the Buckley and Helms amendments might mobilize the full power and authority of the state and its legal apparatus to interfere in this private process, to dictate to the individual citizen who is a woman what she is to do with her body and with her life.[121]

Garrett Hardin joins in Abzug's skepticism. "Let us not forget what Mark Twain once said: 'It is easy to bear adversity—another man's, I mean!' He would have been closer to the target had he finished his remark with these words: 'when the adversity is borne by another person, I mean: especially if that other person is a woman.' "[122] Lawrence Lader records the testimony of abortion activists:

"For us abortion can be a matter of life or death, physical and psychological suffering, and slavery to laws we had no voice in making," stated Female Liberation in Boston.

"The compulsory breeding of women by church and state is nothing more than ecclesiastical and legislative pimpery in which the bodies of all women are utilized for state profit and pleasure," Lana Phelan told the California Conference on Abortion.[123]

Since prochoice arguments seem to make so little entry into the consideration of prolife people, speculation arises among the former as to what the latter's true, motivating insights are. One NARAL publication speculates:

This vindictive, self-righteous attitude shows scorn for women and a feeling that sex is bad and must be punished.

It is ironic that a Church ruled by celibate male priests should lead a movement against contraception and abortion. . . .

Right-to-Life dismisses unwanted pregnancy as a mere annoyance.[124]

Who are the so-called "pro-life" people? They are the COMPULSORY PREGNANCY people, and that's what they should be called. Whose life are they "pro?" Certainly not the life of the woman. Certainly not the life of a child born into poverty. Certainly not the life of a child certain to be born with severe defects. Do they show you women in the death throes of peritonitis? Do they show you the pain, the suicides, the wrecked lives? Do they show you the cost to the taxpayers for raising unwanted children to adulthood? Do they show you the neglected children who go wrong, who fill the jails and perpetuate poverty?

Where is *their* responsibility after they compel a birth?[125]

Also as in the slavery struggle, battle lines are drawn closer to principle than to political realities. When the Senate was debating in 1975 a proposal to deny funding for abortions, Senator Edward Kennedy, whose votes have consistently favored abortion choice, argued that the bill might bar abortions for poor women who had been raped. To the explanation that the number of pregnancies resulting from rape was infinitesimal, Kennedy replied that raped women would take little consolation from such an argument.[126]

A Movement of the People?

But it was more than their arguments that rendered the antislavery partisans so offensive. The movement seems to have had more than its share of idiosyncratic personalities. They seemed to their adversaries to be a strange crowd. John Brown was at once a seer and an unscrupulous freebooter. Lucretia Mott was strident, Angelina Grimké was a prude, John Quincy Adams was embittered. They had a common cause, but rarely the congenial personalities it would take to work harmoniously together. Some among them were distressed at how their style alienated others. "[Catherine] Beecher became the most influential of antifeminists and antiabolitionists, believing they harmed all reform causes by their harsh tactics and radical aims."[127] Many northerners, particularly those in government who were anxious to accommodate the South and preserve the peace, were alarmed by the undiplomatic tone of the Garrisonian abolitionists.[128]

In their fervor the abolitionists, like the feminists, often resorted to symbolic gestures, as when Theodore Weld and Angelina Grimké, abolitionists both, made sure that their wedding was attended by six former slaves of the Grimké family, "our testimony against the horrible prejudice."[129] Slave narratives, engraved portrayals of plantation brutality, and photographs of slaves scarred by beating and mutilation all served the movement as graphic and dramatic—and to their opponents, immensely irritating—propaganda.[130]

Activists against abortion have also appeared, to supporters and adversaries alike, to include more than their share of strident and bizarre personalities. The more flamboyant features of antiabortion efforts, such as vigils and demonstrations at abortoria, have given a theater of display to enough exhibitionist behavior to cause distaste to friends and disgust to foes. And the black Weld-Grimké wedding guests surely had their counterpart in the dead female abortus who was laid before a horrified gathering of representatives from pro- and antiabortion groups, come together for the first time in 1979. "Our unborn sisters were left out of this conference," said the woman who brought the little corpse into the room.[131]

Possibly all such movements need the strident as their first wave of assault. In the aftermath, the abolitionists are given credit:

> . . . They have either been damned as fanatics who incited a needless conflict, or dismissed as a windy rabble whose effusions had little impact on the crisis. They are easier to neglect than understand. Any movement that makes us face the crucial flaw in our own soul is a jarring reminder not only of past failures but of

unfinished responsibilities. . . . They jabbed and provoked an essentially indifferent people into solving its responsibility.[132]

It is too early to hold today's antiabortion leaders in a like perspective. Perhaps, though, Michael Harrington, the socialist leader, was a harbinger when he riled a Planned Parenthood assembly in 1979 with his judgment that the antiabortionists' right-to-life movement was "one of the few genuine social movements of the 1970's."[133]

A Common Summary

After long review of these great interests in conflict one is presented with enough resemblances and parallels to wonder if it is possible to frame a single, common account that would serve as fair description of them both. In broad lines it can, I think, be done.

A mighty storm of controversy broke over the nation. It appeared to find its climax in a lawsuit decided on appeal by the Supreme Court. The legal contest, though, was but one skirmish in a long and perhaps never-abated conflict. On its face the suit was to determine whether a very few individuals could be put at the disposal of those who held them in their power. One party of symbolic protagonists represented a vast cohort of humans, an underclass whose advocates described them as innocent, helpless, easily victimized, and wrongfully subject to the arbitary will of another class of people. This overclass, according to its spokesmen, had long been put upon by its peer-partners, and was newly sensitive to its own dignity and rights and welfare. It would face unthinkable ruin if not left free to dispose of the underclass as its own advantage and good will dictated. It did not even ask encouragement: just neutrality, the freedom to arrange its life as it pleased.

The overclass was willing to stipulate, at the start of its argument, that this particular subjection was an unhappy necessity—tragic, even—which in a saner world might never need to be. But realistically there was no workable way to accept this underclass as their peers, social companions, economic dependents, or partners in destiny. If given their freedom, the members of the underclass would be at a loss to use it for anyone's clear benefit. On any unromantic view of things, their subjection was thus also a shelter from the harsher destiny they might encounter if they were turned out into the give-and-take of our unwelcoming society. Better not to taste, not to know. And so, with reluctance yet responsibility, the prolocutors of the overclass declined the burden of accepting the underclass into equal human fellowship.

As long as one could remember, the underclass had had ambivalent protection under the law, as anyone does whose interests have to depend on others' pleading. Its members had depended for their survival in the past less on the shelter of the law than on the relative indisposition of most people to take advantage of them. Appearing to have hobbled rights, in fact they had no rights, and the Court would soon make this fact law. A time had come when the overclass which held them at its mercy ran short of mercy. Economically, a standard of life was being reached for that the overclass found attractive, did not wish to forfeit, and could only maintain if it did not need to be shared with the underclass.

Religious spokesmen were found who would assure the overclass that Christianity would not condemn its members' self-interest in the matter. Divines had traditionally taken the side of the underclass, though with little rigor. Now some spoke out that no human could treat another as private property; others saw that as doctrinaire, naive, a discredit to world-wise religion. Some said the laws must be judged by a higher law that holds that our human kin who are most imperiled must be most cherished; others argued that religious judgments outrun their writ when they wander onto state property.

All of this debate was for the ears of the overclass; the underclass was neither heard from nor addressed. Those who spoke of the rights of those held in subjection were reproached as too fond of abstract principle, too little responsive to the agonized self-interest of the overclass. And, truth to tell, these advocates of the underclass were not always tasteful or sophisticated.

Both sides set great store by the judgment of the Court, which finally ruled that the members of the underclass were of a lower dignity, too low to come before it for relief, and that how they were dealt with was to be the private concern of the overclass. For the latter, too quick a joy ensued. In time it became clear that the Court was less than supreme when its judgments thwarted the moral mind of the majority—even if that moral opinion was indolently held and inconsistently applied. It is possible that the Court itself was most responsible for arousing many people to pursue the protection of the underclass more ardently and more consistently than had been so for long years past. For those who wished to abolish this peculiar institution, the goal at first became the overthrow of the Court's ruling. Politically, this was as much within their grasp as any measure that conforms to the conscience of most people. But beyond that remained the more distant goal, the costlier fight: to overthrow what the legal rulings dimly stood for: the readiness of many humans to make others forfeit life so that they might pursue theirs in reasonable and self-interested contentment.

This, it seems from the two contests we have reviewed, might fairly stand as brief summary for either.

Two Great Statesmen

Those whose rumination over abortion leads them to chattel slavery for possible and provocative comparison might extend their curiosity further, to study two towering statesmen who involved themselves in this matter of slavery: Thomas Jefferson and Abraham Lincoln. They were two of the most perceptive and well-spoken political leaders America has ever seen. But what makes their treatment of the issue of human bondage especially interesting is that for both men it involved, as abortion does for many today, a collision of high principles. For both men slavery was a moral wrong. For both of them it seemed also a political inevitability.

For Jefferson the clash of principles brought the peculiarly American institution of sovereign local self-government on the state level into conflict with the peculiarly Southern institution which affected some people's rights to life, liberty, and the pursuit of happiness. The bind for Lincoln was between the right of the people to be governed only by their consent and the need for the government to impose the will of the majority, both of which had been established at the founding of the Republic. Each man was a sensitive and pragmatic politican. Neither was disposed to cast away his career by flying in the face of the national will. Yet they stand in history's light quite differently because of the ways they negotiated those conflicts of right and principle. There may be, in their respective ways of honoring two acknowledged but conflicting rights, some matter for our meditation.

Thomas Jefferson

When Thomas Jefferson of Monticello spoke of "my country" he was referring to Virginia, not to the United States. The larger span of his public life was spent in the precincts and politics of that state, more than in the capital and councils of the newer Union of states. A cause dear to him was Virginia's self-determination, her freedom—though in compact with her sister states—to provide for her own welfare in her own way. He was one of the framers of the Union who had shaped it to protect Virginia's autonomy once that had been won.[134]

The states of Jefferson's Union were no thralls. Unlike territorial units within other countries they were not simply subordinated to the national government; indeed, they gave it its powers and warrant. So insistent a design for local freedom was the fruit of remembered experience: that national governments had tended always to take power to themselves and to mistreat the people's more authentically expressed needs, which tended to be better provided for by nearer forms of government.

This protected autonomy, however, was seriously restricted in one way. There was one freedom the states lacked under the Constitution: the freedom to renounce it.[135] The promise to enter the compact of Union was seen as irrevocable, and would surely carry with it some forfeiture of autonomy in favor of the national family and welfare.

Jefferson was among those who saw the promise as binding. In 1787, when James Madison's draft of a proposed Constitution was still under discussion, Jefferson wrote to his younger colleague from Virginia: "It is my principle that the will of the Majority should always prevail." Yet in the same letter the same Jefferson also writes: "I own I am not a friend to very energetic government. It is always oppressive. . . . No country should be long without a rebellion."[136] Earlier that same year he had observed to Madison, commenting on the popular form of government they were establishing:

> The mass of mankind under this form of government enjoys a precious degree of liberty and happiness. It has it's [sic] evils too: the principal of which is the turbulence to which it is subject. . . . Even this evil is productive of good. It prevents the degeneracy of government, and nourishes a general attention to the public affairs. I hold it that a little rebellion now and then is a good thing, and as necessary in the political world as storms in the physical.[137]

Jefferson sounds as if he were indulgent towards dissenting and even departing fellow citizens. Indeed, in the same letter he speculated that if the inhabitants of Virginia's land claim to the west of the Alleghenies were to declare themselves independent, Virginians were hardly likely to take up arms against their brothers there. Jefferson's position, as stated early, seems to have been that he would neither secede nor prevent secession by force. In all respects, he sought a government that was freely accepted by the governed.

In 1798 Jefferson found himself sitting as vice-president of the United States amid an otherwise Federalist-dominated government. Even in this disgruntled time he did not favor violation of the Union:

> If to rid ourselves of the present rule of Massachusetts and Connecticut, we break the Union, will the evil stop there? Suppose the New England States alone cut off, will our nature be changed? Are we not men still to the south of that, and with all the passions of men? Immediately, we shall see a Pennsylvania and a Virginia party arise in the residuary confederacy, and the public mind will be distracted with the same party spirit. What a game too will the one party have in their hands, by eternally threatening the other that unless they do so and so, they will join their northern neighbors. . . . An association of men who will not quarrel with one another is a thing which never yet existed, from the greatest confederacy of nations to a town meeting or a vestry.[138]

That was in 1798. In 1817, years after he had gained the presidency and then retired back to Virginia, Jefferson still insisted on union. "The first principle of republicanism is, that the *lex-majoris partis* is the fundamental law of every society of individuals of equal rights; to consider the will of the society enounced by the majority of a single vote, as sacred as if unanimous, is the first of all lessons in importance, yet the last which is thoroughly learnt. This law once disregarded, no other remains but that of force, which ends necessarily in military despotism."[139] At this point he is taking the middle line between autonomy and compact. One must acquiesce to one's political partners, but one must believe that over time a rational presentation of one's needs—those of the citizen before the state, those of the state before the Union—would eventually be honored.

But within a few short years, Jefferson was to be alarmed by the struggle between North and South over Missouri and what Missouri stood for. He had long been outraged by the willingness of John Marshall's Supreme Court to overturn state laws as violative of the Federal Constitution; it had been his early view, to the contrary, that states might strike down federal laws they rejected. Now the North was doing battle over the admission of Missouri, to the north of the Maxon-Dixon line, as a slave state. Jefferson, who saw the prerogatives of Virginia in the balance, in partnership with the southern states, entered the fray and began himself to consider secession by the South. Among the most awful possible specters of a future in which the states lost their autonomy to the Congress was the possibility of a law proclaiming that "the condition of all men within the United States shall be that of freedom."[140]

Here was the crunch. Jefferson, who had for years propounded the pragmatic necessity of yielding to a political majority, now found his sticking point. In one respect it was the right of states to self-determination. But in another respect there was an entirely different principle at stake: the right of some to hold others in slavery. Thomas Jefferson was willing to forego the United States if it meant that he and his fellow planters from Virginia, whose comfort rested entirely on the possession of numerous slaves, would be obliged to give those blacks their freedom or, worse still, to dwell beside them in their freedom.[141] When faced with what he saw as a threat to the legitimate needs and claims of his fellow Virginians, and citizens of other states, to govern their own lives, he was willing to ignore that they enjoyed this freedom, in Virginia and elsewhere, at the cost of others whose needs and claims he felt less compellingly.

Slavery was another matter that concerned him throughout his long career. In 1781, at the close of the Revolutionary War, he wrote in his *Notes on Virginia*:

> The whole commerce between master and slave is a perpetual exercise of the most boisterous passions, the most unremitting despotism on the one part, and degrading submission on the other. . . . Can the liberties of a nation be thought secure when we have removed their only firm basis, a conviction in the minds of the people that these liberties are of the gift of God? That they are not to be violated but with his wrath? Indeed, I tremble for my country when I reflect that God is just; that his justice cannot sleep forever; that considering numbers, nature and natural means only, a revolution of the wheel of fortune, an exchange of situation is among possible events; that it may become possible by super-natural interference! The Almighty has no attribute which can take side with us in such a contest. But it is impossible to be temperate and to pursue this subject through the various considerations of policy, of morals, or history natural and civil. We must be con-tented to hope they will force their way into every one's mind. I think a change already perceptible, since the origin of the present revolution. The spirit of the master is abating, that of the slave rising from the dust, his conditions mollifying, the way I hope preparing, under the auspices of heaven, for a total emancipation, and that this is disposed, in the order of events, to be with the consent of the masters, rather than by their extirpation.[142]

In this matter Jefferson was to be deceived. Five years later, in 1786, when he was on embassy to Paris, he found himself having to explain to his intellec-tual friends how it was that his native Virginia had just passed a slave law without any provision for emancipation, even gradual:

> There wanted not in that assembly men of virtue enough to propose, and talents to vindicate this clause. But they saw that the moment of doing it with success was not yet arrived, and that an unsuccessful effort, as too often happens, would only rivet still

closer the chains of bondage, and retard the moment of delivery to this oppressed description of men. What a stupendous, what an incomprehensible machine is man! Who can endure toil, famine, stripes, imprisonment or death itself in vindication of his own liberty, and the next moment be deaf to all those motives whose power supported him thro' his trial, and inflict on his fellow man a bondage, one hour of which is fraught with more misery than ages of that which he rose in rebellion to oppose. But we must await with patience the workings of an overruling providence.[143]

Here was a matter of heartfelt importance wherein Thomas Jefferson was never able to carry with him anything resembling a majority of his fellow burgesses in Virginia, but one in which he was always unwilling for Virginia to be overruled by a national majority. His political actions in service of his antislavery tenets were increasingly indecisive. In drafting the Declaration of Independence he omitted mention of property in his enumeration of natural rights, purposely depriving slavery of at least that document's blessing. He drafted a constitution for Virginia which provided for gradual emancipation; it was rejected. His was the principal hand in codifying Virginia laws, but then he made the slave code and the laws concerning free blacks more onerous for blacks in several ways. In 1784 he sponsored an ordinance to forbid slavery across the Alleghenies; it failed in Congress by one vote. After that, he forbore to contradict proslavery sentiment.[144] "He had learned that, while many Virginians deplored slavery and professed to wish nothing so much as to be delivered from its hated embrace, when a plan for eliminating slavery was proposed they became strangely immobilized."[145]

John Chester Miller sees Jefferson himself as immobilized:

> Jefferson asked to be judged by his acts rather than by his words. But on the issue of slavery in America he emerges with greater luster if he is judged by his words rather than by his acts. For here he signally failed to live up to his own precepts: "To do whatever is right, and leave the consequences to Him who has the disposal of them," and to "give up money, give up fame, give up science, give up earth itself and all it contains, rather than do an immoral act." In the antislavery movement, except for the abolition of the slave trade in 1808, he chose—or, as he said, was constrained to choose by imperious circumstances beyond his control—to philosophize about the moral evil of slavery, to warn his countrymen of the divine chastizement they were inviting by their intransigence, and to plant ideas in his wide-ranging correspondence which he hoped others would bring to fruition. By so doing, he played a part congenial to the retiring, studious, and literary side of his character. His refusal to follow up the *Notes on Virginia* with an active assault upon slavery never ceased to occasion regret among the later abolitionists: as William Lloyd Garrison said, if Jefferson had acted upon his theories of the rights of man "what an all-conjuring influence must have attended his illustrious example." Whatever

the tenor of Jefferson's words, his "illustrious example"—and nothing in that regard was more telling than the fact that he remained a slaveowner all his life—tended to countenance the institution he abhorred.[146]

Jefferson very credibly stated that he abhorred slavery. He stated this in private, however (his only public assertions appeared in his *Notes on Virginia*, which he had never wished to have published, and had printed only after a pirated translation came out). The public unpopularity of this view kept him discreetly silent on the subject until, late in life, he saw this principle of universal human rights conflict with that other principle he cherished, that of Virginia's autonomy. When it came to a choice of whether he and his peers would award human rights to the negroes he had confessed should have them by divine right, or whether he and his peers would vindicate their own right to pursue their own threatened welfare, he abandoned the principle that would have cost him much. Possibly the best comment on Jefferson's irresolute dedication to the slaves' cause came from John Quincy Adams, a successor and the son of his predecessor, who wrote in his diary after reading Jefferson's posthumous writings:

> He saw the gross inconsistency between the principles of the Declaration of Independence and the fact of negro slavery, and he could not, or would not, prostitute the faculties of his mind to the vindication of that slavery which from his soul he abhorred. He would have introduced a flaming denunciation of slavery into the Declaration of Independence, but the discretion of his colleagues struck it out. He did insert a most eloquent and impassioned argument against it in his *Notes on Virginia*; but on that very account the book was published almost against his will. He projected a plan of general emancipation in his revision of the Virginian laws, but finally presented a plan of leaving slavery precisely where it was. And in his memoirs he leaves a posthumous warning to the planters, that they must at no distant day emancipate their slaves, or that worse will follow; but he withheld the publication of his prophecy till he should himself be in the grave.[147]

Abraham Lincoln

Abraham Lincoln was also a man who loved peace, and yet his presidency was one entirely identified with war. On the day of his inauguration word was received that Fort Sumter was under attack; on the afternoon of the day of his death he had received from General Grant his report on the surrender at Appomattox. So circumscribed was his time of highest service by this most desperate of struggles, a struggle which dealt also with the principles of justice and freedom.

On the subject of slavery Lincoln was a moderate, more so than many of his Republican supporters. In his 1854 debates with Stephen Douglas, for example, he had said: "Well I too, go for saving the Union. Much as I hate slavery, I would consent to the extension of it rather than see the Union dissolved, just as I would consent to any *great* evil, to avoid a *greater* one."[148] As candidate he argued, not for the abolition of slavery, but for a limit to its spread into the new territories and states in the hope that, if not enlarged, it might wither. As president he would insist that he lacked desire, intention, and authority to set slaves free. Unlike Roger Taney, he was aware of his limitations and did not imagine he could settle the slavery question. The two men were especially dissimilar in that Taney seized an opportunity to (as he imagined) resolve it, while Lincoln faced his with dread.

He admitted he had no clear or untroubled proposal for eradicating slavery, and in 1854 he certainly did not wish to see the slaves as his equals. He saw no possibility of deportation or of emancipation. What then to do?

> I would not hold one in slavery, at any rate; yet the point is not clear enough for me to denounce people upon. What next? Free them and make them politically and socially, our equals? My own feelings will not admit of this; and if mine would, we well know that those of the great mass of white people will not. Whether this feeling accords with justice and sound judgment, is not the sole question, if indeed, it is any part of it. A universal feeling, whether well or ill-founded, can not safely be disregarded. We can not, then, make them equals. It does seem to me that systems of gradual emancipation might be adopted; but for their tardiness in this, I will not undertake to judge our brethren of the south.[149]

Lincoln was every bit as pragmatic a politician as Jefferson, who in his opinion "was, is, and perhaps will continue to be the most distinguished politician of our history."[150] Unlike Jefferson, he had not as a young man formulated his own clear condemnation of slavery. But as he matured he began to see it as evil. Quite opposite from Jefferson, however, instead of putting the rights of slaves in conflict with the freedoms of citizens, he began to ground his argument against slavery in the very principle of the consent of the governed:

> I trust I understand, and truly estimate the right of self-government. My faith in the proposition that each man should do precisely as he pleases with all that is exclusively his own, lies at the foundation of the sense of justice there is in me. I extend the principle to communities of men, as well as to individuals. . . . The doctrine of self-government is right—but it has no just application, as here attempted. Or perhaps I should rather say that whether it has such just application depends upon whether a negro is *not* or *is* a man. If he is *not* a man, why in that case, he who *is* a man may, as a matter of self-government, do just as he pleases with him. But if the negro *is* a man, is it not to that extent, a total destruction of self-government, to say that he too shall not govern himself? When the white man governs himself that is self-government; but when he governs himself, and also governs *another* man, that is more

than self-government—that is despotism. . . .

No man is good enough to govern another man, *without that other's consent.* [151]

Six years after saying that, he found himself leading his people to war against their brethren who had answered the call of Jefferson Davis to defend Thomas Jefferson's principles of state autonomy and the consent of the governed. Lincoln would not allow, however, that this was what men were dying for. In the greatest of his speeches, the second inaugural, he came to define the true issue as slavery. In 1861, when he uttered his first inaugural, he had defined the Union as the great issue. It was to enforce the Union's laws in all the states, and not to tamper with slavery, that he saw himself headed toward confrontation. By 1865, however, he saw that the deep issue was slavery.

Both parties deprecated war; but one of them would *make* war rather than let the nation survive; and the other would accept war rather than let it perish. And the war came. One eighth of the whole population were colored slaves, not distributed generally over the Union, but localized in the Southern part of it. These slaves constituted a peculiar and powerful interest. All knew that this interest was, somehow, the cause of the war. To strengthen, perpetuate, and extend this interest was the object for which the insurgents would rend the Union, even by war; while the government claimed no right to do more than restrict the territorial enlargement of it. [152]

He had been meditating on slavery, though quietly. In 1855 he chided his friend, Judge George Robertson of Lexington, Kentucky, for an earlier speech on the gradual disappearance of slavery:

When we were the political slaves of King George, and wanted to be free, we called the maxim that "all men are created equal" a self-evident truth; but now we have grown fat, and have lost all dread of being slaves ourselves, we have become so greedy to be *masters* that we call the same maxim "a self-evident lie." The fourth of July has not quite dwindled away; it is still a great day—*for burning fire-crackers!*

That spirit which desired the peaceful extinction of slavery, has itself become extinct, with the *occasion*, and the *men* of the Revolution. Under the impulse of that occasion, nearly half the states adopted systems of emancipation at once; and it is a significant fact, not a single state has done the like since. So far as peaceful, voluntary emancipation is concerned, the condition of the negro slave in America, scarcely less terrible to the contemplation of a free mind, is now as fixed, and hopeless of change for the better, as that of the lost souls of the finally impenitent. [153]

Three years later he was again pondering the problem. He wrote himself a private memorandum entitled "Pro-Slavery Theology":

We will suppose the Rev. Dr. Ross has a slave named Sambo,

and the question is "Is it the Will of God that Sambo shall remain a slave, or be set free?" The Almighty gives no audible answer to the question, and his revelation—the Bible—gives none—or, at most, none but such as admits of a squabble, as to it's [sic] meaning. No one thinks of asking Sambo's opinion on it. So, at last, it comes to this, that Dr. Ross is to decide the question. And while he considers it, he sits in the shade, with gloves on his hands, and subsists on the bread that Sambo is earning in the burning sun. If he decides that God wills Sambo to be free, he thereby has to walk out of the shade, throw off his gloves, and delve for his bread. Will Dr. Ross be actuated by that perfect impartiality, which has ever been considered most favorable to correct decisions?

But, slavery is good for some people!! As a *good* thing, slavery is strikingly peculiar, in this, that it is the only good thing which no man ever seeks the good of, *for himself*.

Nonsense! Wolves devouring lambs, not because it is good for their own greedy maws, but because it is good for the lambs!!![154]

By the time he was president, Lincoln had it clear in his mind that the right to be governed only by one's consent was not the real cause of the Confederacy. It was the Union that was waging war for those governed whose consent had never been solicited. The South fought for its liberty to be a suppressor of liberty.

The world has never had a good definition of the word liberty, and the American people, just now, are much in want of one. We all declare for liberty; but in using the same *word* we do not all mean the same *thing*. With some the word liberty may mean for each man to do as he pleases with himself, and the product of his labor; while with others the same word may mean for some men to do as they please with other men, and the product of other men's labor. . . .

The shepherd drives the wolf from the sheep's throat, for which the sheep thanks the shepherd as a *liberator*, while the wolf denounces him for the same act as the destroyer of liberty, especially as the sheep was a black one.[155]

What Lincoln feared was not that he would, in his effort to relieve oppression, be called a tyrant. He had good nerves. What he feared more was that, in wielding the weapons of coercive authority, he might in fact be imitating his adversaries, fighting for liberty while quenching it. As he explained to a Quaker leader near the end of the war, he found himself much as they did: "Your people—the Friends—have had, and are having, a very great trial. On principle, and faith, opposed to both war and oppression, they can only practically oppose oppression by war."[156]

The Great Difference

Abraham Lincoln consummated the founding of the republic which Jefferson had begun. Like Jefferson, he saw slavery as a blight upon the nation's aspiration to honor freedom. Like Jefferson, he had hoped that through the progress of reasonable discourse human bondage would be repudiated without violence. Like Jefferson, he knew that some forms of obstinate oppression finally yield only to force. He might have written: "Against such a banditti, war had become less ruinous than peace, for then peace was a war on one side only."[157] The words were Jefferson's, written about the Barbary pirates, against whom he had to unleash his navy. But Algerians were one thing; Virginians, quite another. What set Lincoln apart from Jefferson was not the fact that one owned slaves all his life, and the other said—and meant it—that as he would not be a slave, so he would not own one. What set them apart was not that one allowed for men to resist an intrusive government; both believed in that.[158] What set them apart was not that Jefferson began with a clear antislavery insight and gradually abandoned it while Lincoln warmed to his; they were both quite private about what both knew to be politically unacceptable.

What set them apart, in this great matter of human slavery, was that Lincoln was brought to accept what Jefferson refused to accept: that freedom for the oppressed cannot be acquired unless paid for by others. There is no net enlargement of human liberty without accommodation by others. The black slaves could never be awarded human rights, human dignity, human freedom unless their owners forfeited some of their prosperity, and their advocates shed some of their blood. Lincoln finally was brought to see that Virginia's claim to freedom was vitiated because its most free, protected activity was enslavement.

Jefferson was not unaware of his dilemma. During the year of the Missouri Compromise he said: "We have the wolf by the ears, and we can neither hold him, nor safely let him go. Justice is in one scale, and self-preservation in the other."[159] He did not allow himself to see that for justice to be done to another, fewer of the self's advantages can be preserved. There is no free justice.

I offer no contemporary comparisons with what these two statesmen did. One of them declared independence for some. The other gave it to more. It is not yet given to all. But this meditation upon their two responses to struggle and crisis may provide a thought-provoking coda to our consideration of our country's several conflicts over human rights. No rights come easily, or hastily, or abundantly, or painlessly. Those which seem to me to deserve our fiercest devotion are those for any who cannot speak or act on their own behalf. They are likely to be the most exploited. But, more sorrowfully, they are likely to have the most unwitting and, in a manner of speaking, the most high-principled exploiters.

How Much Is a Child Worth?
From Abortion to Infanticide

TWO CRIMINAL TRIALS—the first in the Commonwealth of Massachusetts, the next in the State of California—aroused sharp concern among those who care greatly about abortion. Both defendants were abortionists. Both were supported through their trials by leaders of the abortion movement. Yet each was standing trial, not for abortion, but for manslaughter. Dr. Kenneth Edelin in 1975 and Dr. William Waddill in 1978 were said to have delivered live children, survivors of unsuccessful attempts at abortion. One was accused of having then let the child die through negligence; the other, of having strangled the child.

These were not criminal actions for abortion. Those supportive of abortion, however, correctly saw these men entangled in the contradictions of the law. The law of the land allows a physician to destroy offspring up to the moment of birth. On any occasion, however, when the physician's abortion procedure misfires, if the offspring should emerge still alive and thus, through birth, acquire the status and legal rights of a born child and human person, the law in most states obliges that same physician to reverse his purpose and efforts, and to struggle to save the child's life. The Supreme Court in 1973 had drawn a great line at the moment of birth, after which one comes into the fullness of personal rights and before which none are recognized. Clearly, neither the facts of abortion nor the dispositions of those resorting to it found birth to be so agreeable a moral boundary during the trials in 1975 and 1978 as when they had argued for it in 1973. Later they preferred to envision it as somewhat like a state border, which an officer of one jurisdiction may disregard if he is following a fugitive in hot pursuit.

Birth, for advocates of abortion at the time of its legal establishment, had been proposed as a crucial threshold for human status and rights. Birth, for those who actually procure or perform abortions, is not in fact so decisive. As evidence in the third essay suggests, there is a historical cousinage between abortion and infanticide. Where one is practiced the other exists. Motivations for both are similar. Both are performed by similar personnel. Both are in hot pursuit of the same fugitive.

One of the arguments, persuasive to some and used to gain acceptance for abortion in our day, has been that it is different from infanticide, which kills babies. Abortion, it is said, is a legitimate act of self-determination; infanticide is a heartless outrage on an innocent. Accept the one, and the other will be banished.

Whether there is any ground beneath this position, or any sincerity in it, is a question this chapter aims to address.

The most significant publication on infanticide in our century was published in Leipzig in 1920: *The Permit to Destroy Life Not Worth Living*. It was the work of two authors: Karl Binding, a venerable professor of law at Leipzig and one of Europe's foremost authorities on criminal law; and Alfred Hoche, a distinguished psychiatrist and professor of medicine at Freiburg im Breisgau. It was to become so clearly a classic text that its thesis deserves to be set forth here in some detail.[1]

Binding the jurist begins the exposition. Suicide, he observes, is no crime, either in tradition or in German statutes. No one has a legal right therefore to obstruct a person intent upon suicide. Indeed, a person may employ self-defense to fend off such unrightful coercion, and to protect his own freedom to commit suicide. German law considers this to be a nontransferable right, however. No one, even if requested, may serve as an accessory to another's suicide. But, asks Binding, why need this be so? Might not Germany be well advised to decriminalize certain acts of killing for reasons similar to its allowance of suicide?

Euthanasia offers a painless, possibly swifter relief to someone whom incurable sickness or injury has already destined to die. It does not inflict death, for that is already underway. It merely alleviates the suffering, and this, after all, is one of medicine's purposes. The law should accommodate this kind of service. And German legal history shows a disposition to move in this direction. Earlier laws and present practice seem to impose lighter sanctions on killing, the more willing the victim is.

"Are there," Binding asks, "human lives which have so lost the capacity to benefit that their continuation has lost all value, both for themselves and for society?" In the mines and on the field of battle the lives of promising, vigorous menfolk are lost by hundreds and by thousands. All the while the nation expends enormous care on inmates of mental institutions. There is a jarring dissonance between this squandering of the best and this salvage of the worthless. "There remains no shred of a doubt that there are men living for whom death would come as a relief, as it would also for society, especially the state: the lifting of a burden that serves no useful purpose save as an example of unselfishness."

Binding sets forth three groups of possible beneficiaries of a euthanasia program. *First*, there are those who through illness or injury are unrecoverable, and who with clear minds ask to be given relief. They need not be in pain; hopelessness can exist without pain. "From all standpoints—legal, social, ethical, religious—I can find no grounds for withholding, from those who receive such a request, permission to kill persons who are beyond recovery and wish to die; in fact, I consider this a duty of lawful compassion." *Second*, there are the incurably insane. They have no willingness to live, nor any wish to die. Death would answer no request, but neither would it frustrate any desire. Though they may not find their lives unbearable, such persons are without purpose, and they are a frightfully heavy burden on their kin and on society. Their death creates no gap in anyone's life save, perhaps, that of a mother or a devoted nurse. As they require more and more care, they give rise to a new human way of life: that of vegetating for years or decades, through the course of a life not worth living. There can be no objection to eliminating these people either, though it should always be with consent of their family or guardians. The best time for such a decision is soon after the diagnosis of total idiocy. The *third* category comprises those who have sustained some lethal injury, have lost consciousness, and would, were it regained, face unrelieved misery. For them too Binding thinks release would be a favor, after careful evaluation and, possibly, consent of the family.

How assure that these death decisions will be professional and disinterested? The usual decision, states Binding the jurist, would obviously come from the state. Someone with the right to do so—a sick person (if in category *one* above), his doctor, or a close relative—would submit a request. This would be processed by a government commission composed of a medical doctor, a psychiatrist or a second physician specializing in psychological disorders, and an attorney, plus a nonvoting chairman. This commission could summon witnesses and subpoena evidence. Neither the petitioner nor the attending physician could take part in their deliberations. Once satisfied, the commission would simply rule that, in light of the evidence and in the light of the best scientific judgment, the person's condition is incurable; that there is no doubt of his consent; that there is therefore no reason to prevent his death; which the applicant is then free to arrange as seems best; provided that the sick person still retain the freedom to change his mind, that the death be painless, and that a detailed report on it be filed afterward.

Thus an elaborate procedure was proposed, to ensure that euthanasia would become no haphazard whim. But after the German bureaucracy has been erected, there appears an almost Italianate device for circumventing it. What if, Binding considers, there is no time for all this authorization? Are the doctor and family to be forbidden to act on their compassion? Are they forced to watch helplessly, knowing that the justification for euthanasia is there, but unable to risk acting on it? No. In these unusual cases he would wish the law to forbear punishing those who, even on their own, relieve the incurably afflicted, whether they ask for such relief or are unable to ask for it. And if they act in error? This is indeed a misfortune for the one who perishes, and a sorrow for his family. "But mankind loses so many members by mistake that one more or less hardly weighs on the scale."

Physician Hoche then comes forward. Doctors, he notes, have no code of ethics. They have general obligations, e.g., to heal sickness, to remove or relieve pain, to prolong life. But even these norms have exceptions, as, for instance, when a living child is destroyed at birth or during pregnancy to preserve his mother. These procedures are not legally permitted, but for that matter neither is surgery permitted. However, neither one is sanctioned, provided it is done dutifully, with a higher good in view, according to the rules of the art, with the agreement of the patient or his lawful representative. There will always be a certain loss of life, but "the higher good of restoring a greater number redeems the sacrifice of a lesser number."

This same understanding should apply to the problem under discussion. Physicians carry the onus of knowing their own specialty competently, as well as that of making judgments of value on people's lives. One who has stood at many deathbeds knows that death is not a dread for everyone. For some, medical treatment would be as unwelcome as when an exhausted person who wants to rest is disturbed. Kindness at the wrong times can be a plague.

Hoche agrees that there are lives devoid of value. Some have been so from birth or from earliest childhood; others have been afflicted later in life. These latter have had time to form fond relationships. They therefore have a certain "affection-value." Also, they will need perhaps only twenty or thirty years of care, by contrast with the first group, who may claim fifty to sixty years of care. For both pragmatic reasons, in a state that has to pay an estimated forty million marks per annum to maintain them, the former group should be looked at first. This would free thousands of institutional personnel for work more satisfying than tending these empty human husks.

There may have been times when such human ballast could be carried, but now it is no longer practical.

> Our situation is like that of members of an arduous expedition in whch everyone's fullest effectiveness is indispensably needed for success, with no room for any who function at half-strength, or quarter-, or eighth-. Our task as Germans will for a long while be to marshal a great accumulation of resources, to free every available source of productivity for beneficial purposes. Our present efforts are frustrating the accomplishment of that task, especially when we support all sorts of weaklings and afford care and protection to so many elements who, if not mentally dead, are of little value because of their inability to organize themselves and be useful. These efforts are supporting a deadweight, and have made it thus far impossible (in the eyes of some, possibly even undesirable) to prevent these human defectives from propagating.

There will, of course, be resistance to legalized destruction of lives not worth living: resistance comes from conservative dislike of change, religious scruples, and sentimental emotion.

Hoche acknowledges a conflict between the subjective right to exist and objective expediency and necessity. "Hitherto, due largely to the influence of Christian attitudes, cultures were thought to be more advanced, the more they resolved this conflict in favor of personal survival. But now, viewing the matter from the perspective of a higher morality of state, we cannot deny that in our anxiety to support life at all costs there has been some excess. We had forgotten, because of external [Christian] influence, to take the government on its own terms, as an entity with its own laws and rights, a self-sufficient human organism that, as doctors know, may, in the interests of the welfare of the whole, sacrifice and amputate individual parts that have become unserviceable or detrimental."

The mentally dead must be sloughed off. They require help but give none. They lack the capacity to relate to the world around them, to interact personally with others, or to be self-conscious. They make no claim to life. A false sense of compassion may induce us to project humanity onto them, but this is no more truthful than what is inspiring Europe's contemporary cult of animals. We face a long, slow struggle, Hoche argues, to make the public aware of the meaninglessness of individuals compared with the interests of the whole: to be ready to dispose of those who are of no public usefulness. We need a dose of heroic boldness.

Can we, Hoche is asked, be adequately sure that an individual really has a worthless life? That, he notes, is a question that only a layman would ask. These are the kinds of things doctors can verify "with 100% certitude." He personally considers Binding's proposed government commission as needlessly intrusive upon physicians, but accepts it as a political necessity.

Goethe had described progress as a spiral, and Hoche sees the spiral as an image of the social change he advocates. Once people commonly used to eliminate those born or become inadequate for life. Then came a time when [because of Christianity] it was deemed highly ethical to foster such worthless life. Now we are spiraling back again, but higher: "A new time will come which, from the standpoint of a higher morality, will prevent exaggerated concepts of humanity from spreading, and will keep from being put into practice overestimates of the worth of any mere existence that requires costly sacrifice for its continuance."

Rarely have authors' hopes been so abundantly fulfilled. Binding and Hoche were prophets who would find much honor in their own country, and soon . . .

Their modest proposal, while not entirely new, was certainly not in the mainstream of German thought. Soon after their publication appeared, however, other voices gathered to them. Four years later, for instance, Dr. Fritz Barth brought out in Heidelberg his *Euthanasia: The Problem of Destroying Life Not Worth Living*. In most respects the book is a reprise of Binding and Hoche, and displays how quickly their thesis had gained currency. Where Barth diverges from his predecessors he is even more interesting: their earlier ideas had begun to grow.[2]

Barth classifies three forms of euthanasia. The *first*, "simple euthanasia," consists of the administration of analgesics to ease a painful death. The *second*, "euthanasia in the strict sense," is the administration of a lethal drug, on request, to shorten the process of a painful death. *Third*, and to Barth much the most interesting, is "euthanasia in the wider sense": lethal treatment of someone incapable of requesting it (a child, a mental patient, a comatose patient).

Euthanasia in the wider sense is most often practiced by infanticide. Barth explains that Greeks and Romans alike killed infants to eliminate the blighted or to keep population down. The ancient Aryans, a group for whom there was growing respect in 1924, had given every father the right of life or death over the newborn. The infant would be laid on the earth before him. If he accepted it, he or the midwife would lift the child high; he then sprinkled it with water and named it. If he rejected it, the infant was exposed in the wilds to die. This was the fate of cripples, but healthy children were also exposed. Only one twin or triplet, for example, would be kept: the others were expelled as evidence of their mother's unfaithfulness. Severe poverty was another motive for rejection. Christianity put an end to this infanticide, but it was known later among the Scandinavians and exists today among some primitive tribes, who also expose their sick or their very old.

Binding and Hoche had rooted suicide in the notion of "man as sovereign over his existence and its conditions." Barth begins with one's "right over oneself." But how to move from this principle to the elimination of other people, especially under the frown of religious objections? By distinguishing the subjective from the objective values of life. A life not worth living must be disentitled by objective considerations of eugenics, social hygiene, community biology, and economy (the politicization of science was older than National Socialism). In warfare and industry countless useful lives are forfeited, but to higher national purposes, while many others are wasted as custodial personnel for empty husks of humanity, serving no national purpose at all. "Juridically, then, there is no problem [in eliminating these worthless lives], for life in this case is of no further benefit, and therefore can claim no protection. By 'benefit' we mean, with von Liszt, 'legally protected interest.' Here there is neither a subjective nor an objective interest to be served" by continued existence. With good will on their part, the churches should be able to be brought round in this matter.

Economic considerations, according to Barth, must never enter into an actual decision to destroy an individual. Yet . . . they are not totally to be ignored, either, and Barth does not ignore them. They are, he says, even more significant in time of war, when the nation is under greatest strain. By his reckoning, the care of cripples and idiots is costing the Republic one hundred million marks annually. Half of the 83,400 mental patients are mentally dead, of no productive use to mankind, and would best be eliminated. The money saved could provide the public with the welfare and cultural needs they now cannot afford. Family insurance, for example, might be financed (his proposal is not entirely realistic, since savings would amount to less than two marks per citizen). The orphans or infants or elderly or veterans could occupy the institutions that would be freed up; or, alternatively, they could be offered to families without housing. By giving a boost to natural selection, the nation could shunt funds from wasteful budgeting to many needed cultural amenities. "For this reason, the introduction of euthanasia by the government [euthanasia in the 'wider sense'] is earnestly to be desired."

Having considered the legal and economic aspects of this death program, Barth turns to it as a medical problem. But it is no medical problem: only a legal and religious one that interferes with doctors' work. "We do not really kill the sick, for their usefulness to mankind is virtually zero or even negative. The sick person is not fully capacitated. No, we release him from his pains on humane grounds, and treat him in his own best interests."

As regards religion, it has traditionally allowed killing in abortion, capital punishment, self-defense, and war. Besides, there were the Inquisition and witch-burnings which together, by Barth's most conservative calculation, had claimed ten million victims. What he is proposing is just one more kind of killing for the common good. "In euthanasia we must always give first consideration to the interests of the individual. Next, in second place, the weightiest interests of the community come into question, such as the health and efficiency of the race, the advancement of the public welfare by facilitating free availability of enormous funds hitherto spent uselessly, the deliverance of a great number of families from economic ruin, etc." All this can surely be well described as the *bonum commune*, or "common good" spoken by Aquinas: *occidere hominem non licet nisi publica auctoritate propter bonum commune*: "it is wrong to kill a human being, unless on public authority, for some common good."

Barth's book is, from title page onwards, in heavy debt to his predecessors in Leipzig and Freiburg. But he has carried the argument along. Binding and Hoche had devalued the individual human compared with the human community, but were quite explicit in wanting no initiative to fall to the state in "euthanasia." Barth has eliminated this inconsistency. He wants the government to assume responsibility for a national purge. It is the national budget, more than any household's attempt to make ends meet, that he wants to unburden. And, though he too begins his *plaidoyer* for "euthanasia" by presenting the classic case of the agonized, moribund adult asking for pain relief, once he has made that point he moves more purposefully and less painstakingly to the matter closest to his heart: the handicapped, the crippled, the mentally ill, who do not ask for death but should be disposed of.

Both presentations have the same lineaments, however:

Both begin with the principle of the human right to sovereign self-determination and conclude with the destruction of innocent human beings by others.

Both propose elaborate conditions and procedures: incurable illness or injury; imminent death; insupportable pain; witnessed, written consent; concurrence of family; judgment by commission; protection against conflicts of interest. But likewise both suggest that all of this be dispensable, leaving the doctor alone with his hypodermic to do as he sees fit.

Both claim that financial considerations should not be decisive; but both then make finances their strongest appeal.

Both use coarse, depreciative language when referring to victims: *Menschenballast* (human ballast), *Idioten* (idiots), *Vollidioten* (complete idiots), *Defektmenschen* (human defectives), *Geistestoten* (mentally dead), *Wahnsinnig* (madman), *Blödsinnigen* (imbeciles), *Menschenhulsen* (human husks); only rarely, *Geisteskranken* (mentally ill).

Both present this killing as a "lesser evil," warn supporters that this will be heroic work, and call for a "liberalization" of ethics.

Both reverence the medical and psychiatric professions as scientifically and ethically above reproach or suspicion.

Both call for a more pragmatic ethic in this time of national strain.

Both subject the human individual to the designs and desires of the government, and confound the common good of society with the totalitarian policies of the state.

Both propose death for many categories of people, but have as their prime target the helpless.

Both put a value on human beings that is measured, not by any common human status, but by utilitarian potential for others' advantage.

Both offer no basis for human rights except usefulness to society.

Readers of the previous essays will notice here many echoes in the literature on abortion, but that is not the resonance I would now point out. These writings were the foundation pilings for an infanticide tradition that needs to be known better than it is.

As we have seen, this was one extermination program adopted by Nazi Germany which the churches did attack. In 1934, when the Nazi government was first showing its disposition, the German Catholic bishops had published a protest against "death-assistance and destruction of life not worth living": "The irreconcilability of euthanasia with Christian moral law is established . . . the same holds true for the killing of those with incurable mental illness." What followed is now known. It was not foreseen as it should have been, though. In 1936 Dr. Franz Gurtner, minister of justice, published a conciliatory explanation. "Permission to destroy so-called life not worth living is not the issue. The pivotal question concerns those with severe mental illness, or complete idiots. The National Socialist state strives to prevent the spread of this sort of degeneracy through the body of the people, so that it will recur less and less. But the rigor of the ethical norm which forbids killing need surely not be weakened, when on firm grounds of expediency exceptions are made for the victims of graver illnesses and accidents: victims who had, in the past or in appearance, once been one within the body of the people." That statement, Cardinal Faulhaber of Munich admitted in a letter of protest written four years later, had made him hope there might be no policy of large-scale liquidation. "The development of the last months, which brought a *mass killing* of children entrusted to medical and foster institutions, has destroyed that hope." It had been a foolish hope.[3]

With these earlier German views and policies in mind, let us look at some more contemporary statements in our own time and in our own land. As noted in a previous essay, Cambridge jurist Glanville Williams did not himself advocate infanticide, nor did he sense any swell of political support for it. His treatment of it, however, leads one to conjecture that, had the issue then become active, Williams would have had little reason to refuse it his support.

Infanticide, he notes, is the killing of a newborn child by the parents or with their consent. To kill someone else's child without leave is simply murder. After a historical review that follows standard lines (incidence in classical antiquity, eradication by the church), Williams confesses he finds strange the old Christian idea that infanticide is an especially savage crime. "Infanticide appears to our generation to be a crime less heinous than ordinary murder." He agrees with Dr. Mercier: " 'The victim's mind is not sufficiently developed to enable it to suffer from the contemplation of approaching suffering or death. . . . It leaves no gap in any family circle, deprives no children of their breadwinner or their mother, no human being of a friend, helper or companion.' " Williams then takes the utilitarian model of ethics and bends it to a peculiar shape. If, in seeking the greatest sum of happiness, we consider the happiness prospects of a particular infant, then severely handicapped infants might well be put to death. As a lawyer he realizes this is not permitted, but he says: "I venture to doubt whether society has the right to stand in judgment upon a mother placed in this terrible predicament. . . . Regarded in this spirit, an eugenic killing by a mother, exactly paralleled by the bitch that kills her mis-shapen puppies, cannot confidently be pronounced immoral."

Later, Williams discusses the destruction of handicapped children "on humanitarian grounds—both on account of parents, to whom the child will be a burden all their lives, and on account of the handicapped child itself." To remove this crime from the books would conform to the judgment of juries who hesitate to convict parents for it. He finds appealing the picture drawn by one advocate of infanticide:

> "My personal feeling—and I don't ask anyone to agree with me—is that eventually, when public opinion is prepared for it, no child shall be admitted into the society of the living who would be certain to suffer any social handicap—for example, any physical or mental defect that would prevent marriage or would make others tolerate his company only from a sense of mercy. . . . Life in early infancy is very close to non-existence, and admitting a child into our society is almost like admitting one from potential to actual existence, and viewed in this way only normal life should be accepted."[4]

Behind Professor Williams's position is a firmly held, clearly stated principle. Roman Catholics, he grieved in 1964, "are obsessed with the dogma that you can never do evil so that good may come." He rejects that view, "since to describe the act as sinful when its intention is good begs the question. According to the general opinion, some acts that would otherwise be wrong are rendered rightful by a good purpose, or by the necessity of choosing the lesser of two evils."[5]

This doctrine, that intentions purify actions, or ends justify means, is also a moral starting point for Joseph Fletcher, an ethicist who has had little influence on philosophers and theologians but is widely welcomed among the medical fraternity. Quoting Lenin, he asks, " 'If the end does not justify the means, then in the name of sanity and justice, *what does?*' "[6]

Fletcher wants nothing to do with consistent general norms of action. "Results are what counts, and results are good when they contribute to human well-being." What if this is in defiance of human rights? "I for one am not primarily concerned about any claimed rights to live or to die; I am first of all concerned about human needs and whether they are met by life or by death will depend on the situation. . . . Needs are the moral stabilizers, not rights. The legalistic temper gives first place to rights, but the humanistic temper puts needs in the driver's seat. If human rights conflict with human needs, let needs prevail."

He addresses the obverse issue of infanticide, genetically manipulated reproduction, and is led to contemplate a kind of future *Lebensborn* in which scientists would replace the service role of storm troopers and would breed— for the greatest good of the greatest number—specially hybrid men who could be employed to do dull or unrewarding work, such as testing pollution areas or working on assembly lines or investigating potential avalanches. Work of such large social import should not, he cautions, be left simply in the hands of the scientific guild, for that peer group has rather inward and narrow perspectives. One is put in mind, possibly, of a government commission. In any case, with the expectation that everyone involved will be pursuing good ends with good motives and good results, and that everyone's actions will be ethically tinctured by these, Fletcher can make no sense of what Leon Kass, molecular biologist of the University of Chicago and the National Research Council, is asserting: "Morally, it is insufficient that your motives are good, that your ends are unobjectionable, that you do the procedure 'lovingly,' and even that you may be lucky in the result: you will be engaging in an unethical experiment upon a human subject."[7]

Infanticide, on Fletcher's principles, would have to be judged by its motives and results. To deal, however, with one possible major objection at its root, he has been trying to enumerate what he calls "indicators of humanhood." While one may not be given pause by another's rights, if it could first be established that the one you might wish to eliminate does not even qualify anyway as a human person, then he / she / it has no rights you need to worry about violating. To qualify as a human, on Fletcher's profile, one needs to possess: minimal intelligence, self-awareness, self-control, a sense of time and futurity and the past, the capability to relate to others, concern for others, communication, control of existence, curiosity, change and changeability, balance of rationality and feeling, idiosyncrasy, and neo-cortical function. Thus, for example, a score of 40 on the Stanford-Binet I.Q. test would designate one as "questionably human. Below the 20-mark, not a person." If psychosis has rendered a person helpless, or if coma has broken off communication, one would not be human. Among all of these components, Fletcher sees self-consciousness and relationship with others as especially important, and brain function as the "hominizing trait upon which all the other traits hinge."[8]

A philosophical match for Fletcher the theologian appeared in 1972: Michael Tooley of Stanford University. In an article on abortion and infanticide Tooley sweeps aside as morally insignificant the "cut-off" points that some have marked as limits to permissible abortion, such as quickening or viability or birth. What condition, he asks, must an organism satisfy if it is to have a serious right to life? It has been an unfortunate turn of speech, he says, for people—even philosophers—to refer interchangeably to "persons" and to "human beings"; he would argue that persons are human beings with a right to life, and that not all human beings are so endowed. That right belongs to a human "only if it possesses the concept of a self as a continuing subject of experiences and other mental states, and believes that it is itself such a continuing entity." One can have rights only to what one can consciously comprehend. "It is perfectly clear, I believe, that a newborn baby does not possess the concept of a continuing self, any more than a newborn kitten possesses such a concept. If so, infanticide during a time interval shortly after birth must be morally acceptable." Keep it within the first week or so, and there is little moral problem that the infant has slipped into these inviolable mental states.

297

During the course of his thinking Tooley deals with several problems. For instance, he asserts that one cannot have a right unless he is conceptually capable of having the corresponding desire. Is a child therefore incapable of having a right to property that he cannot conceptually want? Tooley's response is "that he will come to have such a right when he is mature, and that in the meantime no one else has a right to the estate." He is unwilling to propose that in the meantime no one else has a right to his life. Thus property seems more entitled to reverence than owners are. That, though, is not the most serious problem that Tooley is left with. What troubles him, at the end of his argumentation, is whether animals . . . "may not also possess a serious right to life."[9]

This is not a style of argumentation that would find wholehearted acceptance in medical circles. Indeed, if reports are correct, doctors had, all along, without leave from lawyers, theologians, and philosophers, been making it their quiet practice in the nurseries to arrange for unacceptably crippled infants to perish. By coincidence, it was around 1973 that this was brought out into the open. The *New York Times Magazine* for January 30, 1972, carried an article entitled "Doctor, Do We Have a Choice?" Anthony Shaw, a surgeon at the University of Virginia Medical Center, described how he offered parents of children born with Down's syndrome the opportunity to deny their mongoloid children routine surgery needed for survival.

Shaw describes views of colleagues that he finds "simple," "unyielding," "rigid." One of these men would not save any such infant. "He feels that the burden inflicted on the family and on society by the emotional and financial costs involved are too great to justify the procedure." Another cites the Declaration of General and Special Rights of the Mentally Retarded: " 'The mentally retarded person has a right to proper medical care and physical restoration . . . as will enable him to develop his ability and potential to the fullest possible extent, no matter how severe his degree of disability.' " These opposite positions, Shaw says, being based on principle, minimize the surgeon's emotional involvement. His own policy, of saving only those infants whose parents want them, exposes him to considerable emotion. "Standing by and watching a salvageable baby die is the most emotionally exhausting experience I know . . . to stand by in the nursery and watch as dehydration and infection wither a tiny being over hours and days . . . is a terrible ordeal for me and for the hospital staff—much more so than for the parents who never set foot in the nursery."

Shaw is not governed by mere feelings. He notes with regret that "the emotional and financial resources of many families are poured out for helpless retardates," and suggests that perhaps society should assume some responsibility for these life-and-death decisions. Mongoloid children, however, may be more of a burden for the advantaged in society. "Couples who are success-oriented and have high expectations for their children are likely to institutionalize their mentally deficient offspring rather than keep them at home. The argument that mongoloids raised in the home perform better than those raised in an institution is rarely persuasive with such parents." This raises a shadow of doubt over Shaw's belief that his clients make their decision to save or to eliminate based on "the child's ultimate capabilities." His preference would in any case be for mongoloids to be aborted before birth. "It seems to me," he concludes, "that a society which does not provide for its defectives is less than humane."[10]

Two years later Shaw presents his position in a medical journal. He defends parents' right to refuse surgery to their defective infants, though not when it involves only a physical defect without accompanying mental retardation. "Although I personally would not have objected to an abortion in this situation . . . I would not allow an otherwise normal baby with a correctable anomaly to perish for lack of treatment. . . . Although those who believe that all life is sacred, no matter what its level of development, will severely criticize me for the apparent inconsistency of this position, I believe it to be a realistic and human approach to a situation in which no solution is ideal." When the child would be retarded, he would give parents a life-or-death say-so. "Who would say they *must* sign if they don't want a child whose days will be measured by operations, clinic visits and infections?" This leaves the medical staff with the task of complying—sometimes an arduous task. In one case, Shaw recollects, it took a child fifteen days to die. This caused lingering suffering—for the medical staff ("severely demoralized")—and "agony for the parents, who called daily to find out if the baby was still alive."[11]

Shaw is of the view that quality of life is a value that must be balanced against a belief in the sanctity of life. Raymond Duff and A. G. M. Campbell, both at the Yale University School of Medicine, reported at the same time their own misgivings about the sanctity-of-life ethic. Intensive care facilities for newborns can now rescue blighted infants who previously would have perished. But should they? Fourteen percent of the infant deaths in their unit at the Yale–New Haven Hospital were instances when they thought not. As with Shaw, "The parents' or siblings' rights to relief from the seemingly pointless, crushing burdens were important considerations." But Duff and Campbell also give weight, before resolving on death through nontreatment or more direct measures (called a "management option"), to the future of the infant. If the child would have to live in an institution, that might well be "a fate rated worse than death." Some "very defective individuals were considered to have little or no hope of achieving 'meaningful humanhood.' For example, they have little or no capacity to love or be loved."[12]

Duff, in a later interview, recalls a couple who "felt that even minimal obligations to several others in the family could not be met if their money, time and personal resources were spent on the child who could in any case benefit little. . . . Under the circumstances, in their view, death was the better choice. It was a case of how many lives would be wrecked: one of dubious value plus four others, *or* the one of dubious value." Does the decision to destroy, then, Duff is asked, come more typically from the poor? Rarely, he admits.

What of an objective committee to resolve those awesome choices? No. Committee members are usually chosen from the social elite, "distant from the lives of most people" and powerful, in search always of more power. "This tends to corrupt." What of an advocate to speak for the child? No. He and his colleagues would not like any decision-making power to be gathered into such hands. Clearly this is an agonizing work they wish not to relinquish.

What is there in his principles and practice that would keep us from sliding into the policies condoned by Nazi Germany? Duff says he has no idea, save that under the Nazis "decisions were made in high places by people who felt little or no bond whatever with those being killed. Decisions Campbell and I describe were made by persons who had the strongest bonds of affection known to mankind. Families and physicians took into account not only the child's right (to live or to die) but the needs of the family and society and, to some extent, future generations. If we cannot trust these persons to do justice here, can anyone be trusted?"[13]

Shaw, Duff, and Campbell all attribute to Joseph Fletcher their readiness to brave these decisions without any dogmatic presuppositions or principles. Yet another professional who confesses vexation with the ethical notion of the sanctity of life is Milton Heifetz, chief of neurological surgery at a Los Angeles hospital, where policies like those at Virginia and Yale–New Haven have been in force. "This problem of handling the tragically endowed newborn must be faced with honesty and courage." Infants are born without the full potential for human mental and physical qualities. But there is a whole range of such defects; how can we decide which are serious enough to justify destruction? Where should the line be drawn? "We must weigh the validity of that *future subhuman* existence, the right to maintain that life, against the sadness and cruelty imposed on parents living with a subhuman organism." The reader gathers that the burdens faced by those who pay the bills are those most vividly felt. And what of the infant left to die? Was this not cruelty? No, explains Dr. Heifetz, there was no cruelty, no inhumanity. The child was drugged and could not feel what was being done.[14]

Dr. John Freeman is a Baltimore pediatrician who has also published his experiences and views on the treatment of infants born crippled, either mentally or physically. Like Duff and unlike Shaw, he would keep life-and-death decisions over these babies within the reach of attending physicians. Parents' views cannot be objective; they are flung into an unexpected crisis and may be too emotional. Ethical committees, say, of lawyers, clergy, doctors from other specialties, and laypeople would be inept. "Can such people comprehend the enormity of the problems facing the child with a myelomeningocele and his family without first-hand experience? Or will their decisions be emotional and based solely on the 'sanctity of life' rather than on a realistic understanding of the problem?" In some cases Freeman would decide to let a child die through denial of treatment. In others, when the child would survive such medical abandonment, he would think it "more humane" to slay him or her directly, but this is illegal. On balance, though, since more and more physicians are reporting encouraging results when vigorous surgical and medical therapy is given to infants afflicted with myelomeningocele, his "ambiguous" conclusion, based on feelings, is that virtually every such child ought to be given energetic saving treatment.[15]

Since 1973 there have been fewer physicians forthcoming to disclose infanticide practices in their hospitals. It is an activity they undeniably perform, though with no desire to have a critical public looking over their shoulders. The discussion has reverted to the philosophers and theologians. John Fletcher (no relation to Joseph) is a theologian in Washington, D.C., where he serves as in-house bioethicist at the National Institutes of Health. His earlier work on abortion was to be a harbinger of his eventual thoughts on infanticide. In 1972 he published his observations about a group of twenty-five couples who had undergone a program of amniocentesis to ascertain whether their unborn were genetically injured. Three tests came out positive; three abortions and sterilizations ensued. Fletcher's query was as follows. All twenty-five couples had entered the program disposed to abort a handicapped child sooner than give it birth. Did this experience, whatever actually followed for this or that couple—abortion or birth—lessen the affection they bear their children, born or unborn? Did it subvert the deputyship of parents, which is supposed to represent God's cherishing love for all, and did it erode the basic trust which is childhood's earliest need and parenthood's deep duty?

Fletcher's fifty were affluent whites, and he was aware that this made a difference. Their experiences with handicapped children persuaded them that these youngsters led "unfulfilled lives." They wanted their children to have high health and intelligence, "which their life-style requires for a sense of adequacy and success." Lives were to be fulfilled at an upper middle-class standard. Most seemed to share, as did Fletcher, the view that abortion was destroying a life. But it was a life they would not welcome into their home. "These days you have a choice about having a baby," one mother explained. Others spoke of a "right to a good mental life." Another mother said: "The world has enough problems, I don't want to add to them." In general, the couples stood ready to abort for one common reason: to avoid hardship or misery to themselves.

To abort for convenience causes conflict in these men and women: conflict between their own various values, between theirs and society's, and between one another's. These conflicts are somewhat assuaged, Fletcher notices, by an avoidance of conversation with any but medical personnel. Encouraged by this counsel, they are ready "to go to extraordinary lengths to exercise responsible parenthood." Fletcher notes: "I interviewed no parents who came at their roles from highly conscious norms or principles about parenthood and unconditioned caring."

One telltale point in his inquiry was how these couples would tell their healthy children that they would have been destroyed if imperfect; or how they would tell an older, handicapped child that they had contemplated abortion rather than have another like him or her. "One mother gave voice to her sense that an already affected child felt threatened by her visit to the center when she found him hiding in the closet upon returning." One father stated that there was "no good way to explain to your own child that you might have had a part in deciding the end of his life." Most, thought Fletcher, liked to believe "that the child would be so grateful for being born healthy that no real threat would be perceived." His own opinion is that such news can be communicated without serious worry, but it must be forthright: "Nothing could weaken or dissolve the parent-child bond more effectively than children becoming afraid that their parents made such decisions for trivial reasons of personal convenience or because they were forced into it for external societal reasons."

An obvious criticism arises: if this direction is followed, will there not be less tolerance in society for the weak, the imperfect, the unlovely, and the unacceptable? Will this not simply pander to the less noble aspirations of the affluent classes? Only, Fletcher, thinks, "if the therapeutic goals of genetic medicine are displaced by eugenic goals"—a disquieting answer, after he has described genetic medicine as operating for the affluent in the total absence of therapeutic interest or effect.[16]

In an examination of parental and medical attitudes towards defective newborn children, Fletcher notes that the arrival of such an infant is still very traumatic, despite the ability to understand these events scientifically. The "modern, scientific attitude," in fact, seems to have made their acceptance particularly difficult, since it has engendered the expectation that we should be spared such disagreeable turns of fortune. It is, as he had set forth earlier, a direct affront to the affluent to be presented with blighted offspring. Quoting Giannini and Goodman, he finds that "the mongoloid child, the most stigmatized of the retarded, physically and socially, represents an assault to the middle class strivings and aspirations and culturally determined goals. He is seen as a serious impediment to social mobility." Families in developed countries show "an increasing reduction of broad activities to those involved with the personal fulfillment of the adults. Parents, especially in the middle class, expect more intimacy and perfection in their children." So much the worse do those children fare if they fail.

Are there any variants within this widespread rejection of blighted children? Women, it is found, are more accepting than men. Turning to the largely male physicians' profession to ascertain whether they embody this disposition to reject defective newborns, he finds no evidence to say nay. Catholics, according to Zuk's 1959 study, are greatly more accepting of handicapped children. He accepts the explanation that this is "due to the explicit absolution from personal guilt offered by their religious belief," and that a mother might see the child as "a test of her religious faith . . . a special gift from God." It seems not to occur to Fletcher that this is a tradition wherein, by clean contrast with the affluent values that require children to suit their parents' tastes, there has long been the teaching that life is fulfilled by serving others, particularly the afflicted; and that marriage, for better or for worse until death, finds joy in the forfeiture of one's own materialistic and egotistic desires for the sake of the needs of one's closest. The attitude described by Fletcher which arouses the most concern in a reader is that of battering parents, whom one study found possessed of the "conviction, largely unconscious, that children exist to satisfy parental needs." This is exactly the instinct which Fletcher has already described as motivating the abortors.

How are attitudes towards defective newborns affected by the widespread availability of prenatal inspection and abortion? Fletcher finds that practice to be completely acceptable morally, but wonders whether parents might not more readily withdraw care from such newborn sons and daughters "when they know they might have done it only a few months earlier?"

Such a child is born in the face of views produced and hardened by the society Fletcher has characterized thus: "Most parents in our society if given the choice would prefer abortion of an affected fetus to a sick child who requires any but the most trivial treatment. . . . It is ridiculous to give ethical approval to the positive ending of subhuman life *in utero*, as we do in therapeutic abortions for reasons of mercy and compassion, but refuse to approve of positively ending a subhuman life *in extremis*. . . . Does [a parent] have an inalienable right to produce a child that is uneducable?" Fletcher, who supports prenatal slaying, is openly uneasy about where that leads, but unable to conclude with anything more perceptive than that ethicists should "continue to take close readings" of what eugenic medicine is doing to parenting, "to guard against arbitrary and unreasonable erosion of the trust which must exist between newborn and parents." More enlightening is an idea he had earlier had in passing: "that there may be more of a threat to civilization from the strong than from the weak."[17]

Again in 1975 Fletcher returns to the haunting question: is abortion leading to infanticide? "Does the ethical reasoning that is applied to prenatal management bear any relation to decision-making after the birth of the infant?" He wants very much to believe that it does not. He observes that the most trenchant arguments for and against abortion would envision infanticide as a similar moral issue. If one is disposed to reverence or to destroy the unborn, one will do the same to the born. Fletcher, who wants abortion but flinches at infanticide, hopes that three factors will protect handicapped children from "neo-naticide," three protective advantages that come with birth: born children's separate physical existence exerts a stronger moral claim; their afflictions are more open to treatment; and parental loyalty takes firmer hold after birth. Infanticide he rejects. It may brutalize those who perform it, and it would distort the welcoming ambiance of childbirth.

John Fletcher's contribution is important, not because he opposes infanticide, but because he does it so haplessly. He supports abortion as a convenience to the affluent, he imagines that this is consistent with the generosity of parenthood, and then he describes so vividly the evidence that it is not. He concludes with a perfervid exhortation about "visions of the inherent dignity of each member of the human family," and our duty to care for the defenseless "as if the basis of our own dignity depended on the outcome." For this he counts on "the beliefs and values of the religious and humanistic communities that provide our culture with visions of the ultimately desirable." But he has already described so well that the ultimately desirable is socioeconomic comfort. No affronting vision is likely to be visited on that desire by the dozens of religious and humanistic communities which have been defending abortion on demand.[18]

H. Tristram Englehardt, Jr., is both philosopher and physician, associated with the Kennedy Institute at Georgetown University. In 1973 he was pondering the abortion-related question: what is human personhood and when does it begin? His argument begins, so to speak, at each end of life. The Supreme Court has ruled that the unborn are not persons; yet they are undeniably living and human. At the far end of the life span, there is a widely accepted view that a body may still be biologically alive but personally dead if the brain has ceased to function. These two findings Englehardt uses as his warrant, then, to argue that there is human life which is not personal life. For the latter, Englehardt would require what we find in adults: autonomous action, self-awareness, rationality, self-determination. The unborn do not have this. Therefore they are not persons. Therefore they have no intrinsic value or rights. They may have value for others if the others find them attractive, but only if so.

An infant, though born, is not in a substantially different status. "Not only is the fetus not in the strict sense a person, neither is a child until a certain level of consciousness is attained. The infant is still more an 'it' than a 'he' or a 'she.' " Yes, he says, but adults are willing to treat infants *as if* they were persons long enough for them actually to become such. A child has "imputed personhood," and thus still only derivative value and borrowed rights.[19]

In this argument, published for a theological audience, Englehardt clothes a legal ruling with philosophical authority. When writing for a medical audience, also in 1973, he finds in another judgment of the Supreme Court (as he grasps that judgment) a fortunate and creative social doctrine. Believing that the Court had made abortion on demand legitimate only up to the time of viability, instead of up to birth, he sees this as a confirmation of the facts of human development. A newborn infant, though not rational and therefore not a human person, is acted upon *as if it were* an individual. But not much more or less than is the unborn who approaches birth. In the parents' mind the viable fetus "can be appreciated as someone," and by that fact alone begins to be someone. "The question of the time of the emergence of a human person can, thus, be answered in terms of when the organism plays a social role and, within the uncertain range of viability, the exact time can be defined stipulatively in terms of social needs." Englehardt has praise for the Court, which had so uncannily ruled that abortion was appropriate up until the moment that someone began to be concerned for the offspring. Medicine and law and philosophy had clasped one another. "The criterion of viability as a social category is a reminder that medicine is the guardian of human personal, not merely biological, life. If clearly understood, it has the virtue of preserving all the social values which enhance the dignity of the person as the guardian of human personal life (i.e., as opposed to merely biological life)." Quite opposed.[20]

Standing on those grounds Englehardt is inevitably going to turn towards infanticide, and that he soon does. At this point he modifies his approach. In searching for common descriptive features for humankind he does not scan the various stages of development and identify what is enduring. He picks the point of peak development and makes that the norm. Anything significantly less functional than a fully rational adult human is not simply a less rational person: it is no person at all. Then Englehardt reverses the process in assessing infanticide. He does not scan the various genetic afflictions borne by children and ask whether a general license to liquidate would be unacceptable because it would do away with certain ones. Instead he picks the least composed human, the anencephalic born without a brain or a hope of survival, and with this example decides to allow a general freedom to kill defectives. When one seeks a general principle, Englehardt supplies the narrowest possible; when there must be a carefully discriminating policy, he brings in a wholesale permissiveness.

The child cannot decide for himself or herself. At least, Englehardt says, it cannot assert its desires, and so it has no rights. He is arguing that rights derive, not from justice, but from power. "Young children, especially new-born infants, exist for their families and for those who love them." Medical decisions to treat them or to deny care turn, not on any rights, but "on the probability and cost of achieving that future status—a developed personal life." The choice can really fall back on the issue of cost, since parents owe the small child nothing. There is never, in Englehardt's view, a duty to provide extraordinary care, and by that he means costly care. The possibility that one might owe more within the family than to a stranger is not raised precisely because one owes nothing at all to a child who is not yet rational and strong enough to look after his or her own interests. If this be a case of the fittest destroying the less fit, that is no objection since this whole thesis maintains that Darwinian nature should be allowed to take its course.

The very young child, then, has no personhood, no intrinsic value, no rights unto himself. He exists "for his family." There is, however, one injury he is capable of sustaining: what Englehardt calls "the injury of wrongful existence." It can be no injury to slay your unloved infant. But it might be an injury to preserve your loved infant. If children face "lives not worth living," lives of deformity or handicap, then it may be damaging not to relieve them of this future. How can one tell what is not in such a baby's self-interest? Here we are brought back to familiar shores. It is probably best, Englehardt says, to decide "on the basis of the cost and suffering to parents and society." Standing on the firm ground of self-interest and economy, one can hardly go wrong.[21]

Father Richard McCormick is Englehardt's colleague at the Kennedy Institute, but his thoughts on the subject of death decisions originate furlongs away from those we have just reviewed. McCormick stipulates that "every human being, regardless of age or condition, is of incalculable worth. . . . allowing some infants to die does not imply that 'some lives are valuable, others not,' or that 'there is such a thing as a life not worth living.' " He emphasizes that decisions to give injured infants their quittance must be made with reference to the children's good alone, not influenced by the utilitarian perspectives of a technological culture which tends to sum up an individual by his function, by what he can do, rather than by what he is.

From this ideological base, so alien to what this chapter has hitherto recorded, McCormick wends his way forward. Life—biological life—is not our highest good. It is subordinated to spiritual ends: the love of God and neighbor. Put in other words, "the meaning, substance, and consummation of life is found in human *relationships*. . . . Life is a value to be preserved only insofar as it contains some potentiality for human relationships. When in human judgment this potentiality is totally absent or would be, because of the condition of the individual, totally subordinated to the mere effort for survival, that life can be said to have achieved its potential."

Father McCormick contends that when extraordinary medical effort is needed to keep an infant alive one must estimate the quality of life, the "truly human—i.e., relational—potential," to figure out whether it is worth costly inconvenience to others. If the life to be saved were, for instance, to be "painful, poverty-stricken and deprived, away from home and friends, oppressive," the person's human relationships "would be so threatened, strained or submerged that they would no longer function as the heart and meaning of the individual's life as they should." An infant facing such a life could be left to die.[22]

Some critics are wary of letting physicians or family make death decisions for the helpless based on what a burden they might be to others. McCormick concurs with Robert Veatch that if one can sacrifice oneself for others, a similar judgment on one's behalf should be legitimate if made by one's guardians. These custodial choices have to distinguish, not the different value of human *persons*, but the varying value of different *lives*. What constitutes reasonable treatment can be reckoned by costing the financial and psychological burdens on parents and medics, and the quality of interhuman relationships that it might buy. The decision by guardians must be made from the imagined perspective of the infant. McCormick is in agreement with one surgeon's view that "if a severely handicapped child were suddenly given one moment of omniscience and total awareness of his or her outlook for the future, would that child necessarily opt for life? No one has yet been able to demonstrate that the answer would always be 'yes.' " The burden of proof is thereby reversed. It traditionally lay with those who wished the child dead; now it lies with the child himself, and it is to be assessed by those for whom his life would be a burden.[23]

The prospect first raised publicly sixty years ago by Professors Binding and Hoche has recovered from whatever discredit it suffered by massive implementation in the meantime in Germany. In our day and in our country there is broad current support for the elimination of undesirably afflicted newborn children. The support is of two sorts, practical and theoretical. It is perhaps unlikely that physicians were persuaded of it by what philosophers and theologians have been writing about it. Still, their decisions to do these things, for whatever reasons, are very likely given refreshment by the arguments we have seen.

They are unwholesome arguments. To begin with, they proceed like a shell game. One might begin by defending an incurably ill, moribund, pain-wracked adult's freedom to ask for an easy passage into death. One might agree: this seems justified. Let us call it euthanasia, or gracious death. But then we learn abruptly that this title, and its moral seal of approval, have been transferred to an utterly different undertaking: a child who is not ill, not dying, not in pain, is eased into death because his or her physical handicaps will cost the insurance company some money and the parents some hardship. One must say that that is not euthanasia at all, nor is this any argument. It is dishonest flimflam.

Let another example be given; there are many that could. One begins by calling for agreement that each human being has the right to life, to preserve his bodily self. We agree. It follows, then, that in the case of humans not in possession of themselves this great right must be wielded on their behalf by protectors. Yes, we say; that follows. Then, we are asked to conclude, these guardians have in their hands the right to exterminate their protégés at their convenience, for they hold the right to life and death over them. But we object that this does not follow at all. Surely, the argument rejoins, a guardian can rightly perform on his ward's behalf all things that an independent person could perform on his own say-so. No, we say, he surely can not.

What all of these arguments for infanticide conceal or ignore is that fiduciary authority is not untrammeled. I, as an adult, am free to invest my wealth at whatever risk I please, and indeed I am free to lose it and go bankrupt. But I as trustee of my minor nephew am not free to treat his wealth that way. My obligation is to preserve it in trust by cautious decisions, till the day he is mature enough to face those decisions himself. I shall be sent to prison if I treat his money as carelessly as I am free to treat my own. The role of fiduciary is akin to that of president *pro tempore*: one preserves the enterprise, one does not play the part of entrepreneur. As the Supreme Court ruled many years ago, "Parents may be free to become martyrs themselves, but it does not follow that they are free to make martyrs of their children."[24]

It is difficult to see how it would be right to sacrifice children to one's own convenience if it be wrong to sacrifice them to another's altruism. It is a perversion of fiduciary power to turn it destructively upon its rightful beneficiary.

Then one must deal with the repeated argument that the end justifies the means. Even if one were willing to overlook the proclivity of that dialectical vehicle to rumble pell-mell down to chaos, it could have no application in this discussion. Suppose yourself willing to accept that a vehemently worthwhile end could decontaminate an otherwise perverse means. To justify the liquidation of infants one would call for a powerfully desirable end. What end are we offered? The end most consistently proposed throughout the infanticide literature is that families and the state be discharged of a heavy and unwelcome burden of care. The end which they set before themselves is that they free themselves from a burden. Now that is surely not an evil end. But neither is it a significantly good one, or even a good one at all, in any positive sense. It is a neutral end, and among neutral ends the most suspect. There is, for infanticide, no proportionately good end strong enough even to bring the claim of ends justifying means to the test.

Professor Barth in Heidelberg speaks of boosting natural selection. Professor Williams of Cambridge sees balance restored by bitches snapping puppies' spines. Many contemporary savants see in infanticide an acquiescence, even a ministry, to a nature which discards so many zygotes, displants and expels defective fruits of the womb, and destroys many animal young if they come forth crippled. Would it not be in harmony with this natural favor towards the fit if we pinched off the blighted young in the bud? The reply one puts to this misuse of Darwin is that humankind is quite special within nature. When humankind is red in fang and claw, it is almost never up to nature's work but is pursuing purposes of its own. On our hands "natural selection" gloves greed and injustice and revenge. It is the pride of humankind—and the hope of Jewish and Christian faith—that though the race be often to the swift and the battle to the strong, this is said of the dash and the skirmish. The longer course is completed and the campaign won by those who rescue the oppressed, shelter the homeless, redeem the cheated, carry the crippled—not by those whose care is for themselves. We do not take our lesson from a nature that fevers, drowns, and devours. We defy and transfigure nature by finding in her victims our most treasured opportunities.

Another sophistry of the debate is that those who accept infanticide approach the decision bound by no dogmatic principles either way. They are said to be more open to the evidence and the anguish than those who are held at either extreme, who hold that all children are to be saved or that all are expendable. What truly lies behind this affectation of judicious inquiry is unprincipled opportunism. To live by principle is not "to be obsessed with dogma." It is to carry from past experience and the conveyed experience of others a set of general convictions that are always active, always being confirmed, questioned, amended, annulled. To live by principle is a mentally active experience, not a slouching of the mind. We may and do fail our principles, even seriously, but provided we disavow and purge those failures later, the principles survive and so do we: more principled than before. Those who do not discipline their action by principle may not necessarily lead chaotic or inconsistent lives. They may act very consistently. But the consistency is governed in a curious way by precedent. In this frame of mind one is not likely to act in such fashion that one's past behavior can stand condemned. In the more accountable perspective wherein principles can be tested and elaborated by ratification or repentance, one learns by an imperfect past and is not bound to its limits. In the more murky situation described in the infanticide literature, one tends to act on a level of integrity consistent with one's past, but if there be a lapse from it, one tends to adapt more easily to that as to a new and lowered standard. All humans can fail what they hold was right. A tradition of principle is what helps one overcome such failure. Lack of principle denies to one any protection against a downward spiral of degeneracy. The slide from abortion to infanticide is one illustration.

An argument I have not heard on behalf of infanticide is that a good number of churches have spoken out in its favor, or on behalf of the right of the poor to have access to it, or to vindicate it as a woman's right. There has been an ecclesiastical silence, except for Catholics and a few others who inveigh against it. Should, however, a strong and valiant militancy by, say, the American Civil Liberties Union or protection by the federal courts become the trend, I would not expect all the churches and synagogues of the land to remain deaf to these well-tried sources of revelation. Indeed, their indolence in speaking up in support of mercy deaths for unwanted, handicapped infants may be held up to them in reproach, as a gainsaying of the instincts that had once rallied them to defend abortion.

Another assertion that will require auditing is the claim that parents and physicians are well placed, well disposed, and well authorized to make the choice for life or death over infants at risk. As for doctors, it is a responsibility they vindicate in curious ways. It is argued that one must not be aloof or at a distance from such ominous and sensitive matters, emotionally detached or coldly cleaving to some principle. It is doctors who are in the thick of it and therefore can decide best. But it is also argued, contrarily, that one must not be too emotionally involved, with too much of a stake in the outcome, so that one's judgment be riled by tragedy. It is doctors who are objective and self-possessed; they are the ones to rely upon.

Rosalyn Darling has presented findings which raise important questions about the perspective of physicians on chronic handicaps in children. A sample of parents with children of various handicaps (spina bifida, congenital blindness, mongolism, etc.) explained that they had realistically accepted the disappointment, loved their children, and had found supportive comradeship among other parents of handicapped children. They did not conform to the psychoanalysts' theory that the birth of a handicapped child would produce feelings of guilt or denial or projection. They were coping. Most wished that they had not had a crippled child, but none wished not to have the child they now had. Those who were pregnant again were not seeking amniocentesis or abortion. Their target of dissatisfaction was not their children but their doctors. Many had left their original doctors in search of physicians who would take an interest in their children.

Darling then interviewed the doctors, who admitted repeatedly that they had been trained to cure. They felt unprepared to deal with chronic defects or to see that they could offer any positive benefit to those who had them. "A world-view that primarily involves sick people who get better may not leave room for the chronically ill or incurable patient whose defect cannot be 'fixed.' . . . 'Success,' in this view, seems somehow to be equated with complete normalcy of function, and the chronically ill or disabled present a moral dilemma to the physician so oriented. As my findings have indicated, a life defined by physicians as intolerable might come to be defined in a very different way by parents."[25]

And what of parents who decide to have their infants die? Are they not affected by powerful conflicts of interest strong enough to dampen the presumably assertive instincts of protectiveness? Daniel Callahan, who accepts abortion of the handicapped, offers comments that may apply as well to infanticide:

> I am told . . . that we owe it to the fetus to abort it if it has Down's Syndrome. Yet when I read of the actualities of Down's Syndrome it becomes clear that most mongoloids are happy, that many have a minimally adequate intelligence level, that many can be trained for simple jobs, that they are capable of giving and responding to affection. That does not sound like a life of suffering to me. Perhaps, though, it means a life of suffering for the parents. But, if so, then that is a very different matter; a riddance of the mongoloid serves the parents and not necessarily the child himself. That should be said clearly. . . .
>
> Even in the case of Tay-Sachs disease, far more severe than

Down's Syndrome, the suffering of the child itself is apparently not great; the course of the disease brings a mercifully quick degeneration of cognitive and affective faculties; the greatest suffering is on the part of the parents. I, myself, would feel that the parents would have a moral right to turn to abortion in that case and for those reasons. But I would hope that no one would be fooled into thinking that we were really acting for the sake of the child, nor that anyone would be fooled into thinking that we were doing anything other than taking the life of the fetus in order to preserve the welfare of the parents.[26]

I would question both the perceptions and the dispositions of physicians and parents who make "agonizing judgments" that afflicted children would be better off dead. Of all persons they are then the least able to enter into the imagined perspective and interests of the youngster at risk. Instead of calling in a commission of the powerful and the expert, why not assemble a jury of randomly selected handicap victims and their relatives? Better still, let us no longer even entertain the gratuitous and groundless assertion that congenitally defective people would be better dead until someone can come up with the only evidence which could support that claim: evidence that such persons actually do take their own lives. Until suicide reports tell us that handicapped people actually do make "management options" for death in greater proportion than do the thwarted rich, let us not admit any talk of theirs being a life better ended. There is no need to consult the powerful about the purported death wish of their victims. The great have too often been disposed to act as proxies for the awkward in signing away their lives.

Among the many arguments advanced commonly by those who sympathize with infanticide, two are most subtly perverse and require most considered review. One is that these decisions for life or for extinction should consider the quality of life to which the child would be consigned, and the value which that life has. The second is that, being unable to do all good, we must choose those beneficiaries we can most help and abandon the others.

Let us consider this question of life's value. What does value mean? So many things can be valuable to us: a week's holiday from work, a loving parent, a collection of books, a garden with lawn and flowers, strong athletic dexterity, a fine education, a full head of hair, a true friend, shoes that do not leak, a symphony concert, an air conditioner. Even social institutions like the state deal in many varied valuables: a park system, peace between nations, secure retirement benefits, prenatal care, stable banking, clean waterways, reliable pharmaceuticals. The thing about valuable things is that they have such different values. Not only are they unequal; they are sometimes incommensurable. How compare the value of a faithful, loving husband or wife to that of a legal career . . . or that of a second car in the garage? How assess the relative value of full employment and of better railway roadbeds? Or the relative disvalues of juvenile, drug-related crime and a soybean crop failure? How compare the incomparable? Yet we do this all the time, as anyone knows who has deliberated whether to move the family in order to secure a professional promotion, or has sat long on a budget committee.

When we deal in values we are treating of "lesser" and "greater" and "different." And yet we can choose among them. It is said that every thing has its price, and that every person can be bought. But the fundamental measure of value is neither money, nor the work that money represents, nor the portion of our life and time and energy given to the work. The basic measure of value is our own self: how much do I value this thing, this opportunity, this person? What other valued things am I willing to give for it, for her, for him? The medium of barter among valuable things may not always be money, but they all can be and are traded off against one another.

What I mean when I accord you value is that you have a worth for me. Other humans are valued insofar as they serve needs or wants. We possess a calculus whereby to reckon who is worth what. To the scale of other persons' needs I can apply the scale of my own resources, and also the scale of how generously I would yield those resources to meet others' needs, according to how valuable those persons are to me.

When it is not straightforwardly ruthless, but claims to consider children's interests, the argument on selective withholding of treatment from defective newborn children appears to pivot around what value such treatment might have for the infants themselves. A close examination of this value theory, however, discloses that the pivotal value is not internal to the lives and interests of the infants, but derives from what worth those children have for others.

Let me try to illustrate this by comparisons. A while ago a young orderly in a Swedish home for the aged was accused of killing a dozen or more of the residents by offering them carbonated drinks laced with corrosive acid. These old people, he later explained, were leading meaningless lives. What did this "meaningless" mean? Was the young man stating that, in his judgment, the relational potential of these old people was now totally used up, or that it had become totally subordinated to the mere effort for survival? Or was he saying simply that they were more trouble than they were worth? Whatever his drift, he was making a life-and-death judgment that appears to have involved three variables: how much care the old people required; how much relational or spiritual activity so much care would make possible; and how dear these persons were to him. For himself as a staffer, or for the Swedish public whose interests he decided to assert, there seemed to be no adequately "meaningful" outcome from institutional care. The old folks' lives may have had some fundamental value, but no longer enough value to justify continued care. Now, although his statement may appear to have considered the matter from the standpoint and interests of the old men and women, the decisive variable was related, not to them (how much meaningful outcome), but to himself and the public he claimed to represent (how desirable it was to have them around to care for). The measure of meaning was not the victims, but the one who sent them to their deaths.

One remembers similar applications of this value theory. The orderly's judgment about "meaningful life" puts one in mind of *lebensunwertes Leben* (life not worth living), of *Untermenschen* (subhumans fit only for slave labor), and *Mischlinge* (mongrels) first-class and *Mischlinge* second-class, subdivided into "productive" and "nonproductive," "useless eaters" and "antisocials," "racially valueless children" and, to come full circle, defective newborn children. All of these were categories of beings found, in another time and place, not to be leading meaningful lives. It cannot be said that the National Socialists assigned no value to human life. On the contrary, their programs were grounded precisely on an elaborate scale of values. At its base the value system was quite simple. As Hitler once explained to a gathering of general officers, he decided upon the "removal of the Jews from our nation, not because we would begrudge them their existence—we congratulate the rest of the world on their company—but because the existence of our nation is a thousand times more important to us than that of an alien race."[27]

A few decades earlier, liberal reformers in England had been proposing and legislating social policies that, in their way, were also value-responsive. "It was, to illustrate, the law of the land that upon certification of any two doctors, any person might be incarcerated indefinitely for feeblemindedness. Charles Wicksteed Armstrong was saying: 'the nation which first begins to *breed for efficiency*—denying the right of the scum to beget millions of their kind . . . is the nation destined to rule the earth. . . . To diminish the dangerous fertility of the unfit there are three methods: the lethal chamber, segregation and sterilization.' The professor of eugenics at London University was proposing that paupers, tramps, and the insane be left to starve; otherwise the fertile but unfit would continue to reproduce and prevent England from continuing as a world power. A physician with governmental authority who was concerned with mental deficiency tested his theory that it was due to small skulls by operating on children's heads; a fourth of them died. When the National Insurance Act required compulsory contributions from all workers, it provided that workmen could be denied unemployment compensation if they had been discharged for misconduct—insolence, for example. Pensions were withheld from those who had been in prison or had 'persistently failed to work.' "[28]

When one is prepared to assign a variable value to other human beings according as they are expected to rise to a high level of social performance, and then to allot to them a corresponding measure of life's sustenance, this is no ethical refinement. It is the same old business of the runt of the litter getting pushed away from the teat. All too often when we apologize that it would be too unkind to make some creature face so unsatisfying an existence, what we really mean is that we don't want to pay his or her bills.

By evaluating human beings insofar as they are "relational," or by "what they can come to be," or by their "personal or social consciousness," their "quality of life," their "access to higher goods," their potential for attaining a "truly human life," we assign to our fellows a value measured by their active participation in our society. The ideally valuable, "truly human life" appears to belong to a tax-paying adult who earns a living. To the extent that one fails of this ideal, by infancy or senility or criminality or infirmity, one slips down the value scale. Behind all this calculation lurks a readiness to appraise others according as they are pleasant or congenial or contributory towards ourselves, and then to act on this appraisal.

I discern two ethical impediments here. First, in this business of applied values, one appears to be considering three distinct factors: how much this other person needs (burden on the benefactor); how much good it would do this person if helped (benefit to the beneficiary); and how dear this other person is to me (relationship of beneficiary to benefactor). The interplay of all these factors would seem to promise a fair judgment. I must consider how much claim on my own life and resources is being made, how much proportionate gain this will bring my neighbor, and how dear to me my neighbor is or how beholden to him or her I am. But: when one calculates the anticipated benefits to the other person by that person's anticipated social response, then the factor supposedly respecting my neighbor's welfare is turned around and becomes, in effect, an indicator of how productive it is to have that person around. The benefits anticipated are measured, not intrinsically with respect to him or her, but extrinsically with respect to myself and others who stand to gain from a grudging judgment. The calculation is no longer an interplay of interests; it is put entirely at the pleasure of the one in power. The neighbor and the neighbor's future are cast into dependence on how useful I reckon him to be to the rest of us. So when Dr. Tristram Englehardt wants to relieve some infant of the "injury of wrongful existence" or SS Gruppenführer Karl Brandt describes the elimination of "useless eaters" and "undesirable individuals" as an "act of grace," I suspect that this is an injury I should pray for and a grace I should shun. When Dr. Duff designates lives "of dubious value," I hope he will never be in a position to evaluate mine. This concern for "quality of life" is really self-concern bearing the likeness of other-concern.

A second ethical impediment is raised by the readiness to treat persons according as it would be valuable for them. Grant the fact that, even if it were done without selfishness, persons are being evaluated. Quite clearly others *are* more or less valuable according as they become socially productive, or as they realize their "relational potential." What I would still dispute is that we have any ethical warrant to make this value the first basis for our treatment of others.

Let me suggest another way of approach. Rather than designating all human life as valuable, I would propose that all human beings are *not* valuable. They are invaluable. Our fellow human beings are not merely the most valuable things around; they are off the scale, truly incommensurable; not even to be introduced into the rate of exchange whereby we convert the relative values of other things. A human being can be valued, as has been described. But a human being ought also, and more importantly and fundamentally, to be reverenced. Possibly this would support the way some folk have of calling life sacred: not necessarily because of any relationship to God, but because it seems an appropriate category in which to shelter those very precious beings of transcendent goodness. As Simon Peter explained to Simon Magus, there are some things too valuable to have a price.

The governing insight in this assertion that human persons are beyond value—legitimate even without recourse to religious premises—is that mankind is obliged, if they are to live and grow in spirit, to deal with others not simply according to what good that may produce, what use it serves, what response it subsidizes.

We are corrupted morally and destroyed spiritually if we treat others only as they are valuable. We have of course only limited goods and service to dispose of, and fellow human beings whose needs and claims far exceed our where-withal. In matching our resources to their needs we are presented with a most rudimentary social and moral option: whether to exert ourselves to meet those endless neighbor-needs, or whether to adjudicate those needs and claims to serve our pleasure, by calculating their social benefit potential. There is obviously no congruence or conformity between the invaluable persons we confront and the value-benefits we might afford them. But there is a telltale and deep-cleft difference in whether they are the measure of our lives or we the measure of theirs.

This is not, as I say, a religious position, though it might be. The injunction that mankind is to be provided for, from each according to means and to each according to need (an injunction more gracious than all this calculation of values), may be ascribed either to first-century Jewish Christians or nineteenth-century Russian-German atheists. Both were of the mind that it is not enough to run a cost-benefit analysis on one's neighbor (though that is exactly what most Communist powers and some Christian institutions are now doing). In any case, what I know of Christian faith reinforces the conviction that no follower of Jesus, holding in his or her hand the powers of life and death over those less advantaged, should begin to wield such powers by asking how much social yield there will be from any given material investment. We owe things of value to persons beyond value. Indeed, we live by a belief that it is the least able, the least forthcoming, who have strongest claim on our lives and substance.

Virtually every advocate of infanticide on demand has expressed a chafe about the "sanctity-of-life" ethic. The most recent writers propose to ease it aside in favor of a "quality-of-life" ethic. Mere life, they insist, has no absolute, intrinsic value so overriding that it must be accorded precedence over every other good. There are times when life must be laid down rather than injustice be let rule, or great moral harm be suffered, for example. There are even times when one's own self would be personally the worse for life to be prolonged. Thus life's length must be decided with an eye to its higher purposes, relative to personal fulfillment, and not because it is invested with any absolute, religious immunity.

They misconstrue. The ancient notion that life is sacred owes much of its continuance to faith. Yet it is a doctrine that is private to no religion. It does not mean that mere human life is an absolute good before which all others fall. It means that throughout this world, though we are to tame and subdue and use and consume what we need, though all lower living creatures are given into our hands for our increase, before our fellow men and women we must stop short, we must check ourselves. They are not to be used or disposed of. They are to be reverenced. Even when they are put into our power we may not use them for they are too sacred to be used. Nor may we take it on ourselves to decide the quality of their lives, especially for life's forfeiture, for the temptation to do so for our profit is so strong that none of us knows he could resist it. The "quality-of-life" ethic really means that the powerful may resolve that the weak would be happier if no longer a burden to them. The "sanctity-of-life" ethic really means that the powerful must restrain themselves from disencumbering themselves of the weak, for they are precious beyond all other things we would rather have. We are not pure enough to survive if given the spinning, the measuring out, and the shearing short of human fellows' lives.

We must do more, we are told, than merely prolong lives with no concern for their quality. To that we must reply that the personal and moral quality of our lives will be zombied out once we start "merely prolonging" those lives which seem to be of quality. It is essential to the quality of my life that I serve you whatever be the quality of your life. And if that quality is mean, perhaps only my unsubduing service will save you as well as me.

The other major argument we must try to unfang is that of limited resources, emergency times, and critical choices. One is so often reminded that, whatever our disposition to treat our fellows as invaluable, there are still certain situations in which it is both allowable and dutiful to appraise others in a strictly utilitarian way. Triage is the typical situation put forward. At a field hospital in a combat zone, battle will produce casualties that swamp the capacity of the hospital. It becomes an inexorable fact that some must be saved and some left to die. A triage officer stands at the entry, sorting casualties so that the medical facility can accomplish the most practical good. One soldier disastrously wounded has to be set aside in favor of five others who, in the same amount of time, can have their lives saved. The battalion commander is sent in and the assistant cook held back. Officers have priority over enlisted men. Enemy wounded are given last place after one's own comrades, whose survival will help the war effort. Faced with life-and-death needs and inadequate resources, the triage officer does his duty precisely by being ruthlessly utilitarian. The wounded are evaluated; they are treated in accordance with their values to the group and to the struggle. People are sent for saving treatment or left to die on grounds of the payoff that a given amount of care will produce.

About triage as a paradigm of moral choice I would make several observations. First, even when it seems quite justified, it has a way of consuming a person. For a doctor, the fibers of whose self are braided into lifelines of generous concern, it snarls the soul, not simply to lose a patient to death, but to mark him or her for death. It may require uncommonly high and durable virtue to perform this task without making a vice out of necessity. To illustrate: during the Holocaust certain Jewish community leaders, after agonizing at the Nazi order, consented to select numbers of their own communities to be sent to their destruction, in the hope that some others—the right others—might be spared. One such *Aelteste*, leader of the ghetto in Łódź, Poland, explained:

> Now, when we are deporting 10,000 people from the ghetto, I cannot pass over this tragic subject in silence. Unfortunately, in this respect, I received a ruthless order, an order which I had to carry out in order to prevent its being carried out by others.

Within the framework of my possibilities . . . I have tried to
mitigate the severity of the decree. I have settled the matter so
that I assigned for deportation that portion which was for the
ghetto a suppurating abscess. So the list included the ousted
operators of the underground, scum, and all sorts of persons
harmful to the ghetto.[29]

Another in Upper Silesia argued that the Jews should accept from the
Gestapo the onus of selecting the contingents for extermination, so as to
preserve for the community its most helpful elements. First to go, on his lists,
were informers, thieves, and "undesirables"; next went the insane, the sick,
and the defective children.[30] The victims had, by acquiescing in the work,
somehow been contaminated by the mind of the oppressors. Even when
necessity seems to call for it, can a person long deal with his or her neighbors in
this way, calculating their "worth to society," their relational potential, without soon acquiring the perverse habit of mind which one wants to resist but
perhaps cannot?

A closer vignette of triage has been sketched by Dr. Frederic B. Westervelt, Jr., director of the Renal Division at the University of Virginia Medical
Center—down the corridor, so to speak, from where Dr. Shaw's work was
going on. Even years after kidney transplants and dialysis were developed,
less than 10 percent of the needy could be provided with available care. How
to choose that 10 percent? Dr. Westervelt rejects the suggestion that random
lottery would be fairest. The staff judges that these approaches "maintained an
unparalleled 'equality of opportunity,' yet do not fulfill our needs." They
prefer a system of triage, to restore the greatest number to "a useful life worth
living," with the second goal being a public record of efficacy: "an image," as
he calls it. Their purpose, after all, is not merely to prolong individual lives.
"The return to the community of its more visible, articulate, and contributory
members in exchange for its current or projected large expenditures became a
secondary goal." The staff follow "social considerations" in identifying who
best could benefit from the program, "returning to a reasonably happy life,
useful to himself and to others."

What sort of qualities does the triage committee look for? "Motivation,
intelligence, 'the need to prevail,' ability to adhere to broad therapeutic
premises with interpretive flexibility or to adhere to rigid restraints faithfully,
the capacity early to recognize and report deviations from the usual, all these
attributes tend to be found in these persons who because of those same
attributes are vocationally and socially 'successful.' " The image begins to
come clear. Dr. Westervelt's group also prefers patients with access to general
medical care. In other terms this means: "Those higher in the socioeconomic
order are more likely to fall in this category than are their less fortunate
brethren. . . . Thus, in general, selection for dialysis and transplantation has
not so much been prejudicial *against* the socially disadvantaged as prejudiced
in favor of those persons who have, in the eyes of those responsible for triage,
certain attributes of 'survival value.' "

Unfortunately, Dr. Westervelt reports, this favoring of the affluent has led
to criticism, to which he replies, somewhat stung: "A selection process would

be derelict if it did not seek the 'most suitable' of those suitable. . . . Medical criteria must not, of course, serve as a façade behind which other manipulations take place." There seems to be no façade here at all. The best and the brightest are having it all to themselves, right out in the open. If anyone feels stoutly that this is unfair, the renal chief can fall back on a professional principle: "The physician long has been accorded the privilege, even the legal right, of determining to whom he shall and shall not render care, just as the patient may select his own physician." Dr. Westervelt is citing medical ethics, and he proceeds to give this principle a most wonderful explanation. "This stems from a recognition of the phenomenon, hardly unique to medicine, that there must exist personal, behavioral, or even professional incompatibilities which would thwart an effective therapeutic relationship. . . . I do not refer to petty prejudices or differences, but to such that lead to a sense of responsibility, respect, and a conviction that the task is worthwhile, all leading to the needed capacity for extra effort." This, he explains, best supports the morale of his staff (the value circle closes once again). And, as for a random choice of patients, isn't that the sort of "impersonal" treatment medicine has been criticized for?[31]

We owe to Dr. Westervelt's disarming simplicity this portrayal of triage, wherein Charlottesville is so evocative of Łódź and Upper Silesia and all that. People have wondered how the totally physical orientation of medical education could enable doctors to make sophisticated social judgments. The Westervelt report tells us how able some are. One concludes, not just that their training is truly inadequate to their calling, but that there is no training for triage. It may not be a task one can survive.

Another thing about triage: it is so easily invoked. There could be little argument, and little misgiving, that a selection of sorts was necessary for kidney treatment, since there simply were no more machines then to be had. But in a world where medical resources are never likely to satisfy medical needs, is not every day one of triage? Are not all medical practitioners who administer life and death likely to calculate the relative value of their patients? And will this reckoning not be heavily influenced by what this treatment, what this survival would mean to them, the medics? It goes far beyond medicine. Infanticide advocates remind us of the competition for scarce monetary and manpower resources in society. More explicitly, Garrett Hardin has argued that the United States had better leave the poorer nations to starve if it wants to preserve the good life.

A recent newspaper canvass of citizen comment on the "boat people" from Southeast Asia who were frantically seeking asylum elicited a wave of hostile comments from Americans who insisted that our country could not harbor endless waves of feckless refugees. Knowing the devastation that the United States has visited upon the homelands of these people, and that their predecessors here have been some of America's most industrious and self-reliant immigrants, and that our country enjoys such relative abundance among the nations of the earth, what is one to think of these claims that a welcome for these refugees would be wasted? Why is it that the powerful and affluent and engorged of this world are always the most aware that there is not enough to go around, and that there are so many people who will make poor use of what is given them? Why are the lifeboats always being captained by the upper-deck passengers?

And as for the necessity which imposes triage on us: granted the battle, it may be justified to pick some wounded to die because they are less worthwhile. But why grant the battle in the first place? Granted the inadequacy of medical care in poor communities, some people must be left to ail and die who might otherwise be saved. But why grant the inadequacy? The president of the Society of Critical Care Medicine has stated to his colleagues: "As physicians, we pledge ourselves to treat patients and abjure all forms of moralizing at their expense. Triage—deciding which patients to give up on and let die—clearly violates our unconditional Hippocratic commitment to life. Yet, it seems as if every other article in the *New England Journal of Medicine* these days contains some reference to pulling the plug on patients who are presumably hopeless cases. Why? There just isn't enough money anywhere to care for all patients, we are told. Medical care is consuming 8.3 percent of the gross national product. Terrible—that's almost half what we spend on booze, tobacco, and entertainment!"[32]

So often we consent to participate in what we lament as "tragic" decisions that cost other people their lives or well-being without challenging the social injustice that has imposed the tragedy. One is reminded of a proposal submitted to Adolf Eichmann: "There is an imminent danger that not all Jews can be supplied with food in the coming winter. We must seriously consider if it would not be more humane to finish off the Jews, insofar as they are not fit for labor mobilization, with some quick-acting means. In any case this would be more agreeable than to let them die of hunger."[33] There is no triage when the same people who offer humane death are the same ones who cause the imminent danger. And so it so often is.

Behind all this application of value theory there is the possibility of great mischief. This can be seen perhaps by considering the canon drawn up at a conference sponsored by the University of California, San Francisco: "Life-preserving intervention should be understood as doing harm to an infant who cannot survive infancy. . . ." This stands in clean contrast to the stubborn resistance by the Dutch physicians to be drawn into any of the utilitarian programs of the Nazis. Truly human, relational potential was the guiding star over the San Francisco gathering. In Holland they seem to have held, with costly determination, that as doctors they would have to tend patients who would never be cured. They knew their profession was not to produce a healthy, working population, nor to eliminate the stunted. It was their profession to heal whom they could, alleviate the affliction of those they could not, and stand by all whom they served. They would have agreed with advocates of infanticide on demand that death is not the Ultimate Enemy (though perhaps abandonment is). Their dedication was not to human life but to human beings whose lives we heal if we can but still serve if we cannot.

Destruction of the newly born proceeds in the same spirit as destruction of the unborn, the never-born. The motives and weapons and weapon-wielders and betrayals of kinship are alike. It is in barbaric opposition to the humanistic

spirit which knows that life and the living are served at high cost. The spirit
was well expressed by Jean Rostand, the French biologist and philosopher:

> I admit that I am a little disconcerted by the spirit of certain
> books and articles that come my way, when I see that an author is
> trying to take the tragedy out of death (which, as a moralist once
> said, is "the only thing greater than the word that names it"), when
> I read that a person's usefulness to his family or his country should
> be taken into account in deciding whether or not to prolong his
> life, when I realize that, tomorrow, any man may have to justify his
> right to life and prove his organic worthiness. I admit that I am
> scarcely reassured when Fabre-Luce tells us that "all insane,
> vitiated, or degraded life is a profanation," and that, in the future,
> "we shall have to become more and more exacting with regard to
> the conditions of human worthiness." I am even less reassured
> when I think that it might not be men like Fabre-Luce who would
> set the limit of that minimum worthiness. I admit that he frightens
> me a little (and not only because I myself am in my seventies) when
> he writes in his brilliant book, *La Mort a changé*, that "for patients
> beyond the age of ninety, the doctor should be only a helper of
> death, ready to seize the first opportunity."
>
> I admit that I feel uneasy when I hear someone proclaim "the
> right of the more alive over the less alive," because that right is a
> little too much like the right of the fittest or the strongest. I admit
> that I see in all this a slight tinge of Neitzscheanism that is not to
> my liking, and I also see it in certain passages of Teilhard de
> Chardin, where he explains that we must sometimes have the
> courage to abandon stragglers on the road in order to make swifter
> progress toward our goal.
>
> Yes, I admit that I would be repelled and saddened if I wit-
> nessed the development of a social ethic in which the value of
> every life ceased to be infinite, and it was considered perfectly
> logical and natural for a doctor to discontinue a lifesaving perfusion
> or decline to revive a newborn baby. I admit that I would dread
> that excessively rational and realistic society whose advent is now
> being predicted; that society that would mathematically evaluate
> the amount of protection and care that each individual deserved,
> taking into account his age, health, biological fitness, social useful-
> ness, and ability to enjoy life; that society in which everyone would
> receive only his proper portion of medical assistance, and in
> which, after having judged a man to be not worth saving, conscien-
> tious but anonymous experts would sign an order for his death as
> calmly as if it were a routine report. It would be easy, of course—
> and people less "vitalistic" than I am have done so—to contrast the
> traditional, rather sanctimonious respect for human life with the
> savage contempt of it that constantly erupts in our civilization.
> Highways covered with the blood of accident victims, a monstrous
> technology developed for military murder, preparations for an

abominable nuclear or even bacteriological war—in the face of all that, it may seem ridiculous to care about prolonging the life of a patient with irreparable brain damage or an incurable disease, saving a malformed baby, or sparing a criminal sentenced to death. . . .

For my part, I believe that there is no life so degraded, deteriorated, debased, or impoverished that it does not deserve respect and is not worth defending with zeal and conviction. I believe that even if there are good reasons we can give ourselves for sacrificing one life for another, considering the inadequacy of the material means at our disposal, such a sacrifice involves a kind of defeat, because it confirms acceptance of that inadequacy. Above all, I believe that a terrible precedent would be established if we agreed that a life could be allowed to end because it was not worth preserving, since the notion of biological unworthiness, even if carefully circumscribed at first, would soon become broader and less precise. After eliminating what was no longer human, the next step would be to eliminate what was not sufficiently human, and finally nothing would be spared except what fitted a certain concept of humanity.

I have the weakness to believe that it is an honor for a society to desire the expensive luxury of sustaining life for its useless, incompetent, and incurably ill members; I would almost measure a society's degree of civilization by the amount of effort and vigilance it imposes on itself out of pure respect of life. It is noble to struggle unrelentingly to save someone's life, as if he were dear to us, when objectively he has no value and is not even loved by anyone.[34]

Sequelae

In greatest part, this book is both an inquiry into abortion and an examination of a campaign of persuasion on its behalf, a campaign that would have us believe abortion is a necessary and therefore appropriate remedy for certain urgent problems, personal and social. The more I studied that campaign, its premises and arguments and backwash, the more I saw it as a work of dishonesty and death. Just as wife-killing would surely curb the incidence of wife-battering in America, abortion would surely curb some almost unbearable human miseries. Yet somehow each remedy, though it works, is wrong.

Nowhere in these many pages do I set forth an argument against abortion. Before embarking on this study it would not have occurred to me as necessary: why would one need to argue that mothers and fathers and healers should not destroy their unborn young? At the end of this study I doubt that an argument against abortion is decisive, for one sets one's direction in this great matter more by the will than by the mind. In this life we acknowledge and respect those whom we are willing to accommodate. Our basic attitude towards abortion matches our readiness either to address ourselves to others' needs or to eliminate others when their needs burden us too heavily. I sense an obligation to make some simple exposition of my own understanding about abortion, but it will be more an appeal than an argument. Those who do not wish to rearrange their lives to accommodate a child will not readily be brought to see their unborn as endued with rights or as an envoy of joy—at least not by any argument. Those who know that they have nothing more satisfying to do with their lives than to give others life and its hospitality hardly need to have it explained to them that the stranger appearing unbidden at life's entryway must, before all, be bidden welcome.[1]

I hold that the life of every fellow human must be respected, preserved, and even protected. We must defer to others' lives, not simply to gain and repay a like protection from others, nor just to avoid the penalties of the law, nor merely because every human being has a right to his or her life, a right which deserves priority over every other human right, need, or desire. We must defer for still another reason: if we deal unjust injury or violent death to others, we shall bring upon ourselves a death of the spirit—a violent death. Those who kill, die. And they die when they slay, not later.

I hold that, so far as we best can tell, a human person's life begins at conception. Neither birth nor any transition leading up to it serves as a true beginning, unless we talk biological nonsense. Of course an unborn child does not speak or work or give her or his love to others (nor does a newborn child;

nor, for that matter, some people long since born). But it is terribly important that we give the basic protection of life-loyalty to *all* fellow humans, not only to those who suit us as valuable contributors to society. My position is that no one should have the right or power to decide what qualities or what usefulness others must have to avoid being killed. It is enough to be *any* human being, no matter how burdensome or troublesome, to merit the right to life.

Abortion, then—the willful and violent killing of an unborn human being— is homicide. By this neutral term I mean simply the killing of a human. We talk of accidental and deliberate and justifiable homicides. Is there such a thing as a justifiable abortion? Here I would argue that if we claim any honesty we must hew to the same principles in evaluating abortion as govern our judgments on any other form of homicide.

Some maintain that all deliberate killing is wrong. Better, they argue, to accept violence at the hands of others than to take up weapons and end ourselves as death-dealers. Others, likewise committed to life, would say that homicide could be justified under certain conditions, e.g., to protect oneself or some innocent third party from mortal, undeserved attack. On the latter view it might be justifiable to destroy a child were that clearly the only way to save his or her mother's life. But there is no consistent, responsible moral way, from either point of view, to justify the killing of innocent offspring to relieve his or her elders of any inconvenience, no matter how severe the distress.

It is no less savage to abort a deformed child than to exterminate a retarded adult. It is no more justifiable to abort a child in order to conceal adultery than to murder a witness about to give evidence in a trial. One cannot fairly allow a child to be destroyed because he or she was conceived by rape or incest, without also allowing the elimination of illegitimate children.

My argument is straightforward. Abortion is homicide: the destruction of a child. Save for the rare, rare instance when it is a mortal threat to a mother's life to carry her child to birth, there is no abortion that is not the unjust taking of another's life because it is a burden to one's own.

Someone has reckoned that a high percentage of the murders in this country find close family or business associates as victims. We have in us this strange and desperate ability, this selfish madness, to blind our mind's eye towards those nearest us, to see them as insignificant, as nothing really human. We depersonalize our victims before killing them. So with abortion.

In opposing it I am in *no way* insensitive to the plight of mothers who are frightened thirteen-year-olds, or are supporting six children on welfare, or are having to drop out of college because of one night's foolishness. I simply say that these are not misfortunes that justify anyone in raising his or her hand to kill. They are not trivial miseries. But to allege them as cause for abortion reminds me too much of the excuses for the massacre at My Lai, and for the bondage of the slave trade, and for the industrial poisoning at Minamata.

I do not wish to donate on Tuesday to the March of Dimes for medical research on the health of the unborn, and on Thursday to Planned Parenthood to keep crippled children from ever surviving till birth. I want no part of the insanity that sends police into the privacy of homes to stop parents from battering and scalding their four-month-old babies to death, and then uses the same force of law to guarantee the "privacy" of parents to dismember their babies four months before birth. I have no stomach for a society which sees that in many of its homes children are unwanted, and would rather exterminate the children than heal the parents. And though I try to be patient, I do become exasperated when told that since I am a Catholic I have somehow lost my civil right to make public and legal appeal for the lives of the young marked down for death, or that I am imposing my private religious notions on the majority of my fellow citizens, when it is clear to anyone willing to inquire that it is the minority of citizens that presently uses the law to kill.

Women have a right to reproductive freedom, I hear it argued, and I agree: *all* women, even little girls yet unborn who have the right to be free to grow to the age when they in their turn can make love and have babies. Women should have control over their own bodies, it is said, and I agree; but not life-and-death control over the bodies of their children (and in the case of male children, who ever heard of a male part of a female body?). Make abortions illegal, we hear it said, and they will still go on, but in the back streets, and I agree. Yet rape goes on despite our laws; should it no longer be a crime? And if the day came when the nation was no longer willing to go on record that rape was criminal, would there not be more of it? Can anyone who knows that we record 1,500,000 abortions a year in America imagine that most of these would have occurred without the legal protections of 1973? Drive abortion underground, it is said, and young women will die by the septic coathanger. Yes, just as the young women of the Weather Underground who blew themselves up making bombs. I mourn them all, but I mourn more their innocent victims—and differently. Make abortion a criminal act, we hear it said, and only the rich will be able to afford it. Yes, but then the rich have always been better able to afford their vices. I would as soon buy abortions for the poor as buy them heroin. Abortions *will* go on! Why not at least see that they be done cleanly and safely? Yes, say I, and so shall hatred and murder go on, but I shall not use the tax moneys to give sniper-scopes to the Klan or dumdum bullets to the Mafia.

But back to the *point*, the chief point, the much-avoided point, the only point at issue: to abort is to destroy one's son or daughter.

Notes
Preface

1. Letter to the editor, *Newsweek*, 26 July 1976, p. 6C; see John D. Rockefeller III, "No Retreat on Abortion," "My Turn," ibid., 21 June 1976, p. 11.

2. *Philemon's Problem: The Daily Dilemma of the Christian* (Chicago: ACTA, 1973), pp. 78–79; this passage appeared earlier in "The Conservatism of Situation Ethics," *New Blackfriars* (London), October 1966, pp. 7–14.

3. " 'Human Life' and Human Love," *Commonweal* 89, no. 7 (15 November 1968): 245–52.

4. The papers presented at that National Conference on Abortion have been published under my editorship as *Abortion Parley* (Kansas City: Andrews & McMeel, 1980).

Essay 1
Rachel Weeping: The Veterans of Abortion

1. See, for comparisons, Zimmerman's study of 40 mostly young abortors, which is largely congruent with the materials analyzed here: Mary K. Zimmerman, *Passage through Abortion: The Personal and Social Reality of Women's Experiences* (New York: Praeger, 1977). See also Judith G. Smetana, "Beliefs about the Permissibility of Abortion and Their Relationship to Decisions regarding Abortion," *Journal of Population* 2, no. 1 (Spring 1979), 294–305.

2. "Contrary to the popular belief that shame over pregnancy out of wedlock is the major motivation for abortion, we observed that . . . much more important was the woman's rejecting of motherhood with all of its attendant demands. Our impression is that these women tend to be narcissistic and regard the fetus as a competitor for the succorance and dependent care they themselves obviously require." Charles Ford, Pietro Castelnuovo-Tedesco, and Kahlila D. Long, "Women Who Seek Therapeutic Abortion: A Comparison with Women Who Complete Their Pregnancies," *American Journal of Psychiatry* 129, no. 5 (November 1972): 551.

3. Barbara Grizzuti Harrison, "On Reclaiming Moral Perspective," *Ms.*, June 1978, p. 97.

Essay 2
Very Small Fry: Arguments for Abortion

1. *Roe v. Wade*, 410 U.S. 113, 148, 163, 166 (1973); *Doe v. Bolton*, 410 U.S. 179, 197, 192, 199 (1973).

2. 410 U.S. at 143, 144.

3. American Civil Liberties Union Policy No. 247, "Abortion," adopted 25 January 1968. The policy makes clear, however, that the determinative consideration, private and unexaminable, is a woman's *choice*, not her *health*.

4. Stephen Fleck, "A Psychiatrist's Views on Abortion," in David F. Walbert and J. Douglas Butler, eds., *Abortion, Society, and the Law* (Cleveland: Case Western Reserve Press, 1973), p. 181.

5. U.S., Congress, Senate, *Abortion: Hearings on S. J. Res. 119 and S. J. Res. 130 before the Subcommittee on Constitutional Amendments of the Committee on the Judiciary*, 93rd Cong., 2nd sess. vol. 2 (1976), p. 538 (Statement of Frank Johnson).

6. R. Illsley and M. Hall, "Psychosocial Research in Abortion: Selected Issues," in Henry P. David, H. L. Friedman, Jean van der Tak, and M. J. Sevilla, eds., *Abortion in Psychosocial Perspective: Trends in Transnational Research* (New York: Springer, 1978), pp. 11–32.

7. Patricia F. Steinhoff, Roy G. Smith, and Milton Diamond, "Characteristics and Motivations of Women Receiving Abortions," in *Abortion: Hearings* (Senate) 2, pp. 736–39.

8. K. R. Niswander, "Indications and Contraindications," highlights from the 1971 AMA meeting, in *Abortion—A Legal Fact, Audio Digest: Obstetrics and Gynecology* 17 (3 August 1971); quoted in Thomas W. Hilgers and Dennis J. Horan, eds., *Abortion and Social Justice* (New York: Sheed and Ward, 1972), pp. 38–39.

9. 410 U.S. 179 at 192.

10. See Jean Pakter and Frieda Nelson, "Abortion in New York City: The First Nine Months," *Family Planning Perspectives* 3, no. 3 (July 1971): 5–12; "Changing Trends in Birth Patterns over the Last Decade in New York City," presentation at the 101st annual meeting of the American Public Health Association, San Francisco, November 4–8, 1973; J. T. Lanman, S. G. Kohl, and J. H. Bedell, "Changes in Pregnancy Outcome after Liberalization of the New York State Abortion Law," *American Journal of Obstetrics and Gynecology* 118, no. 4 (February 1974): 485–92; D. P. Swartz, "The Harlem Hospital Experience," in Howard J. Osofsky and Joy D. Osofsky, eds., *The Abortion Experience: Psychological and Medical Impact* (Hagerstown, Maryland: Harper & Row, 1973), pp. 94–121; *Population and the American Future*, Report of the Commission on Population Growth and the American Future (New York: Signet, 1972), pp. 174–75.

11. See the *New York Times*, 22 October 1971, p. 21; *Baltimore News-American*, 22 October 1971, reprinted in *Abortion: Hearings* (Senate) 1 (1974), p. 490.

12. Raymond J. Adamek, "Abortion, Personal Freedom, and Public Policy," *Family Coordinator* 23 (1974): 416.

13. For a variety of citations see Alex Barno, "Criminal Abortion Deaths, Illegitimate Pregnancy Deaths, and Suicides in Pregnancy," *American Journal of Obstetrics and Gynecology* 88, no. 3 (1 June 1967): 362, nn. 1–18.

14. *New York Times*, 29 April 1967, p. 34.

15. See Christopher Tietze, *Induced Abortion: 1979* (New York: Population Council, 1979), pp. 91–95. Nineteen abortion-related deaths were reported for 1977: 15 from legally induced abortions, 4 from those illegally induced. See *Abortion Surveillance 1977*, Center for Disease Control (September 1979), pp. 9, 62. There is still some uncertainty in reports of abortion-related maternal mortality, however. In 1975, for example, the CDC reports a total of 47 deaths from abortion, including legal (29), illegal (4), and spontaneous (14), ibid. For that same year another government agency reports 27 deaths, *Vital Statistics of the United States, 1975*, II-Mortality, Part A (National Center for Health Statistics [HEW]), pp. 1–49, 138. Tietze discusses the discrepancies of method and reporting between the agencies, but offers to resolve them by his own extrapolations.

16. Bernard Nathanson, with Richard Ostling, *Aborting America* (Garden City, New York: Doubleday, 1979), p. 193.

17. Ellen Frankfort gives a typical example of this in *Vaginal Politics* (New York: Quadrangle, 1972), pp. 72–73.

18. See Barno, pp. 356–57; *Abortion: Hearings* (Senate) 2, pp. 180–82 (Statement of Alex Barno).

19. See Christopher Tietze and Sarah Lewit, "Joint Program for the Study of Abortion: Early Medical Complications of Abortion," *Studies in Family Planning* 3, no. 6 (June 1972): 97–122; C. Tietze, Jean Pakter, and G. Berger, "Mortality with Legal

Abortion in New York City, 1970–1972," *Journal of the American Medical Association* 225, no. 5 (30 July 1973): 507–509; Henry G. Armitage, Jr., "Comments on a brief filed by certain obstetricians and gynecologists, *amici curiae* in the United States District Court for the District of Rhode Island in the case of *Jane Doe et al.*, Plaintiffs, v. *Richard Israel*, Attorney General of the State of Rhode Island," C. A. No. 5153, 1973, pp. 8–12.

20. See Thomas W. Hilgers, "The Medical Hazards of Legally Induced Abortion," reprinted in *Abortion: Hearings* (Senate) 1, pp. 491–506.

21. *Abortion: Hearings* (Senate) 2, p. 176 (Statement of Carl Tyler).

22. Matthew J. Bulfin, "A New Problem in Adolescent Gynecology," *Southern Medical Journal* 72, no. 8 (August 1979): 967–68.

23. *Hospital Record Study*, a joint publication of the Commission on Professional Hospital Activities in Ann Arbor, Michigan, and IMS America, Ltd., in Ambler, Pennsylvania (1969–1977).

24. Pamela Zekman and Pamela Warwick, "12 Dead after Abortions in State's Walk-In Clinics," *Chicago Sunday Sun-Times*, 19 November 1978, p. 1.

25. Willard Cates, Jr., in the *Washington Star*, 16 February 1978, p. A3. The CDC had predicted up to 90 additional deaths per year; it was able to discover only 4. See Roger Wilkins, "End to Medicaid Funds: A Change in the Social Landscape," *New York Times*, 11 October 1977, p. 24; Julian Gold and W. Cates, Jr., "Restriction of Federal Funds for Abortion: 18 Months Later," *American Journal of Public Health* 69, no. 9 (September 1979): 929–30.

26. See Nathanson, p. 194; Donald P. Warwick, "Foreign Aid for Abortion: Politics, Ethics, and Practice," in James T. Burtchaell, C.S.C., ed., *Abortion Parley* (Kansas City: Andrews & McMeel, 1980), pp. 299–322. In the six-month period following the cut-off of public subsidies for abortion in Illinois, Chicago's Cook County Hospital treated only one patient for infection resulting from a self-induced abortion. Mary Elson, "Time Fades 'Back-Alley' Abortion Fear," *Chicago Tribune*, 2 June 1981, p. 1.

27. Charles B. Goodhart, "Abortion Problems," *Proceedings of the Royal Institution of Great Britain* 42, no. 202 (1972): 384.

28. "Where Paternity Has No Rights," *Times* (London), 26 May 1978, p. 19.

29. "Abortion: The Doctor's Dilemma," *Modern Medicine* 35, no. 9 (24 April 1967): 14–16. See also Samuel A. Nigro, "A Scientific Critique of Abortion as a Medical Procedure," *Psychiatric Annals* 2, no. 9 (September 1972): 22–38.

30. Thomas S. Szasz, "The Ethics of Abortion," *Humanist* 26, no. 5 (September–October 1966): 148.

31. Daniel Callahan, "Abortion: Some Ethical Issues," in Walbert and Butler, p. 96.

32. 410 U.S. 179 at 192.

33. See *Abortion Surveillance 1972*, Center for Disease Control (April 1974), table 19; *Abortion: Hearings* (Senate) 2, p. 336 (Statement of Irving G. Bernstein, University of Minnesota); James H. Ford, "Mass-Produced, Assembly-Line Abortion: A Prime Example of Unethical, Unscientific Medicine," *California Medicine* 117, no. 5 (November 1972): 81.

34. "33,000 Doctors Speak Out on Abortion," *Modern Medicine* 41, no. 10 (31 May 1973): 32.

35. See "Abortion, The Doctor's Dilemma," *Modern Medicine* 35, no. 9 (24 April 1967): 12–32.

36. R. B. Sloane, "The Unwanted Pregnancy," *New England Journal of Medicine* 280, no. 22 (29 May 1969): 1201–13; D. S. Heath, "Psychiatry and Abortion," *Canadian Psychiatry Association Journal* 16 (1971): 55ff.

37. F. J. Kane and J. A. Ewing, "Therapeutic Abortion—Quo Vadimus," *Psychosomatics* 9 (1968): 202ff.; Richard E. Gordon and Katherine K. Gordon, "Social Factors in the Prediction and Treatment of Emotional Disorders of Pregnancy," *American Journal of Obstetrics and Gynecology* 77, no. 5 (May 1959): 1074–83; W. Menninger, "Emotional Factors in Pregnancy," *Bulletin of the Menninger Clinic* 7 (1943): 1ff.

38. See D. D. Youngs and J. R. Niebyl, "Adolescent Pregnancy and Abortion," *Medical Clinics of North America* 59 (1975): 1419ff.; E. Rautanen, R. L. Kantero, and P. Widholm, "Medical and Social Aspects of Pregnancy among Adolescents," *Annales Chirurgiae et Gynaecologiae* 66 (1977): 122ff.

39. Edmund C. Payne et al., "Outcome Following Therapeutic Abortion," *Archives of General Psychiatry* 33, no. 6 (June 1976): 725–33.; Virginia Abernethy, "The Abortion Constellation: Early History and Present Relationships," ibid. 29, no. 9 (1973): 346–350; idem et al., "Identification of Women at Risk for Unwanted Pregnancy," *American Journal of Psychiatry* 132, no. 10 (October 1975): 1027–31; idem, "Unwanted Pregnancy: A Psychological Profile of Women at Risk," in Burtchaell, pp. 161–72.

40. Nathan M. Simon and Audrey G. Senturia, "Psychiatric Sequelae of Abortion, Review of the Literature, 1935–1964," *Archives of General Psychiatry* 15, no. 4 (October 1966): 378–389; E. Hamill and I. M. Engram, "Psychiatric and Social Factors in the Abortion Decision," *British Medical Journal* (1974) no. 1, 229ff.; M. Clark et al., "Sequels of Unwanted Pregnancy," *Lancet* (1968) no. 2, 501ff.; C. M. B. Pare and H. Raven, "Follow-up of Patients Referred for Termination of Pregnancy," ibid. (1970) no. 1, 635ff.

41. Seymour L. Halleck, "Excuse-Makers to the Elite: Psychiatrists as Accidental Social Movers," *Medical Opinion* 7, no. 12 (December 1971): 50.

42. James H. Ford, pp. 80–84; see also Charles V. Ford, Pietro Castelnuovo-Tedesco, and Kahlila D. Long, "Abortion: Is It a Therapeutic Procedure in Psychiatry?" *Journal of the American Medical Association* 218, no. 8 (22 November 1971): 1173–78; "The Right to Abortion: A Psychiatric View," Group for the Advancement of Psychiatry, Report no. 75, 1969.

43. *Abortion: Hearings* (Senate) 2, p. 340 (Statement of Irving C. Bernstein). Professor Zigmund M. Lebensohn, a forthright advocate of abortion choice, testified that in his opinion psychiatry should, with rare exceptions, withdraw entirely from the aborting business. Ibid., pp. 357–91. In England Dr. Myre Sim stated: "If society wants abortion to be easier, it should have the courage to campaign for it honestly and not exploit the psychiatrist, who, I contend, has no factual basis for being associated with the problem." Letter to the editor, *British Medical Journal*, 26 October 1963, p. 1062; see Sim, "Abortion and the Psychiatrist," ibid., 20 July 1963, pp. 145–49, and ensuing correspondence.

44. Stephen Fleck, "Some Psychiatric Aspects of Abortion," *Journal of Nervous and Mental Disease* 151 (1970): 42ff.

45. See Zimmerman, *Passage through Abortion*, pp. 185, 199.

46. Bernstein, pp. 340, 337; see Bergt Jannson, "Mental Disorders after Abortion," *Acta Psychiatrica Scandinavica* 41 (1965): 87–110.

47. Halleck, p. 51. On the possibility of diagnosis of emotional illness being self-fulfilling, see Thomas J. Scheff, *Being Mentally Ill* (Chicago: Alding, 1966).

48. Sidney Bolter, "The Psychiatrist's Role in Therapeutic Abortion: The Unwitting Accomplice," *American Journal of Psychiatry* 119, no. 4 (October 1962): 312–16.

49. *Abortion: Hearings* (Senate) 2, p. 699 (Statement of James E. Welch).

50. Henry P. David, "Abortion in Psychological Perspective," *American Journal of Orthopsychiatry* 41, no. 1 (January 1972): 62; see Jerome Kummer, "Post-abortion

Psychiatric Illness: a Myth?" *American Journal of Psychiatry* 119, no. 10 (April 1963): 980–83.

51. For summaries of these reports, though critical of most research designs, see Simon and Senturia; G. S. Walter, "Psychologic and Emotional Consequences of Elective Abortion," *Obstetrics and Gynecology* 36 (1970): 482ff.; D. Jacobs et al., "Psychological Effects of Therapeutic Abortion," *Contemporary Obstetrics and Gynecology* 5 (1975): 81ff.; B. D. Blumberg and M. S. Golbus, "Psychological Sequelae of Elective Abortion," *Western Journal of Medicine* 123 (1975): 188ff.; C. M. Donovan, "Psychotherapy in Abortion," *Current Psychiatric Therapies* 75 (1975): 77ff.; Hamill and Engram; Pare and Raven; Frank Weston, "Psychiatric Sequelae to Legal Abortion in South Australia," *Medical Journal of Australia* 1 (17 February 1973): 350–54; Joy D. Osofsky, Howard J. Osofsky, and Renga Rajan, "Psychological Effects of Abortion: With Emphasis upon Immediate Reactions and Followup," in Osofsky and Osofsky, pp. 188–205; Robert Athanasiou et al., "Psychiatric Sequelae to Term Birth and Induced Early and Late Abortion: A Longitudinal Study," *Family Planning Perspectives* 5, no. 4 (Fall 1973): 227–31; Mary Ann Lamanna, "Science and Its Uses: The Abortion Debate and Social Science Research," in Burtchaell, pp. 101–58, esp. 121–31.

52. See, for example, Carol Byrne, "Time heals wound, but a scar remains," *Minneapolis Star*, 26 March 1980, pp. 1A, 16A; also private communications to the author from various counselors in Birthright agencies.

53. "Psychological Sequelae of Therapeutic Abortion," editorial, *British Medical Journal* (1976) no. 2, 1239ff.

54. W. C. Brennan observes various techniques of rationalization whereby abortors alleviate guilt, depression, and anxiety: denial of personal responsibility for the pregnancy; denial that the unborn is a victim, by referring to it as a piece of tissue, or characterizing it as an aggressor; portrayal of antiabortion activists as hypocritical, chauvinistic, or morally arrogant; appealing to feminist or Protestant church groups for justification. "Abortion and the Techniques of Neutralization," *Journal of Health and Social Behavior* 15 (1974): 358ff.

55. Nadine Brozan, "For One 19-year-old, a Third Abortion," *New York Times*, 19 September 1979, p. C11.

56. Lance Morrow, "Of Abortion and the Unfairness of Life," Time Essay, *Time*, 1 August 1977, p. 49.

57. Betty Benjamin, "Pro-Choice: Keep Abortion a Private Matter," guest opinion column, *Minneapolis Star*, 31 January 1980, p. 8A.

58. E. F. Lenoski, "Translating Injury Data into Preventive and Health Care Services—Physical Child Abuse," presentation at the 101st annual meeting of the American Public Health Association, San Francisco, November 5, 1973. The linkage between unplanned pregnancy and child abuse is also questioned by the Institute of Medicine report: "Legalized Abortion and the Public Health," (National Academy of Science, 1975); E. W. Pohlman, "Unwanted Contraceptions: Research on Undesirable Consequences," *Eugenics Quarterly* 14 (1967): 143–54; idem, *The Psychology of Birth Planning* (Cambridge, Mass.: Schenkman, 1969).

59. *Abortion: Hearings* (Senate) 1, p. 593 (Statement of C. Stanley Lowell, Americans United for Separation of Church and State).

60. Ibid., p. 106 (Statement of Bella Abzug).

61. Ibid. 2, p. 410 (Statement of James W. Prescott). See H. Forssman and I. Thuwe, "One Hundred and Twenty Children Born after Application for Therapeutic Abortion Refused," *Acta Psychiatrica Scandinavica* 42 (1966): 71–88.

62. *Abortion: Hearings* (Senate) 2, p. 581 (Statement of Leonard Laufe). See also the use of this study by Abzug, ibid. 1, p. 119.

63. See Lamanna. It is perhaps worth noting that Senator Bayh, in the chair when this study was being presented by Dr. Prescott on behalf of abortion freedom, asked if illegitimacy were a controlled factor in the study, and did not receive an answer. *Abortion: Hearings* (Senate) 2, pp. 432–33.

64. *Abortion: Hearings* (Senate) 2, p. 410. For another similar conclusion see Illsley and Hall. Zdeněk Dytrych, Zdeněk Matějček, Vratislav Schüller, Henry P. David, and Herbert L. Friedman, "Children Born to Women Denied Abortion," *Family Planning Perspectives* 7, no. 4 (July/August 1975): 165–71; "Children Born to Women Denied Abortion in Czechoslovakia," in Henry P. David et al., *Abortion in Psychosocial Perspective*, pp. 201–4; Z. Matějček et al., "Children from Unwanted Pregnancies," *Acta Psychiatrica Scandinavica* 57 (1978): 67–90; Z. Matějček et al., "The Prague Study of Children Born from Unwanted Pregnancies," *International Journal of Mental Health* 7 (1979): 63–77; idem, "Follow-up Study of Children Born from Unwanted Pregnancies," *International Journal of Behavioral Development* 3, no. 3 (September 1980): 243–51.

65. Matějček et al., "The Prague Study," p. 75.

66. Matějček et al., "Follow-Up Study," pp. 244, 250.

67. Lamanna, pp. 136–37.

68. Sidney Bolter, p. 315; see also *Abortion: Hearings* (Senate) 2, pp. 391–93 (Statement of Samuel Nigro, Case Western Reserve University).

69. Matějček et al., "The Prague Study," p. 75.

70. David L. Kruegel, "The Validity of Retrospective Reports of Unwanted Births in the United States: Effects of Preference for Children of a Given Sex," *Studies in Family Planning* 6, no. 9 (September 1975): 345–48.

71. E. W. Pohlman, "Change from Rejection to Acceptance of Pregnancy," *Social Science and Medicine* 2 (1968): 337–40.

72. Norman B. Ryder and Charles F. Westoff, *Reproduction in the United States: 1965* (Princeton: Princeton University Press, 1971), pp. 92–93. See also two preliminary reports by Larry Bumpass and Westoff: "The Perfect Contraceptive Population," *Science* 169, no. 3951 (18 September 1970): 1177—82; "Unwanted Births and U.S. Population Growth," *Family Planning Perspectives* 2, no. 4 (October 1970): 9–11. The project, based on the 1965 National Fertility Study, reports on women living with their husbands. Westoff was serving as executive director of the Commission on Population Growth and the American Future, John D. Rockefeller III, chairman, which endorsed abortion on demand.

Desirable, or "ideal," family size seems generally to expand with experience. A Gallup Poll published 4 February 1973 had asked: "What do you think is the ideal number of children for a family to have?" Larger family size (four or more children) was indicated by 12 percent of respondents younger than 30, but nearly twice that proportion of those aged 30–49, 22 percent, chose the larger size.

73. Bumpass and Westoff, "Unwanted Births," p. 10.

74. Charles F. Westoff, "Women's Reactions to Pregnancy," *Family Planning Perspectives* 12, no. 3 (May / June 1980): 135–39. Westoff here describes their more recent and modified categories: "A pregnancy is classified as planned if it was conceived intentionally; unplanned but wanted if the couple wanted a child but conceived it earlier than desired (a timing failure); and unwanted if the pregnancy occurred after the couple had had all the children they wanted. This is the typology most commonly used by demographers conducting fertility surveys. The distinctions made between these concepts are admittedly crude, and imply an unrealistic model of couples behaving with fixed reproductive goals" (p. 136).

75. Planned Parenthood Federation of America, Inc., Annual Report 1979, p. 8.

76. Thus Lawrence Lader of the National Abortion Rights Action League conjec-

tures that "a minimum of 550,000 unwanted births" occur each year in this country. *Abortion II: Making the Revolution* (Boston: Beacon, 1973), p. 20.

77. Philip G. Ney, "Is elective abortion a cause of child abuse?" *Sexual Medicine Today* 4, no. 6 (June 1980): 31. See also, by Ney, "Relationship between Abortion and Child Abuse," *Canadian Journal of Psychiatry* 24, no. 7 (November 1979): 610–20; for dissent from his hypothesis, see W. W. Watters, "Mental Health Consequences of Abortion and Refused Abortion," ibid. 25, no. 1 (February 1980): 68–73.

78. *South Bend Tribune* (Indiana), 6 August 1977.

79. Quoted in National Abortion Rights Action League *Newsletter* 11, no. 5 (July 1979): 1.

80. See Victor Cohn, "Fetuses Aborted to Prevent Child of 'Wrong Sex,' " *Washington Post*, 6 September 1979, pp. A1, A5.

81. John C. Fletcher, "Ethics and Amniocentesis for Fetal Sex Identification," Sounding Board, *New England Journal of Medicine* 301, no. 10 (6 September 1979): 551.

82. Excerpts from correspondence quoted in *National Right to Life News* 5, no. 10 (October 1978): 2.

83. Sidney Callahan, "Talk of 'Wanted Child' Makes for Doll Objects," *National Catholic Reporter*, 3 December 1971, p. 7.

84. Charles V. Ford, Pietro Castelnuovo-Tedesco and Kahlila D. Long, "Women Who Seek Therapeutic Abortion: A Comparison with Women Who Complete Their Pregnancies," *American Journal of Psychiatry* 129, no. 5 (November 1972): 551.

85. Judith G. Smetana, p. 304.

86. Ray E. Helfer, *Diagnostic Process and Treatment Programs* (National Center for Child Abuse and Neglect, 1975 [DHEW Publication OHD 75-69]), p. 28.

87. C. Henry Kempe, "Pediatric Implications of the Battered Baby Syndrome," *Archives of Disease in Childhood* 46 (1971): 30.

88. Brandt F. Steele, "Psychology of Infanticide Resulting from Maltreatment," in Marvin Kohl, ed., *Infanticide and the Value of Life* (Buffalo: Prometheus, 1978), p. 76.

89. 410 U.S. at 156, 157 (1973).

90. Alan Frank Guttmacher, *Life in the Making: The Story of Human Procreation* (New York: Viking, 1933), p. 55.

91. See pp. 155, 175, 176, 180, 188. In reference to a woman who brought 22 children to birth and lost 20 to miscarriage, he says: "In fifteen pregnancies she had a total of 42 children," p. 237.

92. Alan Frank Guttmacher, "Abortion—Yesterday, Today and Tomorrow," in idem, ed., *The Case for Legalized Abortion Now* (Berkeley, California: Diablo, 1967), pp. 1–14.

93. Nathanson, *Aborting America*, pp. 216–17.

94. This is very competently argued by James J. Diamond, "Abortion, Animation, and Biological Hominization," *Theological Studies* 36, no. 2 (June 1975): 305–24.

95. Cyril C. Means, Jr., "The Law of New York Concerning Abortion and the Status of the Foetus, 1664–1968: A Case of the Cessation of Constitutionality," *New York Law Forum* 14, no. 3 (Fall 1968): 411–515; "The Phoenix of Abortional Freedom: Is a Penumbral Ninth-Amendment Right About to Arise from the Ashes of a Fourteenth-Century Common-Law Liberty?" ibid. 17, no. 2 (1971): 335–410.

96. Sissela Bok, "Fetal Research and the Value of Life," in *Research on the Fetus:* Report and Recommendations of the National Commission for the Protection of Human Subjects of Biomedical and Behavioral Research (U.S. Department of Health, Education, and Welfare Publication No. [OS] 76–128, 1975), Appendix, p. 2–7.

97. See *Byrn* v. *New York City Health & Hospitals Corporation*, Brief in

opposition to motions to dismiss appeal, U.S. Supreme Court No. 72-434 (1972); Robert M. Byrn, "Goodbye to the Judeo-Christian Era in Law,"*America* 128, no. 21 (2 June 1973): 511–14; Joseph W. Dellapenna, "The History of Abortion: Technology, Morality, and Law," *University of Pittsburgh Law Review* 40, no. 3 (Spring 1979): 359–428.

98. 410 U.S. 113 at 163 (1973).

99. See Edward A. Langerak, "Abortion: Listening to the Middle," *Hastings Center Report* 9, no. 5 (October 1979): 24–28. Langerak's argument incorporates several "magic moments," but presumes personhood to be represented by adults. See also Laurence Tribe, "The Supreme Court, 1972 Term. Foreword: Toward a Model of Roles in the Due Process of Life and Death," *Harvard Law Review* 87, no. 1 (November 1973): 20–51. Says Tribe: "The only bodies of thought that have purported in this century to locate the crucial line between potential and actual life have been those of organized religious doctrine" (p. 20).

100. See *Abortion: Hearings* (Senate) 1, p. 420 (Statement of Senator Dewey Bartlett).

101. Garrett Hardin, "The History and Future of Birth Control," *Perspectives in Biology and Medicine* 10, no. 1 (Autumn 1966): 12–13.

102. Natalie Shainess, quoted in *Abortion in a Changing World,* Robert E. Hall, ed., 2 vols. (New York: Columbia University Press, 1970), 1: 175.

103. George W. Corner, "An Embryologist's View," ibid., pp. 13–14.

104. See *Abortion: Hearings* (Senate) 1, p. 581 (Statement of Michael M. Levi, obstetrician-gynecologist).

105. Mary Anne Warren, "Can the Fetus be an Organ Farm?" *Hastings Center Report* 8, no. 5 (October 1978): 23.

106. *Abortion: Hearings* (Senate) 1, p. 596 (Statement of Reverend Kenneth E. Grant).

107. Joshua Lederberg, "A Geneticist Looks at Contraception and Abortion," *Annals of Internal Medicine* 67, no. 3, pt. 2 (September 1967): 23–27.

108. Roger Wertheimer, "Understanding the Abortion Argument," *Philosophy and Public Affairs* 1, no. 1 (Fall 1971): 69.

109. Ibid., p. 83.

110. Quoted by Carol Byrne, "Nice children, nice families . . . pregnancy," *Minneapolis Star,* 27 March 1980, p. 5A.

111. Joseph Fletcher, quoted in Hall, *Abortion in a Changing World,* 1:56.

112. Howard I. Diamond, quoted in Norma Rosen, "Between Guilt and Gratification: Abortion Doctors Reveal Their Feelings," *New York Times Magazine,* 17 April 1977, p. 75.

113. "Abortion Error," editorial, *New York Times,* 19 February 1975, p. 34; "Love for Sale," ibid., 2 April 1981, p. A26.

114. Quoted by Sheba Emerson, letter to the editor, *Village Voice,* February 25–March 3, 1981, p. 25. Usages in the *New York Times* show that denial of human status to the unborn occurs when that unborn is unwanted. In June 1981 the *Times* reported the story of a woman pregnant with twins, one of whom had a congenital handicap. Doctors successfully perforated its heart, drained its blood, and killed it. One month later it carried the story of another woman pregnant with twins, one of whom had a urinary blockage. Doctors successfully perforated its bladder, drained its urine, and saved it. The first story described the unborn exclusively as a "fetus." The second referred to "an unborn child," a "fetus," a "baby" (unborn), a "girl" (also unborn). Both operations were deemed "successful." 18 June 1981, p. A1; 27 July 1981, p. D8; 28 July 1981, p. C3; 2 August 1981, p. 21EY.

115. Isaac Asimov, "Coming of Age," foreword, in Jerry Grey, *Enterprise* (New York: Morrow, 1979), p. 7.

116. *New York Times*, 2 June 1977, p. A5. President Carter, when he signed this as a treaty, was expected to ask the Senate to "reserve" this portion from its ratification.

117. H. Tristram Englehardt, Jr., "The Beginnings of Personhood: Philosophical Considerations," *Perkins Journal* (Southern Methodist University Divinity School) 27, no. 1 (Fall 1973): 20–27, quotes at pp. 22, 23; "Viability, Abortion and the Difference Between a Fetus and an Infant," *American Journal of Obstetrics and Gynecology* 116, no. 3 (1 June 1973): 429–34, quotes at p. 432.

118. The Swedish photographer whose images of the unborn have been most widely displayed testifies to this. " 'I get mail from all over the world, enormous amounts of mail. . . . Letters from mothers who send along a photo of a small child, and somehow let it be known that if it weren't for my pictures the baby would have been aborted. It's a tremendous satisfaction.' " Lisbet Nilson, "Profile: Lennart Nilsson," *American Photographer* 5, no. 2 (August 1980): 36.

119. *Abortion in the United States*, A Conference Sponsored by the Planned Parenthood Federation of America, Inc., at Arden House and the New York Academy of Medicine, Mary Steichen Calderone, ed. (New York: Hoeber-Harper, 1958), p. 180. Individual conjectures occur on pp. 164, 171. Alfred Kinsey died in 1956. When published posthumously his study offered no conjectures as to the incidence of criminal abortion nationwide; see Paul H. Gebhard, Wardell B. Pomeroy, Clyde E. Martin and Cornelia V. Christenson, *Pregnancy, Birth and Abortion* (New York: Hoeber-Harper, 1958).

120. Lawrence Lader, *Abortion* (Indianapolis: Bobbs-Merrill, 1966), p. 2.

121. Christopher Tietze, "Induced Abortion and Sterilization as Methods of Fertility Control," in Mindel C. Sheps and Jeanne Clare Ridley, eds., *Public Health and Population Change*, Papers from a 1964 Symposium at the University of Pittsburgh (Pittsburgh University Press, 1965), pp. 400–401.

122. Harold Rosen, *Therapeutic Abortion* (New York: Julian, 1954). Fisher's guess is on p. 6; on p. 219 Rosen refers to it as Fisher's conjecture; by p. 267 he is referring to it as a fact. In a conclusion added to his 1967 edition, Rosen, drawing on Bates and Zawadski, who in turn draw on the Kinsey study and on Taussig, Kopp, and Stix, all obsolete works from the 1930s, suspects that the number may be 90,000 or 750,000, or 1,000,000; *Abortion in America* (Boston: Beacon, 1967), p. 299. Bates and Zawadski note that an accurate statistic is unattainable: "We feel, however, that it is important to select a fairly conservative, commonly agreed upon, although admittedly rough figure, and stay with it." Jerome E. Bates and Edward S. Zawadski, *Criminal Abortion: A Study in Medical Sociology* (Springfield: C. C. Thomas, 1964), p. 3.

123. Lader, *Abortion II*, pp. 20, 29.

124. *Abortion: Hearings* (Senate) 1, pp. 102, 129, 445, 543, 595, 611; 2, p. 571.

125. "Facts About Medicaid Funds For Abortion," Planned Parenthood of New York, 4 March 1981. By contrast, there have been some serious attempts, on a local basis, to ascertain the true frequency of abortion. In Virginia in 1967, for example, a survey of physicians in the state revealed that they had been contacted 10,244 times by persons seeking an abortion, and that in 3,952 cases they had seen evidence of an attempted or completed abortion (an average of less than one abortion per registered physician). See R. W. Jessee and Frederick J. Spencer, "Abortion—The Hidden Epidemic," *Virginia Medical Monthly* 95 (1968): 447–56.

126. *Abortion: Hearings* (Senate) 2, p. 2.

127. Henry P. David, "Abortion: Public Health Concerns and Needed Psychosocial Research," *American Journal of Public Health* 61, no. 3 (March 1971): 510.

128. Charles B. Goodhart, "The Frequency of Illegal Abortion," *Eugenics Review* 55, no. 4 (January 1964): 200; see also his "Estimation of Illegal Abortions," *Journal of Biosocial Science* 1 (1969): 235ff.; "Abortion Problems"; for an alternative reading of British evidence see William H. James, "The Incidence of Illegal Abortion," *Population Studies* (London) 25, no. 2 (July 1971): 327–39.

129. National Center for Health Statistics: Vital Statistics of the U.S., 1969, II, b, 7-124, table 7-5; Summary Report, Final Mortality Statistics, 1970, XXII, 11 (Supplement, 22 February 1974), 6, table 3; Monthly Vital Statistics Report, 1971 Summary Report, Final Mortality Statistics, XXIII, 3 (Supplement, 24 May 1974), 6, table 3.

130. Lader, *Abortion*, p. 3. Lader was not the only proabortionist to give these figures wide circulation. See, for example, Jerome Kummer and Zad Leavy, "Therapeutic Abortion Law Confusion," *Journal of the American Medical Association* 195, no. 2 (10 January 1966): 140–44, who allege more than 1 million abortions annually, and "the tragic wastage of more than 5,000 deaths per year, mostly mothers of young children."

131. Lader cites Ruth Roemer, "Due Process and Organized Health Services," *Public Health Reports* 79, no. 8 (August 1964): 664–72, which in turn depends on Don Harper Mills, "A Medicolegal Analysis of Abortion Statutes," Comment, *Southern California Law Review* 31 (February 1958): 181–99, esp. 182.

132. Tietze does take this occasion to repeat, however, that the Kinsey research sample women "do not constitute a representative sample of the population of the United States." Christopher Tietze and Clyde E. Martin, "Foetal Deaths, Spontaneous and Induced, in the Urban White Population of the United States," *Population Studies* (London) 11, no. 2 (November 1957): 170–76.

133. Reports then indicated that about 100 black women died annually from abortion. Of Dr. Laufe, Sen. Bayh inquired, "Where do you get that 3,000?" Dr. Laufe: "That is an actual data [*sic*] published by Planned Parenthood World Federation." Sen. Bayh: "Well, it has not reached the National Institutes of Health or the Public Health Service yet." See *Abortion: Hearings* (Senate) 2, p. 577; 1, pp. 103, 543, 595, 611.

134. Ibid. 2, p. 543.

135. Christopher Tietze, "Two Years' Experience with a Liberal Abortion Law: Its Impact on Fertility Trends in New York City," *Family Planning Perspectives* 5, no. 1 (Winter 1973): 36–41; "The Effect of Legalization of Abortion on Population Growth and Public Health," ibid. 7, no. 3 (May / June 1975): 123–27; *Abortion: Hearings* (Senate) 2, pp. 1–105.

136. Idem, "Effect of Legalization," p. 123.

137. Raymond Adamek has also noticed that Tietze's thesis on this matter is "rather speculative." "Abortion Policy: Time for Reassessment," in Burtchaell, p. 21.

138. Lance Morrow, "Of Abortion and the Unfairness of Life," p. 49.

139. *Harris* v. *McRae*, 448 U.S. 297, 338 (1980) (Marshall, J., dissenting).

140. See Gebhard et al., pp. 193–94.

141. James Trussell, Jane Menken, Barbara L. Lindheim and Barbara Vaughan, "The Impact of Restricting Medicaid Financing for Abortion," *Family Planning Perspectives* 12, no. 3 (May / June 1980): 120–30. The conclusion of this study raises one question of method. "The goal of our study was to estimate the minimum number of pregnant Medicaid-eligible women who would have obtained abortions in the absence of the Hyde Amendment and to compare this figure with the actual number of abortion recipients. The difference reflects the consequent number of unwanted births that occurred because of the Medicaid restrictions." There are two assumptions here: that the 20 percent of women who did not receive an abortion still actually wanted one but could not afford it; and that when their pregnancy came to term they delivered a

child whom they then did not want. Both assumptions should be treated cautiously. Regarding the first; no desire for a paid service is stable regardless of its cost, for cost has a dynamic interplay with demand. A newly available subsidized service will be desired by some persons who had not previously sought or desired it; when the subsidy is withdrawn some persons will decide that, not only is the service not worth paying for themselves, but they do not wish it at all. The study therefore must be careful when it assumes that after Medicaid was withdrawn the same number of Medicaid-eligible women continued to desire an abortion. Regarding the second assumption: as was noted earlier in this essay (about an earlier Princeton project), one cannot safely conclude that an unfulfilled desire for abortion early in pregnancy invariably leads to an undesired birth at term. See also Willard Cates, Jr., "The Hyde Amendment in Action," *Journal of The American Medical Association* 246, no. 10 (4 September 1981): 1109–1112.

142. Karen Mulhauser, Director's Report, NARAL *Newsletter* 11, no. 6 (August 1979): 3.

143. Idem, NARAL fundraising letter, July 1979.

144. Planned Parenthood Federation of America, *Annual Report* 1979, p. 5.

145. *Abortion: Hearings* (Senate) 1, p. 127 (Statement of Arlie Schardt).

146. Beverly Harrison, "Continuing the Discussion: How to Argue About Abortion: II," *Christianity and Crisis* 37, no. 21 (26 December 1977): 312.

147. Ellie Smeal, NOW recruitment letter, undated.

148. Harris Surveys, July 1977. CBS News / New York Times Polls that same year also reflected a lack of public support for funded abortion, even when the question was appealingly framed. July 1977: "Do you think the government should or should not help a poor woman with her medical bills if she wants an abortion?" Should: 38 percent; should not: 55 percent; no opinion: 7 percent. October 1977: "Do you think the government should or should not help a poor woman with her bills if she wants an abortion?" Should: 47 percent; should not: 44 percent; no opinion: 9 percent. The National Fertility Study had found opinion on government-funded abortion ("Are you in favor of a law which permits a woman to have an abortion even if it has to be at government expense?") to be negative in 1970 (66 percent against), and the Gallup Poll in 1975 showed 57 percent opposed. See "Public Opinion Polls on Abortion Issues 1977–1978," The NARAL Foundation (undated).

149. *Abortion: Hearings* (Senate) 1, p. 553 (Testimony of Congressman Ronald V. Dellums).

150. Jean Henniger, "Abortion: Is It Still an Issue?" *Northwest Magazine, Portland Oregonian*, 28 October 1979, p. NW11.

151. *Times-Picayune* (New Orleans), 22 November 1979, sect. 7, p. 2. For a collection of generally poor surveys see a résumé of 93 congressional polls in *Abortion: Hearings* (Senate) 4 (1976), pp. 14–27 (Statement of NARAL).

152. The full text of the Harris question was as follows:

> In 1973, the U.S. Supreme Court decided that state laws which made it illegal for a woman to have an abortion up to three months of pregnancy were unconstitutional, and that the decision on whether a woman should have an abortion up to three months of pregnancy should be left up to the woman and her doctor to decide. In general, do you favor or oppose the U.S. Supreme Court decision making abortions up to three months of pregnancy legal?

Raymond J. Adamek has already noted that "because it narrowly focuses on the first trimester of pregnancy, the Harris question is an invalid measure of public opinion of the Supreme Court's abortion ruling [the Court had legalized abortion on demand throughout the entire course of pregnancy]." "Abortion Polls," comments and letters, *Public Opinion Quarterly* 42, no. 3 (Fall 1978): 413; for a more extensive critique see his "On the Validity of the Harris Poll's Supreme Court Abortion Decision Questions," a paper presented at the annual meeting of the Midwest Association of Public Opinion Research, October 1978, Chicago, Illinois. Adamek shows that the Harris organization has over the years consistently misstated the 1973 decisions as restricted to the first trimester of pregnancy. The Gallup Poll asked for opinion on a "first-trimester" law in 1969, 1972, and 1974 then discontinued the faulty question, only to reinstate it in 1981. As late as 1979 Harris continued in his misunderstanding: "A substantial 60 to 37 per cent majority of Americans supports the U.S. Supreme Court decision that legalizes abortions performed during the first three months of pregnancy." "Support of Abortions Growing," *Chicago Tribune*, 12 March 1979, sect. 4, p. 3.

After a mistaken question has been repeated so often (1973, 1975, 1976, 1979) one is tempted to think that it represents more than a misunderstanding; at the very least it is professionally incompetent. Abortion advocates who use the Harris results, however, labor under no such misunderstanding of the Court's meaning. Polls like Harris may be playing a part in perpetuating a widespread ignorance of the scope of the law.

In 1975 Judith Blake cast doubt on polls which asked whether the public favored the 1973 abortion decisions: "less than half of American adult respondents were informed about them." "The Supreme Court's Abortion Decisions and Public Opinion in the United States," *Population and Development Review* 3, nos. 1–2 (March / June 1977): 57–59. Indeed, the literature shows a variety of misunderstanding and misstatement about the law. Among the erroneous notions and those who state them:

First Three Months

(1) *Beverly Harrison,* Union Theological Seminary: "The Court . . . limited the option of free choice to the first trimester of pregnancy." "Continuing the Discussion," p. 312.

(2) *The New York Times:* "The Supreme Court ruled 7 to 2 in 1973 that abortions in the first three months of pregnancy were legal and are between a woman and her physician." John Herbers, "Anti-Abortionists' Impact Is Felt in Elections across the Nation," *New York Times,* 20 June 1978, pp. A1, B10.

(3) *Roger M. Williams,* senior editor of *Saturday Review,* discussed "the Supreme Court ruling that gave women an absolute right to have an abortion during the first three months of pregnancy and that severely limited state intervention through the sixth month." "The Power of Fetal Politics," *Saturday Review,* 9 June 1979, p. 12. State intervention through the sixth (and ninth) month cannot inhibit the freedom of a woman to *have* an abortion; it can only require that her own health be safeguarded while having it.

(4) *The Court of Appeal of the State of California:* "The nation's high court determined that parents have a constitutionally protected right to obtain an abortion during the first trimester of pregnancy, free of state interference." *Curlender* v. *Bio-Science Laboratories,* 2 Civ. No. 58192, slip opinion p. 13 (11 June 1980). It is mothers, not parents, who are awarded a right.

(5) *Senator Floyd K. Haskell* of Colorado: "The States are given the authority to determine whether or not abortions are to be available for the stage subsequent to approximately the end of the first trimester." *Abortion: Hearings* (Senate) 1, p. 563.

(6) *President Jimmy Carter:* "The Supreme Court has drawn a line between the first three months of pregnancy, as you know, when abortions are permitted, and the other roughly six months of pregnancy when very tight constraints are placed on the right to have abortions. That is an arbitrary line that is drawn and as President I support the ruling and will enforce it to the best of my ability." Statement at a "town meeting" in Yazoo City, Mississippi, 21 July 1977; see *National Right to Life News* 4, no. 9 (September 1977): 1, 4.

First Six Months

(1) *Reverend Elinor Yeo*, of the Religious Coalition for Abortion Rights: "The Supreme Court handed down its historic decision stating (in simplest terms) that during the first two trimesters of pregnancy the abortion decision is a private one, to be made by individual women or couples and the physicians with whom they take counsel." *Abortion: A Painful Decision* (Washington, D.C.: Religious Coalition for Abortion Rights, 1977), introduction.

(2) *New Republic*: "The Supreme Court found in the Constitution a detailed abortion law that divides pregnancy into 'trimesters' and permits abortions virtually without restrictions in the first two." "The Unborn and the Born Again," editorial, 2 July 1977, p. 5.

(3) *Seth Mydans*, reporter at the trial of Kenneth Edelin (for manslaughter of an infant survivor of abortion): "The court barred states from interfering with a woman's right to an abortion before a fetus became viable." "When Is an Abortion Not an Abortion," *Atlantic Monthly*, May 1975, pp. 72–73.

(4) *New York Post*: "The Supreme Court ruled it permissible up to 24 weeks." Barbara Ross, "Abortion II," 14 February 1979, p. 18.

153. Mulhauser, Director's Report, NARAL *Newsletter* 11, no. 4 (May-June 1979): 3; see also Leslie Bennets, "For Pro-Abortion Group, an 'Aggressive New Campaign,'" *New York Times*, 1 May 1979, p. C22.

154. Lader, "Abortion Opponents' Tactics," column, *New York Times*, 11 January 1978, p. 27.

155. *Constitutional Aspects of the Right to Limit Childbearing*, A Report of the United States Commission on Civil Rights, April 1975, pp. 81–82. The report, written by Mary Berry, slightly alters Gallup's figures, which were actually 51 percent–49 percent.

156. *Abortion: Hearings* (Senate) 1, p. 429.

157. George Vecsey, "Catholics in Survey Endorse Abortion," *New York Times*, 11 November 1979, p. 43; "Public Likes Carter, Survey Finds, More for His Style Than Programs," ibid., 29 July 1977, pp. A1, A22.

158. Louis Harris, "Support of Abortions Growing," *Chicago Tribune*, 12 March 1979, sect. 4, p. 3.

159. These figures combine respondents who said abortion should be illegal always and those who said it should be legal only under certain circumstances.

160. See Judith Blake, "The Supreme Court's Abortion Decisions," pp. 55–57; Peter Skerry, "The Class Conflict over Abortion," *The Public Interest*, no. 52 (Summer 1978), p. 72.

161. Quoted in Enid Nemy, "Conference Scrutinizes 'New Right,'" *New York Times*, 15 September 1980, p. B14.

162. Benjamin, "Pro-Choice," pp. 8A–9A.

163. Judith Blake, "The Supreme Court's Abortion Decisions"; also "The Abortion Decisions: Judicial Review and Public Opinion," in Edward Manier, William Liu, and David Solomon, eds., *Abortion: New Directions for Policy Studies* (Notre Dame: University of Notre Dame Press, 1977), pp. 51–82. The *Redbook* study, after noting that 49 percent of its respondents considered the unborn to be human from conception onwards, 16 percent from the time of quickening, 14 percent from the time of viability and only 12 percent from the moment of birth, dismisses these opinions as theological supposition, digresses about Martin Buber's and Augustine's views about potential humanity and concludes with relief that, in any case, their respondents were not letting their decisions be governed by their prevailing belief that the unborn is a fellow human, for many were still ready to abort. The remainder of the *Redbook* treatment is of similar seriousness.

For other astute comment on opinion surveys see Theodore C. Wagenaar and Ingeborg W. Knol "Attitudes toward Abortion: A Comparative Analysis of Correlates for 1973 and 1975," *Journal of Sociology and Social Welfare* 4, no. 6 (July 1977): 927–44; R. Sauer, "Attitudes to Abortion in America, 1800–1973," *Population Studies* (London) 28, no. 1 (March 1974): 53–67. See also Joseph Tanenhaus and Walter F. Murphy, "Patterns of Public Support for the Supreme Court: A Panel Study," *Journal of Politics* 43 (1981): 24–39, esp. pp. 32–33.

164. *Harris* v. *McRae*, 448 U.S. at 332 (1980), (Brennan, J., dissenting, with whom Marshall and Blackmun, JJ., join); *Id.* at 348, (Blackmun, J., dissenting). It should be noted again here that the issue of who is in the majority and who in the minority has nothing to do with which position is moral or which constitutional. But these admissions by the two chief crafters of *Wade* and *Bolton*, that the 1980 Congress, not the 1973 Court, was expressing a "majoritarian viewpoint," rectify a long misunderstanding.

In addition it ought to be remembered that this pattern of majoritarian rejection of abortion for elective reasons had a long and consistent showing in the surveys. For example, in 1967 *Modern Medicine* conducted a nationwide poll of physicians on whether abortion laws ought to be liberalized. Forty thousand responded, 80 percent affirmatively (psychiatrists were most affirmative; obstetrician-gynecologists, least). But for elective abortion there was very low support: for illegitimacy, 29 percent; socioeconomic reasons, 27 percent; abortion on demand, 14 percent. "Abortion, the Doctor's Dilemma," *Modern Medicine* 35, no. 9 (24 April 1967): 12–32.

165. Quoted by Roger Williams, p. 12.

166. Quoted in David E. Rosenbaum, "Mrs. Harris Favors More Sex Education," *New York Times*, 14 December 1980, p. 31.

167. Linda Greenhouse, " 'Minimal Scrutiny' Leads to a Foreseeable Decision," *New York Times*, 6 July 1980, p. 4E.

168. Maria G. Perez-Reyes and Ruth Falk, "Follow-Up after Therapeutic Abortion in Early Adolescence," *Archives of General Psychiatry* 28, no. 1 (January 1973): 123. It should be noted that the women studied had had elective abortions; they are called therapeutic only because under prevailing North Carolina law a medical reason had to be alleged.

169. Zimmerman, *Passage through Abortion*, pp. 202–3.

170. Yokichi Hayasaka et al., "Japan's 22 Year Experience with a Liberal Abortion Law," in *Abortion: Hearings* (Senate) 2, pp. 677–78.

171. An example: in 1974 Ms. Abzug testified that "there has always been strong support for the view that life does not begin until live birth," ibid. 1, p. 107. Her sentence replicates, word for word, the Supreme Court opinion in *Wade*, 410 U.S. at 160 (1973). However, as Blake observes, the opinion polls had consistently revealed that only one-fifth of American adults hold this view. "Most men and women place both 'human life' and personhood early in the gestational process, and this public definition of the situation may be important in coloring attitudes toward the timing of abortion. Moreover, it is a view that is both at odds with that of the Supreme Court and at variance with what the Court believed public opinion to be." "The Supreme Court's Abortion Decision," p. 54.

172. Some who are personally opposed to abortion, like Mary Segers of Rutgers, and some who hold no principled view but vaguely deplore it, like Daniel Callahan of the Hastings Center, suggest that prolife organizations ought to abandon their push for any political solution, especially through constitutional amendment. They seem not to appreciate that the prolife organizations have quietly taken on a dual function. They continue to argue, on behalf of a small but determined clientele, that abortion is the extermination of human innocents. This is a moral message, and whatever its eventual

persuasiveness and political effect, it is a conviction that has the right to raise its voice. But most (though not all) of these same organizations also serve to orchestrate the much larger body of sentiment that rejects the abortion law fashioned by the Court. This is a lobby that is both moral and political, is majoritarian, and can readily be seen in the fact that many of the proposed "right to life" amendments are designed, not to impose a federal ban on abortion, but simply to remove the federal restraint which blocks the states from governance in the matter. Here the prolife organizations represent a dual constituency—abortion opponents plus the swing-group in the center—and what appears to be a weighty momentum. As the law now stands, all positions except that of abortion on demand are in opposition to the present law, and could be rallied into an imposing coalition. In a sense, the political situation is the exact reverse of what obtained twenty years ago, when the swing-group was successfully courted by abortion advocates in a movement that went considerably beyond what the swing-group really was willing to endorse. See Mary C. Segers, "Abortion Politics and Policy: Is There a Middle Ground?" *Christianity and Crisis* 40, no. 2 (18 February 1980): 21–27; Daniel Callahan, "Abortion and Government Policy," *Family Planning Perspectives* 2, no. 5 (September / October 1979): 275–79; *Abortion: Hearings* (Senate) 4, pp. vii–viii (Senate Joint Resolutions); U.S., Cong., House, *Abortion: Hearings before the Subcommittee on Civil and Constitutional Rights of the Committee on the Judiciary*, 94th Cong., 2nd sess., 1 (1976), pp. 517–639 (House Joint Resolutions).

173. *McRae* v. *Califano*, Brief of the American Jewish Congress, amici curiae, Leo Pfeffer, counsel, p. 6.

174. John M. Swomley, Jr., "Theology and Politics," *Church and State*, November 1976, reprinted by the Religious Coalition for Abortion Rights, with permission of Americans United for Separation of Church and State, pp. 1, 3. Swomley also sees Catholic influence as strong in the past. "It seems clear that one of the chief reasons existing abortion laws have remained on the statute books is the religious teaching of the Roman Catholic Church." "Abortion and Civil Liberty," *Abortion: Hearings* (Senate) 1, p. 683. In addition to his caricature of Catholic teaching, Swomley presents a blurred view of American legal history, which has always dealt with the unborn (albeit inconsistently) as possessed of standing before the law.

175. Frederick S. Jaffe, "Enacting Religious Beliefs in a Pluralistic Society," *Hastings Center Report* 8, no. 4 (August 1978): 15. Jaffe was acknowledged as chief advisor to attorneys who signed the plaintiff's First Amendment brief in *McRae*. His erstwhile colleague at the AGI, Barbara L. Lindheim, has said: "Without the institutional backing of the Catholic Church, the pro-life movement would be a less visible force." *Newsweek*, 5 June 1978, p. 39. For a particularly biased, anti-Catholic treatment, see Jaffe, Lindheim, and Philip R. Lee, *Abortion Politics: Private Morality and Public Policy* (New York: McGraw-Hill, 1981).

176. Quoted in Skerry, p. 74.

177. Henninger, p. NW12.

178. See Nadine Brozan, "Two Fundamentalists Crusade Against Abortion in 20 Cities," *New York Times*, 29 September 1979, p. 46. See also Koop, *The Right to Live, the Right to Die* (Wheaton, Illinois: Tyndale House, 1976).

179. See *Abortion: Hearings* (Senate) 1, pp. 350–58 (Statement of Paul Ramsey); Ramsey, *Ethics at the Edges of Life*, Bampton Lectures in America (New Haven: Yale University Press, 1978); Stanley Hauerwas, "Abortion: Why the Arguments Fail," in Burtchaell, pp. 325–52; Richard John Neuhaus, "Hyde and Hysteria," *Christian Century* 97, no. 28 (10–17 September 1980): 849–50; John Strietelmeier, "Legalized Homicide," editor at large, *Cresset* (Valparaiso University), April 1973. Baruch Brody, "Is Abortion a Religious Issue? Religious, Moral and Sociological Issues: Some Basic Distinctions," *Hastings Center Report* 8, no. 4 (August 1978): 13–16; *Abortion: Hear-*

ings (Senate) 1, pp. 288–318 (Statement of David Bleich); Hadley Arkes, "On the Public Funding of Abortions," in Burtchaell, pp. 239–64; Harold O. J. Brown, "What the Supreme Court Didn't Know," *Human Life Review* 1 (Spring 1975): 5–21; "Abortion: Rights or Technicalities?" ibid. (Summer 1975): 60–74; "Fetal Research II: The Ethical Question," ibid. (Fall 1975): 118–28; "An Evangelical Looks at the Abortion Phenomenon," *America* 135, no. 8 (25 September 1978): 161–64; Stephen R. Valentine, *All Shall Live! Another Quaker Response to the Abortion Dilemma* (Richmond, Indiana: Friends United Press, 1980).

180. C. Eric Lincoln, "Why I Reversed My Stand on Laissez-Faire Abortion," *Christian Century* 90, no. 17 (27 April 1973): 477–78.

181. *McRae* v. *Califano*, Post-Trial Memorandum on the Religious Claims of Intervenor-Defendant Isabel Pernicone, p. 37.

182. Quoted by Jim Castelli, "Sen. Buckley Hits Rights Commission Abortion Report," NC News Service release, 17 April 1975.

183. Richard Schweiker, letter to the editor, *New York Times*, 8 February 1978, in response to Lawrence Lader, "Abortion Opponents' Tactics," ibid., 11 January 1978, p. 27.

184. "A Call to Concern," advertisement, *Christianity and Crisis* 37, no. 14 (3 October 1977): 222–24; *Christian Century* 94, no. 32 (12 October 1977): 912–14.

185. John Bennett, "How to Argue About Abortion," *Christianity and Crisis* 37, no. 18 (14 November 1977): 265.

186. *Abortion: Hearings* (House) 1, p. 337.

187. See, for example, Elizabeth Miller, *Religious Liberty and Abortion*, brochure issued by Religious Coalition for Abortion Rights (1978). Ms. Miller is secretary of the Issue Department, National Ministries, American Baptist Churches, USA.

188. Daniel Callahan, "Abortion and Government Policy," p. 279; "Abortion: Some Ethical Issues," in Walbert and Butler, p. 92.

189. "Do Catholics Have Constitutional Rights?" *Commonweal* 105, no. 24 (8 December 1978): 772.

190. Baruch Brody, "Religious, Moral and Sociological Issues," p. 13.

191. Robert G. Hoyt, "Does the First Amendment Bar the Hyde Amendment?" *Christianity and Crisis* 39, 3 (5 March 1979): 42.

192. Donald Shriver, letter to the editor, *New York Times*, 12 October 1980; "Private Religion, Public Morality," editorial, ibid., 5 October 1980, p. 18E.

193. J. Philip Wogaman, "Does the First Amendment Bar the Hyde Amendment?" *Christianity and Crisis* 39, no. 3 (5 March 1979): 36.

194. Aryeh Neier, "Theology and the Constitution," *Nation*, 30 December 1978, p. 727. Neier was executive director of the ACLU, 1970–78.

195. Laurence H. Tribe, "Toward a Model," pp. 20–51.

196. *Abortion: Hearings* (House) 1, p. 334.

197. Jaffe, "Enacting Religious Beliefs," p. 14.

198. Monroe H. Freedman, letter to the editor, *Nation*, 20 January 1979, p. 34; and 24 February 1979, p. 194; See also his "Abortion-Right Supporters Fight the Wrong Fight," *Los Angeles Times*, 28 March 1979, pt. 2, p. 7, in response to Ira Glasser, "Abortion Funding: A Case of Religious War," ibid., 7 January 1979, pt. 4, p. 5. Glasser, successor to Neier as executive director of the ACLU (of which Freedman, a Hofstra law professor, was a board member), had repeated the argument Neier published in the *Nation*.

199. Leon Lukaszewski, letter to the editor, *Los Angeles Times*, 14 January 1979, pt. 4, p. 4; the writer identifies himself as a member of the ACLU and of the Right to Life League.

200. 410 U.S. at 159, 156–157, 162 (1973).

201. "The Unborn and the Born Again," *New Republic*, p. 6.

202. Callahan, "Abortion: Some Ethical Issues," p. 93.

203. *McRae v. Califano*, Brief of Catholic League for Religious and Civil Rights, amici curiae, p. 24.

204. "Abortion, Religion and Political Life," editorial, *Commonweal* 106, no. 2 (2 February 1979): 37. See also Mary C. Segers, "Does the First Amendment Bar the Hyde Amendment?" *Christianity and Crisis* 39, no. 3 (5 March 1979): 36–38.

205. *Harris v. McRae*, 448 U.S. at 318 (1980); See *McGowan v. Maryland*, 366 U.S. 420, 442 (1961): "The 'Establishment' Clause does not ban federal or state regulation of conduct whose reason or effect merely happens to coincide or harmonize with the tenets of some or all religions. In many instances, the Congress or state legislatures conclude that the general welfare of society, wholly apart from any religious considerations, demands such regulation. Thus, for temporal purposes, murder is illegal. And the fact that this agrees with the dictates of the Judaeo-Christian religions while it may disagree with others does not invalidate the regulation. So too with the questions of adultery, and polygamy. . . . The same could be said of theft, fraud, etc., because those offenses were also proscribed in the Decalogue."

206. *Harris v. McRae, Id.* The trial court had ruled similarly, see *id.* at 297, 298. The French Conseil Constitutionnel in 1975 similarly declined a "secularity" challenge to French abortion law; Mauro Cappelletti and William Cohen, *Comparative Constitutional Law* (Indianapolis: Bobbs-Merrill, 1979), pp. 579–81.

207. *Roe v. Wade*, 410 U.S. at 150 (1973); *Harris v. McRae*, 448 U.S. at 324 (1980).

208. *McDaniel v. Paty*, 435 U.S. 618, 629, 636 (1978) (Brennan, J., concurring). This and all the foregoing points were also made by the trial court which upheld the abortion ordinance of the City of Akron, *Akron Center for Reproductive Health et al. v. City of Akron*, CA C78-155A, 22 August 1979, slip opinion; this is on appeal to the Supreme Court.

The one religious issue left in abeyance is whether denial of subsidized abortion deprives indigent women who seek it because of religious conviction of their right to free exercise of religion. The court in *McRae* declined to resolve this question because none of the plaintiffs asserted legal standing to raise it, 448 U.S. at 320.

209. *New Republic*, "The Unborn and the Born Again," p. 6. Norman Miller has raised the same question, "A New Anti-Catholic Bigotry?" *Wall Street Journal*, 14 December 1978, p. 22; see reply by Ira Glasser ("When human life begins is essentially a religious question"), letter to the editor, ibid., 29 December 1978, p. 8.

210. Patrick Buchanan, "Why Catholics Get Clobbered," *Chicago Tribune*, 18 April 1978, sect. 3, p. 4. See Mary Eisner Eccles, "Abortion: How Members Voted in 1977," *Congressional Quarterly Weekly Report* 36, no. 5 (4 February 1978): 258–67. In an earlier study of abortion-related debate and voting, mention was made of Senators Bartlett, Buckley, Pastore, Kennedy, Javits, and Bellmon; the first four were identified as Catholics, while no religious reference was made to the others; Elizabeth Bowman, "Senate Rejects Anti-Abortion Amendment," ibid. 33, no. 16 (19 April 1975): 814–16.

211. See "The Times is Criticized over Abortion Stories," *New York Times*, 26 April 1978, p. 10.

212. *Reproductive Rights Newsletter* no. 2 (Summer 1978), p. 19; a publication of the New American Movement.

213. See Joan Beck, "A tasteless anti-church tirade—with tax support," column, *Chicago Tribune*, 1 May 1978, p. 2; "Speaking of Good Taste: PP Blunder in Chicago," *National Right to Life News*, June 1978, p. 3; Marcena W. Love, letter to the editor,

Chicago Tribune, 16 May 1978, sect. 3, p. 2.

214. Georgie Anne Geyer, "Abortion Fight Now a Religious War," column, *Phoenix Gazette*, 24 January 1979; the column, circulated by the *Los Angeles Times* Syndicate, was not carried in the *Times* itself.

215. Paul N. McCloskey, Jr., "The Separation of Church and State in the United States: A Cause for Thanksgiving," U.S. Congress, House, Congressional Record, 96th Cong., 1st sess., 1979, p. 152: E5408.

216. See Carl L. Rowan columns in the *Times-Picayune* (New Orleans), 6 February 1979, pt. I, p. 14; 26 March 1979, pt. I, p. 18; 10 October 1979, pt. I, p. 21; 11 November 1979, pt. I, p. 15; 7 February 1980, pt. I, p. 19; and in the *Washington Star*, 10 October 1976, p. F3.

217. "Mother Teresa Speaks Out," *Los Angeles Times*, 12 December 1979, pt. 2, p. 11.

218. Marion B. Blyth, letter to the editor, *Los Angeles Times*, 22 December 1979, pt. 2, p. 4.

219. Liz Smith, column, *New York Daily News*, 27 December 1979, p. 8.

220. Nathanson recounts Lawrence Lader's remarks to him in the 1960s: "Historically every revolution has to have its villain. It really doesn't matter whether it's a king, a dictator, or a tsar, but it has to be *someone*, a person, to rebel against. It's easier for the people we want to persuade to perceive it this way. . . . A single person isn't quite what we want, since that might excite sympathy for him. Rather, a small group of shadowy, powerful people. *Too* large a group would diffuse the focus, don't you see? There's always been one group of people in this country associated with reactionary politics, behind-the-scenes manipulations, socially backward ideas. . . . Not just all Catholics. First of all, that's too large a group, and for us to vilify them all would diffuse our focus. Secondly, we have to convince liberal Catholics to join us, a popular front as it were, and if we tar them all with the same brush, we'll just antagonize a few who might otherwise have joined us and be valuable showpieces for us. No, it's got to be the Catholic *hierarchy*. That's a small enough group to come down on, and anonymous enough so that no names ever have to be mentioned, but everybody will have a fairly good idea whom we are talking about." *Aborting America*, pp. 51–52.

221. Daniel Callahan, "Abortion and Government Policy," p. 279. He says, further: "Widespread attacks upon Roman Catholic bishops by non-Catholics will almost invariably be seen—even by those who totally disagree with the bishops on abortion—as evidence of anti-Catholicism. This is because an attack upon the bishops is an attack upon a major symbol of Catholic belief. Right or wrong, they are still bishops, and are granted respect even when they are believed to be totally wrong and are flagrantly disobeyed. An analogy may underscore the point. Foreign nations hostile to the United States try to make a rhetorical distinction between the nice, decent American people (with whom they have no grudge), and the terrible, vicious, imperialistic American political leaders. Americans rarely accept that distinction. We look at virulent attacks upon our political leaders as evidence of a more pervasive anti-Americanism. A constant emphasis on Catholic opposition to abortion rights—when some other less well-organized groups are no less opposed—can only serve to invoke a sense that anti-Catholicism is still rampant."

222. "The ACLU's Holy War," editorial, *National Review* 31, no. 3 (9 January 1979): 74–76.

223. *Abortion II*. Beacon also published Theodore Rosen's *Therapeutic Abortion* and presently has another abortion book in preparation.

224. See *New York Times*, 10 April 1970, pp. 1, 42; 11 April 1970, pp. 1, 17; 23 April 1970, p. 36; 4 May 1970, p. 36 (letter); 5 June 1970, p. 40; 24 June 1970, p. 35; 4 November 1970, p. 19.

225. See Peter Skerry, "The Class Conflict over Abortion." See also Judith Blake and Jorge H. del Pinal, "Predicting Polar Attitudes toward Abortion in the United States," in Burtchaell, pp. 29–56.

226. See a very thoughtful column by Jane Adams, "Hers," *New York Times*, 2 October 1980, p. C2

227. Hauerwas, pp. 344–45.

228. See Dean M. Kelley, " 'Let Them Eat Cake,' Says the Supreme Court," *Christian Century* 97, no. 27 (August 27–September 3, 1980): 820–24. Kelley is the NCC executive for religious and civil liberty. The NCC brief asks the Court not to address the "religious establishment" claims in *McRae*.

229. Edward D. Schneider and Gordon R. Payne, letters to the editor, ibid., no. 28 (10–17 September 1980): 852–54. The editorial criticized was "The New Left Exploits Abortion," by James M. Wall, ibid., no. 25 (July 30–August 6, 1980).

230. Richard Neuhaus, "Hyde and Hysteria," pp. 849–50.

231. *Beal* v. *Doe*, 432 U.S. 438, 462 (1977), repeated in *Harris* v. *McRae*, 448 U.S. at 33 (1980). In *Poelker* v. *Doe*, decided concurrently with *Beal*, the Court upheld a mayor who introduced prolife measures in St. Louis after being elected with this among his campaign promises; here too Justice Marshall opined against the electorate.

232. Judith Randal, "No Abortions for the Poor," column, *Washington Star*, 10 December 1973, reproduced in *Abortion: Hearings* (Senate) 1, p. 136.

233. *The Abortion Rights Crisis* (Washington, D.C.: Religious Coalition for Abortion Rights, n.d.).

234. Laurie Johnston, "Abortion Foes Gain Support as They Intensify Campaign," *New York Times*, 23 October 1977, sect. 1, p. 1.

235. Louis Tyrer, vice president of Planned Parenthood, quoted in *Milwaukee Journal*, 6 June 1979; Judie Brown, spokesperson for the National Right to Life Committee, quoted in *New York Times*, 23 October 1977, sect. 1, p. 24.

236. Gloria Steinem, "Now That It's Reagan," Feminist Notes, *Ms.*, January 1981, p. 31.

237. "A Call to Concern."

238. See James Tunstead Burtchaell, C.S.C., "A Call and a Reply," advertisement, *Christianity and Crisis* 37, no. 17 (14 November 1977): 270–71; *Christian Century* 94, no. 37 (16 November 1977): 1074–75.

239. See the *Portland Oregonian*, 25 March 1970, p. 16; an earlier Packwood bill proposed to grant decreasing exemptions to a limit of three children, ibid., 9 January 1970, p. 17, and 12 April 1970, p. 2F. Packwood later abandoned this as a strategy of population control, ibid., 24 August 1971, p. 17. It should be remembered that bills like these, without cosponsors, are usually more of a gesture than a political plausibility.

240. See ibid., 10 March 1970, p. 4; 24 April 1970, p. 1.

241. Todd Engdahl, "Packwood's Stands bring . . . Donations," ibid., 14 June 1975, p. 24.

242. See A. Robert Smith, "Packwoods Reveal Planned Adoption," ibid., 22 July 1970, sect. 2, p. 3; also *Oregon Journal*, 7 January 1971, p. 4; ibid., 13 January 1971, sect. 3, p. 1.

243. "200 Cattle Deaths Stir Packwood," *Oregon Journal*, 26 August 1969, p. 5.

244. *Portland Oregonian*, 20 August 1979, p. 7.

245. Peter A. Sistrom, "Running on Empty," *Willamette Week* (Portland), 27 October 1980, p. 2.

246. Richard Colby, "Sen. Packwood Predicts Long, Tough Fight for Pro-Abortion Lobbyists," *Portland Oregonian*, 5 February 1978, p. D5.

247. Sandra McDonough, "Abortion Issue Fills Packwood Coffers," column,

ibid., 20 April 1980.

248. The *Official 1980 General Voters' Pamphlet*, issued to all citizens by the Oregon secretary of state, allows every candidate equal space in which to put forward his or her qualifications and views. See also Sandra McDonough, "Packwood's Media Campaign Package Avoids Controversy," *Portland Oregonian*, 24 August 1980, p. C1.

249. See Peter A. Sistrom, "Bob P.A.C.wood's Money," *Willamette Week*, 10 December 1979, p. 1; also McDonough, "Abortion Issue."

250. See McDonough and Sistrom. A suit by former Representative Charles Porter under the Oregon Corrupt Practices Act was dismissed for want of standing: Porter was a candidate in the Democratic primary and thus never directly faced Packwood at the polls. There has been talk of charges for mail fraud, but no known complaints have been filed.

251. Morton Mintz, "Election '80 Was Record Year for PACs, Especially Those on Right," *Washington Post*, 27 January 1981, p. A4. Note that these figures reach back cumulatively before calendar 1980.

252. Sissela Bok, "Ethical Problems of Abortion," *Hastings Center Studies* 2, no. 1 (January 1974): 33.

253. *Legal Abortion: Arguments Pro & Con*, brochure (Washington, D.C.: NARAL Foundation, 1978).

254. Minnette Doderer, quoted in John Herbers, "Anti-Abortionists' Impact Is Felt in Elections Across the Nation," *New York Times*, 20 June 1978, pp. A1, B10.

255. "A Call to Concern," p. 222.

256. Advertisement by Planned Parenthood of New York City, *New York Times*, 3 October 1980, p. A17.

257. Karen Mulhauser, fundraising letter for NARAL, 13 July 1979.

258. Faye Wattleton, quoted in Helen Epstein, "Abortion: An Issue That Won't Go Away," *New York Times Magazine*, 30 March 1980, p. 56.

259. Howard I. Diamond, quoted in Norma Rosen, "Between Guilt and Gratification," p. 74.

260. Clifford M. Turner, letter to the editor, *Nation*, 20 January 1979, p. 34.

261. Eleanor Smeal, recruitment letter for NOW, 1979.

262. Senator George McGovern, quoted in Steven V. Roberts, "McGovern in Battle—for Survival," *New York Times*, 15 September 1980, p. A16.

263. "The Abortion Decision," editorial, *Commonweal* 97, no. 19 (16 February 1973): 435–36. Six years later, when *Wade* talk had led to Hyde talk, this liberal, antiabortion journal had a scolding for both sides. "The recent action of the National Right to Life Committee in choosing a 1980 'hit list' consisting almost entirely of liberal Congressmen, as well as the movement's performance in the recent election, raises the question whether 'right-to-life' will become nothing more than 'life-to-the-right,' a manipulative adjunct to the new right-wing politics. Of course, the left sees the abortion movement that way. It makes little effort to understand the position of abortion opponents, writing them off as 'absolutist,' a curious adjective that one never finds applied to those who will brook no anti-Semitism, no sexual inequality, or no corporate bribery." "Abortion, Religion and Political Life," editorial, ibid. 106, no. 2 (2 February 1979): 37.

264. *National Catholic Reporter*, 17 October 1980, p. 12; see also ibid., 27 March 1981, p. 14; 24 April 1981, p. 32.

265. Ruth Ann Hanley, "Do Right-to-Lifers Care Only About the Unborn?" editorial, *The Communicator* (Indiana Right-to-Life newsletter) 5, no. 5 (June 1980): 2.

266. *National Right to Life News*, September 1977, p. 13.

267. Mary S. Segers, "Abortion Politics and Policy: Is There a Middle Ground?" *Christianity and Crisis* 40, no. 2 (18 February 1980): 26.

268. Bill Raspberry, "A liberal who battles abortion," column, *Chicago Tribune*, 29 January 1980, p. 15.

269. Mary Claire Blakeman, "Young Protesters' New Target: Abortion," *Los Angeles Times*, 16 September 1980, sect. 2, p. 7.

270. Barbara Grizzuti Harrison, "Some can see both sides of the abortion issue," *Chicago Tribune*, 1 June 1980, sect. 12, pp. 1, 6.

271. See "A New Breed of Right-To-Lifers?" *National Catholic Reporter* 16, no. 35 (18 July 1980): 23.

272. Mary Meehan, "The Other Right-to-Lifers," *Commonweal* 107, no. 1 (18 January 1980): 13–16; see also John Garvey, "Pro-life means more than anti-abortion," *U.S. Catholic* 45, no. 3 (March 1980): 35–37; also Juli Loesch, "Abortion and an Attempt at Dialogue," *America* 140, no. 11 (24 March 1979): 234–36.

273. "Morality and Abortion," editorial, *Chicago Defender*, 9 August 1980, p. 27.

274. *Respect Life* (Washington, D.C.: Committee for Pro-Life Activities, 1979 and 1980).

275. Jim Wallis, "Coming Together on the Sanctity of Life," editorial, *Sojourners* 9, no. 11 (November 1980): 3. The issue title is: "Abortion: What Does It Mean To Be Pro-Life?"

276. *New Republic*, "The Unborn and the Born Again," p. 5.

277. Anne Crittenden, "A Colloquy on the Sanger Spirit," *New York Times*, 18 September 1979, p. B8.

278. See Madeline Gray, *Margaret Sanger: A Biography of the Champion of Birth Control* (New York: Richard Marek, 1979). Sanger propounded an entire population plan wherein a special department of the federal government, directed by scientists, would direct and control immigration and birth rates and distribution of people across the country. Mental and moral degenerates (the mentally ill and criminals) would be given their choice of sterilization or lifelong segregation in compulsory farmwork battalions. Those with lesser sorts of degeneracy, including the poor, the illiterate, the retarded, and the unemployable, would be segregated "as long as necessary for the strengthening and development of moral conduct," under governmental "medical protection." She thus envisioned "fifteen or twenty millions of our population" mobilized, "defending the unborn against their own disabilities." Sanger, "A Plan For Peace," *Birth Control Review* 16, no. 4 (April 1932): 107–8.

279. See *Abortion: Hearings* (Senate) 1, p. 260 (Statement of Barbara McNeel, seminary professor of human relations and educational psychology).

280. "The fetus in utero is of course perfectly viable providing he is left alone. . . . In induced abortion it is the physician's action which causes the lack of viability. It seems like an aberration that the very act which makes the fetus non-viable should find its justification for some in the fact that the resulting fetus is precisely non-viable. The fact that an adult who cannot swim is not viable hardly seems a sufficient justification for throwing him overboard and thus making him non-viable." André E. Hellegers, "The Beginnings of Personhood: Medical Considerations," *Perkins Journal* (Southern Methodist University Divinity School) 27, no. 1 (Fall 1973): 14.

281. *Abortion: Hearings* (Senate) 1, p. 151 (Statement of former Senator Ernest Gruening of Alaska).

282. "Abortion Attempt Turns into Birth; Baby's 'Fine'," *Chicago Sun-Times*, 23 March 1981, p. 25.

283. *Abortion: Hearings* (Senate) 2, p. 303 (Statement of Jean Margaret Horrobin, University of Minnesota).

284. Ibid. 2, p. 765 ("Albert Schweitzer and Abortions," statement of Hans Zellweger, University of Iowa).

285. Ibid. 2, p. 593 (Statement of James F. Crow, University of Wisconsin).

286. Ibid. 2 p., 765 (Zellweger).

287. "Abortion, Politics and Tolerance," editorial, *New York Times*, 6 July 1980, p. 16E.

288. "Abortion: A Contemporary Issue Affecting Mentally Retarded Citizens," Report of the Ad Hoc Task Force on Abortion, The Association for Retarded Citizens (Arlington, Texas, 1980), p. 29.

289. *New York Times*, 30 September 1980, p. A15; see other ads in this series, 22 September, p. A23; 3 October, p. A17; 14 October, p. B17; 22 October, p. C32. Another series commenced in June 1981.

290. A further item of note regarding this advertisement: an inquiry revealed that the reported statistic of 63,000 teenage pregnancies in New York State had been secured from the New York Department of Health and Social Programs, and included both married and unmarried women; pregnancies that were desired and undesired; miscarriages, births, and induced abortions. In brief, the statistic reports every instance of pregnancy occurring to a woman under 20 years of age. It is an undifferentiated figure, and is obviously used here in a way intended to mislead the reader into a distorted impression of unwanted pregnancy.

291. James C. Hyatt, "Protection for Unborn? Work-Safety Issue Isn't as Simple as It Sounds," *Wall Street Journal*, 2 August 1977, pp. 1, 27; *Research on the Fetus*; *New York Times*, 18 June 1978, p. 17.

292. See Karen Mulhauser, executive director of NARAL, fund-raising letter, 1979; Judy Klemesrud, "Complacency on Abortion: A Warning to Women," *New York Times*, 23 January 1978, p. A18.

293. *Time*, 31 July 1978, p. 66.

294. Sissela Bok, "Ethical Problems of Abortion," pp. 33–52; "Fetal Research and the Value of Life."

295. See advertisement for Animal Welfare Institute, *New York Times*, 11 July 1980, p. A9; Greenpeace brochure, 1980; Whale Protection Fund letter, 1980.

296. See advertisements for the Millenium Guild in *New York Times*, 7 October 1980, p. B14, and by the New England Anti-Vivisection Society, ibid., 21 August 1980, p. 42.

297. See advertisement for the Humane Society of New York, *New York Times*, 6 November 1976, p. 46.

298. *New York Times*, 19 December 1980, p. A28.

Essay 3
Die Buben sind unser Unglück! The Holocaust and Abortion

1. Brenda M. Dissel, letter to the editor, *Harvard Magazine* 80, no. 4 (March–April 1978): 9–10.

2. Robert M. Byrn, "Confronting Objections to an Anti-Abortion Amendment," *America* 134, no. 24 (19 June 1976): 533–34.

3. Roger M. Williams, "The Power of Fetal Politics," *Saturday Review*, 9 June 1979, p. 15. Months earlier, in an article of comparable concern, Williams had castigated the Allied governments for rejecting requests to halt the Holocaust by bombing rail centers or the extermination camps themselves. "What about losses among the inmate population—killing the very people you were trying to save? Without question there would have been inmate deaths, perhaps dozens of them. Whether those deaths would have been justifiable in the process of rendering Auschwitz inoperable poses a difficult ethical question. Those who argue for bombing the camp obviously thought the answer to be yes, and I agree with them. . . . It seems

fair to assume that, if any of the suggested targets had been bombed, some and perhaps many lives would ultimately have been saved. The point can be argued eternally. What appears beyond argument, a third of a century after those cataclysmic events, is that the bombing should have been done for larger symbolic reasons. Faced with the gigantic, systematic eradication of an entire people, the United States had a transcending moral obligation to act, and to act in a way that would be felt by the oppressor and honored by history. The worst sin was to do nothing but talk, because talk was powerless against the madness of the Final Solution." "Why wasn't Auschwitz bombed?" *Commonweal* 105, no. 23 (24 November 1978): 751. On the bombing requests, see also Raul Hilberg, *The Destruction of the European Jews* (New York: Harper, 1979), pp. 543,.771; Nora Levin, *The Holocaust: The Destruction of European Jewry 1933–1945* (New York: Crowell [1968]), p. 674.

4. Cited in Linda Ambrose, "The McRae Case: A Record of the Hyde Amendment's Impact on Religious Freedom and Health Care," *Family Planning / Population Reporter* 7, no. 2 (April 1978): 29.

5. Gloria Steinem, "The Nazi Connection: If Hitler Were Alive, Whose Side Would He Be On?" Feminist Notes, *Ms.*, October 1980, pp. 88–90; "The Nazi Connection: Authoritarianism Begins at Home," ibid., November 1980, pp. 14–24. See, in a similar vein, Bernice Glatzer Rosenthal, "Stalin, 'Right To Life' Leader," column, *New York Times*, 8 October 1980, p. A27. She concludes: " 'Right-To-Lifers' would impose upon Americans the life of grim asceticism, renunciation, and endless toil characteristic of totalitarian societies, which sacrifice the individual to the state."

6. Eugene J. Fisher, "The Uniqueness of Christian-Jewish Dialogue in the United States and Canada," *Ecumenical Trends* 8, no. 10 (November 1979): 160.

7. Bernard Nathanson, with Richard Ostling, *Aborting America* (Garden City, New York: Doubleday, 1979), p. 183.

8. *Reproductive Rights Newsletter* no. 2 (Summer 1978), p. 5; a publication of the New American Movement.

9. Frederic Wertham, *A Sign for Cain* (New York: Macmillan, 1966), p. 140.

10. See Lucy Dawidowicz, *The War against the Jews, 1933–1945* (New York: Holt, Rinehart and Winston, 1975), pp. 402–403; Hilberg, p. 767; Levin, pp. 715–18.

11. Wertham, p. 158; Leo Alexander, "Medical Science under Dictatorship," *New England Journal of Medicine* 241, no. 2 (14 July 1949): 40.

12. Lt. Gen. von dem Bach-Zelewsky, quoted in Leo Alexander, "War Crimes and their Motivation: The Socio-Psychological Structure of the SS and the Criminalization of a Society," *Journal of Criminal Law and Criminology* 39 (1948–1949): 312.

13. Alexander Mitscherlich and Fred Mielke, *Doctors of Infamy: The Story of the Nazi Medical Crimes*, trans. Heinz Norden (New York: Henry Schuman, 1949), p. 51.

14. Dawidowicz, p. 118.

15. Clarissa Henry and Marc Hillel, *Of Pure Blood*, trans. Eric Mossbacher (New York: McGraw-Hill, 1976), p. 149.

16. See Gitta Sereny, *Into That Darkness: From Mercy Killing to Mass Murder* (New York: McGraw-Hill, 1974), pp. 98–99.

17. *Trials of War Criminals before the Nuernberg Military Tribunals under Control Council Law No. 10* (Nuernberg, October 1946–April 1949), vol. 1, "The Medical Case," p. 40 (cited hereafter as *Nuernberg Trials*).

18. Alexander Mitscherlich and Fred Mielke, *The Death Doctors*, trans. James Cleugh (London: Elek, 1962), p. 261.

19. Levin, p. 297.

20. Hilberg, p. 213.

21. See Dawidowicz, p. 185; Hilberg, p. 654.

22. These definitions were first set forth in the Law for the Protection of German Blood and German Honor, incorporated into what were known as the Nuremberg Laws of 1935. Dawidowicz, pp. 63–69.

23. Ibid., p. 12.

24. Levin, pp. 607–8. See also Eugene Levai, *Black Book of the Martyrdom of Hungarian Jewry*, ed. Lawrence Davis (Zurich and Vienna: Central European Times and Panorama, 1948), pp. 31–32; also Jenö [Eugene] Levai, ed., *Eichmann in Hungary: Documents* (Budapest: Pannonia, 1961), p. 54, which quotes a 1939 book, *Die jüdische Weltpest*: "Adolf Hitler has asserted that all cultured nations regard Jews as trichina and bacilli."

25. Hilberg, pp. 12–13.

26. Ibid., pp. 151, 149.

27. Levin, p. 245.

28. Mitscherlich and Mielke, *Doctors of Infamy*, p. 81.

29. *Nuernberg Trials*, 1:868.

30. Hilberg, p. 657.

31. Hilberg, p. 643; see also Dawidowicz, p. 99.

32. Hilberg, p. 132.

33. Sereny, p. 170.

34. Ibid., pp. 100–101.

35. Ibid., pp. 208–9. The story of this man Blau is an affecting subplot. An acquaintance of commandant Stangl from the past, he was saved to be a camp worker. Two favors to him are recorded. On the day when he discovered his own 80-year-old father among the morning's transport, as a special consideration he was permitted to spare his father the gas chamber by taking him aside and shooting him. Later he and his wife were themselves saved from being shot by a prior warning that enabled them to poison themselves. This would exemplify a less "depersonalized" treatment of a Jewish captive. Ibid., pp. 207–9.

36. Ibid., pp. 203, 200–201, 232–33.

37. *Nuernberg Trials*, 1:58.

38. Hans Günther, *Ritter, Tod und Teufel* (Munich: Lehmann, 1928), cited in Henry and Hillel, pp. 24–25. This was not an ideal that was pursued invariably. Himmler, himself neither blond nor blue-eyed, was of Mongolian extraction from a family resident earlier in Hungary. Once, when witnessing an execution at Minsk, he discerned a blond youth of about 20 in a batch to be liquidated, interrogated him earnestly to find if he might have some gentile ancestry, and then consigned him to the machine guns unhappily when he could find none. See ibid., p. 25; Hilberg, p. 218.

39. See, for example, Levai, *Eichmann*, p. 141.

40. Dawidowicz, p. 115; Leo Alexander, "Destructive and Self-Destructive Trends in Criminalized Society: A Study of Totalitarianism," *Journal of Criminal Law and Criminology* 39 (1948–1949): 557.

41. Helmut Krausnick, Hans Buchheim, Martin Broszat, and Hans-Adolf Jacobsen, *Anatomy of the SS State*, trans. Richard Barry, Marian Jackson, and Dorothy Long (London: Collins, 1968), p. 13.

42. Ibid., p. 18.

43. Ibid., pp. 12, 9.

44. Hilberg, p. 11; Wertham, p. 189; Bert Honolka, *Die Kreuzelschreiber: Aerzte ohne Gewissen; Euthanasie im Dritten Reich* (Hamburg: Rütten & Loening, 1961), pp. 122–23.

45. Hannah Arendt, *Eichmann in Jerusalem: A Report on the Banality of Evil*, rev. ed. (New York: Viking Press, Compass Edition, 1965), pp. 85, 1–8; Dawidowicz, p. 153; Hilberg, pp. 216, 619, 652; Levin, pp. 207, 248, 262, 297, 547; *Nuernberg*

Trials, 1:867–68; Gerald Reitlinger, *The Final Solution: The Attempt to Exterminate the Jews of Europe, 1939–1945* (London: Valentine, Mitchell, 1953), pp. 116–17; 129; Leo Alexander, "The Molding of Personality under Dictatorship: The Importance of the Destructive Drives in the Socio-Psychological Structure of Nazism," *Journal of Criminal Law and Criminology* 40 (1949–1950): 11–14.

46. See Dawidowicz, p. 132; Henry and Hillel, pp. 110–12; Hilberg, p. 151; Mitscherlich and Mielke. *Death Doctors*, p. 233; idem, *Doctors of Infamy*, p. 92; *Nuernberg Trials* 1:822, 844; Reitlinger, p. 129; Sereny, p. 50.

47. Sereny, p. 74. One German prelate, Dr. Hilfrich, bishop of Limburg, explicitly rejected the expression and its assumptions, in a hot letter of protest to the minister of justice. Hilfrich was one of the most vociferous critics of Nazi killing programs. See *Nuernberg Trials*, 1:845–46.

48. Levin, p. 301; Mitscherlich and Mielke, *Doctors of Infamy*, pp. 93ff., 100ff.; *Nuernberg Trials*, 1:817.

49. *Nuernberg Trials*, 1:855, 814, 892–95.

50. Ibid., 2:135–36. See also Mitscherlich and Mielke, *Death Doctors*, pp. 265–69, for Brandt's argument that modern medicine and a strong sense of humanity combine to override literal interpretations of the doctor's Hippocratic Oath not to administer poison to a patient even when requested.

51. *Nuernberg Trials*, 1:873.

52. Ibid., p. 870. The visitor was Lt. Kurt Gerstein, whose later attempts to warn the Vatican and the Jewish community were fictionalized in *The Deputy*.

53. Levai, *Eichmann*, pp. 216–17; *Nuernberg Trials*, 1:809–11.

54. Levin, p. 258; Alexander, "War Crimes," p. 314. The officer from *Einsatzgruppe D* also exercised care that the non-Jewish population was not disturbed; by dint of special exertions his group was able to shoot 9,600 persons "in time to permit Christmas celebrations in a city without Jews."

55. Hilberg, pp. 541–42, 668, 249.

56. Rudolf Höss, *Commandant of Auschwitz*, trans. Constantine FitzGibbon (Cleveland and New York: World, 1959), p. 167: Levai, *Black Book*, p. 442.

57. Dawidowicz, p. 153; Hilberg, p. 216.

58. Hilberg, pp. 113, 151.

59. Reitlinger, pp. 485–86.

60. Alexander, "Molding of Personality," p. 19; "War Crimes," pp. 315, 318, 323–24.

61. Arendt, pp. 48–49; see also pp. 85ff. where she comments on the *Sprachregelung* (language restrictions) that bound those who shared the Holocaust secret.

62. Ibid., p. 69.

63. *Nuernberg Trials*, 1:816.

64. Ibid., p. 542.

65. Ibid., p. 957.

66. Höss, p. 160.

67. See Hilberg, pp. 46ff.

68. Levin, p. 295.

69. Wertham, pp. 166–67.

70. *Nuernberg Trials*, 1:815; see also Honolka, pp. 141–45.

71. *Nuernberg Trials*, 1:970–72; see also Mitscherlich and Mielke, *Doctors of Infamy*, p. 161.

72. *Nuernberg Trials*, 1:956–57.

73. Hilberg, pp. 214–15, 648.

74. Sereny, p. 52; Mitscherlich and Mielke, *Death Doctors*, p. 257.

75. Höss, p. 94; see also Alexander, "Molding of Personality," pp. 11–12.

76. Arendt, p. 289. In another respect, Alexander discusses the position of Nazi women who, by their moral support, gave ideological justification to their partners while themselves remaining "uninvolved." "Molding of Personality," pp. 15–16.

77. Mitscherlich and Mielke, *Doctors of Infamy*, p. 152.

78. Sereny, pp. 89–90.

79. Levai, *Black Book*, p. 189.

80. Ibid., p. 176.

81. Sereny, pp. 37–39, 164.

82. Alexander, "Medical Science," p. 44. Gebhardt became president of the German Red Cross.

83. *Nuernberg Trials*, 1:737–38.

84. Mitscherlich and Mielke, *Death Doctors*, p. 248.

85. Arendt, pp. 290–91.

86. Dawidowicz, p. 70.

87. *Nuernberg Trials*, 1:540–41.

88. Ibid., 2:6–9.

89. Ibid., p. 15; see also pp. 72–73. A note in the file of Sievers' Ahnenerbe Society reads: "After all, we are not conducting these tests for the sake of some scientific notion, but to be of practical service to the troops, and beyond them, to the whole German people." Mitscherlich and Mielke, *Doctors of Infamy*, p. 77.

90. *Nuernberg Trials*, 1:970–73; 2:126–29.

91. Hilberg, p. 399. Pierre Laval, when the German who was negotiating the removal of refugee Jews from France remarked that the business was slightly unsavory, snapped: "Well, what am I to do? I offered these foreign Jews to the Allies, but they didn't take them off my hands." Ibid., p. 408.

92. *Nuernberg Trials*, 2:42–43; see Ivy's statement in Mitscherlich and Mielke, *Doctors of Infamy*, pp. x–xiii.

93. Robert Coles, "American Amok," *New Republic*, 27 August 1966, p. 15; reprinted in *The Mind's Fate* (Boston, Toronto: Atlantic-Little, Brown, 1975), pp. 18–19.

94. Henry and Hillel, p. 150.

95. Ibid., passim; *Nuernberg Trials*, 1:676–78. Rascher was shot and his wife hanged when Himmler, proud sponsor to their children, found they had been adopted, not bred.

96. Wertham, p. 186; *Nuernberg Trials*, 1:702–3.

97. Höss, introduction, p. 24.

98. Ibid., pp. 38–39, 50, 72, 162–63, 172–73. Lord Russell observes: "He was, like so many of his fellow fiends, a great family man. So many of these SS men appear to have had a schizophrenic capacity for sentiment and sadism, but that was, doubtless, because the latter was all just part of their job. The stoker, whose duty it was to look after the fires in the concentration camp crematorium, could gather round the Christmas tree with his young children after lunch on Christmas Day, and a few minutes later glance at his watch and hurry away to be in time for the evening shift. Höss was also a lover of animals as were other Nazi villains. One of the officials in Ravensbrück concentration camp, known as 'the women's hell,' carried out the cruelest physical and mental tortures on the women inmates in his charge. When he was convicted by a War Crimes Tribunal in 1947, and sentenced to death by hanging, many of his relatives and friends wrote to say that 'dear, kind Ludwig could do no harm to any animal,' and that when his mother-in-law's canary died he 'tenderly put the birdie in a small box, covered it with a rose, and buried it under a rosebush in the garden,' " Ibid., introduction, p. 25.

99. Sereny, pp. 30, 51, 122–24, 133, 136–38, 229, 272, 350.

100. Arendt, p. 109.

101. Ibid., p. 51.

102. See Mitscherlich and Mielke, *Death Doctors*, pp. 17–19; *Doctors of Infamy*, pp. 94–95; Levai, *Eichmann*, pp. 284–86. Various medical associations and even the German Red Cross were co-opted.

103. *Nuernberg Trials*, 1:827, 826; see also pp. 817, 894.

104. Hilberg, p. 210.

105. Wertham, p. 157.

106. Arendt, p. 127.

107. Höss, pp. 94, 141, 163.

108. Krausnick et al., p. 374.

109. Sereny, pp. 171, 209; see also pp. 101, 136–37, 155.

110. Reitlinger, pp. 131, 139, 208–9; Levin, pp. 242–44; Arendt, p. 101.

111. *Nuernberg Trials*, 2:139.

112. Hilberg, p. 651.

113. Levin, p. 238.

114. Levin, p. 205; see also *Nuernberg Trials*, 1:866–67.

115. Reitlinger, p. 297. Said one officer at the talk, "We were rather surprised." On the cultivation of "hardness" in the SS, see Krausnick et. al., pp. 334–39.

116. Hilberg, p. 562; Arendt, p. 106.

117. Mitscherlich and Mielke, *Doctors of Infamy*, pp. 93–95; Wertham, p. 191; Krausnick et al., pp. 371ff. To the contrary, see Alexander, "War Crimes," p. 321.

118. Levin, p. 245; Höss, pp. 94–95; Krausnick et al., p. 375.

119. Mitscherlich and Mielke, *Doctors of Infamy*, pp. 17, 26.

120. Ibid., pp. 24, 48, 153.

121. Alexander, "Molding the Personality," p. 8; "Destructive, Self-Destructive Trends," p. 563.

122. Arendt, pp. 287–88.

123. Alexander, "Medical Science," pp. 40–41; Mitscherlich and Mielke, *Doctors of Infamy*, pp. 98–99.

124. Reitlinger, p. 133.

125. Wertham, pp. 182–83.

126. Alexander, "Medical Science," p. 40; Wertham, p. 180.

127. Wertham, pp. 169–71.

128. See Arendt, p. 108; Höss, pp. 161ff.

129. Levin, p. 207. For a chronicle of the progressive destruction in Hungary, see Levai, *Black Book*, pp. 9–27.

130. Henry and Hillel, pp. 36–38.

131. Quoted from his table conversation on 22 July 1942, ibid., p. 148. See also Sereny, p. 62; Levai, *Eichmann*, pp. 208–10.

132. Henry and Hillel, pp. 82–83.

133. Ibid., p. 111.

134. Ibid., pp. 200–201; 145–49; Sereny, p. 99.

135. Sereny, p. 62.

136. Levai, *Eichmann*, pp. 210–20; Alexander, "War Crimes," p. 40; *Nuernberg Trials*, 1:713, 721.

137. Alexander, "War Crimes," p. 42; Sereny, p. 95.

138. Arendt, p. 108; see also Alexander, "War Crimes," p. 40; Levin, pp. 297–302.

139. Wertham, p. 152.

140. Krausnick et al., pp. 369–71.

141. Alexander, "Medical Crimes," pp. 44–45.

142. See Henry and Hillel, pp. 69–70; Levai, *Black Book*, pp. 27, 37; Hilberg, 439, 614, 643–46; Wertham, pp. 141–50.

143. Honolka, p. 36.

144. *Nuernberg Trials*, 1:856.

145. Alexander, "Medical Science," p. 39; Reitlinger, pp. 132–33.

146. Adolf Dorner, *Mathematik in Dienste der Nationalpolitischen Erziehung* (Frankfurt, 1935), quoted in Alexander, "Molding the Personality," pp. 7–8; see also Mitscherlich and Mielke, *Death Doctors*, p. 234. Other questions in this textbook ask the pupils to calculate how much poison gas it would take to kill all inhabitants of various-sized cities.

147. Dawidowicz, p. 36; Levin, p. 15.

148. Alexander, "Medical Science," p. 42.

149. Ibid., p. 40; Hilberg, pp. 618, 627; Sereny, pp. 49–50.

150. Alexander, "Medical Science," p. 44; see also his "Sociopsychologic Structure of the SS: Psychiatric Report of Nuremberg Trials for War Crimes," *Archives of Neurology and Psychiatry* 59 (1948): 622–34; "War Crimes: Their Social-Psychological Aspects," *American Journal of Psychiatry* 105, no. 3 (September 1948): 170–77.

151. "Jahresversammlung des Vereins Bayerischer Psychiater, München, 18–19 Juli 1931," in *Allgemeine Zeitschrift für Psychiatrie* 96 (1932): 370–73.

152. Henry and Hillel, p. 112.

153. Alexander, "Medical Science," p. 43.

154. Henry and Hillel, pp. 174–75.

155. Alexander, "Medical Science," p. 40; Wertham, p. 181.

156. Arendt, p. 296; see also Sereny, pp. 17–18, 30, 37, 58–59, 62–63, 68–69, 73–75, 141–42; Levin, pp. 301, 686–87, 743; Mitscherlich and Mielke, *Doctors of Infamy*, pp. 106–10; *Death Doctors*, pp. 256–57; *Nuernberg Trials*, 1:814–15, 872–73; 2:136; Honolka, pp. 62–63. Interestingly, in November 1938, on the occasion of *Kristallnacht*, an organized anti-Jewish riot, the German ambassador in Washington reported to Berlin that he was not surprised "that the Catholic bishops' campaign against Germany is waged more bitterly than before." Hilberg, p. 25.

157. Levai, *Black Book*, passim, especially pp. 14, 19, 25, 91–93, 117–22, 145, 148–52, 178–81, 197–211, 217–26, 292–93, 360–61, 372–73.

158. Hilberg, pp. 662–69. Hilberg illustrates this by one memorable story of the pathetic attempts to appease the oppressor in the Latvian town of Shavel. "The *Judenrat* [Jewish council] had been asked three times whether any births had occurred in the ghetto, and each time it had denied that there were any births. Now, however, the Jewish leadership was confronted with twenty pregnancies. It decided to use persuasion and, if need be, threats on the women to submit to abortions. One woman was in her eighth month; the *Judenrat* decided that in this case a doctor would induce premature birth and that a nurse would kill the child. (A doctor objected to doing the job himself.) The nurse would be told to proceed in such a way that she would not know the nature of her act" (pp. 664–65).

159. Ibid., pp. 666–67.

160. Dawidowicz, p. 304; see also Hilberg, p. 146; Levin, p. 207; Reitlinger, pp. 64–65. Höss of Auschwitz was puzzled by what he saw as callous indifference of Jewish *Kapos* towards their kindred inmates (pp. 168–69).

161. Reitlinger, pp. 160–61.

162. Arendt, pp. 118, 133. On this issue of resistance to the Holocaust see Walter Laqueur, *The Terrible Secret: Suppression of the Truth about Hitler's "Final Solution"* (Boston: Little, Brown, 1980).

163. See Audrie Girdner and Anne Loftis, *The Great Betrayal: The Evacuation of the Japanese-Americans during World War II* (New York: Macmillan, 1969), p. 205.

164. Ibid., p. 34.

165. Alan R. Bosworth, *America's Concentration Camps* (New York: Norton, 1967), p. 33.

166. Girdner and Loftis, pp. 63, 17, 115, 254, 358; Bosworth, pp. 187, 216.

167. Girdner and Loftis, pp. 27, 73–74, 444, 477.

168. Ibid., pp. 237–38.

169. Ibid., pp. 16–17, 22–23.

170. Ibid., pp. 252–53; Bosworth, pp. 13–18, 39.

171. Girdner and Loftis, pp. 59–62, 74–75, 90. The architect of this legislation, California Attorney General Webb, had made it clear that their basis was "race undesirability." The Constitution had been written by white people, for white people, and the Fourteenth Amendment was intended to naturalize the Negro. It was repellant to think, he said, that it was intended to make citizens of all other peoples of color born in the United States. Bosworth, p. 222.

172. Girdner and Loftis, pp. 17, 30, 120, 328–29, 105, 360; Bosworth, p. 216.

173. Girdner and Loftis, pp. 26, 61, 92–93, 104, 107–8, 358–61; Bosworth, pp. 38–39, 221.

174. Girdner and Loftis, p. 201; also pp. 201–36.

175. Ibid., p. 368.

176. Ibid., p. 103.

177. Ibid., pp. 477–78. Another study of the American concentration camp decision, early and detailed, is Morton Grodzins, *Americans Betrayed: Politics and the Japanese Evacuation* (Chicago: University of Chicago Press, 1949).

178. Michael Herr, *Dispatches* (New York: Avon, 1978), pp. 222, 60–61.

179. Kenneth M. Stampp, *The Peculiar Institution: Slavery in the Ante-Bellum South* (New York: Random House, Vintage Books, 1965), pp. 5, 235. It is, on the other hand, not well known that in the entire South less than 3,000 whites before the Civil War owned 100 or more blacks; three-quarters of them owned no slaves at all (pp. 30–33).

180. Ibid., chap. 4, "To Make Them Stand in Fear," especially p. 190; also p. 129.

181. Ibid., pp. 201, 203.

182. Ibid., pp. 11, 347.

183. Ibid., p. 345.

184. See Dickran H. Boyajian, *Armenia: The Case for a Forgotten Genocide* (Westwood, N.J.: Educational Book Crafters, 1972). Said Hitler in 1939: "Who, after all, speaks today of the annihilation of the Armenians? The world believes in success only."

185. Garrett Hardin, *Mandatory Motherhood: The True Meaning of "Right to Life"* (Boston: Beacon, 1974), pp. 11–15.

186. Quoted in a discussion transcribed in Robert Hall, ed., *Abortion in a Changing World*, Proceedings of an International Conference convened by the Association for the Study of Abortion, at Hot Springs, Virginia, 17–20 November 1968, 2 vols. (New York: Columbia University Press, 1970), 1:175.

187. Nathanson, *Aborting America*, p. 188; also his "Deeper into Abortion," *New England Journal of Medicine* 291, no. 22 (28 November 1974): 1189–90.

188. See Malcolm Potts, Peter Diggory, and John Peel, *Abortion* (Cambridge: At the University Press, 1977), p. 200; Paul Ramsey, *Ethics at the Edges of Life: Medical and Legal Intersections*, The 1975 Bampton Lectures in America (New Haven: Yale University Press, 1978), pp. 108–9; John T. Noonan, Jr., *A Private Choice: Abortion in America in the Seventies* (New York: Free Press, 1979), p. 149; *Research on the Fetus*: Report and Recommendations of the National Commission for the Protection of Human Subjects of Biomedical and Behavioral Research (U.S. Department of Health,

Education, and Welfare Publication No. [OS] 76–127, 1975).

189. Henry P. David, "Abortion: Public Health Concerns and Needed Psychosocial Research," *American Journal of Public Health* 61, no. 3 (March 1971): 515.

190. George Allardice Riddell, *Medico-Legal Problems* (London: H. K. Lewis, 1929), p. 35.

191. 410 U.S. 113, 164, 165 (1973).

192. Noonan, *A Private Choice*, p. 140; Glanville Williams, *The Sanctity of Life and the Criminal Law*, The 1956 James S. Carpenter Lectures at Columbia Law School (New York: Knopf, 1957), p. 12.

193. *Floyd* v. *Anders*, 440 F. Supp. 535, 539 (D. So. Car. 1977); see also Glanville Williams, "The Legalization of Medical Abortion," *Eugenics Review* 56, no. 1 (April 1964): 21.

194. Lawrence Lader, *Abortion* (Indianapolis: Bobbs-Merrill, 1966), p. 16.

195. *New York Post*, 13 February 1979, p. 31.

196. *Burns* v. *Alcala*, 420 U.S. 575 (1975).

197. *Research on the Fetus*, Appendix (DHEW Publication No. [OS] 76–128), p. 3–3. Compare this with the reported attitudes of UCLA medical researchers toward their patient–subjects: "Once diagnosed as terminally ill, the patient is no longer a human being but a research subject with a disease to be fitted to a protocol (experimental plan)." Paul Jacobs, "UCLA Researchers Reprimanded," *Portland Oregonian*, 28 December 1980, p. A16.

198. Quoted in Hall, *Abortion in a Changing World*, 1:48; see also p. 56.

199. Williams, *Sanctity of Life*, pp. 226, 215.

200. Charles Mercier, *Crime and Criminals* (London: University of London Press, 1918), pp. 196–97; *Crime and Insanity* (London: 1911), pp. 212–13; quoted in Williams, *Sanctity of Life*, pp. 217, 18.

201. Paul Ramsey, "Protecting the Unborn," *Commonweal* 100, no. 13 (31 May 1974): 308; Raymond S. Duff and A. G. M. Campbell, "Moral and Ethical Dilemmas in the Special-Care Nursery," *New England Journal of Medicine* 289, no. 17 (25 October 1973): 892.

202. See Thomas B. Littlewood, *The Politics of Population Control* (Notre Dame: University of Notre Dame Press, 1977), p. 134 and passim; Peter Skerry, "The Class Conflict over Abortion," *Public Interest*, no. 52 (Summer 1978): 69–84.

203. Paul Ramsey, *Ethics*, pp. 207, 230; "Feticide / Infanticide upon Request," *Religion in Life* 39, no. 2 (Summer 1970): 177, reprinted in *Child and Family* Reprint Booklet Series, 1978, p. 69.

204. Daniel Callahan, "Abortion: Some Ethical Issues," in David F. Walbert and J. Douglas Butler, eds., *Abortion, Society and the Law* (Cleveland: Case Western Reserve University Press, 1973), pp. 100–101.

205. Richard Stith, "In Response to Those Who Ask Why I Care About Abortion," *The Cresset* (Valparaiso University), December 1973, p. 8.

206. See, for instance, the following items in the *New York Times*: "No Constitutional Shortcut on Abortion," editorial, 21 March 1981, p. 16; Walter Sullivan, "Onset of Human Life: Answer on Crucial Moment Elusive," 4 May 1981, p. B12; compare "Love for Sale," editorial, 2 April 1981, p. A26; Harold M. Schmeck, Jr., "Life of Baby is Apparently Saved By Doses of Vitamin Before Birth," 15 May 1981, p. B16; *Idem*, "Therapy in the Womb Rescues Unborn Lives," 26 May 1981, p. C1. A recent editorial clarifies the *Times* position. Abortion law must not be grounded on whether or not "human life begins when a sperm and an egg unite to form a zygote"; according to the *Times* this is a widely known fact, but it is not the fact which should control abortion law. What really matters is: "when does this society deem an abortion to be homicide?" The status and rights of the unborn should derive, not from whether it is human (it

clearly is), but from whether society wants it to survive. Soma Golden, "Once Again, the Abortion Puzzle," editorial notebook, 18 May 1981, p. A18.

207. Williams, *Sanctity of Life*, p. 147.

208. George Will, "Discretionary Killing," *Newsweek*, 20 September 1976, p. 96.

209. Nathanson, *Aborting America*, p. 177.

210. Callahan, in Walbert and Butler, p. 96. For example, James V. Neel, advocating abortion of the genetically defective, entitles his article: "Some Genetic Aspects of Therapeutic Abortion," *Perspectives in Biology and Medicine* 11, no. I (Autumn 1967): 129–35.

211. See Maria G. Perez-Reyes and Ruth Falk, "Follow-up after Therapeutic Abortion in Early Adolescence," *Archives of General Psychiatry* 28, no. 1 (January 1973): 123.

212. James H. Ford, "Mass-Produced, Assembly-Line Abortion: A Prime Example of Unethical, Unscientific Medicine," *California Medicine* 117, no. 5 (November 1972): 82; see also Samuel A. Nigro, "A Scientific Critique of Abortion as a Medical Procedure," *Psychiatric Annals* 2, no. 9 (September 1972): 23.

213. Tom Clark, "Religion, Morality and Abortion: A Constitutional Appraisal," *Loyola University of L.A. Law Review* 2, no. 1 (1969): 9.

214. Nathanson, *Aborting America*, p. 101.

215. Lawrence Lader, *Abortion II: Making the Revolution* (Boston: Beacon, 1973), p. 43.

216. *Roe* v. *Wade*, 410 U.S. 113, 163 (1973).

217. *Commonwealth* v. *Edelin*, 359 N.E. 2d 4 (1976).

218. *National Abortion Rights Action League Newsletter* 11, no. 5 (July 1979): 1.

219. Jacqueline Darroch Forrest, Christopher Tietze, and Eileen Sullivan, "Abortion in the United States 1976–1977," *Family Planning Perspectives* 10, no. 5 (September / October 1978): 278.

220. "33,000 Doctors Speak Out on Abortion," *Modern Medicine* 41, no. 10 (14 May 1973): p. 31.

221. At a hearing 3 August 1977, in *McRae* v. *Mathews*, before Judge Dooling, U.S. District Court, Eastern District of N.Y.

222. Nathanson, *Aborting America*, pp. 190–91.

223. *Research on the Fetus*, Appendix, p. 7–3.

224. *Chicago Sun-Times*, 19 November 1978.

225. Ramsey, *Ethics*, p. 241; Englehardt, in *Journal of Pediatrics* 83 (1973): 170ff.

226. Thomas Szasz, "The Ethics of Abortion," *Humanist* 26, no. 5 (September–October 1966): 148.

227. E. Fuller Torrey, ed., *Ethical Issues in Medicine* (Boston: Little, Brown, 1968), p. viii; see also p. 77.

228. *Roe* v. *Wade*, 410 U.S. 113, 163, 165, 167 (1973); *Doe* v. *Bolton*, 410 U.S. 179, 199 (1973).

229. ACLU Policy No. 247: Abortion (1968).

230. *Roe* v. *Wade*, 410 U.S. at, 152, 153 (1973).

231. Lader, *Abortion II*, p. 12.

232. 410 U.S. at 209–221 (1973).

233. *U.S.* v. *Vuitch*, 305 F. Supp. 1032, 1035 (D.C.D.C. 1969).

234. See Noonan, *Private Choice*, pp. 13–19, 90–95.

235. Georgie Anne Geyer, *Portland Oregonian*, 11 May 1978, p. D5.

236. Anthony Shaw, "Doctor, Do We Have a Choice?" *New York Times Magazine*, 30 January 1972, pp. 44–54. Elsewhere Shaw describes medical help which temporarily staves off a clinically imposed death as "palliative treatment." "Dilemmas

of 'Informed Consent' in Children," *New England Journal of Medicine* 289, no. 17 (25 October 1973): 886. An interesting side note: the drugs used to eliminate newborns are the same that were used in the Nazi "euthanasia" program; see Ramsey, *Ethics*, p. 196.

237. *Research on the Fetus*, Appendix, p. 4–7; see also Willard Gaylin and Marc Lappé, "Fetal Politics: The Debate on Experimenting with the Unborn," *Atlantic Monthly*, May 1975, p. 69; " 'Live' Abortus Research Raises Hackles of Some, Hopes of Others," *Medical World News* 14, no. 36 (5 October 1973): 33. Lappé shows further sensitivity to matters of individual protection when he notes, as "perhaps the most vexing consequence" of the 1973 abortion decisions, that there can no longer be any legally consistent recourse against women who allow their unborn to be blighted by harmful drugs, growth-retarding smoking, and other injurious treatment; see his "The Moral Claims of the Unwanted Fetus," *Hastings Center Report* 5, no. 2 (April 1975): 11–13.

238. *Research on the Fetus*, Appendix, p. 1–31.

239. 410 U.S. 179, 208 (1973).

240. Robert A. Bennett, letter to the editor, *New England Journal of Medicine* 292, no. 9 (27 February 1975): 484.

241. Potts et al., p. 236.

242. Williams, "Euthanasia and Abortion," *University of Colorado Law Review* 38 (1966): 189.

243. Excerpt from an interview recorded in 1978 by a student, in the author's files.

244. See " 'Live' Abortus Research Raises Hackles of Some, Hopes of Others," *Medical World News* 14, no. 36 (5 October 1973): 36.

245. Gaylin and Lappé, pp. 66–71. This view is not always held consistently. For instance, one line the Court drew with a firm stroke was at the moment of birth: the human born is from that instant acknowledged as a person. Gaylin and Lappé, however, like the National Commission for the Protection of Human Subjects of Biomedical and Behavioral Research, call that "an arbitrary line."

246. Nathanson, "Deeper into Abortion," p. 1189; see also his *Aborting America*, pp. 245–47.

247. Quoted in Seth Mydans, "When Is an Abortion Not an Abortion," *Atlantic Monthly*, May 1975, p. 72.

248. Quote in Ramsey, *Ethics*, p. 206.

249. Edmund Overstreet, in *American Journal of Psychiatry* 127, no. 9 (March 1971): 1160; see also his "Experience with the New California Law" in Hall, 1:137–42.

250. Jo Ann Levine, "British Abortionist 'Outside' Society," *Christian Science Monitor*, 19 July 1969.

251. *Congressional Record*, 96th Cong., 1st sess., 19 June 1979, S8079.

252. Mulhauser, Letter to the NARAL Membership, 13 July 1979.

253. Lader, *Abortion II*, p. 223.

254. See also Barbara Ross, "Abortion-II," *New York Post*, 14 February 1979, p. 8.

255. *Doe v. Bolton*, 410 U.S. 179, 196, 197 (1973).

256. Robert F. Drinan, [S.J.], "The Abortion Decision," *Commonweal* 97, no. 19 (16 February 1973): 439. Drinan, writing immediately after the rulings, mistakenly sees this medical authority as limited by the Court to the first trimester of pregnancy.

257. See Harriet F. Pilpel and Ruth J. Zuckerman, "Abortion and the Rights of Minors," in Walbert and Butler, pp. 293–95.

258. Ramsey, *Ethics*, pp. 59–60.

259. Williams, "Euthanasia and Abortion," p. 180.

260. ACLU Policy No. 247, adopted 1968. This was not, of course, the legal

position taken by the Union in respect of racial integration. A contrasting view is taken by David L. Bazelon, while chief judge of the U.S. Court of Appeals, D.C. Circuit, "The Morality of the Criminal Law," *Southern California Law Review* 49 (1976): 385: "I would ask: is the conduct in question viewed by the society as both a moral wrong and a breach of some minimum condition of social existence? In other words, although not every act regarded as immoral by the dominant community should be made criminal, no act should be made criminal if it is not viewed as immoral. I believe that the criminal code should define only the minimum conditions of each individual's responsibility to the other members of society in order to maximize personal liberty. . . . Furthermore, in spite of contrary assertions by historians and political scientists, such decisions are not simply the product of the ebb and flow of personalities, pressures, and interests. *These decisions, like all great constitutional decisions, are statements of moral principle.* In the words of Judge Elbert Tuttle, '[T]he only way the law has progressed from the days of the rack, the screw and the wheel is the development of moral concepts. . . . ' " (pp. 385, 398–99). An editorial in *Commonweal* adopts a similar position: "What a society values it protects with laws. In that sense civil rights, minimum wage and welfare bills have a moral dimension in that they witness to the national community's concern for every member; and state laws restricting abortion at least testified to some consensus that life in process is *life* and must be protected." *Commonweal* 97, no. 19 (3 February 1973): 435.

261. *Research on the Fetus*, Appendix, p. 3–12.

262. See Lader, *Abortion II*, pp. 42–43, 75.

263. Kenneth R. Niswander, "Abortion Practices in the United States: A Medical Viewpoint," in Walbert and Butler, p. 209; see also S. Bolter, "The Psychiatrist's Role in Therapeutic Abortion: The Unwitting Accomplice," *American Journal of Psychiatry* 119, no. 4 (October 1962): 312–16.

264. Seymour Halleck, "Excuse-Makers to the Elite: Psychiatrists as Accidental Social Movers," *Medical Opinion* 7, no. 12 (December 1971): 50; article excerpted from *Politics of Therapy* (New York; Science House, 1972); see also Ford, pp. 80–84.

265. The best elaborated statement on this is the *Report of the Commission on Population Growth and the American Future*, a group and a document initiated by John D. Rockefeller III to attract national support for his lifelong conviction that the need to curb population growth was an imperative that should override lesser ethical considerations. See *Population and the American Future* (New York: New American Library, Signet Edition, 1972).

266. Williams, "Euthanasia and Abortion," p. 199; Potts et al., p. 203.

267. Enid Nemy, "From Saving Lives to Ending Them: Why Many Nurses Shun Abortion Duty," *New York Times*, 1 February 1972, p. 32.

268. Nathanson, *Aborting America*, p. 141.

269. Ibid., pp. 138, 136–37, 161.

270. Shaw, "Doctor," p. 54.

271. Norma Rosen, "Between Guilt and Gratification: Abortion Doctors Reveal Their Feelings," *New York Times Magazine*, 17 April 1977, pp. 73, 74, 78.

272. Joseph Fletcher, "Ethical Aspects of Genetic Controls: Designed Genetic Changes in Man," *New England Journal of Medicine* 285, no. 14 (30 September 1971): 776–83; reprinted in "Genetic Engineering," *Humanhood: Essays in Biomedical Ethics* (Buffalo: Prometheus, 1979), see pp. 89–90. Lader designates Fletcher as "the foremost philosopher of [abortion law] repeal." *Abortion II*, p. 90.

273. Geyer, p. D5; Marcia Kramer, "Ethical Issues in Neonatal Intensive Care: An Economic Perspective," in Albert H. Jonsen and Michael J. Garland, eds., *Ethics of Newborn Intensive Care* (Berkeley: Institute of Governmental Studies, University of California, 1976), pp. 75–93.

274. Henry P. David, "Abortion: A Continuing Debate," *Family Planning Perspectives* 10, no. 5 (September-October 1978): 313–16.

275. Stephen Fleck, "A Psychiatrist's View on Abortion," in Walbert and Butler, p. 182.

276. Potts et al., pp. 227–28.

277. Quoted by Barbara Ross, "Abortion-II," *New York Post*, 14 February 1979, p. 16.

278. Williams, "The Law of Abortion," *Current Law Problems* 5 (1952): 147.

279. James J. Kilpatrick, "Abortion: A Poor Presidential Issue," *Washington Star*, 18 September 1976.

280. *Population and the American Future*, p. 173.

281. "They did not consciously suppress affection for the fetus or deny there was a human life at stake." John Fletcher, "The Brink: The Parent-Child Bond in the Genetic Revolution," *Theological Studies* 33, no. 3 (September 1972): 457–85.

282. Perez-Reyes and Falk, pp. 120–26. See also Mary K. Zimmerman, *Passage through Abortion: The Personal and Social Reality of Women's Experiences* (New York: Praeger, 1977).

283. Potts et al., pp. 3, 545.

284. Ruth Tiffany Barnhouse, letter to the editor, *New England Journal of Medicine* 292, no. 9 (27 February 1975): 485.

285. Interviewed in Charlotte L. Rosenberg, "The Abortion Revolution: Don't Rush It," *Medical Economics* 5, no. 5 (5 March 1973): 31–45.

286. Garrett Hardin, "Abortion and Human Dignity," in Sharon Robbins and Bruce Granger, *Having a Wonderful Abortion* (New York: Exposition, 1971), pp. 145–46; see Norman St. John-Stevas, *The Right to Life* (London: Hodder and Stoughton, 1963), pp. 22, 19.

287. Williams, *Sanctity of Life*, p. 15.

288. Williams, ibid., pp. 14–15; Garrett Hardin, "The History and Future of Birth Control," *Perspectives in Biology and Medicine* 10, no. 1 (Autumn 1966): 7.

289. See Madeleine Simms and Keith Hindell, *Abortion Law Reformed* (London: Peter Owen, 1971); Anthony Hordern, *Legal Abortion: The English Experience* (Oxford: Pergamon [1971]); Potts et al., pp. 277–97; Ramsey, *Ethics*, pp. 51–58.

290. See James C. Mohr, *Abortion in America: The Origins and Evolution of National Policy, 1800–1900* (New York: Oxford, 1978); Lader, *Abortion II*; Ramsey, *Ethics*; Noonan, *Private Choice*; *Research on the Fetus*.

291. See *Pediatric Research* 7 (1973): 309. Also, *Journal of Endocrinology and Metabolism* 37 (1973): 74; 42 (1976): 612.

292. Robbins and Granger, p. 63. Apropos of this, authors have been remarking on the significantly increased incidence of child abuse since the decriminalization of abortion.

293. Nathanson, *Aborting America*, p. 182.

294. Williams, *Sanctity of life*, p. x.

295. Michael Tooley, "Infanticide and Abortion," *Philosophy and Public Affairs* 1, no. 2 (Fall 1972): 37–65.

296. Milton Heifetz, *The Right to Die* (New York: Putnam, 1975), pp. 51–56.

297. Shaw, "Doctor."

298. F. Raymond Marks, "The Defective Newborn: An Analytic Framework for a Policy Dialogue," in Jonsen and Garland, pp. 97–125; see also Ramsey, *Ethics*, pp. 230–31. Dr. Joshua Lederberg, of Stanford, has suggested that while public policy is constrained by emotional bias and taste, the point where individuals of our species become measurably human beings—and logically begin to have a right to survive—is at about the first year after birth, with the acquisition of language. "A Geneticist

Looks at Contraception and Abortion," *Annals of Internal Medicine* 65, no. 3, pt. 2 (September 1967): 25–27. Glanville Williams writes: "Regarded in this spirit, an eugenic killing by a mother, exactly paralleled by the bitch that kills her mis-shapen puppies, cannot confidently be pronounced immoral. And where this certainty is lacking, should not liberty prevail?" At the close of his book Williams suggests that elimination of handicapped children might be a good thing to legalize, though he finds (in 1957) only insignificant public support for such a suggestion. Williams, *Sanctity of Life*, pp. 349–50. He is, on this subject, not a bulwark of principle.

299. John M. Freeman, "To Treat or Not to Treat: Ethical Dilemmas of Treating the Infant with a Myelomeningocele," *Clinical Neurosurgery* 20 (1973): 134–46. Cited in D. M. Forrest, "Modern Trends in the Treatment of Spina Bifida," *Proceedings of the Royal Society of Medicine* 60 (1967): 763–67.

300. Reported by Eunice Kennedy Shriver in a dedicatory speech at Chisholm, Minnesota, 8 February 1973.

301. Gilbert Cant, "Deciding When Death is Better Than Life," *Time*, 16 July 1973, pp. 36–37.

302. See Littlewood, pp. 113ff.

303. Ibid., pp. 200–202, citing Ron Wiggins, "Growth Is a Curse in Fecundity," *Palm Beach Post*, 23 July 1975.

304. Geneticist James V. Neel, for example, points out that "early abortion based on prenatal diagnosis can be viewed as the modern counterpart of infanticide based on congenital defect." "Ethical Issues Resulting from Pre-Natal Diagnosis," in Maureen Harris, ed., *Early Diagnosis of Human Genetic Defects: Scientific and Ethical Considerations*, Fogarty International Center Proceedings 6 (Washington: U.S. Government Printing Office, 1972), p. 221.

305. Gaylin and Lappé, p. 66.

306. Duff and Campbell, p. 892.

307. John Updike, *Couples* (New York: Knopf, 1968), p. 380.

308. Rosenberg, p. 39.

309. *Modern Medicine*, 14 May 1973, p. 35.

310. Nathanson, *Aborting America*, p. 112.

311. See Pamela Zeckman, Pamela Warrick et al., "The Abortion Racketeers," *Chicago Sun-Times*, 13, 17, 19, 12, 29, 18 November 1978.

312. Ibid., 17 November 1978.

313. Williams, "Legalization," p. 25.

314. Neel, pp. 133–34.

315. *Washington Post*, 2 June 1977, p. 13.

316. *NARAL Newsletter* 11, no. 4 (May–June 1979): 2.

317. Jesse Jackson, black leader in Chicago, has opposed "the use of federal funds for a policy of killing infants. The money would be much better expended to meet human needs. I am therefore urging that the Hyde Amendment be supported in the interest of a more humane policy and some new directions in caring for the most precious resource we have—our children." In a speech, 6 September 1977. Joining in objections to funded abortion as a genocidal policy are the Council of La Raza, the Nation of Islam, the Southern Christian Leadership Conference, the Progressive National [Black] Baptists' Convention, and ethnic leaders Cesar Chavez, Constance Redbird Uri, and Dick Gregory.

318. Quoted in Noonan, *Private Choice*, p. 111.

319. "Abortion: The Doctor's Dilemma," *Modern Medicine* 35, no. 9 (24 April 1967): 12–32. Psychiatrists were most desirous of change; least were obstetrician-gynecologists. Grounds which were decisively not reckoned legitimate were "illegitimacy" (supported by only 29 percent), "socioeconomic" (27 percent), and "on demand"

(14 percent). This correlates interestingly with the National Fertility Study in 1965, to which American women replied that abortion should be permitted for health reasons (87 percent) or deformity (50 percent) or rape (52 percent), but not for illegitimacy (13 percent), economic reasons (11 percent), or on demand (8 percent). See Norman Ryder and Charles Westoff, *Reproduction in the United States, 1965* (Princeton: Princeton University Press, 1971), pp. 269–70.

320. Johan W. Eliot, Robert E. Hall, J. Robert Willson, and Carolyn Houser, "The Obstetrician's View," in Hall, 1:85–95.

321. Vatican II, Constitution on the Church in the Modern World, 7 December 1965, par. 27; quoted in *Documentation on the Right to Life and Abortion* (Washington: U.S. Catholic Conference, 1974), pp. 71–72.

322. "Human Life in Our Day," pastoral letter of the National Conference of Catholic Bishops, 15 November 1968; quoted in *Documentation*, p. 69.

323. Albert Outler, "The Beginnings of Personhood: Theological Considerations," *Perkins Journal* (Southern Methodist University Divinity School) 27, no. 1 (Fall 1973): 31–32.

324. Harold O. J. Brown, "An Evangelical Looks at the Abortion Phenomenon," *America* 135, no. 8 (25 September 1976): 164.

325. Charles E. Curran, "Abortion: Law and Morality in Contemporary Catholic Theology," *Jurist* 33, no. 2 (Spring 1973): 182–83.

326. *Research on the Fetus*, Appendix, p. 3–12.

327. National Catholic News Service release, 28 June 1978. See also "A Life 'Cut Short,' " *America* 139, no. 2 (15–22 July 1978): 23.

328. John Moore and John Pamperin, "Abortion and the Church," *Christian Century* 87, no. 20 (20 May 1970): 629–31.

329. See James Wilkinson, "A Doctor Speaks on Abortion," *London Express*, 25 January 1967; also Potts et al., p. 289.

330. *Aborting America* is the story of Nathanson's change; see also other contrasting stories in Rosen, pp. 70–80.

331. Russell L. McIntyre, "Abortion: Perceptions of the Clinical Perspective," *Dialog* 17, no. 2 (Spring 1978): 106.

332. C. Eric Lincoln, "Why I Reversed My Stand on Laissez-Faire Abortion," *Christian Century* 90, no. 17 (25 April 1973): 477–79. Lincoln thinks the state should, as guardian of public welfare and policy, rediscover an interest in regulating abortion. For the medical profession he has much blame: "A decision about abortion is not properly the doctor's responsibility unless a medical problem is involved, and most abortions currently demanded are not even remotely 'medical.' Since the physician was not a party to the procreative act, his role in determining the consequences of that act is questionable. We have made of medicine a convenient façade. We have made of the doctor a mere functionary and accessory—a scapegoat for the clergy, the judiciary, the pregnant woman and her partner in the act, for all the rest of us who turn away from personal and social accountability. This is social progress?"

333. *Chicago Sun-Times*, 3 December 1978. See, however, Charles Bayer, "Confessions of an Abortion Counselor," *Christian Century* 87, no. 20 (20 May 1970): 624–26, who while continuing to refer women for abortions was uneasy that the Clergy Consultation Service was not answering "the hard questions."

334. See, for instance, the advocacy in Beverly Harrison, "Toward a Just Social Order," *Journal of Current Social Issues* 15, no. 1 (Spring 1978): 63–70; Sarah Weddington, "The Woman's Right of Privacy," *Perkins Journal* 27, no. 1 (Fall 1973): 35–41 (Weddington was appellant's attorney in *Roe* v. *Wade*).

335. See release by *Washington Post* News Service, 1 March 1977; also column by Joan Beck, *Chicago Tribune*, 20 August 1976.

336. See 39 Bundesverfassungsgericht 1 (25 February 1975), available in Robert E. Jonas and John D. Gorby, "Translation of the German Federal Constitutional Court Decision," *John Marshall Journal of Practice and Procedure* 9 (1976): 605, 641, 642, 643, 645, 662; Ernst Benda, "The Impact of Constitutional Law on the Protection of Unborn Life: Some Comparative Remarks," *Human Rights* 6 (1977): 227; *Nuernberg Trials*, 2:181–82; also Donald Kommers, "Abortion and the Constitution: United States and West Germany," *American Journal of Comparative Law* 25 (1977): 225. Somewhat more permissive legislation which permits abortion in certain circumstances was passed by the German Parliament in 1976, and has not yet sustained a test of its constitutionality. See *Bulletin* (Press and Information Office of the Federal Government, Bonn) 6 (27 May 1980). Laws restrictive of abortion in the Federal Republic have been upheld by the European Human Rights Commission: see *Yearbook of the European Convention on Human Rights, 1978*, Resolution D H (78) 1 of the Committee of Ministers, Brueggeman Case, p. 638.

Essay 4
Eliza and Lizzie Scott, and Infants Roe and Doe: How They Fared— Slavery and Abortion in America

1. *Dred Scott v. John F. A. Sandford*, 19 Howard 393, 412, 413, 409 (1857). The defendant's surname, Sanford, was wrongly spelled throughout the case report.

2. *Roe v. Wade*, 410 U.S. 113, 157, 162 (1973). Jane Roe is the plaintiff-appellant's pseudonym. Reference is made below also to *Wade's* companion case, *Doe v. Bolton*, 410 U.S. 179 (1973).

3. 19 Howard at 405.

4. See Don E. Fehrenbacher, *The Dred Scott Case: Its Significance in American Law and Politics* (New York: Oxford University Press, 1978), pp. 305–21. I owe much to the thoroughness and sagacity of Fehrenbacher's study.

5. 410 U.S. at 153, 208 (1973), (Burger, C.J., concurring.) The point is repeated often in the Court's opinion, *id*. at 150, 154, 155, 162, 189.

6. 19 Howard at 454, 455.

7. Thomas L. Shaffer, "Brothers in Law," review of *The Brethren*, by Bob Woodward and Scott Armstrong, in *Review of Politics* 43, no. 1 (January 1981): 133.

8. "[A]bolition, with all its annoyances and offenses against our peace and safety, has resulted in our moral reassurance,—in the establishing, to our own perfect conviction, our right to the labor of our slaves, and in relieving us from all that doubt, that morbid feeling of weakness in respect to the moral of our claim, which was undoubtedly felt so long as we forebore the proper consideration of the argument. Twenty years ago, few persons in the South undertook to justify Negro Slavery, except on the score of necessity. Now, very few persons in the same region, question their perfect right to the labor of their slaves,—and more,—their moral obligation to keep them still subject, as slaves, and to compel their labor, so long as they remain the inferior beings which we find them now, and which they seem to have been from the beginning." W. Gilmore Simms, "The Morals of Slavery," *Southern Literary Messenger*, 1837, reprinted in *The Pro-Slavery Argument, as Maintained by the Most Distinguished Writers of the Southern States* (Philadelphia: Lippincott, Grambo, 1853), p. 179. The struggle had caused the respective sides to articulate their positions more sharply.

9. See Louis Filler, *The Crusade against Slavery, 1830–1860* (New York: Harper & Brothers, 1960), pp. 247–48.

10. Charles Warren, *The Supreme Court in United States History*, 3 vols., rev.

ed. (Boston: Little, Brown, 1923),3:79.

11. Derrick A. Bell, Jr., ed., *Race, Racism, and American Law* (Boston: Little, Brown, 1973), p. 21.

12. 410 U.S. at 116.

13. U.S., Congress, Senate, *Abortion: Hearings on S.J.Res. 119 and S.J.Res. 130 before the Subcommittee on Constitutional Amendments of the Committee on the Judiciary*, 93rd Cong., 2nd sess., vol. 1 (1974), p. 123, (Statement of Bella S. Abzug).

14. For the most reliable analyses of public opinion on abortion see the studies of Judith Blake: "Abortion and Public Opinion: The 1960–1970 Decade," *Science* 171, no. 3971 (12 February 1971): 540–49; "Elective Abortion and our Reluctant Citizenry: Research on Public Opinion in the United States," in Howard J. Osofsky and Joy D. Osofsky, eds., *The Abortion Experience: Psychological and Medical Impact* (Hagerstown: Harper & Row, 1973), pp. 447–67; "The Supreme Court's Abortion Decisions and Public Opinion in the United States," *Population and Development Review* 3, nos. 1–2 (March–June 1977): 45–62; "The Abortion Decisions: Judicial Review and Public Opinion," in Edward Manier, William Liu, and David Solomon, eds., *Abortion: New Directions for Policy Studies* (Notre Dame: University of Notre Dame Press, 1977), pp. 51–82; and idem and Jorge H. del Pinal, "Predicting Polar Attitudes toward Abortion in the United States," in James Tunstead Burtchaell, C.S.C., ed., *Abortion Parley* (Kansas City: Andrews & McMeel, 1980), pp. 27–56.

Many advocates of abortion have not been absorbing what the polls have been disclosing. For instance, Bella Abzug, testifying at Senate hearings in 1974, presented a summary of the polls by ACLU official Arlie Schardt who concluded that most Americans agreed with *Wade* and *Bolton*. See *Abortion: Hearings* (Senate) 1, pp. 122, 123, 127. Linda Greenhouse writes, with more caution: ". . . the Court has entangled itself in the political process—exactly what the Justices wish to avoid. The Court usually has a well-developed instinct for self-preservation; if it finds itself moving uncomfortably far away from a perceived consensus, it tends to pull back and wait for the Legislative and Executive Branches to set the tone by setting policy. Some Justices may believe that their 1973 *Roe* v. *Wade* decision, making abortion a constitutional right, was as far in the van of a national consensus as the Court should prudently get." " 'Minimal Scrutiny' Leads to a Foreseeable Decision," *New York Times*, 6 July 1980, p. 4E. Karen Mulhauser, executive director of the National Abortion Rights Action League, admits: "The country wasn't with us." Quoted in Roger M. Williams, "The Power of Fetal Politics," *Saturday Review*, 9 June 1979, p. 12.

15. See David W. Louisell and John T. Noonan, Jr., "Constitutional Balance," in Noonan, ed., *The Morality of Abortion: Legal and Historical Perspectives* (Cambridge: Harvard University Press, 1970), pp. 220–60.

16. 19 Howard at 404, 405.

17. *Id.* at 410. The Court's opinion passes over the fact that white women and children, though citizens, did not share in the political sovereignty (indeed, there were some legal acts impossible for them which a black man could perform); that alien men, not American citizens, enjoyed most rights under the Constitution; and that ships and corporations had been acknowledged as legal persons entitled to sue. The Taney Court had decided (with Taney himself delivering the opinion), in *Louisville, Cincinnati and Charleston Railroad* v. *Letson*, 2 Howard 497 (1844), that "A corporation . . . seems to us to be a person . . . and therefore entitled, for the purpose of suing and being sued, to be deemed a citizen." *Id.* at 555. On the inconsistency in the framers' minds on blacks, see Fehrenbacher, pp. 17–18.

18. 19 Howard at 425, 426. John Noonan has pointed out that "although Taney only needed to decide that the descendants of slaves were not 'citizens,' he went further and denied that these people had *any* rights under the Constitution. He

thereby denied their rights as *persons* under the Fifth Amendment." Review of Fehrenbacher, *Arizona State Law Journal* 1 (1979): 284.

19. 410 U.S. at 156, 157.

20. *Id.* at 152–162.

21. 19 Howard at 409, 407.

22. 410 U.S. at 163.

23. See Fehrenbacher's critique, pp. 335–88.

24. See John Connery, S.J., *Abortion: The Development of the Roman Catholic Perspective* (Chicago: Loyola University Press, 1977).

25. Justice Blackmun also has difficulties in keeping "animation" and "quickening" unconfused. For a more thorough treatment of this history see Joseph W. Dellapenna, "The History of Abortion: Technology, Morality and the Law," *University of Pittsburgh Law Review*, 40, no. 3 (Spring 1979): 359–428.

26. See the rectification of this treatment in James C. Mohr, *Abortion in America: The Origins and Evolution of National Policy, 1800–1900* (New York: Oxford University Press, 1978), pp. 29–31, 164–66, 216, and passim.

27. Sperm had, of course, long been known to be reproductive. Hence a more appropriate primitive view of the unborn was not, as Justice Blackmun reconstructs it, a "part of the mother," but an implant of the father.

28. See John T. Noonan, Jr., *A Private Choice* (New York: Free Press, 1979).

29. 19 Howard at 620, 621, (Curtis, J., dissenting.)

30. *Id.* at 538, (McLean, J., dissenting.)

31. 410 U.S. at 174, (Rehnquist, J., dissenting.)

32. *Id.* at 219, 220, (White, J., dissenting, joined by J. Rehnquist.)

33. 19 Howard at 550.

34. See Fehrenbacher, pp. 307–12; Noonan, *A Private Choice*, p. 45.

35. *Report of the Special Committee of the House of Representatives of South Carolina, on so much of the Message of his Excellency Gov. Jas. H. Adams, as Relates to Slavery and the Slave Trade* (Charleston: Walker Evans, 1857), p. 3. On the pleadings in *Dred Scott* see Fehrenbacher, p. 302.

36. Lance Morrow, "On Abortion and the Unfairness of Life," *Time*, 1 August 1977, p. 49.

37. Daniel Callahan, "Abortion and Government Policy," *Family Planning Perspectives* 11, no. 5 (September–October 1979): 275. See also Mary C. Segers, "Abortion: The Last Resort," *America* 133, no. 21 (27 December 1975): 457.

38. *Register of Debates in Congress*, 20th Cong., 1st sess., 4, p. 974 (10 January 1828).

39. Thornton Stringfellow, *The Bible Argument: or, Slavery in the Light of Divine Revelation*, reprinted in E. N. Elliott, ed., *Cotton Is King, and Pro-Slavery Arguments* (Augusta, Georgia: Pritchard, Abbot & Loomis, 1860), p. 521.

40. Thomas R. Dew, *Review of the Debate in the Virginia Legislature of 1831 and 1832* (Richmond: T. W. White, 1832), reprinted in *The Pro-Slavery Argument*, p. 292.

41. *"Negro Slavery Not Unjust," A Speech by Charles O'Conor at the Union Meeting, at the Academy of Music, New York City, Dec. 19, 1859 (New York Tribune* pamphlet).

42. [David Christy], *Cotton Is King: or the Culture of Cotton, and its Relation to Agriculture, Manufactures and Commerce; to the Free Colored People; and to Those Who Hold That Slavery Is in Itself Sinful* (Cincinnati: Moore, Wilstach, Keys, 1855), pp. 21–22. Another partisan argued similarly: "These states could not, therefore, like the northern and northeastern states, emancipate the slave, or place him upon a footing with the white, and extend to him the right of suffrage and all other political

rights which belong to the free white citizen, without the most serious fears, not only of lessening, in a very sensible degree, the political influence and weight of the white portion of the population, but *much worse*—of raising up, within their own borders, a rival power which, at a future and not very distant day, might show itself a determined and formidable antagonist to the dominion, and even the existence, of the ruling race." "A South Carolinian" [Henry Middleton], *Economical Causes of Slavery in the United States, and Obstacles to Abolition* (London: Robert Hardwicke, 1857), p. 32.

43. Thomas R. Dew, in *The Pro-Slavery Argument*, pp. 377–78.

44. "Amor Patriae," *The Blasphemy of Abolition Exposed: Servitude, and the Rights of the South Vindicated; A Bible Argument* (New York: n.p., 1850), p. 13.

45. *New York Times*, 27 November 1977, pp. 1, 29.

46. [Middleton], p. 45.

47. "Amor Patriae," p. 17.

48. "How far [Benjamin] Franklin's influence failed to promote the humane object he had in view, may be inferred from the fact, that forty-seven years after Pennsylvania struck off the shackles from her slaves, and thirty-eight after he issued his Appeal [for funds to help free blacks], one-third of the convicts in her penitentiary were colored men, while few of the other free States were more fortunate; and some of them even worse—one-half of New Jersey's convicts being colored men. . . . Unfortunately, the free colored people persevered in their evil habits. . . . Thus the free colored people themselves, ruthlessly threw the car of emancipation from the track, and tore up the rails upon which, alone, it could move." [Christy], pp. 17–18. See also Albert Deutsch, "The First U.S. Census of the Insane (1840) and Its Use as Pro-Slavery Propaganda," *Bulletin of the History of Medicine* 15 (1944): 469ff.; Filler, p. 96.

49. Samuel Tyler, *Memoir of Roger Brooke Taney, LL.D.*, 2nd ed. (Baltimore: Murphy, 1876), pp. 660–64; Fehrenbacher, p. 428.

50. *Scott, a Man of Color* v. *Emerson*, 15 Missouri Reports 576, 587 (1852).

51. Chancellor Harper, *Memoir on Slavery*, reprinted in *The Pro-Slavery Argument*, pp. 48–49.

52. [Middleton], pp. 39–40.

53. Dew, p. 459.

54. Ibid., p. 451; Elliott, *Cotton Is King, and Pro-Slavery Arguments*, p. ix.

55. Harper, in *The Pro-Slavery Argument*, pp. 50–51.

56. *Abortion: Hearings* (Senate) 1, p. 110.

57. "Statement of Social Principles," II, (D), *Journal of the 1972 General Conference of the United Methodist Church*, John L. Schreiber, ed., (n.p., 1972), 2:1058.

58. John D. Rockefeller III, "No Retreat on Abortion," *Newsweek*, 21 June 1976, p. 11.

59. *Abortion: Hearings* (Senate) 2, pp. 588–89 (Statement of Garrett Hardin); Garrett Hardin, *Mandatory Motherhood: The True Meaning of "Right to Life"* (Boston: Beacon, 1974), pp. 98–100.

60. *Abortion: Hearings* (Senate), 1, p. 106.

61. Ibid. 2, p. 540 (Statement of Frank Johnson).

62. Vivian Lindermayer and Eric Lindermayer, "Continuing the Discussion; How to Argue About Abortion: II," *Christianity and Crisis* 37, no. 21 (26 December 1977): 318.

63. *Beal* v. *Doe*, 432 U.S. 438, 456 (1977), (Marshall, J., dissenting.)

64. *Id.* at 463, (Blackmun, J., dissenting, joined by JJ. Brennan and Marshall) this dissent applies also to the companion cases *Maher* v. *Roe, id.* at 464, and *Poelker* v. *Doe, id.* at 519.

65. See James B. Sellers, *Slavery in Alabama* (University, Alabama: University

of Alabama Press, 1950), pp. 344–45. Also Kenneth M. Stampp, *The Peculiar Institution: Slavery in the Ante-Bellum South* (New York: Random House, Vintage Edition, 1956), pp. 8–9.

66. M. T. Wheat, *The Progress and Intelligence of Americans; Collateral Proof of Slavery*, 2nd ed. (Louisville: n.p., 1862).

67. John Campbell, *Negro-Mania: Being an Examination of the Falsely Assumed Equality of the Various Races of Men* (Philadelphia: Campbell & Power, 1851), pp. 6, 11.

68. Harper, in *The Pro-Slavery Argument*, p. 14.

69. Fehrenbacher, p. 355.

70. O'Conor, p. 12.

71. [Middleton], p. 20.

72. Ibid., p. 21.

73. Rev. John H. Caldwell, *Slavery and Southern Methodism: Two Sermons Preached in the Methodist Church in Newman, Georgia* (Printed for the Author, 1865), pp. 18–19.

74. Hodge's *Essays and Reviews*, quoted in George D. Armstrong, *The Christian Doctrine of Slavery* (New York: Charles Scribner, 1857), p. 108.

75. Sissela Bok, "Fetal Research and the Value of Life," in *Research on the Fetus*: Report and Recommendations of the National Commission for the Protection of Human Subjects of Biomedical and Behavioral Research (U.S. Department of Health, Education, and Welfare Publication No. [OS] 76–128, 1975), Appendix, p. 2–7.

76. *Abortion: Hearings* (Senate) 1, pp. 408–10 (Statement of Robert Veatch).

77. Ibid. 1, p. 257 (Statement of Bishop James Armstrong of the United Methodist Church); p. 268 (Statement of Ms. Jane Stitt of the Presbyterian Church in the United States).

78. See, for example, *Report: H. R., So. Carolina*, pp. 30–31, where the resumption of slave importation is recommended (in 1857), so as to hold down the price of cotton from 15 cents a pound to 10 cents.

79. [Christy], pp. 14, 28–34.

80. Stampp, p. 5.

81. Ibid., pp. 29–30.

82. *Report: H.R., So. Carolina*, p. 53.

83. See, for example, Bella Abzug, in *Abortion: Hearings* (Senate) 1, pp. 119–20; Bentley Glass, "It's an Individual Choice," *Wall Street Journal*, 26 October 1976, p. 26.

84. Christopher Tietze, *Induced Abortion: 1979*, 3rd ed. (New York: Population Council, 1979), pp. 35, 59.

85. Rev. Rufus Wm. Bailey, *The Issue Presented in a Series of Letters on Slavery* (New York: John S. Taylor, 1837), pp. 18, 21, 57–58.

86. Charles K. Whipple, *Relations of Anti-Slavery to Religion* (New York: American Anti-Slavery Society, 1856), p. 1; Filler, pp. 23–24.

87. George D. Armstrong, *Christian Doctrine of Slavery*, p. 136; Armstrong was a Presbyterian pastor in Norfolk, Virginia.

88. Filler, pp. 13, 17, 28ff., 232, 261–63, 278.

89. See W. E. B. DuBois, ed., *The Negro Church* (Atlanta: Atlanta University Press, 1903), p. 22; Stampp, p. 345.

90. Armstrong, p. 144.

91. Wendell Phillips Garrison and Francis Jackson Garrison, *William Lloyd Garrison, 1805–1879; The Story of His Life Told by His Children* (Boston: Houghton, Mifflin, 1889), 3:12–13.

92. H. Mattison, *The Impending Crisis of 1860: or the Present Connection of the*

Methodist Episcopal Church with Slavery, and Our Duty in Regard to It (New York: Mason Bros., 1858), pp. 5ff. See also Lucius C. Matlack, *The History of American Slavery and Methodism, from 1780 to 1849: and History of the Wesleyan Methodist Connection of America* (New York: n.p., 1849).

93. Mattison, p. 41.

94. Caldwell, pp. 33–34.

95. See Lawrence Lader, *Abortion II: Making the Revolution* (Boston; Beacon, 1973), chap. 4, "Referral Services, The Gentle (And Not So Gentle) Lawbreakers," pp. 42ff; also Bernard N. Nathanson, with Richard N. Ostling, *Aborting America* (Garden City, N.Y.: Doubleday, 1979), pp. 26, 42–43, 66, 81, 94.

96. See Judith Blake, "The Abortion Decisions," in Manier, Liu, and Solomon, pp. 51ff.

97. See Nathanson, pp. 31, 51–52; see index, s.v. "Roman Catholic Church."

98. 122 *Congressional Record*, 94th Cong., 2nd sess., 28 April 1976, S6129–6130.

99. National Catholic News Service release, 11 September 1980.

100. *New York Times*, "The Archbishop and Abortion," 19 September 1980, p. A26.

101. *The Book of Resolutions of the United Methodist Church, 1968* (Nashville: Methodist Publishing House, 1968), Approved Resolution on Responsible Parenthood, p. 50—see also p. 96; *Journal of the General Conference of the United Methodist Church*, John L. Schreiber, ed. (1972), 2:1058; idem, ed., 1976, 2:1176–77; *The Book of Discipline of the United Methodist Church* (Nashville: Methodist Publishing House, 1980), par. 71G, p. 91. The church's only express misgiving about future abortion use is that there might not be enough widespread availability of contraception; but for the Christian use of contraception the Statement of Social Principles offers no guidance.

102. Paul Ramsey, "Feticide / Infanticide Upon Request," *Religion in Life* 39, no. 2 (Summer 1970): 172–73.

103. *The Works of William H. Seward*, ed. George E. Baker (New York: Redfield, 1853), 1:66, 74–75.

104. John Weiss, *The Life and Correspondence of Theodore Parker* (New York: Appleton, 1864), 2:146; Theodore Parker, *The Trial of Theodore Parker, for the "Misdemeanor" of a Speech in Faneuil Hall against Kidnapping, before the Circuit Court of the United States, at Boston, April 3, 1855, with the Defense* (Boston: by the author, 1855), pp. 188–89, 213–14 (see also pp. 10–11, 16).

105. Weiss, 2:185–86; Fehrenbacher, p. 554. The brief of counsel against Dred Scott before the Missouri Supreme Court had also railed against "higher law demagogues," *Scott, a Man of Color* v. *Emerson*, 15 Missouri Reports 576, 577–581 (1852); Norris, for Plaintiff.

106. See Filler, pp. 15–16, 163, 202, 216; Lawrence Lader, *The Bold Brahmins, New England's War against Slavery: 1831–1963* (New York: Dutton, 1961), pp. 55–56, 101ff., 117, 164.

107. Filler, p. 28; see also pp. 74, 100–101.

108. Ibid., pp. 209–10.

109. Harper, in *The Pro-Slavery Argument*, p. 5.

110. *Congressional Globe*, 31st Cong., 1st sess. (1850), p. 258.

111. Bailey, p. 39. He also writes: "Christian masters, and ministers of the Gospel, especially, were actively engaged with much success, until a set of gentlemen from abroad, interfered, saying, 'Sirs, you are altogether behind the age. This slavery is a sin and the only way to treat sin is to leave it off. Therefore, immediate abolition is the true doctrine, and these slaves are your fellow citizens.' This doctrine could not be received—and when it is officiously, and pertinaciously and imprudently urged, the

slaveholder says to the abolitionist, leave my home, Sir,—you shall not be permitted to speak to me or my family" (p. 35).

112. *Congressional Globe*, 34th Cong., 1st sess. (1856), Appendix, p. 5.

113. *Register of Debates in Congress*, 20th Cong., 1st sess., (1828) 4, 974–75, speech of William Drayton, Member from South Carolina.

114. *Southern Agriculturalist* 2 (1829): 575–76, quoted in Stampp, p. 423.

115. Simms, in *The Pro-Slavery Argument*, p. 183.

116. "Amor Patriae," p. 11.

117. Jackson *Mississippian*, 17 September 1858, quoted in Stampp, p. 272.

118. Campbell, p. 546.

119. [Middleton], p. 53.

120. NARAL fund appeal letter, July 1979.

121. *Abortion: Hearings* (Senate) 1, pp. 100–102.

122. Garrett Hardin, *Mandatory Motherhood*, p. 28.

123. Lader, *Abortion II*, p. 81.

124. Leaflet distributed for the NARAL Foundation, October 1978.

125. NARAL advertisement, *New York Times*, 16 July 1978, p. E5.

126. *Congressional Quarterly Weekly Report* 33 (1975), pp. 815–16.

127. Filler, pp. 42–43; see also p. 276.

128. Ibid., pp. 258–59. Filler quotes, ibidem, a Kentucky Senator sympathetic to union: "[The South] had some cause to complain of a few old women and fanatical preachers and madmen in the Northern States, who were always agitating this question, but nine out of ten of the Northern people were sound upon the subject. . . . They were willing to accord to the slaveholder and the slave States all their constitutional rights."

129. Lader, *Bold Brahmins*, p. 67.

130. Filler, p. 161.

131. Juli Loesch, "Abortion and an Attempt at Dialogue," *America* 140, no. 11 (24 March 1979): 234–36.

132. Lader, *Bold Brahmins*, p. 269.

133. Ann Crittenden, "A Colloquy in the Sanger Spirit," *New York Times*, 18 September 1979, p. B8.

134. The Constitution of the United States of America was unprecedented in its respect for the continuing autonomy of the member states. It was (and is) an extraordinary arrangement among nations for a general government to abide such robust privileges in any of its constituent fractions. The Constitution itself required adhesion by all belonging states, and ratification of amendments by three of every four. It was an unusual thought that the entire might of the executive, the legislature, and the courts could be called to heel by arrangements between the member states. Federal officers—president, vice-president, and senators—were chosen by the states through electors and legislatures. The states retained their own militiae and police, while denying to the federal government both standing army and national constabulary. The new union was a federation of states that were sovereign, not subordinate. They reserved to themselves the privilege of all sovereigns: not to be hailed into court save by their own consent. In one sense the states enjoyed a sovereignty that was even more primal. The general government held only those powers expressly delegated by the states, whereas the states were free to assume practically any civil powers. Still more: at the outset the federal government was obliged to yield to the people an unheard-of set of freedoms. They were to be free of a national religion and of interference in religion by the government; they could assemble, speak, and publish as they pleased; and the writ of *habeas corpus* ran the length of the land. Yet these restraints which the states imposed upon the national government they did not lay upon themselves

uniformly until the adoption of the Fourteenth Amendment nearly a century later.

135. An individual citizen might come and go through naturalization and expatriation (voluntary or involuntary). Yet for the states there was no such symmetry. Provision was made for accession to the Union, but none for secession or expulsion. By entering the Union, a state became bound by kinship to all others. The freedom if its territory then belonged by right to the people of every other state, for its land was now somehow part of the common heritage of all Americans.

136. Letter of 20 December 1787, in *The Papers of Thomas Jefferson*. ed. Julian P. Boyd et al. (Princeton: Princeton University Press, 1950–55), 12:442.

137. Letter of 30 January 1787, in Boyd, 11:93.

138. Letter to John Taylor, 1 June 1798, in *The Writings of Thomas Jefferson*, ed. Paul Leicester Ford, 10 vols. (New York: G. P. Putnam's Sons, 1892–99), 7:264–65.

139. Letter to Baron F. H. Alexander von Humboldt, 13 June 1817, in Ford (1899), 10:89.

140. Letter to Albert Gallatin, 26 December 1820, in Ford, 12:185. "Are our slaves to be presented with freedom and a dagger?" he wrote to John Adams, 21 January 1821, ibid., p. 198.

141. See John Chester Miller, *The Wolf by the Ears: Thomas Jefferson and Slavery* (New York: Free Press, 1977), pp. 23–26.

142. *Notes on Virginia*, Memorial Edition (Washington: Thomas Jefferson Association, 1903), 2:225–28.

143. Letter to Jean Nicolas Demeunier, 26 June 1786, in Boyd, 10:63.

144. William W. Freehling credits Jefferson with enough pragmatism to do what he could. By eliminating slavery from the North, keeping it out of the West, and abolishing the slave trade, he at least made slavery "a crippled, restricted" institution. But Jefferson can be given little responsibility for emancipation in the North; he supported the Northwest Ordinance of 1787 but fought to allow the extension of slavery throughout his Louisiana Purchase; and the abolition of slave trade in 1808 was Congress's work. "The Founding Fathers and Slavery," *American Historical Review* 77 (1972): 81–93. See also William Cohen, "Jefferson and the Problem of Slavery," *Journal of American History* 56 (1969): 503–26.

145. Miller, p. 18.

146. Ibid., pp. 277–78.

147. *Memoirs of John Quincy Adams*, ed. Charles Francis Adams (Philadelphia: Lippincott, 1876), 8:299–300. A further Adams comment: "Although Jefferson was not inclined in his last days to avow his perseverance in his opinions upon negro slavery, he was willing to let them loose after his death—the motive for which appears to be to secure to himself posthumous fame as a prophet" (p. 238).

148. Speech at Peoria, 16 October 1854, in *The Collected Works of Abraham Lincoln*, ed. Roy P. Basler (New Brunswick, New Jersey: Rutgers University Press, 1953), 2:270.

149. Ibid., pp. 255–56. On Lincoln's intransigent refusal to allow extension of slavery in the territories, see Richard N. Current, *The Lincoln Nobody Knows* (New York: McGraw-Hill, 1958), chap. 4, "The Man Who Said No," pp. 76–103.

150. Speech in Peoria, 16 October 1854, in Basler, 2:249.

151. Ibid., pp. 265–66.

152. 4 March 1865, ibid., 8:332.

153. Letter to George Robertson, 15 August 1855, ibid., 2:318.

154. Fragment on Pro-Slavery Theology, 1 October 1858(?), ibid., 3:204–5.

155. Address at Baltimore Sanitary Fair, 18 April 1964, ibid., 7:301–2.

156. Letter to Eliza P. Gurney, 4 September 1864, ibid., 7:535.

157. Letter to John Wayles Eppes, 11 September 1813, in Ford, 9:396.

158. During the War with Mexico, when Lincoln served his only term in Congress, he said this to the House of Representatives: "Any people anywhere, being inclined and having the power, have the *right* to rise up, and shake off the existing government, and form a new one that suits them better. This is a most valuable,—a most sacred right—a right, which we hope and believe, is to liberate the world. Nor is this right confined to cases in which the whole people of an existing government, may choose to exercise it. Any portion of such people that *can, may* revolutionize, and make their *own*, of so much of the territory as they inhabit. More than this, a *majority* of any portion of such people may revolutionize, putting down a *minority*, intermingled with, or near about them, who may oppose their movement. Such minority, was precisely the case, of the tories of our own revolution." Speech in the U.S. House of Representatives, in Basler, 1:438–39.

159. Letter to John Holmes, 22 April 1820, in Ford, 12:159.

Essay 5
How Much is a Child Worth? From Abortion to Infanticide

1. Karl Binding & Alfred Hoche, *Die Freigabe der Vernichtung lebensunwerten Lebens: Ihr Mass und ihre Form* (Leipzig: Felix Meiner, 1920).

2. Fritz Barth, *Euthanasie: Das Problem der Vernichtung lebensunwerten Lebens* (Heidelberg: Paul Braus, 1924).

3. See Bert Honolka, *Die Kreuzelschreiber: Aerzte ohne Gewissen; Euthanasie im Dritten Reich* (Hamburg: Rütten & Loening, 1961), pp. 92–93.

4. Glanville Williams, *The Sanctity of Life and the Criminal Law*; The 1956 James S. Carpentier Lectures at the Columbia Law School (New York: Knopf, 1957), pp. 13–20, 349–50. Williams quotes Millard S. Everett, *Ideals of Life* (New York, 1954), p. 347.

5. Williams, "The Legalization of Medical Abortion," *Eugenics Review* 56, no. 1 (April 1964): 22; *Sanctity of Life*, p. 198.

6. Joseph Fletcher, *Situation Ethics* (Philadelphia: Westminster, 1966), p. 121.

7. Fletcher, "Ethical Aspects of Genetic Controls," *New England Journal of Medicine* 285, no. 14 (30 September 1971): 776–83.

8. Fletcher, "Indicators of Humanhood: A Tentative Profile of Man," *Hastings Center Report* 2, no. 5 (November 1972): 1–4; "Four Indicators of Humanhood—The Enquiry Matures," ibid. 4, no. 6 (December 1974): 4–7; see James T. Burtchaell, C.S.C., letter to the editor, ibid. 3, no. 1 (February 1973): 13.

9. Michael Tooley, "Abortion and Infanticide," *Philosophy and Public Affairs* 1, no. 2 (Fall 1972): 37–65; quotations at pp. 44, 63, 49, 64.

10. Anthony Shaw, "Doctor, Do We Have a Choice?" *New York Times Magazine*, 30 January 1972, pp. 44–54.

11. Shaw, "Dilemmas of 'Informed Consent' in Children," *New England Journal of Medicine* 289, no. 17 (25 October 1973): 885–90.

12. Raymond S. Duff and A. G. M. Campbell, "Moral and Ethical Dilemmas in the Special-Care Nursery," *New England Journal of Medicine* 289, no. 17 (25 October 1973): 890–94.

13. Beverley Kelsey, "Which Infants Should Live? Who Should Decide? An Interview with Dr. Raymond S. Duff," *Hastings Center Report* 5, no. 2 (April 1975): 5–8.

14. Milton Heifetz, *The Right to Die* (New York: Putnam, 1975), pp. 50–54, 64; see chap. 6, "The Tragic Newborn," pp. 43–72.

15. John M. Freeman, "To Treat or Not to Treat: Ethical Dilemmas of Treating

the Infant with a Myelomeningocele," *Clinical Neurosurgery* 20 (1973): 134–46; see also his *Practical Management of Myelomeningocele* (Baltimore: University Park Press, 1974); and "The Shortsighted Treatment of Myelomeningocele: A Long-Term Case Report," *Pediatrics* 53, no. 3 (March 1974): 311–13.

16. John C. Fletcher, "The Brink: The Parent-Child Bond in the Genetic Revolution," *Theological Studies* 33, no. 3 (September 1972): 457–85; quotations from pp. 466, 464, 470, 474, 478, 483.

17. John C. Fletcher, "Attitudes towards Defective Newborns," *Hastings Center Studies* 2, no. 1 (January 1974): 21–32.

18. John C. Fletcher, "Abortion, Euthanasia, and Care of Defective Newborns," *New England Journal of Medicine* 292, no. 2 (9 January 1975): 75–78. In this article Fletcher begins himself to advocate the removal of defective newborns "for whom death is the desirable outcome." With pain relief, denial of treatment "does no harm."

19. H. Tristram Englehardt, Jr., "The Beginnings of Personhood: Philosophical Considerations," *Perkins Journal* (Southern Methodist University Divinity School) 27, no. 1 (Fall 1973): 20–27. Englehardt's argument is circular—doubly so, in fact. He stipulates, without grounds, that mature functions define personhood, and then defines out all humans who are not yet mature. It is as if one were to ask what is a Freemason, then choose Shriners as the defining model, and then conclude that Masons at lower degrees of initiation are not truly Masons, only potential ones, for want of the red fez. Also, he bases his separation of human and personal life on two findings: one legal, by a Court that had neither the intention nor the capacity to decide a philosophical question; the other medical, which aimed at verifying, not when a person died within a living human body, but when the rationality of a human organism stopped. The Harvard doctors and the Ad Hoc Committee of the American Electroencephalographic Society on EEG Criteria for Determination of Cerebral Death had no more ambition to speak to a philosophical matter than did the nine justices. Engelhardt simply begins by accepting that the unborn is human but not personal, and constructs upon that an argument concluding that the unborn is human but not personal. This is of interest not because it is a contribution to philosophy, but because doctors who read it kill.

20. Engelhardt, "Viability, Abortion, and the Difference between a Fetus and an Infant," *American Journal of Obstetrics and Gynecology* 116, no. 3 (1 June 1973): 429–34.

21. Englehardt, "Ethical Issues in Aiding the Death of Small Children," in Marvin Kohl, ed., *Beneficent Euthanasia* (Buffalo: Prometheus, 1975), pp. 180–92; see also his "Bioethics and the Process of Embodiment," *Perspectives in Biology and Medicine* 18, no. 4 (Summer 1975): 486–500; and letter to the editor, *Journal of Pediatrics* 83, no. 1 (July 1973): 170–71.

22. Richard A. McCormick, S.J., "To Save or Let Die: The Dilemma of Modern Medicine," *Journal of the American Medical Association* 229, no. 2 (8 July 1974): 172–76. Also his "Human Life and Human Rights," in Alan D. Falconer, ed., *Understanding Human Rights* (Dublin: Irish School of Ecumenics, 1980), pp. 74–84.

23. McCormick, "The Quality of Life, The Sanctity of Life," *Hastings Center Report* 8, no. 1 (February 1978): 30–36; for a presentation harmonious with that of McCormick, see Paul Johnson, "Selective Nontreatment of Defective Newborns: An Ethical Analysis," *Linacre Quarterly* 47, no. 1 (February 1980): 39–53. The remainder of this chapter follows closely an earlier article of mine. James T. Burtchaell, "How Much Should A Child Cost? A Response to Paul Johnson," *Linacre Quarterly* 47, no. 1 (February 1980): 54–63.

24. *Prince* v. *Massachusetts*, 321 U.S. 158, 170 (1944).

25. Rosalyn Benjamin Darling, "Parents, Physicians and Spina Bifida," *Hastings*

Center Report 7, no. 4 (August 1977): 10–14. For a review of how some physicians eliminate handicapped infants, either by drugs or by starvation ("we don't feed them"), see R. B. Zachary, "Life with Spina Bifida," *British Medical Journal* (1977), no. 2, 1460–62. Says Zachary: "It has often been said by those who oppose abortion that the disregard for the life of a child in the uterus would spill over into postnatal life. This suggestion has been 'pooh-poohed,' yet in spina bifida there is a clear example of this. The equanimity with which the life of a 17-week-gestation spina bifida is terminated after the finding of a high level of *x*-fetoprotein in the amniotic fluid has, I think, spilled over to a similar disregard for the life of the child with spina bifida after birth. . . . The attitude of mind that would eliminate all the severely handicapped reminds me of the poster issued by Christian Aid some years ago, which said, 'Ignore the hungry and they will go away'—to their graves." Zachary is professor of pediatric surgery in Sheffield, England.

26. Daniel Callahan, "Who Should Be Born: Is Procreation a Right?" Quoted by John Fletcher, "The Brink," p. 482.

27. Lucy S. Dawidowicz, *The War against the Jews, 1933–1945* (New York: Holt, Rinehart and Winston, 1975), p. 163.

28. See James T. Burtchaell, "Reheating the Mutton Chop of Chesterton," *Review of Politics* 40, no. 4 (October 1978): 500, reviewing Margaret Canovan, *G. K. Chesterton: Radical Populist* (New York: Harcourt Brace Jovanovich, 1977).

29. Dawidowicz, pp. 291–92. See also Isaiah Trunk, *Jewish Responses to Nazi Persecution*, trans. Gabriel Trunk (New York: Stein and Day, 1979), pp. 229–34.

30. Dawidowicz, p. 299.

31. Frederic B. Westervelt, Jr., "The Selection Process as Viewed from Within: A Reply to Childress," *Soundings* 53, no. 4 (Winter 1970): 356–62.

32. Louis R. M. Del Guercio, "The Hippocratic Oath Hasn't Been Amended, But Vigilance Is Needed," *New York Times*, 2 September 1977, p. A21.

33. Dawidowicz, p. 162.

34. Jean Rostand, *Humanly Possible: A Biologist's Notes on the Future of Mankind*, trans. Lowell Bair (New York: Saturday Review Press, 1973), pp. 89–90. By way of contrast, see a collection of recent essays which reproduces, in most of its elements, the proposals of Binding, Hoche, and Barth: Marvin Kohl, ed., *Infanticide and the Value of Life* (Buffalo: Prometheus, 1978).

Sequelae

1. What follows was in part first published as "Abortion: Another Point of View," in Ann Landers, ed., *The Ann Landers Encyclopedia A to Z* (Garden City, New York: Doubleday, 1978), pp. 6–10.

Index

INDEX

Christian Action Council, 107
Christian Century, 343
Christy, David, 363, 365
Clark, Chase, 190
Clark, M., 328
Clark, Richard, 121
Clark, Tom, 203, 355
Clarke, Homer, 266
Clergy Consultation Service on
  Abortion, 213, 235, 267, 360
Cohen, William, 368
Cohn, Victor, 331
Coke, Thomas, 266
Colby, Richard, 343
Coles, Robert, 164, 171, 350
College of Obstetricians and
  Gynaecologists (U.K.), 222
Commission on Population Growth and
  the American Future, x, 218, 326,
  330, 357
Commonweal, 109, 128, 340, 341, 344,
  357
Congregationalists, 107, 265, 267
*Congressional Quarterly Weekly
  Report*, 113, 341, 367
Connery, John, 363
Conti, Leonardo, 146
Contraception, xvi, 3–6, 15, 23, 207
Corner, George W., 332
Council of La Raza, 359
Craigg, Joyce, 34
Crittenden, Anne, 345, 367
Crow, James F., 345
Csapo, A.I., 196
Culver, John C., 121
Curlender v. *Bio-Science Laboratories*,
  336
Curran, Charles E., 232, 360
Current, Richard N., 368
Curtis, Benjamin, 251, 270, 271, 363

Darling, Rosalyn Benjamin, 309, 370
David, Henry P., 70, 93, 196, 217,
  328, 333, 354, 357
David, Henry P.; Friedman, H.L.;
  van der Tak, Jean; and Sevilla, M.J.,
  326
Davis, Jefferson, 285
Dawidowicz, Lucy, 347, 348, 350, 352,
  371
Decker, David, 67

Del Guercio, Louis R.M., 371
Dellapenna, Joseph W., 83, 332, 363
Dellums, Ronald V., 92, 94, 335
Demeunier, Jean Nicolas, 368
Deutsch, Albert, 364
Dew, Thomas R., 363, 364
De Witt, John L., 190, 192
Diamond, Howard I., 127, 216, 332,
  344
Diamond, James J., 331
Dies, Martin, 191
Disciples of Christ, 193, 230
Dissel, Brenda M., 346
Doderer, Minnette, 126, 344
Donovan, C.M., 329
Dorner, Adolf, 352
Douglas, Stephen, 283
Douglas, William, 207
Downey, Connie, 254
Drayton, William, 253, 367
Drinan, Robert F., 212, 356
DuBois, W.E.B., 365
Duff, Raymond S. and Campbell,
  A.G.M., 299, 300, 313, 354, 359, 369
Dytrych, Zdeněk; Matějček, Zdeněk;
  Schüller, Vratislav; David, Henry P.;
  and Friedman, Herbert L., 54, 74,
  75, 330

Eccles, Mary Eisner, 341
Edelin, Kenneth, 86, 205, 208, 211,
  288, 337
Commonwealth v. *Edelin*, 355
Ehrlich, Paul, 122
Eichmann, Adolf, 155–58, 166, 167,
  171, 172, 174, 318, 348, 349, 351
Eichner, Edward, 49
Eidelman, Norma, 34
Eliot, Johan W.; Hall, Robert E.;
  Wilson, J. Robert; and Houser,
  Carolyn, 360
Elliott, E.N., 363, 364
Ellis, Havelock, 196
Elson, Mary, 327
Emerson, Shelba, 332
Endre, Lazlo, 162
Engdahl, Todd, 343
Englehardt, Jr., H. Tristram, 206, 209,
  303–05, 313, 333, 355, 370
Episcopalians, 117, 230, 265, 267
Eppes, John Wayles, 368

Nott, Josiah C., 260

O'Conor, Charles, 363, 365
Ohlendorf, Otto, 168
Olivarez, Graciela, 131
O'Rourke, Joseph, 101
Orthodox, 231
Osofsky, Howard J. and Joy D., 326, 329, 362
Outler, Albert, 107, 232, 360
Overstreet, Edmund, 356

Packwood, Bob, 122–24, 267, 343, 344
Pakter, Jean and Nelson, Frieda, 326
Pare, C.M.B. and Raven, H., 328, 329
Parker, Theodore, 270, 366
Parkes, A.S., xiii
Pastore, John, 341
Paul VI, xvi, 123
Payne, Edmund C., 328
Payne, Gordon R., 343
Peek, Mary, 141
Percy, Charles H., 92
Perez-Reyes, Maria G. and Falk, Ruth, 104, 219, 338, 355, 358
Pernicone, Isabel, 340
Pfannenstiel, Prof., 154
Pfannmüller, Hermann, 162
Phelan, Lana, 275
Pierce, Franklin, 273
Pilpel, Harriet, 213, 356
del Pinal, Jorge H., 343, 362
Planned Parenthood, ix, xvi, 2, 10, 14, 20, 27, 32, 34, 54, 62, 74, 77, 82, 91–94, 96, 98, 106, 113, 114, 121, 125–27, 133, 135, 138, 139, 141, 202, 209, 213, 214, 224, 229, 277, 322, 330, 333, 335, 341, 343, 344
Planned Parenthood v. Danforth, 138
Planned Parenthood Association v. Fitzpatrick, 139
Planned Parenthood Association of Kansas City, Mo. v. Ashcroft, 139
Planned Parenthood League of Massachusetts v. Bellotti, 139
Plessy v. Ferguson, 244
Poelker v. Doe, 343, 364
Pohlman, E.W., 54, 329, 330
Population Council, 125
Population Resource Center, 228
Porter, Charles, 344

Potts, Malcolm, 196, 197, 209, 215, 218–20
Potts, Malcolm; Diggory, Peter; and Peel, John, 353, 356–58
Presbyterians, 107, 230, 231, 261, 262, 264, 265, 267, 365
Prescott, James W., 74, 329, 330
von Preysing, Konrad, 183
Prince v. Massachusetts, 370
Pro-Lifers for Survival, 130
Protestants, 35, 85, 99, 101, 107, 108, 117, 119, 122, 125, 147, 183, 223, 237

Quakers, 193, 230, 265, 267

Rajan, Renga, 329
Ramsey, Paul, 107, 201, 213, 232, 339, 353–56, 358, 366
Randal, Judith, 121, 343
Rappeport, Michael and Labaw, Patricia, 98
Rascher, Sigmund, 145, 165, 166, 171, 181, 350
Rashbaum, William, 216
Raspberry, Bill, 130, 345
Rauschning, Hermann, 146
Rautanen, E.; Kantero, R.L.; and Widholm, P., 328
Reagan, Ronald, 245, 343
Redbook, 100–02, 337
Rees, Thomas M., 99
Rehnquist, William, 251, 363
Reitlinger, Gerald, 156, 173, 349, 351, 352
Reles, Abe, 176, 227
Religious Coalition for Abortion Rights, 78, 108, 121, 211, 337, 339, 340, 343
Reproductive Rights Newsletter, 113, 142, 341, 347
Riddell, George Allardice, 197, 354
Right to Life League, 340
Robbins, Sharon and Granger, Bruce, 224, 358
Roberts, Steven V., 344
Robertson, George, 285, 368
Rockefeller Foundation, xi
Rockefeller, III, John D., ix–xi, xvii, 257, 325, 330, 357, 364
Rockefeller, Nelson, 244
Roemer, Ruth, 334

About the Author

James Tunstead Burtchaell, C.S.C., is a noted scholar and teacher, with degrees from Cambridge University, the Pontificia Universita Gregoriana in Rome, Catholic University of America, and the University of Notre Dame. Appointed to the position of University Provost at Notre Dame in 1970, Father Burtchaell oversaw much of the educational and social aspects of student life at Notre Dame. Though he resigned from the position in 1977, Father Burtchaell is still an active member of the university's Department of Theology.

Father Burtchaell has served as the president of the American Academy of Religion and is the author or editor of numerous works, including *Philemon's Problem; Marriage Among Christians: A Curious Tradition;* and *Abortion Parley.*